COMPUTER CONFLUENCE

Exploring Tomorrow's Technology

second edition

COMPUTER CONFLUENCE

Exploring Tomorrow's Technology

George Beekman

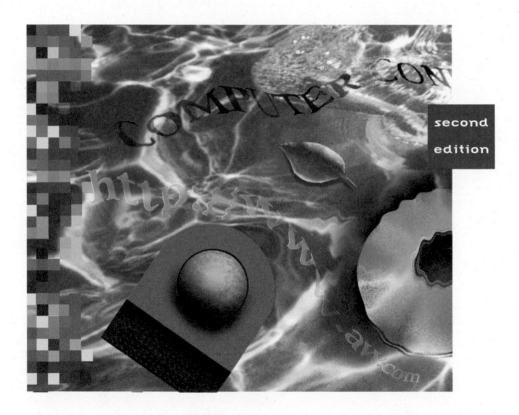

second edition

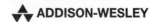
ADDISON-WESLEY

Addison-Wesley is an imprint of Addison Wesley Longman

Menlo Park, California • Reading, Massachusetts • New York • Harlow, England
Don Mills, Ontario • Sydney • Mexico City • Madrid • Amsterdam

Senior Acquisitions Editor	Maureen Allaire
Project Manager	Adam Ray
Developmental Editor	Sue Ewing
Production Editor	Jean Lake
Assistant Editor	Heide A. Chavez
Visual Design Manager	Don Kesner
Cover Design	Yvo Riezebos Design
Cover Illustration	Yvo Riezebos
Text Design	Vargas Williams Design
Illustrations	17th Street Studios
Photo Editor	Kathleen Cameron
Art Supervisor	Carol Ann Smallwood
Copy Editor	Barbara Conway
Manufacturing Supervisor	Janet Weaver
Marketing Manager	Melissa Baumwald
Composition	Thompson Type
Film	H&S Graphics
Printing and Binding	R. R. Donnelley & Sons Company

Library of Congress, Cataloging-in-Publication Data

Beekman, George.
    Computer confluence : exploring tomorrow's technology / George
Beekman.
      p.   cm.
   Includes index.
   ISBN 0-8053-2466-6. -- ISBN 0-8053-2289-2
    1. Computers. I. Title.
  QA76.5.B3652 1997   96-38494
  004--DC20   CIP
      3   4   5   6   7   8   9   10 - DOW - 00 99 98 97

To Sue,

my companion and my inspiration . . .
yesterday, today, and tomorrow

CD-ROM. Included free with every new copy of the book, this digital companion to the main text offers state-of-the-art 3-D animation, thought provoking video clips, interactive tutorials, self-assessment quizzes, and software application demos. The CD is an expansion of the content in the main text and serves as a complementary learning tool, making *Computer Confluence* a complete learning package.

World Wide Web Site (http://www.aw.com/bc/cc). This is an exciting way to find additional content via the Internet, fully integrating the traditional printed textbook with the world of the Web. Each new copy of the book includes a free subscription to up-to-the-minute news and activities that complement the book and its content. The *Computer Confluence* Web site consists of regularly updated pages, including late-breaking news, as well as Web links and forums for both students and professors. This is a key component of this supplement package.

Annotated Instructor's Edition. This special edition with annotations by Michael Johnson is provided free to instructors. It contains annotations for lecture preparation and includes information not found in the Instructor's Manual. The annotations include *Perspective Notes* to share with the students, *Technical Notes* to help elaborate on more complex issues, *Teaching Tips* for helpful hints on how to present the material in a "new" way, and *Quotes* that are pertinent to the material at hand. Test Bank, Transparency, and PowerPoint references are also included.

Instructor's Manual and Printed Test Bank. Written by George Beekman and Lisa Miller, these supplements to the lecture material are provided free to instructors. The Instructor's Manual extends the information in both the text and the Annotated Instructor's Edition with behavioral objectives, chapter overviews, key terms, and class outlines. The Printed Test Bank includes multiple choice, true/false, matching, completion, and situation essay questions, totaling about 2000 test items.

On-line Testing and Computerized Test Bank. This easy-to-use program allows instructors to generate tests, edit questions, and administer exams with several on-line testing options. Grading is done automatically, and analysis for each test is included. The complete system is provided free to text adopters.

PowerPoint Presentation Lecture Support Software. This is an interactive instructional support presentation created in Microsoft PowerPoint that allows instructors to customize lectures using art and main points from the text. The Annotated Instructor's Edition thoroughly references the presentation, making the software easy to use, even for a first-timer!

Color Transparency Acetates. This collection of full-color acetates provides you with excellent visual support in your lectures, bringing the art, diagrams, and application screens from the text to your classroom. Each acetate is page referenced to the text for ease of class planning.

Videotapes. Benjamin/Cummings makes available to qualified adopters free videotapes from our library of commercially produced tapes. Use this valuable resource to enhance your lectures on concepts presented in the text. Your Addison Wesley Longman sales representative has details about this offer.

Software. Your school may qualify for full-version software licenses. Ask your Addison Wesley Longman sales representative for more information.

Brief Table of Contents

PART ONE

Approaching Computers   1
Hardware and Software Fundamentals

PART TWO

Using Computers   97
Essential Applications

PART THREE

Exploring with Computers   201
Networks and Gateways

PART FOUR

Mastering Computers   255
From Algorithms to Intelligence

PART FIVE

Living with Computers   313
Into the Information Age

Detailed Table of Contents

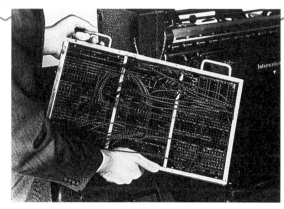

PART TWO Using Computers 97
Essential Applications

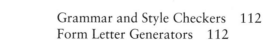

PART THREE

Exploring with Computers 201
Networks and Gateways

PART FOUR   Mastering Computers   255
From Algorithms to Intelligence

Chapter 16
Inventing the Future   384

Preface

onfluence **1:** a coming or flowing together, meeting, or gathering at one point (a happy *confluence of weather and scenery*) **2a:** the flowing together of two or more streams **b:** the place of meeting of two streams **c:** the combined stream formed by conjunction

—Merriam Webster's Collegiate Dictionary,

Electronic Edition

When powerful forces come together, change is inevitable. As the 20th century comes to a close, we're standing at the confluence of three powerful technological forces: computers, telecommunications, and electronic entertainment. The computer's digital technology is showing up in everything from telephones to televisions, and the lines that separate these machines are eroding. This digital convergence is rapidly—and radically—altering the world's economic landscape. Startup companies and industries are emerging to ride the waves of change, while older organizations reorganize, regroup, and redefine themselves to keep from being washed away.

Smaller computers, faster processors, smarter software, larger networks, new communication media—in the world of information technology, it seems like change is the only constant. In less than a human lifetime, this technological cascade has transformed virtually every facet of our society—and the transformation is just beginning. As old technologies merge and new technologies emerge, far-fetched predictions routinely come true. This headlong rush into the high-tech future poses a formidable challenge for all of us: How can we extract the knowledge we need from the deluge of information? What must we understand about information technology to successfully navigate the waters of change that carry us into the future? *Computer Confluence: Exploring Tomorrow's Technology* is designed to aid travelers on their journey into that future.

What Is Computer Confluence?

Computer Confluence is more than a textbook; it's the confluence of three information sources: an illustrated textbook, a multimedia CD-ROM, and a timely World Wide Web site on the Internet. This integrated learning package takes advantage of the unique strengths of three media types:

- *Computer Confluence,* the text. In spite of the talk about a paperless future, a book's user interface still has many advantages: You can read it under a tree or on the subway, you can bend the corners and scribble in the margins, you can study the words and pictures for hours without suffering from eyestrain or backache. A well-written text can serve as a learning tool, a reference work, a study guide, and even a source of motivation and inspiration. A textbook is no substitute for a good teacher, but a good textbook can almost always make a good teacher better. This book is an updated, expanded, and refined version of *Computer Currents,* which has served as an information age guidebook for thousands of students since its publication in 1994.

- *Computer Confluence,* the CD-ROM. A CD-ROM may not be as warm and friendly as a good book, but it can deliver video, audio, animation, and other dynamic media that can't be printed on paper. A well-designed CD-ROM can encourage exploration through interactivity. The *Computer Confluence* CD-ROM supplements and reinforces the printed material in the book with state-of-the-art 3-D animation, audio, and video. It also includes a software sampler for hands-on experimentation and interactive study materials that provide immediate student feedback.

- *Computer Confluence,* the Web site (http://www.aw.com/bc/cc). The information in computer books and CD-ROMs has a short shelf life. The Internet makes it possible to publish up-to-the-minute news and information regularly and link that information to other sources around the world. The Internet can also serve as a communication conduit for on-line discussion and research. An extensive collection of timely, media-rich Web pages keeps the information in *Computer Confluence* current. The regularly updated pages include late-breaking news, multimedia tidbits, and links to the most important computer and information technology sites, all organized by chapter and topic. The Web site also includes discussion areas where students, instructors, and authors can meet on-line.

Computer Confluence presents computers and information technology on three levels:

- Explanations: *Computer Confluence* clearly explains what a computer is and what it can (and can't) do; it explains the basics of information technology clearly and concisely.

- Applications: *Computer Confluence* clearly illustrates how computers and networks can be used as practical tools to accomplish a wide variety of tasks and solve a wide variety of problems.

- Implications: *Computer Confluence* puts computers in a human context, illustrating how information technology affects our lives, our world, and our future.

Who Is Computer Confluence For?

Computer Confluence: Exploring Tomorrow's Technology is especially designed for the introductory computer class for college freshmen—nonmajors and majors. *Computer Confluence* is also appropriate for many introductory computer science classes, discipline-specific computer courses offered through other departments, high school courses, and adult education courses. *Computer Confluence* can also serve as a self-study guide for anyone who's motivated to understand the changing technological landscape.

Most introductory computer courses are divided into lecture and lab sections. In some courses the labs cover computer applications like Microsoft Excel, Word-Perfect, and ClarisWorks; in some courses the labs cover Internet tools like electronic mail and the World Wide Web; a few courses include programming with langauges like BASIC, Pascal, C, and Java. Since this book focuses on concepts rather than keystrokes, it can be used in courses that teach any combination of lab applications and tools. The Benjamin/Cummings SELECT Lab Series includes specially designed hands-on modules covering the most popular applications and programming languages. There are dozens of books covering applications and programming languages that can be used for the lab segment of this course.

How Is Computer Confluence Organized?

The book consists of 16 chapters organized into five broad sections:

1. *Approaching Computers: Hardware and Software Fundamentals*
2. *Using Computers: Essential Applications*
3. *Exploring with Computers: Networks and Gateways*
4. *Mastering Computers: From Algorithms to Intelligence*
5. *Living with Computers: Into the Information Age*

Part 1 provides the basics: a brief historical perspective, a nontechnical discussion of computer basics, and an overview of hardware and software options. These chapters quickly introduce key concepts that recur throughout the book, putting the student on solid ground for understanding future chapters. Part 2 covers the most important and widely used computer applications, including word processing, spreadsheets, graphics, multimedia tools, and databases. These applications, like those in Parts 3 and 4, are presented in terms of concepts and trends rather than keystrokes. Part 3 explores the world of networks, from simple interoffice LANs to the massive global infrastructure that's evolving from the Internet. Part 4 describes the process and the problems of creating software, including software in the curious field of computer science known as artificial intelligence. Part 5 explores the far-reaching impact of computers on our work, our homes, our society, and our future.

Throughout the five parts, the book's focus gradually flows from the concrete to the controversial and from the present to the future. Individual chapters have a similarly expanding focus. After a brief introduction, each chapter flows from concrete concepts that provide grounding for beginners toward abstract, future-oriented questions and ideas.

Each chapter includes instructional aids to help students master the material quickly. Key terms are highlighted in boldface type for quick reference; secondary terms are italicized. All important terms are defined in context, in a glossary at the end of the text, and in the CD-ROM's hypertext glossary. Each chapter begins with a list of objectives and ends with a chapter summary; a list of key terms; collections of review questions, discussion questions, and projects; and an annotated list of sources and resources for students who want more information or intellectual stimulation.

Throughout *Computer Confluence* special focus boxes complement the text:

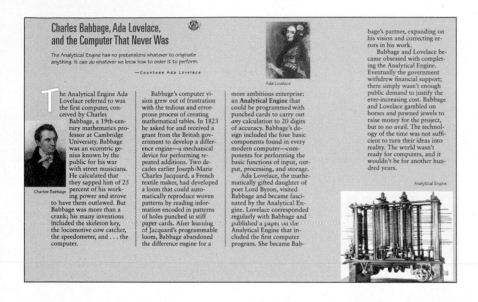

Charles Babbage, Ada Lovelace, and the Computer That Never Was

The Analytical Engine has no pretensions whatever to originate anything. It can do whatever we know how to order it to perform.

—Countess Ada Lovelace

The Analytical Engine Ada Lovelace referred to was the first computer, conceived by Charles Babbage, a 19th-century mathematics professor at Cambridge University. Babbage was an eccentric genius known by the public for his war with street musicians. He calculated that they sapped him of 25 percent of his working power and strove to have them outlawed. But Babbage was more than a crank; his many inventions included the skeleton key, the locomotive cow catcher, the speedometer, and . . . the computer.

Babbage's computer vision grew out of frustration with the tedious and error-prone process of creating mathematical tables. In 1823 he asked for and received a grant from the British government to develop a difference engine—a mechanical device for performing repeated additions. Two decades earlier Joseph-Marie Charles Jacquard, a French textile maker, had developed a loom that could automatically reproduce woven patterns by reading information encoded in patterns of holes punched in stiff paper cards. After learning of Jacquard's programmable loom, Babbage abandoned the difference engine for a

more ambitious enterprise: an **Analytical Engine** that could be programmed with punched cards to carry out *any* calculation to 20 digits of accuracy. Babbage's design included the four basic components found in every modern computer—components for performing the basic functions of input, output, processing, and storage.

Ada Lovelace, the mathematically gifted daughter of poet Lord Byron, visited Babbage and became fascinated by the Analytical Engine. Lovelace corresponded regularly with Babbage and published a paper on the Analytical Engine that included the first computer program. She became Bab-

bage's partner, expanding on his vision and correcting errors in his work.

Babbage and Lovelace became obsessed with completing the Analytical Engine. Eventually the government withdrew financial support; there simply wasn't enough public demand to justify the ever-increasing cost. Babbage and Lovelace gambled on horses and pawned jewels to raise money for the project, but to no avail. The technology of the time was not sufficient to turn their ideas into reality. The world wasn't ready for computers, and it wouldn't be for another hundred years.

Charles Babbage

Ada Lovelace

Analytical Engine

Human Connection boxes at the beginning of all chapters feature stories of personalities who made an impact on the world of computing, and in some cases, people whose lives were transformed by computers and information technology.

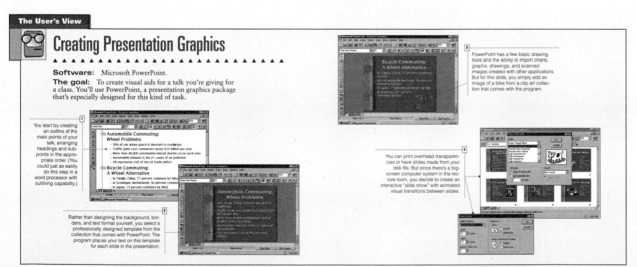

The User's View

Creating Presentation Graphics

▲ ▲ ▲ ▲ ▲ ▲ ▲ ▲ ▲ ▲ ▲ ▲ ▲ ▲ ▲ ▲ ▲ ▲ ▲ ▲

Software: Microsoft PowerPoint.

The goal: To create visual aids for a talk you're giving for a class. You'll use PowerPoint, a presentation graphics package that's especially designed for this kind of task.

You start by creating an outline of the main points of your talk, arranging headings and subpoints in the appropriate order. (You could just as easily do this step in a word processor with outlining capability.)

Rather than designing the background, borders, and text format yourself, you select a professionally designed template from the collection that comes with PowerPoint. The program places your text on this template for each slide in the presentation.

PowerPoint has a few basic drawing tools and the ability to import charts, graphs, drawings, and scanned images created with other applications. But for this slide, you simply add an image of a bike from a clip art collection that comes with the program.

You can print overhead transparencies or have slides made from your disk file. But since there's a big-screen computer system in the lecture room, you decide to create an interactive "slide show" with animated visual transitions between slides.

User's View boxes show the reader, through screens and text, what it's like to work with computer applications without getting bogged down in the details of button pushing. Most featured applications are available on both Windows and Macintosh platforms.

Throughout the book, icons indicate links to supplementary material on the CD-ROM and the World Wide Web.

Rules of Thumb boxes provide practical, nontechnical tips for avoiding the pitfalls and problems created by computer technology. How can you use graphics effectively and tastefully in a computer document? How can you minimize the health hazards of extended computer use? How can you protect your data from viruses and other software risks? What's the best way to communicate effectively with electronic mail? These are the types of questions that are answered in Rules of Thumb boxes.

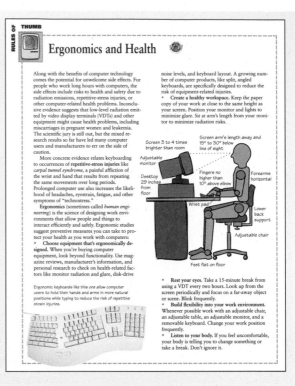

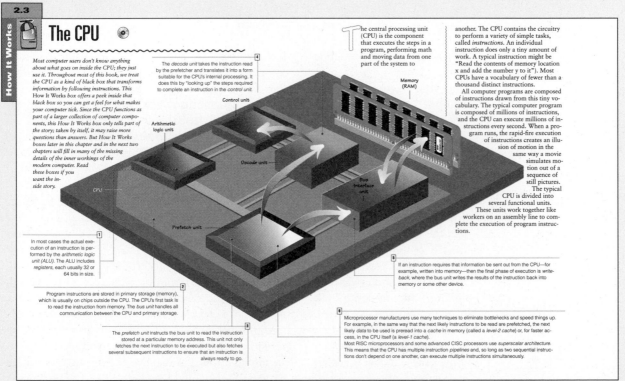

How It Works boxes are designed to provide additional technical material for courses and students who need it. How does the CPU execute a program? Why does a color image look different on the screen than on a printout? How does compression make files smaller? How can messages be encrypted? Students will find answers to these kinds of questions in the How It Works boxes. For classes where this kind of technical detail isn't necessary, students can safely skip these boxes without missing any critical information. How It Works boxes are numbered to make it easy for instructors to create customized reading assignments by specifying which are required and which are optional.

A Word to Instructors

When *Computer Currents* was published in 1994, most introductory computer classes were taught using command-line software on hardware that couldn't support any form of multimedia. Few introductory books even mentioned the Internet, few students used e-mail, and the World Wide Web was a well-kept secret. Today's computer user takes the graphical user interface for granted. Most new software is delivered on CD-ROMs, and multimedia computers are commonplace. The Internet has become fashionable, e-mail is taught and used in hundreds of introductory classes, and World Wide Web URLs are even showing up in television commercials.

This kind of change threatens to make even the most successful introductory computer classes irrelevant. How do we provide timely information on a subject about which last year's news seems remarkably old? How can we be sure that a freshman-level Introduction to Computers class won't seem like a History of Computers class by the time those freshmen graduate? How do we design courses that provide students with practical, expansive, lasting knowledge about computers and information technology?

It's no longer enough to teach students the fundamentals of programming in assembly language or BASIC and call them "computer literate." Nor can we assume that students who know WordPerfect and Lotus 1-2-3 keystrokes are properly equipped to survive and prosper in the information age. Even today's e-mail programs and the World Wide Web browsers will probably look like antiques in a few short years. In fact, any hands-on experience is likely to have a short useful life unless it's accompanied by material that provides a broader context.

Computer Confluence is designed to provide that context. Like the first edition, the book emphasizes big ideas, broad trends, and the human aspects of technology—the critical concepts that tend to remain constant even while hardware and software change. But even big ideas and broad trends change over time. For example, the last few years have seen the Internet and interactive multimedia move from the fringe to the center of our collective computer consciousness. *Computer Confluence* has been rewritten to reflect those changes. The Internet is introduced in the first chapter and covered extensively throughout the book; Chapter 10 provides a chapter-long, in-depth look at the Internet and related technologies. Chapter 7 has been revised and expanded to provide more clear, comprehensive, and current coverage of hypermedia and interactive multimedia.

But *Computer Confluence* doesn't just *talk* about the Internet and multimedia—it *uses* these technologies to deliver information that is more expansive, more interactive, and more current than what can be provided by a book alone. The massive storage capacity of a CD-ROM makes it possible to include supplementary text, animated illustrations, interactive exercises, and audio and video clips for anyone with access to a multimedia-ready computer. The CD-ROM runs on Windows and Macintosh machines, so students can use it on their own computers, even computers that aren't the same kind you use in your labs. The *Computer Confluence* Web site provides your students with timely updates and cross-links to other resources via modem or direct connection to the Internet. Your students don't need to have access to CD-ROM drives and the World Wide Web to benefit from *Computer Confluence;* they can easily master the material in the book without using other media. But the additional material on the CD-ROM and the Web can make their learning experiences more interesting, exciting, and timely.

The *Computer Confluence* book, CD-ROM, and Web site, when combined with your guidance and instruction, can provide students with unprecedented resources for understanding the technologies that are shaping their future. Hopefully, many of those students will use their knowledge to take an active part in shaping that future.

A Word to the Student

If you're like most students, you aren't taking this course to read about computers—you want to *use* them. That's sensible. You can't really understand computers without some hands-on experience, and you'll be able to apply your computer skills to a wide variety of future projects.

But it's a mistake to think that you're computer savvy just because you can use a PC to write term papers and surf the Internet. It's important to understand how people use and abuse computer technology, because that technology has a powerful and growing impact on your life. (If you can't imagine how your life would be different without computers, read the vignette called "Living Without Computers" in Chapter 1.) Even if you have lots of computer experience, future trends are almost certain to make much of that experience obsolete—probably sooner than you think. In the next few years, computers are likely to take on entirely new forms and roles because of breakthroughs in artificial intelligence, voice recognition, virtual reality, interactive multimedia, networking, and cross-breeding with telephone and home entertainment technologies. If your knowledge of computers stops with a handful of PC and Internet applications, you may be standing still while the world changes around you.

When you're cascading through white water, you need to be able to use a paddle, but it's also important to know how to read a map, a compass, and the river. *Computer Confluence: Exploring Tomorrow's Technology* is designed to serve as a map, compass, and book of river lore to help you ride the information waves into the future.

Computer Confluence will help you understand the important trends that will change the way you work with computers and the way computers work for you. This book discusses the promise and the problems of computer technology without overwhelming you with technobabble.

Computer Confluence is intentionally nontechnical and down to earth. Occasional ministories bring concepts and speculations to life. Illustrations and photos make abstract concepts concrete. Quotes add thought-provoking and humorous seasoning.

Whether you're a hard-core hacker or a confirmed computerphobe, there's something for you in *Computer Confluence*. Dive in!

Navigating Computer Confluence (Read Me First!)

Here are a few pointers to aid you on your journey through *Computer Confluence:*

- **Know your boxes.** Text chapters include several types of boxes, each of which is designed to be read in a particular way.

  User's View boxes show you what it's like to be in the driver's seat of some of the most powerful and popular software on the market today. Even if you have experience with the software, take a little time to look over these boxes. Some key concepts are introduced in the User's View boxes. A UV symbol like this **UV** in the main text means "This is a good time to look over the User's View box."

  Rules of Thumb boxes provide practical tips on everything from designing a publication to protecting your personal privacy. These popular boxes bring computer concepts down to earth with useful suggestions and concrete facts that can save you time, money, and peace of mind.

  How It Works boxes, new in this edition, are for those readers who want—or need—to know more about what's going on under the hood. These illustrated boxes use words and pictures to take you a little deeper into the inner workings of the machinery without getting bogged down in technical detail. The CD-ROM includes multimedia versions of many of these How It Works boxes; video, audio, and animation can make it easier to visualize and understand technical concepts. If your course objectives or personal curiosity don't motivate you to explore the How It Works material, that's OK; you can skip every How It Works box and still understand the rest of the material in *Computer Confluence.* Think of *Computer Confluence* without the How It Works boxes as *Computer Confluence Lite.*

- **Watch for media road signs.** You don't need a CD-ROM drive and an Internet connection to explore *Computer Confluence*—you don't even need a computer. But if you have access to these tools, they can make your journey more interesting. As you're reading the text, look for icons pointing you toward other media:

  This icon means that the CD-ROM contains information related to this section of the book. It may be an animated illustration, a video clip, a software demonstration, or an interactive exercise. Use the CD-ROM's Multimedia Study Guide to find the chapter and section. The study guide is organized through a table of contents that matches the text; you can explore any chapter or subject by clicking on its name. If you're feeling more adventurous than hurried, you can explore the material on the CD-ROM by navigating your way through a 3-D Virtual Computing Center.

This icon means that there's material in the *Computer Confluence* World Wide Web site (http://www.aw.com/bc/cc) related to this section of the book. The *Computer Confluence* Web site includes in-depth discussions and essays on relevant topics, updates to time-sensitive material, multimedia illustrations or examples, and links to dozens of other interesting and useful Web sites. If you're in a hurry, you'll need to exercise some self-discipline; it's easy to spend hours following your curiosity around the Web.

One cautionary note: the CD-ROM and Web sites are revised regularly, so the icons in this book may not reflect the exact contents of the other media. Be sure to take time to look for items not referenced in the book.

- **Read it and read it again.** If possible, read each chapter twice: once for the big ideas and the second time for more detailed understanding. You may also find it helpful to survey each chapter's outline in the table of contents before reading the chapter for the first time.

- **Don't get stuck.** If a concept seems unclear on the first reading, make a note and move on. Sometimes ideas make more sense after you've seen the bigger picture. If you still don't understand the second time through, check the CD-ROM and the Web site for further clarification. When in doubt, ask questions.

- **Remember that there's more than one way to learn.** Some of us learn best by reading, others learn best by exploring interactive examples, still others learn best by discussing ideas with others, on line or in person. *Computer Confluence* offers you the opportunity to learn in all of these ways. Use the learning tools that work best for you.

- **Don't try to memorize every term the first time through.** Computer jargon can be overwhelming if you tackle it all at once. Throughout the text, key terms are introduced in boldface, and secondary terms are italicized. Use the Key Terms list at the end of each chapter to review and the glossary to recall any forgotten terms. The CD-ROM contains an interactive cross-referenced version of the glossary so that you can quickly find any term without searching through the book.

- **Don't overanalyze examples.** *Computer Confluence* is designed to help you understand concepts, not memorize keystrokes. You can learn the nuts and bolts of working with computers in labs. The examples in this text may not match the applications you learn in your lab, but the concepts are similar.

- **Get your hands dirty.** If possible, try the applications while you're reading about them. When you read about word processing in *Computer Confluence,* get some firsthand word processing experience. Your reading and your lab work will reinforce each other and help solidify your newfound knowledge. The CD-ROM contains demonstration versions of many popular applications.

- **Study together.** There's plenty to discuss here, and discussion is a great way to learn.

Acknowledgments

Writing a book requires countless hours of working alone, but it isn't just solo work. This book is undeniably a team effort. I'm deeply grateful to all of the people who've helped bring *Computer Confluence* together. Their names may not be on the cover, but their high-quality work shows in every detail of this project.

I'll start by saying thanks again to the marvelous Benjamin/Cummings team that worked with me to put together the first edition. If it hadn't been for the vision, talent, and hard work of these folks, the original *Computer Currents* wouldn't have been such a big success, and there wouldn't even *be* a second edition. I was doubly fortunate to have many of those same people back to help me turn *Computer Currents* into *Computer Confluence*. Because of our experience working together on the first edition, we were able to accomplish things that couldn't have happened with an uninitiated group.

I owe a special thank you to Maureen Allaire, who served as Senior Acquisitions Editor and guiding light throughout the transition from *Computer Currents* to *Computer Confluence*. Maureen's vision, enthusiasm, clarity, hard work, and talent energized the project and kept it on track. Maureen and I were fortunate to have Adam Ray join the team as Project Manager for the second edition. Adam brought a wealth of experience—experience that he intelligently applied to every aspect of this project. Assistant Editor Heide A. Chavez, Project Editor Kathy Yankton, and Administrative Assistant Kathleen Conant skillfully helped track the myriad details and demands of the project.

The second edition was my first opportunity to work with Sue Ewing, a seasoned developmental editor with a marvelous gift for helping an author turn a rough project into a coherent manuscript that's ready for copy editing and production. Copy Editor Barbara Conway, with her amazing eye for detail and talent for making muddy passages clear, took up where Sue left off. Production Editor Jean Lake, who won an award for her work on the first edition, deserves *several* awards for her superhuman efforts in bringing everything together the second time around. If it weren't for Jean, Manufacturing Coordinator Janet Weaver never would have been able to turn all these grand ideas into a beautiful bound book.

The artistic realization of the book—the way it *looks*—is the results of the work of a talented team skillfully coordinated by Visual Design Manager Don Kesner. Art Editor Carol Ann Smallwood exhibited outstanding artistic vision and patience turning my vague descriptions, scratchy sketches, and indecisive mumblings into art. Photo Editor Kathleen Cameron convinced me that she could probably find a photo of just about anything. The folks at Vargas Williams Design are responsible for the excellent text design and layout of the book. Yvo Riezebos somehow managed to pull all of the conflicting demands for the cover into a coherent work of art.

I want to especially thank Gary Brent, an exceptionally talented writer, educator, programmer, and computer expert at Scottsdale Community College in Arizona. Gary contributed almost all of the material for the How It Works boxes in this book and served as a valued consultant, technical advisor, and co-conspirator throughout the project. Thanks also to Paul Thurrott, who worked with Gary, and to April Brent, who graciously agreed to take on more of the responsibilities at home (including caring for their new baby) so Gary could put in countless extra hours on this project. I'm delighted that Gary and Gene Rathswohl are coauthoring an expanded business edition of *Computer Confluence* with me.

The *Computer Confluence* CD-ROM and Web pages were produced by a team of Oregon wizards headed by Mark Dinsmore and Dave Trenkel, two former students who morphed into multimedia professionals. Mark's technical expertise, design talent, problem-solving skills, insatiable curiosity, and endless energy made him an ideal multimedia project coordinator. Dave's crystal clear tutorials, stunning 3-D animations, and intelligent electronic music rival the best in the business. Web researcher Greg Klein, graphic designer Delores Dinsmore, and 3-D modeler Ben Beekman each brought a unique set of talents to the team and the project. Other Oregonians who contributed to *Computer Confluence* include my OSU colleagues Mike Johnson and Sherry Clark, who managed to find time in their impossibly busy schedules to annotate the instructor's edition, produce a myriad of ancillary materials, and help construct the Web site. Their contributions are greatly appreciated.

All of these talented people did great work on *Computer Confluence*, but you aren't likely to hear them bragging about it. Fortunately, Melissa Baumwald, Michael Smith, Lianne Shayer, and the rest of the Benjamin/Cummings Marketing Team did a wonderful job of getting the good words out to the academic community and the world.

Because of a corporate reorganization, many of the people at Benjamin/Cummings who worked on this book are moving on to new challenges. I'll miss working with all of them; they've become a sort of long-distance family to me. I know they'll bring a tremendous amount of talent and energy to their new endeavors. I wish them all the best.

There are others who contributed to *Computer Confluence* in all kinds of ways, including critiquing chapters, answering technical questions, tracking down obscure references, guiding me through difficult decisions, and being there when I needed support. There's no room here to detail their contributions, but I want to thank the people who gave time, energy, talent, and support during the years that this book was under development, including Peter Harris, Walter Rudd, Cherie Pancake, Bruce D'Ambrosio, Bernie Feyerherm, Clara Knutson, Sheryl Parker, Rajeev Pandey, Clay Cowgill, Dave Stuve, Jan Dymond, Marilyn Wallace, Claudette Hastie-Baehrs, Shjoobedebop, SMILE, Breitenbush, Oregon Public Broadcasting, and KLCC. Thanks also to all the hardware and software companies whose cooperation made my work easier. And most of all, thanks to Susan, Ben, and Johanna, whose patience, support, love, and sacrifice inspired me every day through all these years.

Reviewers

Thanks to all of the dedicated educators who reviewed the manuscript at various stages of development; *Computer Confluence* is a significantly more valuable educational tool as a result of your ideas, suggestions, and constructive criticism.

William Allen
University of Central Florida
Orlando, Florida

Frederick Bounds
DeKalb College
Dunwoody, Georgia

David Bozak
SUNY Oswega
Oswega, New York

Gary Brent
Scottsdale Community College
Scottsdale, Arizona

Judy Cameron
Spokane Community College
Spokane, Washington

Mark Ciampa
Volunteer State Community College
Gallatin, Tennessee

Daniel Combellick
Scottsdale Community College
Scottsdale, Arizona

H. E. Dunsmore
Purdue University
Lafayette, Indiana

Joseph Fahs
Elmira College
Elmira, New York

Pat Fenton
West Valley College
Saratoga, California

David Fickbohm
Golden Gate University
San Francisco, California

Blaine Garfolo
San Francisco State University
San Francisco, California

Wade Graves
Grayson County College
Denison, Texas

Ananda Gunawardena
University of Houston - Downtown
Houston, Texas

Dale Gust
Central Michigan University
Mt. Pleasant, Michigan

Michael Hansen
Midlands Technical College
Columbia, South Carolina

Sally Ann Hanson
Mercer County Community College
Doylestown, Pennsylvania

Trevor Jones
Duquesne University
Pittsburgh, Pennsylvania

Fred Klappenberger
Computer Information Science
Anne Arundel City College
Arnold, Maryland

Pat Mattsen
St. Cloud University
St. Cloud, Minnesota

Vicki McCullough
Palomar College
San Marcos, California

J. Michael McGrew
Ball State University
Muncie, Indiana

Doris McPherson
Schoolcraft College
Livonia, Michigan

Linda Wise Miller
University of Idaho
Moscow, Idaho

William Moates
Indiana State University
Terre Haute, Indiana

Gerhard Plenert
Brigham Young University
Provo, Utah

Loreto Porte
Hostos City College
Bronx, New York

Mike Quinn
Oregon State University
Corvallis, Oregon

Jennifer Sedelmeyer
Broome City College
Binghamton, New York

Raoul Smith
Northeastern University
Boston, Massachusetts

Randy Stolze
Marist College
Poughkeepsie, New York

Tim Sylvester
Maricopa City College
Tempe, Arizona

Patricia Wermers
North Shore City College
Andover, Massachusetts

Alan Whitehurst
Brigham Young University
Provo, Utah

Melissa Wiggins
Mississippi College
Clinton, Mississippi

Floyd Jay Winters
Manatee City College
Bradenton, Florida

Rich Yankosky
Frederick City College
Frederick, Maryland

The Computer Confluence TechSuite Edition

Build a custom edition of *Computer Confluence,* Second Edition, for your lab course by combining the text with one or more selections from our SELECT Lab Series. The SELECT Lab Series offers dozens of proven and class-tested material, from Windows and DOS software applications textbooks to Internet activities, multimedia, CD-ROMs, and computer-based training. Your customized choice of textbooks will be sent to the bookstore, combined in a TechSuite, allowing students to purchase all books in one convenient package. Students gain a wide range of hands-on computer experiences, including the Internet, World Wide Web, word processing, spreadsheets, databases, programming, presentation graphics, and integrated packages. Instructors can add their own class notes or syllabi to create a unique learning package that has been tailored to match their individual course objectives.

Instructors choose what they want, and we customize the TechSuite to fit their needs. All materials from the SELECT Lab Series are also available separately.

Your Addison Wesley Longman representative will be happy to work with you and your bookstore manager to provide the most current "menu" of SELECT Lab Series offerings, outline the ordering process, and provide pricing, ISBNs, and delivery information. Or, visit our Web site at **http://www.aw.com/bc/is**

PART ONE

APPROACHING COMPUTERS

HARDWARE AND SOFTWARE FUNDAMENTALS

COMPUTERS IN CONTEXT

Charles Babbage, Ada Lovelace, and the Computer That Never Was

The Analytical Engine has no pretensions whatever to originate anything. It can do whatever we know how to order it to perform.

—Countess Ada Lovelace

Ada Lovelace

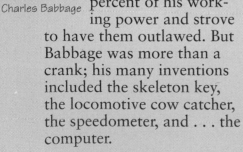

Charles Babbage

The Analytical Engine Ada Lovelace referred to was the first computer, conceived by Charles Babbage, a 19th-century mathematics professor at Cambridge University. Babbage was an eccentric genius known by the public for his war with street musicians. He calculated that they sapped him of 25 percent of his working power and strove to have them outlawed. But Babbage was more than a crank; his many inventions included the skeleton key, the locomotive cow catcher, the speedometer, and . . . the computer.

Babbage's computer vision grew out of frustration with the tedious and error-prone process of creating mathematical tables. In 1823 he asked for and received a grant from the British government to develop a difference engine—a mechanical device for performing repeated additions. Two decades earlier Joseph-Marie Charles Jacquard, a French textile maker, had developed a loom that could automatically reproduce woven patterns by reading information encoded in patterns of holes punched in stiff paper cards. After learning of Jacquard's programmable loom, Babbage abandoned the difference engine for a

more ambitious enterprise: an **Analytical Engine** that could be programmed with punched cards to carry out *any* calculation to 20 digits of accuracy. Babbage's design included the four basic components found in every modern computer—components for performing the basic functions of input, output, processing, and storage.

Ada Lovelace, the mathematically gifted daughter of poet Lord Byron, visited Babbage and became fascinated by the Analytical Engine. Lovelace corresponded regularly with Babbage and published a paper on the Analytical Engine that included the first computer program. She became Babbage's partner, expanding on his vision and correcting errors in his work.

Babbage and Lovelace became obsessed with completing the Analytical Engine. Eventually the government withdrew financial support; there simply wasn't enough public demand to justify the ever-increasing cost. Babbage and Lovelace gambled on horses and pawned jewels to raise money for the project, but to no avail. The technology of the time was not sufficient to turn their ideas into reality. The world wasn't ready for computers, and it wouldn't be for another hundred years.

Analytical Engine

Computers are so much a part of modern life that we hardly notice them. But computers are everywhere, and we'd certainly notice them if they suddenly stopped working. Imagine . . .

LIVING WITHOUT COMPUTERS

You wake up with the sun well above the horizon and realize your alarm clock hasn't gone off. You wonder if you've overslept. You have a big research project to finish today. The face of your digital wristwatch stares back at you blankly. The TV and radio are no help; you can't find a station on either one. You can't even get the time by telephone, because it doesn't work either.

The morning newspaper is missing from your doorstep. You'll have to guess the weather forecast by looking out the window. No music to dress by this morning—your CD player refuses your requests. How about some breakfast? Your automatic coffee maker refuses to be programmed; your microwave oven is on strike, too.

You decide to go out for breakfast. Your car won't start. In fact the only cars moving are at least 15 years old. The lines at the subway are unbelievable. People chatter nervously about the failure of the subway's computer-controlled scheduling device.

You duck into a fast-food outlet and find long lines of people waiting while cashiers handle transactions by hand. Still, you're hungry, so you decide to wait and join the conversation that's going on around you. People seem more interested in talking to each other since all the usual tools of mass communication have failed.

You're down to a couple of dollars in cash, so you stop after breakfast at an automated teller machine. Why bother?

You return home to wait for the book you ordered by overnight mail. You soon realize that you're in for a long wait; planes aren't flying because

3

Computers (above) are used to track Olympic test results in Atlanta. San Francisco's Bay Area Rapid Transit (BART) District (right) is a 75-mile automated train system. An automatic fare collection system tracks entry and exit points, calculates fares, and takes tickets without human intervention. The centralized Operations Control Center is used to perform supervisory control of train operations, remote control of electrification, ventilation, and emergency response systems.

air-traffic-control facilities aren't working. You head for the local library to see if the book is in stock. Of course, it's going to be tough to find since the book catalog is computerized.

As you walk home you speculate on the implications of a worldwide computer failure. How will people function in high-tech, high-rise office buildings that depend on computer systems to control everything from elevators to humidity? Will electric power plants be able to function without computer control? What will happen to patients in computerized medical facilities? What about satellites that are kept in orbit by computer-run control systems? Will the financial infrastructure collapse without computers to process and communicate transactions? Will the world be a safer place if all computer-controlled weapons are grounded?

Our story could go on, but the message should be clear enough by now. Computers are everywhere, and our lives are affected in all kinds of ways by their operation—and nonoperation. It's truly amazing that computers have infiltrated our lives so thoroughly in such a short time.

COMPUTERS IN PERSPECTIVE: AN EVOLVING IDEA

Consider the past and you shall know the future.

—Chinese Proverb

While the computer has been with us for only about half a century, its roots go back to a time long before Charles Babbage conceived of the Analytical Engine. This extraordinary machine is built on centuries of insight and intellectual effort.

Before Computers

Computers grew out of a human need to quantify. Early humans were content to count with fingers or rocks. As cultures became more complex, so did their counting tools. The abacus, the Arabic number system, and the concept of zero are only three examples of early calculating tools. Each of these ideas spread rapidly and had an immediate and profound effect on society.

The Analytical Engine had no impact on the development of calculating tools until a century after its invention, when it served as a blueprint for the first *real* programmable computer. Virtually every computer in use today follows the basic plan laid out by Babbage and Lovelace.

The Information-Processing Machine

Like the Analytical Engine, the computer is a machine that changes information from one form to another. All computers take in information (**input**) and give out information (**output**), as shown in this figure.

Input   Computer   Output

Because information can take many forms, the computer is an incredibly versatile tool, capable of everything from computing federal income taxes to guiding the missiles those taxes buy. For calculating taxes, the input to the computer might be numbers representing wages, other income, deductions, exemptions, and tax tables, and the output might be the number representing the taxes owed. If the computer is deploying a missile, the inputs might be radio and radar signals for locating the missile and the target, and the output might be electrical signals to control the flight path of the missile. Amazingly enough, the same computer could be used to accomplish all these tasks.

How can a machine be so versatile? The computer's flexibility isn't hidden in hardware—the physical parts of the computer system. The secret is **software**, or **programs**—the instructions that tell the hardware what to do to transform the input **data** (information in a form it can read) into the necessary output.

Whether a computer is doing a simple calculation or producing a complex animation, a program controls the process from beginning to end. In effect, changing programs can turn the computer into a different tool. Because it can be programmed to perform various tasks, the typical modern computer is a *general-purpose* tool.

The First Real Computers

Although Ada Lovelace predicted that the Analytical Engine might someday compose music, the scientists and mathematicians who designed and built the first working computers a century later had more modest goals: to create machines capable of doing repetitive mathematical calculations. Here are some landmark examples:

- In 1939 a young German engineer named Konrad Zuse completed the first programmable, general-purpose digital computer—a machine he built from electric relays to automate the process of doing engineering calculations. "I was too lazy to calculate and so I invented the computer," Zuse recalls. In 1941 Zuse and a friend asked the German government for funds to build a faster *electronic* computer using vacuum tubes to help crack enemy codes. The Nazi military establishment turned him down, confident that their aircraft could quickly win the war without the aid of sophisticated calculating devices. (As you'll read in the profile of Alan Turing later in the book, the British government used Colossus, a special-purpose electronic computer, to crack Nazi codes, allowing them to eavesdrop on even the most secret German messages throughout most of the war!)

- In 1939 Iowa State Professor John Atanasoff, seeking a tool to help his graduate students solve long, complex differential equations, developed what could have been the first electronic digital computer, the Atanasoff-Berry Computer (ABC). His university never bothered to patent Atanasoff's ground-breaking machine, and Atanasoff never managed to turn it into a fully operational product. The International Business Machines Corporation responded to his queries by telling him "IBM will never be interested in an electronic computing machine."

J. Presper Eckert (middle) and CBS News Correspondent Walter Cronkite (right) confer while UNIVAC 1 tallies votes in the 1952 presidential election. After counting 5 percent of the votes, UNIVAC correctly predicted that Eisenhower would win the election, but CBS cautiously chose to withhold the prediction until all votes were counted. Today networks commonly announce winners based on computer projections while many people are still voting.

- Harvard professor Howard Aiken was more successful in financing the automatic general-purpose calculator he was developing. In 1944, with a million dollars from IBM, he completed the Mark I. This 51-foot-long, 8-foot-tall monster used noisy electromechanical relays to calculate five or six times faster than a person could, but it was far slower than a modern $5 pocket calculator.

- After consulting with Atanasoff and studying the ABC, John Mauchly teamed up with J. Presper Eckert to help the U.S. effort in World War II by constructing a machine to calculate trajectory tables for new guns. The machine was the ENIAC (Electronic Numerical Integrator and Computer), a 30-ton behemoth with 18,000 vacuum tubes that failed at an average of once every seven minutes. When it *was* running it could calculate 500 times faster than the existing electromechanical calculators—about as fast as a modern pocket calculator. Nevertheless, it failed in its first mission: It wasn't completed until two months after the end of the war. Still, it convinced its creators that large-scale computers were commercially feasible. After the war Mauchly and Eckert started a private company and created UNIVAC 1, the first general-purpose commercial computer. UNIVAC I went to work for the US Census Bureau in 1951.

Evolution and Acceleration

Computer hardware evolved rapidly from those early days, with new technologies replacing old every few years. Historians marked major hardware changes in the first decades of the computer age by defining **four generations of computers.** UNIVAC I and other computers in the early 1950s were, according to this common classification scheme, *first-generation* computers. This was the era of machines built around *vacuum tubes*—light-bulb-sized glass tubes that housed switching circuitry. First-generation machines were big, expensive, and finicky. Only the largest of institutions could afford a computer, not to mention the climate-controlled computer center needed to house it and the staff of technicians needed to program it and keep it running. But with all their faults, first-generation computers quickly became indispensable tools for scientists and engineers.

The *transistor,* invented in 1948, could perform the same function as a vacuum tube by transferring electricity across a tiny resistor. Transistors were first used in a computer in 1956, an event generally viewed as the beginning of the computer's *second generation.* Computers that used transistors were radically smaller, more reliable, and less expensive than tube-based computers. Because of improvements in software at about the same time, these machines were also much easier and faster to program and use. As a result, computers became more widely used in business as well as in science and engineering.

But America's fledgling space program needed computers that were even smaller and more powerful than the second-generation machines, so researchers developed technology that allowed them to pack hundreds of transistors into a single **integrated circuit** on a tiny **silicon chip.** By the mid-1960s transistor-based computers were replaced by smaller, more powerful *third-generation* machines built around the new integrated circuits. Integrated circuits rapidly replaced early transistors for the same reasons that transistors superseded vacuum tubes:

- *Reliability.* Machines built with integrated circuits were less prone to failure than their predecessors because the chips could be rigorously tested before installation.

- *Size.* Single chips could replace entire circuit boards containing hundreds or thousands of transistors, making it possible to build much smaller machines.

- *Speed.* Because electricity had shorter distances to travel, the smaller machines were markedly faster than their predecessors.

- *Efficiency.* Since chips were so small, they used less electrical power. As a result, they created less heat.

- *Cost.* Mass production techniques made it easy to manufacture inexpensive chips.

Just about every breakthrough in computer technology since the dawn of the computer age has presented similar advantages over the technology it replaced.

The relentless progress of the computer industry is illustrated by *Moore's Law:* In 1965 Gordon Moore, the Chairman of Intel, predicted in jest that the power of a silicon chip of the same price would double every year or two for at least two decades. So far Moore's prediction has been uncannily accurate!

These three devices define the first three computer generations. The vacuum tube (left) housed a few switches in a space about the size of a light bulb. The transistor (middle) allowed engineers to pack the same circuitry in a semiconductor package that was smaller, cooler, and much more reliable. The first silicon chips (right) packed several transistors worth of circuitry into a speck much smaller than a single transistor. Today a single chip the size of your fingernail (below) can contain the equivalent of millions of transistors.

The Microcomputer Revolution

The inventions of the vacuum tube, the transistor, and the silicon chip had impacts on society, which is why they're used as computer-generational boundaries by many historians. But none of these had a more profound effect than the invention in 1969 of the first **microprocessor**—the critical components of a complete computer housed on a tiny silicon chip. The invention of the microprocessor marked the beginning of the *fourth generation* of computers—and, for all practical purposes, the end of an era when it made sense to count computer generations. The microprocessor's invention caused immediate and radical changes in the appearance, capability, and availability of computers.

The research and development costs for the first microprocessor were tremendous. But once the assembly lines were in place, silicon computer chips could be mass-produced cheaply. The raw materials were certainly cheap enough; silicon is the second most common element (behind oxygen) in the Earth's crust. It's the main ingredient in beach sand, among other things.

American companies soon flooded the marketplace with watches and pocket calculators built around inexpensive microprocessors. The economic effect was immediate: Mechanical calculators and slide rules became obsolete overnight, electronic

The microcomputer revolution didn't just increase the number of computers in offices; it opened up entirely new possibilities for computer habitats. The marine biologist above uses a laptop computer to record research notes and analyze data in the field. The student shown to the right, like millions of other students worldwide, uses a desktop computer for research, writing, problem solving, and leisure activities. Computer-driven display systems are important fixtures in meeting rooms, like the one shown on the far right. It's getting harder to find a workplace that doesn't have at least one computer.

hobbyists became wealthy entrepreneurs, and California's San Jose area gained the nickname Silicon Valley when dozens of microprocessor manufacturing companies sprouted and grew there.

The **microcomputer revolution** began in the mid-1970s when companies like Apple, Tandy, and Commodore introduced low-cost, typewriter-sized computers as powerful as many of the room-sized computers that had come before. **Personal computers,** or **PCs,** as **microcomputers** have come to be known, are now common in offices, factories, homes, schools, and just about everywhere else. Since chip manufacturers have been so successful at obeying Moore's Law, microcomputers have steadily increased in speed and power over the last two decades. At the same time, personal computers have taken over many tasks formerly performed by large computers, and every year people find new, innovative ways to harness these tiny workhorses. Large computers changed the world during the 1950s and 1960s—an era of *institutional computing*. But small computers had an even greater impact during the decades that followed—the *personal computer era*. Still, desktop computers haven't completely replaced big computers, which have also evolved. Today's world is populated with a variety of computers, each particularly well suited to specific tasks.

COMPUTERS TODAY: A BRIEF TAXONOMY

Invention breeds invention.

—Ralph Waldo Emerson

People today work with mainframe computers, supercomputers, workstations, notebook computers, palmtop computers, embedded computers, and, of course, PCs. Even though they're based on the same technology, these machines have important differences. In this section we'll briefly examine the main categories of computers.

Terminals like the one in the photo to the left make it possible for ticket agents all over the world to send information to a single mainframe computer like the one shown above.

Mainframes and Supercomputers

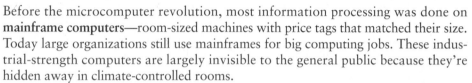

Before the microcomputer revolution, most information processing was done on **mainframe computers**—room-sized machines with price tags that matched their size. Today large organizations still use mainframes for big computing jobs. These industrial-strength computers are largely invisible to the general public because they're hidden away in climate-controlled rooms.

But the fact that you can't see them doesn't mean you don't use them. When you make an airline reservation or deposit money in your bank account, a mainframe computer is involved in the transaction. Your travel agent and your bank teller communicate with a mainframe using a computer **terminal**—a combination keyboard and screen that transfers information to and from the computer. The computer might be in another room or another country.

Mainframe computers are capable of communicating with several users simultaneously through a technique called **timesharing**. For example, a timesharing system allows travel agents all over the country to make reservations using the same computer and the same information at the same time.

Timesharing also makes it possible for users with diverse computing needs to share expensive computing equipment. Many research scientists and engineers, for example, need more computing power than they can get from personal computers. Their computing needs might require a powerful mainframe computer. A timesharing machine can simultaneously serve the needs of scientists and engineers in different departments working on a variety of projects.

Many researchers can't even get the computing power they need from a mainframe computer; their calculation-intensive work simply can't be performed fast enough on a traditional "big iron." These power-users need to have access to the fastest, most powerful computers made. Super-fast, super-powerful computers are called **supercomputers** or **high-performance computers**. These powerful machines are discussed in more detail in the last chapter.

Until a few years ago people commonly referred to another class of multiuse machine called the *minicomputer*. According to traditional definitions, minicomputers were smaller and less expensive than mainframes but larger and more powerful than personal computers. But most of today's mainframes are no bigger than yesterday's minicomputers, and most desktop computers are more powerful than those early minis. By most accounts the minicomputer is history.

Scientists and engineers use supercomputers like the Cray T3E because of their speed. The T3E can perform up to 1.3 trillion calculations per second.

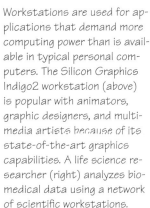

Workstations are used for applications that demand more computing power than is available in typical personal computers. The Silicon Graphics Indigo2 workstation (above) is popular with animators, graphic designers, and multimedia artists because of its state-of-the-art graphics capabilities. A life science researcher (right) analyzes biomedical data using a network of scientific workstations.

Workstations and PCs

For many applications the minicomputer has been replaced by a *server*—a computer especially designed to provide software and other resources to other computers over a network. (Networks and servers are discussed later in this chapter and in Chapters 9 and 10.) For other applications the minicomputer has been replaced by the **workstation**—a high-end desktop computer with massive computing power at a fraction of the cost. Workstations are widely used by scientists, engineers, Wall Street analysts, animators, and others whose work involves intensive computation. While many workstations are capable of supporting multiple users simultaneously, in practice they're often used by only one person at a time.

Of course, like many computer terms, *workstation* means different things to different people. Some people refer to all desktop computers and terminals as workstations. Those who reserve the term for the most powerful desktop machines admit that the line separating personal computers and workstations is fading. As workstations become less expensive and personal computers become more powerful, the line becomes as much a marketing distinction as a technical one. It's becoming harder and harder to find a definition for *workstation* that excludes the most powerful personal computers.

Most computer users don't need the power of a scientific workstation to do their day-to-day business. A modern personal computer has plenty of computing power for word processing, accounting, and other common applications. No surprise there—today's personal computers are far more powerful than the mainframes that dominated the world of computing a *human* generation ago. A personal computer, as the name implies, is almost always dedicated to serving a single user.

(A word about terminology: The term *personal computer* occasionally generates confusion because in 1981 IBM named its first desktop computer the IBM Personal Computer. To some people the term *personal computers* or *PCs* means only IBM computers or machines compatible with IBM hardware. But in this book the term is used to describe any general-purpose single-user computer.)

Portable Computers

A few years ago the terms *personal computer* and *desktop computer* were interchangeable; virtually all PCs were desktop computers. Today, however, one of the fastest growing segments of the PC market involves machines that aren't tied to the desktop—**portable computers**.

Of course, portability is a relative term. A decade ago "portable" computers were 20-pound suitcases with fold-out keyboards and small TV-like screens. Those machines were portable only in the sense that they could be moved from one desk to another. Today those "luggable" computers have been replaced by flat-screen, battery-powered **laptop computers** that are so light you can rest one on your lap while you work or carry it like a small briefcase when it's closed. A typical older laptop weighs around ten pounds and resembles a briefcase when closed. Today's laptop, commonly called a **notebook computer,** weighs much less and can be carried like a notebook *inside* a briefcase, with room to spare. A **subnotebook computer** is smaller still—about the size of a hardbound book, and just barely big enough for a touch-typeable keyboard. **Hand-held (palmtop) computers** small enough to be tucked into a jacket pocket serve the needs of users who value mobility over a full-sized keyboard and screen. Many of these tiny devices are designed as much for communication as for computing; they're often called **personal digital assistants** or *personal communicators.* Size notwithstanding, most portable computers in all their variations are general-purpose computers built around microprocessors similar to those that drive desktop models. But portability comes at a price—portable computers generally cost more than comparable desktop machines.

Embedded Computers and Special-Purpose Computers

Not all computers are general-purpose machines. Many are **special-purpose (dedicated) computers** that perform specific tasks, ranging from controlling the temperature and humidity in a high-rise office building to monitoring your heart rate while you work out. **Embedded computers** enhance all kinds of consumer goods: wristwatches, game machines, stereos, video cassette recorders, ovens, and even automobiles. Embedded computers are also widely used in industry, the military, and science for controlling a variety of hardware devices, including robots.

Most special-purpose computers are, at their core, similar to general-purpose personal computers. But unlike their desktop cousins, these special-purpose machines

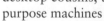

Portable computers come in a variety of sizes. IBM's line of ThinkPad computers (above right) includes a subnotebook with a foldout keyboard, a standard notebook-sized model for basic business applications, and a multimedia model with a large screen and CD-ROM drive. Hewlett Packard's OmniBook palmtop (left) has a tiny keyboard and runs on AAA batteries. Sony's Magic Link (right) is a combination computer and communication device that uses a pen rather than a keyboard for input.

Embedded computers are so common in today's world that they're all but invisible. These photos show three examples of embedded computers that aren't hidden away inconspicuously. BOB, the Breathing Observation Bubble (above left), is a high-tech underwater scooter with extensive computer controls. This rental car (above right) includes a special navigation computer that can continually display its current location on maps using data beamed from government satellites. As the cyclist (right) pedals and steers this stationary VR Bike, she sees a virtual landscape unfold on the screen in front of her. When she climbs a hill, pedal resistance builds; when she races down the other side, a cool breeze blows through her hair.

typically have their programs etched in silicon so they can't be altered. When a program is immortalized on a silicon chip it becomes **firmware**—a hybrid of hardware and software.

COMPUTER CONNECTIONS: THE NETWORK REVOLUTION

It is not proper to think of networks as connecting computers. Rather they connect people using computers to mediate. The great success of the Internet is not technical, but its human impact.

—Dave Clark, Internet pioneer, now a senior research scientist at MIT

We've seen how breakthroughs in switching, storage, and processor technology have produced new types of computers. Each of these technological advances had an impact on our society as people found new ways to put computers to work. Most historians stopped counting computer generations after the microcomputer became commonplace; it was hard to imagine another breakthrough having as much impact as the tiny microprocessor. But while the world was still reeling from the impact of the microcomputer revolution, another information technology revolution was quietly building up steam: a **network revolution.** If current trends continue, we may look back on the 1990s as the beginning of the era of *interpersonal computing*.

The Emergence of Networks

The first computers were large, expensive, self-contained machines that could only process one job at a time. As demand for computing power grew, computer scientists searched for ways to make scarce computer resources more accessible. The invention of timesharing in the 1960s allowed multiple users to connect to a single mainframe computer through individual terminals. When personal computers started replacing terminals, many users found they had all the computing power they needed on their desktops. Still, there were advantages to linking some of these computers together in *local area networks*. When clusters of computers were networked, they could share scarce, expensive resources. For example, a single high-speed printer could meet the needs of an entire office if it was connected to a network. As a bonus, people could use computers to send and receive messages electronically through the networks.

The advantages of electronic communication and resource sharing were multiplied when smaller networks were joined into larger networks. Emerging telecommunication technology eventually allowed *wide area networks* to span continents and oceans. Banks, government agencies, and other large, geographically distributed institutions gradually built information processing systems to take advantage of long distance networking technology. But for most computer users outside of these organizations, networking wasn't the norm. People saw computers as tools for doing calculations, storing data, and producing paper documents—not as communication tools.

There were exceptions: A few visionary computer scientists and engineers, with financial backing from the U.S. government, built an experimental network called ARPANET in 1969. This ground-breaking network would become the **Internet**—the global collection of networks that is radically transforming the way the world uses computers.

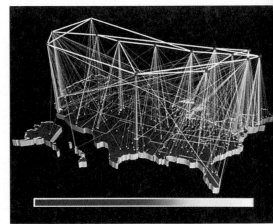

This computer-generated 3-D map represents major Internet connections in the United States. You can view an animated video version of this map on the World Wide Web.

The Internet Explosion

In its early years the Internet was the domain of researchers, academics, and government officials. It wasn't easy to use; users had to know cryptic commands and codes that only a programmer could love. In the 1990s Internet software took giant leaps forward in usability. The biggest changes came with the development of the **World Wide Web,** a vast tract of the Internet accessible to just about anyone who could point to buttons on a computer screen. *The Web*, as it's often called, led the Internet's transformation from a text-only environment into a multimedia landscape incorporating pictures, sounds, animation, and even video.

These changes have resulted in profound changes in the Internet's population. The Internet today isn't just for scholars and scientists. It's used by mom-and-pop businesses and multinational corporations who want to communicate with their customers and track economic conditions; by kindergarteners and college students doing research and exploration; by consumers and commuters who need access to timely information; by families and friends who just want to stay in touch. All kinds of people are signing onto the Internet, and they're doing it in record numbers. Why? Reasons vary, but most people connect to the Internet because it gives them the power to do things that they couldn't easily do otherwise. Using the Internet you can

- send a message to one or 1001 people, around town or around the world, and receive replies as quickly as the recipients can read the message and type a response

- quickly explore vast libraries of research material, ranging from classic scholarly works to contemporary reference works

- study material that's designed to supplement this book, including late-breaking news, interactive study aids, and multimedia simulations that can't be printed on paper

- shop for obscure items that you can't find elsewhere

- browse through all kinds of fascinating information sources and discover worlds of knowledge that you might not have known about otherwise

Using browser software like Netscape Navigator, you can explore the World Wide Web site for this book by typing in its URL (or World Wide Web address) and clicking on labeled buttons.

- find instant answers to time-sensitive questions like "What's the weather like in Boston right now?" or "What software do I need to make my new computer work with my new printer?" or "Who won this morning's Olympic high-diving competition?" or "What did Bill Gates say on National Public Radio's *All Things Considered* last night?" or "Where in the world is the Federal Express package I sent last night?"

- participate in discussions or play games with people all over the globe who share your interests; if you have the right equipment, you might be able to set aside your keyboard and communicate through live audio-video links

- publish your own writings, drawings, photos, and multimedia works so they can be viewed by Internet users all over the world

The Internet has become so pervasive that many people believe we'll soon use computers mostly as gateways to the Internet. In fact, several companies are gambling on that notion by developing and marketing low-cost, stripped-down computers designed to function as **Internet terminals** (or, as they're sometimes called, *Network Computers,* or simply NCs). These terminals cost less than half the price of a typical PC because they don't contain all of the hardware necessary in a computer that's designed to work by itself. An Internet terminal can't do much by itself; like a TV, it's designed to retrieve information from elsewhere. But unlike a TV, an Internet terminal also allows you to send and receive information; it's a two-way connection to the wired world.

Whether you use a terminal, a personal computer, or a high-powered workstation, you can connect to the Internet either through a direct connection—one that's hard-wired through a business, school, or government— or through an indirect connection using the telephone system. But as ties between the computer and communication industries grow, we may start connecting to the Internet through cable TV systems using special-purpose computers called **set-top boxes.** Who knows? Future homes and businesses may have dozens of computers, electronic devices, even appliances continually connected to the Internet, monitoring all kinds of

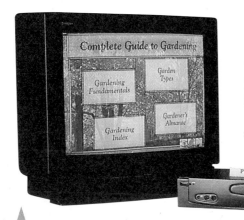

Millions of homes may soon be connecting to the Internet through televisions using set-top boxes like this Pippen model from Apple.

data that can have an impact on our lives and our livelihoods. Whatever happens, it's clear that the Internet is going to play an increasing role in our future.

LIVING WITH COMPUTERS

> There may still be plenty of stragglers who have yet to nuzzle up to computers, but there is no one unaffected by the explosion of computer technology.
>
> —Steven Levy, technology writer

The proliferation of computers and networks today is transforming the world rapidly and irreversibly. More than any other recent technological breakthrough, the development of the computer is responsible for profound changes in society. Of course, computer scientists and computer engineers aren't responsible for all the technological turbulence. Developments in fields as diverse as telecommunications, genetic engineering, medicine, and atomic physics contribute to the ever-increasing rate of social change. But researchers in all of these fields depend on computers to produce their work.

In less than a human lifetime, computers have evolved from massive, expensive, error-prone calculators like the Mark I and ENIAC into a myriad of dependable, versatile machines that have worked their way into just about every nook and cranny of modern society. The pioneers who created and marketed the first computers didn't foresee the spectacular advances in computer technology that came about in the decades that followed. Thomas Watson, Sr., the founding father of IBM, declared in 1953 that the world wouldn't need more than five computers! And the early pioneers certainly couldn't have predicted the extraordinary social changes that resulted from the computer's rapid evolution. In the time of UNIVAC, who could have imagined Nintendo and Netscape?

Technological breakthroughs encourage further technological change, so we can expect the *rate* of change to continue to increase in coming decades. In other words, the technological and social transformations of the past five decades may be dwarfed by the changes that occur over the next half century. It's just a matter of time, and not very much time, before today's state-of-the-art computers look as primitive as ENIAC looks to us today. Similarly, today's high-tech society just hints at a future world that we haven't begun to imagine.

What do you *really* need to know about computers today? The remaining chapters of this book provide answers to that question. Here's an overview of what you can expect from those chapters.

Explanations

You don't need to be a computer scientist to coexist with computers. But your encounters with technology will make more sense if you understand a few basic computer concepts. Computers are evolving at an incredible pace, so many of the details of hardware and software change every few years. But most of the underlying concepts remain constant as computers evolve. If you understand the basics, you'll find that it's a lot easier to keep up with the changes.

Applications

Many people define *computer literacy* as the ability to *use* computers. But because computers are so versatile, there's no one set of skills that you can learn to become computer literate in every situation. **Application programs,** also known simply as

By 1500 BC papyrus, libraries, clay tablets, abacus

600 AD printing press invented by Bi Shing

9th century Buddhist text is first known printed book

11th century movable type, decimal number system, musical notation

12th century modern abacus

15th century Gutenberg's printing press

16th century algebraic symbols, lead pencil

17th century calculus, Pascal's calculator, probability, binary arithmetic, newspapers, mailboxes

18th century typewriter, three-color printing, industrial revolution

19th century automated loom, Analytical Engine, telegraph, vacuum tube, cathode ray tube, telephone, color photograph, Hollerith's data processing machine, radio, sound recordings

Early 20th century assembly-line automated production, analog computer, television, motion pictures

1939 Atanasoff creates the first digital computer

1939 Zuse completes first programmable, general-purpose computer

1943 Turing's Colussus computer breaks Nazi codes

1944 Aiken completes the Mark I

1945 Von Neumann proposes storing programs as data

1946 Mauchly and Eckert design ENIAC

1947 Shockley, Brittain, and Ardeen invent the transistor

1949 Orwell writes 1984, a novel about totalitarianism and computers

1951 Univac I is delivered to U.S. Census Bureau

1954 IBM makes first mass-produced computer

1956 first computer operating system

1956 Bell labs build first transistorized computer

1956 computerized banking begins

1957 USSR launches Sputnik

1959 Jack Kilby and Robert Noyce develop the integrated circuit

1960 laser invented

1962 DEC introduces minicomputer

1962 first timesharing operating system

1963 Doug Engelbart patents mouse

1964 first prosecuted computer crime

1967 software first sold separately

1969 first nationwide network (Arpanet)

1969 first person on moon

1969 first microprocessor

1970 ROM developed

1972 first home computer game

1974 first microcomputer

1974 first computer-controlled industrial robot

1975 Cray-1 supercomputer is introduced

1977 Xerox pioneers graphical user interface

1977 Apple introduces the Apple II

1978 first spreadsheet program

1979 Pac Man appears

1981 IBM introduces its first personal computer

1984 Apple introduces the Macintosh

1984 Volkswagen loses hundreds of millions to computer fraud

1986 desktop publishing takes off

1986 Connection Machine massively parallel computer introduced

1988 Internet worm cripples 6000 computers for two days

1989 Word Wide Web created

1990 Hewlett-Packard and others introduce pocket computers

1990 Microsoft introduces Windows 3.0 for IBM-compatible computers

1991 IBM, Apple and Motorola team up to develop next generation of Power PC machines

1991 many PC makers launch multimedia products

1992 several pen-based computers and hand-held communications devices introduced

1993 computer companies, phone companies, and cable TV companies form alliances to create new interactive media

1994 Apple introduces Power Macintosh using CPU developed by IBM

1994 White House announces its World Wide Web page

1994 Intel replaces thousands of Pentium processors because of bugs

1995 U.S. Justice Department settles antitrust suit with Microsoft

1995 Microsoft introduces Windows 95 with $200 million marketing campaign

1996 Several companies introduce network computers for Internet access

} The floodgates are open, and information technology ideas are flowing faster all the time.

applications, are the software tools that allow a computer to be used for specific purposes. Many computer applications in science, government, business, and the arts are far too specialized and technical to be of use or of interest to people outside the field. On the other hand, some applications are so flexible that they can be used by all kinds of people. Regardless of your background or aspirations, you can almost certainly benefit from knowing a little about these applications.

- *Word processing and desktop publishing. Word processing* is a critical skill for anyone who communicates in writing. It's far and away the number one application used by students. *Desktop publishing* uses the personal computer to transform written words into polished, visually exciting publications.

- *Spreadsheets and other number-crunching applications.* In business the electronic *spreadsheet* is the personal computer application that pays the rent, or at least calculates it. If you work with numbers of any kind, spreadsheets and statistical software can help you turn those numbers into insights.

- *Databases for information storage and retrieval.* If word processors and spreadsheets are the most popular PC applications, *databases* reign supreme in the world of mainframes. Of course, databases are widely used on PCs, too. As libraries, banks, and other institutions turn to databases for information storage, the average person has more reasons to learn the basics of databases.

- *Computer graphics.* Computers aren't limited to working with text and numbers; they're capable of producing all kinds of graphics, from the charts and graphs produced by spreadsheets to realistic 3-D animation. As graphics tools become more accessible, visual communication skills become more important for all of us.

- *Multimedia and hypermedia.* Many of the computing industry's visionaries have their sights focused on these two related technologies. *Multimedia* tools for PCs make it possible to combine audio and video with traditional text and graphics, adding new dimensions to computer communication. *Hypermedia* tools focus on the interactive capabilities of computers. Unlike books, videos, and other linear media, which are designed to be experienced from beginning to end, hypermedia allow users to explore a variety of paths through information sources. The combination of multimedia and hypermedia has an almost unimaginable potential for transforming the way we see and work with information.

- *Telecommunication and networking.* A network connection is a door into a world of electronic mail, on-line bulletin boards, database services, hypermedia publishing ventures, and other new forms of communication. If current trends continue, *telecommunication*—long distance communication—may be the single most important function of computers in the not-too-distant future. The multipurpose global communication web known as the Internet may become as important in our lives as the telephone system, the postal service, and broadcast television are today.

- *Artificial intelligence. Artificial intelligence* is the branch of computer science that explores using computers in tasks that require intelligence, imagination, and insight—tasks that have traditionally been performed by people rather than machines. Until recently, artificial intelligence was mostly an academic discipline—a field of study reserved for researchers and philosophers. But that research is paying off today with commercial applications that exhibit intelligence—applications that you may be using soon.

- *General problem solving.* People use computers to solve problems. Most people use software applications written by professional programmers. But some kinds of problems can't easily be solved with off-the-shelf applications; they require at least some custom programming. *Programming languages* aren't applications;

Computer Time Line

These *Time* covers symbolize changes in the way people saw and used computers as they evolved through the last half of this century. Notice that the beginning of each new "era" doesn't mean the end of the old ways of computing; today we live in a world of institutional, personal, and interpersonal computing.

| 1950 | 1975 | 1995 |

Institutional Computing Era
(Starting approximately 1950)

Characterized by a few large, expensive mainframe computers in climate-controlled rooms; controlled by experts and specialists; used mainly for data storage and calculation.

Personal Computing Era
(Starting approximately 1975)

Characterized by millions of small, inexpensive micro-computers on desktops in offices, schools, homes, factories, and almost every where else; controlled mostly by independent users; used mostly for document creation, data storage, and calculation.

Interpersonal Computing Era
(Starting approximately 1995)

Characterized by networks of interconnected computers in offices, homes, schools, vehicles, and almost everywhere else; controlled by users (clients) and network operators; used mostly for communication, document creation, data storage, and calculation.

In the early 1950s the first computers were changing the military and a few government agencies and big businesses. By 1980 the microcomputer revolution was transforming offices, schools, and some homes. In the 1990s the network revolution is likely to have an even bigger impact on our society.

they're tools that allow you to build and customize applications. Many computer users find their machines become more versatile, and valuable, when they learn a little about programming.

Implications

Even if you never touch a personal computer, computer technology will continue to have a growing impact on your life and your world. People all around you use PCs to manage finances and schedules, to write letters and novels, to draw maps and illustrations, to publish newspapers and political manifestos, to store addresses and musical scores, to send messages across town and around the world. Computers routinely save lives in hospitals, keep space flights on course, and predict the weekend weather.

The future is rushing toward you, and computer technology is a big part of it. It's exciting to consider the opportunities arising from advances in artificial intelligence, multimedia, robotics, and other cutting-edge technologies of the electronic revolution—opportunities in the workplace, the school, and the home. But it's just as important to pay attention to the potential risks, including

- the threat to personal privacy posed by large databases

- the hazards of high-tech crime and the difficulty of keeping data secure
- the risks of failure of computer systems
- the threat of automation and the dehumanization of work
- the abuse of information as a tool of political and economic power
- the dangers of dependence on complex technology

For better *and* for worse, we'll be coexisting with computers till death do us part. As with any relationship, a little understanding can go a long way. The remaining chapters of this book will help you gain the understanding you need to survive and prosper in a world of computers.

SUMMARY

While the basic idea behind a computer goes back to Charles Babbage's 19th-century plan for an Analytical Engine, the first real computers were developed during the 1940s. Computers have evolved at an incredible pace since those early years, becoming consistently smaller, faster, more efficient, more reliable, and less expensive. At the same time, people have devised all kinds of interesting and useful ways to put computers to work to solve problems.

Computers today, like their ancestors, are information-processing machines designed to transform information from one form to another. When a computer operates, the hardware accepts input data from some outside source, transforms the data by following instructions called software, and produces output that can be read by a human or by another machine.

Computers today come in all shapes and sizes, with specific types being well suited for particular jobs. Mainframe computers and supercomputers provide more power and speed than smaller desktop machines, but they are expensive to purchase and operate. Timesharing makes it possible for many users to work simultaneously at terminals connected to these large computers. At the other end of the spectrum, workstations, personal computers, and a variety of portable devices provide computing power for those of us who don't need a mainframe's capabilities. Microprocessors aren't just used in general-purpose computers; they're embedded in appliances, automobiles, and a rapidly growing list of other products.

Connecting to a network enhances the value and power of a computer—it can share resources with other computers and facilitate electronic communication with other computer users. Some networks are local to a particular building or business; others connect users at remote geographic locations. The Internet is an interconnected collection of networks that spans the globe. Businesses, public institutions, and individuals are rushing to connect their computers and other devices to the Internet, and people are finding new ways to take advantage of the global network every day. As the Internet grows and changes, it will play an increasingly important role in our lives.

Computers and information technology have changed the world rapidly and irreversibly. It's easy to list dozens of ways that computers make our lives easier and more productive. Personal computer applications like word processing, desktop publishing, spreadsheets, graphics, and databases continue to grow in popularity. Computer networks are emerging as important communication tools. Emerging technologies like artificial intelligence offer promise for future applications. At the same time, computers threaten our privacy, our security, and perhaps our way of life. As we rush into the information age, our future depends on computers and on our ability to understand and use them in productive, positive ways.

Chapter Review

Key Terms

Analytical Engine
application program (application)
data
embedded computer
firmware
four generations of computers
hand-held (palmtop) computer
hardware
high-performance computer
input
integrated circuit
Internet

Internet terminal
laptop computer
mainframe computer
microcomputer
microcomputer revolution
microprocessor
network revolution
Network Computer (NC)
notebook computer
output
personal computer (PC)
personal digital assistant

portable computer
program
set-top box
silicon chip
software
special-purpose (dedicated)
    computer
subnotebook computer
supercomputer
terminal
timesharing
workstation
World Wide Web

Review Questions

1. Provide a working definition of each of the key words listed above. Check your answers in the glossary.

2. List several ways you interact with computers in your daily life.

3. Why was the Analytical Engine never completed during Charles Babbage's lifetime?

4. Outline the evolution of the computer from World War II to the present.

5. How are hardware and software related?

6. What is the most important difference between a computer and a calculator?

7. What is the difference between a mainframe and a microcomputer? What are the advantages and disadvantages of each?

8. What kinds of computer applications require the speed and power of a supercomputer? Give some examples.

9. What types of computers typically employ timesharing?

10. List several common personal computer applications.

11. Why is it important for people to know about and understand computers?

12. Describe some of the benefits and drawbacks of the computer revolution.

Discussion Questions

1. What do people mean when they talk about the computer revolution? What is revolutionary about it?

2. How do you feel about computers? Examine your positive and negative feelings.

3. What major events *before* the 20th century influenced the development of the computer?

4. Suppose Charles Babbage and Ada Lovelace had been able to construct a working Analytical Engine and develop a factory for mass-producing it. How do you think

the world would have reacted? How would the history of the 20th century been different as a result?

5. How would the world be different today if a wrinkle in time transported a modern desktop computer system, complete with software and manuals, onto the desk of Herbert Hoover? Adolph Hitler? Albert Einstein?

6. The automobile and the television set are two examples of technological inventions that changed our society drastically in ways that were not anticipated by their inventors. Outline several positive and negative effects of each of these two inventions. Do you think, on the balance, that we're better off as a result of these machines? Why or why not? Now repeat this exercise for the computer.

7. Should all students be required to take at least one computer course? Why or why not? If so, what should that course cover?

8. Computerphobia—fear or anxiety related to computers—is a common malady among people today. What do you think causes it? What, if anything, should be done about it?

9. In your opinion what computer applications offer the most promise for making the world a better place? What computer applications pose the most significant threats to our future well-being?

Projects

1. Start a collection of news articles, cartoons, or television segments that deal with computers. Does your collection say anything about popular attitudes toward computers?

2. Trace computer-related articles through several years in the same magazine. Do you see any changes or trends?

3. Develop a questionnaire to try to determine people's attitudes about computers. Once you have people's answers to your questions, summarize your results.

4. Take an inventory of all the computers you encounter in a single day. Be sure to include embedded computers such as those in cars, appliances, entertainment equipment, and other machines.

Sources and Resources

Periodicals

Byte (general and technical), *PC* (IBM-compatible), *PC World* (IBM-compatible), *PC/Computing* (IBM-compatible), *Windows Magazine* (IBM-compatible), *Compute!* (IBM-compatible), *Macworld* (Macintosh), *MacUser* (Macintosh). Because the world of personal computers changes so rapidly, computer users depend on magazines to keep them up to date on hardware and software developments. The average computer owner is interested mainly in information related to one type of machine, so most of these magazines target brand-specific audiences.

Computerworld, Infoworld, PC Week, MacWeek. These weekly newspapers provide up-to-the-week news on computers, emphasising corporate applications.

Wired. This trend-setting monthly is billed as "the first consumer magazine for the digital generation to track technology's impact on all facets of the human condition." Some of the best writers and thinkers in the field contribute to this thought-provoking magazine. *Wired* isn't for everybody, though. The ultra-hip, in-your-face style and bold design has led some to suggest that it should be called *Weird*.

Whole Earth Review. This eclectic quarterly includes everything from ecology to anthropology, but it has superb coverage of cutting-edge technologies like artificial life and virtual reality.

Books

Jargon: An Informal Dictionary of Computer Terms, by Robin Williams with Steve Cummings (Berkeley, CA: Peachpit Press, 1993) and *Illustrated Computer Dictionary for Dummies,* by Dan Gookin, Wally Wang, and Chris Van Buren (Foster City, CA: IDG Books, 1993). It sometimes seems like the computer industry makes three things: hardware, software, and jargon. These two friendly, readable dictionaries do a masterful job of defining and demystifying the jargon so you can better understand the other two. The differences between these two books reflect the background of the authors: *Jargon* does an especially good job on graphics and Macintosh-related terminology, while the Dummies dictionary is especially strong on IBM PC technology and terminology.

InfoCulture: The Smithsonian Book of Information Age Inventions, by Steven Lubar (Boston: Houghton Mifflin Company, 1993). This illustrated social history of our modern technological culture takes a broad view of the communication, entertainment, and information-processing industries. Lubar clearly explains how emerging technologies work, how we use them, and how they change our lives. Like a visit to a good museum, this book can fill you with fresh insights and stimulate your curiosity at the same time.

The Dream Machine: Exploring the Computer Age, by Jon Palfreman and Doren Swade (London: BBC Books, 1991). This book, designed to accompany a BBC TV documentary, is filled with photos and text describing the evolution of the computer from its earlier days.

The History of Computers, by Les Freed (Emeryville, CA: Ziff-Davis Press, 1995). This illustrated paperback traces high points of the computer's evolution from Pascal's 15th century calculators to the present. This isn't a complete scholarly history; plenty of important milestones are missing. Still, it's a colorful and readable overview with plenty of interesting facts and photos.

Fire in the Valley: The Making of the Personal Computer, by Paul Freiberger and Michael Swaine (Berkeley, CA: Osborne/McGraw-Hill, 1984). This book chronicles the early years of the personal computer revolution. The text occasionally gets bogged down in details, but the photos and quotes from the early days are fascinating.

Accidental Empires: How the Boys of Silicon Valley Make Their Millions, Battle Foreign Competition, and Still Can't Get a Date, by Robert X. Cringely (Reading, MA: Addison-Wesley, 1992). Robert X. Cringely is the pen-name for *InfoWorld's* computer-industry gossip columnist. In this opinionated, irreverent, and highly entertaining book, Cringely discusses the past, present, and future of the volatile personal computer industry. When you read the humorous, colorful characterizations of the people who run this industry, you'll understand why Cringely doesn't use his real name. A 1996 PBS TV show and video, caled Triumph of the Nerds, is based loosely on this book.

The Difference Engine, by William Gibson and Bruce Sterling (New York: Bantam, 1991). How would the world of the 19th-century be different if Charles and Ada had succeeded in constructing the Analytical Engine 150 years ago? This imaginative mystery novel takes place in a world where the computer revolution arrived a century early. Like other books by these two pioneers of the "cyberpunk" school of science fiction, *The Difference Engine* is dark, dense, detailed, and thought-provoking.

Videos

The Machine That Changed the World (available from Films for the Humanities and Sciences, Princeton, NJ). This five-part PBS television special on video is one of the best treatments of the history of computing available. The series contains hours of fascinating footage covering everything from the Analytical Engine to virtual reality.

World Wide Web Pages

Some of the best sources and resources on computers and information technology are on the Internet's World Wide Web. For example, the Boston Computer Museum's Web site (http://net.org) is a wonderful source of information about the past, present, and future of computers. But the Web is changing quickly, and new sites are appearing every day. The *Computer Confluence* Web pages includes up-to-date links to many of the best computer-related resources on the Web. To find them, open your Web browsing software, enter the address `http://www.aw.com/bc/cc`, follow the on-screen buttons to the table of contents, select a chapter, and click on the links that interest you.

HARDWARE
BASICS
Inside the Box

Thomas J. Watson, Sr., and the Emperor's New Machines

There is no invention—only discovery.

—Thomas J. Watson, Sr.

Thomas J. Watson, Sr.

As president or, as he has been called, the "emperor" of IBM, Thomas J. Watson, Sr., created a corporate culture that fostered both invention and discovery. In 1914 he joined the ailing Computing-Tabulating-Recording Company as a salesman. The company specialized in counting devices that used punched cards to read and store information. Ten years later Watson took it over, renamed it International Business Machines, and used a firm leadership style to chart a course for the company that eventually turned it into the dominant force in the computer industry.

Thomas Watson has been called autocratic. He de-manded unquestioning allegiance from his employees and enforced a legendary dress code that forbade even a hint of color in a shirt. But in many ways Watson ran his company like a family, rewarding loyal employees with uncommon favors. During the depression he refused to lay off workers, choosing instead to stockpile surplus machines. As if to prove that good deeds don't go unrewarded, the director of the newly formed Social Security Administration bought Watson's excess stock.

Watson's first involvement with computers was providing financial backing for Howard Aiken's Mark I, the pioneering electrome-chanical computer developed in the early 1940s at Harvard. But he stubbornly refused to develop a commercial computer, even as UNIVAC I achieved fame and commercial contracts for the fledgling Sperry company.

Shortly after Watson retired from the helm of IBM in 1949, his son, Thomas Watson, Jr., took over. (The younger Watson led IBM into the computing field with a vengeance, eventually building a computing empire that dwarfed all competitors.) When Watson Senior died of a heart attack in 1956 at the age of 82, he still held the title of chairman of IBM.

After decades of unquestioned dominance in the computer industry, IBM today struggles to maintain its reputation as the industry leader. The conservative giant has been slow to adjust to the rapid-fire changes in the computer industry, making it possible for smaller, more nimble companies to seize emerging markets. Massive losses forced IBM to reorganize, replace many of its leaders, and abandon the company's long-standing no-layoffs policy. (IBM also recently abandoned the legendary dress code, opting for a more casual image.) But in spite of recent difficulties, IBM maintains its position as the number one computer hardware company.

Computers schedule airlines, predict the weather, play music, control space stations, and keep the world's economic wheels spinning. How can one kind of machine do so many things?

To understand what *really* makes computers tick you would need to devote considerable time and effort to studying computer science and computer engineering. Most of us don't need to understand every detail of a computer's inner workings, any more than a parent needs to explain wave and particle physics when a child asks why the sky is blue. We can be satisfied with simpler answers, even if those answers are only approximations of the technical truth. We'll spend the next three chapters exploring answers to the question, "How do computers do what they do?"

The main text of each of these chapters will provide simple, nontechnical answers and basic information. How It Works boxes use text and graphics to dig deeper into the inner workings of the computer. Depending on your course, your learning style, and your level of curiosity, you may read these boxes as they appear in the text, read them after you've completed the basic material in the chapter, or (if you don't need the technical details) skip them altogether. If your questions aren't answered in these chapters, use the Sources and Resources section at each chapter's end as a jumping off point for further explorations. No matter how much you know about computers, there's always more to learn. So let's get started.

WHAT COMPUTERS DO

Stripped of its interfaces, a bare computer boils down to little more than a pocket calculator that can push its own buttons and remember what it has done.

—Arnold Penzias, in *Ideas and Information*

The simple truth is that computers can *really* do only four things:

1. *Receive input.* They accept information from the outside world.

2. *Process information.* They perform arithmetic or logical (decision-making) operations on information.

3. *Produce output.* They communicate information to the outside world.

4. *Store information.* They move and store information in the computer's memory.

These four basic functions are responsible for everything computers do. Every computer system contains hardware components that specialize in each of these four functions:

- **Input devices** accept input from the outside world. The most common input device, of course, is the keyboard. But computers can accept input signals from a variety of other devices, including pointing devices like mice and trackballs.

- **Output devices** send information to the outside world. Most computers use a TV-like video monitor as their main output device and some kind of printer to produce paper printouts.

- A **processor,** or **central processing unit** (CPU), processes information, performing all the necessary arithmetic calculations and making basic decisions based on information values. The CPU is, in effect, the computer's "brain."

- **Storage devices** are used to store information. **Primary storage,** the computer's **memory,** is used to store programs and data that need to be instantly accessible to the CPU. **Secondary storage** media, including disks and tape drives, serve as long-term storage media. A secondary storage device like a disk drive can be thought of as a combination input and output device, because the computer sends information out to the storage device (output) and later retrieves that information from it (input).

These components, when combined, make up the hardware part of a computer system. Of course, the system isn't complete without software. But for now we'll concentrate on hardware. In this chapter we'll focus on the central processing unit and the computer's primary storage; these components are at the center of all computing operations. In the next chapter we'll look at the input, output, and secondary storage devices—**peripherals** that round out the computer system. Since every computer hardware component is designed either to transport or to transform information, we'll start with a little bit of information about information.

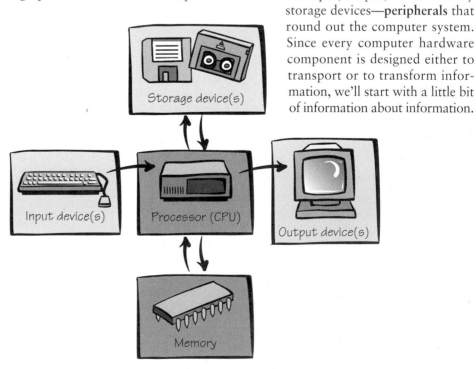

The basic components of every computer system include the central components (the CPU and primary memory, shown here in GREEN) and peripherals (input, output, and secondary storage devices, shown in ORANGE and YELLOW).

Storage device(s)

Input device(s)   Processor (CPU)   Output device(s)

Memory

A BIT ABOUT BITS

Even the most sophisticated computer is really only a large, well-organized volume of bits.

—David Harel, in *Algorithmics: The Spirit of Computing*

The term **information** is difficult to define because it has many meanings. According to many traditional definitions, information is communication that has value because it informs. People who subscribe to this definition often say that computers turn raw *data,* which has no value in its current form, into *information,* which is valuable. Many beginning textbooks use this model to emphasize the computer's role as a business data processing machine. But in our modern interconnected world, where one computer's output might be another's input, it's difficult to draw a hard line between worthless data and valuable information.

In the language of communication and information theory, the term *information* can be applied to just about anything that can be communicated, whether it has value or not. By this definition, which is the one we'll be using in this book, information comes in many forms. The words, numbers, and pictures on this page are symbols representing information. If you underline this sentence, you're adding new information to the page. The sounds and moving pictures that emanate from a television set are packed with information, too. (Remember, not all information has value.)

In the world of computers, information is **digital:** It's made up of discrete units—that is, units that can be counted—so it can be subdivided. In many situations people need to reduce information to simpler units to use it effectively. For example, a child trying to pronounce an unfamiliar word can sound out each letter individually before tackling the whole word.

A computer doesn't understand words, numbers, pictures, musical notes, or even letters of the alphabet. Like a young reader, a computer can't process information without dividing it into smaller units. In fact, computers can only digest information that has been broken into bits. A **bit** (*b*inary dig*it*) is the smallest unit of information. A bit can have one of two values: on or off. You can also think of these two values as yes and no, zero and one, black and white, or just about anything else you want to call them.

If we think of the innards of a computer as a collection of microscopic on/off switches, it's easy to understand why computers process information bit by bit. Each switch can be used to store a tiny amount of information: a signal to turn on a light, for example, or the answer to a yes/no question.

Remember Paul Revere's famous midnight ride? His co-conspirators used a pair of lanterns to convey a choice between two messages, "One if by land, two if by sea"—a **binary** choice. It's theoretically possible to send a message like this with just one lantern. But "One if by land, zero if by sea" wouldn't have worked very well unless there was some way to know exactly when the message was being sent. With two lanterns, the first lantern could say "Here is the message" when it was turned on. The second lantern communicated the critical bit's worth of information: land or sea. If the revolutionaries had wanted to send a more complex message, they could have used more lanterns ("Three if by subway!").

In much the same way, a computer can process larger chunks of information by treating groups of bits as units. For example, a collection of 8 bits, called a **byte,** can represent 256 different messages ($256 = 2^8$). If we think of each bit as a light that can be either on or off, then we can make different combinations of lights represent different messages. (Computer scientists usually speak in terms of 0 and 1 instead of

Binary Numbers

The MITS Altair, the first personal computer, came with no keyboard or monitor. It could only be programmed by using a bank of binary switches for input; binary patterns of lights provided the output.

I n a computer all information—program instructions, pictures, text, sounds, or mathematical values—is represented by patterns of microscopic switches. In most cases these groups of switches represent numbers or numerical codes.

The easiest kind of switch to manufacture is an on/off toggle switch: It has just two settings, on and off, like an ordinary light switch. That's the kind of switch that's used in every modern computer.

Binary arithmetic follows the same rules as ordinary decimal arithmetic. But with only two digits available for each position, you have to borrow and carry (manipulate digits in other positions) more often. Even adding 1 and 1 results in a two-digit number, 10.

Multiplication, division, negative numbers, and fractions can also be represented in binary, but most people find them messy and complicated compared to decimal arithmetic.

1

The use of switches to represent numbers would be easy to understand if the switches each had 10 settings (0 through 9). The decimal number 67 might look like this:

on and off, but the concept is the same either way.) The computer has an advantage over Paul Revere in that it sees not just the number of lights turned on, but also their order, so 01 (off-on) is different from 10 (on-off).

Building with Bits

What does a bit combination like 01100110 mean to the computer? There's no single answer to that question; it depends on context and convention. A string of bits can be interpreted as a number, a letter of the alphabet, or almost anything else.

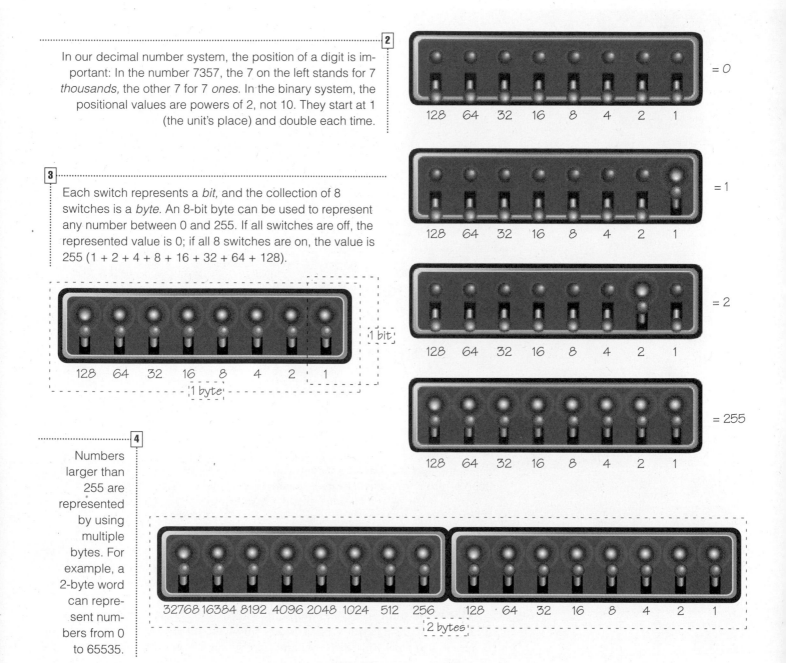

2 In our decimal number system, the position of a digit is important: In the number 7357, the 7 on the left stands for 7 *thousands,* the other 7 for 7 *ones.* In the binary system, the positional values are powers of 2, not 10. They start at 1 (the unit's place) and double each time.

128 64 32 16 8 4 2 1   = 0

128 64 32 16 8 4 2 1   = 1

128 64 32 16 8 4 2 1   = 2

3 Each switch represents a *bit,* and the collection of 8 switches is a *byte.* An 8-bit byte can be used to represent any number between 0 and 255. If all switches are off, the represented value is 0; if all 8 switches are on, the value is 255 (1 + 2 + 4 + 8 + 16 + 32 + 64 + 128).

128 64 32 16 8 4 2 1

1 bit

1 byte

128 64 32 16 8 4 2 1   = 255

4 Numbers larger than 255 are represented by using multiple bytes. For example, a 2-byte word can represent numbers from 0 to 65535.

32768 16384 8192 4096 2048 1024 512 256   128 · 64 32 16 8 4 2 1

2 bytes

Bits as Numbers

Because computers are built from switching devices that reduce all information to 0s and 1s, they represent numbers using the *binary number system*—a system that denotes all numbers with combinations of two digits. Like the ten-digit decimal system we use every day, the binary system has clear, consistent rules for every arithmetic operation.

There was a time when working with binary arithmetic was a necessary part of using a computer. But today's computers include software that converts decimal numbers into binary numbers automatically, and vice versa. As a result, the computer's binary number processing is completely hidden from the user.

In the binary number system, every number is represented by a unique string of 0s and 1s.

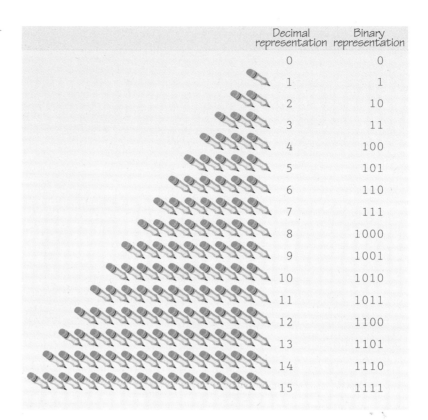

	Decimal representation	Binary representation
	0	0
	1	1
	2	10
	3	11
	4	100
	5	101
	6	110
	7	111
	8	1000
	9	1001
	10	1010
	11	1011
	12	1100
	13	1101
	14	1110
	15	1111

Bits as Codes

Today computers work at least as much with text as with numbers. To make words, sentences, and paragraphs fit into the computer's binary-only circuitry, people have devised codes that represent each letter, digit, and special character as a unique string of bits.

The most widely used code, **ASCII** (an abbreviation of American Standard Code for Information Interchange, generally pronounced "as-kee"), represents each character as a unique 8-bit code. Out of a string of 8 bits, 256 unique ordered patterns can be made—enough to make unique codes for all letters (upper- and lowercase) and numbers, and a wide variety of special characters.

As the world shrinks and our information needs grow, many computer users are finding that ASCII's 256 unique characters simply aren't enough, and new coding schemes are being developed. To facilitate multilingual computing, manufacturers are likely to switch eventually from ASCII to a more information-rich coding scheme, such as **UniCode**'s 65,000-character set.

Of course, today's computers work with more than characters. A group of bits can also represent colors, sounds, quantitative measurements from the environment, or just about any other kind of information that's likely to be processed by a computer. We'll explore other types of information later.

Bits as Instructions in Programs

So far we've dealt with the ways bits can be used to represent data—information from some outside source that's processed by the computer. But another kind of information is just as important to the computer: the programs that tell the computer what to do with the data we give it. The computer stores programs as collections of bits, just as with data.

Programs, like characters, are represented in binary notation through the use of codes. For example, the code 01101010 might tell the computer to add two numbers together. Other groups of bits—instructions in the program—would contain codes that tell the computer where to find those numbers and where to store the result. You'll learn more about how these computer instructions work in later chapters.

Bits, Bytes, and Buzzwords

Trying to learn about computers by examining their operation at the bit level is a little like trying to learn about how people look or act by studying individual human cells; there's plenty of information there, but it's not the most efficient way to find out what you need to know. Fortunately, people can use computers without thinking about bits. Some bit-related terminology *does* come up in day-to-day computer work, though. Specifically, most computer users need to have at least a casual understanding of these terms:

- **Byte:** a grouping of 8 bits. If you work mostly with words, you can think of a byte as one character of ASCII-encoded text.

- **K (kilobyte)** (sometimes called *KB*): about 1000 bytes of information. For example, about 5K of storage is necessary to hold 5000 characters of ASCII text. (Technically, 1K is 1024 bytes, because 1024 is 2^{10}, which makes the arithmetic easier for binary-based computers. For those of us who don't think in binary, 1000 is close enough.)

- **MB (megabyte)** (sometimes called *meg*): approximately 1000K, or 1 million bytes.

- **GB (gigabyte)** (sometimes called *gig*): approximately 1000MB.

- **TB (terabyte):** approximately 1 million megabytes. This astronomical unit of measurement applies to the largest storage devices commonly available today.

People use the abbreviations K, MB or meg, and GB or gig when describing the capacity of some of the computer components we'll discuss in this chapter and the next. A computer might, for example, be described as having 16MB of memory and a hard disk as having a 1GB storage capacity. The same terms are used to quantify sizes of computer *files*. A **file** is an organized collection of information, such as a term paper or a set of names and addresses, stored in a computer-readable form. For example, the text for this chapter is stored in a file that occupies about 50K of space on a disk.

Character	ASCII binary code
A	0 1 0 0 0 0 0 1
B	0 1 0 0 0 0 1 0
C	0 1 0 0 0 0 1 1
D	0 1 0 0 0 1 0 0
E	0 1 0 0 0 1 0 1
F	0 1 0 0 0 1 1 0
G	0 1 0 0 0 1 1 1
H	0 1 0 0 1 0 0 0
I	0 1 0 0 1 0 0 1
J	0 1 0 0 1 0 1 0
K	0 1 0 0 1 0 1 1
L	0 1 0 0 1 1 0 0
M	0 1 0 0 1 1 0 1
N	0 1 0 0 1 1 1 0
O	0 1 0 0 1 1 1 1
P	0 1 0 1 0 0 0 0
Q	0 1 0 1 0 0 0 1
R	0 1 0 1 0 0 1 0
S	0 1 0 1 0 0 1 1
T	0 1 0 1 0 1 0 0
U	0 1 0 1 0 1 0 1
V	0 1 0 1 0 1 1 0
W	0 1 0 1 0 1 1 1
X	0 1 0 1 1 0 0 0
Y	0 1 0 1 1 0 0 1
Z	0 1 0 1 1 0 1 0
0	0 0 1 1 0 0 0 0
1	0 0 1 1 0 0 0 1
2	0 0 1 1 0 0 1 0
3	0 0 1 1 0 0 1 1
4	0 0 1 1 0 1 0 0
5	0 0 1 1 0 1 0 1
6	0 0 1 1 0 1 1 0
7	0 0 1 1 0 1 1 1
8	0 0 1 1 1 0 0 0
9	0 0 1 1 1 0 0 1

The capital letters and numeric digits are represented in the ASCII character set by 36 unique patterns of 8 bits. (The remaining 92 ASCII bit patterns represent lowercase letters, punctuation characters, and special characters.)

THE COMPUTER'S CORE: THE CPU AND MEMORY

There's a runaway market for bits.

—Russell Schweickart, astronaut

It may seem strange to think of automated teller machines, video game consoles, and supercomputers as bit processors. But whatever it looks like to the user, a digital computer is at its core a collection of on/off switches designed to transform information from one form to another. The user provides the computer with patterns of bits—input—and the computer follows instructions to transform that input into a different pattern of bits—output—to return to the user.

Representing the World's Languages

The United States has long been at the center of the computer revolution; that's why the ASCII character set was originally designed to include only English-language characters. ASCII code numbers range from 0 to 127. This isn't enough to handle all the characters used in the languages of Western Europe, including accents and other diacritical marks.

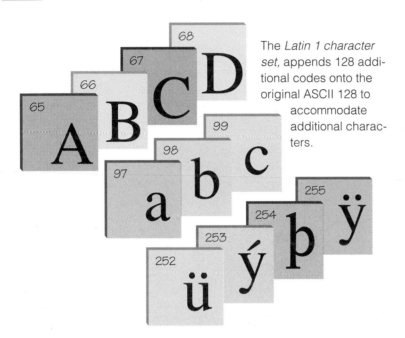

The *Latin 1 character set,* appends 128 additional codes onto the original ASCII 128 to accommodate additional characters.

Computer keyboards for East Asian languages don't have one key for each character. Using phonetic input, a user types a pronunciation for a character using a western-style keyboard and then chooses the character needed from a menu of characters that appear on the screen. Some menu choices can be made automatically by the software based on common language usage patterns.

The CPU: The Real Computer

The transformations are performed by the central processing unit (CPU) or processor. Every computer has a CPU to interpret and carry out the instructions in each program, to do arithmetic and logical data manipulations, and to communicate with all the other parts of the computer system. A modern CPU is an extraordinarily complex collection of electronic circuits. When all of those circuits are built into a single silicon chip, as they are in most computers today, that chip is referred to as a *microprocessor.* In a typical desktop computer, the CPU is housed along with other chips and electronic components on a **circuit board.** (The circuit board that contains a desktop computer's CPU is sometimes called the *motherboard.*)

Both the ASCII and Latin 1 character sets can use 8 bits—1 byte—to represent each character, but there's no room left for the characters used in languages like Greek, Hebrew, Hindi, and Arabic, each of which has its own 50-to-150-character alphabet or syllabary. East Asian languages like Chinese, Japanese, and Korean present bigger challenges for computer users. Chinese alone has nearly 50,000 distinct characters, of which about 13,000 are in current use.

Most major new software applications and operating systems are designed to be transported to different languages. To make a software application work in different languages involves much more than translating the words. For example, some languages write from right-to-left or top-to-bottom. Pronunciation, currency symbols, dialects, and other variations often make it necessary to produce customized software for different regions even when the same language is spoken.

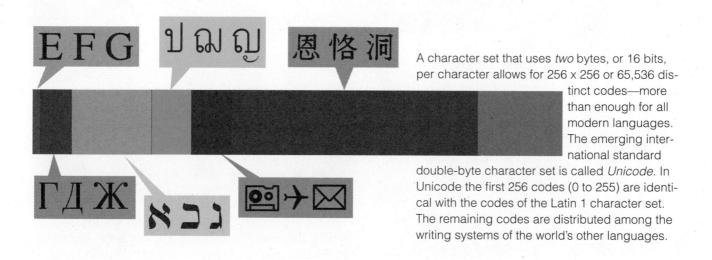

A character set that uses *two* bytes, or 16 bits, per character allows for 256 x 256 or 65,536 distinct codes—more than enough for all modern languages. The emerging international standard double-byte character set is called *Unicode*. In Unicode the first 256 codes (0 to 255) are identical with the codes of the Latin 1 character set. The remaining codes are distributed among the writing systems of the world's other languages.

There are many different kinds of CPUs in common use today; when you choose a computer, the type of CPU in the computer is an important part of the decision. While there are many variations in design among these chips, only two factors are important to a casual computer user: compatibility and speed.

Compatibility

Not all software is **compatible** with every CPU; that is, software written for one processor may not work with another. Every processor has a built-in *instruction set*—a vocabulary of instructions the processor can execute. CPUs in the same *family* are generally designed so newer processors can process all of the instructions

The Intel Pentium Pro CPU chip shown here (foreground) at about normal size reveals intricate circuitry when highly magnified (background).

The main circuit board of a typical PC contains the CPU, memory, and several other important chips and components.

handled by earlier models. For example, Intel's Pentium chip is *backward compatible* with the 486, 386, and 286 chips that preceded it, so it can run most software written for those older CPUs. But software written for the Power PC family of processors used in Macintosh computers won't run on the Intel processors found in most IBM-compatible computers; the Intel processors simply can't understand programs written for the Power PC CPUs. Similarly, the Macintosh Power PC processor can't run Windows software without some help from software or an additional processor. In Chapter 4 you'll see how software can overcome some incompatibility problems. But in general, compatibility is a function of the CPU.

Speed

There's a tremendous variation in how fast different processors can handle information. A computer's speed is determined in part by the speed of its internal *clock*—the timing device that produces electrical pulses to synchronize the computer's operations. Computers are often described in terms of their clock speeds, measured in units called *megahertz (MHz)*. But clock speed by itself doesn't adequately describe how fast a computer can process words, numbers, or pictures. Speed is also determined by the **architecture** of the processor—the design that determines how individual components of the CPU are put together on the chip. In fact, the architecture of the entire computer system is an important part in the speed equation.

From a user's point of view, the important point is that faster is better. Most computer applications, such as word processing, are more convenient to use on a faster machine. Many applications that use graphics and computations, such as some statistical programs and graphic design programs, *require* faster machines to produce results in any reasonable amount of time.

Because speed is so important, engineers and computer scientists are constantly developing techniques for speeding up a computer's ability to manipulate and move bits. In the interest of speed, many computer manufacturers are switching from *CISC* to *RISC* processors. Most of today's computers have complex instruction sets that include instructions that are seldom, if ever, used. Research has shown that these complex instruction set computer (CISC) processors are slower and less efficient than processors designed to execute fewer instructions. Today many supercomputers, workstations, and personal computers use **reduced instruction set computer (RISC)** processors. The most widely publicized example of a RISC processor is the Power PC processor developed by IBM in partnership with Apple and Motorola. Virtually all modern Macintoshes use a Power PC processor, and IBM and other manufacturers offer desktop machines built around this family of chips. Because of its RISC design, the Power PC processor is typically able to perform faster than a CISC chip with a similar clock speed. But the Power PC family of chips is relatively young, and hardware and software engineers are still developing better ways to take advantage of its radical new design. At the same time, Intel engineers have incorporated many speed-enhancing techniques, including a few RISC tricks, into the CISC-based Pentium and Pentium Pro processors built into most modern PCs. As a result, the speed differences between Power PC and Pentium systems are, at this point, relatively small.

Popular CPU families
and their systems

These CPU families . . .

are used in the computers from these manufacturers.

Intel
Pentium family

IBM/Motorola
Power PC family

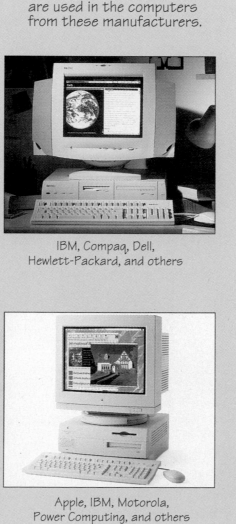

IBM, Compaq, Dell,
Hewlett-Packard, and others

Apple, IBM, Motorola,
Power Computing, and others

The CPU

Most computer users don't know anything about what goes on inside the CPU; they just use it. Throughout most of this book, we treat the CPU as a kind of black box that transforms information by following instructions. This How It Works box offers a peek inside that black box so you can get a feel for what makes your computer tick. Since the CPU functions as part of a larger collection of computer components, this How It Works box only tells part of the story; taken by itself, it may raise more questions than answers. But How It Works boxes later in this chapter and in the next two chapters will fill in many of the missing details of the inner workings of the modern computer. Read these boxes if you want the inside story.

4 The *decode unit* takes the instruction read by the prefetcher and translates it into a form suitable for the CPU's internal processing. It does this by "looking up" the steps required to complete an instruction in the *control unit*.

Control unit

Arithmetic logic unit

Decode unit

CPU

Prefetch unit

1 In most cases the actual execution of an instruction is performed by the *arithmetic logic unit (ALU)*. The ALU includes *registers,* each usually 32 or 64 bits in size.

2 Program instructions are stored in primary storage (memory), which is usually on chips outside the CPU. The CPU's first task is to read the instruction from memory. The *bus unit* handles all communication between the CPU and primary storage.

3 The *prefetch unit* instructs the bus unit to read the instruction stored at a particular memory address. This unit not only fetches the next instruction to be executed but also fetches several subsequent instructions to ensure that an instruction is always ready to go.

The central processing unit (CPU) is the component that executes the steps in a program, performing math and moving data from one part of the system to another. The CPU contains the circuitry to perform a variety of simple tasks, called *instructions*. An individual instruction does only a tiny amount of work. A typical instruction might be "Read the contents of memory location x and add the number y to it"). Most CPUs have a vocabulary of fewer than a thousand distinct instructions.

All computer programs are composed of instructions drawn from this tiny vocabulary. The typical computer program is composed of millions of instructions, and the CPU can execute millions of instructions every second. When a program runs, the rapid-fire execution of instructions creates an illusion of motion in the same way a movie simulates motion out of a sequence of still pictures.

The typical CPU is divided into several functional units. These units work together like workers on an assembly line to complete the execution of program instructions.

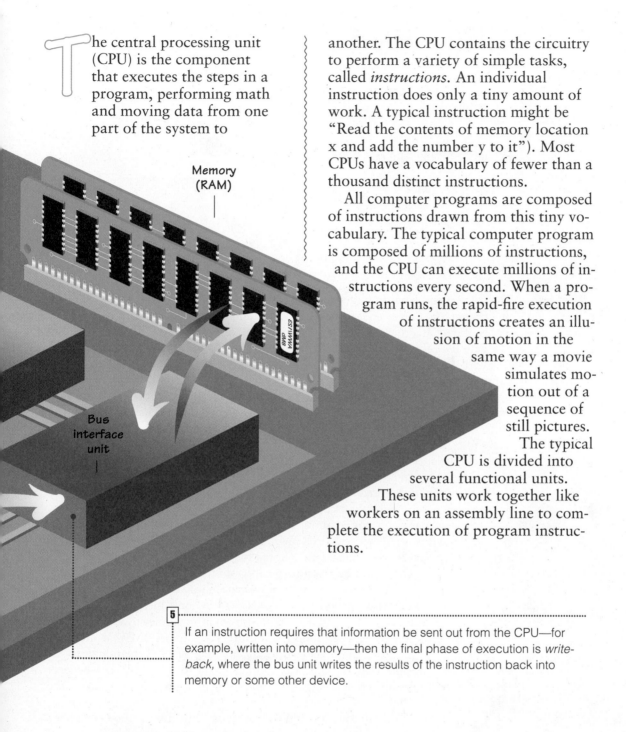

Memory (RAM)

AMWA1LSS
dM8

Bus interface unit

5 ⋯⋯⋯⋯⋯⋯⋯⋯⋯⋯⋯⋯⋯⋯⋯⋯⋯⋯⋯⋯⋯⋯⋯⋯⋯⋯⋯⋯⋯⋯⋯

If an instruction requires that information be sent out from the CPU—for example, written into memory—then the final phase of execution is *write-back,* where the bus unit writes the results of the instruction back into memory or some other device.

6 ⋯⋯

Microprocessor manufacturers use many techniques to eliminate bottlenecks and speed things up. For example, in the same way that the next likely instructions to be read are prefetched, the next likely *data* to be used is preread into a *cache* in memory (called a *level-2 cache*) or, for faster access, in the CPU itself (a *level-1 cache*).

Most RISC microprocessors and some advanced CISC processors use *superscalar architecture.* This means that the CPU has multiple instruction *pipelines* and, so long as two sequential instructions don't depend on one another, can execute multiple instructions simultaneously.

One common trick for improving a computer's performance is to put more than one processor in a computer. Many personal computers, for example, have specialized subsidiary processors that take care of mathematical calculations or graphics displays. Most supercomputers have several full-featured processors that can divide jobs into pieces and work in parallel on the pieces. This kind of processing, known as **parallel processing,** may soon be commonplace throughout the computing world.

Primary Storage: The Computer's Memory

"What's one and one and one and one and one and one and one and one and one and one and one?"

"I don't know," said Alice. "I lost count."

"She can't do addition," said the Red Queen.

—Lewis Carroll, in *Through the Looking Glass*

The CPU's main job is to follow the instructions encoded in programs. But like Alice in *Through the Looking Glass,* the CPU can handle only one instruction and a few pieces of data at a time. The computer needs a place to store the rest of the program and data until the processor is ready for them. That's what RAM is for.

RAM (random access memory) is the most common type of primary storage, or computer memory. RAM chips contain circuits that can be used to store program instructions and data temporarily. Each RAM chip is divided by the computer into many equal-sized memory locations. Memory locations, like houses, have unique addresses, so the computer can tell them apart when it is instructed to save or retrieve information. You can store a piece of information in any RAM location—you can pick one at random—and the computer can, if so instructed, quickly retrieve it. Hence the name random access memory.

The information stored in RAM is nothing more than a pattern of electrical current flowing through microscopic circuits in silicon chips. This means that when the power goes off, for whatever reason, the computer instantly forgets everything it was remembering in RAM. In technical terms RAM is called **volatile memory** because information stored there is not held permanently.

This could be a serious problem if the computer didn't have another type of memory to store information that's too important to lose. This **nonvolatile memory** is called **ROM** (read-only memory) because the computer can only read information from it; it can never write any new information on it. All modern computers include ROM that contains startup instructions and other critical information. The information in ROM was etched in when the chip was manufactured, so it is available whenever the computer is operating, but it can't be changed except by replacing the ROM chip.

ROM isn't always hidden away on chips inside the computer's chassis. Many home video game machines use removable **ROM cartridges** as permanent storage devices for games and other programs.

Other types of memory are available. *EPROM* (Erasable Programmable Read-Only Memory) is used in most PCs to store boot-up information, but it's too slow and difficult to change to be used for common memory tasks. *Flash RAM* chips are fast and can be erased and rewritten repeatedly, but they're still too expensive to replace RAM and other common storage media. Until prices come down or new technologies emerge, most computers will continue to depend on RAM and ROM. (The last chapter explores emerging memory technologies.)

The ROM cartridge inserted into this video game machine stores a game program in a permanent, unchangeable form.

Slots and ports allow the CPU to communicate with the outside world via peripheral devices. Here a circuit board is beinginserted into a slot. Several ports are visible on the back of the console.

A portable computer typically has one or more slots to accommodate credit-card-sized PC cards like this one.

Buses, Ports, and Peripherals

In a typical desktop computer, the CPU and memory chips are attached to circuit boards along with other key components. Information travels between components through groups of wires called **buses**. Buses typically have 8, 16, or 32 wires; a bus with 16 wires is called a *16-bit bus* because it can transmit 16 bits of information at once, twice as many as an 8-bit bus. Just as multilane freeways allow masses of cars to move faster than they could on single-lane roads, wider buses can transmit information faster than narrower buses. Newer, more powerful computers have wider buses so they can process information faster.

Some buses connect to **slots** inside the computer's housing. Users can customize their computers by inserting special-purpose circuit boards (usually called *cards* or just *boards*) into these slots. Other buses connect to external **ports**—sockets on the outside of the computer chassis. Because portable computers don't have room for full-sized cards, many have slots for **PC cards**—credit-card-sized cards that contain memory or peripherals. (When these cards were first released, they were known as PCMCIA cards. One writer suggested that this stood for "People Can't Memorize Computer Industry Acronyms." Thankfully, the name was shortened to PC cards.)

Slots and ports make it easy to add external devices, or peripherals, to the computer system so the CPU can communicate with the outside world and store information for later use. Without peripherals, CPU and memory together are like a brain without a body. Some peripherals, such as keyboards and printers, serve as communication links between people and computers. Other peripherals link the computer to other machines. Still others provide long-term storage media. In the next chapter we'll explore a variety of input, output, and storage peripherals.

Memory ⊙

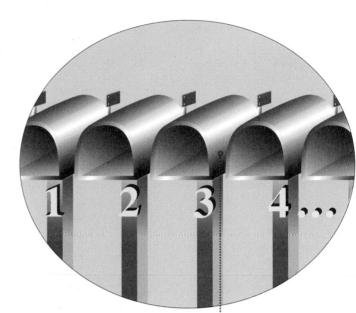

Memory is the work area of the CPU. Think of memory as millions of tiny storage cells, each of which can contain a single byte of information. The information in memory could be program instructions, numbers for arithmetic, codes representing text characters, a part of a picture, or other kinds of data.

Each byte has an address that identifies it and helps the CPU keep track of where things are stored. A typical personal computer has from 16 to 64 million bytes (16 to 64 megabytes) of memory.

2 Memory locations are like mailboxes. Each mailbox represents one address and holds 1 byte of information.

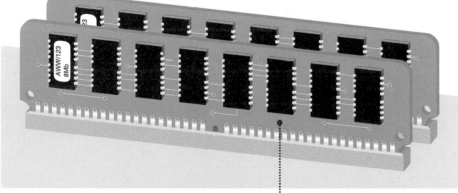

1 Memory chips are usually grouped together on small circuit boards called *SIMMs* (single in-line memory modules) and *DIMMs* (dual in-line memory modules) and are plugged into the main system board. This part represents a group of two SIMMs in a circuit board.

The CPU can *only* see into and access memory. Memory addresses make up the CPU's entire world, so any program that needs to be executed or data that needs to be modified must make its way into memory. Memory is composed of storage cells called *bytes*.

Most computer systems use *memory-mapped I/O,* where information for input and output are stored in special areas of memory. For example, information to be displayed on the monitor screen is written into a special range of memory addresses that is continually scanned by the video subsystem.

RAM

3
The executing instructions help the system start up and tell it how to *load* the operating system—copy it from disk into memory.

cpu

ROM

5
Once executing instructions are loaded into memory, the CPU is able to execute them.

4
When you turn on the computer, the CPU automatically begins executing instructions stored in read-only memory (ROM). On most computer systems, ROM also contains parts of the operating system. The firmware programs in ROM are sometimes called the *BIOS* (basic input/output system).

SUMMARY

Whether it's working with words, numbers, pictures, or sounds, a computer is manipulating patterns of bits—binary digits of information that can be stored in switching circuitry and represented by two symbols. Groups of bits can be treated as numbers for calculations using the binary number system. Bits can be grouped into coded messages that represent the alphabetic characters, pictures, colors, sounds, or just about any other kind of information. Even the instructions computers follow—the software programs that tell the computer what to do—must be reduced to strings of bits before the computer accepts them. Byte, kilobyte, megabyte, and other common units for measuring bit quantities are used in descriptions of memory, storage, and file size.

The central processing unit (CPU) follows software instructions to perform the calculations and logical manipulations that transform input data into output. Not all CPUs are compatible with each other; each is capable of processing a particular set of instructions, so a program written for one family of processors can't be understood by a processor from another family. Engineers are constantly improving the clock speed and architecture of CPUs, making computers capable of processing information faster. The fastest computers today use some combination of RISC processing and parallel processing.

The CPU uses RAM (random access memory) as a temporary storage area—a scratch pad—for instructions and data. Another type of primary storage, ROM (read-only memory), contains unchangeable information that serves as reference material for the CPU as it executes program instructions.

The CPU and main memory are housed in silicon chips on one or more circuit boards inside the computer. Buses connect to slots and ports that allow the computer to communicate with peripherals.

Chapter Review

Key Terms

architecture
ASCII
binary
bit
bus
byte
central processing unit (CPU)
circuit board
compatible
digital
file
GB (gigabyte)

information
input device
K (kilobyte)
MB (megabyte)
memory
nonvolatile memory
output device
parallel processing
PC card
peripheral
port
primary storage

processor
RAM (random access memory)
RISC (reduced instruction set computer)
ROM (read-only memory)
ROM cartridge
secondary storage
slot
storage device
TB (terabyte)
Unicode
volatile memory

Review Questions

1. Provide a working definition of each of the key words listed above. Check your answers in the glossary.

2. Draw a block diagram showing the major components of a computer and their relationship. Briefly describe the function of each component.

3. Think of this as computer input: 123.4

   This might be read by the computer as a number or a set of ASCII codes. Explain how these concepts differ.

4. Why is information stored in some kind of binary format in computers?

5. Why can't you normally run Macintosh software on a PC with an Intel Pentium CPU?

6. Clock speed is only one factor in determining a CPU's processing speed. What is another?

7. How does a RISC processor differ from a CISC processor?

8. Explain how parallel processing can increase a computer's speed; use an example or a comparison with the way people work if you like.

9. What is the difference between RAM and ROM? What is the purpose of each?

10. What is the difference between primary and secondary storage?

Discussion Questions

1. Why are computer manufacturers constantly releasing faster computers? How do computer users benefit from the speed increases?

2. How is human memory similar to computer memory? How is it different?

Projects

1. Collect computer advertisements from newspapers, magazines, and other sources. Compare how the ads handle discussions of speed. Evaluate the usefulness of the information in the ads from a consumer's point of view.

2. Interview a salesperson in a computer store. Find out what kinds of questions people ask when buying a computer. Develop profiles for the most common types of computer buyers. What kinds of computers do these customers buy, and why?

Sources and Resources

Books

How Computers Work, by Ron White (Emeryville, CA: PC/ Computing/Ziff-Davis Press, 1995). This first-in-a-series book clearly illustrates with beautiful pictures and clear writing how each component of a modern personal computer system works. If you're interested in looking under the hood, this is a great place to start. The book was produced on a Macintosh, but its explanations and illustrations are based on IBM-compatible computers. The latest edition includes a Windows-compatible CD-ROM called *How Multimedia Computers Work,* which uses animation, video, and sound to bring many of the concepts in the book to life.

How MACs Work, Bestseller Edition by John Rizzo and K. Daniel Clark (Emeryville, CA: Ziff-Davis Press, 1997). This book covers the basics of Macintosh anatomy in the same style as *How Computers Work,* but without the CD-ROM.

The Soul of a New Machine, by Tracy Kidder (Boston: Atlantic–Little, Brown, 1981). This award-winning book provides a journalist's inside look at the making of a new computer, including lots of insights into what makes computers (and computer people) tick.

Big Blues: The Unmaking of IBM, by Paul Carroll. (Crown) and *Computer Wars: The Fall of IBM and the Future of Global Technology,* by Charles H. Ferguson (Times Books). In recent years the post-Watson IBM has lost much of its power and influence; these two books explore that period of decline.

Ideas and Information: Managing in a High-Tech World, by Arno Penzias (New York: Norton, 1989). A highly intelligent and readable discussion of the relationship between computer technology and the people who develop and use it. This book is full of insights and examples to make computer hardware and software easier to understand.

World Wide Web Pages

Most computer hardware manufacturers have World Wide Web pages on the Internet. Use a web browser like Netscape Navigator to visit some of these sites for information about the latest hardware from these companies. It's not hard to guess the web addresses of computer companies; most follow the pattern suggested by these examples:

http://www.ibm.com

http://www.apple.com

http://www.compaq.com

The *Computer Confluence* Web site will guide you to these and other hardware pages of interest.

3

HARDWARE
BASICS
Peripherals

Steve Wozniak, Steve Jobs, and the Garage That Grew Apples

It's not like we were all smart enough to see a revolution coming. Back then, I thought there might be a revolution in opening your garage door, balancing your checkbook, keeping your recipes, that sort of thing. There are a million people who study markets and analyze economic trends, people who are more brilliant than I am, people who worked for companies like Digital Equipment and IBM and Hewlett-Packard. None of them foresaw what was going to happen, either.

—Steve Wozniak

What Steve Wozniak ("the Woz") and all those other people failed to foresee was the personal computer revolution—a revolution that he helped start. Wozniak, a brilliant engineer with an eye for detail, worked days as a calculator technician at Hewlett-Packard; he was refused an engineer's job because he lacked a college degree. At night he designed and constructed a scaled-down state-of-the-art computer system that would fit the home hobbyist's budget. When he completed the computer in 1975, he offered it to Hewlett-Packard, and they turned it down.

Wozniak took his invention to the Homebrew Computer Club in Palo Alto, where it caught the imagination of another college dropout, Steven Jobs. A free-thinking visionary, Jobs persuaded Wozniak to quit his job in 1976 to form a company and market the machine, which they named the Apple I. Jobs raised $1300 in seed capital by selling his Volkswagen, and Apple Computer, Inc., was born in Jobs' garage.

With the help and considerable financial backing of businessman A. C. Markkula, the two Steves turned Apple into a thriving business. Wozniak created the Apple II, a more refined machine for consumers, and invented the first personal computer disk operating system so computers wouldn't be dependent on cassette tapes for storage. More interested in engineering than management, Wozniak allowed Jobs to assume the leadership role in the company. Because it put computing power within everyone's

After reading this chapter, you should be able to:

~~~~~~

- List several examples of input devices and explain how they can make it easier to get different types of information into the computer
- List several examples of output devices and explain how they make computers more useful
- Explain why a typical computer has different types of storage devices
- Diagram how the components of a typical computer system fit together and interact

reach, the Apple II became popular in businesses, homes, and especially schools. Apple became the first company in American history to join the Fortune 500 in less than five years. Still in his mid-twenties, Jobs was running a corporate giant. But troubled times were ahead for Apple.

When IBM introduced its PC in 1982, it quickly overshadowed Apple's presence in the business world, where people were accustomed to working with IBM mainframes. Other companies developed PC clones, treating the IBM PC as a standard—a standard that Apple refused to accept. Inspired by a visit to Xerox's Palo Alto Research Center (PARC), Jobs worked with a team of Apple engineers to develop the Macintosh, a futuristic computer he hoped would leapfrog IBM's advantage. When Jobs insisted on fo-

cusing most of Apple's resources on the Macintosh, Wozniak resigned to pursue noncomputer interests.

However, businesses failed to embrace the Mac, and Apple's stockholders grew uneasy with Jobs's controversial management style. In 1985, a year and a half after the Macintosh was introduced, Jobs was ousted from power by president John Sculley. Jobs went on to form NeXT, a company that produced powerful,

easy-to-use UNIX workstations and now produces software. He also owns Pixar, the computer animation company that captured the public's attention with *Toy Story*, the first computer-generated full-length motion picture. Today Apple still struggles to increase its market share in a world dominated by IBM-compatible PCs. At the same time, Apple retains a reputation for innovation.

Steve Wozniak and Steve Jobs

The Apple II's phenomenal success wasn't due to a powerful processor or massive memory; the machine had at its core a relatively primitive processor and only 16K of memory. The Apple II was more than a processor and memory; it included a keyboard, a monitor, and disk and tape drives for storage. While other companies sold computer kits to tinkerers, the two Steves delivered complete computer systems to hobbyists, schools, and businesses. They recognized that a computer isn't complete without peripherals.

In this chapter we'll complete the tour of hardware we started in the last chapter. We've seen the CPU and memory at the heart of the system unit; now we'll explore the peripherals that radiate out from those central components. We'll start with input devices, then move on to output devices, and finish with a look at external storage devices. As usual, the main text will provide the basic overview; if you want or need to know more about the inner workings, consult the How It Works boxes scattered throughout the chapter.

INPUT: FROM PERSON TO PROCESSOR

The computer is by all odds the most extraordinary of the technological clothing ever devised by man, since it is an extension of our central nervous system. Beside it the wheel is a mere hula hoop . . . .

—Marshall McLuhan, in *War and Peace in the Global Village*

The nuts and bolts of information processing are usually hidden from the user, who sees only the input and output, or as the pros say, *I/O*. This wasn't always the case. Users of the first computers communicated 1 bit at a time by flipping switches on massive consoles or plugging wires into switchboards; they had to be intimately familiar with the inner workings of the machines before they could successfully communicate with them. In contrast, today's users have a choice of hundreds of input devices that make it easy to enter data and commands into their machines. Of all these devices, the most familiar is the computer keyboard.

The Omnipresent Keyboard

Typing letters, numbers, and special characters with a computer **keyboard** is similar to typing on a standard typewriter keyboard. But unlike a typewriter, the computer responds by displaying the typed characters on the screen at the position of the line or rectangle called the **cursor.** Some keys—*cursor (arrow) keys,* the *Delete key,* or the *Enter key, function keys (f-keys),* and others—send special commands to the computer, and these keys may have different names or meanings on different computer systems. Some of the most important keys are shown in the User's View box to the right.   UV

In spite of nearly universal acceptance as an input device, the QWERTY keyboard (named for the first row of letter keys) seems strangely out of place in a modern computer system. The original arrangement of the keys, chosen to reduce the likelihood of jammed keys on early typewriters, stays with us a century later, forcing millions of people to learn an awkward system just so they can enter text into their computers. Many improvements to the basic keyboard design have been conceived, tested, and shown to be superior and easier to learn than the classic QWERTY keyboard. But technological traditions die hard, and few people are willing or able to use nonstandard keyboards today. Still, as alternative input devices emerge, the role of the keyboard is changing.

The User's View

Working with a Keyboard
▲ ▲

Keyboarding on a computer is pretty much like typing, except that certain keys send codes that have special meaning to the computer or terminal. This figure shows a typical keyboard on an IBM-compatible PC. Keyboards for Macintoshes and other types of systems have a few differences but operate on the same principles.

Function keys (f-keys), labeled F1, F2, and so on, send signals to the computer that have no inherent meaning. The function of these keys depends on the software being used. F1 might mean "Save file" to one program and "Delete file" to another. In other words, function keys are programmable.

Backspace on a PC tells the computer to delete the character just typed (or the one to the left of the cursor on the screen, or the currently selected data.)

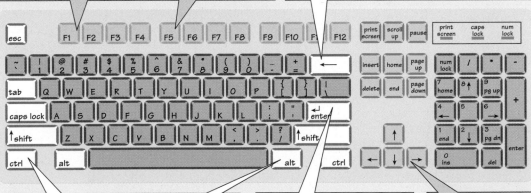

Control and Alt are modifier keys that cause nothing to happen by themselves but change the meaning of other keys. When you hold down a modifier key while pressing another key, the combination makes that other key behave differently. For example, typing S while holding down the Control key might send a command to save the current document.

Enter sends a signal telling the computer or terminal to move the cursor to the beginning of the next line on the screen. For many applications, this key also "enters" the line just typed, telling the computer to process it.

Cursor (arrow) keys are used to move the cursor up, down, left, or right.

Pointing Devices

Millions of computer users today use their keyboards mostly for entering text and numeric data. For other traditional keyboard functions, like sending commands and positioning the cursor, they use a **mouse.** The mouse is designed to move a pointer around the screen and point to specific characters or objects. The most common type of mouse has a ball on its underside that allows it to roll around on the desktop. As the mouse moves, the pointer on the screen mimics the mouse's motion.

Working with a Mouse

▲ ▲

As you slide the mouse across your desktop, a pointer echoes your movements on the screen. You can **click** the mouse—press the button while the mouse is stationary—or **drag** it—move it while holding the button down. (On a two-button mouse, the left button is usually used for clicking and dragging.) These two techniques can be used to perform a variety of operations.

Clicking the Mouse:

If the pointer points to an on-screen button, clicking the mouse presses the button.

⚠ You still have items in your Out Basket.

Do you want to send the items before disconnecting?

[Don't Send]   [Cancel]   [**Send**]

If the pointer points to a picture of a tool or object on the screen, clicking the mouse selects the tool or object; for example, clicking on the pencil tool allows you to draw with the mouse.

If the pointer points to a part of a text document, it turns from an arrow into an I-beam; clicking repositions the flashing cursor.

Jack fell down and I
Jill came tumbling
after.

Dragging the Mouse:

If you hold the button down while you drag the mouse with a selected graphic tool (like a paintbrush), you can draw by remote control.

If you drag the mouse from one point in a text document to another, you select all the text between those two points so you can modify or move it. For example, you might select this movie title so you could italicize it.

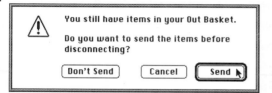
The zany Duck Soup I captured the Marx Brothers at their peak.

You can drag the mouse to select a command from a menu of choices. For example, this command would italicize the text you selected above.

Style	
✓Plain Text	⌘T
Bold	⌘B
Italic	⌘I
Underline	⌘U
Strike Thru	
Outline	
Shadow	
Condense	
Extend	
Superscript	⇧⌘+
Subscript	⇧⌘-
Text Color	▶
Define Styles...	

The mouse has one or more buttons that can be used to send signals to the computer, conveying messages like "Perform this command," "Activate the selected tool," and "Select all the text between these two points." The User's View box above shows a few examples. **UV**

Millions of computer users function efficiently without the use of a mouse. Still, there's clear evidence that this plastic rodent can make us more productive—so much so that it's virtually impossible to find a new computer today that doesn't come with a mouse as standard equipment. There's an exception: The mouse is impractical as a pointing device on portable computers, because these machines are often used where there's no room for a mouse to roam across a desktop. Portable computer manufacturers provide a variety of alternatives to the mouse as a general-purpose pointing device:

- The **trackball** is something like an upside-down mouse. It remains stationary while the user moves the protruding ball to control the pointer on the screen. (Trackballs are also available as space-saving mouse alternatives for desktop machines.)

- The **touch pad** is a small flat panel that's sensitive to light pressure. The user moves the pointer by dragging a finger across the pad.

- The **track point** is a tiny handle that sits unobtrusively in the center of the keyboard, responding to finger pressure by moving the mouse in the direction it's pushed. It's like a tiny embedded joystick (see below).

Other pointing devices offer advantages for specific types of computer work (and play). Here are some examples:

- The **joystick** is a gearshift-like device that's a favorite controller for arcade-style computer games.

- The **graphics tablet** is particularly popular with artists and designers. The best touch tablets are pressure sensitive, so they can send different signals depending on how hard the user presses on the tablet with a stylus.

- The **touch screen** can respond when the user points to or touches different screen regions. Computers with touch screens are frequently used in places where many users are unfamiliar with computers, such as in public libraries, airports, and stores.

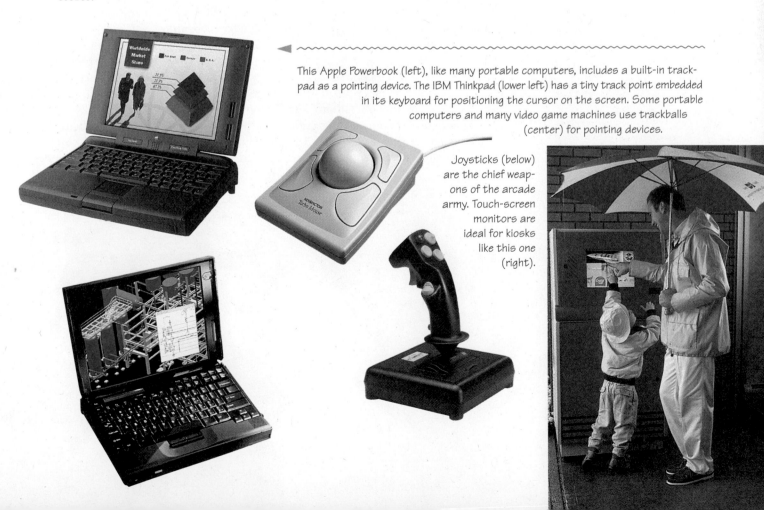

This Apple Powerbook (left), like many portable computers, includes a built-in track-pad as a pointing device. The IBM Thinkpad (lower left) has a tiny track point embedded in its keyboard for positioning the cursor on the screen. Some portable computers and many video game machines use trackballs (center) for pointing devices.

Joysticks (below) are the chief weapons of the arcade army. Touch-screen monitors are ideal for kiosks like this one (right).

Reading Tools

In spite of their versatility, pointing devices are woefully inadequate for the input of text and numbers into computers, which is why the mouse hasn't replaced the keyboard on the standard personal computer. Still, there are alternatives to typing large quantities of data. Some input devices provide the computer with limited ability to "read" directly from paper, converting printed information into bit patterns that can be processed by the computer. Some reading devices are uniquely qualified for specific everyday tasks:

Computers use specialized input devices to read information stored as optical marks, bar codes, and specially designed characters.

- **Optical-mark readers** use reflected light to determine the location of pencil marks on standardized test answer sheets and similar forms.

- **Bar-code readers** use light to read universal product codes (UPCs), inventory codes, and other codes created out of patterns of variable-width bars.

- **Magnetic-ink character readers** read those odd-shaped numbers printed with magnetic ink on checks.

- **Wand readers** use light to read alphabetic and numeric characters written in a specially designed typeface found on many sales tags and credit card slips. People can read text created in this typeface, too. In many stores wand readers are attached to **point-of-sale (POS) terminals.** These terminals send information scanned by the wand to a mainframe computer. The computer determines the item price, calculates taxes and totals, and records the transaction for future use in inventory, accounting, and other areas.

When wand readers are used to recognize words and numbers at a POS terminal, the computer is performing **optical character recognition (OCR)**. Point-of-sale OCR is a far cry from reading the *New York Times* or *Huckleberry Finn*. A computer *can* read text from a book, newspaper, magazine, or letter, but the process requires artificial intelligence techniques, and it's far from foolproof. Recognizing handwriting is even more difficult, but the technology is progressing rapidly. Handwriting recognition and OCR are described in more detail in a later chapter.

Handwritten text analysis is critical in a **pen-based computer.** This keyboardless machine accepts input from a stylus applied directly to a flat-panel screen. It electronically simulates a pen and pad of paper. In addition to serving as a pointing de-

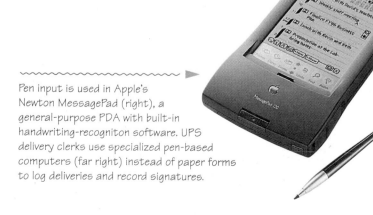

Pen input is used in Apple's Newton MessagePad (right), a general-purpose PDA with built-in handwriting-recogniton software. UPS delivery clerks use specialized pen-based computers (far right) instead of paper forms to log deliveries and record signatures.

Hand-held scanners (left), flatbed scanners (center), and sheet-fed scanners (right) serve the same purpose: to capture and digitize images from external paper sources.

vice, the pen can be used as a writing stylus, but only if the computer's software can decipher the user's handwriting. As OCR technology improves, pen-based systems are becoming popular with information workers who spend lots of time filling out forms and with people who lack typing skills. But many people think the real future of pen-based technology is in *personal digital assistants (PDAs),* which will serve as pocket-sized organizers, notebooks, appointment books, and communication devices for people on the go.

Digitizing the Real World

Before a computer can recognize handwriting, it must first **digitize** the information—convert it into a digital form that can be stored in the computer's memory. Since real-world information comes in so many forms, a variety of input devices have been designed for capturing and digitizing information.

A **scanner** is an input device that can make a digital representation of any printed image. Scanners are available in several sizes and shapes. The most common models today are *flatbed scanners,* which look and work like photocopy machines. Hand-held scanners look like tiny vacuum cleaners for sucking images from paper. One type of *sheet-fed scanner* is designed to sit between your keyboard and monitor, turning on whenever you insert paper into a slot. Some scanners can capture color images; less expensive models convert images to shades of gray. Regardless of its type or capabilities, however, a scanner converts photographs, drawings, charts, and other printed information into bit patterns that can be stored and manipulated in a computer's memory using software described in Chapter 7.

In the same way, a **digital camera** can be used to capture snapshots of the real world as digital images. Unlike a scanner, a digital camera isn't limited to capturing flat printed images; it can record anything that a normal camera can. A digital camera looks like a normal camera. But instead of capturing images on film, a digital

Digitizing the Real World

We live in an *analog* world, where we can perceive smooth, continuous changes in color and sound. Modern *digital* computers store all information as discrete binary numbers. To store analog information, such as an analog sound or image, in a computer we must *digitize* it—convert it from analog to digital form.

Scanners

A typical desktop scanner contains a camera similar to the kind found in many video camcorders. The scanner camera moves back and forth across an original image, recording for each sample the intensities of red, green, and blue light at that point. (Human eyes have receptors for red, green, and blue light; all colors are perceived as combinations of these three.)

A single byte is commonly used to represent the intensity of each color component; a 3-byte (24-bit) code represents the color for each sample. The scanner sends each digital code to the computer where it can be stored and manipulated.

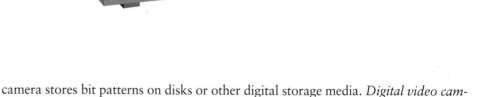

camera stores bit patterns on disks or other digital storage media. *Digital video cameras* can capture video signals in the same way; digital video is used for multimedia (Chapter 7) and desktop videoconferencing (Chapter 9).

Audio digitizers contain circuitry to digitize sounds from microphones and other audio devices. Digitized sounds can be stored in a computer's memory and modified with software described in Chapter 8. Of course, audio digitizers can capture spoken words as well as music and sound effects. But digitizing spoken input isn't the same thing as converting speech into text. Like scanned text input, digitized voice input requires artificial intelligence software to be correctly interpreted by the computer as words. The promise and problems of automated speech recognition will be described in a later chapter.

The visual equivalent of the audio digitizer is the *video digitizer.* A video digitizer is a collection of circuits that can capture input from a video camera, video cassette recorder, television, or other video source and convert it to a digital signal that

Digitizing involves using an input device, such as a desktop scanner or audio board, to take millions of tiny *samples* of the original. A sample of an image might be one pinpoint-sized area of the image; each sample from an audio source is like a brief recording of the sound at a particular instant.

The value of a sample can be represented numerically and therefore stored on a computer. A representation of the original image or sound can be reconstructed by assembling all the samples in sequence.

Audio Digitizers

Digital audio is commonplace today; the CD player is really a computer system designed to translate digital information on a compact disc into analog signals that can be amplified and sent to speakers.

In digital audio recording using a personal computer, sound waves vibrate the diaphragm of a microphone connected to the computer, usually through a sound card. The position of the microphone diaphragm is sampled frequently—as much as 44,000 times each second—and its level is stored as a number.

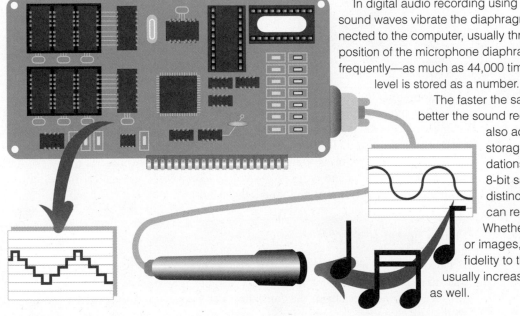

The faster the sampling frequency, the better the sound recording. Better sound is also achieved by using more storage to represent finer gradations of the sound level. An 8-bit sample can represent 256 distinct levels; a 16-bit sample can represent 65,536 levels. Whether digitizing sounds or images, attempts to increase fidelity to the original will usually increase storage requirements as well.

can be stored in memory and displayed on computer screens. Chapter 7 describes a variety of video applications for computers.

Sensing devices designed to monitor temperature, humidity, pressure, and other physical quantities provide data used in robotics, environmental climate control, weather forecasting, medical monitoring, biofeedback, scientific research, and hundreds of other applications.

Computers can accept input from a variety of other sources, including manufacturing equipment, telephones, communication networks, and other computers. New input devices are being developed all the time as technologies evolve and human needs change. By stretching the computer's capabilities, these devices stretch our imaginations to develop new ways of using computers. We'll consider some of the more interesting and exotic technologies later; now we'll turn our attention to the output end of the process.

Digital cameras turn real-world scenes into digital images that can be stored and manipulated by the computer.

OUTPUT: FROM PULSES TO PEOPLE

We swim in a sea of information.

—Gary Snyder, poet

A computer can do all kinds of things, but none of them are worth anything to us unless we have a way to get the results out of the box. A variety of output devices give computers the power to convert their internal bit patterns into a form that humans can understand. The first computers were limited to flashing lights, teletypewriters, and other primitive communication devices. Most computers today produce output through two main types of devices: *video monitor screens* for immediate visual output and *printers* for permanent paper output.

Screen Output

A **video monitor,** or **video display terminal (VDT),** makes it possible for a computer user to see input characters as they're typed, but it also serves as an output device for receiving messages from the computer. Early computer monitors were designed to display characters—text, numbers, and tiny graphic symbols. Today's monitors are as likely to display graphics, photographic images, animation, and video as they are to display text and numbers. Because of the monitor's ever-expanding role as a graphical output device, computer users need to know a bit about the factors that control image size and quality.

The monitor is connected to the computer by way of the *video adapter,* which is a circuit board inside the main system unit. An image you see on the monitor exists inside the computer in *video memory,* or *VRAM,* a special portion of RAM dedicated to holding video images. The more video memory a computer has, the more detail it can present in a picture. The typical personal computer has between 2 and 8 megabytes of video memory.

Monitor size, like television size, is usually measured as the length of a diagonal line across the screen; a typical desktop monitor today is about 15 inches. Images on a monitor are composed of tiny dots, called **pixels** (for picture elements). A square inch of an image on a typical monitor is a grid of dots about 72 pixels on each side. Such a monitor is sometimes said to have a **resolution** of 72 dots per inch (dpi). The higher the resolution, the closer together the dots.

Another way to talk about *resolution* is to refer to the total number of pixels displayed on the screen. Assuming that two monitors are the same size, the one that displays the dots closest together displays more pixels—and has a sharper, clearer display. When describing resolution in this way, people usually indicate the number of columns and rows of pixels rather than the total number of pixels. For example, a 1024x768 image is composed of 1024 columns by 768 rows of pixels, for a total of 786,432 pixels. The most common monitor resolution today is 640x480, but higher-resolution monitors are quickly becoming the norm.

Resolution isn't the only factor in determining image quality. Computer monitors are limited by *color depth*—the number of different colors they can display at the same time. Color depth is sometimes called *bit depth* because a wider range of colors per pixel takes up more bits of space in video memory. For example, on a **monochrome monitor,** an image uses 1 bit of memory for each pixel, because each pixel can display two possible colors (usually black and white); the color depth is two. If each pixel is allotted 8 bits of memory, the resulting image can have up to 256 different colors on-screen at a time. (There are 256 unique combinations of 8 bits to use as color codes.) In other words, 8-bit color, typical of desktop computers today, has a color depth of 256. Many graphics professionals use 24-bit color, or *true color,* because it allows more than 16 million color choices per pixel—more than enough for photo-realistic images.

Monochrome monitors can only display monochrome images. **Gray-scale monitors** (which can display black, white, and shades of gray but no other colors) and color monitors (which can display a range of colors) have greater color depth. Sometimes the color depth is appended to the resolution to give a concise description of the video capability: 800x600x256 means an 800x600-pixel display composed of up to 256 different colors.

Many computer systems can display different combinations of resolution and color depth on the same *multisynch* monitor. Since there's a fixed amount of video memory in the system, an increase in color depth means a decrease in resolution. For example, a computer system might be able to switch a monitor's display back and forth from 800x600x16M to 1280x1024x16.

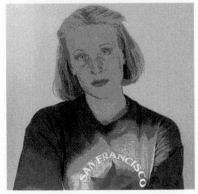

These four images show the same photograph displayed in four different bit depths: 1 bit, 4 bit, 8 bit, and 16 bit.

Color Video

The colors in some CRT video images glow because the monitor is a luminous source of light using *additive color synthesis*—colors are formed by adding together different amounts of red, green, and blue light.

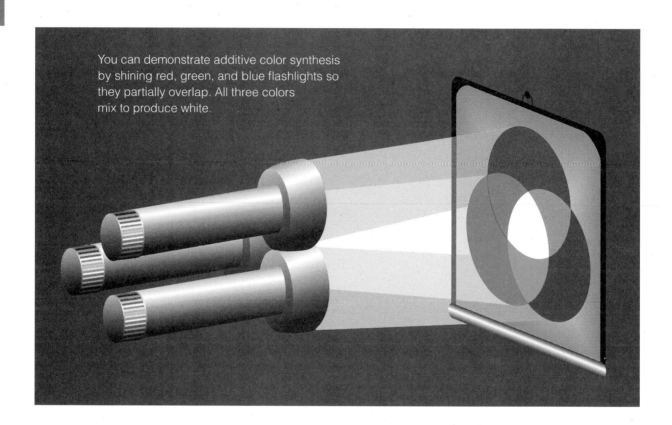

You can demonstrate additive color synthesis by shining red, green, and blue flashlights so they partially overlap. All three colors mix to produce white.

Most monitors fall into one of two classes: television-style **CRT (cathode ray tube) monitors** and flat-panel **LCD (liquid crystal display) monitors**. Because of their clarity, speedy response time, and low cost, CRTs are the overwhelming favorite for desktop computers. Lighter, more compact LCDs dominate the portable computer market and are also widely used in *overhead projection panels* and *video projectors*. But as LCDs improve in quality and come down in price, they are turning up on more and more desktops. Both types are available in color, gray-scale, or monochrome models in a variety of sizes. As you might expect, large color monitors are considerably more expensive than small monochrome models. They also require more video memory.

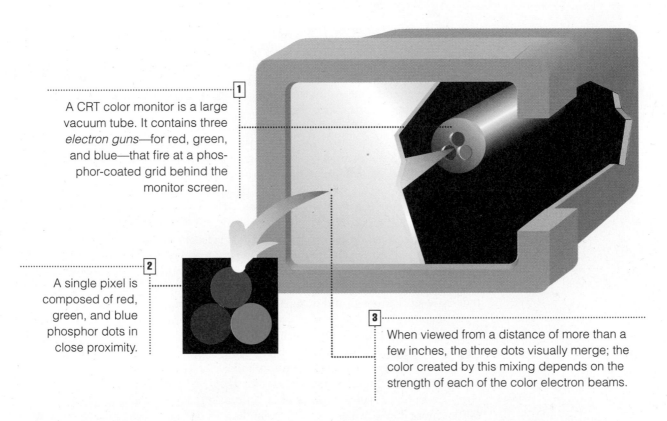

1 A CRT color monitor is a large vacuum tube. It contains three *electron guns*—for red, green, and blue—that fire at a phosphor-coated grid behind the monitor screen.

2 A single pixel is composed of red, green, and blue phosphor dots in close proximity.

3 When viewed from a distance of more than a few inches, the three dots visually merge; the color created by this mixing depends on the strength of each of the color electron beams.

Like television sets, computer monitors *refresh* or update their images many times per second. If a monitor refreshes its image fewer than 70 times per second (70 hertz), the flicker may be enough to cause eye strain, headaches, and nausea.

Many monitors slow down their refresh rates if the resolution is increased, so if you're shopping for a monitor, buy one with a refresh rate of more than 70 hertz at the maximum resolution you expect to be using.

This LCD projector allows the presenter to show a roomful of people the images displayed on her computer screen.

Paper Output

Output displayed on a monitor is immediate but temporary. A **printer** allows a computer user to produce a **hard copy** on paper of any information that can be displayed on the computer's screen. Printers come in several varieties, but they all fit into two basic groups: *impact printers* and *nonimpact printers*.

Impact printers include line printers and dot-matrix printers. Printers of this type share one common characteristic: They form images by physically striking paper, ribbon, and print hammer together, the way a typewriter does. **Line printers** are used by mainframes to produce massive printouts; these speedy, noisy beasts hammer out hundreds of lines of text per second. You've undoubtedly seen plenty of form letters, bills, and report cards printed with line printers. Because they're limited to printing characters, line printers are inadequate for applications like desktop publishing, where graphics are an essential ingredient in the finished product.

Dot-matrix printers print text and graphics with equal ease. Instead of printing each character as a solid object, a dot-matrix printer uses pinpoint-sized hammers to transfer ink to the page. The printed page is a matrix of tiny dots, some white and some black (or, for color printers, other colors). It's almost as if the computer were hammering bits directly on the page. The final printout might be a picture, text, or a combination of the two. With most dot-matrix printers you have to sacrifice print quality for flexibility. A typical dot-matrix printer produces printouts with resolution—relative closeness of dots—of less than 100 dots per inch (dpi), so the dots that make up characters and pictures are obvious to even casual readers.

Except for those applications where multipart forms need to be printed, **nonimpact printers** are gradually replacing impact printers in most offices. **Laser printers** use the same technology as photocopy machines: A laser beam creates patterns of electrical charges on a rotating drum; those charged patterns attract black toner and transfer it to paper as the drum rotates. **Ink-jet printers** spray ink directly onto paper. Both types typically produce output with much higher resolution—usually 600 or more dots per inch—than is possible with dot-matrix models. At these resolutions it's hard to tell with the naked eye that characters are, in fact, composed of

Dot matrix printers (left), ink jet printers (middle), and laser printers (right), provide different forms of hard copy output.

Color Printing

Printed colors can't be as vivid as video colors because printed images don't produce light like a video monitor does; they only *reflect* light. Most color printers use *subtractive synthesis* to produce colors: Various amounts of cyan (light blue), magenta (reddish purple), yellow, and black pigments are mixed to create a color.

Most printers, like monitors, are *raster* devices—they form images from little dots. The resolution of raster printers is normally measured in dots per inch (dpi). Typical laser printers have resolutions of between 300 and 1200 dpi.

More expensive printers have resolutions of 1200 to 5000 dpi.

Matching on-screen color with printed color is difficult because monitors use additive color synthesis to obtain the color, whereas printers use subtractive synthesis. Monitors are able to display more colors than printers, though printers can display a few colors that monitors can't. But the range of colors that humans can perceive extends beyond either technology.

You can demonstrate subtractive synthesis by painting overlapping areas of cyan, magenta, and yellow ink. The combination of all three is black; combinations of pairs produce red, green, and blue, which are the secondary colors of the subtractive system.

dots. Because of their ability to print high-resolution text and pictures, nonimpact printers are widely used in publishing and other graphics-intensive applications.

For certain scientific and engineering applications, a **plotter** is more appropriate than a printer for producing hard copy. A plotter is, in effect, an automated drawing tool that can produce finely scaled drawings by moving the pen and/or the paper in response to computer commands.

Output You Can Hear

Computer output isn't all visual. Computers can produce sounds, too. *Synthesizers,* which are little more than specialized computers designed to generate sounds electronically, can be used to produce music, noise, or anything in between. Many personal computers have built-in synthesizers for producing sounds that go beyond the basic beep. On IBM-compatible multimedia computers, these built-in synthesizers are included in *sound cards* along with other audio hardware; all Macintoshes include sound synthesis capabilities without additional boards. Just about any

Ergonomics and Health

Along with the benefits of computer technology comes the potential for unwelcome side effects. For people who work long hours with computers, the side effects include risks to health and safety due to radiation emissions, repetitive-stress injuries, or other computer-related health problems. Inconclusive evidence suggests that low-level radiation emitted by video display terminals (VDTs) and other equipment might cause health problems, including miscarriages in pregnant women and leukemia. The scientific jury is still out, but the mixed research results so far have led many computer users and manufacturers to err on the side of caution.

More concrete evidence relates keyboarding to occurrences of **repetitive-stress injuries** like *carpal tunnel syndrome,* a painful affliction of the wrist and hand that results from repeating the same movements over long periods. Prolonged computer use also increases the likelihood of headaches, eyestrain, fatigue, and other symptoms of "technostress."

Ergonomics (sometimes called *human engineering*) is the science of designing work environments that allow people and things to interact efficiently and safely. Ergonomic studies suggest preventive measures you can take to protect your health as you work with computers:

- **Choose equipment that's ergonomically designed.** When you're buying computer equipment, look beyond functionality. Use magazine reviews, manufacturer's information, and personal research to check on health-related factors like monitor radiation and glare, disk-drive

Ergonomic keyboards like this one allow computer users to hold their hands and arms in more natural positions while typing to reduce the risk of repetitive strain injuries.

noise levels, and keyboard layout. A growing number of computer products, like split, angled keyboards, are specifically designed to reduce the risk of equipment-related injuries.
- **Create a healthy workspace.** Keep the paper copy of your work at close to the same height as your screen. Position your monitor and lights to minimize glare. Sit at arm's length from your monitor to minimize radiation risks.

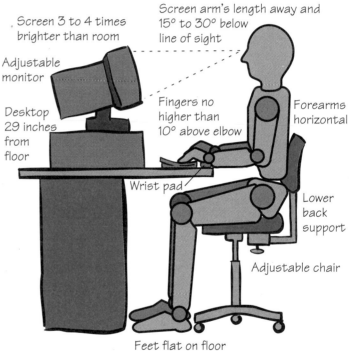

Screen 3 to 4 times brighter than room

Screen arm's length away and 15° to 30° below line of sight

Adjustable monitor

Desktop 29 inches from floor

Fingers no higher than 10° above elbow

Forearms horizontal

Wrist pad

Lower back support

Adjustable chair

Feet flat on floor

- **Rest your eyes.** Take a 15-minute break from using a VDT every two hours. Look up from the screen periodically and focus on a far-away object or scene. Blink frequently.
- **Build flexibility into your work environment.** Whenever possible work with an adjustable chair, an adjustable table, an adjustable monitor, and a removable keyboard. Change your work position frequently.
- **Listen to your body.** If you feel uncomfortable, your body is telling you to change something or take a break. Don't ignore it.

Laurie Anderson is one of many musicians who relies heavily on computers and synthesizers for composing and performing music.

computer can be connected to a stand-alone synthesizer so the computer has complete control of the instrument. And with appropriate hardware, a computer can play digital recordings of all kinds of sounds. Of course, to produce any kind of sound, the computer needs to include or be attached to one or more speakers. Chapter 7 explores sound output applications in more detail.

Controlling Other Machines

In the same way many input devices convert real-world sights and sounds into digital pulses, many output devices work in the other direction, taking bit patterns and turning them into nondigital movements or measurements. Robot arms, telephone switchboards, transportation devices, automated factory equipment, spacecraft, and a host of other machines and systems accept their orders from computers. And, of course, computers can send information directly to other computers, bypassing human interaction altogether. The possibilities for computer output are limited only by the technology and the human imagination, both of which are stretching further all the time.

Computers control the movements of this and every spacecraft.

SECONDARY STORAGE: INPUT AND OUTPUT

A retentive memory may be a good thing, but the ability to forget is the true token of greatness.

—Elbert Hubbard

Some computer peripherals are capable of performing both input and output functions. These devices, which include tape and disk drives, serve as *secondary storage* for the computer. Unlike RAM, which forgets everything whenever the computer is turned off, and ROM, which can't learn anything new, secondary storage devices allow the computer to record information semipermanently, so it can be read later by the same computer or by another computer.

Magnetic Tape

Tape drives are common storage devices on most mainframe computers and some personal computers. The reason for the widespread use of **magnetic tape** as a storage medium is clear: A typical magnetic tape can store massive amounts of information in a small space at a relatively low cost. The spinning tape reels that symbolized computers in so many science fiction movies have mostly been replaced by tape cartridges on modern mainframes. **Digital audio tape (DAT)** is the preferred tape for storage on small computers.

Magnetic tape has one clear limitation: Tape is a **sequential access** medium. Whether a tape holds music or computer data, the user must zip through information in the order in which it was recorded. Retrieving information from the middle of a tape is far too time-consuming for most modern computer applications because people expect immediate response to their commands. As a result, magnetic tape is used today mostly for backup of data and a few other operations that aren't time sensitive.

Magnetic Disks

Fortunately there's a readily available alternative to tape as a storage medium: the **magnetic disk.** A computer's **disk drive** can rapidly retrieve information from any part of a magnetic disk without regard for the order in which the information was recorded, in the same way you can quickly select any track on an audio compact disc (CD). Because of their **random access** capability, disks are far and away the most popular media for everyday storage needs.

Most computer users are familiar with the **diskette** (or **floppy disk**)—a small, magnetically sensitive, flexible plastic wafer housed in a plastic case. Most personal computers include at least one disk drive that allows the computer to write to and read from diskettes. As a result, diskettes are an almost universal currency for transferring information between machines and for packaging commercial software.

Diskettes are inexpensive, convenient, and reliable, but they lack the storage capacity and drive speed for many large jobs. Most users rely on hard disks as their primary storage devices. A **hard disk** is a rigid, magnetically sensitive disk that spins rapidly and continuously inside the computer chassis or in a separate box connected to the computer housing; this type of hard disk is never removed by the user. While a typical diskette has a storage capacity of between 1 and 3MB, a hard disk might hold hundreds or thousands of megabytes of information. Information can be transferred quickly to and from a hard disk much faster than with a diskette.

To fill the gap between low-capacity diskettes and nonremovable hard disks, many manufacturers have come up with high-capacity transportable storage solu-

A technician removes a tape from a tape drive. Tape reels like this one have been replaced at most institutions by smaller, more reliable cartridges.

This portable ZIP drive can store roughly 100 megabytes of information—about 70 diskettes' worth—on a removable disk cartridge about the size of a standard diskette.

tions. Usually referred to by brand names (such as SyQuest Cartridges, Bernoulli Cartridges, and Zip Cartridges) or by the generic term **removable media,** these disks generally use a modified form of the technology used in hard disks. One popular type, called **magneto-optical (MO) disks,** use a combination of magnetic disk technology and optical disk technology.

Optical Disks

As multimedia applications become more commonplace, even the large storage capacity of a hard disk can be quickly gobbled up by sounds, color pictures, video sequences, and other storage-intensive items. For these kinds of applications, **optical disks** provide an attractive storage alternative. An **optical disk drive** uses laser beams rather than magnets to read and write bits of information on the disk surface. While they currently aren't as fast as magnetic hard disks, optical disks have considerably more room for storing data. People who use optical disks often talk in terms of gigabytes.

CD-ROM (compact *disc—read*-only *memory*) drives are optical drives capable of reading CD-ROMs—data disks that are physically identical to musical compact discs. (The similarity of audio and data CDs is no accident; it makes it possible for CD-ROM drives to play music CDs under computer control.) A CD-ROM can hold the contents of an encyclopedia, including pictures, with room to spare for sounds and video clips. One secretary typing 90 words per minute, 8 hours per day, would take more than 8 years to type enough text to fill a single CD-ROM. But since CD-ROM drives are read-only devices, they can't be used as secondary storage devices; instead, they're widely used to read commercially pressed CD-ROMs containing everything from multimedia games to massive reference libraries.

Drives capable of writing on a blank CD have come down in price in recent years, making it possible for even small organizations to produce their own CD-ROMs. These **CD-R drives** are a type of **WORM (write once, read many) drive.** They write digital information onto blank

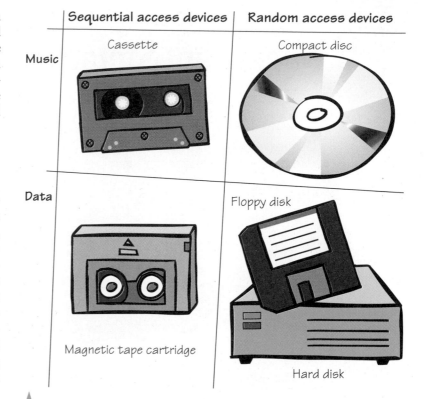

Sequential access devices	Random access devices
Music Cassette	Compact disc
Data Magnetic tape cartridge	Floppy disk / Hard disk

Most stereo systems include sequential access devices—cassette decks—and random access devices—compact disc players. The advantages of random access are the same for stereos as for computers.

| 1 CD-ROM | 450 1440K diskettes | 500 books (text only) |

A single CD-ROM can hold far more information than traditional magnetic storage media—about 500 books worth of text. Newer DVD-ROMs (Digital Video Disk—Read Only Memory) are the same size as CD-ROMs but can hold between 5 and 20 times more information!

Secondary Storage

Over the history of computing many devices have been invented to permanently store data. Magnetic and optical disks are two of the most important of those devices in use today.

Magnetic Disks

Both hard disks and floppy disks are coated with a magnetic oxide similar to the material used to coat cassette and video tapes. The read/write head of a disk drive is similar to the record/play head on a tape recorder; it magnetizes parts of the surface to record information. The difference is that a disk is a *digital* medium—binary numbers are read and written. The typical hard disk consists of several platters, each accessed via a read/write head on a moveable *armature*. The magnetic signals on the disk are organized into concentric *tracks;* the tracks in turn are divided into *sectors*. This is the traditional scheme used to construct addresses for data on the disk.

Hard disks spin much faster than floppy disks and have a higher storage density (number of bytes per square inch). The read/write head of a hard disk glides on a thin cushion of air above the disk and never actually touches the disk.

(or partially filled) optical disks, but they can't erase the information once it's burned in. A CD-ROM created on a CD-R drive can be read with a standard CD-ROM drive. Organizations often use these drives to make archival copies of large data files. The drives are also useful for creating master copies of CD-ROMs for duplication and distribution.

While a CD-ROM drive has become standard equipment in most modern multimedia computers, a new standard is emerging that may eventually replace the traditional CD-ROM drive. The *Digital Video Disk (DVD)* is the same size as a standard CD-ROM, but can hold between 3.8 and 17 gigabytes of information, depending on the way the information is stored. DVD players are marketed as devices for playing movies in home entertainment systems; full-length digital movies are packaged in DVD format. But **DVD-ROM** drives (which can also read standard CD-ROMs) are also produced as high-capacity computer peripherals.

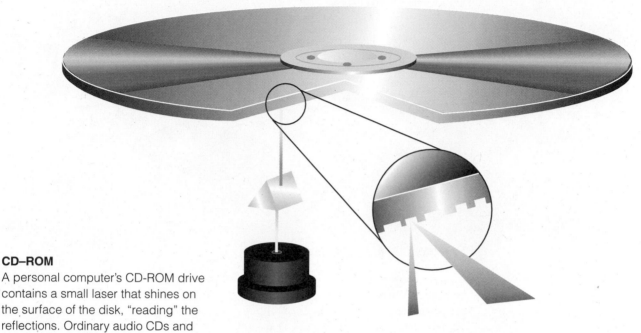

CD–ROM

A personal computer's CD-ROM drive contains a small laser that shines on the surface of the disk, "reading" the reflections. Ordinary audio CDs and computer CD-ROMs have similar formats. (That's why you can play an audio CD with a CD-ROM drive.) In each case, information is represented optically—the bottom surface of the CD, under a protective layer of plastic, is coated with a reflective metal film. A laser burns unreflective pits into the film to record data bits. Once a pit is burned, it can't be smoothed over and made shiny again; that's why ordinary CD-ROMs are read-only. Recent advances in optical storage technology are making rewritable CDs more affordable and commonplace.

Computer Systems: The Sum of Its Parts

A typical computer system might have several different input, output, and storage peripherals connected to the main computer housing. From the computer's point of view, it doesn't matter which of these devices is used at any given time. Each input device is just another source of electrical signals; each output device is just another place to send signals; each storage device is one or the other, depending on what the program calls for. Read from here, write to there—the CPU doesn't care; it dutifully follows instructions. Like a stereo receiver, the computer is oblivious to which input and output devices are attached and operational, as long as they're compatible.

A typical desktop computer system includes a computer and several peripheral devices.

Systems Without Boundaries

Unlike a stereo system, which has clearly defined boundaries, a computer system can be part of a **network** that blurs the boundaries between computers. When computers are connected in a network, one computer can, in effect, serve as an input device for another computer, which serves as an output device for the first computer. Networks can include hundreds of different computers, each of which might have access to all of the peripherals on the system. Many public and private networks span the globe by taking advantage of satellites, fiber optic cables, and other communication technologies. Using a peripheral called a *modem*, a computer can connect to a network through ordinary phone lines. The rise in computer networks is making it more difficult to draw lines between individual computer systems. If you're connected to the Internet, your computer is, in effect, just a tiny part of a global system of interconnected networks. In Chapters 9 and 10 we'll look more closely at computer networks in general and the Internet in particular.

The Missing Piece

In the span of a few pages, we've surveyed a mind-boggling array of computer hardware. In truth we've barely scratched the surface. Nonetheless, all this hardware is worthless without software to drive it. In the next chapter we'll take a look at the software that makes a computer system come to life.

SUMMARY

A computer with just a CPU and internal memory is of limited value; peripherals allow that computer to communicate with the outside world and store information for later use. Some peripherals are strictly input devices. Others are output devices. Some are external storage devices that accept information from *and* send information to the CPU.

The most common input devices today are the keyboard and the mouse. But a variety of other input devices can be connected to the computer. Trackballs, touch-sensitive pads, touch screens, and joysticks provide alternatives to the mouse as a pointing device. Bar-code readers, optical-mark readers, and magnetic ink readers are designed to recognize and translate specially printed patterns and characters. Scanners and digital cameras convert photographs, drawings, and other analog images into digital files that can be processed by the computer. Sound digitizers do the same thing to audio information. All input devices are designed to do one thing: convert information signals from an outside source into a pattern of bits that can be processed by the computer.

Output devices perform just the opposite function: They accept strings of bits from the computer and transform them into a form that is useful or meaningful outside the computer. Video monitors, including CRTs and LCDs, are almost universally used to display information continually as the computer functions. A variety of printers are used for producing paper output. Sound output from the computer, including music and synthesized speech, is delivered through audio speakers. Output devices also allow computers to control other machines.

Unlike most input and output peripherals, storage devices like disk drives and tape drives have two-way communication with the computer. Because of their high-speed random access capability, magnetic disks—high-capacity hard disks, inexpensive diskettes, and a variety of removable media—are the most common forms of secondary storage on modern computers. Sequential access tape devices are generally used only to archive information that doesn't need to be accessed often. While optical disks today are used mostly as high-capacity read-only media, they may become the preferred interactive storage medium as the technology improves and the associated costs go down.

The hardware for a complete computer system generally includes at least one processor, main memory, one or more secondary storage devices, and several I/O peripherals for communicating with the outside world. Network connections make it possible for computers to communicate with one another directly. Networks blur the boundaries between individual computer systems. With the hardware components in place, a computer system is ready to receive and follow instructions encoded in software.

Chapter Review

Key Terms

bar-code reader	dot-matrix printer	keyboard
CD-R drive	drag	laser printer
CD-ROM	DVD-ROM	LCD (liquid crystal display) monitor
click	ergonomics	line printer
CRT (cathode ray tube) monitor	graphics tablet	magnetic disk
cursor	gray-scale monitor	magnetic-ink character reader
digital audio tape (DAT)	hard copy	magnetic tape
digital camera	hard disk	magneto-optical disks
digitize	impact printer	monochrome monitor
diskette (floppy disk)	ink-jet printer	mouse
disk drive	joystick	nonimpact printer

optical character recognition (OCR)
optical disk
optical disk drive
optical-mark reader
pen-based computer
pixel
plotter
point-of-sale (POS) terminal
printer

random access
removable media
repetitive-stress injuries
resolution
scanner
sensing device
sequential access
tape drive
touch screen

touch pad
trackball
track point
video display terminal (VDT)
video monitor
wand reader
WORM (write once, read many)
    drive

Review Questions

1. Provide a working definition of each of the key words listed above. Check your answers in the glossary.

2. List five input devices and three output devices that might be attached to a personal computer. Describe a typical use of each.

3. Name and describe three special-purpose input devices that are commonly used by people in public places like stores, banks, and libraries.

4. The mouse is impractical for use as a pointing device on a laptop computer. Describe at least three alternatives that are more appropriate.

5. What are the advantages of CRT monitors over LCDs?

6. Name at least two hardware devices that use LCDs because using a CRT would be impractical.

7. What are the advantages of nonimpact printers like laser printers over impact printers? Are there any disadvantages?

8. Some commonly used peripherals can be described as both input and output devices. Explain.

9. What is the difference between sequential access and random access storage devices? What are the major uses of each?

10. What is the main advantage of CD-ROM as a storage medium when compared with magnetic disks? What is the main disadvantage?

Discussion Questions

1. If we think of the human brain as a computer, what are the input devices? What are the output devices? What are the storage devices?

2. What kinds of new input and output devices do you think future computers might have? Why?

Projects

1. The keyboard is the main input device for computers today. If you don't know how to touch-type, you're effectively handicapped in a world of computers. Fortunately, many personal computer software programs are designed to teach keyboarding. If you need to learn to type, try to find one of these programs and use it regularly until you are a fluent typist.

2. Using the inventory of computers you developed in Project 4 in Chapter 1, determine the major components of each (input devices, output devices, storage, and so on).

3. Visit a bank, store, office, or laboratory. List all the computer peripherals you see, categorizing them as input, output, and storage devices.

4. Using the inventory of computers you developed in Project 4 in Chapter 1, determine the major components of each (input devices, output devices, storage, and so on).

5. Using computer advertisements in magazines, newspapers, and catalogs, try to break down the cost of a computer to determine, on the average, what percentage is for the system unit (including CPU, memory, and disk drives) and what percentage is for input and output devices. How does this percentage change as the price of the system goes up?

Sources and Resources

Books

West of Eden, by Frank Rose (New York: Viking Penguin, 1990). This book chronicles the early history of Apple Computer and its transition from garage supplier of home-grown computers to a Fortune 500 company that is still shaping the future of computing. It is a fascinating inside look at the people who drove Apple computer in the 1980s.

Steve Jobs & The NeXT Big Thing, by Randall E. Stross (New York: Athenium, 1993). This is the story of Steve Job's next bid to alter the direction of computing after leaving Apple Computer. This book discusses the difficulty of repeating past success in Silicon Valley, even for a man as powerful as Steve Jobs. The story of NeXT is a series of missteps, disasters, and massive quarterly losses featuring a cast of world-famous characters.

Disclosure, by Michael Crichton. This book-turned-movie gives an inside look at a fictional Seattle corporation that manufactures computer peripherals. Even though the author has clearly tampered with credibility for the sake of a suspenseful plot, the story still provides insights into the roles money and power play in today's high-stakes computer industry.

How Computers Work, by Ron White (Emeryville, CA: PC/Computing/Ziff-Davis Press, 1994) and *How Macs Work,* by John Rizzo and K. Daniel Clark (Emeryville, CA: Ziff-Davis Press, 1993). These two books, described at the end of Chapter 2, provide clear explanations of the inner workings of most commonly used personal computer peripherals.

The Computer User's Survival Guide, by Joan Stigliani (Sebastopol, CA: O'Reilly & Associates, 1995), *Zap! How your computer can hurt you—and what you can do about it,* by Don Sellers (Berkeley, CA: Peachpit Press, 1994), and

25 Steps to Safe Computing, by Don Sellers (Berkeley, CA: Peachpit Press, 1995). If you do much computer work (or play), you owe it to yourself to learn about the inherent dangers. These books can help you understand the health hazards of computing. *The Computer User's Survival Guide* provides clear, detailed descriptions of a wide range of medical problems that might result from improper computer use and suggests a variety of treatments and preventative measures. *Zap!* covers the same ground in a little less detail. If you don't think you'll bother to read even *Zap!*'s 150 illustrated pages, try *25 Steps to Safe Computing* by the same author; it presents the essential tips in condensed form.

EMF Handbook, by Stephen Prata (Corte Madera, CA: The Waite Group, 1993). This little book focuses on electromagnetic fields, the controversial research about their impact on our health, and what you can do to minimize your personal risk.

The Underground Guide to Laser Printers, by the Editors of Flash Magazine (Berkeley, CA: Peachpit Press, 1993). This little book covers the ins, outs, and abouts of laser printers: how they work, how to fix them, how to recycle cartridges, how to make toner, how to choose paper—even how to print T-shirt transfers.

Scanning the Professional Way, by Sybil Ihrig and Emil Ihrig. (Berkeley, CA: Osborne McGraw-Hill, 1995). It's easy to to use a scanner, but it isn't always easy to get high-quality scans. This illustrated book covers scanner use from the basics to advanced tips and techniques.

World Wide Web Pages

Most computer peripheral manufacturers have World Wide Web pages. The *Computer Confluence* Web site will guide you to many of the most interesting pages.

SOFTWARE BASICS
The Ghost in the Machine

John von Neumann Invents the Invisible

All experience shows that technological changes profoundly transform political and social relationships.

—John von Neumann

John von Neumann

John von Neumann was one of the greatest mathematicians of the 20th century, making fundamental contributions to mathematical logic, quantum theory (by his 20s), numerical weather prediction, and flowcharting. Von Neumann ordered his life mathematically, using concepts from the mathematical theory of games that he developed. His head was filled with so many ideas and he was so busy that he allowed himself only five hours of sleep per night. He saw great possibilities for applying abstract concepts like mathematics to the affairs of people.

During World War II von Neumann consulted for the U.S. military in weather fore-

casting, ballistics, operations research, and atomic weapons. One of the world's most knowledgeable authorities on computers, he was eager to promote research on computers to further their use. He became technical advisor to J. Presper Eckert and John Mauchly, who were searching for an alternative to the plug boards and patch cords used to program ENIAC. In 1945 he wrote a first draft of a paper that drew on the ideas developed by these three men. The paper called for storing the computer's program instructions with the data in memory. Every computer created since has been based on the *stored-program concept* described in that paper.

While working on the atomic bomb after World War II ended, von Neumann wit-nessed many bomb explosions first hand, oblivious to possible radiation dangers. His faith in technology caused him to overlook the potential risks brought on by that technology. Shortly after he was appointed chairman of the Atomic Energy Commission in 1955, he learned that he had bone cancer, probably caused by his heavy exposure to radiation during years of atomic testing. He kept working through the pain right to the end in 1957.

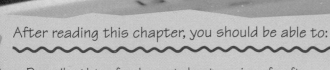

After reading this chapter, you should be able to:

- Describe three fundamental categories of software and their relationship
- Explain the relationship of algorithms to software
- Discuss the factors that make a computer application a useful tool
- Describe the role of the operating system in a modern computer system

- Outline the evolution of user interfaces from early machine-language programming to futuristic virtual reality interfaces
- Compare character-based user interfaces with graphical user interfaces, and explain the trade-offs involved in choosing a user interface

The communication gap...

Person with problems to solve

Computer— only knows zeros and ones

Communication gap

Person with problems to solve

Software: the link between human and computer

Computer— only knows zeros and ones

Chapters 2 and 3 told only part of the story of how computers do what they do. Here's a synopsis of our story so far:

On one side we have a person—you, me, or somebody else; it hardly matters. We all have problems to solve—problems involving work, communication, transportation, finances, and more. Many of these problems cry out for computer solutions.

On the other side we have a computer—an incredibly sophisticated bundle of hardware capable of performing all kinds of technological wizardry. Unfortunately the computer *recognizes only zeros and ones*.

A great chasm separates the person who has a collection of vague problems from the stark, rigidly bounded world of the computer. How can humans bridge the gap to communicate with the computer?

That's where software comes in. Software allows people to communicate certain kinds of problems to computers and makes it possible for computers to communicate solutions back to those people.

Modern computer software didn't just materialize out of the atmosphere. Just as computer hardware has continually evolved to make computers faster and more powerful, software has steadily improved to make computers more responsive and easier to use.

In a sense von Neumann, Eckert, and Mauchly established the software industry by liberating programmers from the tyranny of hardware. Instead of flipping switches and patching wires, today's programmers write *programs*—sets of computer instructions designed to solve problems—and feed them into the computer's memory through input devices like keyboards and mice. These programs are the computer's software. Because software is stored in memory, a computer can switch from one task to another and then back to the first, without a single hardware modification. For instance, the computer that serves as a word processor for writing this book can, on command, turn almost instantly into an accounting spreadsheet, a telecommunications terminal, a musical instrument, or a game machine.

What is software, and how can it transform a mass of circuits into an electronic chameleon? This chapter provides some general answers to that question along with a few specific details about each of the three major categories of software:

- *compilers and other translator programs,* which allow programmers to create other software

- *software applications,* which serve as productivity tools to help computer users solve problems

- *system software,* which coordinates hardware operations and does behind-the-scenes work the computer user seldom sees

PROCESSING WITH PROGRAMS

The programmer, like the poet, works only slightly removed from pure thought-stuff. He builds castles in the air, creating by exertion of the imagination. Yet the program construct, unlike the poet's words, is real in the sense that it moves and works, producing visible outputs separate from the construct itself.

—Frederick P. Brooks, Jr., in *The Mythical Man Month*

Software is invisible and complex. To make the basic concepts clear, we'll start our exploration of software with a down-to-earth analogy.

Food for Thought

Think of the hardware in a computer system as the kitchen in a short-order restaurant: It's equipped to produce whatever output a customer (user) requests, but it sits idle until an order (command) is placed. Robert, the computerized chef in our imaginary kitchen, serves as the CPU, waiting for requests from the users/customers. When somebody provides an input command—say, an order for a plate of French toast—Robert responds by following the instructions in the appropriate recipe.

As you may have guessed, the recipe is the software. It provides instructions telling the hardware what to do to produce the output desired by the user. If the recipe is correct, clear, and precise, the chef turns the input data—eggs, bread, and other ingredients—into the desired output—French toast. If the instructions are unclear or if the software has **bugs,** or errors, the output may not be what the user wanted.

For example, suppose Robert has this recipe:

Suzanne's French Toast Fantastique

1. Combine 2 slightly beaten eggs with 1 teaspoon vanilla extract, ½ teaspoon cinnamon, and ⅔ cup milk.
2. Dip 6 slices of bread in mixture.
3. Fry in small amount of butter until golden brown.
4. Serve bread with maple syrup, sugar, or tart jelly.

This seemingly foolproof recipe has several trouble spots. Since step 1 doesn't say otherwise, Robert might include the shells in the "slightly beaten eggs." Step 2 says nothing about separating the six slices of bread before dipping them in the batter; Robert would be within the letter of the instruction if he dipped all six at once. Step 3 has at least two potential bugs. Since it doesn't specify *what* to fry in butter, Robert might conclude that the *mixture* should be fried rather than the bread. Even if Robert decides to fry the bread, he may let it overcook waiting for the *butter* to turn golden brown, or he may wait patiently for the top of the toast to brown while the bottom quietly blackens. Robert, like any good computer, just follows instructions.

A Fast, Stupid Machine

The most useful word in any computer language is "oops."

—David Lubar, in *It's Not a Bug, It's a Feature*

Our imaginary automated chef may not seem very bright, but he's considerably more intelligent than a typical computer's CPU. Computers are commonly called "smart machines" or "intelligent machines." In truth a typical computer is incredibly limited, capable of doing only the most basic arithmetic operations (such as $7 + 3$ and $15 - 8$) and a few simple logical comparisons ("Is this number less than that number?" "Are these two values identical?").

Computers *seem* smart because they can perform these operations and comparisons quickly and accurately. A typical desktop computer can do thousands of calculations in the time it takes you to pull your pen out of your pocket. A well-crafted program can tell the computer to perform a sequence of simple operations that, when taken as a whole, produce an animated display, print a term paper, or simulate a game of pinball. Amazingly, everything you've ever seen a computer do is the result of a sequence of extremely simple arithmetic and logical operations done very quickly. The challenge for software developers is to devise instructions that put those simple operations together in ways that are useful and appropriate.

Suzanne's recipe for French toast isn't a computer program; it's not written in a language that a computer can understand. But it could be considered an **algorithm**— a set of step-by-step procedures for accomplishing a task. A computer program generally starts as an algorithm written in English or some other human language. Like Suzanne's recipe, the initial algorithm is likely to contain generalities, ambiguities, and errors.

The programmer's job is to turn the algorithm into a program by adding details, hammering out rough spots, testing procedures, and correcting errors. For example, if we were turning Suzanne's recipe into a program for our electronic-brained short-order cook, we might start by rewriting it like the recipe shown here.

Suzanne's French Toast Fantastique

1. Prepare the batter by following these instructions:
   1a. Crack 2 eggs so whites and yolks drop in bowl; discard shells.
   1b. Beat eggs slightly with wire whip, fork, or mixer.
   1c. Mix in 1 teaspoon vanilla extract, ½ teaspoon cinnamon, and ⅔ cup milk.
2. Place small amount of butter in frying pan and place on medium heat.
3. For each of 6 pieces of bread, follow these steps:
   3a. Dip slice of bread in mixture.
   3b. For each of the two sides of the bread do the following steps:
      3b1. Place the slice of bread in the frying pan with this (uncooked) side down.
      3b2. Wait 1 minute and then peek at underside of bread; if lighter than golden brown, repeat this step.
   3c. Remove bread from fry pan and place on plate.
4. Serve bread with maple syrup, sugar, or tart jelly.

We've eliminated much of the ambiguity from the original recipe. Ambiguity, while tolerable (and sometimes useful) in conversations between humans, is a source of errors for computers. In its current form the recipe contains far more detail than any human chef would want but not nearly enough for a computer. If we were programming a computer (assuming we had one with input hardware capable of recognizing golden brown French toast and output devices capable of flipping the bread), we'd need to go into excruciating detail, translating every step of the process into a series of absolutely unambiguous instructions that could be interpreted and executed by a machine with a vocabulary smaller than that of a two-year-old child!

The Language of Computers

Every computer processes instructions in a native **machine language.** Machine language uses numeric codes to represent the most basic computer operations—adding numbers, subtracting numbers, comparing numbers, moving numbers, repeating instructions, and so on. Early programmers were forced to write every program in a machine language, tediously translating each instruction into binary code. This process was an invitation to insanity; imagine trying to find a single mistyped character in a page full of zeros and ones! Today most programmers use programming languages like BASIC, COBOL, and C++ that fall somewhere between natural human languages and precise machine languages. These languages make it possible for scientists, engineers, and business people to solve problems using familiar terminology and notation rather than cryptic machine instructions. For a computer to understand a program written in one of these languages, it must use a translator program to convert the English-like instructions to the zeros and ones of machine language.

To clarify the translation process, let's go back to the kitchen. Imagine a recipe translator that allows our computer chef to look up phrases like "fry until golden brown." Like a reference book for beginning cooks, this translator fills in all the details of testing and flipping foods in the frying pan, so Robert understands what to do whenever he encounters "fry until golden brown" in any recipe. As long as our computer cook is equipped with the translator, we don't need to include so many details in each recipe. We can communicate at a higher level. The more sophisticated the translator, the easier the job of the programmer. The most common type of translator program is called a **compiler,** because it compiles a complete translation of the program in a high-level computer language before running the program. But there are other types of translators, as you'll see later in the book.

Programming languages have steadily evolved during the last few decades. Each new generation of languages makes the programming process easier by taking on, and hiding from the programmer, more of the detail work. The computer's unrelenting demands for technical details haven't gone away; they're just handled automatically by translation software. As a result, programming is easier and less error-prone. As translators become more sophisticated, programmers can communicate in computer languages that more closely resemble **natural languages**—the languages people speak and write every day.

Even with state-of-the-art computer languages, programming requires a considerable investment of time and brain power. (You'll see why when we take a closer look at programming in a later chapter.) Fortunately most tasks that required programming two decades ago can now be accomplished with easy-to-use software applications—tools like word processors, spreadsheets, and graphics programs. Programming languages are still used to solve problems that can't be handled with off-the-shelf software applications, but most computer users manage to do their work without programming. Programming today is done mainly by professional software developers who use programming languages to create and refine the applications and other programs used by computer users every day.

SOFTWARE APPLICATIONS: TOOLS FOR USERS

> The computer is only a fast idiot, it has no imagination; it cannot originate action. It is, and will remain, only a tool to man.
>
> —American Library Association reaction to the UNIVAC computer exhibit at the 1964 New York World's Fair

Software applications allow users to control computers without thinking like programmers. We'll turn our attention now to applications.

Consumer Applications

Chapter 1 included a description of the most important types of computer applications—applications we'll be exploring in detail in succeeding chapters of this book:

- word processing and desktop publishing (Chapter 5)
- spreadsheets and other number-crunching applications (Chapter 6)
- computer graphics and multimedia (Chapter 7)
- databases for information storage and retrieval (Chapter 8)
- telecommunications and networking (Chapters 9 and 10)

Just about everyone who works with personal computers uses software that fits into one or more of these categories. Computer stores, software stores, and mail-order houses sell thousands of different software titles. The process of buying computer software is similar to the process of buying music software (CDs or cassettes) to play on a stereo system. But there are some important differences:

- A computer software package generally includes printed **documentation**—tutorial manuals and reference manuals that explain how to use the software. Many programs today are so easy to use that it's possible to put them to work without reading the manuals. And most modern software packages have some kind of **on-line documentation:** *Help screens* appear when the user asks for more information. Still, it's rare to find a software package that doesn't include at least one manual of instructions.

- Most software companies continually work to improve their products by removing bugs and adding new features. As a result, new *versions* of most popular programs are released every year or two. To distinguish between versions, program names are generally followed by version numbers, such as 4.0 in ClarisWorks 4.0. Most companies use decimals to indicate minor revisions and whole numbers to indicate major revisions. For example, Painter 3.1 includes only a few more features than Painter 3.0, but Painter 4.0 is significantly different than version 3.1. Not all software follows this convention; for example, Microsoft Windows 3.1 was followed by Windows 95. When you buy a software program, you generally buy the current version. When a new version is released, you can **upgrade** your program to the new version by paying an upgrade fee to the software manufacturer.

- A computer software buyer must be concerned with **compatibility.** When you buy a music cassette, you don't need to specify

Most modern computer software provides some kind of on-line help on demand. Microsoft Windows provides context-sensitive help—help windows whose contents depend on what else is currently on the screen.

Executing a Program

Most programs are composed of millions of simple instructions. Here we'll observe the execution of a tiny part of a running program: a series of instructions that perform some arithmetic. The machine instructions are similar to those in actual programs, but the details have been omitted. The computer has already loaded (copied) the program from disk into main memory so that the CPU can see it.

The CPU automatically fetches and executes instructions in sequence—from a series of consecutive memory addresses—unless it's told to "jump" somewhere else. The CPU is about to read the next instruction from memory location 100. This instruction and the ones that follow (in locations 101, 102, and 103) tell the CPU to read a couple of numbers from memory (locations 2000 and 2001), add them together, and store the result back into memory (location 2002). Translated into English, the instructions look like this:

(100) Get (read) the number at memory address 2000 (not the number 2000, but the number stored in location 2000) and place it in register A.

(101) Get the number at memory address 2001 and place it in register B.

(102) Add the contents of registers A and B, placing the result in register C.

(103) Write (copy) the number in register C to memory address 2002.

For this example, let's suppose that memory location 2000 contains the number 7 and memory location 2001 contains 9.

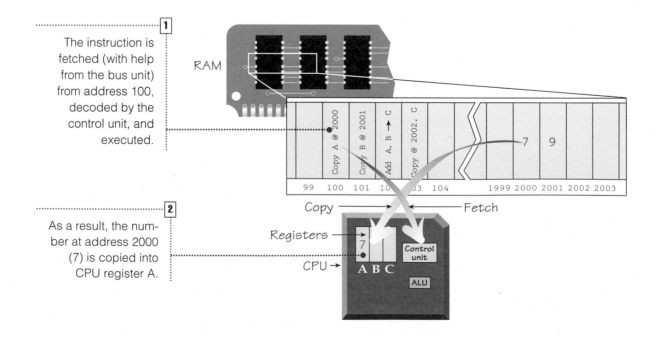

1 The instruction is fetched (with help from the bus unit) from address 100, decoded by the control unit, and executed.

2 As a result, the number at address 2000 (7) is copied into CPU register A.

RAM

Copy A @ 2000 | Copy B @ 2001 | Add A, B → C | Copy @ 2002 , C | | 7 | 9

99   100   101   102   103   104   1999 2000 2001 2002 2003

Copy ——→   ←—— Fetch

Registers

CPU →   A B C   Control unit   ALU

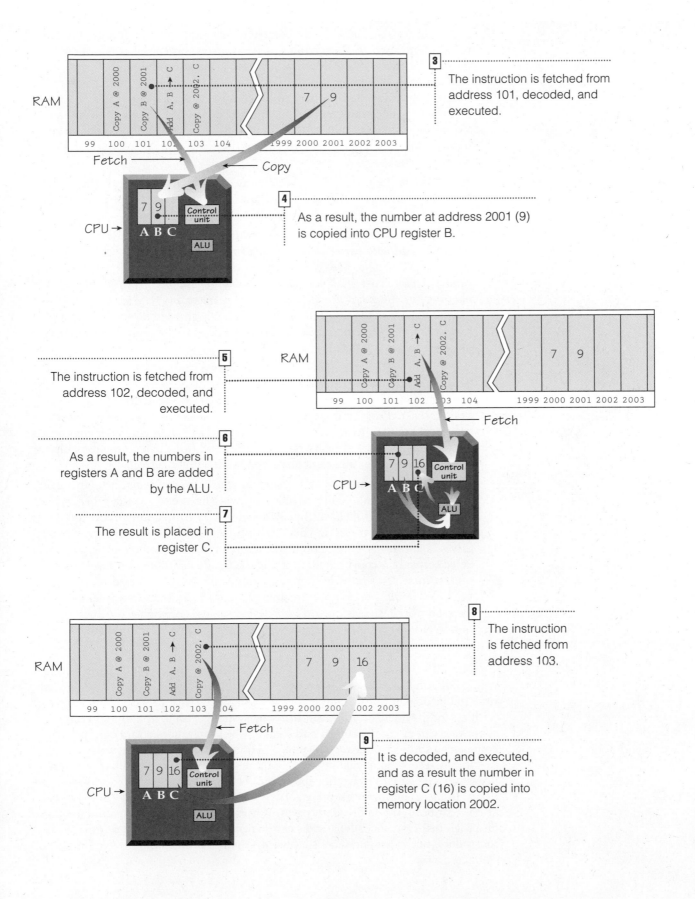

3 The instruction is fetched from address 101, decoded, and executed.

Fetch → | Copy

CPU →

4 As a result, the number at address 2001 (9) is copied into CPU register B.

5 The instruction is fetched from address 102, decoded, and executed.

RAM

← Fetch

6 As a result, the numbers in registers A and B are added by the ALU.

CPU →

7 The result is placed in register C.

8 The instruction is fetched from address 103.

RAM

← Fetch

CPU →

9 It is decoded, and executed, and as a result the number in register C (16) is copied into memory location 2002.

the brand of your cassette player because all manufacturers adhere to common industry standards. But no complete, universal software standards exist in the computer world, so a program written for one type of computer system probably won't work on another. Software packages contain labels with statements such as "Requires Macintosh with 4MB of memory running System 7.0 or later" or "Runs on IBM-compatible computers with Windows 9x." (An x in a version specification generally means "substitute any number" so "Window 9x" means "Windows ninety-*something*.") These demands should not be taken lightly; without compatible hardware and software, most software programs are worthless.

• According to the warranties printed on many software packages, the applications might be worthless even if you have compatible hardware and software. Here's the first paragraph from a typical "Limited Warranty":

This program is provided "as is" without warranty of any kind. The entire risk as to the result and performance of the program is assumed by you. Should the program prove defective, you—and not the manufacturer or its dealers—assume the entire cost of all necessary servicing, repair, or correction. Further, the manufacturer does not warrant, guarantee, or make any representations regarding the use of, or the result of the use of, the program in terms of correctness, accuracy, reliability, currency, or otherwise, and you rely on the program and its results solely at your own risk.

Why do software companies hide behind nonwarranties like this? In short, because nobody's figured out how to write error-free software. Remember our problems providing Robert with a fool-proof set of instructions for producing French toast? Programmers who write applications such as word processing programs must try to anticipate and respond to all combinations of commands and actions performed by users under any conditions. Given the difficulty of this task, most programs work amazingly well, but not perfectly.

• When you buy a typical computer software package, you're not actually buying the software. Instead you're buying a **software license** to use the program on a single machine. While licensing agreements vary from company to company, most include limitations on your right to copy disks, install software on hard drives, and transfer information to other users. Virtually all commercially marketed software is **copyrighted,** so it can't be *legally* duplicated for distribution to others; some disks (mostly games) are physically **copy-protected,** so they can't be copied *at all*. Because programming is so difficult, software development is incredibly expensive. Most software developers use copyrights and copy protection to ensure that they sell enough copies of their products to recover their investments and stay in business to write more programs.

Not all software is copyrighted and sold through commercial channels. Electronic bulletin boards (see Chapter 9), user groups, and other sources commonly offer **public domain software** (free for the taking) and **shareware** (free for the trying, with a send-payment-if-you-keep-it honor system). Public domain software and shareware can be legally copied and shared. The same can't be said of copyrighted commercial software—the overwhelming majority of software in use today.

It may seem strange that anyone would pay several hundred dollars for a product that comes with no warranty and dozens of legal restrictions about how you can use it. In fact the rapidly growing software industry has spawned dozens of programs that have sold millions of copies. Why do so many people buy and use these hit programs? Of course, the answer varies from person to person and from product to product. But in general most successful software products share two important characteristics:

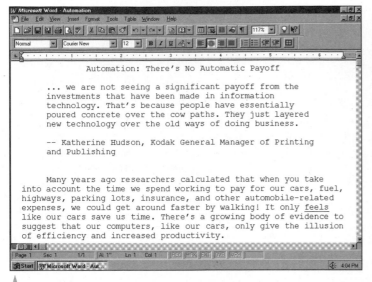

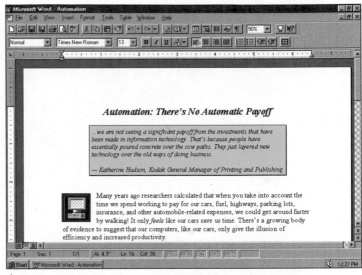

> Entering text with a word processor is similar to typing with a standard typewriter; the computer screen displays an image of the page being typed.

> The word processor makes it easy to rearrange and change the appearance of the text—even add a picture—before printing the final document. No typewriter can do this.

1. *Most successful software applications are built around visual metaphors of real-world tools.* Word processors and drawing programs turn part of the screen into a sheet of paper; desktop publishing programs make the screen look like a designer's drafting table; spreadsheets resemble accountant's ledger sheets. But if these programs merely mimicked their real-world counterparts, people would have no compelling reason to use them.

2. *Most popular computer applications are successful because they extend human capabilities in some way, allowing users to do things that can't be done easily, or at all, with conventional tools.* Word processors allow writers to edit and format documents in ways that aren't possible with a typewriter or pencil. An artist using a graphics program can easily add an other-worldly effect to a drawing and just as easily remove it if it doesn't look right. Spreadsheet programs allow managers to project future revenues based on best guesses and then instantly recalculate the bottom line with a different set of assumptions. Software applications that extend human capabilities are the driving force behind the computer revolution.

Integrated Applications and Suites: Multipurpose Software

While most software packages specialize in a particular application—word processing, graphics, or whatever—**integrated software** packages include several applications designed to work well together. ClarisWorks, Microsoft Works, and other popular integrated packages generally include most or all of these application types:

- word processing
- database
- spreadsheet
- graphics
- telecommunications

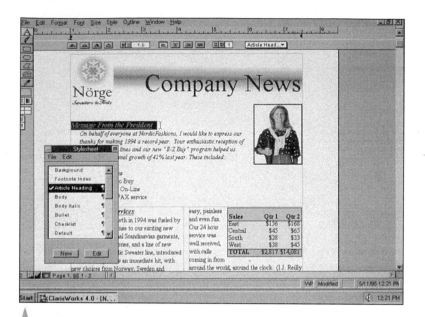

With an integrated software package like ClarisWorks, you can easily create a table and graphical chart to include in a report—and watch the chart change automatically whenever you change the figures in the table.

The parts of an integrated package may not have all the features of their separately packaged counterparts, but integrated packages still offer several advantages:

- They cost considerably less than the total cost of purchasing individual programs that perform all of the separate functions.

- They allow quick and easy transfer of data among applications. Many include *interapplication communication* features, so, for example, changes in a financial spreadsheet are automatically reflected in a graphic table embedded in a word-processed memo.

- They apply a similar *look and feel* to all of their applications, so users don't need to memorize different commands and techniques for doing different tasks. Many commands apply across all applications in an integrated package, making it easy for users to learn new applications without starting over.

- The best integrated programs blur the lines between applications so you don't need to think so much about what tool to use—you can focus on the task at hand. For example, you can create a table full of calculations right in the middle of a typed letter without explicitly switching from a word processor to a spreadsheet.

These advantages aren't unique to integrated packages. Unified command structures and interapplication communication are built into many operating systems today, as you'll see later in the chapter. And many software companies offer **application suites** (or *office suites*)—bundles containing several application programs that are also sold as separate programs. For example, the Microsoft Office Professional suite includes Microsoft Word (a word processor), Excel (a spreadsheet program), PowerPoint (a presentation graphics program), and Access (a database program). Microsoft has designed these applications so they have similar command structures and interapplication communication. The price of a suite like Microsoft Office is generally less than the total price of individual applications purchased separately but more than the cost of an integrated package like Microsoft Works. Suites generally have more features than integrated programs but also make greater demands on system memory, disk storage, the CPU, and the user who must learn all those extra commands and options. Suites offer flexibility and power for serious users who have the hardware to handle them. But many computer novices, casual users, mobile users, budget-conscious consumers, and businesses opt for integrated packages in the name of simplicity and economy.

Vertical-Market and Custom Software

Because of their flexibility, word processors, spreadsheets, databases, and graphics programs are used in homes, schools, government offices, and all kinds of businesses. But many computer applications are so job specific that they're of little interest or use to anybody outside a given profession. Medical billing software, library cataloging software, restaurant management software, and other applications designed specifically for a particular business or industry are sometimes called **vertical-market applications.**

Vertical-market applications tend to cost far more than mass-market applications, because companies that develop the software have very few potential customers through which to recover their development costs. In fact some **custom applications** are programmed specifically for single clients. For example, the software used to control the space shuttle was developed with a single customer—NASA—in mind.

NASA scientists use custom software to recreate a Martian environment.

SYSTEM SOFTWARE:
THE HARDWARE-SOFTWARE CONNECTION

Originally, operating systems were envisioned as a way to handle one of the most complex input/output operations: communicating with a variety of disk drives. But, the operating system quickly evolved into an all-encompassing bridge between your PC and the software you run on it.

—Ron White, in *How Computers Work*

Whether you're programming or using an application, software is taking care of many details of computing for you. When you're typing a paper or writing a program, you don't need to concern yourself with the parts of the computer's memory that hold your document, the segments of the word processing software currently in the computer's memory, or the output instructions sent by the computer to the printer. These details, and hundreds of others, are handled behind the scenes by **system software,** a class of software that includes the *operating system* and *utility programs.* (By some definitions, system software also includes compilers and other translator programs.)

What the Operating System Does

Virtually every general-purpose computer today, whether timesharing supercomputer or laptop PC, depends on an **operating system (OS)** to keep hardware running efficiently and to make the process of communication with that hardware easier. Operating system software runs continuously whenever the computer is on, even when users are working with software applications. In essence the operating system provides an additional layer of insulation between the user and the bits-and-bytes world of computer hardware. Because the operating system stands between the software application and the hardware, application compatibility is often defined by the operating system as well as the hardware.

The operating system, as the name implies, is a system of programs that perform a variety of technical operations, including

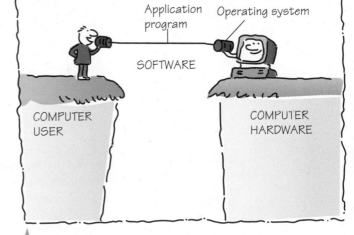

The user's view: When a person uses an application, whether a game or an accounting program, the person doesn't communicate directly with the computer hardware. Instead the user interacts with the application, which depends on the operating system to manage and control hardware.

- *Communicating with peripherals.* Some of the most complex tasks performed by a computer involve communicating with screens, printers, disk drives, and other peripheral devices. A computer's operating system always includes programs that transparently take care of the details of communication with peripherals.

- *Coordinating concurrent processing of jobs.* Large, multiuser computers often work on several jobs at the same time—a technique known as **concurrent processing.** State-of-the-art parallel processing machines use multiple CPUs to process jobs simultaneously. But a typical computer has only one processor, so it must work on several projects by rapidly switching back and forth between projects. The computer takes advantage of idle time in one process (for example, waiting for input) by working on another program. (Our computerized chef, Robert, might practice concurrent processing by slicing fruit while he waits for the toast to brown.) A timesharing computer practices concurrent processing whenever multiple users are connected to the system. The computer quickly moves from terminal to terminal, checking for input and processing each user's data in turn. Concurrent processing is becoming increasingly common in personal computer operating systems that allow **multitasking.** If a PC has multitasking capabilities, the user can issue a command that initiates a process (for example, to print this chapter) and continue working with other applications while the computer follows through on the command.

- *Memory management.* When several jobs are being processed concurrently, the operating system must keep track of how the computer's memory is being used and make sure that no job encroaches on another's territory. Memory management is accomplished in a variety of ways, from simple schemes that subdivide the available memory equally between jobs to elaborate schemes that temporarily swap information between the computer's memory and external storage devices. One common technique for dealing with memory shortages is to set aside part of a hard disk as *virtual memory.* Thanks to the operating system, this chunk of disk space looks just like internal memory to the CPU, even though access time is slower.

- *Resource monitoring, accounting, and security.* Many multiuser computer systems are designed to charge users for the resources they consume. These systems keep track of each user's time, storage demands, and pages printed, so accounting programs can calculate and print accurate bills. Even in environments where billing isn't an issue, the operating system should monitor resources to ensure the privacy and security of each user's data.

- *Program and data management.* In addition to serving as a traffic cop, a security guard, and an accountant, the operating system acts as a librarian, locating and accessing files and programs requested by the user and by other programs.

Utility Programs

Even the best operating systems leave a certain amount of housekeeping to other programs and to the user. **Utility programs** serve as tools for doing system maintenance and some repairs that aren't automatically handled by the operating system. Utilities make it easier for users to copy files between storage devices, to repair damaged data files, to translate files so that different programs can read them, to guard against *viruses* and other potentially harmful programs (as described in the chapter on computer security and risks), and to perform countless other important, if unexciting, tasks. Many utility programs can be invoked directly by the operating system, so they appear to the user to be part of the operating system. For example, a printer driver that allows a computer to communicate with a particular printer works behind the scenes whenever the user requests that a document be printed. Some utility programs are included with the operating system; others are sold as separate products.

Where the Operating System Lives

Some computers—mostly game machines and special-purpose computers—store their operating systems permanently in ROM (read-only memory) so they are ready to go to work as soon as they are turned on. But since ROM is unchangeable, these machines can't have their operating systems modified or upgraded without hardware transplants. Most computers include only part of the operating system in ROM—the remainder of the operating system is loaded into memory in a process called **booting.** (The term *booting* is used because the computer seems to pull itself up by its own bootstraps.)

Most of the time the operating system works behind the scenes, taking care of business without the knowledge or intervention of the user. But occasionally it's necessary for a user to communicate directly with the operating system. For example, when you boot a personal computer, the operating system steps into the foreground, waiting for instructions from you. If you issue a command to open a graphics application, the operating system locates the program, copies it from disk into memory, turns the screen over to the application, and then accepts commands from the application while you draw pictures on the screen.

Interacting with the operating system, like interacting with an application, can be intuitive or challenging. It depends on something called the *user interface.* Because of its profound impact on the computing experience, the user interface is a critically important component of almost every piece of software.

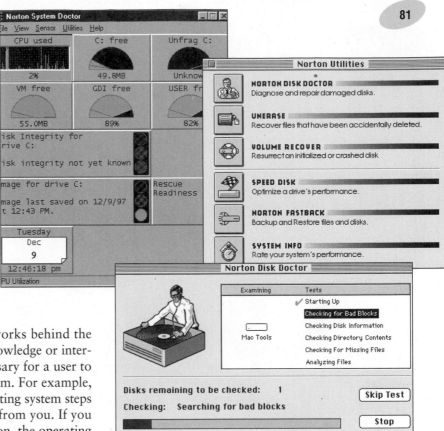

A typical commercial utility package includes software tools for recovering damaged files, repairing damaged disks, and improving disk performance. (Software: Norton Utilities from Symantec, Windows, and Macintosh versions.)

THE USER INTERFACE: THE HUMAN-MACHINE CONNECTION

The anthropologist Claude Levi-Strauss has called human beings tool makers and symbol makers. The user interface is potentially the most sophisticated of these constructions, one in which the distinction between tool and symbol is blurred.

— Aaron Marcus and Andries van Dam, user interface experts

Early computer users had to spend tedious hours writing and debugging machine-language instructions. Later users programmed in languages that were easier to understand but still technically challenging. Today users spend much of their time working with preprogrammed applications like word processors that simulate and amplify the capabilities of real-world tools. As software evolves, so does the **user interface**—the look and feel of the computing experience from a human point of view.

Probably the easiest way to understand the importance of user interfaces is to see how we might accomplish a simple task using different user interfaces. We'll look at the user interface of:

The Operating System

ost of what you see on screen when you use an application program, and most of the common tasks you have the program perform, such as saving and opening files, are being performed by the operating system at the application's request.

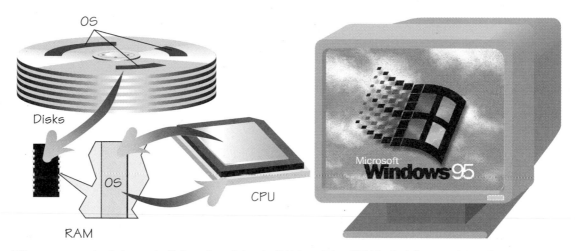

When a computer is turned off, there's nothing in RAM and the CPU isn't doing anything. The operating system (OS) programs must be in memory and running on the CPU before the system can function. When you turn on the computer, the CPU automatically begins executing instructions stored in ROM. These instructions help the system boot, and the operating system is loaded from disk into part of the system's memory.

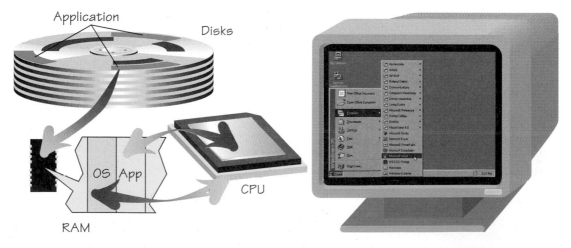

Using the mouse, you "ask" the operating system to load a word processing application program into memory so it can run.

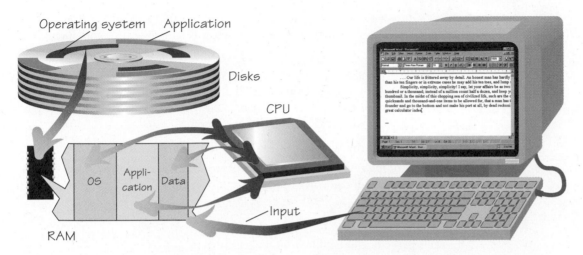

The loaded application occupies a portion of memory, leaving that much less for other programs and data. The OS remains in memory so it can provide services to the application program, helping it to display on-screen menus, communicate with the printer, and perform other common actions. Because the OS and application are in constant communication, *control*—the location in memory where the CPU is reading program instructions—jumps all around. If the application calls the OS to help display a menu, the application tells the CPU, "Go follow the menu display instructions at address x in the operating system area; when you're done, return here and pick up where you left off."

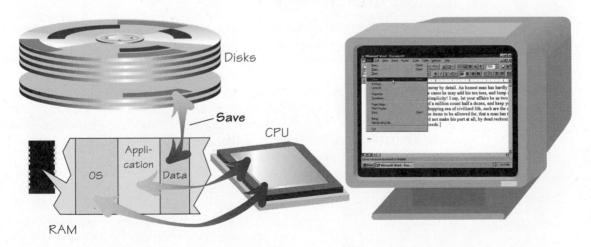

To avoid losing your data file when the system is turned off, you save it to the disk—write it into a file on the disk for later use. The OS handles communication between CPU and the disk drive, ensuring that your file doesn't overwrite other information. (Later, when you reopen the file, the OS locates it on the disk and copies it into memory so the CPU—and, therefore, any program—can see it and work with it.)

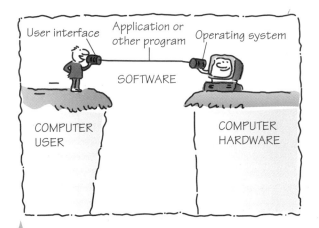

The user's view revisited: The user interface is the part of the computer system that the user sees. A well-designed user interface hides the bothersome details of computing from the user.

- MS-DOS—the operating system that's standard equipment in millions of older IBM-compatible computers (computers that are functionally identical to an IBM personal computer and therefore capable of running IBM-compatible software)

- Apple's Macintosh—the most popular alternative to IBM-compatible computers

- Microsoft Windows—software that provides a Macintosh-like user interface for most newer IBM-compatible computers

In each case we'll use the word processing application WordPerfect to print a term paper we created in an earlier session. This term paper, stored as a file on the hard disk, is a WordPerfect document. In general, a **document** is a file created with an application. For each example we'll perform a series of steps:

1. Locate either the WordPerfect application or the document on the hard disk.

2. **Open** (or *load*) the application (copy it from disk into memory so we can use it), and open the document.

3. Print the document.

4. Close the application.

5. Delete the document file from the hard disk.

Before we begin, a disclaimer and a reminder:

- *The disclaimer:* This comparison is intended to compare different types of interfaces—not to establish a champion in the ongoing brand-name wars.

- *The reminder:* The examples shown here, like the other User's View examples in this book, are designed to give you a *feel* for the software, not to provide how-to instructions. If you want to learn how to use the software, refer to the manuals that accompany the software or to other books on the subject, some of which are listed at the ends of chapters in this book.

A Character-based User Interface: MS-DOS

MS-DOS (Microsoft Disk Operating System, sometimes called just DOS) is the most widely used general-purpose operating system in the world. When IBM chose *PC-DOS*—the IBM brand of MS-DOS—as the operating system for its first personal computer in 1981, almost all computer displays were defined in terms of characters. A typical computer monitor displayed 24 eighty-column lines of text, numbers, and/or symbols. The computer sent messages to the monitor telling it which character to display in each location on the screen. To comply with this hardware arrangement, MS-DOS was designed with a **character-based interface**—a user interface based on characters rather than graphics.

Today tens of thousands of applications are MS-DOS-compatible. (People used to just say IBM-compatible, but as you'll see, that phrase doesn't necessarily mean the same thing anymore.) Most applications shield the user from the behind-the-scenes work of the operating system. When it is necessary to communicate directly with the operating system (to start up an application, for example), the user carries on a dialog through the MS-DOS **command-line interface.** With a command-line interface the user types commands and the computer responds. Some MS-DOS-compatible applications have a command-line interface, but it's more common for applications to have a **menu-driven interface** that allows users to choose commands from on-screen lists called **menus.** The User's View box illustrates two different character-based interfaces: the command-line interface of MS-DOS and the menu-driven interface of WordPerfect, a popular word processing application. **UV**

The User's View

Using Character-based Interfaces

▲ ▲

Software: MS-DOS and WordPerfect.

The goal: To open a term paper created with a word processor, print it, and delete it from the hard disk. (The *other* goal: to experience command-line and menu-driven character-based interfaces.)

1

When you turn on the computer, the MS-DOS operating system displays a **prompt** (`C:\>`) and a flashing cursor, and waits for you to type a command. You type `dir /w` to see a list of items in drive C's **directory.**

2

MS-DOS displays a list of items on the hard disk, including files and *subdirectories*— collections of files that have been grouped together—followed by another C-prompt saying the operating system is waiting for another command.

3

To open the paper you must first open the application program that created it: WordPerfect. The application is stored in the subdirectory *wp61,* so you type `cd wp61` to change to that directory.

4

You type `wp` then press Enter to open WordPerfect.

5

WordPerfect lets you choose commands from menus hidden in a **menu bar** at the top of the screen. The words in the menu bar— *File, Edit,* and the rest— are the names of the menus. You can use the mouse or keyboard to show menu choices and select commands.

6

You select the Open command from the file menu and choose the file called `privacy.wp6`.

7

The file is loaded from disk into the computer's memory, and the first part of the term paper appears on the screen.

8

You select the Print command to print the term paper.

9

You select the Exit command to close the word processing application and return to the MS-DOS prompt.

10

To delete the file you just printed, you enter the command `DEL` followed by the file name. You accidentally misstype a character.

11

The operating system doesn't recognize the command, so it responds with "Bad command or filename"— an **error message** telling you you've done something wrong.

12

You type the command correctly, the file is deleted.

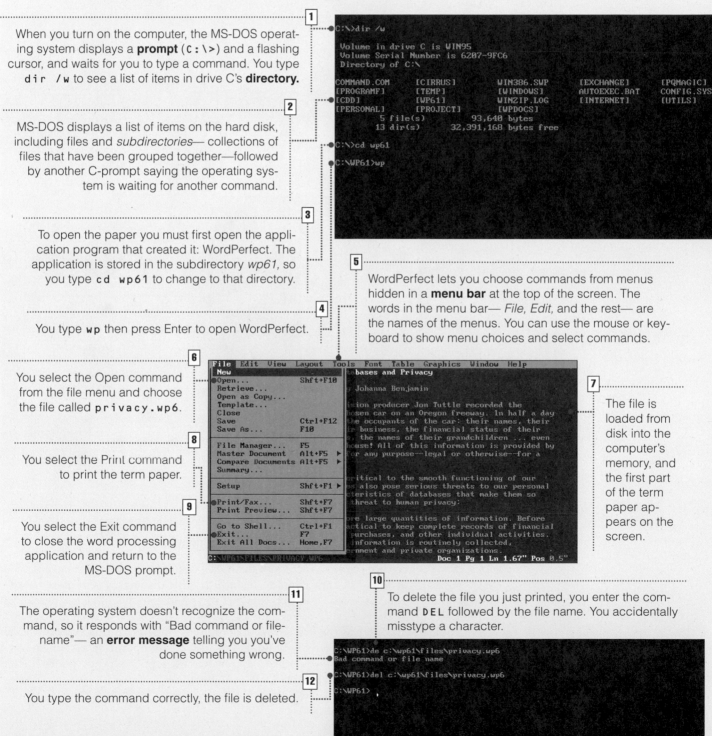

The User's View

Using a Macintosh GUI

▲▲▲▲▲▲▲▲▲▲▲▲▲▲▲▲▲▲▲▲▲▲▲▲▲

Software: Macintosh System 7.5 and WordPerfect.

The goal: To print and delete a term paper file, this time with a graphical user interface—a GUI.

1 When you turn on the Macintosh, you see a visual representation of a **desktop** with a menu bar at the top.

5 When you hold the mouse button down while pointing to the File menu, a pull-down menu appears like a window shade. To open the selected folder, you drag the mouse down until the pointer points to the Open command and release the button to choose that command.

2 An open window shows the contents of the hard disk called Macintosh HD.

3 Each icon in the window represents a **folder** containing other files.

4 The term paper icon is in a folder called School Work. You move the mouse so that the pointer points to the School Work icon and click the mouse button. It darkens to indicate that it has been *selected.*

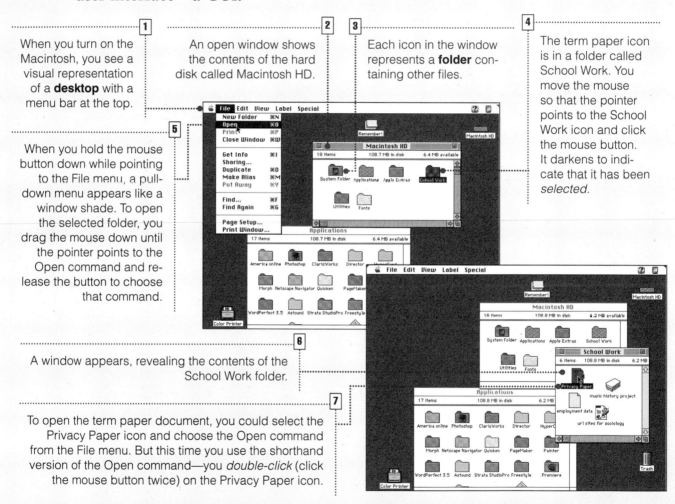

6 A window appears, revealing the contents of the School Work folder.

7 To open the term paper document, you could select the Privacy Paper icon and choose the Open command from the File menu. But this time you use the shorthand version of the Open command—you *double-click* (click the mouse button twice) on the Privacy Paper icon.

Graphical User Interfaces: Macintosh and Windows

In the years since the introduction of the IBM-PC, hardware advances have made it possible for low-cost computers to include graphic displays. A computer with a graphic display is not limited to displaying rows and columns of characters; it can individually control every dot on the screen. When it was introduced in 1984, the Apple Macintosh was the first low-cost computer whose operating system was designed with a graphic display in mind. The **Macintosh operating system** sports a **graphical user interface**—sometimes abbreviated **GUI,** pronounced "gooey"—that is radically different from the MS-DOS command-line interface.

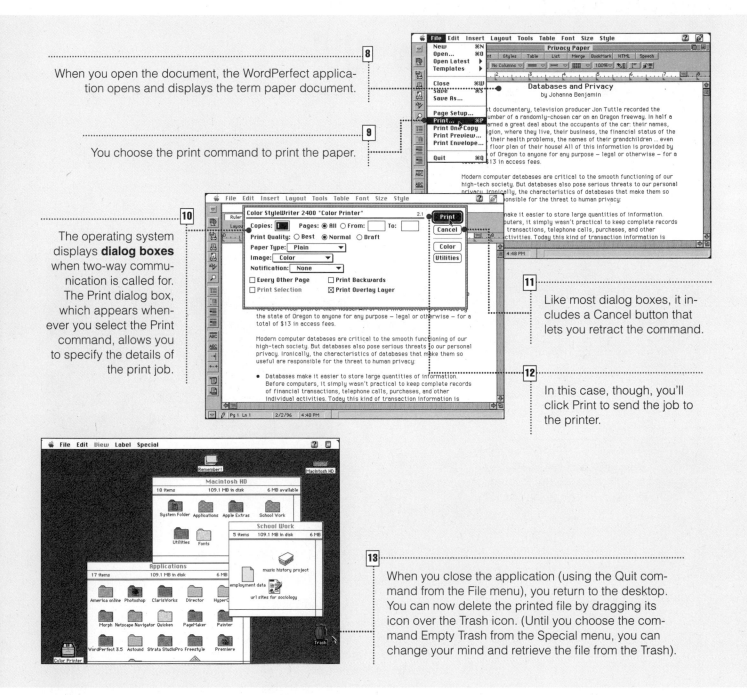

8

When you open the document, the WordPerfect application opens and displays the term paper document.

9

You choose the print command to print the paper.

10

The operating system displays **dialog boxes** when two-way communication is called for. The Print dialog box, which appears whenever you select the Print command, allows you to specify the details of the print job.

11

Like most dialog boxes, it includes a Cancel button that lets you retract the command.

12

In this case, though, you'll click Print to send the job to the printer.

13

When you close the application (using the Quit command from the File menu), you return to the desktop. You can now delete the printed file by dragging its icon over the Trash icon. (Until you choose the command Empty Trash from the Special menu, you can change your mind and retrieve the file from the Trash).

Instead of reading typed commands and file names from a command line, the Macintosh operating system determines what the user wants by monitoring movements of the mouse. With the mouse the user points to pictures, known as **icons,** that represent files, folders (collections of files), and disks. Documents are displayed in **windows**—framed areas that can be opened, closed, and rearranged with the mouse. The user selects commands from **pull-down menus** at the top of the screen. Because this kind of graphical user interface doesn't require users to memorize commands, it allows users who are new to a program to be up and running in a fraction of the time it takes to learn a command-line system. This User's View box shows a simple Macintosh session. **UV**

Using a Windows GUI
▲ ▲

Software: Microsoft Windows and WordPerfect for Windows.

The goal: To print the term paper one more time, this time with Windows.

1 Like the Macintosh, Windows presents a graphical display made up of icons and windows.

2 You can launch programs using the same techniques used in the Macintosh example, but many users prefer to use the Start Menu to select the application.

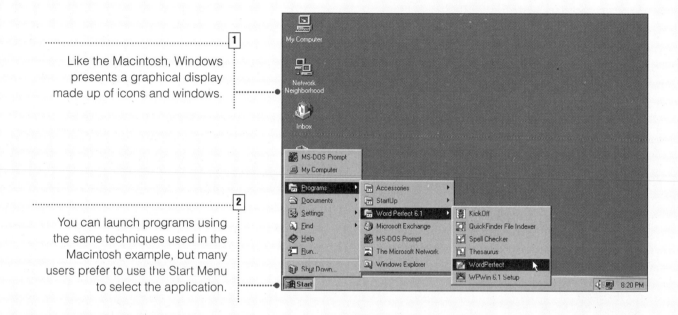

As you can see, working with a Macintosh is a very different experience than working with an IBM-compatible computer running MS-DOS. But the difference has less to do with the *hardware platform*—the hardware on which the software runs—than with the software itself. In fact, today people often use the term **platform** to describe the combination of hardware *and* operating system software upon which application software is built. In the case of the Macintosh, the distinction is moot, since every Macintosh includes the Macintosh operating system. But on IBM-compatible machines, the software part of the platform determines whether the user works with characters and typed commands or a GUI with many of the features that made the Macintosh popular.

Ironically the Macintosh's biggest competitor in the graphical user interface market is a product from Microsoft, the company that produces MS-DOS. Originally **Microsoft Windows** (commonly called Windows, or just Win) was a type of program, known as a **shell,** that put a Macintosh-like face on MS-DOS. The Windows shell stood between the user and the operating system, translating mouse movements and other user input into commands that could be recognized by MS-

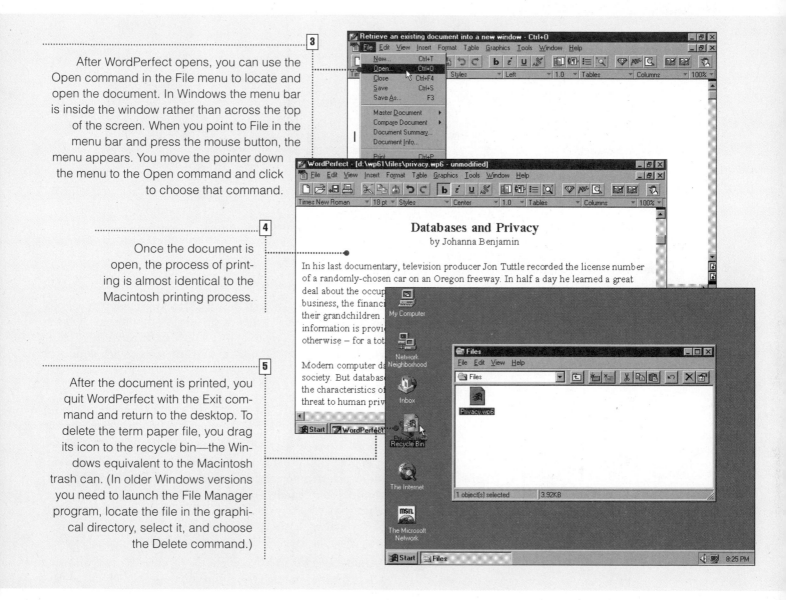

After WordPerfect opens, you can use the Open command in the File menu to locate and open the document. In Windows the menu bar is inside the window rather than across the top of the screen. When you point to File in the menu bar and press the mouse button, the menu appears. You move the pointer down the menu to the Open command and click to choose that command.

4 Once the document is open, the process of printing is almost identical to the Macintosh printing process.

5 After the document is printed, you quit WordPerfect with the Exit command and return to the desktop. To delete the term paper file, you drag its icon to the recycle bin—the Windows equivalent to the Macintosh trash can. (In older Windows versions you need to launch the File Manager program, locate the file in the graphical directory, select it, and choose the Delete command.)

DOS. Windows 3.1 and its predecessors don't completely hide their MS-DOS roots, but they do shield users from most of the details of DOS. With the introduction of Windows 95, Microsoft completed the transition of Windows from an operating system shell into an operating system similar in many ways to the Mac OS. Compare the Windows session shown in this User's View box with the earlier MS-DOS and Macintosh sessions. **UV**

Why WIMP Won

Make things as simple as possible—but no simpler.

—Albert Einstein

In these three examples we did the same job with different versions of the same application and produced the same output. In the case of MS-DOS and Windows, we even used the same hardware platform. But from the user's point of view, the

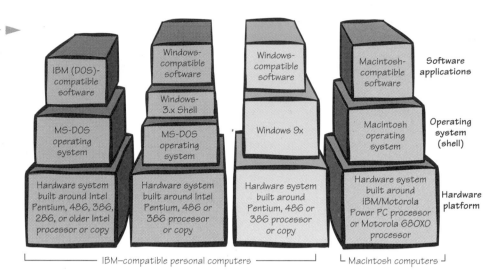

IBM—compatible personal computers   Macintosh computers

Compatibility Issues: Hardware Platforms and Software Environments. Most personal computers today are built on one of two hardware platforms: the Intel-based platform used in IBM-compatible PCs and the Motorola-based Macintosh platform. Among IBM-compatible computers, many include the Windows 3.x shell along with the MS-DOS operating system. Most new systems include Windows 95, an operating system that replaces both Windows 3.x and MS-DOS. Most software today is sold as DOS-compatible, Windows 3.x-compatible, Windows 95-compatible, or Macintosh-compatible because these four hardware/software environments dominate the market.

Macintosh and Windows sessions have more in common, even though they involve different hardware. The critical difference between these sessions and the DOS session are in the user interfaces. This is more than just a difference between working with pictures and working with words. Graphical user interfaces with *w*indows, *i*cons, *m*enus, and *p*ointing devices (collectively known as *WIMP*) offer several clear advantages from the user's point of view:

- *They're intuitive.* Visual metaphors like trash cans and folders are easier for people to understand and learn than typed commands. Users feel safe learning by trial and error because it's usually easy to predict the results of each action.

- *They're consistent.* People who use multiple applications on non-GUI systems are often faced with inconsistent interfaces that require them to keep reference manuals handy to look up commands. GUI applications have the same user interface as their operating systems, so users don't need to learn new ways of doing things whenever they switch applications. Many Macintosh and Windows users have mastered dozens of applications without ever consulting a manual.

- *They're forgiving.* Almost every dialog box includes a Cancel button, allowing the user to say, in effect, "Never mind." The Undo command can almost always take back the last command, restoring everything the way it was before the current command was issued.

- *They're protective.* When you're about to do something that may have unpleasant consequences (such as replacing the revised version of your term paper with an older version), the software opens a dialog box, reminding you to make sure you're doing what you want before you proceed.

- *They're flexible.* Users who prefer to keep their hands on the keyboard can use keyboard shortcuts instead of mouse movements to invoke most commands. Most actions can be accomplished in several different ways; each user can, in effect, customize the user interface.

Of course, all of this user-friendliness doesn't come free. Graphical user interfaces and friendly operating systems generally require more expensive graphics display systems, more memory, more disk space, and faster processors. MS-DOS and other command-line operating systems have minimal hardware requirements when compared to just about any GUI operating system or shell. But as hardware goes down in price and up in speed, efficiency arguments become less convincing.

GUIs Today

The computer industry is rallying behind graphical user interfaces. Almost all new personal computer systems today include either Windows or the Macintosh operating system. But these aren't the only GUI operating systems on the market today. Some others worth noting include

- IBM's *OS/2* is a high-powered operating system that can run most applications developed for both DOS and Windows. OS/2 is installed on millions of PCs, and many experts argue that it is technically superior to Microsoft Windows. But IBM's marketing of OS/2 has so far been no match for Microsoft's massive Windows campaign.

- Microsoft *Windows NT* is a variant of the Windows operating system aimed at networked computers that need features not found in Windows 3.x or Windows 9x. NT's multitasking capabilities and security controls make it a popular operating system for *servers*—systems that serve data and programs to networked PCs. NT is also distinguished from Windows 9x by its ability to run on a variety of processors—not just the Intel x86 family. NT's hardware requirements are stiff, but as more powerful systems become commonplace, NT is showing up on more PC desktops in the workplace.

- *UNIX*, a powerful and popular operating system that runs on everything from high-end PCs to mainframes. At its heart, UNIX is a command-line, character-based operating system. But several companies market UNIX variations and shells with state-of-the-art graphical interfaces. UNIX is the dominant operating system for workstations and many minicomputers and mainframes, and it's the native language of the Internet, but it's still relatively uncommon as a PC operating system. (You'll learn more about UNIX in Chapter 10.)

Of course, millions of older PCs don't have the hardware power to support *any* GUI. But many DOS applications and shells mimic modern GUIs within the limitations of the older hardware—the DOS version of WordPerfect in our User's View is a good example.

Still, the trends are unmistakable. Today's market for new PC hardware and software is dominated by two platforms: Windows, in all its variations, and the Macintosh. While the Macintosh commands a hefty share of specialized markets like graphic design, publishing, music, multimedia, and education, it runs a distant second to Windows in the massive corporate market.

To compete in a Windows-dominated world, Apple offers **emulation** options to make Windows and DOS software run on Macintoshes. One technique involves *software emulation*; a software program creates a *simulated* Windows machine in the Mac, translating all Windows-related instructions into signals the Mac's operating system and CPU can understand. But translation takes time, so software emulation isn't adequate when speed is critical. The other solution, *hardware emulation,* involves adding a circuit board containing an Intel-compatible CPU and additional PC hardware. This board effectively puts a second computer in the Mac's system unit. Emulation technology isn't unique to the Macintosh; there are emulation programs, for example, that allow Windows and Mac programs to run on UNIX-based Sun workstations. Emulation blurs the lines between platforms and allows users to avoid having to choose a single OS and user interface.

When we step back from the details of specific products and scan the big picture, one thing is clear: The graphical user interface is the interface of choice for computer users today. If current trends continue, command-line user interfaces will soon be as foreign to most computer users as FORTRAN, COBOL, and machine language are today.

RULES OF THUMB

Computer Consumer Concepts

The best computer for your specific needs is the one that will come on the market immediately after you actually purchase some other model.

—Dave Barry, humorist

This book's appendix, CD-ROM, and Internet Web Site contain lots of specific information about the nuts and bolts of buying hardware and software to make your own computer system. Of course, *any* brand-specific advice on choosing computer equipment is likely to be dated within a few months of publication because of the rapid rate of change in the computer marketplace. Still, some general principles remain constant while the technology races forward. Here are nine consumer criteria worth considering, even if you have no intention of buying your own computer.

•   **Cost.** Obviously, this is the bottom line. Buy what you can afford, but be sure to allow for extra memory, extended warranties, peripherals (printer, extra storage devices, modem, cables, speakers, and so on) and, above all, software. If you join a user group or connect to an on-line service (described in Chapters 9 and 10), you'll be able to meet some of your software needs at low (or no) cost. But you'll almost certainly need some commercial software, too. Don't be tempted to copy copyrighted software from your friends or public labs; software piracy is theft, prosecutable under federal laws. (Choosing

software isn't easy, but many of the periodicals listed at the end of Chapter 1 publish regular reviews to help you sort out the good stuff. If possible, try before you buy.)

•   **Capability.** Is it the right tool for the job? If you plan to do color graphics and desktop publishing, make sure your machine has enough memory and disk storage to support the resource-intensive applications you'll need. If you want to take advantage of state-of-the-art multimedia programs, consider only machines that meet *the latest* multimedia standards. If you want to *create* state-of-the-art multimedia programs, you'll probably need a powerful computer that can handle audio and video input as well as output. Be sure the machine you buy can do the job you need it to do, now and in the foreseeable future.

•   **Capacity.** Buy a computer that's powerful enough to meet your needs. Make sure the processor is fast enough to handle your demands and that the memory and external storage capacity are sufficient for the jobs you'll be doing—and are easily upgradable as your needs grow. Consult periodicals and software packages for minimum requirements.

•   **Customizability.** Computers are versatile, but they don't all handle all jobs with equal ease. If you'll be using word processors, spreadsheets, and other mainstream software packages, just about any computer will do. If you have off-the-beaten-path needs (video editing, instrument monitoring, and so on),

Tomorrow's User Interfaces

I hate computers. Telepathy would be better.

—John Perry Barlow, writer and cofounder of the Electronic Frontier Foundation

As attractive and popular as today's graphical user interfaces are, they're not likely to reign forever. Future user interfaces will be built around technologies that are still in development today. Here are some likely candidates:

•   *The end of applications.* As more programs take advantage of interapplication communication, the boundaries between individual applications are likely to blur. Future computer users may not think in terms of word processors, spreadsheets, and such; they'll just use their computers like we use pencils today—as all-purpose tools.

choose an *open system* (with slots and ports) that can be customized.

- **Compatibility.** Will the software you plan to use run on the computer you're considering? Most popular computers have a good selection of compatible software, but if you have specific needs, such as being able to take your software home to run on Mom's computer, study the compatibility issue carefully. Total compatibility isn't always possible or necessary. A typical IBM-compatible computer, for example, probably won't run *every* "IBM-compatible" program, but it will almost certainly run the mainstream applications that most users need. Many people don't care if all their programs will run on another kind of computer; they just need *data* compatibility—the ability to move documents back and forth between systems on disk or through a network connection. It's common, for example, for IBM users and Macintosh users to send documents back and forth over a network without any loss of data.

- **Connectivity.** In today's networked world it's short-sighted to see your computer as just a self-contained information appliance. Make sure you include a high-speed modem and/or network connection in your system so you can take full advantage of the communication capabilities of your computer. (Chapters 9 and 10 describe network communication in detail.)

- **Convenience.** Just about any computer can do most common jobs, but which is the most convenient for you? Do you value portability over having all the peripherals permanently connected? Is it important to you to have a machine that's easy to install and maintain so you can take care of it yourself?

Or do you want to choose the same kind of machine as the people around you so you can get help easily when you need it? Which user interface makes the kind of work *you'll* be doing easiest?

- **Company.** If you try to save money by buying an off-brand computer, you may find yourself the owner of an orphan computer. High-tech companies can, and frequently do, vanish overnight. Make sure you'll be able to get service and parts down the road.

- **Curve.** Most models of personal computers seem to have a useful life span of just a few years—if they survive the first year or two. If you want to minimize your financial risk, avoid buying a computer during those early years in a model's life, when little compatible software is available. Also avoid buying a computer that's over the hill; you'll know it because most software developers will have abandoned this model for greener CPUs. In the words of Alexander Pope, "Be not the first by whom the new are tried, nor yet the last to lay the old aside."

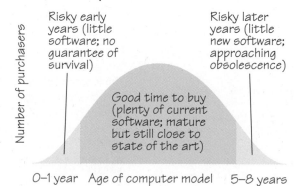

Computer consumer's curve

Risky early years (little software; no guarantee of survival)

Risky later years (little new software; approaching obsolescence)

Good time to buy (plenty of current software; mature but still close to state of the art)

Number of purchasers

0–1 year   Age of computer model   5–8 years

- *Natural-language interfaces.* It's just a matter of time before we'll be able to communicate with computers in English, Spanish, Russian, Japanese, or some other natural language. Today many computers can reliably read subsets of the English language or can be trained to understand spoken English commands and text. Tomorrow's machines should be able to handle much day-to-day work through a natural-language interface, written or spoken. Natural-language processing lies in the domain of artificial intelligence, discussed in a later chapter.

- *Agents.* Artificial intelligence research being done today may lead to intelligent *agents* that "live" in our computers and act as digital secretaries, anticipating our requests, filling in details in our work, searching networks for critical information, and adjusting the computerized workspace to fit our needs. The last chapter of this book describes agents and other futuristic user interface technologies, including the technology of virtual reality.

- *Virtual realities.* Further into the future many experts predict that user interfaces will become so sophisticated that we'll be hard-pressed to detect the difference

Virtual reality hardware and software are used in a variety of unusual applications. Engineers in a virtual reality chamber (top left) watch simulated waves pound against an imaginary boat to see what kind of deck-mounted structures can best withstand battering. High-tech gamers (above) wearing special goggles are immersed in a 3-D environment that responds to their every move. Scientist at CERN (top right) flies through the virtual prototype of the site for a future experiment in particle acceleration.

between the real world outside the computer and the **virtual reality** created by the computer, except that the virtual reality will allow us to do things that can't be done on the physical plane. Some computer games today provide surprisingly convincing simulations of the experience of driving a car or flying a plane. These games represent the tip of a gigantic iceberg of research into virtual reality software. More sophisticated virtual reality interfaces can be achieved today with specially designed hardware—for input, a glove or body suit equipped with motion sensors, and for output, a helmet with eye-sized screens whose views change as the helmet moves. This equipment, when coupled with appropriate software, allows the user to explore an artificial world of data as if it were three-dimensional physical space.

The best-known example of the kind of virtual reality researchers are working toward is the Holodeck on TV's *Star Trek*. The Holodeck can create absolutely convincing simulations of anything from a Sherlock Holmes detective story to a 24th-century antimatter generator. No keyboards or screens are in sight; the user interface is a three-dimensional artificial world full of people, places, and things—real or imaginary—that can be seen, touched, talked to, and controlled by one or more "users." Far fetched? Absolutely. Possible? Maybe. When? Don't sell your keyboard for a while. . . .

SUMMARY

Software provides the communication link between human and computer. Because software is *soft*—stored in memory rather than hard-wired into the circuitry—it can easily be modified to meet the needs of the computer user. By changing software, you can change a computer from one kind of tool into another.

Most software falls into one of three broad categories: compilers and other translator programs, software applications, and system software. A compiler is a software tool that allows programs written in English-like languages like BASIC and C to be translated into the zeros and ones of the machine language the computer understands. A compiler frees the programmer from the tedium of machine-language programming, making it easier to write quality programs with fewer bugs. But even with the best translators, programming is a little like communicating with an alien species. It's a demanding process that requires more time and mental energy than most people are willing or able to invest.

Fortunately software applications make it easy for most computer users today to communicate their needs to the computer without learning programming. Applications simulate and extend the properties of familiar real-world tools like typewriters, paint brushes, and file cabinets, making it possible for people to do things with computers that would be difficult or impossible otherwise. Integrated software packages combine several applications in a single unified package, making it easy to switch between tools. For situations when a general commercial program won't do the job, programmers for businesses and public institutions develop vertical-market and custom packages.

Whether you're writing programs or simply using them, the computer's operating system is functioning behind the scenes, translating your software's instructions into messages that the hardware can understand. An operating system serves as the computer's business manager, taking care of the hundreds of details that need to be handled to keep the computer functioning. A timesharing operating system has the particularly challenging job of serving multiple users concurrently, monitoring the machine's resources, keeping track of each user's account, and protecting the security of the system and each user's data. Many of those system-related problems that the operating system can't solve directly can be handled by utility programs.

Applications, utilities, programming languages, and operating systems all must, to varying degrees, communicate with the user. A program's user interface is a critical factor in that communication. User interfaces have evolved over the years to the point where sophisticated software packages can be operated by people who know little about the inner workings of the computer. A well-designed user interface shields the user from the bits and bytes, creating an on-screen façade or shell that makes sense to the user. Today the computer industry has moved away from the tried-and-true command-line interfaces toward a friendlier graphical user interface that uses windows, icons, mice, and pull-down menus in an intuitive, consistent environment. Tomorrow's user interfaces are likely to depend more on voice, three-dimensional graphics, and animation to create an artificial reality.

Chapter Review

Key Terms

algorithm	emulation	operating system (OS)
application suite (office suite)	error message	platform
booting	folder	prompt
bug	graphical user interface (GUI)	public domain software
character-based interface	icon	pull-down menu
command-line interface	integrated software	shareware
compatibility	machine language	shell
compiler	Macintosh operating system	software license
concurrent processing	menu	system software
copy-protected software	menu bar	upgrade
copyrighted software	menu-driven interface	user interface
custom application	Microsoft Windows	utility program
desktop	MS-DOS	vertical-market application
dialog box	multitasking	virtual reality
directory	natural language	window
document	on-line documentation	
documentation	opening a file	

Review Questions

1. Define or describe each of the key terms listed above. Check your answers in the glossary.

2. What is the relationship between a program and an algorithm?

3. Most computer software falls into one of three categories: compilers and other translator programs, software applications, and system software. Describe and give examples of each.

4. Which must be loaded first into the computer's memory, the operating system or software applications? Why?

5. Write an algorithm for changing a flat tire. Check your algorithm carefully for errors and ambiguities. Then have a classmate or your instructor check it. How did your results compare?

6. Describe several functions of a single-user operating system. Describe several additional functions of a multiuser operating system.

7. What does it mean when software is called IBM-compatible or Macintosh-compatible? What does this have to do with the operating system?

8. Why is the user interface such an important part of software?

9. What is a graphical user interface? How does it differ from a command-line interface? What are the advantages of each?

Discussion Questions

1. In what way is writing instructions for a computer more difficult than writing instructions for a person? In what way is it easier?

2. How would using a computer be different if it had no operating system? How would programming be different?

3. Speculate about the user interface of a typical computer in the year 2010. How would this user interface differ from those of today's computers?

4. If you had the resources to design a computer with a brand new user interface, what would your priorities be? Make a rank-ordered list of the qualities you'd like to have in your user interface.

Projects

1. Write a report about available computer applications in your field of study or in your chosen profession.

2. Take an inventory of computer applications available in your computer lab. Describe the major uses for each application.

3. Research different personal computer systems from a consumer's point of view. Include software and peripherals in your analysis.

Sources and Resources

Books

How Software Works, by Ron White (Emeryville, CA: Ziff-Davis Press, 1993). This book by the author of *How Computers Work* focuses on software. With the same graphical approach that combines rich computer-generated illustration with terse, readable explanations, *How Software Works* turns software into something concrete. It's IBM-specific, but the underlying processes are mostly universal.

The Little Mac Book, by Robin Williams (Berkeley, CA: Peachpit Press, 1995) and *The Little Windows 95 Book,* by Kay Yarborough Nelson (Berkeley, CA: Peachpit Press, 1995). These highly acclaimed guides succinctly and clearly introduce first-time users to the Macintosh and Windows OSs. They're ideal for people who don't want to spend a lot of time reading long manuals. If you can't find one of these, there are dozens of other beginner books for learning the basics of working with personal computer operating systems.

Tog on Interface, by Bruce Tognazzini (Reading, MA: Addison-Wesley, 1992). A witty and thought-provoking collection of ideas on user interfaces from a long-time "evangelist" for Apple developers, now at Sun Microsystems.

The Art of Human-Computer Interface Design, edited by Brenda Laurel (Reading, MA: Addison-Wesley, 1990). This entertaining, provocative, and highly informative book is filled with essays by the experts on what makes a user interface work or not work. Chapters cover everything from menus and icons to virtual reality.

Designing the User Interface: Strategies for Effective Human-Computer Interaction, by Ben Schneiderman (Reading, MA: Addison-Wesley, 1992). This book thoroughly explores the issues that face anyone designing a user interface, whether it's a simple application program, a complex hypermedia document, or a virtual reality environment. In a style that's both academic and approachable, Schneiderman discusses everything from input and output hardware to the ultimate social impact of the technology.

Silicon Mirage: The Art and Science of Virtual Reality, by Steve Aukstakalnis and David Blatner (Berkeley, CA: Peachpit Press, 1992). This book provides accessible answers to the question, "What's virtual reality all about?" It includes explanations of the basic technology, descriptions of present and future applications, and discussions of social and technological issues raised by VR.

How Virtual Reality Works, by Joshua Eddings (Emeryville, CA: Ziff-Davis Press, 1994). In the graphically rich style of *How Computers Work,* this book illustrates the basics of VR technology and shows many present and future applications.

World Wide Web Pages

Software companies, like hardware companies, have established their presence on the Net. Most of the companies use addresses that follow the formula http://www.companyname.com. Examples include http://www.microsoft.com, http://www.claris.com, and http://www.corel.com. Content varies from company to company; you might find technical support, product descriptions, demo software, software updates, and user tips on a typical software home page. For more software information, check the home pages of publishers that specialize in computer books. For example Peachpit Press (http://www.peachpit.com) includes sample chapters from several popular software books on its home pages. As usual, the *Computer Confluence* home page provides up-to-date links to a variety of valuable Web resources.

PART TWO

USING COMPUTERS

ESSENTIAL

APPLICATIONS

5

WORKING WITH WORDS

Mark Twain Goes for Broke

This newfangled writing machine has several virtues. It piles an awful stack of words on one page. It don't muss things or scatter ink blots around. Of course it saves paper.

—Mark Twain

In 1874 Mark Twain bought a Remington Type-Writer for $125. One year later he became the first author in history to submit a typewritten manuscript: *The Adventures of Tom Sawyer.*

Twain later invested almost $200,000 (the equivalent of $1.5 million today) in the promising new Paige typesetting technology. He wrote, "All the other wonderful inventions of the human brain sink pretty nearly into commonplaces contrasted with this awful mechanical miracle. Telephones, telegraphs, locomotives, cotton gins, sewing machines, Babbage calculators, Jacquard looms, perfecting presses, all mere toys, simplicities! The Paige Compositor marches alone and far in the land of human inventions," and on a more down-to-earth level, "This typesetter does not get drunk."

The Paige might very well have transformed publishing, as Twain predicted, had not Ottmar Mergenthaler invented the Linotype machine at about the same time. Because of the Linotype, Twain's promising publishing machine was obsolete at its inception, and Twain was forced into bankruptcy.

Linotypes dominated the industry until the 1960s, when electronic typesetting with mainframe computers took over. Now mainframe publishing systems are rapidly being displaced by personal computers. From

Mark Twain

Early computers were no threat to typewriters; they were too unfriendly, inconvenient, inflexible, and expensive to be used by anyone but highly skilled experts. The special-purpose "word processing machines" used by clerical workers in the 1960s represented a big step forward, but they were a far cry from the state-of-the-art word processing programs on today's personal computers. Word processing software available today is easier to learn, easier to use, and more powerful than anyone might have imagined a few decades ago.

Anyone who has used a computer as a word processor knows that it's far more than a fancy typewriter. The entire writing process is transformed by modern word processing software. Instead of suffering through the painful and disjointed process of typing and retyping in pursuit of a "clean" draft, a writer can focus on developing ideas and let the machine take care of the details of laying out the words neatly on the page. Today's word processing technology makes it possible and fun for just about any literate person to communicate effectively in writing. More than any other software application, word processing is a tool for everybody.

In this chapter we'll take a writer's view of word processing, from the first stages of entering text right on through to printing the final document. We'll consider advanced software tools for working with words, from outliners and idea processors to sophisticated reference tools. Finally we'll see how desktop publishing technology is transforming the entire publishing process and providing more people with the power to communicate in print.

THE WORD PROCESSING PROCESS

I . . . cannot imagine now that I ever wrote with a typewriter.

—Arthur C. Clarke, author and scientist

simple word processors to professional desktop publishing systems, small computers are rapidly and radically transforming the entire publishing process.

Working with any word processor (a common way of referring to word processing software) involves several steps:

99

- entering text
- editing text
- formatting the document
- proofreading the document
- saving the document on disk
- printing the document

Early word processing systems generally forced users to follow these steps in a strict order. Some systems still in use today—mainly on mainframes and other time-sharing systems—segregate these processes into steps that can't easily be mixed. But modern word processing systems provide all of the necessary tools in a single, seamless software package. Most users of word processors today switch freely between editing and formatting, in some cases doing both at the same time. Still, for our discussion it makes sense to consider these as separate processes.

Entering Text

Entering text using a word processor is similar to using a typewriter but simpler. As you type on the computer keyboard, your text is displayed on the screen and stored in the computer's RAM. Since random access memory is not a permanent storage medium, it's important to regularly **save** your work—that is, make a disk file containing your work in progress. That way if the power fails, or if the computer fails, or if you accidentally erase part of the text, you can restart the machine (if necessary) and *open* the saved version of your document—copy it back from a floppy or hard disk into the computer's memory. If you save your work on a diskette, you can take a break and later return to your computer (or another one like it at a different location), open your document, and start where you left off.

The User's View box shows a sample of entering text with Microsoft Word, a modern word processing program. Like most of the applications featured in this book, Microsoft Word is available in almost identical versions for both Macintosh and Windows-compatible computers. **UV**

Editing Text

All word processing applications allow you to do basically the same thing: write and refine a document on screen until it's good enough to commit to paper. If you're working with a modern **WYSIWYG** (short for *w*hat *y*ou *s*ee *i*s *w*hat *y*ou *g*et and pronounced "wizzy-wig") word processor, the arrangement of the words on the screen represents a close approximation of the arrangement of words on the printed page.

A modern word processor makes it easy to **edit text.** You can change and re-arrange your work in all kinds of ways that aren't possible with typewriters or pencils. With a word processor you can easily

- **navigate** to different parts of the document by scrolling or by using a **Find command** to locate a particular word or phrase
- **insert text** at any point in the document
- **delete text** from any part of the document
- **move text** from one part of the document to another section of the same document or to another document
- **copy text** from one part of a document and duplicate it in another section of the document or in a different document
- **search and replace** selected words or phrases throughout a document

The User's View

Entering Text

▲ ▲

Software: Microsoft Word.

The goal: To produce a copy of a classic work to be read in an English class presentation.

1 A word processing document starts as an empty window.

2 A flashing **cursor** (sometimes called an **insertion bar**) indicates your location in the document. As you type, the cursor moves to the right, leaving a trail of text in its wake. At the same time, those characters are stored in the computer's memory. If you mistype a character or string of characters, you can press Delete or Backspace to eliminate the typos.

3 Because of a feature called **word wrap,** the word processor automatically transports any words that won't fit on the current line to the next line along with the cursor. The only time you need to press Return or Enter is when you want to *force* the program to begin a new line— such as at the end of a paragraph.

4 As you type, the topmost lines **scroll** out of view to make room on the screen for the new ones. The text you've entered is still in memory, even though you can't see it on the screen.

5 You can retrieve it anytime by scrolling backward through the text. In this respect, a word processor document is like a modern version of ancient paper scrolls.

6 Every few minutes you select the Save command to save your document in a disk file containing your work so far. This provides insurance against accidental erasure of the text you've entered.

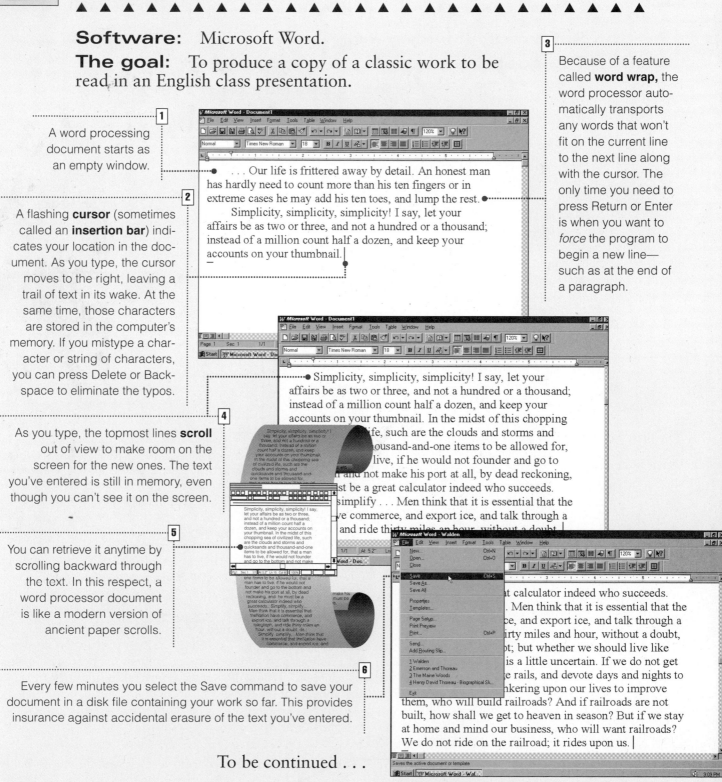

To be continued . . .

Editing Text

▲ ▲

Software: Microsoft Word.

The goal: To edit the text you have entered.

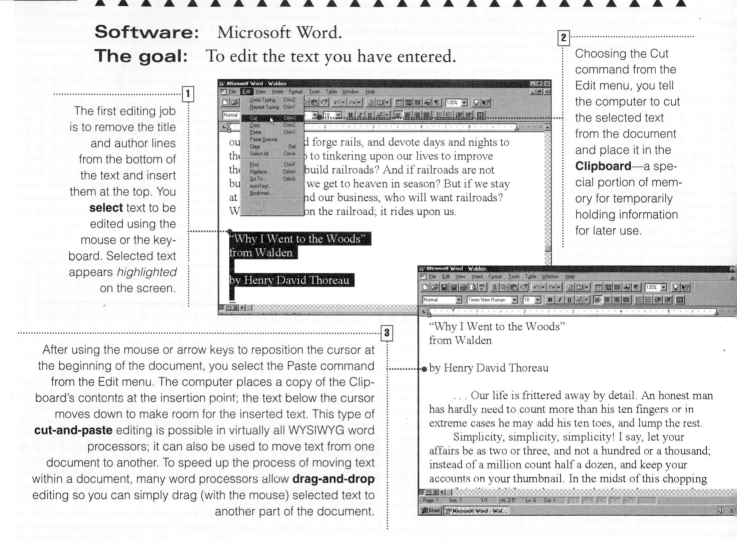

1 The first editing job is to remove the title and author lines from the bottom of the text and insert them at the top. You **select** text to be edited using the mouse or the keyboard. Selected text appears *highlighted* on the screen.

2 Choosing the Cut command from the Edit menu, you tell the computer to cut the selected text from the document and place it in the **Clipboard**—a special portion of memory for temporarily holding information for later use.

3 After using the mouse or arrow keys to reposition the cursor at the beginning of the document, you select the Paste command from the Edit menu. The computer places a copy of the Clipboard's contents at the insertion point; the text below the cursor moves down to make room for the inserted text. This type of **cut-and-paste** editing is possible in virtually all WYSIWYG word processors; it can also be used to move text from one document to another. To speed up the process of moving text within a document, many word processors allow **drag-and-drop** editing so you can simply drag (with the mouse) selected text to another part of the document.

Professional word processing programs contain sophisticated variations on these basic editing features. But even with this basic set of features, you can go a long way toward eliminating the drudgery that plagued writers in the precomputer era.

The User's View box above shows a brief editing session with a short document. As you'll see in this example, a word processor streamlines the process of making changes. Of course, real-world editing often involves several sessions of writing and rewriting. The bigger the editing job, the more a word processor can help. **UV**

Formatting Text

When you're editing text, you only need to concern yourself with the words. But before you print your document, you'll need to consider the *format* of the document—

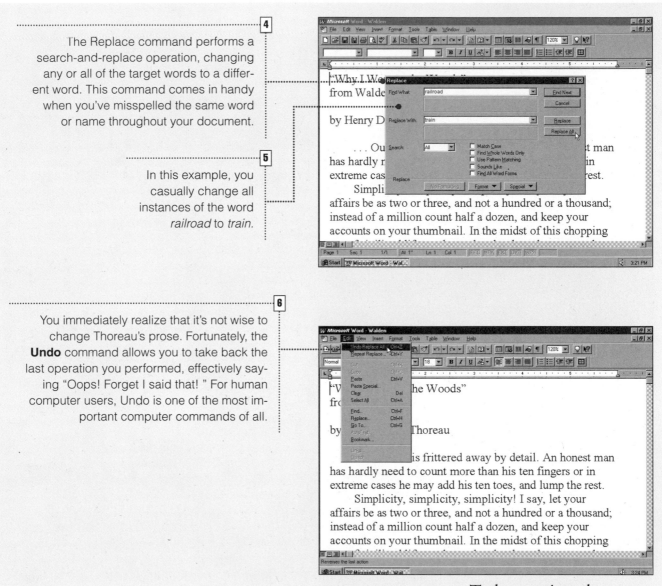

4

The Replace command performs a search-and-replace operation, changing any or all of the target words to a different word. This command comes in handy when you've misspelled the same word or name throughout your document.

5

In this example, you casually change all instances of the word *railroad* to *train*.

6

You immediately realize that it's not wise to change Thoreau's prose. Fortunately, the **Undo** command allows you to take back the last operation you performed, effectively saying "Oops! Forget I said that! " For human computer users, Undo is one of the most important computer commands of all.

To be continued . . .

how the words will look on the page. **Text formatting** commands allow you to control the format and style of the document. Character-based systems (such as most programs running on IBM-compatibles without Windows) generally don't provide the full range of formatting options available on WYSIWYG systems, and when they do they're more challenging to use. Still, most modern word processors allow users to control the formats of individual characters, lines, or paragraphs, as well as complete documents.

Formatting Characters

The format of the characters that you print is determined largely by your printer. Most modern printers can print text in a variety of point sizes, typefaces, and styles that aren't possible with typewriters. Characters are traditionally measured by **point size,** with one point equal to 1/72 inch. Most documents, including this book, use

These fonts represent just a few of the hundreds of type-faces available for personal computers and printers today. The two symbol fonts given, Symbol and Zapf Ding-bats, provide special charac-ters not available with other fonts.

Examples of	12-point size	24-point size
Serif fonts	Times Courier	**Times** Courier
Sans-serif fonts	Helvetica Avant Garde	**Helvetica** **Avant Garde**
Script fonts	*Zapf Chancery* *Kuenstler Script*	*Zapf Chancery* *Kuenstler Script*
Display fonts	Regular Joe Birch Remedy	Regular Joe Birch Remedy
Symbol fonts	Συμβολ ✳❀□❄ ❂✳■	Συμβολ ✳❀□❄ ❂✳■

smaller point sizes for text to fit more information on each page and larger point sizes to make titles and headings stand out.

In the language of typesetters, a **font** is a size and style of **typeface.** For example, the typeface known as Helvetica includes many fonts, one of which is 12-point Hel-vetica bold. In the world of personal computing, the distinction isn't quite so clear; many people use the terms *font* and *typeface* interchangeably.

Whatever you call them, you have hundreds of choices of typefaces for most modern computers. **Serif fonts,** like those in the Times family, are embellished with serifs—fine lines at the ends of the main strokes of each character. **Sans serif fonts,** like those in the Helvetica family, have plainer, cleaner lines. Typewriters and fonts that mimic typewriters, like those in the Courier family, produce characters that al-ways take up the same amount of space, no matter how skinny or fat the characters are. In contrast, **proportionally spaced fonts** allow more room for wide characters like w's than for narrow characters like i's.

Formatting Lines and Paragraphs

Many formatting commands naturally apply to more than a few characters or words: those that control margins, space between lines, indents, tab stops, and justi-fication. **Justification** refers to the alignment of text on a line. Four justification

5.1

Font Technology

When a computer displays a character on a monitor or prints it on a laser, ink-jet, or dot-matrix printer, the character is nothing more than a collection of dots in an invisible grid. *Bit-mapped fonts* store characters in this way, with each pixel represented as a black-or-white bit in a matrix. A bit-mapped font usually looks fine on screen in the intended point size but doesn't look smooth when printed on a high-resolution printer or enlarged on screen.

This bit-mapped font suffers from pixellation when enlarged.

Most computer systems now use scalable outline fonts to represent type in

This outline for the lowercase letter *a* retains its original shape at any size or resolution.

memory until it is displayed or printed. A scalable font represents each character as an outline that can be scaled—increased or decreased in size without distortion. Curves and lines are smooth and don't have stair-stepped, jagged edges when they're resized. The outline is stored inside the computer or printer as a series of mathematical statements about the position of points and the shape of the lines connecting those points.

Downloadable fonts (soft fonts) are stored in the computer system (not the printer) and downloaded to the printer only when needed. These fonts usually have matching screen fonts and are easily moved to different computer systems. Most importantly, you can use the same downloadable font on many printer models.

Laser printers are really dedicated computer systems that contain their own CPU, RAM, ROM, and specialized operating system. *Printer fonts* are stored in the printer's ROM and are always available for use with that printer, but you may not be able to achieve WYSIWYG if your computer doesn't have a screen font to match your printer font. And if you move your document to a different computer and printer, the same printer font may not be available on the new system.

Fonts are most commonly available in two scalable outline forms: Adobe Postscript and Apple/Microsoft TrueType. Because Apple and Microsoft supply TrueType downloadable fonts with their operating systems, TrueType fonts are more popular among general computer users. Postscript fonts usually require additional software but are the standard among many graphics professionals. Postscript is actually a complete page description language particularly well suited to the demands of professional publishers.

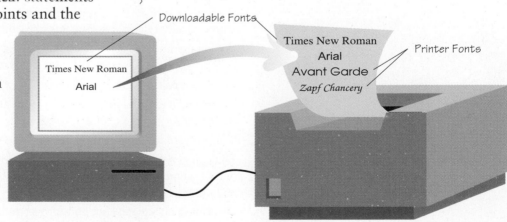

Downloadable Fonts

Times New Roman
Arial

Times New Roman
Arial
Avant Garde
Zapf Chancery

Printer Fonts

Most word processors provide four different options for justifying text.

This text illustrates centered justification. For centered text both margins are ragged. Centered text is often used for titles.

This text illustrates left justification. For left-justified text the left margin is smooth and the right margin is ragged.

This text illustrates right justification. For right-justified text the right margin is smooth and the left margin is ragged.

This text illustrates full justification. For fully justified text, spaces between words are adjusted to make both m a r g i n s smooth.

choices are commonly available: *left justification* (with a smooth left margin and ragged right margin), *right justification*, *full justification* (both margins are smooth), and *centered justification*.

Word processors vary as to how they handle these formatting commands. Some, like Microsoft Word, apply them to paragraphs you have selected. Others, like WordPerfect, apply them to blocks of text marked by beginning and ending codes. Both approaches give you control over the final look of every line of text.

Formatting the Document

Some formatting commands are applied to entire documents. For example, Word's Page Setup command allows you to control the margins that apply throughout the document. Other commands allow you to specify the content, size, and style of **headers** and **footers**—blocks that appear at the top and bottom of every page, displaying repetitive information like chapter titles, author names, and automatically calculated page numbers. The User's View box demonstrates some basic text formatting operations using Microsoft Word. **UV**

High-end word processing programs often provide a great deal of formatting flexibility. Here are some examples:

- You can define **style sheets** containing custom styles for each of the common elements in a document (for example, you can define a style called "subhead" as a paragraph that's left-justified, boldface, 12-point Helvetica font with standard margins, and apply that style for every subhead in the document without re-selecting all three of these commands for a new subhead. If you decide later to change the subheads to 14-point Futura, your changes in the subhead style are automatically reflected throughout the doucment.)

- You can define alternate headers, footers, and margins so that left- and right-facing pages can have different margins, headers, and footers.

- You can create documents with variable-width multiple columns.

- Using **automatic footnoting** saves you from having to place footnotes and endnotes.

- Using **automatic hyphenation** divides long words that fall at the ends of lines.

- You can generate table-of-contents and indexes for books and other long works (with human help for making judgments about which words belong in the index and how they should be arranged).

- You can easily create, edit, and format multicolumn tables.

The User's View

Formatting Text

▲▲▲▲▲▲▲▲▲▲▲▲▲▲▲▲▲▲▲▲▲▲▲▲▲

Software: Microsoft Word.

The goal: To change the look of the text you've entered and edited.

1
To italicize the title *Walden,* you select the characters to be changed ...

2
... choose the Font command from the Format menu ...

3
... and then select the *Italic* font style in the Font dialog box.

4
You can center text by selecting the text ...

5
... and clicking the center button.

6
You can see a miniature picture of your final output by selecting the *Print Preview* command from the File menu.

7
If it looks right, you can select the Print command or click on the printer icon to produce a hard copy.

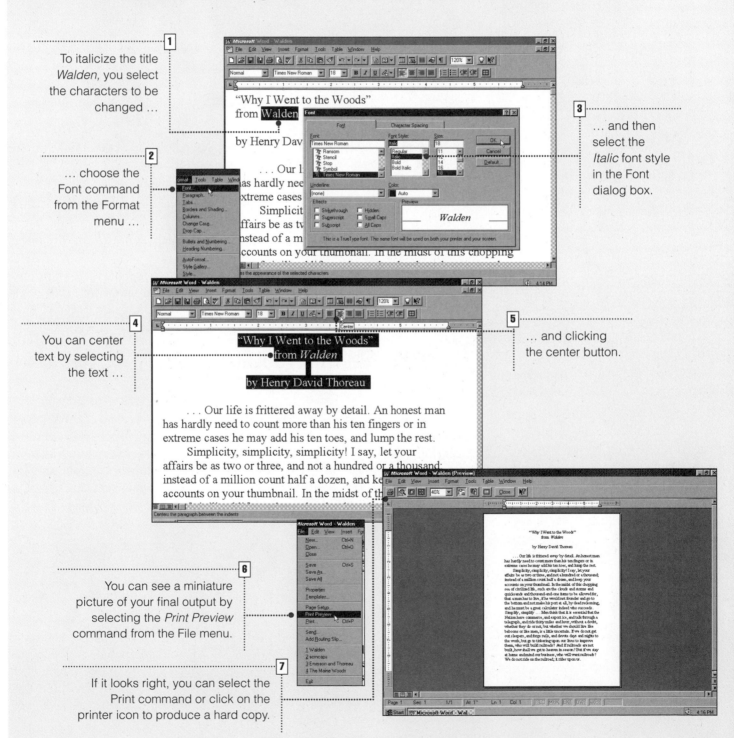

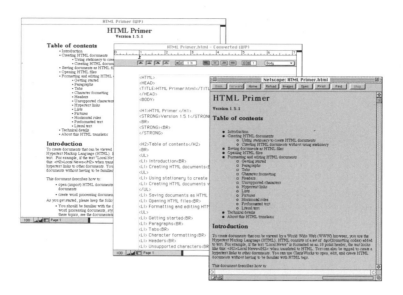

ClarisWorks is one of many word processors that can save documents in HTML format so they can be published on the World Wide Web. The screen shown on the left is a formatted ClarisWorks document. The center screen shows the same document saved in HTML format. Notice how embedded codes have replaced the formatting in the document. The screen on the right shows what the HTML document looks like as a web page.

- You can attach hidden text, pop-up notes, or auditory notes that can be seen or heard without showing up in the final printed document.

- You can incorporate graphics created with other applications.

- Automatic editing features catch and correct common typing errors (such as *THe* instead of *The*) on the fly.

- Coaching or help features walk you through complex document formatting procedures.

- You can convert formatted documents to *HTML (HyperText Markup Language)* or other formats used for publishing documents on the Internet's World Wide Web, as discussed in Chapter 10.

THE WORDSMITH'S TOOLBOX

Word processing doesn't need to be limited to basic editing and formatting. A typical word processor might include a built-in *outliner, spelling checker, thesaurus,* and *indexer.* But even word processors that don't include those features can be enhanced with stand-alone programs specifically designed to accomplish the same things. We'll examine a few of these tools next.

Outliners and Idea Processors

> If any man wishes to write in a clear style, let him first be clear in his thoughts.
>
> —Johann W. von Goethe

For many of us, the hardest part of the writing process is collecting and organizing our thoughts. Many traditional English-class techniques for preparing to write—outlines, 3x5 note cards, and the like—involve so much additional work that they often seem to add another layer to the problem. But when computer technology is applied to these time honored techniques, they're transformed into high-powered tools for extending our minds and streamlining the process of turning vague thoughts into solid prose.

Word Processing Is Not Typing

If you're already a touch typist, your typing skills will help you become proficient at word processing quickly. (If you're *not* a touch typist, see Project 1, Chapter 3.) Unfortunately, a few typing skills are counterproductive on a modern word processor. Here's a short list of new word processing habits to replace outmoded typing habits:

• **Use the Return or Enter key only when you must.** Let the computer's automatic word wrap handle routine end-of-line business.

• **Use tabs and margin guides, not the spacebar, to align columns.** WYSIWYG is a matter of degree, and text that looks perfectly aligned on screen may not line up on paper if you depend on your eyes and the spacebar.

• **Don't underline.** Use *italics* and **boldface** for emphasis. Italicize book and journal titles.

• **Use only one space after a period.** Most type experts agree that proportionally spaced fonts look better if you avoid double spaces.

• **Take advantage of special characters.** Bullet (•), em dash (—), curly quotes (" "), and other nontypewriter characters make your work look more professional, and they don't cost a thing.

Idea processors take a variety of forms, but most are built around the concept of **outlining**. At first glance an outliner looks like a word processor. The difference lies in the underlying structure: While word processors are designed to manipulate characters and words, outliners are organized around hierarchies or levels of ideas. Most outliners are particularly effective at performing three functions:

• arranging information into levels, so that each heading can be fleshed out with more detailed subheads, which can then be broken into smaller pieces

• rearranging ideas and levels so that subideas are automatically moved with their parent ideas

• hiding and revealing levels of detail as needed, so that you can examine the forest, the trees, or an individual leaf of your project

For a project that requires research, an outliner can be used as a replacement for 3x5 note cards. Ideas can be collected, composed, refined, rearranged, and reorganized much more efficiently when they're stored in an outline. When the time comes to turn research into a research paper, the notes don't need to be retyped; they can be exported to your word processor and polished with standard text-editing techniques. If the outliner is built into the word processor, the process of organizing blends seamlessly into the writing process, and the line between notes and finished product blurs to the point where it almost disappears.

Outliners aren't just used for preparing to write. Many people use them for preparing speeches, to-do lists, schedules, and anything else that requires prioritizing and organization. On the other hand, many people find the hierarchical outline form confining and difficult to use. Fortunately idea processors come in other forms. Many visual thinkers find they work best with graphical idea processors that allow

The word processor's Outline view allows you to examine and restructure the overall organization of the document while showing each topic in as much detail as you need. When you move headlines, the attached subheads and paragraphs follow automatically. (Software: Microsoft Word.)

them to draw their ideas as nodes on a chart with arrows connecting related ideas. Idea charts may resemble tree charts with many branches or look more like free-form clusters. Some idea processors allow users to switch back and forth between text view and graphics view.

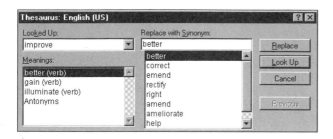

An on-line thesaurus puts synonyms at your fingertips. In this case the computer is providing synonyms for the word improve. (Software: Microsoft Word.)

Synonym Finders

The classic synonym finder, or **thesaurus,** is an invaluable tool for finding just the right word, but it's not particularly user friendly. A computerized thesaurus is another matter altogether. With a good on-screen thesaurus, it's a simple matter to select a word and issue a command for a synonym search. The computerized thesaurus provides almost instant gratification, displaying all kinds of possible replacements for the word in question. If you find a good substitute in the list, you can indicate your preference with a click or a keystroke; the software even makes the substitution for you. It couldn't be much simpler.

Digital References

Writers rely on dictionaries, quotation books, encyclopedias, atlases, almanacs, and other references. Most of these traditionally printed resources are now available in digital form. These electronic references offer advantages and disadvantages when compared with their hard-copy counterparts.

The biggest advantage of the electronic form is speed; searching for subjects or words by computer is usually faster than thumbing through a book. Well-designed references make it easy to jump between related topics in search of elusive facts. In addition, copying quotes electronically takes a fraction of the time it takes to retype information from a book. Of course, this kind of quick copying makes plagiarism easier than ever and may tempt more writers to violate copyright laws.

Some references lose something in the translation to electronic form. Because pictures, maps, and drawings take up so much disk space, they're often removed or modified in computerized references. Disk capacity problems largely disappear when reference books are stored on optical CD-ROM disks. In fact, many CD-ROM references take advantage of the massive disk capacity by including sounds, animation, video,

Students can save time searching for facts in computerized reference books, like those included in Microsoft Bookshelf.

and other forms of information that aren't possible in books. Multimedia references are discussed in more detail in Chapter 7.

Spelling Checkers

It's a darn poor mind that can only think of one way to spell a word.

—Andrew Jackson

While many of us sympathize with Jackson's point of view, the fact remains that correct spelling is an important part of most written communication. That's why most word processors today include a built-in **spelling checker.** Spelling checkers come in different forms, but they all essentially do the same thing: compare the words in your document with words in a disk-based dictionary. Every word that's not in the dictionary is flagged as a suspect word—a potential misspelling. In many cases the spelling checker suggests the corrected spelling and offers to replace the suspect word. Ultimately, though, it's up to you to decide whether the flagged word is, in fact, spelled incorrectly.

Most spelling checkers offer several choices for each suspect word:

- replace the word with the suggested alternative
- replace the word with another alternative typed by the user
- leave the word alone (used when the word is spelled correctly, but it's not in the dictionary because it's an obscure word, a specialized term, or a proper name)
- leave the word alone and add it to the dictionary so that it won't be flagged next time (used when the word is spelled correctly, it's not in the dictionary, and it's a regular part of the user's written vocabulary)

The most common spelling checkers are *batch spelling checkers;* they check all of the words in your document in a batch when you issue the appropriate command. Some people prefer *interactive spelling checkers* that check every word as it's typed, beeping or flashing each time a word is typed incorrectly.

While spelling checkers are wonderful aids, they can't replace careful proofreading by alert human eyes. When you're using a spelling checker, it's important to keep two potential problems in mind:

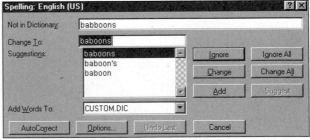

Most spelling checkers offer a user several choices for handling words that aren't in the dictionary. (Software: Microsoft Word.)

1. *Dictionary limitations and errors.* No dictionary includes every word, so you have to know what to do with unlisted words—proper names, obscure words, technical terms, foreign terms, colloquialisms, and other oddities. If you add words to your spelling checker's dictionary, you run the risk of adding an incorrectly spelled word, making future occurrences of that misspelling invisible to the spelling checker and to you.

2. *Errors of context.* The biggest limitation of today's spelling checkers is their lack of intelligence in dealing with a word's context. The fact that a word appears in a dictionary does not guarantee that it is correctly spelled in the context of the sentence. The following passage, for example, contains eight spelling errors, none of which would be detected by a typical spelling checker:

I wood never have guest that my spelling checker would super seed my editor as my mane source of feed back. I no longer prophet from the presents of an editor while I right.

Grammar and Style Checkers

The errors in the preceding quote would have slipped by a spelling checker, but many of them would have been detected by a **grammar and style checker.** In addition to checking spelling, grammar-and-style-checking software analyzes each word in context, checking for errors of context ("I wood never have guest"), common grammatical errors ("Ben and me went to Boston"), and stylistic foibles ("The book that is most popular"). In addition to pointing out possible errors and suggesting improvements, it can analyze prose complexity using measurements like sentence length and paragraph length. This kind of analysis is useful for determining whether your writing style is appropriate for your target audience.

Grammar-and-style-checking software is, at best, imperfect. A typical program misses many true errors while flagging correct passages. Still, it can be a valuable writing aid, especially for students who are mastering the complexities of a language for the first time. But software is no substitute for practice, revision, editing, and a good English teacher.

> Grammar-and-style-checking software flags possible errors and makes suggestions about how they might be fixed. (Software: Microsoft Word.)

Form Letter Generators

Congratulations, Mr. <lastname>! You may already have won!

Most word processors today have **mail merge** capabilities for producing personalized form letters. When used with a database containing a list of names and addresses, a word processor can quickly generate individually addressed letters and mailing labels. Many programs can incorporate custom paragraphs based on the recipient's personal data, making each letter look as if it were individually written. The uses and abuses of this kind of technology are discussed in Chapter 8.

> Businesses rely on desktop publishing technology to produce in-house newsletters, brochures, advertising materials, training manuals, periodicals, and books.

THE DESKTOP PUBLISHING STORY

Freedom of the press belongs to the person who owns one.
—A. J. Liebling, the late media critic for *The New Yorker*

Just as word processing changed the writer's craft in the 1970s, the world of publishing was radically transformed in the 1980s with the introduction of desktop publishing. Publishing—traditionally an expensive, time-consuming, error-prone process—has rapidly become an enterprise that just about anyone with a computer and a little cash can undertake. Poor Richard could publish quite an almanac with today's technology.

What Is Desktop Publishing?

The process of producing a book, magazine, or other publication includes several steps:

1. Writing text.
2. Editing text.
3. Producing drawings, photographs, and other graphics to accompany the text.
4. Designing a basic format for the publication.
5. Typesetting text.
6. Arranging text and graphics on pages.
7. Typesetting and printing pages.
8. Binding pages into a finished publication.

In traditional publishing, many of these steps required expensive equipment, highly trained specialists to operate the equipment, and *lots* of time.

With modern **desktop publishing** (DTP) technology, the bulk of the publishing process can be accomplished with tools that are small, affordable, and easy to use. A desktop publishing system generally includes a computer with a graphical user interface, desktop publishing software, and a laser printer or other high-resolution printer. It's now possible for a single person with a modest equipment investment to do all the writing, editing, graphic production, design, page layout, and typesetting for a desktop publication. Of course, few individuals have the skills to handle all these tasks, so most publications are still the work of teams that include writers, editors, designers, artists, and supervisors. But even if the titles remain the same, each of these jobs is changing because of desktop publishing technology.

The first steps in the publishing process involve producing **source documents**—articles, chapters, drawings, maps, charts, and photographs that are to appear in the publication. Desktop publishers generally use standard word processors and graphics programs to produce most source documents. Scanners are used to transform photos and hand-drawn images into computer-readable documents. **Page-layout software** is used to combine the various source documents into a coherent, visually appealing publication. Pages are generally laid out one at a time on screen, although most programs have options for automating many of the steps in producing long documents. The User's View box shows how a simple publication is created with page-layout software. **UV**

A typical desktop publishing system includes a personal computer, a high-resolution printer, a scanner, and a variety of software programs.

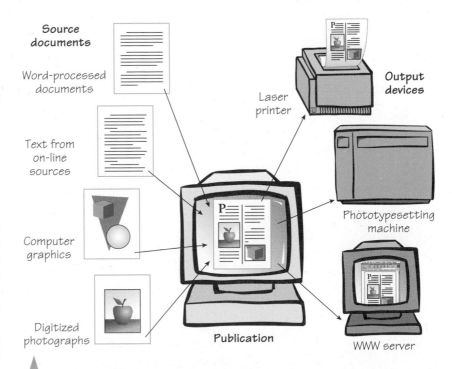

Source documents

Word-processed documents

Text from on-line sources

Computer graphics

Digitized photographs

Publication

Laser printer

Output devices

Phototypesetting machine

WWW server

Source documents are merged in a publication document, which can be printed on a laser printer, printed on a high-resolution photo typesetter, or even published on the World Wide Web.

Desktop Publishing

▲▲▲▲▲▲▲▲▲▲▲▲▲▲▲▲▲▲▲▲▲▲▲▲▲▲

Software: Ofoto scanning software, Aldus PageMaker page-layout software.

The goal: To create a publication that includes a collection of class projects and presentations and a variety of graphic illustrations.

1 The first step is to create and collect source documents. The articles are all word processor files, so they're ready to go. The pictures are a mixture of computer graphics files and hand-drawn images. You start by using a scanner with Ofoto scanning software to convert these drawings into graphics files.

2 After the source documents are ready, you open PageMaker to design and lay out the pages.

3 You start the page-layout process by creating a new document and specifying the number and size of its pages.

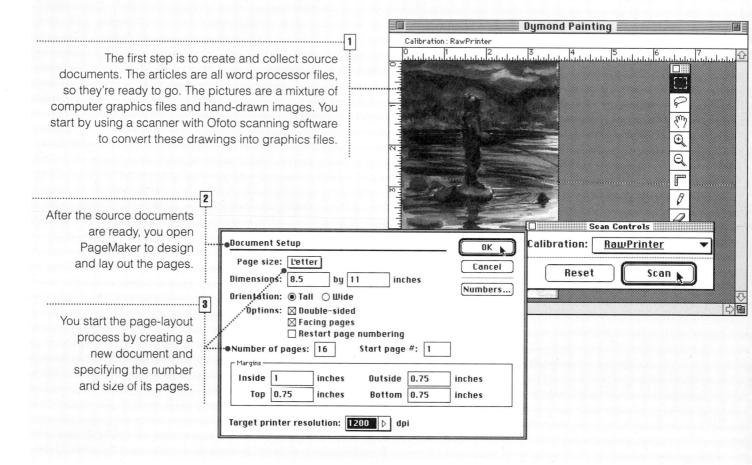

When a document is created with page-layout software, it can be printed on a variety of high-resolution output devices. Most black-and-white desktop publications are printed on laser printers capable of producing output with a resolution of about 600 dots per inch (dpi). Output of 600 dpi is sufficiently sharp for most applications, but it's far less than the 1200 dpi that's the traditional minimum for professional typesetting. High-priced devices, often called *phototypesetting machines* or *imagesetters*, allow desktop publications to be printed at 1200 dpi or higher. Many desktop publishers who need typeset-quality output prefer to rely on outside **service bureaus** to print their final **camera-ready** pages—pages that are ready to be photographed and printed.

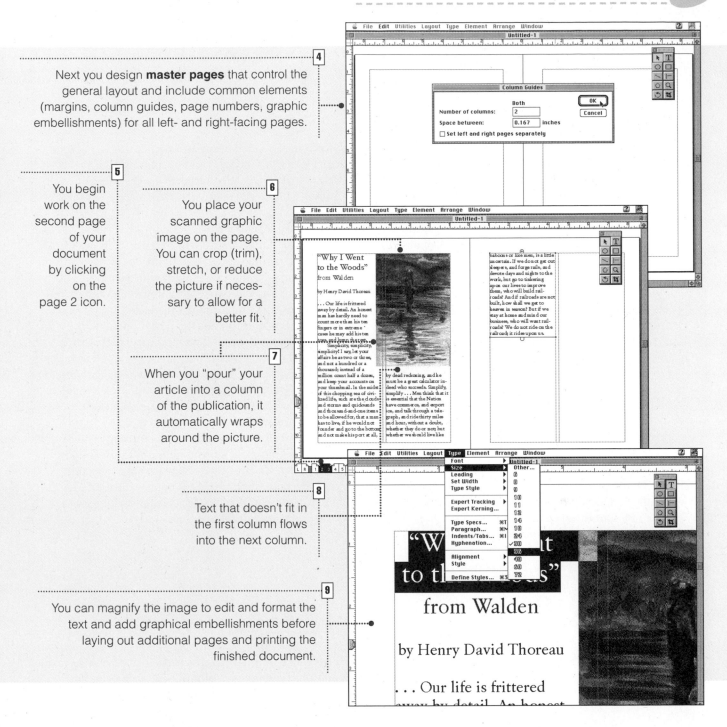

4 Next you design **master pages** that control the general layout and include common elements (margins, column guides, page numbers, graphic embellishments) for all left- and right-facing pages.

5 You begin work on the second page of your document by clicking on the page 2 icon.

6 You place your scanned graphic image on the page. You can crop (trim), stretch, or reduce the picture if necessary to allow for a better fit.

7 When you "pour" your article into a column of the publication, it automatically wraps around the picture.

8 Text that doesn't fit in the first column flows into the next column.

9 You can magnify the image to edit and format the text and add graphical embellishments before laying out additional pages and printing the finished document.

Desktop publishing has quickly become the standard procedure for producing black-and-white pamphlets, periodicals, and books with near typeset quality. The tools provide graphic designers with control over virtually every element of the design, right down to the spacing between each pair of letters (*kerning*) and the spacing between lines of text (*leading*). For users without background in layout and design, most desktop publishing packages include **templates**—professionally designed "empty" documents that can easily be adapted to specific user needs. Even without templates it's possible for beginners to create professional-quality black-and-white publications with a modest investment of money and time.

Beyond DESKTOP Tacky!

Many first-time users of WYSIWYG word processors and desktop publishing systems become intoxicated with the power at their fingertips. It's easy to get carried away with all those fonts, styles, and sizes, and create a document that makes supermarket tabloids look tasteful. While there's no substitute for a good education in the principles of design, it's easy to avoid tacky looking documents if you follow a few simple guidelines:

• **Plan before you publish.** Design (or select) a simple, visually pleasing format for your document and use that format throughout the document.

• **Use appropriate fonts.** Limit your choices to one or two fonts and sizes per page, and be consistent throughout your document. Serif fonts like this one generally are good choices for paragraphs of text; the serifs gently guide the reader's eye from word to word. Sans serif fonts, like the headings in this book, work well for headings and titles. Make sure all your chosen fonts work properly with your printer.

• **Don't go style-crazy.** Avoid overusing italics, boldface, underlines, and other styles for emphasis. *When in doubt, leave it out.*

• **Look at your document through your readers' eyes.** Make every picture say something. Don't try to cram too much information on a page. Don't be afraid of white space. Use a format that speaks clearly to your readers. Make sure the main points of your document stand out. Whatever you do, do it for the reader.

• **Learn from the masters.** Study the designs of successful publications. What makes them work? Use design books, articles, and classes to develop your aesthetic skills along with your technical skills. With or without a computer, publishing is an art.

• **Know the limitations of the technology.** Desktop publishing technology makes it possible for anyone to produce high-quality documents with a minimal investment of time and money. But today's technology has limitations; for many applications, desktop publishing is no match for a professional design artist or typesetter. If you need the best, work with a pro.

• **Remember the message.** Fancy fonts, tasteful graphics, and meticulous design can't turn shoddy ideas into words of wisdom or lies into the truth. The purpose of publishing is communication; don't try to use technology to disguise the lack of something to communicate.

The process becomes more complicated when color is introduced. *Spot color*—the use of a single color (or sometimes two) to add interest to a mostly monochrome document—is relatively easy, assuming you have access to a color printer or imagesetter. But *full color* desktop publishing, including color photos, drawings, and paintings, means dealing with the inconsistencies of different color output devices. Because printers and monitors use different types of color-mixing technologies (as described in the How It Works boxes in Chapter 3), what you see on the screen isn't always what you get when you print it out. It's even difficult to get two monitors (or two printers) to produce images with exactly the same color balance. Still, color desktop publishing is big business, and advances in color-matching technology are making it easier all the time. And with an ever-increasing number of inexpensive color printers on the market, color desktop publishing is rapidly becoming the norm.

Why Desktop Publishing?

In less than a decade, desktop publishing has become a standard operating procedure for thousands of professional publishers, large and small. More than any other application, desktop publishing was responsible for the initial acceptance of computers with graphical user interfaces by large corporations. Why has desktop publishing enjoyed such wide acceptance by businesses? The reasons are clear.

First and foremost, desktop publishing saves money. Publications that used to cost hundreds or thousands of dollars to produce through outside publishing services can now be produced in-house for a fraction of their former cost. What's more, desktop publishing saves time. The turnaround time for a publication done on the desktop can be a few days instead of the weeks or months it might take to publish the same thing using traditional channels. Finally, desktop publishing can reduce the quantity of publication errors. Quality control is easier to maintain when documents are produced in-house.

The real winners in the desktop publishing revolution might turn out to be not big businesses but everyday people with something to say. With commercial TV networks and newspapers increasingly controlled by a few giant corporations, many media experts worry that the free press guaranteed by our First Amendment is seriously threatened by a de facto media monopoly. Similarly, the book-publishing industry is dominated by a few conglomerates with cautious publishing patterns that avoid unpopular and controversial books.

Desktop publishing technology offers new hope for every individual's right to publish. Writers, artists, and editors whose work is shunned or ignored by large publishers and mainstream media now have affordable publishing alternatives. The number of small presses and alternative, low-circulation periodicals is steadily increasing as publishing costs go down. If, as A. J. Liebling suggested, freedom of the press belongs to the person who owns one, that precious freedom is now accessible to more people than ever before.

Tomorrow's Word Tools

What's over the horizon for wordsmiths? Based on current trends and research, several possibilities exist.

The End of Desktop Publishing Software?

Ironically many experts predict that the thriving desktop publishing software industry may decline, or even disappear, in the coming decade. While these predictions may be farfetched, they're based on some important trends in the industry today.

As word processors grow in sophistication, they absorb more and more of the features formerly available only in page-layout software. Many word processors available today are capable of producing professional-quality books and periodicals, complete with graphics. It seems likely that the line between word processors and page-layout programs will blur in coming years.

Of course, desktop publishing software is becoming more sophisticated, too, incorporating features essential to discriminating professionals. The publishing industry now uses desktop computers for a variety of tasks beyond basic page layout—tasks that can't be accomplished with word processors alone.

Another common prediction is that desktop publishing—and paper publishing in general—will be replaced by paperless electronic media. As you'll see in later chapters, digital media *are* likely to eclipse paper for many applications. Programs as diverse as ClarisWorks, Microsoft Word, and Pagemaker already allow you to save your documents in HTML formats so they can be published on the Internet's World Wide Web for a potential audience of millions. But paper still offers advantages for countless communication tasks. The printed word isn't going away anytime soon.

Groupware for Writing and Editing

As we've seen, the publishing process involves a variety of tasks, from writing and editing to drawing and design. A typical publication project involves several writers working in conjunction with editors, artists, and other specialized professionals. Modern computer networks make it possible for all these people to work together on the same set of computer documents using **groupware**—software designed to be used by work groups rather than individuals. Software companies are developing software specifically to facilitate communication between writers, editors, and other publication professionals.

Using groupware, several writers might work simultaneously on the same master document. Each writer can monitor and make suggestions concerning the writing of any other writer on the team. Editors can "blue pencil" corrections and attach notes directly to the electronic manuscript. Editing notes might resemble on-screen sticky-notes, or they might be audio notes spoken by the editor. Either way, the notes attach to the document so they can be read or heard by any or all the writers—even those who are on the other side of the continent. At the same time graphic artists and designers can work in tandem on the visual aspects of the publication. When the text and drawings are completed, they can easily be merged into a completed document using page-layout software.

Electronic Dictation

Changes in output devices—graphic screens and high-resolution printers—have had a tremendous impact on writing and publishing software in the last decade. As a result, the major bottlenecks in most modern desktop publishing systems are on the input side. Many experts predict that the next big advances will occur as a result of emerging input devices.

For millions of computer users, the mouse has taken over many of the functions of the keyboard. For a small but rapidly growing population, pen-based systems provide an alternative tool for entering text. Ultimately, though, most writers long for a computer that can accept and reliably process speech input—a *talkwriter*.

Speech-recognition software systems are showing up in products, but today's systems are severely limited. It takes a great deal of intelligence to understand the intricacies of our language, and no machine available today is smart enough or powerful enough to rise to the challenge consistently. Still, research in this area is progressing rapidly, and hardware and software breakthroughs happen every year. Word processors that can reliably recognize human speech are almost certainly in your future.

Intelligent Word Processors

Speech recognition is just one aspect of artificial intelligence research that's likely to end up in future word processors. Many experts foresee word processors able to anticipate the writer's needs, acting as an electronic editor or coauthor. Today's grammar and style checkers are primitive forerunners of the kinds of electronic writing consultants that might appear in a few years. Here are some possibilities:

- As you're typing a story, your word processor reminds you (via a pop-up message on the screen or an auditory message) that you've used the word *delicious* three times in the last two paragraphs and suggests that you choose an alternative from the list shown on the screen.

- Your word processor continuously analyzes your style as you type, determines your writing habits and patterns, and learns from its analysis. If your writing tends to be technical and formal, the software modifies its thesaurus, dictionary, and other tools so they're more appropriate for that style.

- You're writing a manual for a large organization whose documentation has specific style guidelines. Your word processor modifies your writing as you type so that it conforms to the organizational style.

- You need some current figures to support your argument on the depletion of the ozone layer. You issue a command, and the computer does a quick search of the literature in a library database and reports back to you a few seconds later with several relevant facts.

All these examples are technically possible now; some are incorporated into systems being developed in research laboratories. The trend toward intelligent word processors is clear. Nevertheless, you're in for a long wait if you're eager to buy a system with commands such as Clever Quote, Humorous Anecdote, and Term Paper.

SUMMARY

Even though the computer was originally designed to work with numbers, it quickly became an important tool for processing text. Today the word processor has all but replaced the typewriter as the tool of choice for committing words to paper.

Word processing is far more than typing text into a computer. Word processing software allows the writer to use commands to edit text on the screen, eliminating the chore of retyping pages until the message is right. Other commands allow the writer to control the format of the document: typefaces, spacing, justification, margins, columns, headers, footers, and other visual components. WYSIWYG word processors make it possible to see the formatted pages on the screen before printing them on paper. Most professional word processing programs automate footnoting, hyphenation, and other processes that are particularly troublesome to traditional typists.

Many advanced word processing functions are available as part of high-end word processing programs or as stand-alone special-purpose applications. Outlining software turns the familiar outline into a powerful, dynamic, organizational tool. Spelling checkers and grammar and style checkers partially automate the proofreading process, although they leave the more difficult parts of the job to literate humans. On-line thesauruses, dictionaries, and other computer-based references automate reference work. Production of specialized documents like personalized form letters and full-length illustrated books can be simplified with other word processing tools.

As word processors become more powerful, they take on many of the features previously found only in desktop publishing software. Still, many publishers use word processors and graphics programs to create source documents that can be used as input for page-layout programs. The combination of the graphical user interface (GUI), desktop publishing software, and the high-resolution printer has revolutionized the publishing process by allowing publishers and would-be publishers to produce professional-quality text-and-graphics documents at a reasonable cost. Amateur and professional publishers everywhere use desktop publishing technology to produce everything from comic books to reference books. The near-overnight success of desktop publishing may foreshadow other changes in the way we communicate with words as new technologies like groupware, voice recognition, and intelligent word processors emerge.

Chapter Review

Key Terms

automatic footnoting	idea processor	selecting text
automatic hyphenation	inserting text	serif font
camera-ready	insertion bar	service bureau
Clipboard	justification	source document
copying text	mail merge	spelling checker (batch or
cursor	master pages	interactive)
cut-and-paste	moving text	style sheet
deleting text	navigating	template
desktop publishing (DTP)	outlining	text editing
drag-and-drop	page-layout software	text formatting
Find command	point size	thesaurus
font	proportionally spaced font	typeface
footer	sans serif font	Undo command
grammar and style checker	saving a document	word wrap
groupware	scrolling	WYSIWYG
header	search and replace	

Review Questions

1. Define or describe each of the key words above. Check your answers in the glossary.

2. How is word processing different from typing?

3. What happens to your document when you turn the computer off? What should you do if you want to work on the document later?

4. Explain the difference between text editing and text formatting. Give several examples of each.

5. What is scrolling, and how is it useful?

6. When do you use the Enter or Return key in word processing?

7. What are the different ways that a paragraph or line of text can be justified? When might each be appropriate?

8. How is working with an outliner (or idea processor) different from a word processor?

9. What is a font, and how is it used in word processing and desktop publishing?

10. Describe three different ways a spelling checker might be fooled.

11. How does desktop publishing differ from word processing?

12. List several advantages of desktop publishing over traditional publishing methods.

13. What are the three most important components of a desktop publishing system?

14. Is it possible to have a computer publishing system that is not WYSIWYG? Explain.

Discussion Questions

1. Which of the word processing features and software categories described in this chapter would be the most useful to you as a student? How do you think you would use them?

2. What do you think of the arguments that word processing reduces the quality of writing because (1) it makes it easy to write hurriedly and carelessly, and (2) it puts the emphasis on the way a document looks rather than what it says?

3. Many experts fear that desktop publishing technology will result in a glut of unprofessional, tacky-looking publications. Others fear it will result in a glut of slick-looking documents full of shoddy ideas and dangerous lies. How do you feel about each of these fears?

4. Like Gutenberg's development of the movable type printing press more than 500 years ago, the development of desktop publishing puts powerful communication tools in the hands of more people. What impact will desktop publishing technology have on the free press and the free exchange of ideas guaranteed in the United States Constitution? What impact will the same technology have on free expression in other countries?

Projects

1. Using advertisements, hands-on demonstrations, and personal experience, compare the features of two or more popular word processing programs. (You may include the word processing modules of integrated software packages

like ClarisWorks in your comparison.) What are the advantages and disadvantages of each program from a student's point of view?

2. Research one or more of your favorite local or national publications to find out how computers are used in their production.

3. Use a word processing system or a desktop publishing system to produce a newsletter, brochure, or flyer in support of an organization or cause that is important to you.

Sources and Resources

Books

Most word processing and desktop publishing books are hardware- and software-specific—they're designed to be used with a specific version of a specific program on a specific machine running a specific operating system. If you need a book to get you started, choose one that fits your system. Make sure the book is an introductory tutorial, not a substitute for the software reference manual or a collection of "power user" tips. If possible, browse before you buy.

Everyone's Guide to Successful Publications: How to Produce Powerful Brochures, Newsletters, Flyers, and Business Communications, Start to Finish, by Elizabeth W. Adler (Berkeley, CA: Peachpit Press, 1993). This thorough and extremely readable book may be the best single source of information for anyone interested in creating brochures, newsletters, catalogs, manuals, posters, reports, and other publications. Unlike most desktop publishing books, this one guides you through the entire process, from planning, writing, and design through printing and distribution. True to its title, this book is an invaluable resource for beginners and experienced publishers alike.

The Non-Designer's Design Book, by Robin Williams (Berkeley: Peachpit Press, 1994), *Looking Good in Print: A Guide to Basic Design for Desktop Publishing,* by Roger C. Parker (Chapel Hill, NC: Ventana Press, 1990) and *Collier's Rules for Desktop Design and Typography,* by David Collier (Reading, MA: Addison-Wesley, 1991). These three books cover the nontechnical side of desktop publishing. Now that you know the mechanics, how can you make your work look good? Williams provides a friendly introduction to the basics of design and page layout in her popular, down-to-earth style. Parker clearly describes the basic design tools and techniques and then applies them in sample documents ranging from brochures to books. Collier's book is more concise, colorful, and contemporary than the other two; most topics are covered in bold, two-page spreads that go beyond the basics.

A Blip in the continuum, by Robin Williams (Berkeley: Peachpit Press, 1995).Once you've learned the design basics from one of the books listed above, you might want to spend some time in this bold little book. Williams demonstrates how it sometimes pays to break time-honored rules by using contemporary "grunge" fonts to create bold, in-your-face layouts. A Macintosh-compatible disk of fonts is included.

How Desktop Publishing Works, by Pamela Pfiffner and Bruce Fraser (Emeryville, CA: Ziff-Davis Press, 1994). Want to know more about desktop publishing technology? This full-color, lavishly illustrated book clearly explains the tools and processes of publishing without getting overly technical. It includes sections on history, graphics, type, color, hardware, and prepress.

Bugs in Writing, by (Reading, MA: Addison Wesley, 1994). This entertaining little book is designed to help computer science and computer information systems students—who presumably already know how to debug their programs—debug their prose. It's a friendly, readable tutorial that can help almost anybody to be a better writer.

The Elements of Style, by William Strunk, Jr., and E. B. White. (New York: Macmillan Publishing Co., Inc.) If you want to improve your writing, this book is the classic.

Periodicals

Publish! This monthly provides cover-to-cover desktop publishing coverage. (All the brand-specific monthlies mentioned at the end of Chapter 1 also regularly discuss word processing and desktop publishing.)

World Wide Web Pages

The Web is full of fascinating resources for publishers, writers, and page designers. Some, like http://www.adobe.com, are obvious; others are harder to find but no less useful. Check the *Computer Confluence* Web site for links to the best pages.

6

CALCULATION, VISUALIZATION, AND SIMULATION

Dan Bricklin and Mitch Kapor Count on Computers

In terms of the success of VisiCalc, I don't feel I have to repeat it. But it is nice to be able to realize you've done something very worthwhile.

— Dan Bricklin

Mitch Kapor

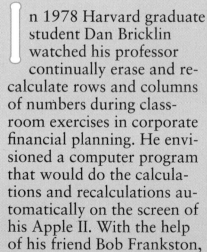

In 1978 Harvard graduate student Dan Bricklin watched his professor continually erase and re-calculate rows and columns of numbers during class-room exercises in corporate financial planning. He envi-sioned a computer program that would do the calcula-tions and recalculations au-tomatically on the screen of his Apple II. With the help of his friend Bob Frankston, an MIT student, he developed VisiCalc, the first computer spread-sheet program. Almost overnight this revolutionary software changed the world of per-

sonal computing. Before VisiCalc, personal comput-ers were used mostly to mimic the functions of main-frames. But VisiCalc was a unique tool—one that pro-vided managers with capa-bilities they never had before. Many analysts believe VisiCalc was respon-sible for the early success of the Apple II, and the desk-top computer in general, in the business world.

After IBM introduced the IBM PC in 1981, many VisiCalc-inspired spreadsheet programs were competing for the software dollars of businesses. One of those programs was developed by Mitch Kapor, an idealistic young entrepreneur who

had worked for a VisiCalc distributor and tested a release of VisiCalc. In 1983 Kapor's start-up company, Lotus, released a powerful, easy-to-use integrated spread-sheet/graphics package called 1-2-3 that quickly established itself as *the* standard spread-sheet on IBM-compatible computers. By backing a solid software product with an expensive marketing cam-paign and a support program that made it easier for nontechnical corporate users to get training and help, Lotus established new stan-dards for software success. Quickly 1-2-3 became the most successful software product the computer indus-try had ever seen.

Dan Bricklin

Today 1-2-3 has been eclipsed by Microsoft Excel, a graphical spreadsheet program developed first for the Macintosh and later for Windows. The original VisiCalc program was purchased by Lotus and discontinued. After an unsuccessful trade-secret-theft lawsuit against Lotus, VisiCalc's parent company faded into obscurity. In 1995 IBM purchased Lotus and began integrating Lotus products into the IBM software line.

What happened to Bricklin and Kapor? Both left their original companies for other computer ventures. Bricklin still develops innovative software, including pen-based systems and multimedia authoring tools. Kapor is the cofounder of and spokesperson for the Electronic Frontier Foundation, an organization dedicated to protecting human rights and the free flow of information on the Internet.

Computers were originally created to calculate, and today's machines are still widely used for numeric computations. Numbers are at the heart of applications ranging from accounting to statistical analysis. The most popular number-crunching application is the spreadsheet, conceived by Bricklin and institutionalized by Lotus. Executives, engineers, scientists, and others use the spreadsheet for the same reason: It allows them to create and work with simulations of real-world situations.

A well-designed simulation, whether constructed with a spreadsheet or another software application, can help people achieve a better understanding of the world outside the computer. Computer simulations have their limitations and risks, too. In this chapter we'll explore the world of number manipulation and computer simulation, starting with the spreadsheet.

THE SPREADSHEET: SOFTWARE FOR SIMULATION AND SPECULATION

Compare the expansion of business today to the conquering of the continent in the 19th century. The spreadsheet in that comparison is like the transcontinental railroad. It accelerated the movement, made it possible, and changed the course of the nation.

—Mitch Kapor

More than any other type of personal computer software, the spreadsheet has changed the way people do business. In the same way a word processor can give a computer user control over words, **spreadsheet software** allows the user to take control of numbers, manipulating them in ways that would be difficult or impossible otherwise. A spreadsheet program can make short work of tasks that involve repetitive calculations: budgeting, investment management, business projections, grade books, scientific simulations, checkbooks, and so on. A spreadsheet can also reveal hidden relationships between numbers, taking much of the guesswork out of financial planning and speculation.

The Malleable Matrix

The goal was that it had to be better than the back of an envelope.

—Dan Bricklin

Almost all spreadsheet programs are based on a simple concept: the malleable matrix. A spreadsheet document, called a **worksheet,** typically appears on the screen as a grid of numbered **rows** and alphabetically lettered **columns.** The box representing the intersection of a row and a column is called a **cell.** Every cell in this grid has a unique **address** made up of a row number and column letter. For example, the cell in the upper-left corner of the grid is called cell A1 (column A, row 1). All the cells are empty in a new worksheet; it's up to the user to fill them. Each cell can contain a numeric value, an alphabetic label, or a formula representing a relationship between numbers in other cells.

Values (numbers) are the raw material used by the spreadsheet software to perform calculations. Numbers in worksheet cells can represent wages, test scores, weather data, polling results, or just about anything that can be quantified.

To make it easier for people to understand the numbers, most worksheets include **labels** at the tops of columns and at the edges of rows, such as "Monthly Wages," "Midterm Exam 1," "Average Wind Speed," and "Final Approval Rating." To the computer these labels are meaningless strings of characters. The label "Total Points" doesn't tell the computer to calculate the total and display it in an adjacent cell; it's just a road sign for human readers.

To calculate the total points (or the average wind speed or the final approval rating) the worksheet must include a **formula**—a step-by-step procedure for calculating the desired number. The simplest spreadsheet formulas are arithmetic expressions using +, −, *, and / to represent addition, subtraction, multiplication, and division. For example, cell B5 might contain the formula =(B2+B3)/2. This formula tells the computer to add the numbers in cells B2 and B3, divide the result by 2, and display the final result in the cell containing the formula, cell B5. You don't see the

The worksheet may be bigger than what appears on your screen. The program allows you to scroll horizontally and vertically to view the larger matrix. (After Z, columns are labeled with double letters: AA, AB, and so on.)

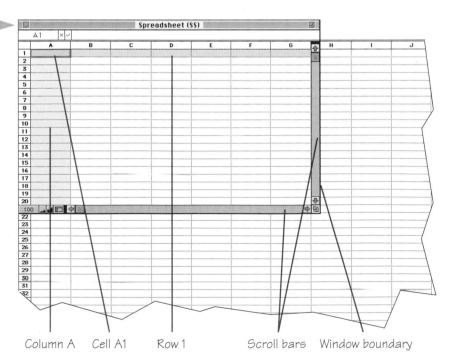

Column A   Cell A1   Row 1   Scroll bars   Window boundary

formula in cell B5; you just see its effect. It doesn't matter whether the numbers represent test scores, dollars, or nothing at all; the computer obediently calculates their average and displays the results. If either number in cell B2 or B3 changes, the number displayed in that cell automatically changes, too. The User's View on the next page illustrates how you might create a simple worksheet. [UV]

Different brands of spreadsheets are distinguished by their features and their user interfaces. In spite of their differences, all popular spreadsheet programs work in much the same way. It's rare to find a spreadsheet that doesn't have most or all of these features:

- *Automatic replication of values, labels, and formulas.* Most worksheets contain a great deal of repetition: Budgetary amounts remain constant from month to month; exam scores are calculated the same way for every student in the class; a scheduling program refers to the same seven days each week. Many spreadsheet commands streamline entry of repetitive data, labels, and formulas. Commands vary between programs, but all **replication** commands are, in essence, flexible extensions of the basic copy-and-paste functions found in other software. Probably the most commonly used replication commands are the Fill Down and Fill Right commands illustrated in the User's View example. Formulas can be constructed with *relative references* to other cells, as in the example, so they refer to different cells when replicated in other locations, or as *absolute references* that don't change when copied elsewhere.

- *Automatic recalculation.* **Automatic recalculation** is one of the spreadsheet's most important capabilities. It not only allows for the easy correction of errors but also makes it easy to try out different values while searching for solutions. For large, complicated worksheets, recalculation can be painfully slow, so most spreadsheets allow you to turn off the automatic recalculation feature and recalculate the worksheet only when you need it.

- *Predefined functions.* The first calculators made computing a square root a tedious and error-prone series of steps. On today's calculators a single press of the square-root button tells the calculator to do all of the necessary calculations to produce the square root. Spreadsheet programs contain built-in **functions** something like the calculator's square-root button. A function in a formula instructs the computer to perform some predefined set of calculations. For example, the formula =SQRT(C5) calculates the square root of the number in cell C5. Modern spreadsheet applications have large libraries of predefined functions. Many, like SUM, AVERAGE (or AVG), MIN, and MAX, represent simple calculations that are performed often in all kinds of worksheets. Others automate complex financial, mathematical, and statistical calculations that would be extremely difficult to do manually. The IF function allows the worksheet to decide what to do based on the contents of other cells, giving the worksheet logical decision-making capability. (For example: If the number of hours worked is greater than 40, calculate pay using the overtime schedule.) Like the calculator's square-root button, these functions can save time and reduce the likelihood of errors.

- *Macros.* A spreadsheet's menu of functions, like the menu in a fast-food restaurant, is limited to the most popular selections. For situations where the built-in functions don't fill the bill, most spreadsheets allow the user to capture sequences of steps as reusable **macros**—custom-designed procedures that you can add to the existing menu of options. Some programs insist that you type macros using a special *macro language;* others allow you to turn on a *macro recorder* that captures every move you make with the keyboard and mouse, recording those actions in a macro transcript. Later you can ask the computer to carry out the instructions in that macro. Suppose, for example, you use the same set of calculations every month when preparing a statistical analysis of environmental

Creating a Simple Worksheet

▲ ▲

Software: Microsoft Excel.

The goal: To create a computerized version of a worksheet showing projected expenses for one college student's fall term. The design of the worksheet is based on this hand-drawn planning version.

Expenses	Sept	Oct	Nov	Dec	Total
Tuition and Fees					
Books					
Rent					
Utilities					
Food					
Transportation					
Odds and Ends					
Total Monthly expenses					

1

The first step is to type descriptive labels for the worksheet title and to label the rows and columns. Typing appears in the **current** or **active cell**—the cell containing the cursor—and in the long window above the worksheet, called the **console** or **formula bar.** You move from cell to cell by clicking with the mouse or by navigating with the keyboard.

2

To make room for row labels, you widen the first column by dragging its border to the right.

3

After typing the labels you type numeric values to represent dollar values for each category in each month.

4

To change cell formats so numbers are displayed with dollar signs, you select the **range** (rectangular block) of cells by dragging between cells B3 and F11, two opposite corners of the rectangle, . . .

5

. . . choose the Cells command from the Format menu . . .

6

. . . and then select the Currency format to change the appearance of all values in the range.

7 You enter a formula to calculate the total expenses for September in cell B11: =sum(B3:B9). When you press Enter, the formula in the cell is replaced by the calculated value—the sum of the numbers in cells B3 through B9. (The formula is still visible in the formula bar whenever cell B11 is active.)

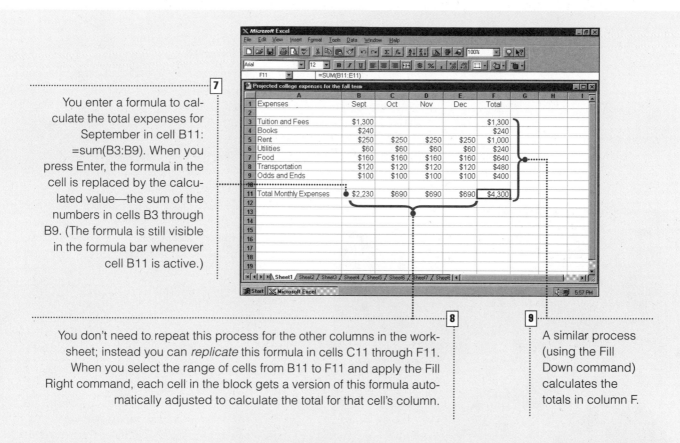

8 You don't need to repeat this process for the other columns in the worksheet; instead you can *replicate* this formula in cells C11 through F11. When you select the range of cells from B11 to F11 and apply the Fill Right command, each cell in the block gets a version of this formula automatically adjusted to calculate the total for that cell's column.

9 A similar process (using the Fill Down command) calculates the totals in column F.

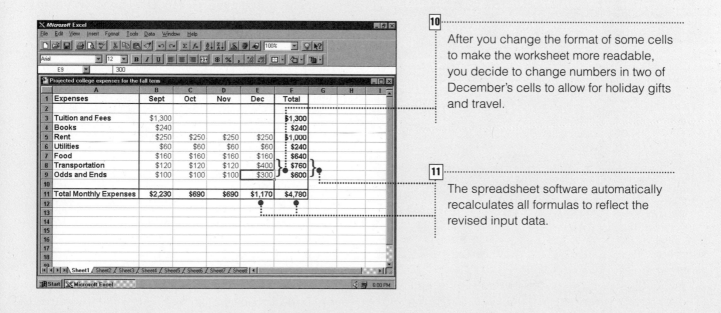

10 After you change the format of some cells to make the worksheet more readable, you decide to change numbers in two of December's cells to allow for holiday gifts and travel.

11 The spreadsheet software automatically recalculates all formulas to reflect the revised input data.

data. Without macros you'd have to repeat the same sequence of keystrokes, mouse clicks, and commands each time you created the monthly report. But by creating a macro called, for instance, Monthstats, you can effectively say "Do it again!" by issuing the Monthstats command.

- *Templates.* Even with functions and macros, the process of creating a complex worksheet from scratch can be intimidating. Many users take advantage of worksheet **templates** that contain labels and formulas but no data values. These reusable templates produce instant answers when you fill in the blanks. Some common templates are packaged with spreadsheet software; others are marketed separately. When templates aren't available, users can create their own or commission programmers to write them. Whatever its origin, a well-designed template can save considerable time, effort, and anguish.

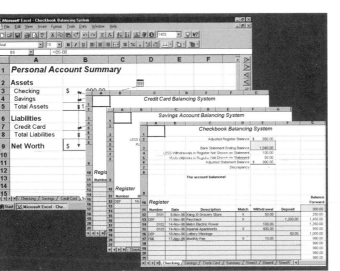

All of these worksheets are linked together into a single 3-D worksheet.

- *Linking.* Sometimes a change in one worksheet produces changes in another. For example, a master sales summary worksheet for a business should reflect changes in each department's sales summary worksheet. Most spreadsheet programs allow you to create **automatic links** between worksheets, so when values change in one, all linked worksheets are updated automatically. Some programs, like Lotus 1-2-3, can create three-dimensional worksheets by stacking and linking several two-dimensional sheets.

- *Database capabilities.* Database software is discussed in detail in Chapter 8. For now it's sufficient to mention that many spreadsheet programs can perform basic database functions: storage and retrieval of information, searching, sorting, report generation, mail merge, and such. With these features, a spreadsheet can serve users whose database needs are modest. For those who require a full-featured database management system, spreadsheet software might still be helpful; many spreadsheet programs support automatic two-way communication with database software.

"What If?" Questions

The purpose of computation is not numbers but insight.

—R. W. Hamming

A spreadsheet program is a versatile tool, but it's especially valuable for answering **"What if?"** questions: "What if I don't complete the third assignment? How will that affect my chances for getting an A?" "What if I put my savings in a high-yield, tax-sheltered IRA account with a withdrawal penalty? Will I be better off than if I leave it in a low-yield passbook account with no penalty?" "What if I buy a car that gets only 10 miles per gallon instead of a car that gets 40? How much more will I pay altogether for fuel over the next four years?" Because it allows you to change numbers and

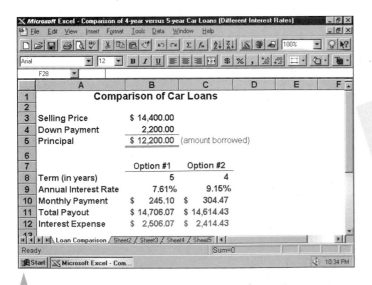

This worksheet compares two different car loans for total interest expense: a five-year loan at 7.61%, and a four-year loan at 9.15%. The cells whose contents appear in color (blue or red) contain formulas that compute results based on the contents of the worksheet. The four-year loan, even though it has a higher interest rate, is a slightly better choice.

Avoiding Spreadsheet Pitfalls

Spreadsheet errors are easy to make and easy to overlook. When creating a worksheet, you can minimize errors by following a few basic guidelines:

- **Plan the worksheet before you start entering values and formulas.** Think about your goals, and design the worksheet to meet those goals.
- **Make assumptions as accurate as possible.** Answers produced by a worksheet are only as good as the assumptions built into the data values and formulas. A worksheet that compares the operating costs of a gas guzzler and a gas miser must make assumptions about future trips, repair costs, and above all, gasoline prices. The accuracy of the worksheet is tied to all kinds of unknowns, including the future of Middle East politics. The more accurate the assumptions, the more accurate the predictions.
- **Double-check every formula and value.** Values and formulas are input for worksheets, and input determines output. Computer professionals often describe the dark side of this important relationship with the letters **GIGO**—garbage in, garbage out. One highly publicized spreadsheet transcription error for Fidelity Investments resulted in a $2.6 billion miscalculation because of a single missing minus sign! You may not be working with values this big, but it's still important to proofread your work carefully.

- **Make formulas readable.** If your software allows you to attach names to cell ranges, use meaningful names in formulas. It's easier to create and debug formulas when you can use readily understandable language like payrate*40+1.5*payrate*(hoursworked–40) instead of a string of characters like C2*40+1.5*C2*(D2–40).
- **Check your output against other systems.** Use another program, a calculator, or pencil and paper to verify the accuracy of a sampling of your calculations.
- **Build in cross-checks.** Compare the sum of row totals with the sum of column totals. Does everything add up?
- **Change the input data values and study the results.** If small input adjustments produce massive output changes, or if major input adjustments result in little or no output changes, something may be wrong.
- **Take advantage of preprogrammed functions, templates, and macros.** Why reinvent the wheel when you can buy a professionally designed vehicle?
- **Use a spreadsheet as a decision-making aid, not a decision maker.** Some errors aren't obvious; others don't show up immediately. Stay alert and skeptical.

instantly see the effects of those changes, spreadsheet software streamlines the process of searching for answers to these questions.

Some spreadsheet programs include **equation solvers** that turn "What if?" questions around. Instead of forcing you to manipulate data values until formulas give you the numbers you're looking for, an equation solver allows you to define an equation, enter your target value, and watch while the computer determines the necessary data values. For example, an investor might use an equation solver to answer the question, "What is the *best* mix of these three stocks for minimizing risk while producing a 10 percent return on my investment?"

Tomorrow's Spreadsheet?

As revolutionary as VisiCalc was when it was introduced in 1979, it simply couldn't meet the demands of today's spreadsheet user. Even the original 1-2-3 looks primitive and underpowered next to modern graphic spreadsheets designed for Windows and the Macintosh. It's unlikely that spreadsheets have reached the end of their evolutionary path. What's next?

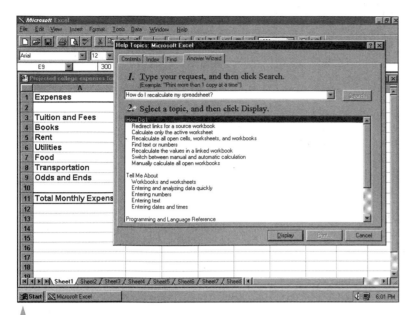

Excel's on-line help uses simple artificial intelligence techniques to guide users through complex procedures.

Modern versions of Lotus 1-2-3 include user help functions that incorporate the kinds of multimedia technology described in Chapter 7. Microsoft Excel and other spreadsheets are beginning to incorporate artificial intelligence to guide users through complex procedures. (A very simple example is shown in the next User's View box.) To help users check complex worksheets for consistency of entries and formula logic, future spreadsheets are likely to include *validators*—the equivalent of spelling and grammar checkers for spreadsheets.

Further down the road spreadsheets may disappear into the background along with other applications. Today's massive, feature-laden spreadsheets may be replaced by smaller software tools that can be combined into custom applications. Users will work with words, numbers, and other types of data without having to think about separate word processors, spreadsheets, and other applications. From the user's point of view, the focus will be more on the data than the tools. But until that happens, spreadsheets will continue to evolve into tools that better meet the needs of millions of users.

SPREADSHEET GRAPHICS: FROM DIGITS TO DRAWINGS

Our work . . . is to present things that are as they are.

—Frederick II (1194–1250), King of Sicily

Most spreadsheet programs include charting commands that can turn worksheet numbers into charts and graphs automatically. Stand-alone charting programs create charts from any collection of numbers, whether stored in a worksheet or not. The process of creating a chart is usually as simple as filling in a few blanks in a dialog box.

Creating Charts from Numbers

The growth in the national debt seems more real as a line shooting toward the top of a graph than as a collection of big numbers on a page. The federal budget makes more (or less?) sense as a sliced-up dollar pie than as a list of percentages. The correct chart can make a set of stale figures come to life, awakening our eyes and brains to trends and relationships that we might not have otherwise seen.   **UV**

Most spreadsheet and charting programs offer a variety of basic chart types and options for embellishing charts. The differences among these chart types are more than aesthetic; each chart type is well suited for communicating particular types of information. **Pie charts** show the relative proportions of the parts to a whole. **Line charts** are most often used to show trends or relationships over time or to show relative distribution of one variable through another. (The classic bell-shaped normal

The User's View

Charting with a Spreadsheet

▲ ▲

Software: Microsoft Excel.

The goal: To create a chart to bring your budget into focus.

1 To chart the breakdown totals from your budget, you'll use two ranges of cells: One contains the column of totals (F3 through F9) . . .

2 . . . and another contains the category names for those totals (A3 through A9).

4 After verifying the selected ranges in the first Chart Wizard step, you select the 3-D Pie chart type.

3 After selecting both ranges, you click on the Chart Wizard icon on the button bar. Chart Wizard walks you through the process of creating a chart by presenting a series of five dialog boxes.

5 The next dialog box, Step 3, offers several choices of 3-D pie charts. You choose the one that shows percentage values.

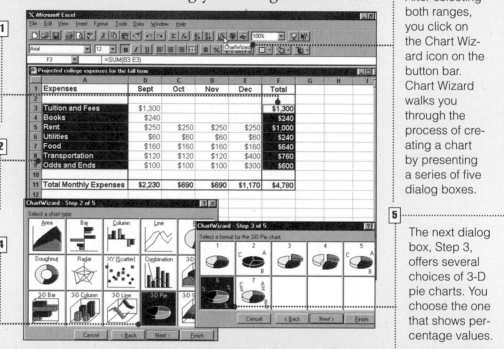

6 Step 4 lets you specify that the data is in columns, not rows, and that the first selected column contains chart labels, not data.

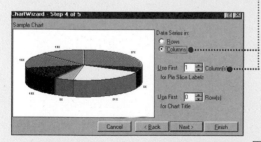

7 Step 5 allows you to add a title and a legend.

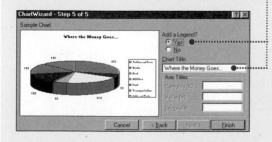

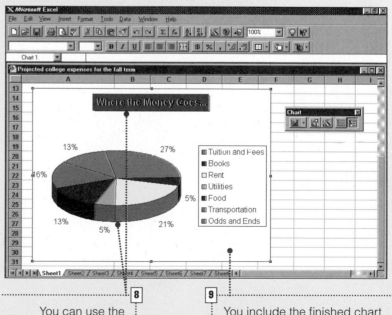

8 You can use the program's graphics tools to fine-tune the chart's appearance.

9 You include the finished chart on the same page as the worksheet. If you change a value in the worksheet, the chart is automatically updated.

The line chart and bar chart shown here were created with specialized charting software that offers more flexibility than most spreadsheet programs. (Software: Deltagraph Professional.) The scatter chart shown here was generated from data in an educational geographical database program. (Software: USA GeoGraph.)

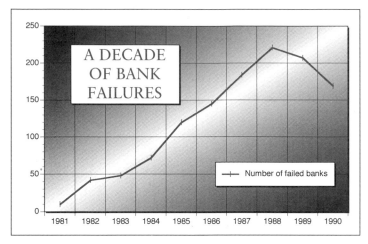

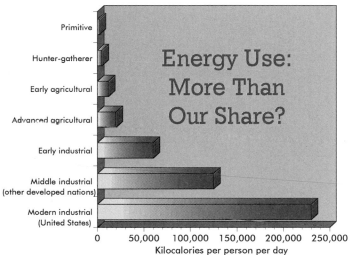

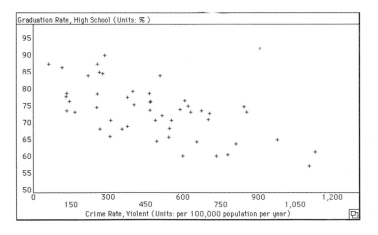

curve is a line chart.) **Bar charts** and *column charts* (like bar charts except with vertical bars) are similar to line charts, but they're more appropriate when data falls into a few categories. Bars can be stacked in a **stack chart** that shows how proportions of a whole change over time; the effect is similar to a series of pie charts. **Scatter charts** are used to discover, rather than display, a relationship between two variables. A well-designed chart can convey a wealth of information, just as a poorly designed chart can confuse or mislead.

RULES OF THUMB

Making Smart Charts

A chart can be a powerful communication tool if it's designed intelligently. If it's not, the message may miss the mark. Here are some guidelines for creating charts that are easy to read and understand.

- **Choose the right chart for the job.** Think about the message you're trying to convey. Pie charts, bar charts, line charts, and scatter charts are not interchangeable.

- **Keep it simple, familiar, and understandable.** Use charts in magazines, books, and newspapers as models.

- **Strive to reveal the truth, not hide it.** Whether accidentally or intentionally, many computer users create charts that convey misinformation. Changes in the scale or dimensions of a chart can completely transform the message, turning information into propaganda.

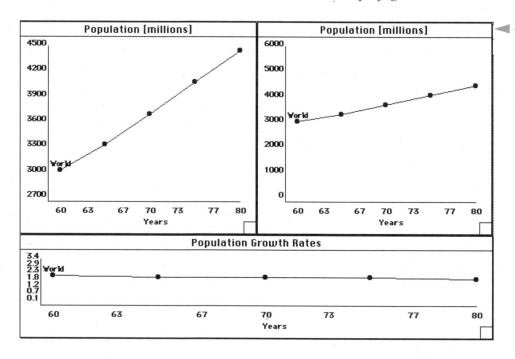

These charts are based on identical data; only the values on the vertical axes have been changed to distort the facts. (Software: PEMD Discovery.)

STATISTICAL SOFTWARE: BEYOND SPREADSHEETS

An IBM electronic calculator speeds through thousands of intricate computations so quickly that on many complex problems, it's just like having 150 extra engineers...

—IBM, ad showing dozens of slide-rule-toting engineers in *National Geographic*, February 1952

Spreadsheet software is remarkably versatile, but no program is perfect for every task. Other types of number-manipulation software are available for those situations in which spreadsheets don't quite fit the job.

Money Managers

Spreadsheet software has its roots in the accountant's ledger sheets, but spreadsheets today are seldom used for accounting and bookkeeping. Accounting is a complex concoction of rules, formulas, laws, and traditions, and creating a worksheet to handle the details of the process is difficult and time consuming. Instead of relying on general-purpose spreadsheets for accounting, most businesses (and many households) use professionally designed **accounting and financial management software.**

Whether practiced at home or at the office, accounting involves setting up *accounts*—monetary categories to represent various types of income, expenses, assets, and liabilities—and keeping track of the flow of money between those accounts. An accountant routinely records *transactions*—checks, cash payments, charges, and other activities—that move money from one account to another. Accounting software automatically adjusts the balance in every account after each transaction. What's more, it records every transaction so that the history of each account can be retraced, step by step. This *audit trail* is a necessary part of business financial records, and it's one reason accountants use special-purpose accounting packages rather than spreadsheet programs. In addition to keeping records, financial management software can automate check writing, bill paying, budgeting, and other routine money matters. Periodic reports and charts can provide detailed answers to questions like "Where does the money go?" and "How are we doing compared to last year?" You can even subscribe to a service that allows your personal finance software to communicate with your bank's computer through a modem, so it's easier than ever to track transactions, balance your checkbook, and monitor your money in a timely fashion.

Most accounting and financial management programs don't calculate income taxes, but they *can* export records to programs that do. **Tax preparation software** works like a prefabricated worksheet. As you enter numbers into the blanks in on-screen forms, other blanks are filled automatically by the program. Every time a number is entered or changed, the bottom line is recalculated automatically. When the forms are completed, they're ready to print, sign, and mail to the Internal Revenue Service. Some taxpayers bypass paper forms altogether by sending the completed forms *electronically* to the IRS.

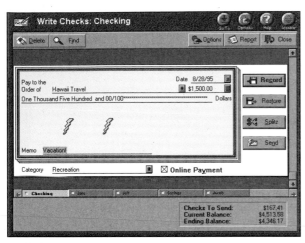

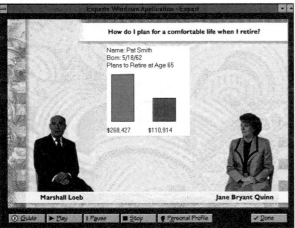

Inexpensive financial management programs for homes and small businesses make the accounting process easier to understand by simulating checks and other familiar documents on the screen. Above: Quicken allows you to print checks or send them electronically through participating banks. Below: Quicken can also provide financial advice from experts using digital video.

Automatic Mathematics

Most of us seldom do math more complicated than filling out our tax forms. But higher mathematics is an essential part of the work of many scientists, researchers, engineers, architects, economists, financial analysts, teachers, and other professionals. Mathematics is a universal language for defining and understanding natural phenomena as well as a tool used to create all kinds of products and structures. Whether or not we work with it directly, our lives are constantly being shaped by mathematics.

Many professionals and students whose mathematical needs go beyond the capabilities of spreadsheets depend on symbolic **mathematics processing software** to grapple with complex equations and calculations. Mathematics processors make it easier for mathematicians to create, manipulate, and solve equations, in much the same way word processors help writers. Features vary from program to program, but a typical mathematics processor can do polynomial factoring, symbolic and numeric calculus, real and complex trigonometry, matrix and linear algebra, and three-dimensional graphics.

Mathematics processors generally include an interactive question-and-answer mode, a programming language, and tools for creating interactive documents that combine text, numerical expressions, and graphics. Although mathematics processors have only been available for a few years, they've already changed the way professionals use mathematics and the way students learn it. By handling the mechanics of mathematics, these programs allow people to concentrate on the content and implications of their work.

Statistics and Data Analysis

Yet to calculate is not in itself to analyze.

—Edgar Allan Poe, 1841

One branch of applied mathematics that has become more important in the computer age is statistics—the science of collecting and analyzing data. Modern computer technology provides us with mountains of data—census data, political data, consumer data, economic data, sports data, weather data, scientific data, and more. We often refer to the data as statistics ("The government released unemployment statistics today"), but the numbers by themselves tell only part of the story. The analysis of those numbers—the search for patterns and relationships among them—can provide meaning for the data ("Analysts note that the rise in unemployment is confined to cities most heavily impacted by defense cutbacks"). Statisticians in government, business, and science depend on computers to make sense of raw data.

Do people who live near nuclear power plants run a higher cancer risk? Does the current weather pattern suggest the formation of a tropical storm? Are rural voters more likely to support small-town candidates? These questions can't be answered with absolute certainty; the element of chance is at the heart of statistical analysis. But **statistical analysis software** can suggest answers to questions like these by testing the strength of data relationships. Statistical software can also produce graphs showing how two or more variables relate to each other. Statisticians can often uncover trends by browsing through two- and three-dimensional graphs of their data, looking for unusual patterns in the dots and lines that appear on the screen. This kind of visual exploration of data is an example of one of the fastest growing computer applications: *scientific visualization.*

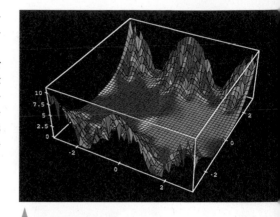

An abstract mathematical relationship is easier to understand when turned into a visible object with high-level mathematical software. (Software: Mathematica.)

The 3-D scatter charts below show the relationship among three variables: latitude, longitude, and population density in the United States. In the chart on the left, the relationship isn't clear. But when the "structure" is rotated and viewed from a different angle, as in the middle picture, it makes more sense. The final picture spells out the pattern by adding a surface. It is clear from this plot that the population is spread unevenly across the country.

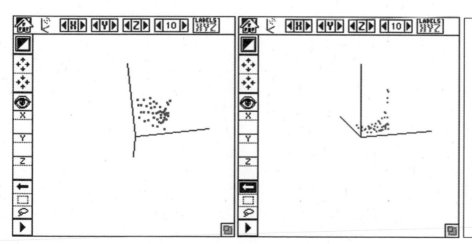

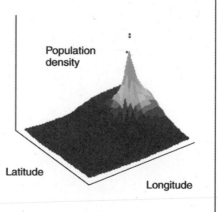

Scientific Visualization

> The wind blows over the lake and stirs the surface of the water. Thus, visible effects of the invisible are manifested.
>
> —The I Ching

Inside two simulated molecules in Argonne National Laboratory's Cave Automatic Virtual Environment, computer scientist David Levine investigates how one molecule "docks" into another. His research uses advanced computers to understand how proteins form string-like molecules that are related to Alzheimer's disease and rheumatoid arthritis.

Scientific visualization software uses shape, location in space, color, brightness, and motion to help us understand relationships that are invisible to us. Like mathematical and statistical software, scientific visualization software is no longer confined to mainframes and supercomputers; some of the most innovative programs are developed for use on high-end personal computers and workstations, working alone or in conjunction with more powerful computers. Scientific visualization takes many forms, all of which involve graphical representation of numerical data. The numbers can be the result of abstract equations, or they can be data gleaned from the real world. Either way, turning the numbers into pictures allows researchers and students to see the unseeable, and sometimes, as a result, to know what was previously unknowable. Here are two examples:

- Astronomer Margaret Geller of Harvard University created a three-dimensional map of the cosmos from data on the locations of known galaxies. While using her computer to "fly through" this three-dimensional model, she saw something that no one had seen before: the mysterious clustering of galaxies along the edges of invisible bubbles.

- Dr. Mark Ellisman of the University of California, San Diego, School of Medicine used a 30-foot electron microscope to collect data from cells of the brain and enter it into a supercomputer, which rendered a 3-D representation of the brain cell. When Ellisman's team displayed the data on a graphic workstation, they saw several previously undiscovered aberrations in brains of patients who had Alzheimer's disease—aberrations that may turn out to be clues for discovering the cause and cure for this disease.

In these examples and hundreds of others like them, visualization helps researchers see relationships that might have been obscure or even impossible to grasp without computer-aided visualization tools.

CALCULATED RISKS: COMPUTER MODELING AND SIMULATION

> No man's knowledge here can go beyond his experience.
>
> —John Locke

Whether part of a simple worksheet or a complex set of equations, numbers often symbolize real-world phenomena. Computer **modeling**—the use of computers to create abstract models of objects, organisms, organizations, and processes—can be done with spreadsheets, mathematical applications, or standard programming languages. Most of the applications discussed in this chapter are examples of computer modeling. A business executive who creates a worksheet to project quarterly profits and losses is trying to model the economic world that affects the company. An engineer who uses a mathematics processor to test the stress capacity of a bridge is modeling the bridge mathematically. Even a statistician who starts by examining data collected in the real world creates statistical models to describe the data.

Flight simulator games for home computers like Outpost Cuba (left) are simplified versions of flight simulators used to train military pilots (right). Both varieties allow users to test their wings without risking their necks.

Computer models aren't always serious; most computer games are models. Chess boards, pinball games, battlefields, sports arenas, ant colonies, cities, medieval dungeons, interplanetary cultures, mythological societies—they've all been modeled in computer games. In classrooms, students use computer models to travel the Oregon Trail, explore nuclear power plants, invest in the stock market, and dissect digital frogs.

Whether it's created for work, education, or play, a computer model is an *abstraction*—a set of concepts and ideas designed to mimic some kind of system. But a computer model isn't static; it can be put to work in a computer **simulation** to see how the model operates under certain conditions. A well-designed model should behave like the system it imitates.

Suppose, for example, an engineer constructs a computer model of a new type of airplane to test how the plane will respond to human commands. In a typical flight simulation, the "pilot" controls the plane's thrust and elevator angle by feeding input data to the model plane. The model responds by adjusting air speed and angle of ascent or descent, just as a real plane would. The pilot responds to the new state of the aircraft by adjusting one or more of the controls, which causes the system to respond by revising the aircraft's state again. This **feedback loop,** where plane and pilot react to data from each other, continues throughout the simulation.

A flight simulator might have a graphical user interface that makes the computer screen look and act like the instrument panel of a real plane so that it can be run interactively by human pilots. Or it might display nothing more than numbers representing input and output values, and the input values might be generated by a simulated pilot—another computer model! Either way, it can deliver a wealth of information about the behavior of the plane, provided the model is accurate.

Computer Simulations: The Rewards

We are reaching the stage where problems that we must solve are going to become insolvable without computers. I do not fear computers; I fear the lack of them.

—Isaac Asimov, scientist and science fiction writer

Computer simulations are widely used for research in the physical, biological, and social sciences and in engineering. Schools, businesses, and the military also use simulations for training. There are many reasons:

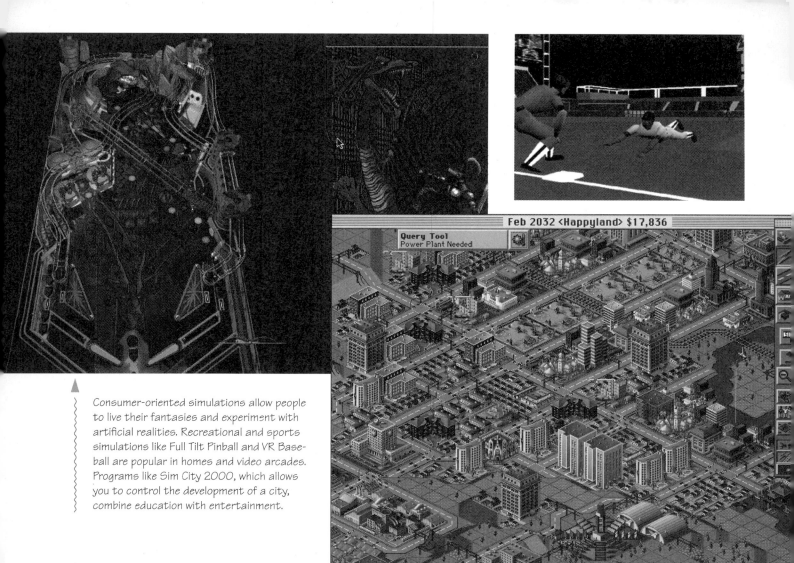

Feb 2032 <Happyland> $17,836

Query Tool
Power Plant Needed

Consumer-oriented simulations allow people to live their fantasies and experiment with artificial realities. Recreational and sports simulations like Full Tilt Pinball and VR Baseball are popular in homes and video arcades. Programs like Sim City 2000, which allows you to control the development of a city, combine education with entertainment.

- *Safety.* While it's safer to learn piloting skills sitting in front of a computer than actually flying in the air, it's still possible to learn to fly without a computer simulation. Some activities, however, are so dangerous that they aren't ethically possible without computer simulations. How, for example, can scientists study the effects of a nuclear power plant meltdown on the surrounding environment? Until a meltdown occurs, there's only one practical answer: computer simulation.

- *Economy.* It's far less expensive for an automobile manufacturer to produce a digital model of a nonexistent car than to build a prototype out of steel. The computer model can be tested for strength, handling, and efficiency in a series of simulations *before* the company builds and tests a physical prototype. The cost of the computer model is small when compared to the possible expense of producing a defective car.

- *Projection.* Without computers it could take decades for biologists to determine whether the rising deer population on an island threatens other species, and by the time they discover the answer, it would be too late to do anything about it. A computer model of the island's ecosystem would speed up natural biological processes, so their effects over several generations could be measured in a matter of minutes. A computer simulation can, in effect, serve as a time machine for exploring one or more possible futures.

- *Visualization.* Computer models make visualization possible, and visualization allows researchers and students to see and understand relationships that might otherwise go unnoticed. Computer models can speed time up or slow it down; they can make subatomic particles big and the universe small.

- *Replication.* In the real world it can be difficult or impossible to repeat a research project with slightly different conditions. But this kind of repetition is an important part of serious research. An engineer needs to fine-tune dimensions and angles to achieve peak performance. A scientist studies the results of one experiment and develops a new hypothesis that calls for further testing. An executive needs to test a business plan under a variety of economic scenarios. If the research is conducted on a computer model, replication is just a matter of changing input values and running a new simulation.

Computer Simulations: The Risks

The down side of computer simulation can be summed up in three words: *Simulation isn't reality.* The real world is a subtle and complex place, and capturing even a fraction of that subtlety and complexity in a computer simulation is a tremendous challenge.

GIGO Revisited

The accuracy of a simulation depends on how closely its mathematical model corresponds to the system being simulated. Mathematical models are built on assumptions, many of which are difficult or impossible to verify. Some models suffer from faulty assumptions; others contain hidden assumptions that may not even be obvious to their creators; still others go astray simply because of clerical or human errors.

The highly publicized 1974 Club of Rome study, summarized in the book *The Limits of Growth,* used the most powerful computers available at the time to model the environmental and economic impact of human activity on earth. Months after the study was released, a researcher discovered a misplaced decimal point in one key equation that threw many calculations off by a factor of ten! Correcting the error didn't negate the report's overall conclusions, but it did raise many questions about the study. Bad input in a complex simulation can come from numerous sources, and "garbage in, garbage out" is a basic rule of simulation.

Making Reality Fit the Machine

Simulations are computation intensive. Today's personal computers can run modest simulations, but they're hopelessly underpowered for medium-to-large simulations. Most scientists and engineers who work extensively with mathematical models depend on workstations, mainframes, or supercomputers to run simulations. Even Apple, the personal computer manufacturer, used a Cray supercomputer to model future Apple machines. (Fittingly, Seymour Cray claimed to use an Apple computer to help him design Cray machines!)

Some simulations are so complex that researchers need to simplify models and streamline calculations to get them to run on the best hardware available. Even when there's plenty of computing power available, researchers face a constant temptation to reshape reality for the convenience of the simulation. In one classic example a U.S. Forest Service computer model reduced complex old-growth forests to "accumulated capital." Aesthetics, ecological diversity, and other hard-to-quantify factors didn't exist in this model.

Sometimes this simplification of reality is deliberate; more often it's unconscious. Either way, information can be lost, and the loss may compromise the integrity of the simulation and call the results into question.

Scientific Computing

Computers have long been used to analyze and visualize scientific data collected through experiments and observation. A computer can also serve as a virtual laboratory that simulates a physical process without real-world experiments. Of course, an inaccurate simulation can give incorrect results.

The problem of accurate simulation helped initiate the study of *chaos* and *fractals*. Chaos is now a vast field of study with applications in many disciplines.

The "Chaos Game" illustrates how computers can quickly complete repetitive tasks in experiments that would otherwise be impractical or impossible. You could perform the first few steps of such an experiment with pencil, paper, and ruler, like this:

1 Draw three widely separated points on the paper to form a triangle; label the points A, B, and C. Draw a random starting point anywhere on the paper. This will be the first "current" point.

2 Repeat the following process four times: randomly choose from among points A, B, and C, and draw a new point halfway (on an imaginary straight line) between the current point and the chosen point. The newly drawn point then becomes the new current point.

3 If you use a simple computer program to plot 100,000 repeats of step 2 (excluding the first few points from the drawing), you'll see a pattern emerge rather than a solid mass of dots. This pattern, called a Sierpinski gasket, is a fractal—an object in which pieces are miniatures of the whole figure. You will see a pattern like this.

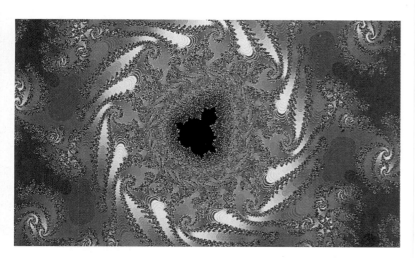

The Mandelbrot Set, discovered by the mathematician Benoit Mandelbrot (who coined the term fractal) while he was working at IBM's Thomas J. Watson Research Facility, is one of the most famous fractals to emerge from the theory of chaos.

Because some fractal formulas mimic the patterns of natural objects, such as coastlines and mountains, chaos has found applications in computer-generated scenery and special effects for movies and television shows.

The Illusion of Infallibility

Risks can be magnified because people take computers seriously. For many people information takes on an air of respectability if it comes from a computer. Computer-generated reports tend to be emphasized, often at the expense of other sources of knowledge. Executives use worksheets to make decisions involving hundreds of jobs and millions of dollars. Politicians decide the fate of military weapons and endangered species based on summaries of computer simulations. Doctors use computer models to make life-and-death decisions involving new drugs and treatments. All these people, in some sense, are placing their trust in computer simulations. Many of them trust the data precisely *because* it was generated by a computer.

A computer simulation, whether generated by a PC spreadsheet or churned out by a supercomputer, can be an invaluable decision-making aid. The risk is that the people who make decisions with computers will turn over too much of their decision-making power to the computer. The Jedi Master in the motion picture *Star Wars* understood the danger when he encouraged Luke Skywalker in the heat of battle to turn off his computer simulation rather than let it overpower his judgment. His admonition was simple: "Trust your feelings."

SUMMARY

Spreadsheet programs, first developed to simulate and automate the accountant's ledger, are widely used today in business, science, engineering, and education. Spreadsheet software can be used for tracking financial transactions, calculating grades, forecasting economic conditions, recording scientific data—just about any task that involves repetitive numeric calculations. Spreadsheet documents, called worksheets, are grids with individual cells containing alphabetic labels, numbers, and formulas. Changes in numeric values can cause the spreadsheet to update any related formulas automatically. The responsiveness and flexibility of spreadsheet software make it particularly well suited for providing answers to "What if?" questions.

Most spreadsheet programs include charting commands to turn worksheet numbers into a variety of graphs and charts. The process of creating a chart from a spreadsheet is automated to the point that human drawing isn't necessary; the user simply provides instructions concerning the type of chart and the details to be included in the chart.

Number crunching often goes beyond spreadsheets. Specialized accounting and tax preparation software packages perform specific business functions without the aid of spreadsheets. Symbolic mathematics processors can handle a variety of higher mathematics functions involving numbers, symbols, equations, and graphics. Statistical analysis software is used for data collection and analysis. Scientific visualization can be done with math processors, statistical packages, graphics programs, or specialized programs designed for visualization.

Modeling and simulation are at the heart of most applications involving numbers. When people create computer models, they use numbers to represent real-world objects and phenomena. Simulations built on these models can provide insights that might be difficult or impossible to obtain otherwise, provided that the models reflect reality accurately. If used wisely, computer simulation can be a powerful tool to help people understand their world and make better decisions.

Chapter Review

Key Terms

accounting and financial
  management software
active cell
address
automatic link
automatic recalculation
bar chart
cell
column
console
current cell
equation solver
feedback loop

formula
formula bar
function
GIGO
label
line chart
macro
mathematics processing software
modeling
pie chart
range
replication
row

scatter chart
scientific visualization software
simulation
spreadsheet software
stack chart
statistical analysis software
tax preparation software
template
value
"What if?" question
worksheet

Review Questions

1. Define or describe each of the key terms above. Check your answers using the glossary.

2. In what ways are word processors and spreadsheet programs similar?

3. What are some advantages of using a spreadsheet to maintain a budget over using a calculator? Are there any disadvantages?

4. If you enter =B2+C2 in cell B1 of a worksheet, the formula is replaced by the number 125 when you press the Enter key. What happened?

5. Using the worksheet from question 4, you change the number in cell B2 from 55 to 65. What happens to the number in cell B1? Why?

6. Explain the difference between a numeric value and a formula.

7. What is a spreadsheet function and how is it useful?

8. What is the difference between a spreadsheet program and a financial management program?

9. Describe or draw examples of several different types of charts, and explain how they're typically used.

10. Describe several software tools used for numeric applications too complex to be handled by spreadsheets. Give an example of an application of each.

11. List several advantages and disadvantages of using computer simulations for decision making.

Discussion Questions

1. Spreadsheets are sometimes credited with legitimizing the personal computer as a business tool. Why do you think they had such an impact?

2. Why do you think errors in spreadsheet models go undetected? What can you do to minimize the risk of spreadsheet errors?

3. The statement "Computers don't make mistakes, people do" is often used to support the reliability of computer output. Is the statement true? Is it relevant?

4. Are computer simulations misused? Give some examples and explain your answer.

5. Before spreadsheets, people who wanted to use computers for financial modeling had to write programs in complex computer languages to do the job. Today spreadsheets have replaced those programs for many financial applications. Do you think spreadsheets will be replaced by some easier-to-use software tool in the future? If so, try to imagine what it will be like.

Projects

1. Use a spreadsheet or a financial management program to develop a personal budget. Try to keep track of all your income and outgo for the next month or two, and record the transactions with your program. At the end of that time, evaluate the accuracy of your budget and discuss your reactions to the process.

2. Use a spreadsheet to search for answers to a "What if" question that's important to you. Possible questions: What if I lease a car instead of buying it—am I better off? What if I borrow money for school—how much does it cost me in the long run?

3. Develop a multiple-choice questionnaire for determining public attitudes on an issue that's important to you. Use a computer to analyze, summarize, and graphically represent the results, trying to be as fair and accurate in your summary as you can.

4. Use a spreadsheet to track your grades in this (or another) class. Apply weightings from the course syllabus to your

individual scores, calculating a point total based on those weightings.

5. Choose a controversial issue—environmental, economic, or other—and locate numeric data related to the issue. Develop a set of charts and graphs that argues effectively for one point of view. Using the same data, create visuals to support the other point of view. Compare audience reactions (and your reactions) to both presentations.

Sources and Resources

Books

Books covering basic spreadsheet operations number in the hundreds—far too many to review here. Almost all these books are software and hardware specific. Some are intended to be used as reference manuals; some are collections of tips, hints, and shortcuts; others are collections of sample documents that can be used as templates; still others are overviews or hands-on tutorials for beginners. If you're new to spreadsheets, start with a book in the last category. Look for one that fits your system and that's readable and easy to understand.

How to Lie with Statistics, by Darrell Huff (New York: Norton, 1954). This 40-year-old book has more relevance in today's computer age than it did when it was written.

The Visual Display of Quantitative Information and *Envisioning Information,* by Edward R. Tufte (Cheshire, CT: Graphics Press, 1983 and 1990, respectively). These two stunningly beautiful books should be required reading for anyone who creates charts, graphs, or other visual aids. For that matter they should be read by anyone who *reads* charts, graphs, and other visual aids.

Elements of Graphic Design, by Stephen M. Kosslyn (New York: W. H. Freeman and Comany, 1948). This handy book is smaller, more affordable, and more accessible than the Tufte books. It's packed with useful tips for designing charts and graphs that communicate clearly, with plenty of examples comparing charts done the wrong way with charts done correctly.

Visualization of Natural Phenomena, by Robert Wolff and Larry Yaeger (New York: Telos/Springer-Verlag, 1993). This oversized book is a visually captivating overview of scientific visualization via computers. It's fun to browse through the stunning images even if you don't read the text. A CD-ROM is included.

World Wide Web Pages

The Internet was created as a tool for scientific researchers and engineers. Today the Web is filled with sites that deal with mathematics, statistics, scientific visualization, and simulation. The *Computer Confluence* Web pages include links to many of the best sites in government, education, and private corporations.

GRAPHICS, HYPERMEDIA, AND MULTIMEDIA

Doug Engelbart Explores Hyperspace

If you look out in the future, you can see how best to make right choices.

—Doug Engelbart

Doug Engelbart

O n a December day in 1950, Doug Engelbart looked out into the future and saw what no one had seen before. Engelbart had been thinking about the growing complexity and urgency of the world's prob lems and wondering how he could help solve those problems. In his vision of the future, Engelbart saw computer technology augmenting and magnifying human mental abilities, providing people with new powers to cope with the urgency and complexity of life.

Engelbart decided to dedicate his life to turning his vision into reality. Unfortunately the rest of the world wasn't ready for Engelbart's vision. His farsighted approach didn't match the prevailing ideas of the time, and most of the research community denounced or ignored Engelbart's work. In 1951 there were only about a dozen computers in the world, and those spent most of their time doing military calculations. It was hard to imagine ordinary people using computers to augment their personal productivity. So Engelbart put together the Augmentation Research Center to create working models of his visionary tools.

In 1968 he demonstrated his Augment system to an auditorium full of astonished computer professionals and changed forever the way people think about computers. A large screen showed a cascade of computer graph- ics, text, and video images, controlled by Engelbart and a coworker several miles away. "It was like magic," recalls Alan Kay, one of the young computer scientists in the audience. Augment introduced the mouse, video display editing (the forerunner to word processing), mixed text and graphics, windowing, outlining, shared-screen video conferencing, computer conferencing, groupware, and hypermedia. Although Engelbart used a large computer, he was really demonstrating a futuristic "personal" computer—an interactive multimedia workstation for enhancing individual abilities.

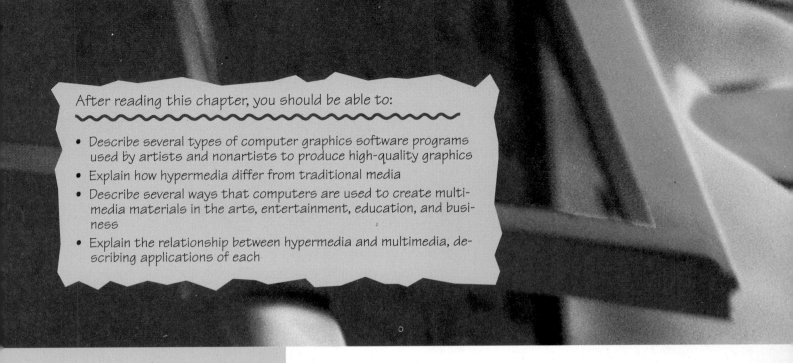

After reading this chapter, you should be able to:

~~~~~~

- Describe several types of computer graphics software programs used by artists and nonartists to produce high-quality graphics
- Explain how hypermedia differ from traditional media
- Describe several ways that computers are used to create multimedia materials in the arts, entertainment, education, and business
- Explain the relationship between hypermedia and multimedia, describing applications of each

Today many of Engelbart's inventions and ideas have become commonplace. He is widely recognized for one small part of his vision: the mouse. But Engelbart hasn't stopped looking into the future. He now heads the Bootstrap Institute, a nonprofit think tank dedicated to helping organizations make decisions with the future in mind. In a world where automation can dehumanize and eliminate jobs, Engelbart is still committed to replacing automation with augmentation. But now he focuses more on the human side of the equation, helping people chart a course into the future guided by intelligent, positive vision. He talks about turning organizations into "networked improvement communities" and demonstrates ways to "improve the improvement process." If anyone understands how to build the future from a vision, Doug Engelbart does.

By combining live-action video with long-distance text editing and idea processing, Doug Engelbart showed that the computer could be a multiple-media communication tool with fantastic potential. Today the personal computer is living up to that potential. Graphics programs allow artists, designers, engineers, publishers, and others to create and edit visual images. Hypermedia documents guide users through information along uniquely personal trails rather than traditional start-to-finish paths. Interactive multimedia tools combine text, graphics, animation, video, and sound in computer-controlled packages. In this chapter we'll look into these cutting-edge technologies and see how they can augment human abilities.

FOCUS ON COMPUTER GRAPHICS

~~~~~~

Actually, a root word of technology, techne, originally meant "art." The ancient Greeks never separated art from manufacture in their minds, and so never developed separate words for them.

—Robert Pirsig, in Zen and the Art of Motorcycle Maintenance

Chapter 6 demonstrated how spreadsheet programs, statistical programs, and other mathematical software create *quantitative* graphics—charts and graphs generated from numbers. These programs help business people, scientists, and engineers who lack the time or talent to create high-quality drawings by hand. But computer graphics today go far beyond pie charts and line graphs. In this section we'll explore a variety of graphical applications, from simple drawing and painting tools to complex programs used by professional artists and designers.

Painting: Bit-Mapped Graphics

One must act in painting as in life, directly.

—Pablo Picasso

When it's used with compatible software, a pen on a pressure-sensitive tablet can simulate the feel of a paint-brush on paper. As the artist presses harder on the tablet, the line becomes thicker and denser on the screen.

An image on a computer screen is made of a matrix of **pixels**—tiny dots of white, black, or color arranged in rows. The words, numbers, and pictures we see are nothing more than patterns of pixels created by software. Most of the time the user doesn't directly control those pixel patterns; software creates the patterns automatically in response to commands. For example, when you press the "e" key while word processing, software constructs a pattern that appears on the screen as an "e." Similarly, when you issue a command to create a bar chart from a spreadsheet, software automatically constructs a pixel pattern that looks like a bar chart. Automatic graphics are convenient, but they can also be restrictive. When you need more control over the details of the screen display, another type of graphics software might be more appropriate.

Painting software allows you to "paint" pixels on the screen with a pointing device. A typical painting program accepts input from a mouse, joystick, trackball, touchpad, or pen, translating the pointer movements into lines and patterns on screen. A professional artist might prefer to work with a pen on a pressure-sensitive tablet because it can, with the right software, simulate a traditional paintbrush more accurately than other pointing devices.

A painting program typically offers a palette of tools on screen. Some tools mimic real-world painting tools, while others can do things that are difficult, even impossible, on paper or canvas. The User's View box on page 148 shows some examples. **UV**

Painting programs create **bit-mapped graphics** (or, as they're sometimes called, **raster graphics**)—pictures that are, to the computer, simple maps showing how the pixels on the screen should be represented. For the simplest bit-mapped graphics, a single bit of computer memory represents each pixel. Since a bit can contain one of two possible values, 0 or 1, each pixel can display one of two possible colors, usually black or white.

Higher-quality pictures can be produced by allocating more memory per pixel, so each pixel can display more possible colors or shades. **Gray-scale graphics** allow each pixel to appear as black, white, or one of several shades of gray. A gray-scale program that assigns 8 bits per pixel allows up to 256 different shades of gray to appear on the screen—more than the human eye can distinguish.

Realistic color graphics require even more memory. Today's low-end multimedia computers typically have hardware to support 8-bit color, allowing 256 possible colors to be displayed on the screen at a time—enough to display rich images, but not enough to *exactly* reproduce most photographs. Photo-realistic color requires hardware that can display millions of colors at a time—24 or 32 bits of memory for each pixel on the screen.

The number of bits devoted to each pixel—called **color depth** or **bit depth**—is one of two technological factors limiting an artist's ability to create realistic on-screen images with a bit-mapped graphics program. The other factor is **resolution**—the density of the pixels, usually described in *dots per inch*, or *dpi*. Not surprisingly, these are also the two main factors controlling image quality in monitors, as de-

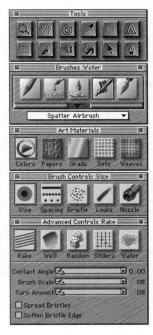

Professional painting programs like Fractal Design Painter allow artists and nonartists alike to use tools that work like real-world painting tools. The palettes on the right show a few of the hundreds of tools and options available on Painter's palettes; the three images above show snapshots of a work-in-progress created with those tools.

scribed in Chapter 3. But some graphic images are destined for the printer after being displayed on screen, so the printer's resolution comes into play, too. When displayed on a 72-dpi computer screen—on an Internet World Wide Web page, for example—a 72-dpi picture looks fine. But when printed on paper, that same image lacks the fine-grain clarity of a photograph. Diagonal lines, curves, and text characters have tiny "jaggies"—jagged, stair-step-like bumps that advertise the image's identity as a collection of pixels.

Most painting programs get around the jaggies by allowing you to store an image at 300 dots per inch or higher, even though the computer screen can't display every pixel at that resolution and normal magnification. Of course, high-resolution pictures demand more memory and disk space. But for many applications the results are worth the added cost. The higher the resolution, the harder it is for the human eye to detect individual pixels on the printed page.

Practically speaking, resolution and bit depth limitations are easy to overcome with today's technology. Using high-end Macintosh and Windows PCs with professional paint programs like Fractal Design's Painter, artists are able to produce works that convincingly simulate water colors, oils, and other natural media. And with similar hardware, bit-mapped image editing software can even be used to edit photographic images.

Digital Image Processing: Photographic Editing by Computer

Like a picture created with a high-resolution paint program, a digitized photograph or a photograph captured with a digital camera is a bit-mapped image. **Digital image processing software** allows the user to manipulate photographs and other high-resolution images with tools similar to those found in paint programs. Digital image processing software like Adobe Photoshop is in many ways similar to professional paint software like Painter—both are tools for editing high-resolution bit-mapped images.

Digital image processing software makes it easier for photographers to remove unwanted reflections, eliminate "red eye," and brush away facial blemishes—to perform the kinds of editing tasks that were routinely done with magnifying glasses and tiny brushes before photographs could be digitized. But digital photographic editing is far more powerful than traditional photo retouching techniques. With image

Painting with a Computer

▲ ▲

Software: ClarisWorks.

The goal: To draw a picture of a computer—a simple image to be displayed on the screen. You'll use ClarisWorks, an integrated software package. In addition to word processing, spreadsheet, and database tools, ClarisWorks includes a variety of graphics tools, including painting tools that are ideal for this project.

1 When you open a new document for painting, you see a blank page beside a *tool panel*—a collection of buttons representing tools.

2 You click on the painting button to turn the mouse pointer into a paintbrush.

3 As you drag the brush around the window, it leaves a black trail.

4 Your cartoon sketch has a little too much personality, so you double-click on the eraser tool to clear the page.

5 You decide to draw the outlines of the computer monitor and CPU box using the rounded-rectangle tool. Like the other shape tools, the rounded-rectangle tool can draw shapes that are filled with a selected paint pattern and color.

6 Because you want the shapes to be hollow outlines, you select the Transparent Fill icon from the Pattern menu. The Pattern menu is a **pop-up menu**—it pops into view when you click on the Fill Pattern icon.

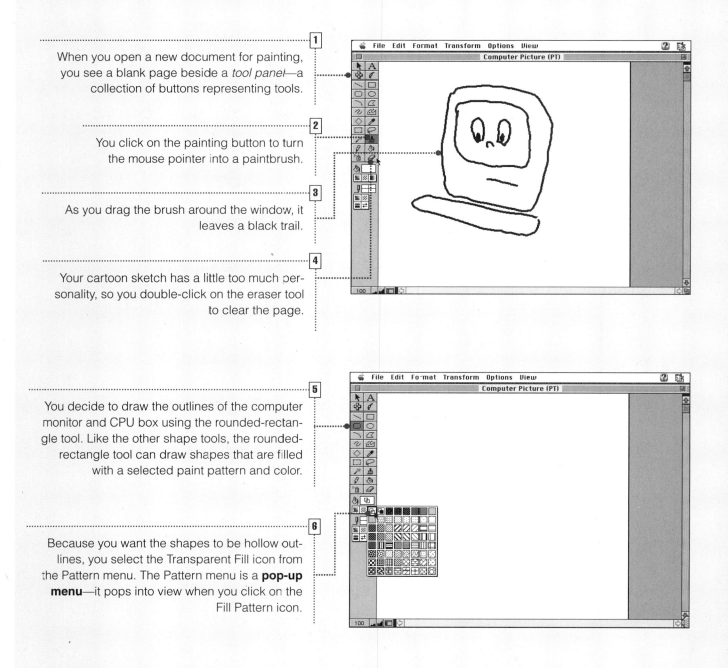

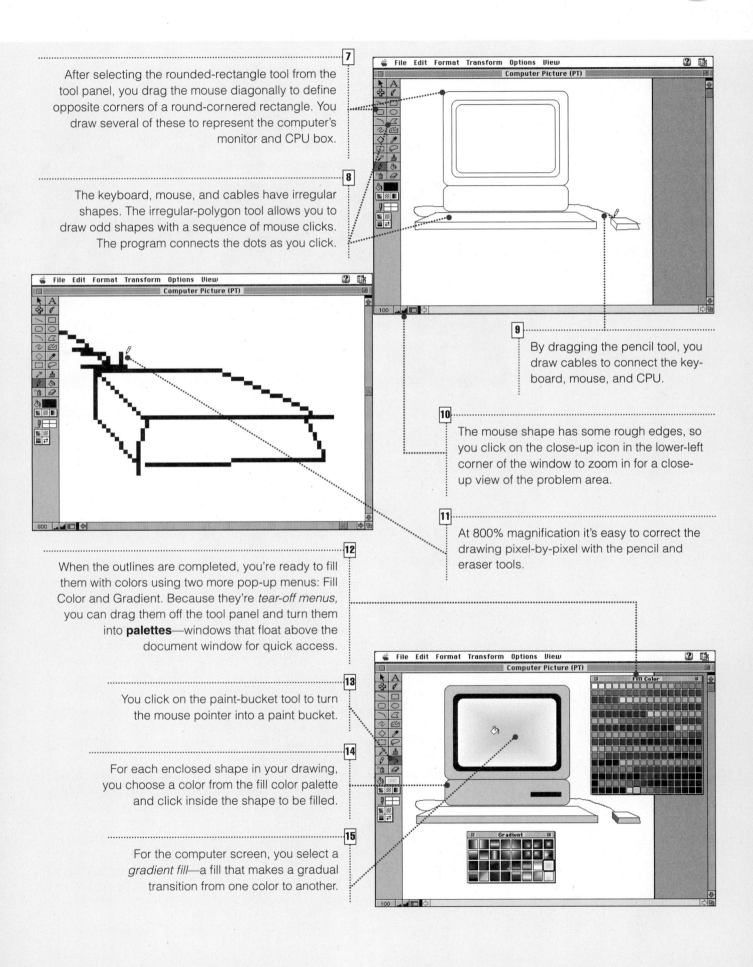

7

After selecting the rounded-rectangle tool from the tool panel, you drag the mouse diagonally to define opposite corners of a round-cornered rectangle. You draw several of these to represent the computer's monitor and CPU box.

8

The keyboard, mouse, and cables have irregular shapes. The irregular-polygon tool allows you to draw odd shapes with a sequence of mouse clicks. The program connects the dots as you click.

9

By dragging the pencil tool, you draw cables to connect the keyboard, mouse, and CPU.

10

The mouse shape has some rough edges, so you click on the close-up icon in the lower-left corner of the window to zoom in for a close-up view of the problem area.

11

At 800% magnification it's easy to correct the drawing pixel-by-pixel with the pencil and eraser tools.

12

When the outlines are completed, you're ready to fill them with colors using two more pop-up menus: Fill Color and Gradient. Because they're *tear-off menus,* you can drag them off the tool panel and turn them into **palettes**—windows that float above the document window for quick access.

13

You click on the paint-bucket tool to turn the mouse pointer into a paint bucket.

14

For each enclosed shape in your drawing, you choose a color from the fill color palette and click inside the shape to be filled.

15

For the computer screen, you select a *gradient fill*—a fill that makes a gradual transition from one color to another.

Photographer Richard Wahlstrom used image editing software to create this advertising "photograph" from the photographic images shown at the bottom of the picture.

processing software it's possible to distort and *combine* photographs, creating fabricated images that show no evidence of tampering. Supermarket gossip tabloids routinely use these tools to create sensationalistic cover photos. Many experts question whether photographs should be allowed as evidence in the courtroom now that photos can be doctored so convincingly.

Drawing: Object-Oriented Graphics

Because high-resolution paint images and photographs are stored as bit maps, they can make heavy storage and memory demands. Another type of graphics program can economically store pictures with virtually *infinite* resolution, limited only by the capabilities of the output device. **Drawing software** stores a picture, not as a collection of dots, but as a collection of lines and shapes. When you draw a line with a drawing program, the software doesn't record changes in a pixel map. Instead, it calculates and remembers a mathematical formula for the line. A drawing program stores shapes as shape formulas and text as text. Because pictures are collections of lines, shapes, and other objects, this approach is often called **object-oriented graphics** or **vector graphics.** In effect, the computer is remembering "a blue line segment goes here and a red circle goes here and a chunk of text goes here" instead of "this pixel is blue and this one is red and this one is white. . . ."

Many drawing tools—line, shape, and text tools—are similar to painting tools in bit-mapped programs. But the user can manipulate objects and edit text without affecting neighboring objects, even if the neighboring objects overlap. On screen, an object-oriented drawing looks similar to a bit-mapped painting. But when it's printed, a drawing appears as smooth as the printer's resolution allows. (Of course, not all drawings are designed to be printed. You may, for example, use a drawing program to create images for publication on the Internet. Because many Internet applications work only with bit-mapped images, you'll probably convert the drawings to bit maps before they're displayed.) **UV**

The User's View

Drawing with a Computer

▲ ▲

Software: ClarisWorks.

The goal: To find the best way to fit your furniture into the space available in your new room. Your furniture is heavy, but you can easily create digital scale models that weigh nothing. It's easier to drag these drawings around a floor plan than to move their real-world counterparts.

1 After opening a ClarisWorks document for drawing, you turn on the Rulers option so you can scale your drawing at 2 feet per inch.

2 Using the rectangle tool from the tool panel, you draw a rectangle representing the room's floor plan.

3 When you click on the rectangle, a square handle appears at each corner. Handles allow you to adjust the shape of an object until it's exactly right.

4 You tear off palettes so you can easily change colors, patterns, and line widths. For each shape you draw, you'll select colors and patterns from the three palettes.

5 Using the rectangle, rounded-rectangle, and straight-line tools, you drag the doorway, rug, bed, couch, bookshelf, desk, chair, and (of course) computer, using the program's invisible Autogrid option to snap the shapes into alignment.

6 The Group command allows you to group several objects so you can manipulate them as a single object. You group the desk, chair, and computer into a single object so you can rotate it and move it around in the room. In the same way you move the bed, the couch, and the bookshelf until you're satisfied with an arrangement for the furniture.

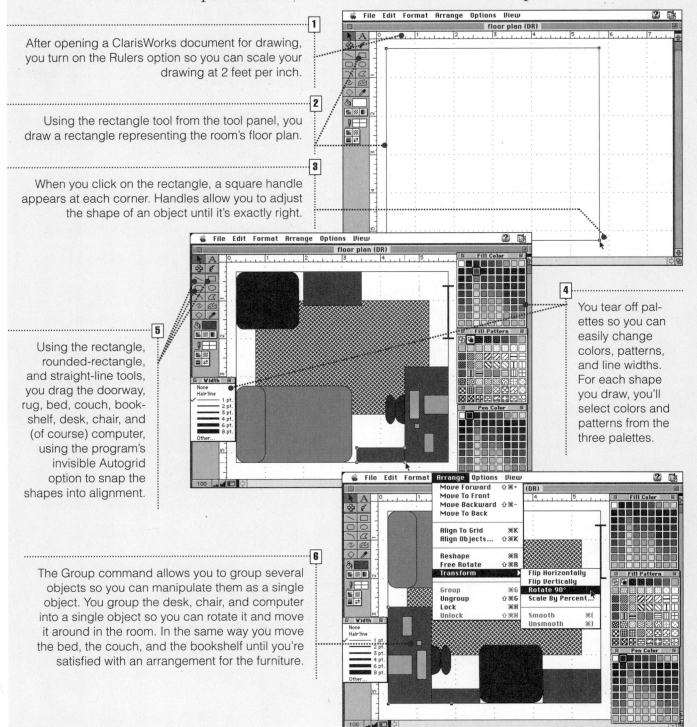

Many professional drawing programs, including Adobe Illustrator and Macromedia Freehand, store images using **PostScript**—a standard **page-description language** for describing text fonts, illustrations, and other elements of the printed page. PostScript is built into many laser printers and other high-end output devices, so those devices can understand and follow PostScript instructions. PostScript-based drawing software constructs a PostScript program as the user draws. This program provides a complete set of instructions for reconstructing the picture at the printer. When the user issues a Print command, the computer sends PostScript instructions to the printer, which uses those instructions to construct the grid of microscopic pixels that will be printed on each page. Most desktop publishing software uses PostScript in the same way.

Pixels versus Objects How do you edit a picture? It depends on what you're doing and how the picture is stored.		
The task . . .	**Using bit-mapped graphics**	**Using object-oriented graphics**
Moving and removing parts of pictures	Easier to work with regions rather than objects (note), especially if those objects overlap	Easier to work with individual objects or groups of objects, even if they overlap
Working with shapes	Shapes stored as pixel patterns can be edited with eraser and drawing tools	Shapes stored as math formulas can be transformed mathematically
Magnification	Magnifies pixels for fine detail editing	Magnifies objects, not pixels
Text handling	Text "dries" and can't be edited, but can be moved as a block of pixels When paint text "dries" it can't be edited like other text	Text can always be edited Draw text always can be changed
Printing	Resolution of printout can't exceed the pixel resolution of the stored picture	Resolution is limited only by the output device
Working within the limits of the hardware	Photographic quality is possible but requires considerable memory and disk storage	Complex drawings require considerable computational power for reasonable speed

Artists created these images using computers. The image on the left has textures typical of bit-mapped graphics and the one on the right has the kind of crisp lines often found in object-oriented graphics.

Object-oriented drawing and bit-mapped painting each offer advantages for certain applications. Bit-mapped image editing programs give artists and photo editors unsurpassed control over textures, shading, and fine detail; they're widely used for creating screen displays (for example, in video games, multimedia presentations, and Internet Web pages), for simulating natural paint media, and for embellishing photographic images. Object-oriented drawing and illustration programs are a better choice for creating printed graphs, charts, and illustrations with clean lines and smooth shapes. Some integrated programs like ClarisWorks include both drawing and painting modules, allowing you to choose the right tool for each job. A growing number of programs merge features of both in a single application, blurring the distinction and offering new possibilities for amateur and professional illustrators.

This personal computer system from the *Computer Confluence CD-ROM* is a 3-D model created on a Macintosh using Strata Studio Pro 3-D modeling software. The images on the left are shown in wire frame view; the ones on the right have been fully rendered to add surface textures.

3-D Modeling Software

Working with a pencil, an artist can draw a three-dimensional scene on a two-dimensional page. Similarly, an artist can use a drawing or painting program to create a scene that appears to have depth on a two-dimensional computer screen. But in either case the drawing lacks true depth; it's just a flat representation of a scene. With **3-D modeling software** graphic designers can create three-dimensional objects with tools similar to those found in conventional drawing software. You can't touch a 3-D computer model; it's no more real than a square, a circle, or a letter created with a drawing program. But a 3-D computer model can be rotated, stretched, and combined with other model objects to create complex 3-D scenes.

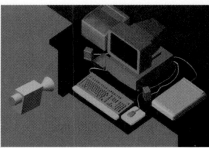

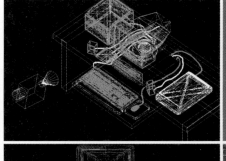

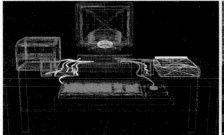

Creating Smart Art

Modern graphics software isn't just for professional artists. Just about anybody can use it to create pictures and presentations. Here are some guidelines to help you make the most of the computer as a graphic tool:

• **Overcome art anxiety.** For many of us the hardest part is getting started. We are all programmed by messages we received in our childhood, which for many of us included "You aren't creative" and "You can't draw." Fortunately a computer can help us overcome this early programming and find the artist that's locked within us. Most drawing and painting programs are flexible, forgiving, and fun. Allow yourself to experiment; you'll be surprised at what you can create if you're patient and playful. (For more help you might want to read *Overcoming Art Anxiety,* mentioned in the Sources and Resources section at the end of the chapter.)

• **Choose the right tool for the job.** Is your artwork to be displayed on the computer screen or printed? Does your output device support color? Would color enhance the finished work? Your answers to these questions will help you determine which software and hardware tools are most appropriate. As you're thinking about options, don't rule out low-tech tools. The best approach may not involve a computer, or it may involve some combination of computer and nonelectronic tools.

• **Borrow from the best.** Art supply stores sell **clip art**—predrawn images that artists can legally cut out and paste into their own pictures or posters. Computer artists have hundreds of digital clip art collections to choose from, with a difference: Computer clip art images can be cut, pasted, and edited electronically. Some computer clip art collections are in the public domain (free); others can be licensed for a small fee. Computer clip art comes in a variety of formats, and it ranges from simple line drawings to scanned color photographs. If you have access to a scanner, you can create your own digitized clip art from traditional photos and drawings.

• **Don't borrow without permission.** Computers, scanners, and digital cameras make it all too easy to create unauthorized copies of copyrighted photographs, drawings, and other images. There's a clear legal and ethical line between using public domain or licensed clip art and pirating copyrighted material. If you use somebody else's creative work, make sure you have written permission from the owner.

• **Protect your own work.** Copyright laws aren't just to protect other people's work. If you've created something that's marketable, consider copyrighting it. The process is easy and inexpensive, and it might help you to get credit (and payment) where credit is due.

Illustrators who use 3-D software appreciate its flexibility. A designer can create a 3-D model of an object, rotate it, view it from a variety of angles, and take two-dimensional "snapshots" of the best views for inclusion in final printouts. Similarly, it's possible to "walk through" a 3-D environment that exists only in the computer's memory, printing snapshots that show the simulated space from many points of view. For many applications the goal is not a printout but an animated presentation on a computer screen or videotape. Animation software, presentation graphics software, and multimedia authoring software (all described later in this chapter) can display sequences of screens showing 3-D objects being rotated, explored, and transformed. Many modern television and movie special effects involve combinations of live action and simulated 3-D animation. Techniques pioneered in films like *Jurassic Park* make it almost impossible for audiences to tell clay and plastic models from computer models.

CAD/CAM: Turning Ideas into Products

3-D graphics also play an important role in the branch of engineering known as **computer-aided design (CAD)**—the use of computers to design products. CAD software allows engineers, designers, and architects to create designs on screen for products ranging from computer chips to public buildings. Today's software goes far beyond basic drafting and object-oriented graphics. It allows users to create three-dimensional "solid" models with physical characteristics like weight, volume, and center of gravity. These models can be rotated and viewed from any angle. The computer can evaluate the structural performance of any part of the model by applying imaginary force to the object. Using CAD an engineer can crash-test a new model of an automobile before it ever leaves the computer screen. CAD tends to be cheaper, faster, and more accurate than traditional design-by-hand techniques. What's more, the forgiving nature of the computer makes it easy to alter a design to meet the goals of a project.

Computer-aided design is often linked to **computer-aided manufacturing (CAM)**. When the design of a product is completed, the numbers are fed to a program that controls the manufacturing of parts. For electronic parts the design translates directly into a template for etching circuits onto chips. The emergence of CAD/CAM has streamlined the design and manufacturing process. The combination of CAD and CAM is often called **computer-integrated manufacturing (CIM)**; it's a major step toward the fully automated factory.

This abstract image is actually a computer-aided design, created by the designer shown below the image.

Presentation Graphics: Bringing Lectures to Life

One common application for computer graphics today is the creation of visual aids—slides, transparencies, graphics displays, and handouts—to enhance presentations. While drawing and painting programs can create these aids, they aren't as useful as programs designed with presentations in mind.

Presentation graphics software helps to automate the creation of visual aids for lectures, training sessions, sales demonstrations, and other presentations. When broadly defined, presentation graphics software includes everything from spreadsheet charting programs to animation editing software. But presentation graphics programs are most commonly used for creating and displaying a series of on-screen "slides" to serve as visual aids for presentations. Slides might include photographs, drawings, spreadsheet-style charts, or tables. These different graphical elements are usually integrated into a series of **bullet charts** that list the main points of a presentation. Slides can be output as 35mm color slides, overhead transparencies, or handouts. Presentation graphics programs can also display "slide shows" directly on computer monitors or LCD projectors, including animation and video clips along with still images. **UV**

Because they can be used to create and display on-screen presentations with animated visual effects and video clips, presentation graphics programs like PowerPoint are sometimes called *multimedia presentation tools*. These programs *do* make it easy for nonartists to combine text, graphics, and other media in simple multimedia presentations. But as you'll see, true *multimedia authoring tools* are more flexible and powerful than are basic slide presentation programs.

We'll turn our attention now to several types of media that go beyond the limitations of the printed page or the static screen; then we'll see how multimedia authoring software can combine these diverse media types to produce dynamic, interactive documents.

Creating Presentation Graphics

▲ ▲

Software: Microsoft PowerPoint.

The goal: To create visual aids for a talk you're giving for a class. You'll use PowerPoint, a presentation graphics package that's especially designed for this kind of task.

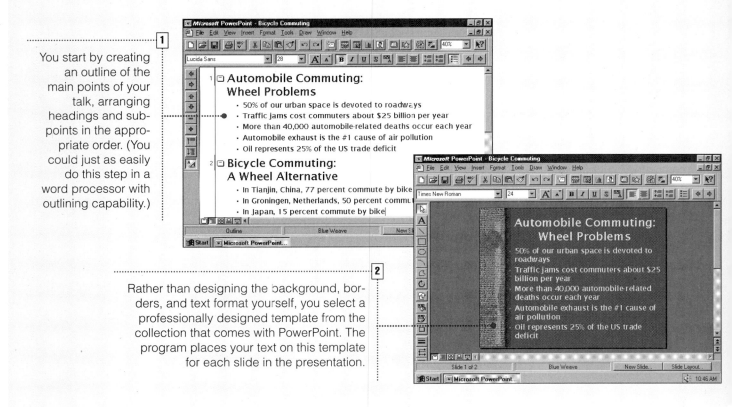

1 You start by creating an outline of the main points of your talk, arranging headings and sub-points in the appropriate order. (You could just as easily do this step in a word processor with outlining capability.)

2 Rather than designing the background, borders, and text format yourself, you select a professionally designed template from the collection that comes with PowerPoint. The program places your text on this template for each slide in the presentation.

DYNAMIC MEDIA: BEYOND THE PRINTED PAGE

The aim of every artist is to arrest motion, which is life, by artificial means and hold it fixed so that a hundred years later, when a stranger looks at it, it moves again since it is life.

—William Faulkner

Most modern personal computer applications—painting and drawing programs, word processors, desktop publishers and so on—are designed to produce paper documents. But many types of modern media can't be reduced to pixels on printouts because they contain dynamic information—information that changes over time or in

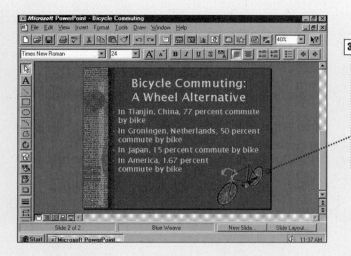

3 PowerPoint has a few basic drawing tools and the ability to import charts, graphs, drawings, and scanned images created with other applications. But for this slide, you simply add an image of a bike from a clip art collection that comes with the program.

4 You can print overhead transparencies or have slides made from your disk file. But since there's a big-screen computer system in the lecture room, you decide to create an interactive "slide show" with animated visual transitions between slides.

response to user input. Just as text and graphics serve as the raw materials for desktop publishing, dynamic media like animation, video, audio, and hypertext are important components of interactive multimedia projects.

Animation: Graphics in Time

Creating motion from still pictures—this illusion is at the heart of all **animation.** Before computers, animated films were hand-drawn, one still picture, or **frame,** at a time. Modern computer graphics technology has transformed both amateur and professional animation by allowing many of the most tedious aspects of the animation process to be automated.

In its simplest form computer-based animation is similar to traditional frame-by-frame animation techniques—each frame is a computer-drawn picture, and the

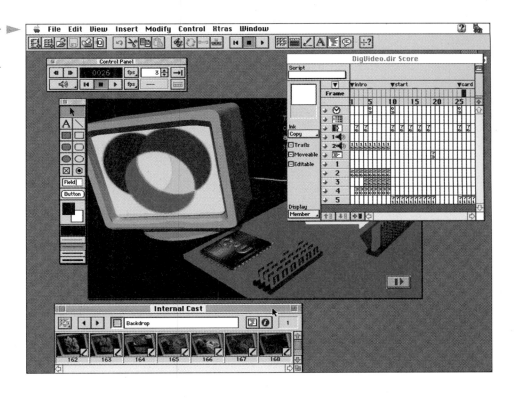

Macromedia's Director is a popular multimedia program with powerful animation capabilities. The frames in the Cast window (below) show several different views of an object as it moves through the timeline shown in the Score Window (above). You'll find the completed animation in the Digital Video How It Works section of the Computer Confluence CD-ROM.

computer displays those frames in rapid succession. But computer animation programs, even the low-priced packages aimed at the home market, contain software tools that can do much more than flip pages. They can take much of the tedium out of animation by automating repetitive processes. Instead of drawing every frame by hand, an animator can create key frames and objects and use software to help fill in the gaps. The most powerful animation programs include tools for working with animated objects in three dimensions, adding depth to the scene on the screen.

Desktop Video: Computers and TV

Most animated sequences are made of drawings, whether created with a computer or a pen and brush. But a growing number of multimedia applications can also use video footage to put motion into presentations. On-screen digital movies can add realism and excitement to educational, training, presentation, and entertainment software. System extensions like Apple's cross-platform *QuickTime* make it possible for any multimedia-capable computer to display digital video clips without additional hardware.

Conventional television and video images are stored and broadcast as analog (smooth) electronic waves. Within the next decade that's likely to change as the television and video industries switch to **digital video** storage and transmission. Because digital video can be reduced to a series of numbers, it can be edited, stored, and played back without any loss of quality. Digital video, like text, numbers, and computer graphics, can be treated as data by computers and combined with other forms of data.

For an added sense of realism, Broderbund's *In the First Degree* seamlessly blends video footage with still photographs and interactive controls. The net result is a game that feels like a high-quality television drama—with you playing the leading role.

Until digital video becomes the standard, multimedia producers will use **video digitizers** to convert analog video signals into digital data. Some video digitizers can import signals from televisions, videotapes, video cameras, and other sources and display them on the computer's screen in *real time*—at the same time they're created or imported—along with computer controls and other graphic images. Other video digitizers are designed to capture video sequences and convert them into digital "movies" that can be stored, edited, and played on computer screens at a later time without external video equipment. Some Macintosh models have built-in video digitizers; for most other computers, video digitizers must be installed as add-on cards.

Once the video clips are digitized, they can be transformed using a variety of software tools. For example, Morph and Elastic Reality make it easy to create **morphs**—video clips in which one image metamorphoses into another. Programs like VideoPaint and Painter make it possible to digitally paint a few frames—say, with a polka-dotted sky—and have the painting effects automatically applied to the other frames. Video editing software like Adobe Premiere allows you to splice together scenes, insert visual transitions, superimpose titles, create special effects, and add a musical soundtrack. After it's edited the video clip can be imported into a multimedia document or "printed" on a master videotape.

But digital movies can make heavy hardware demands; even a short full-screen video clip can quickly fill a large hard disk. To save storage space and to allow the processor to keep up with the quickly changing frames, many digital movies are displayed on computer screens in small windows with fewer than the standard video rate of 30 frames per second. In addition, **data compression** software and hardware are used to squeeze data out of movies so they can be stored in smaller spaces, usually with only a slight loss of image quality. General data compression software can be used to reduce the size of almost any kind of data file; specialized *image compression software* is generally used to compress graphics and video files. System extensions like *QuickTime* include several common software compression schemes. But the best compression schemes involve specialized hardware as well as software.

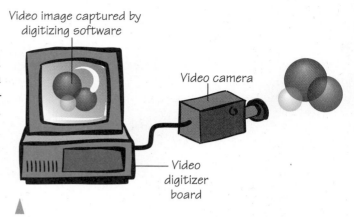

Video image captured by digitizing software

Video camera

Video digitizer board

Video digitizers allow you to capture analog video images as digital data that can be stored and manipulated in the computer's memory.

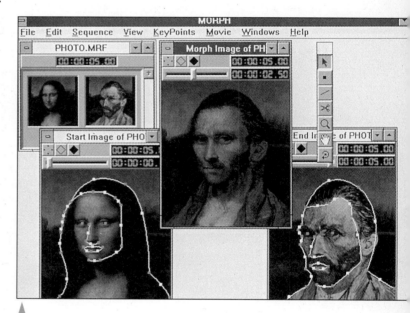

Morphing software was used to create the portrait in the center by mathematically combining the two images on opposite sides of the screen. (Software: Morph)

Even highly compressed video clips gobble up storage space quickly, so most digital movies are stored on CD-ROM and other high-capacity storage media. As compression and storage technologies continue to improve, digital movies will become larger, longer, smoother, and more common in everyday computing applications. In fact, compression hardware may soon become standard equipment in multimedia computers.

Professionals in the motion picture, television, and video industries create their products using graphic workstations that cost hundreds of thousands of dollars. Today it's possible to put together a Macintosh- or Windows-based system that can perform most of the same functions for a fraction of the cost. These systems wouldn't meet the needs of Steven Spielberg, but they satisfy thousands of individuals, schools, and small businesses with smaller budgets. If current trends continue,

Data Compression

A full-screen 256-color photograph or painting takes about a megabyte of storage—the same as the complete text from a typical paperback book! Graphic images, digital video, and sound files can consume massive amounts of storage space on disk and in memory; they can also be slow to transmit over computer networks. Data compression technology allows large files to be temporarily squeezed so they take less storage space and network transmission time. Before they can be used, compressed files must be decompressed. (In the physical world many companies "compress" goods to save storage and transportation costs: When you "just add water" to a can of concentrated orange juice, you're "decompressing" the juice.)

All forms of compression involve removing bits; the trick is to remove bits that can be replaced when the file can be restored. Different compression techniques work best for different types of data.

Suppose you want to store or transmit a large text file. Your text compression software might follow steps similar to these shown here:

1 Each character in the uncompressed ASCII file occupies 8 bits; a seven-character word—*invoice,* for example—requires 56 bits of storage.

i   n   v   o   i   c   e

(space)   p   a   y   a   b   l   e

Portion of a dictionary		
A	oooooooo	ooooooo●
a	oooooooo	ooooo●●o
aback	oooooooo	ooooo●●●
abacus	oooooooo	ooooo●oo
. . .		
invoice	oo●oo●o●	oo●●●oo●
invoiced	oo●oo●o●	oo●●●●o●
invoke	oo●oo●o●	oo●●●o●●
. . .		
pay	o●o●●o●o	●o●oooo●
payable	o●o●●o●o	●o●oooo●o
. . .		
zygote	●●●●●●●●	●●●●●●●●

2 A 2-byte binary number can contain code values ranging from 0 to 65,535—enough codes to stand for every commonly used word in English. This partial code dictionary shows the code values for a few words, including *invoice* and *payable.*

3 To compress a file using a code dictionary, the computer looks up every word in the original file, in this example, *invoice* and *payable.* It replaces each word with its 2-byte code value. In this example they are % 9 and V ú. The seven-character word now takes up only 16 bits—less than one-third of its original size.

4 In a compressed file, these 2-byte code values would be used to store or transmit the information for *invoice* and *payable,* using fewer bits of information either to increase storage capacity or to decrease transmission time.

%   9   V   ú

To reverse the process of compression, the same dictionary (or an identical one on another computer) is used to decompress the file, creating an exact copy of the original. All the tedious dictionary lookup is performed quickly by a computer program.

Most modern compression programs usually work on patterns of bits rather than English words. For example, one type of digital video compression stores values for pixels that *change* from one frame to the next; there's no need to repeatedly store values for pixels that are the same in every frame.

For example, the only pixels that change in these 2 pictures are the ones that represent the unicycle and the shadows. In general, compression works because most raw data files contain redundancy that can be "squeezed out."

Lossless compression systems allow a file to be compressed and later decompressed without any loss of data; the decompressed file will be an identical copy of the original file. Popular lossless compression systems include ZIP/PKZIP (DOS/Windows), StuffIt (Macintosh), tar (UNIX), and GIF (general graphics).

A *lossy* system can usually achieve better compression than a lossless one but may lose some information in the process; the decompressed file isn't always identical to the original. This is tolerable in many types of sound, graphics, and video files, but not for most program and data files. JPEG is a popular lossy compression system for graphics files.

MPEG is a popular compression system for digital video. An MPEG file takes just a fraction of the space of an uncompressed video file. Because decompression programs demand time and processing power, playback of compressed video files can sometimes be jerky or slow. Some computers get around the problem with MPEG hardware boards that specialize in compression and decompression, leaving the CPU free for other tasks. *Hardware compression* is likely to be built into most computers as multimedia becomes more commonplace.

The original photographic image (above) is clear with an uncompressed size of 725 KB. The image on the right shows the visible lossy effect of aggressive JPEG compression. But the size of the compressed file is only 19 KB.

low-cost systems will transform the video industry in the same way that desktop publishing has revolutionized the world of the printed word.

The Synthetic Musician: Computers and Audio

It's easy to play any musical instrument: all you have to do is touch the right key at the right time and the instrument will play itself.

—J. S. Bach

Sound and music can turn a visual presentation into an activity that involves the ears, the eyes, and the whole brain. For many applications, sound puts the *multi* in *multimedia*. Computer sounds can be digitized—digitally recorded—or **synthesized**—synthetically generated. PCs with *sound cards* (see Chapter 3) and Macintoshes (which have sound hardware already built in) can produce sounds that go far beyond the basic beeps of early computers; most of them can also digitize sounds.

Digitized Sounds as Computer Data

Any sound that can be recorded can be captured with an **audio digitizer** and stored as a data file on a diskette, hard disk, or other computer storage medium. Digitized sound data, like other computer data, can be loaded into the computer's memory and manipulated by software. Sound editing software can change a sound's volume and pitch, add special effects like echoes, remove extraneous noises, even rearrange musical passages. Sound data is sometimes called *waveform audio* because this kind of editing often involves manipulating a visual image of the sound's waveform. To play a digitized sound, the computer must load the data file into memory, convert it to an analog sound, and play it through a speaker.

Recorded sound can consume large amounts of space on disk and in memory. Sound data compression, like image compression, saves space, but can compromise quality. Even without compression, PC waveform audio recordings usually lack the crystal-clear fidelity of compact disc recordings. The difference is due to differences in *sampling rate*—the number of sound "snapshots" the recording equipment takes each second. Because of its high sampling rate, a CD's sound closely approximates the original analog sound. Most PCs can't duplicate CD audio quality without additional hardware.

This waveform is a visual representation of the digitized phrase "I am not a crook," ready for editing. The section highlighted in black is the word "not." Pressing Delete will turn the sound bite into "I am a crook!" (Software: Soundedit 16.)

CD Audio

A computer can also play sounds from standard audio CDs using a CD-ROM drive connected to headphones or amplified speakers. Sounds are stored on CDs, not in the computer's memory. When the sounds are stored on CDs, software needs to contain only *commands* telling the CD-ROM drive what to play and when to play it.

The advantages of CD audio are obvious: The sound quality is high and the storage costs are low. Of course, this approach requires CD-ROM hardware and a CD containing the necessary music or sounds. Since CD-ROM is a read-only medium, CD sound is "listen-only"—there's no way for the user to record sounds. But for music appreciation, language instruction, interactive music videos, and other applications that can take advantage of commercial recordings, CD-based audio is a sound alternative.

MIDI

Multimedia computers can also control a variety of electronic musical instruments and sound sources using **MIDI** (Musical Instrument Digital Interface)—a standard interface that allows electronic instruments and computers, regardless of type or

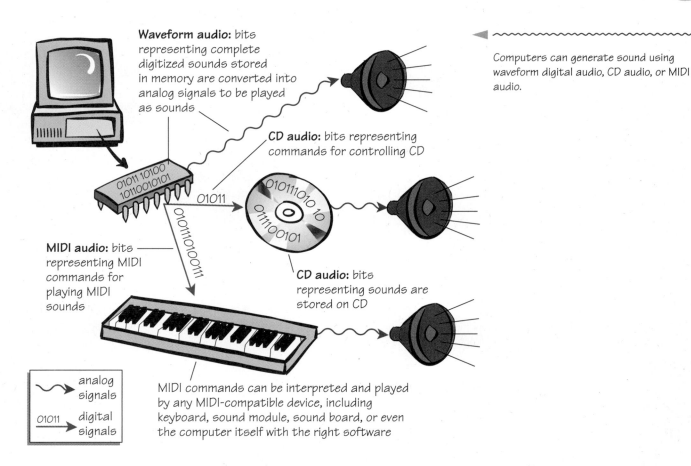

Waveform audio: bits representing complete digitized sounds stored in memory are converted into analog signals to be played as sounds

CD audio: bits representing commands for controlling CD

MIDI audio: bits representing MIDI commands for playing MIDI sounds

CD audio: bits representing sounds are stored on CD

Computers can generate sound using waveform digital audio, CD audio, or MIDI audio.

analog signals

01011 digital signals

MIDI commands can be interpreted and played by any MIDI-compatible device, including keyboard, sound module, sound board, or even the computer itself with the right software

brand, to communicate with each other and work together. In the same way that PostScript is the common language of desktop publishing hardware, MIDI is the universal language of electronic music hardware. MIDI is used to send commands to instruments and sound sources—commands that, in effect, say "play this sound at this pitch and this volume for this amount of time. . . ."

MIDI commands like this can be interpreted by a variety of music *synthesizers* (electronic instruments that synthesize sounds using mathematical formulas), *samplers* (instruments that can digitize, or sample, audio sounds, turn them into notes, and play them back at any pitch), and hybrid instruments that play sounds that are part sampled and part synthesized. But most multimedia PCs can also interpret and execute MIDI commands using sounds built into their sound boards or stored in software form. Whether the sounds are played back on external instruments or internal devices, the computer doesn't need to store the entire recording in memory or on disk; it just has to store commands to play the notes in the proper sequence. A *MIDI file* containing the MIDI messages for a song or soundtrack takes just a few kilobytes of memory.

Nonmusicians can use ready-to-play *clip music* MIDI files for multimedia productions. But anyone with even marginal piano-playing skills and **sequencing software** can create MIDI music files. Sequencing software turns a computer into a musical composition, recording, and editing machine. The computer records MIDI signals as a musician plays each part on a keyboard. The musician can use the computer to layer instrumental tracks, substitute instrument sounds, edit notes, cut and paste passages, transpose keys, and change tempos, listening to each change as it's made. The finished composition can be played by the sequencing software or

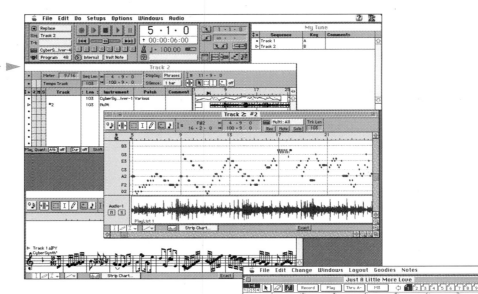

Sequencing software is like a cross between a multitrack tape recorder and a word processor. A sequencer allows a single person to compose, edit, and combine several MIDI parts into a complete instrumental composition. Amateur and professional musicians use sequencing software for composition, recording, and performance. Studio Vision Pro allows you to add digital audio tracks to MIDI sequences, allowing your computer to serve as a complete recording studio.

Music publishing software can turn a MIDI file into a musical score, ready for publishing. For many musicians and publishers, this kind of software has eliminated the tedious and error-prone process of transcribing musical scores by hand. (Software: Encore.)

In the modern music studio, computer keyboards and music keybcards often sit side-by-side.

exported to any other MIDI-compatible software, including a variety of multimedia applications.

With the appropriate software, a computer can be used as an aid for composing, recording, performing, music publishing, and music education. Just as computer graphics technology has changed the way many artists work, electronic music technology has transformed the world of the musician. What's more, computer music technology has the power to unleash the musician in the rest of us.

Hypertext and Hypermedia

Word processors, drawing programs, and most other applications today are **WYSIWYG**—*w*hat *y*ou *s*ee (on the screen) *i*s *w*hat you *g*et (on the printed page). But as Doug Engelbart has demonstrated for decades, WYSIWYG isn't always necessary or desirable. If a document doesn't need to be printed, it doesn't need to be structured like a paper document. If we want to focus on the relationship of ideas rather than the layout of the page, we may be better off with another kind of document—a dynamic, cross-referenced super document that takes full advantage of the computer's interactive capabilities.

Since 1945 when President Roosevelt's science advisor, Vannevar Bush, first wrote about such an interactive cross-referenced system, computer pioneers like Doug Engelbart and Ted Nelson have pushed the technology toward that vision. Early efforts were called **hypertext** because they allowed textual information to be linked in *nonsequential* ways. Conventional text media like books are linear, or *sequential:* They are designed to be read from beginning to end. A hypertext document contains *links* that can lead readers quickly to other parts of the document or to other related documents. Hypertext invites readers to cut their own personal trails through information.

If this book were a hypertext document, you might click on the name Doug Engelbart in the previous paragraph to learn more about Engelbart. You would be transported to the profile at the beginning of this chapter that describes Engelbart's visionary work. After reading that profile you might want to return to this section and continue reading about hypertext. On the other hand, you might want to learn more about Alan Kay, the computer scientist quoted in Engelbart's profile. Clicking on Kay's name would transport you to the profile at the beginning of the final chapter. From that point you could continue to explore topics related to Alan Kay or return here to learn more about hypertext. With a comprehensive, well-designed hypertext reference, you could follow your curiosity just about anywhere by pointing and clicking.

Hypertext first gained widespread public attention in 1987 when Apple introduced HyperCard. Because HyperCard can combine text, numbers, graphics, animation, sound effects, music, and other media in hyperlinked documents, it is often described not as a hypertext system, but as a **hypermedia** system. (Depending on how it's used, the term *hypermedia* might be synonymous with *interactive multimedia*.)

The newest hotbet of hypertext activity is the World Wide Web on the Internet. As you'll see in Chapter 10, hypertext on the Web allows readers to jump between documents all over the Internet just as easily as HyperCard users jump between cards in a HyperCard stack. Like HyperCard, the Web has spawned countless hypermedia

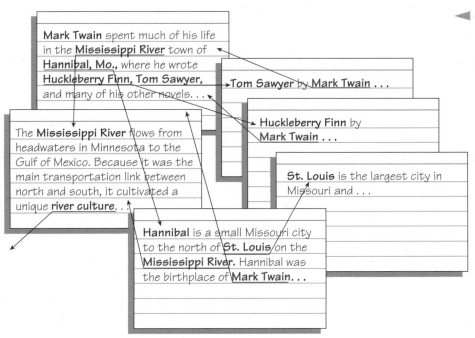

While you're reading about Mark Twain, you might become curious about his hometown in Missouri, his novels, or the river that inspired those novels. Your explorations of 19th-century Hannibal, Missouri, might lead you to explore other Mississippi River towns of the time, or it might inspire you to learn more about midwestern geography. Hypertext puts you in control.

documents, many of them created by educators, students, and hobbyists. But in spite of its popularity, hypertext isn't likely to replace paper books any time soon. People who work with hypermedia today face several problems:

Interactivity and Multiplicity: the Two Dimensions of Multimedia

- Hypermedia documents can be disorienting and leave readers wondering what they've missed. When you're reading a book, you always know where you are and where you've been in the text. That's not necessarily true in hypermedia.

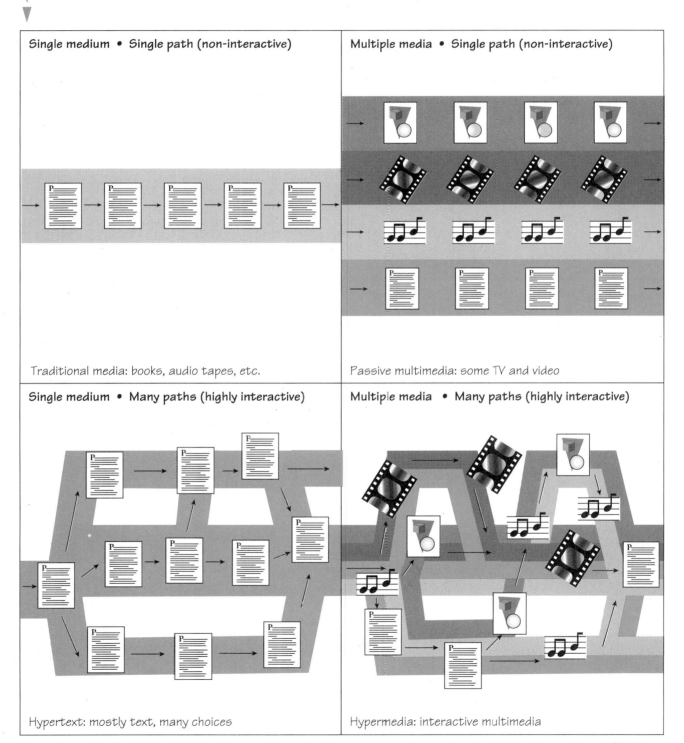

Single medium • Single path (non-interactive)

Traditional media: books, audio tapes, etc.

Multiple media • Single path (non-interactive)

Passive multimedia: some TV and video

Single medium • Many paths (highly interactive)

Hypertext: mostly text, many choices

Multiple media • Many paths (highly interactive)

Hypermedia: interactive multimedia

- Hypermedia documents don't always have the links readers want. Hypermedia authors can't build every possible connection into their documents, so some readers are frustrated because they can't easily get "there" from "here."

- Hypermedia documents don't encourage scribbled margin notes, highlighting, or turned page corners for marking key passages. Some hypermedia documents provide buttons for making "bookmarks" and text fields to add personal notes, but they aren't as friendly and flexible as traditional paper markup tools.

- Hypermedia hardware can be hard on humans. Most people find that reading a computer screen is more tiring than reading printed pages. Many complain that extended periods of screen-gazing cause eyestrain, headache, backache, and other ailments. It's not easy to stretch out under a tree or curl up in an easy chair with a desktop computer, and many hypermedia documents require hardware not found in portable computers.

- The art of hypermedia is still in its infancy. Every new art form takes time to develop. How can writers develop effective plot lines if they don't know what path their readers will choose through their stories? This is just one of the hundreds of questions that hypermedia authors are struggling with.

Still, hypermedia is not all hype. As the art matures, advances in software and hardware design will take care of many of these problems. Even today hypermedia documents provide extensive cross-referencing, flexibility, and instant keyword searches that simply aren't possible with paper media.

Later in this chapter you'll see how hypermedia documents are created with HyperCard. In Chapter 10 you'll explore the world's biggest hypermedia network, the Internet's World Wide Web.

INTERACTIVE MULTIMEDIA: EYE, EAR, HAND, AND MIND

A good interactive title chooses the best information from all the media at its disposal and combines them into something indefinable yet powerful.

—Denise Caruso, multimedia writer

We live in a world rich in sensory experience. Information comes to us in a variety of forms: pictures, text, moving images, music, voice, and more. As information-processing machines, computers are capable of delivering information to our senses in a variety of forms. Until recently, computer users could work with only one or two forms of information at a time. Today's multimedia computers, however, allow users to work with information-rich documents that intermix a wide variety of audio-visual media.

Interactive Multimedia: What Is It?

The term **multimedia** generally means using some combination of text, graphics, animation, video, music, voice, and sound effects to communicate. By this definition, an episode of "Sesame Street" or the evening news might be considered multimedia. In fact, computer-based multimedia tools are used heavily in the production of "Sesame Street," the evening news, and hundreds of other television programs. Entertainment industry professionals use computers to create animated sequences,

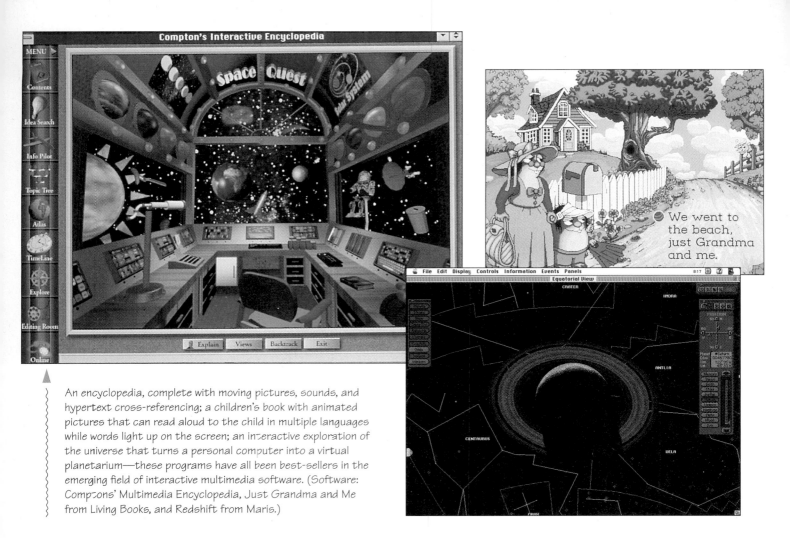

An encyclopedia, complete with moving pictures, sounds, and hypertext cross-referencing; a children's book with animated pictures that can read aloud to the child in multiple languages while words light up on the screen; an interactive exploration of the universe that turns a personal computer into a virtual planetarium—these programs have all been best-sellers in the emerging field of interactive multimedia software. (Software: Comptons' Multimedia Encyclopedia, Just Grandma and Me from Living Books, and Redshift from Maris.)

display titles, construct special video effects, synthesize music, edit sound tracks, coordinate communication, and perform dozens of other tasks crucial to the production of modern television programs and motion pictures.

So when you watch a typical TV program, you're experiencing a multimedia product. Every second that you watch, the program bombards you with millions of bits of information. But television and video are *passive* media—they pour information into our eyes and ears while we sit and take it all in. We have no control over the information flow. Modern personal computer technology allows information to move in both directions, turning multimedia into **interactive multimedia.** Unlike TV, radio, and video, interactive multimedia allow the viewer/listener to take an active part in the experience. The best interactive multimedia software puts the user in charge, allowing that person to control the information flow.

Interactive multimedia software is delivered to consumers on a variety of platforms. Multimedia computers—Macintosh and Windows machines with high-quality color displays, relatively fast processors, large memories, CD-ROM drives, speakers, and sound cards—are everywhere. Thousands of interactive multimedia programs are available on CD-ROM through bookstores, software stores, and other retail channels. As you'll see in Chapters 9 and 10, interactive multimedia materials are also available through the Internet and other on-line sources.

Many multimedia software titles are designed to be used with television sets and controlled by game machines and other types of *set-top boxes* from Nintendo, Sega, Sony, Apple, and other companies. We'll soon be seeing set-top boxes that, to varying degrees, turn the television into a two-way communication device.

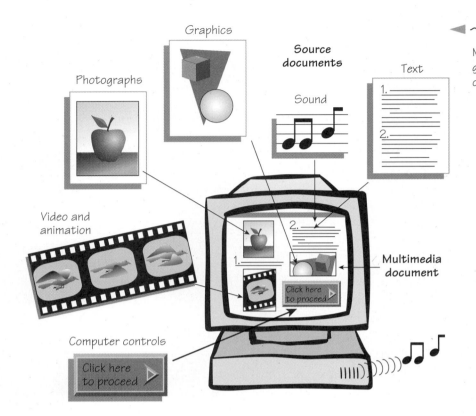

Graphics

Photographs

Source
documents

Text

Sound

Multimedia authoring software glues together media captured and created with
other applications.

Video and
animation

Multimedia
document

Computer controls

Multimedia Authoring: Making Mixed Media

Set-top boxes make it possible for people who don't own personal computers to *use*, but not *create*, interactive multimedia software. But with a multimedia-ready computer you can do more than just experience interactive multimedia documents. With **multimedia authoring software** you can create and edit multimedia documents. Like desktop publishing, interactive multimedia authoring involves combining source documents—including graphics, text files, video clips, sounds—in an aesthetically pleasing format that communicates. Multimedia authoring software, like page layout software, serves as a glue that binds documents created and captured with other applications. But since a multimedia document can change in response to user input, authoring involves specifying not just what? and where? but also when? and why?

Authoring programs vary widely in capabilities, price, and user interface. Some are designed for professionals; others are designed for children; many are used by both. Probably the most widely used interface for authoring tools is the card-and-stack interface originally introduced with Apple's HyperCard. Because it's easy to learn and relatively intuitive, the card-and-stack metaphor (or something similar) is used by a number of authoring systems, including SuperCard, Oracle Media Objects, HyperStudio, ToolBook, and LinkWay.

According to this metaphor, a multimedia document is a *stack*—a virtual stack of index cards. Each screen, called a *card*, can contain graphics, text, and **buttons**— "hot spots" that respond to mouse clicks. Buttons can be programmed to transport the user to another card, play music, open dialog boxes, launch other applications, rearrange information, perform menu operations, send messages to hardware devices, or do other things. The User's View box shows part of the process of creating an interactive document with one of these authoring tools. **UV**

Multimedia Authoring

▲ ▲

Software: HyperCard.

The goal: To produce an interactive multimedia display on computers for a class project. After an introductory screen, the user will see a picture of a computer with instructions to click on each component.

1 You start by creating a map showing the overall plan—a flowchart showing how all of the screens and media elements are tied together.

2 A title screen opens the presentation.

3 A button will play an audio introduction and reveal the main screen, a picture of a computer system

4 Each computer component in this picture will have a hidden button. When the user clicks on a component, a video presentation will describe and demonstrate the component.

5 Visible buttons will allow the user to get help, view references, and exit the presentation.

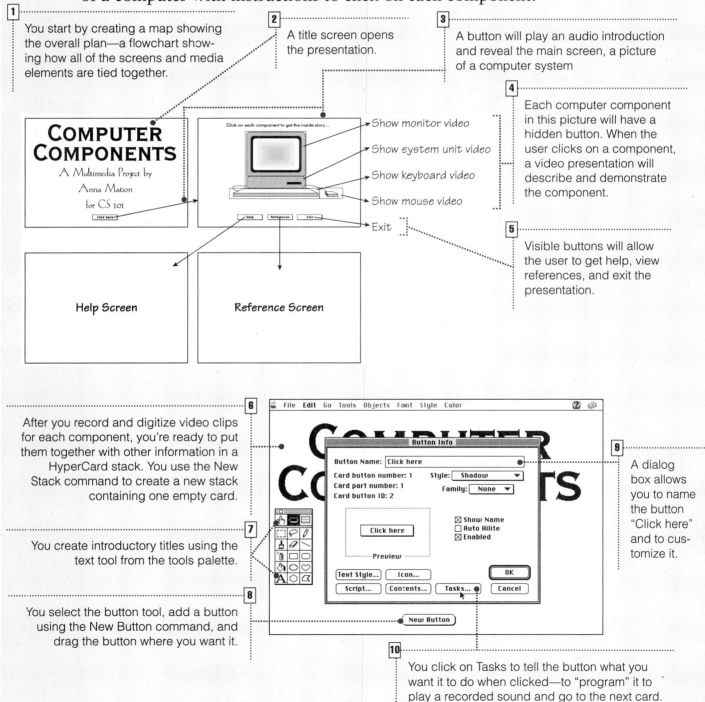

6 After you record and digitize video clips for each component, you're ready to put them together with other information in a HyperCard stack. You use the New Stack command to create a new stack containing one empty card.

7 You create introductory titles using the text tool from the tools palette.

8 You select the button tool, add a button using the New Button command, and drag the button where you want it.

9 A dialog box allows you to name the button "Click here" and to customize it.

10 You click on Tasks to tell the button what you want it to do when clicked—to "program" it to play a recorded sound and go to the next card.

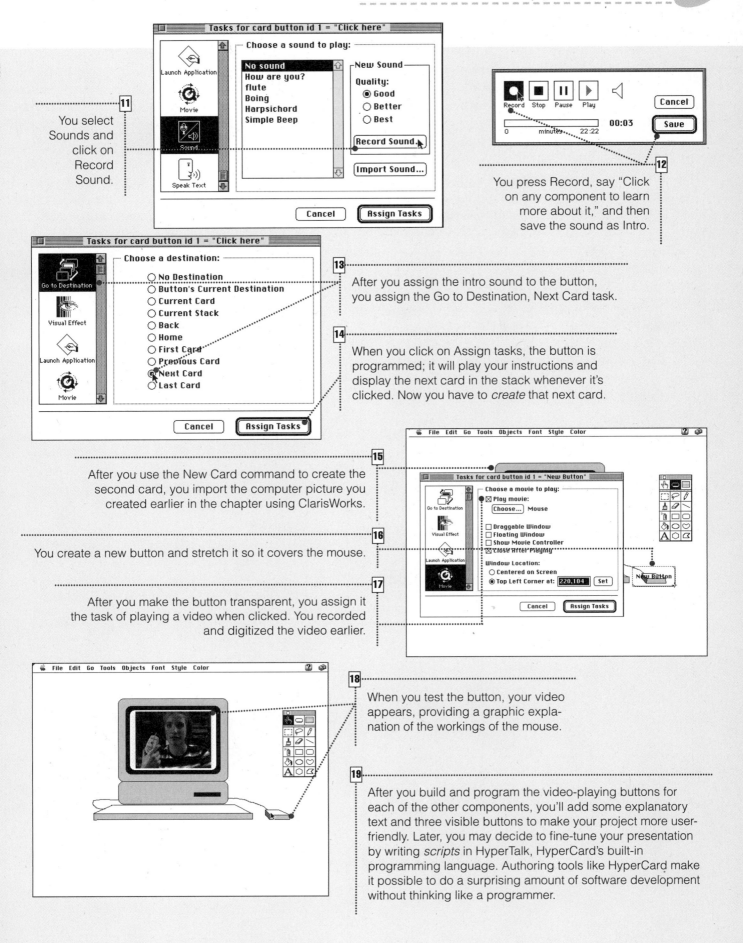

11 You select Sounds and click on Record Sound.

12 You press Record, say "Click on any component to learn more about it," and then save the sound as Intro.

13 After you assign the intro sound to the button, you assign the Go to Destination, Next Card task.

14 When you click on Assign tasks, the button is programmed; it will play your instructions and display the next card in the stack whenever it's clicked. Now you have to *create* that next card.

15 After you use the New Card command to create the second card, you import the computer picture you created earlier in the chapter using ClarisWorks.

16 You create a new button and stretch it so it covers the mouse.

17 After you make the button transparent, you assign it the task of playing a video when clicked. You recorded and digitized the video earlier.

18 When you test the button, your video appears, providing a graphic explanation of the workings of the mouse.

19 After you build and program the video-playing buttons for each of the other components, you'll add some explanatory text and three visible buttons to make your project more user-friendly. Later, you may decide to fine-tune your presentation by writing *scripts* in HyperTalk, HyperCard's built-in programming language. Authoring tools like HyperCard make it possible to do a surprising amount of software development without thinking like a programmer.

Making Interactive Multimedia Work

Whether you're creating a simple presentation or a full-blown multimedia extravaganza, your finished product will communicate more effectively if you follow a few simple guidelines:

• **Be consistent.** Group similar controls together and keep a consistent visual appearance throughout the presentation.

• **Make it intuitive.** Use graphical metaphors to guide viewers and make your controls do what they look like they should do.

• **Strive for simplicity.** A clean, uncluttered screen is more inviting than a crowded one—and easier to understand, too.

• **Keep it lively.** If your presentation doesn't include motion, sound, and lots of user interaction, it probably should be printed and distributed as a paper.

• **The message is more important than the media.** Your goal is to communicate information, not saturate with sensations. Don't let the bells and whistles get in the way of your message.

• **Put the user in the driver's seat.** Include controls for turning down sound, bypassing repetitive animation, and turning off annoying features. Provide navigation aids, search tools, bookmarks, on-line help, and "where am I?" feedback. Never tell the user "You can't get there from here."

• **Let real people test your presentation.** The best way to find out if your presentation works is to test it on people who aren't familiar with the subject. If they get lost or bored, find out why and fix it.

Multimedia authoring software today puts a great deal of power into the hands of computer users, but it doesn't solve all of the technical problems in this new art form. Many of the problems with hypertext and hypermedia outlined earlier are even more serious when multiple media are involved. What's more, current technology hasn't lived up to the hype; multimedia consumers spend far too much time installing, loading, and waiting, and the results often aren't worth the wait. Still, the best multimedia productions transcend these problems and show the promise of this emerging technology.

Interactive Media: Visions of the Future

For most of recorded history, the interactions of humans with their media have been primarily passive in the sense that marks on paper, paint on walls, even motion pictures and television, do not change in response to the viewer's wishes. [But computers can] respond to queries and experiments—so that the message may involve the learner in a two-way conversation.

—Alan Kay

For hundreds of thousands of years, two-way, interactive communication was the norm: One person talked, another responded. Today television, radio, newspapers, magazines, and books pour information into billions of passive people every day.

For many people, one-way, passive communication has become more common than interactive discourse.

According to many experts, interactive multimedia technology offers new hope for turning communication back into a participation sport. With interactive multimedia software, the audience is a part of the show. Interactive multimedia tools can give people control over the media—control traditionally reserved for professional artists, film makers, and musicians. The possibilities are far-reaching, especially when telecommunication enters the picture. Consider these snapshots from a not-too-distant future:

- Instead of watching your biology professor flip through overhead transparencies, you control a self-paced, interactive presentation complete with video footage illustrating key concepts.

- In your electronic mailbox you find a "letter" from your sister. The letter shows her performing all the instrumental parts for a song she composed, followed by a request for you to add a vocal line.

- Your favorite TV show is an interactive thriller that allows you to control the plot twists and work with the main characters to solve mysteries.

- You share your concerns about a proposed factory in your hometown at the televised electronic town meeting. Thousands of others respond to questions from the mayor by pressing buttons on their remote control panels. The overwhelming citizen response forces the city council to reconsider the proposal.

Of course, the future of interactive multimedia may not be all sunshine and roses. Many experts fear that these exciting new media possibilities will further remove us from books, other people, and the natural world around us. If television today can mesmerize so many people, will tomorrow's interactive multimedia TVs cause even more serious addiction problems? Or will interactive communication breathe new life into the media and the people who use them? Will interactive electronic media make it easier for abusers of power to influence and control unwary citizens, or will the power of the push button create a new kind of digital democracy? Will interactive digital technology just turn "sound bites" into "sound bytes," or will it unleash the creative potential in the people who use it? For answers, stay tuned.

SUMMARY

Computer graphics today encompass more than quantitative charts and graphs generated by spreadsheets. Bit-mapped painting programs allow users to "paint" the screen with a mouse, pen, or other pointing device. The software stores the results in a pixel map, with each pixel having an assigned color. The more possible colors and the higher the resolution (pixel density), the more the images can approach photorealism. Object-oriented drawing programs also allow users to draw on the screen with a pointing device, with the results stored as collections of geometric objects rather than as maps of computer bits.

Bit-mapped graphics and object-oriented graphics each offer advantages in particular situations; tradeoffs involve storage, printing, editing, and ease of use. Both types of graphics have applications outside the art world. Bit-mapped graphics are used in high-resolution digital image processing software for on-screen photo editing. Object-oriented graphics are at the heart of 3-D modeling software and computer-aided design (CAD) software used by architects, designers, and engineers. Presentation graphics software, which may include either or both graphics types, automates the process of creating slides, transparencies, handouts, and computer-based presentations, making it easy for nonartists to create visually attractive presentations.

Computers today aren't limited to working with static images; they're widely used to create and edit documents in media that change over time or in response to user interaction. For animation and digital video work, PCs mimic many of the features of expensive professional workstations at a fraction of the cost. Similarly, today's personal computers can perform a variety of sound and music editing tasks that used to require expensive equipment and numerous musicians.

The interactive nature of the personal computer makes it possible to create nonlinear documents that allow users to take individual paths through information. Early nonlinear documents were called hypertext because they could contain only text. Today authoring systems like HyperCard allow users to create or explore hypermedia documents—interactive documents that mix text, graphics, sound, and moving images with on-screen navigation buttons.

Today's multimedia computer systems make a new kind of software possible—software that uses text, graphics, animation, video, music, voice, and sound effects to communicate. Interactive multimedia documents are available for desktop computers, video game machines, set-top boxes connected to televisions, and networks. Regardless of the hardware, interactive multimedia software allows the user to control the presentation rather than just watch or listen passively. Only time will tell whether these new media will live up to their potential for enhancing education, training, entertainment, and cultural enrichment.

Chapter Review

Key Terms

animation
audio digitizer
bit-mapped (raster) graphics
bullet chart
button
clip art
color depth (bit depth)
computer-aided design (CAD)
computer-aided manufacturing (CAM)
computer-integrated manufacturing (CIM)
data compression

digital image processing software
digital video
drawing software
frame
gray-scale graphics
hypermedia
hypertext
interactive multimedia
MIDI
morph
multimedia
multimedia authoring software
object-oriented (vector) graphics

page-description language
painting software
palette
pixel
pop-up menu
PostScript
presentation graphics software
resolution
sequencing software
synthesized sound
3-D modeling software
video digitizer
WYSIWYG

Review Questions

1. Define or describe each of the key terms above. Check your answers using the glossary.

2. What is the difference between bit-mapped graphics and object-oriented graphics? What are the advantages and disadvantages of each?

3. What two technological factors limit the realism of a bit-mapped image? How are these related to storage of that image in the computer?

4. How is digital image processing of photographs related to bit-mapped painting?

5. Describe several practical applications for 3-D modeling and CAD software.

6. Why is image compression an important part of digital video technology?

7. Describe three different technologies for adding music or other sounds to a multimedia presentation. Describe a practical application of each sound source.

8. How do hypertext and other hypermedia differ from linear media?

9. Describe several practical applications for hypermedia.

10. What are the main disadvantages of hypermedia when compared to conventional media such as books and videos?

11. Is it possible to have hypermedia without multimedia? Is it possible to have multimedia without hypermedia? Explain your answers.

12. How does presentation graphics software differ from multimedia authoring software? Give an example of a practical application of each.

Discussion Questions

1. How does modern digital image processing technology affect the reliability of photographic evidence? How does digital audio technology affect the reliability of sound recordings as evidence? How should our legal system respond to this technology?

2. Scanners, video digitizers, and audio digitizers make it easier than ever for people to violate copyright laws. What, if anything, should be done to protect intellectual property rights of the people who create pictures, videos, and music? Under what circumstances do you think it's acceptable to copy sounds or images for use in your own work?

3. Do you think hypermedia documents will eclipse certain kinds of books and other media? Which ones? Why?

4. Thanks to modern electronic music technology, one or two people can make a record that would have required dozens of musicians 20 years ago. What impact will electronic music technology ultimately have on the music profession?

5. Try to answer each of the questions posed at the end of the section called "Interactive Media: Visions of the Future."

Projects

1. Draw a familiar object or scene using a bit-mapped painting program. Draw the same object or scene with an object-oriented drawing program. Describe how the process changed using different software.

2. Create visual aids for a speech or lecture using presentation graphics software. In what ways did the software make the job easier? What limitations did you find?

3. Create an interactive hypermedia document using Hyper-Card, ToolBook, or some other authoring tool. Test your document on several people and describe the results.

4. Compose an original music composition using a synthesizer, a computer, and a sequencer. Describe the experience.

5. Review several interactive multimedia titles. Discuss their strengths and weaknesses as communication tools. In what ways did their interactivity enhance their usefulness? (Extra challenge: Make your review interactive.)

Sources and Resources

Books

Most of the best graphics applications books are software-specific. When you decide on a software application, choose books based on your chosen software.

The Computer Artist's Handbook, by Lillian F. Schwartz with Laurens R. Schwartz (New York: Norton, 1992). A pioneer in the field of computer art has produced a beautiful overview of the field, covering everything from drawing and perspective to computer analysis of traditional art masterpieces.

Overcoming Art Anxiety, by Betty Edwards. If you're convinced you have no artistic ability, give this book a try; you might surprise yourself.

Information Illustration, by Dale Glasgow (Reading, MA: Addison-Wesley, 1994). A professional illustrator shows you, through a series of real-world projects, how he uses his computer to create graphic illustrations that communicate clearly.

How Computer Graphics Work, by Jeff Prosise (Emeryville, CA: Ziff-Davis Press, 1994); *How Music and Computers Work,* by Erik Holsinger (Emeryville, CA: Ziff-Davis Press, 1994); *How Multimedia Works,* by Erik Holsinger (Emeryville, CA: Ziff-Davis Press, 1994). These three books follow the formula for Ziff's successful *How Computers Work:* Simple, clear, brief explanations accompanied by lavish full-color diagrams and drawings. They don't answer every question, but they do a good job covering the basics. *How Music and Computers Work* includes an audio CD containing interviews, sound samples, and music.

Multimedia Illustrated: The Full-Color Guide to How It All Works, by Nat Gertler (Indianapolis: Que, 1994). This book is similar in layout, design, and style to *How Multimedia Works.* It doesn't go quite as deep into the technology behind multimedia, but it has an additional section containing tips on creating multimedia documents. The book comes with a CD-ROM full of clip media samples.

Multimedia Demystified: A Guide to the World of Multimedia, by Apple Computer (New York: Random House, 1994). In spite of its corporate sponsorship, this book is packed with valuable information for anyone interested in the business of multimedia, regardless of platform. It's structured like a hypermedia document, with color-coded cross links to other parts of the book.

Multimedia Power Tools, by Peter Jerram, Michael Gosney, and others (New York: Random House, 1996). This massive book-CD combination provides one of the most complete and valuable overviews of the field you will find anywhere. It won't make you an instant expert, but it is a solid starting place.

The Desktop Multimedia Bible, by Jeff Burger (Reading, MA: Addison-Wesley, 1993) and *Multimedia for Decision Makers: a Business Primer,* by Jeff Burger (Reading, MA: Addison-Wesley, 1994). Even though it's a bit dated, *The Desktop Multimedia Bible* still provides clear explanations of the science and technology that make multimedia possible. *Multimedia for Decision Makers* is less technical but equally well written. It can help managers and other decision makers cut through the jargon so they can avoid making expensive and embarrassing multimedia mistakes.

Multimedia: Gateway to the Next Millennium, edited by Rober Aston and Joyce Schwartz (Boston: AP Professional, 1994). This is an informative series of essays and articles discussing the present and future of the emerging new media and their role in our society.

HyperCard 2.3 in a Hurry: the Fast Track to Multimedia, by George Beekman (Berkeley, CA: Peachpit Press and Belmont, CA: Wadsworth, 1996). This self-teaching guide is designed to get beginners up to speed with HyperCard, the original hypermedia authoring tool for Macintoshes. The author is a great guy.

Becoming a Computer Musician, by Jeff Bowen (Indianapolis: Sams Publishing, 1994). Most books about computers and music are too technical for beginners or too specific for general readers. Bowen's book/CD-ROM provides a simple interactive introduction for anyone with a Mac or PC, a MIDI keyboard, and an interest in putting them together to create music.

The Desktop Musician: Creating Music on your Computer, by David M. Rubin (Berkeley, CA: Osborne McGraw-Hill, 1995). This book is an excellent introduction to MIDI and digital audio, written from a musician's perspective. There are thorough reviews of most of the popular MIDI software packages, and demos on the accompanying CD-ROM.

The Computer Music Tutorial, by Curtis Roads (Cambridge, MA: The MIT Press, 1996). Not for the faint-hearted, this highly technical 1200+ page book covers nearly every aspect of creating music on the computer. The focus is on the mathematics and algorithms behind various computer synthesis techniques.

The Photographer's Digital Studio: Transferring Your Photos into Pixels, by Joe Farace (Berkeley, CA: Peachpit Press, 1996). If you're an experienced photographer who wants to move out of the darkroom into the computer room, this book will help you make the move. Hardware, software, file formats, and techniques are covered in detail.

Designing Multimedia: A Visual Guide to Multimedia and Online Graphic Design, by Lisa Lopuck (Berkeley, CA: Peachpit Press, 1996) and *Interactivity by Design: Creating and Communicating with New Media,* by Ray Kristof and Amy Satran (Mountain View, CA: Adobe Press, 1995). These two beautiful books are designed to help multimedia authors with the many issues related to design. Lopuck's book is more comprehensive, but both are full of good ideas.

Periodicals

Verbum (P.O. Box 15439, San Diego, CA 92115, 619/233-9977). This avant garde magazine covers the electronic art world. It's a visually stylish periodical that demonstrates by example how computers and art go together. *Verbum Interactive,* an occasional computer-based version of the magazine, includes animation, video, and CD-audio (requires a Macintosh and a CD-ROM drive).

CD-ROM Today. This monthly magazine includes news and reviews for CD-ROM consumers. A cross-platform CD-ROM comes with every issue so you can try demos of the software reviewed in the magazine.

NewMedia Magazine (901 Mariner's Island Blvd., Suite 365, San Mateo, CA 94404, 415/573-5190). This lively monthy magazine covers computer-related multimedia with news, reviews, feature articles, and lots of graphics. It's probably the best single periodical for anyone serious about multimedia authoring.

Keyboard and *Electronic Musician.* These two magazines are among the best sources for up-to-date information on computers and music synthesis.

World Wide Web Pages

The Web is known as the multimedia part of the Internet, and there are plenty of Web sites for learning about—and experiencing first hand—a variety of mixed media. The *Computer Confluence* Web pages will link you to multimedia hardware and software companies and pages that demonstrate state-of-the-art multimedia on the Web.

DATABASE APPLICATIONS AND IMPLICATIONS

Bill Gates Rides the Digital Wave

The goal is information at your fingertips.

—Bill Gates

In the early days of the personal computer revolution, Bill Gates and Paul Allen formed a company called Microsoft to produce and market a version of the BASIC programming language for microcomputers. Microsoft BASIC quickly became the standard language installed in virtu-

Bill Gates and Paul Allen

ally every desktop computer on the market.

BASIC was important, but Microsoft's biggest break came when IBM went shopping for an operating system for its new personal computer. Gates purchased an operating system from a small company, reworked it to meet IBM's specifications, named it MS-DOS (for *Microsoft Disk Operating System*), and offered it to IBM. The IBM PC became an industry standard, and Microsoft found itself owning the operating system that kept most of the PCs in the world running.

Today Bill Gates and Microsoft dominate the personal computer software industry, selling operating systems, programming languages, and applications programs for a variety of

desktop computers. Microsoft has over 8000 employees and more than a billion dollars in annual revenues—almost half the total revenue in PC software worldwide. Software has made the youthful Gates the richest American and one of the wealthiest people on earth.

All this success is not without controversy. Critics argue that Gates uses unethical business practices to ruthlessly stomp out competition. Many of Microsoft's biggest customers confide that they mistrust Gates and fear a Microsoft monopoly. Even the Federal Trade Commission has repeatedly investigated Microsoft's business practices for possible violations of antitrust laws.

According to writer Steven Levy, Gates "has the

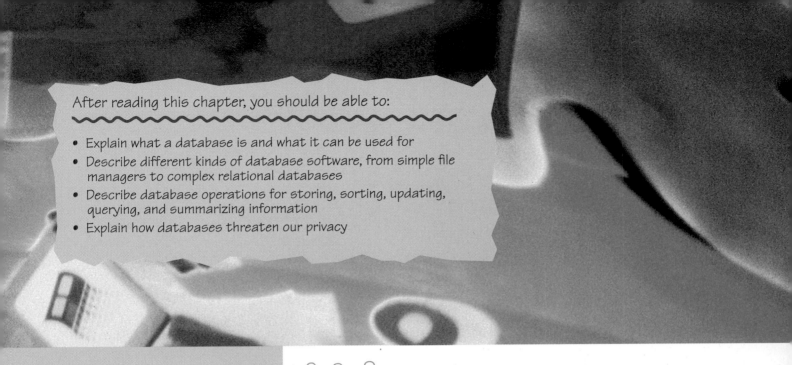

After reading this chapter, you should be able to:

- Explain what a database is and what it can be used for
- Describe different kinds of database software, from simple file managers to complex relational databases
- Describe database operations for storing, sorting, updating, querying, and summarizing information
- Explain how databases threaten our privacy

obsessive drive of a hacker working on a tough technical dilemma, yet has an uncanny grasp of the marketplace, as well as a firm conviction of what the future will be like and what he should do about it." The future, says Gates, will be digital. Even the pictures on our walls will be high-definition digital reproductions of paintings and photographs that can be changed at the touch of a button. Unbelievable? Not if you've been to the $10 million Gates mansion and viewed his digital collection!

To prepare for this all-digital future, Microsoft is quietly buying the electronic rights to hundreds of works of literature, art, and cinema. At the same time, Gates tirelessly evangelizes for Microsoft products in particular and computer technology in general—technology that makes computers easier to use and more accessible to everybody, so we all can have "information at our fingertips."

Bill Gates

We live in an information age. We're bombarded with information by television, radio, newspapers, magazines, books, and computers. It's easy to be overwhelmed by the sheer quantity of information we're expected to deal with each day. Computer applications like word processors and spreadsheets can aggravate the problem by making it easier for people to generate more documents full of information.

A *database program* is an information manager that can help alleviate information overload. Databases make it possible for people to store, organize, retrieve, communicate, and manage information in ways that wouldn't be possible without computers. To control the flood of information, people use databases of all sizes and shapes—from massive mainframe database managers that keep airlines filled with passengers to computerized appointment calendars on palmtop computers and public database kiosks in shopping malls.

First the good news: "Information at your fingertips" can make your life richer and more efficient in a multitude of ways. Ready cash from street-corner machines, instant airline reservations from any telephone, catalog shopping with overnight mail-order delivery, exhaustive reference searches in seconds—none of these conveniences would be possible without databases.

Now the bad news: Much of the information stored in databases is *your* data, and you have little or no control over who has it and how they use it. Ironically the database technology that liberates us in our day-to-day lives is, at the same time, chipping away at our privacy. We'll explore both sides of this important technology in this chapter.

THE ELECTRONIC FILE CABINET: DATABASE BASICS

The next best thing to knowing something is knowing where to find it.

—Samuel Johnson

We'll start by looking at the basics of databases. Like word processors, spreadsheets, and graphics programs, database programs are applications—programs for turning computers into productive tools. If a word processor is a computerized typewriter and a spreadsheet is a computerized ledger, we can think of a database program as a computerized file cabinet.

While word processors and spreadsheets generally are used to create printed documents, database programs are designed to maintain databases—collections of information stored on computer disks. A database can be an electronic version of a phone book, a recipe file, a library's card catalog, an inventory file stored in an office file cabinet, a school's student grade records, a card index containing the names and addresses of business contacts, or a catalog of your compact disc collection. Just about any collection of information can be turned into a database.

What Good Is a Database?

Why do people use computers for information-handling tasks that can be done with index cards, three-ring binders, or file folders? Computerized databases offer several advantages over their paper-and-pencil counterparts:

- *Databases make it easier to store large quantities of information.* If you have only 20 or 30 compact discs, it makes sense to catalog them in a notebook. If you have 2000 or 3000, your notebook may become as unwieldy as your CD collection. With a computerized database your complete CD catalog could be stored on a single diskette. The larger the mass of information, the bigger the benefit of using a database.

- *Databases make it easier to retrieve information quickly and flexibly.* While it might take a minute or more to look up a phone number in a card file or telephone directory, the same job can be done in seconds with a database. If you look up 200 numbers every week, the advantage of a database is obvious. That advantage is even greater when your search doesn't match your file's organization. For example, suppose you have a phone number on a scrap of paper and you want to find the name and address of the person with that number. That kind of search may take hours if your information is stored in a large address book or file alphabetized by name, but the same search is almost instantaneous with a computerized database.

- *Databases make it easy to organize and reorganize information.* Paper filing systems force you to arrange information in one particular way. Should your book catalog be organized by author, by title, by publication date, or by subject? There's a lot riding on your decision, because it takes time if you decide to rearrange everything later. With a database you can instantly switch between these organizational schemes as often as you like; there's no penalty for flexibility.

- *Databases make it easy to print and distribute information in a variety of ways.* Suppose you want to send letters to hundreds of friends inviting them to your post-graduation party. You'll need to include directions to your place for out-of-towners but not for hometowners. A database, when used with a word processor, can print personalized form letters, including extra directions for those who need them, and print preaddressed envelopes or mailing labels in a fraction of the time it would take you to do it by hand and with less likelihood of error. You can even print a report listing invitees sorted by zip code so you can suggest possible car pools. (If you want to bill those who attend the party, your database can help with that, too.)

Database Anatomy

As you might expect, there's a specialized vocabulary associated with databases. Unfortunately some terms take on different meanings depending on their context, and different people use these words in different ways. We'll begin by charting a course through marketing hype and technical terminology to find our way to the definitions most people use today.

For our purposes a **database** is a collection of information stored in an organized form in a computer, and a **database program** is a software tool for organizing storage and retrieval of that information. A variety of programs fit this broad definition, ranging from simple address book programs to massive inventory-tracking systems. We'll explore the differences between types of database programs later in the chapter, but for now we'll treat them as if they were more or less alike.

Many terms that describe the components of database systems grew out of the file cabinet terminology of the office. A database is composed of one or more files. A **file** is a collection of related information; it keeps that information together the way a drawer in a file cabinet does. If a database is used to record sales information for a company, a separate file might contain the relevant sales data for each year. For an address database, separate files might hold personal and business contacts. It's up to the designer of the database to determine whether or not information in different categories is stored in separate files on the computer's disk.

The term *file* sometimes causes confusion because of its multiple meanings. A disk can contain application programs, system programs, utility programs, and documents, all of which are, from the computer's point of view, files. But for database users the term *file* usually means a file that is part of a database—a specific kind of file. In this chapter *file* refers specifically to a data file created by a database program.

A database file is a collection of records. A **record** is the information relating to one person, product, or event. In the library's card catalog database, a record is equivalent to one card. In an address book database, a record contains information about one person. A compact disc catalog database would have one record per CD.

Each discrete chunk of information in a record is called a **field**. A record in the library's card catalog database would contain fields for author, title, publisher, address, date, and title code number. Your CD database could break records into fields by title, artist, and so on.

The type of information a field can hold is determined by its *field type*. For example, the author field in the library database would be defined as a *text field*, so it could contain text. The field specifying the number of copies of a book would be defined as a *numeric field*, so it could contain only numbers—numbers that can be used to calculate totals and other arithmetic formulas, if necessary. A date-of-purchase field might be a *date field* that could contain only dates. In addition to these standard field types, many database programs allow fields to contain graphics, digitized photographs, sounds, or even video clips. **Computed fields** contain formulas similar to spreadsheet formulas; they display values calculated from values in other numeric fields. For example, a computed field called GPA might contain a formula for calculating a student's grade point average using the grades stored in other fields.

Most database programs provide you with more than one way to view the data, including *form views* that show one record at a time and *list views* that display several records in lists similar to a spreadsheet. In any view, fields can be rearranged without changing the underlying data. **UV**

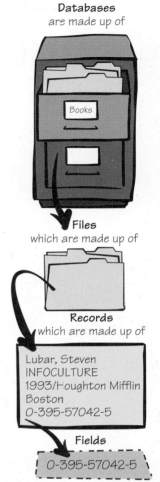

Databases
are made up of

Files
which are made up of

Records
which are made up of

Lubar, Steven
INFOCULTURE
1993/Houghton Mifflin
Boston
0-395-57042-5

Fields

0-395-57042-5

These two screens show the list and form views of a database.

Building a Database

▲▲▲▲▲▲▲▲▲▲▲▲▲▲▲▲▲▲▲▲▲▲▲

Software: Claris FileMaker Pro.

The goal: To create an Addresses database file to replace your tattered address book, the bundle of business cards in your desk drawer, and the scribbled list of numbers posted by your phone.

1

To create a new Addresses database file, you must first define fields by typing a name and specifying a field type for each one. In addition to including text fields for last name, first name, and other information, you add two date fields: one for birthday and one that will automatically display the most recent modification date for each record. You also include a *picture field* and two *value lists*—restricted fields that can only contain values from lists specified by you.

2

The program creates a standard form-style layout for data entry, but it could be easier to use.

3

You modify the layout by rearranging fields and labels and changing their formats.

4

You type information into the first record of the reformatted layout, using the Tab key to move from field to field.

5

The Category and Frequent Call fields use mouse clicks to select the appropriate values.

6

You can fill in the Picture field later with a scanned photograph.

7

When you're through, you use the New Record command to store this record in the data file and replace it on the screen with a new empty record.

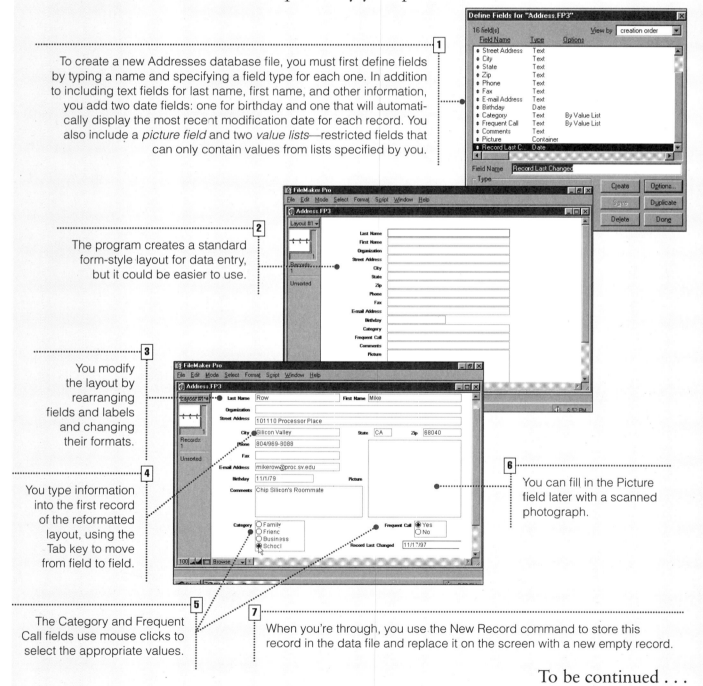

To be continued . . .

Database Operations

> Information has value, but it is as perishable as fresh fruit.
>
> —Nicholas Negroponte, founder and director
> of the MIT Media Lab

Once the structure of a database is defined, it's easy to get information in; it's just a matter of typing. Typing may not even be necessary if the data already exists in some computer-readable form. Most database programs can easily **import** or receive data in the form of text files created with word processors, spreadsheets, or other databases. When information changes or errors are detected, records can be modified, added, or deleted.

The challenging part of using a database is retrieving information in a timely and appropriate manner. Information is of little value if it's not accessible. One way to find information is to **browse** through the records of the database file just as you would if they were paper forms in a notebook. Most database programs provide keyboard commands, on-screen buttons, and other tools for navigating quickly through records. But this kind of electronic page turning offers no particular advantage over paper, and it's painfully inefficient for large files.

Fortunately most database programs include a variety of commands and capabilities that make it easy to get the information you need when you need it.

Database Queries

The alternative to browsing is to ask the database for specific information. In database terminology, an information request is called a **query**. A query may be a simple **search** for a specific record (say, one containing information on Abraham Lincoln) or a request to **select** *all* the records that match a set of criteria (for example, records for all U.S. presidents who served more than one term). Once you've selected a group of records, you can browse through it, produce a printout, or do just about anything else you might do with the complete file.

Sorting Data

Sometimes it's necessary to rearrange records to make the most efficient use of data. For example, a mail-order company's customer file might be arranged alphabetically by name for easy reference, but it must be rearranged in order by zip code to qualify for postal discounts on catalog mailings. A **sort** command allows you to arrange records in alphabetic or numeric order based on values in one or more fields.

Printing Reports, Labels, and Form Letters

In addition to displaying information on the screen, database programs can produce a variety of printouts. The most common type of database printout is a **report**—an ordered list of selected records and fields in an easy-to-read form. Most business reports arrange data in tables with rows for individual records and columns for selected fields; they often include summary lines containing calculated totals and averages for groups of records.

Database programs can also be used to produce mailing labels and customized form letters. Many database programs don't actually print letters; they simply **export data** or transmit the necessary records and fields to word processors with **mail merge** capabilities, which then take on the task of printing the letters. ▪

Complex Queries

Queries may be simple or complex, but either way they must be precise and unambiguous. With appropriate databases, queries could be constructed to find

Selecting, Sorting, and Reporting

▲ ▲

Software: Claris FileMaker Pro.

The goal: To create a postable printout of names and phone numbers for frequently called entries from your Addresses database so you have quick access to important phone numbers.

Last name	First name	Phone
Row	Mike	804/969-8088
Feyerham	Bernie	413-2879
Parker	Sheryl	821-0719
Knutson	Clara	772-1503
Alvarez	Joe	954-3324
Reigelman	Laurel	818/444-5745
Savage	JoAnn and Jim	754-1212
Westfall	Rosalind	255-2558
Cochrane	Lynn	808-8245
Holmes-Swanson	Anna Marie	322-2877
Dengler	Chelsea	422-7014
Putnam	Matthew	265-1215
Heisner	Philbert	802/433-7348
Cadliz	Asa	314/442-1811

1 Creating a report like this one involves selecting the desired records, designing a layout for the report, sort ng the records in the appropriate order, and printing the report.

2 When you select the Find command, the screen displays an empty form. If you type values into the fields, the program will locate records with fields that match those values. The field you want to match, though, is not a typed field; it's the Frequent Call check box.

3 You click Yes in that check box and the Find button.

4 The program indicates that 19 of 109 records were selected because they had Frequent Call checked. You can now work with this collection of records.

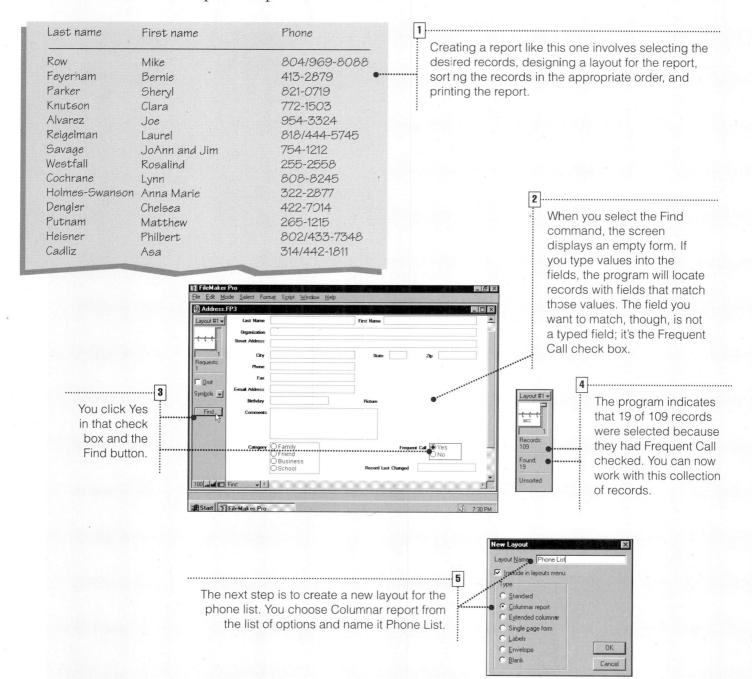

5 The next step is to create a new layout for the phone list. You choose Columnar report from the list of options and name it Phone List.

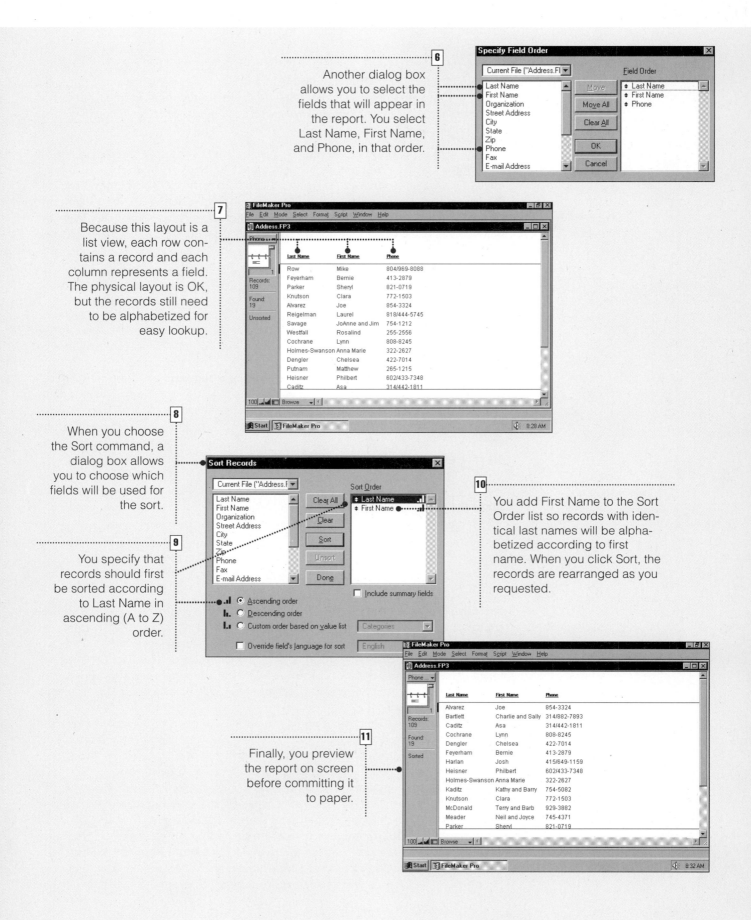

6 Another dialog box allows you to select the fields that will appear in the report. You select Last Name, First Name, and Phone, in that order.

7 Because this layout is a list view, each row contains a record and each column represents a field. The physical layout is OK, but the records still need to be alphabetized for easy lookup.

8 When you choose the Sort command, a dialog box allows you to choose which fields will be used for the sort.

9 You specify that records should first be sorted according to Last Name in ascending (A to Z) order.

10 You add First Name to the Sort Order list so records with identical last names will be alphabetized according to first name. When you click Sort, the records are rearranged as you requested.

11 Finally, you preview the report on screen before committing it to paper.

- in a hospital's patient database, the names and locations of all of the patients on the hospital's fifth and sixth floors
- in a database of airline flight schedules, the least expensive way to fly from Boston to San Francisco on Tuesday afternoon
- in a politician's database, all voters who contributed more than $1000 to last year's legislative campaign and who wrote to express concern over gun control laws since the election

These may be legitimate targets for queries, but they aren't expressed in a form that most database programs can understand. The exact method for performing a query depends on the user interface of the database software. Most programs allow the user to specify the rules of the search by filling in a dialog box or a blank on-screen form. Some require the user to type the request using a special **query language** that's more precise than English. For example, to view the records for males between 18 and 35, you might type

```
Select * From Population Where
Sex = M and Age > 18 and Age < 35
```

Many database programs include programming languages so queries can be included in programs and performed automatically when the programs are executed. While the details of the process vary, the underlying logic is consistent from program to program.

Most modern database management programs support **SQL**—the standard for programming complex queries. Because SQL is available for many different database management systems, programmers and sophisticated users don't need to learn new languages when they work with different hardware and software systems. Users are usually insulated from the complexities of the query language by graphical user interfaces that allow point-and-click queries. UV

Special-Purpose Database Programs

> The best way to organize information is the way that reveals what we want to communicate.
>
> —Richard Saul Wurman, author of *Information Anxiety*

Specialized database software is preprogrammed for specific data storage and retrieval purposes. The CD-ROM databases used in many libraries are examples of special-purpose database programs. Users of special-purpose databases don't generally need to define file structures or design forms because these details have been taken care of by the designers of the software. In fact, some special-purpose database programs are not even sold as databases; they have names that more accurately reflect their purposes.

For example, an *electronic phone directory* can pack millions of names and phone numbers onto a single CD-ROM. Using an electronic phone directory for the U.S. you can track down phone numbers of people and businesses all over the United States—even if you don't know where they are. You can look up a person's name if you have the phone number or street address You can generate a list of every dentist in town—any town. Then using another type of specialized database, an *electronic street atlas*, you can pinpoint each of your finds on a freshly printed map.

Geographical information systems (GIS) go beyond simple mapping programs. A GIS allows a business to combine tables of data, such as customer sales lists, with demographic information from the census bureau and other sources. The right combination can reveal valuable strategic information. For example, a stock brokerage

Querying a CD-ROM Database

▲ ▲

Software: ProQuest Periodical Abstracts CD-ROM.

Goal: To locate recent articles discussing the impact of computers on personal privacy. You'll use the library's ProQuest Periodical Abstracts CD-ROM, an electronic reference that packs abstracts for articles from hundreds of magazines onto a 5-inch optical disk.

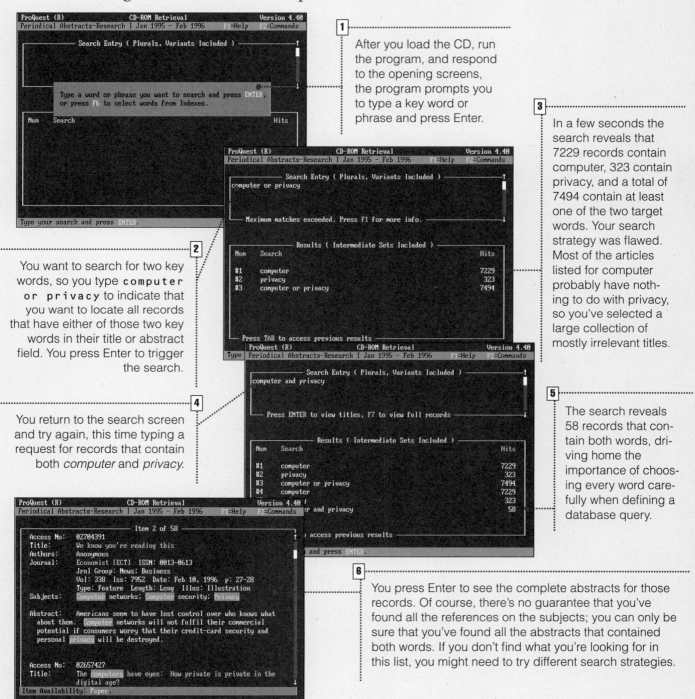

1 After you load the CD, run the program, and respond to the opening screens, the program prompts you to type a key word or phrase and press Enter.

2 You want to search for two key words, so you type **computer or privacy** to indicate that you want to locate all records that have either of those two key words in their title or abstract field. You press Enter to trigger the search.

3 In a few seconds the search reveals that 7229 records contain computer, 323 contain privacy, and a total of 7494 contain at least one of the two target words. Your search strategy was flawed. Most of the articles listed for computer probably have nothing to do with privacy, so you've selected a large collection of mostly irrelevant titles.

4 You return to the search screen and try again, this time typing a request for records that contain both *computer* and *privacy*.

5 The search reveals 58 records that contain both words, driving home the importance of choosing every word carefully when defining a database query.

6 You press Enter to see the complete abstracts for those records. Of course, there's no guarantee that you've found all the references on the subjects; you can only be sure that you've found all the abstracts that contained both words. If you don't find what you're looking for in this list, you might need to try different search strategies.

The Language of Database Queries

Years ago, the number of incompatible database languages made it difficult for people using different applications to access the same database. In the mid-1970s, IBM's E. F. Codd proposed a standardized Structured English Query Language, which evolved into SQL. Contrary to popular belief, SQL is not an acronym for "Structured Query Language"—SQL is far more than a query language. With SQL, users and programmers can employ the same language to access databases from a wide variety of vendors.

SQL combines the familiar database concepts of tables, rows (records) and columns (fields), and the mathematical idea of a *set*. We'll illustrate a simple SQL command using the Rental Vehicles database from Clem's Transportation Rental ("If it moves, we rent it.") Here's a complete listing of the database records:

Vehicle_ID	Vehicle_Type	Transport_Mode	Num_Passengers	Cargo_Capacity	Rental_Price
1062	Helicopter	Air	6	500	$1,250.00
1955	Canoe	Water	2	30	$5.00
2784	Automobile	Land	4	250	$45.00
0213	Unicycle	Land	1	0	$10.00
0019	Minibus	Land	8	375	$130.00
3747	Balloon	Air	3	120	$340.00
7288	HangGlide	Air	1	5	$17.00
9430	Sailboat	Water	8	200	$275.00
8714	Powerboat	Water	4	175	$210.00
0441	Bicycle	Land	1	10	$12.00
4759	Jet	Air	9	2300	$2,900.00

can pinpoint the best locations for branch offices based on average incomes and other neighborhood data; a cable TV company can locate potential customers who live close to existing lines. Because they can display geographic and demographic data on maps, they allow users to see data relationships that might be invisible in table form.

Many specialized database programs are sold as **personal information managers (PIMs)** or **electronic organizers.** A personal information manager can automate some or all of these functions:

- *Address/phone book.* PIM address books provide options for quickly displaying specific records and printing mailing labels, address books, and reports. Some include automatic phone-dialing options and fields for recording phone notes.

A typical SQL statement filters the records of a database, capturing only those that meet the specific criteria. For example, suppose you wanted to list the ID numbers and types of the vehicles that traveled on land and cost less than $20.00 per day. The SQL statement to perform this task would look like this:

```
SELECT Vehicle_ID, Vehicle_Type

FROM Rental_Vehicles

WHERE Transport_Mode = 'Land'
AND

Rental_Price < 20.00 ;
```

In a *Venn (set) diagram,* the selection looks like this:

In English this SQL statement says "Show me (from the Rental Vehicles database) the vehicle IDs and vehicle types for those vehicles that travel by land and cost less than $20.00 per day to rent."

Two rows in the database meet these criteria, the unicycle and bicycle:

```
0213 Unicycle

0441 Bicycle
```

The selection rules for SQL are consistant and understandable whether queries are simple or complex. This simple example is designed to give you an idea of how they work.

Vehicles renting for under $20 a day

Land vehicles

Land vehicles renting for under $20 a day

- *Appointment calendar.* A typical PIM calendar allows you to enter appointments and events and display or print them in a variety of formats, ranging from one day at a time to a monthly overview. Many include built-in alarms for last-minute reminders.

- *To-do list.* Most PIMs allow users to enter and organize ongoing lists of things to do and archive lists of completed tasks.

- *Miscellaneous notes.* Some PIMs accept diary entries, personal notes, and other hard-to-categorize tidbits of information.

PIMs are popular among people with busy schedules and countless contacts. They're easier to understand and use than general-purpose database programs, and they offer distinct advantages in speed and flexibility over their leather-bound paper

Personal Information Management software can help you keep track of appointments, phone numbers, and to-do lists, as long as your computer is nearby—or you can find a way to carry the data with you. The Timex Data Link watch can download critical data by reading flashes of light from the PC screen, transferring the facts and figures into a "remote personal information manager" on your wrist.

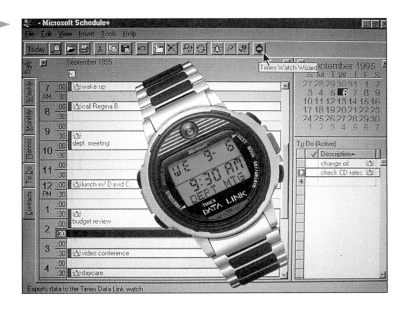

counterparts. For people on the go, PIMs work especially well with notebook and laptop computers. But PIMs aren't for everybody; many people find that the standard features built into personal information management software don't meet their needs or match their style. Personal information management is, in the end, personal.

BEYOND THE BASICS:
DATABASE MANAGEMENT SYSTEMS

When we try to pick out anything, we find it hitched to everything else in the universe.

—John Muir, first director of the National Park Service

So far we've used simple examples to illustrate concepts common to most database programs. This oversimplification is useful for understanding the basics, but it's not the whole story. In truth database programs range from simple mailing label programs to massive financial information systems, and it's important to know a little about what makes them different as well as what makes them alike.

From File Managers to Database Management Systems

Technically speaking, many consumer databases and personal information managers programs aren't really database managers at all; they're file managers. A **file manager** is a program that allows users to work with one file at a time. A true **database management system (DBMS)** is a program or system of programs that can manipulate data in a large collection of files, cross-referencing between files as needed. A database management system can be used interactively, or it can be controlled directly by other programs. A file manager is sufficient for mailing lists and other common data management applications. But for many large, complex jobs, there's no substitute for a true database management system.

Consider, for example, the problem of managing student information at a college. It's easy to see how databases might be used to store this information: a file containing one record for each student, with fields for name, student ID number, address, phone, and so on. But a typical student generates far too much information to store practically in a single data file.

Most schools choose to keep several files containing student information: one for financial records, one for course enrollment and grade transcripts, and so on. Each of these files has a single record for each student. In addition, a school must maintain class enrollment files with one record for each class and fields for information on each student enrolled in the class. Three of these files might be organized like this:

Transcript file

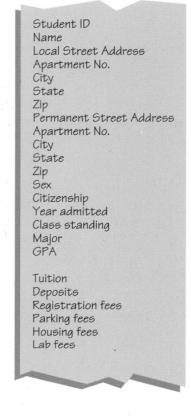

Student ID
Name
Local Street Address
Apartment No.
City
State
Zip
Permanent Street Address
Apartment No.
City
State
Zip
Sex
Citizenship
Year admitted
Class standing
Major
GPA

(Course 1 information)
Department
Number
Credits
Grade
Date

(Course 2 information)
Department

Financial info file

Student ID
Name
Local Street Address
Apartment No.
City
State
Zip
Permanent Street Address
Apartment No.
City
State
Zip
Sex
Citizenship
Year admitted
Class standing
Major
GPA

Tuition
Deposits
Registration fees
Parking fees
Housing fees
Lab fees

Class list file

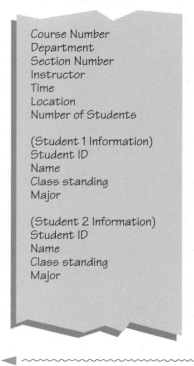

Course Number
Department
Section Number
Instructor
Time
Location
Number of Students

(Student 1 Information)
Student ID
Name
Class standing
Major

(Student 2 Information)
Student ID
Name
Class standing
Major

Student information is duplicated in several different files of this inefficient, error-prone database.

In the database above, each of the three separate files contains basic information about every student. This redundant data not only occupies expensive storage space but also makes it difficult to ensure that student information is accurate and up to date. If a student moves to a different address, several files must be updated to reflect this change. The more changes, the greater the likelihood of a data-entry error.

With a database management system there's no need to store all this information in every file. The database can include a basic student file containing demographic information—information that's unique for each student. Because the demographic information is stored in a separate file, it doesn't need to be included in the financial information file, the transcript file, the class list file, or any other file. The student ID number, included in each file, serves as a **key field;** it unlocks the relevant student information in the Student file when it's needed elsewhere. The Student ID field is, in effect, shared by all files that use data from this file. If the student moves, the change of address need only be recorded in one place. Databases organized in this way are called *relational databases*.

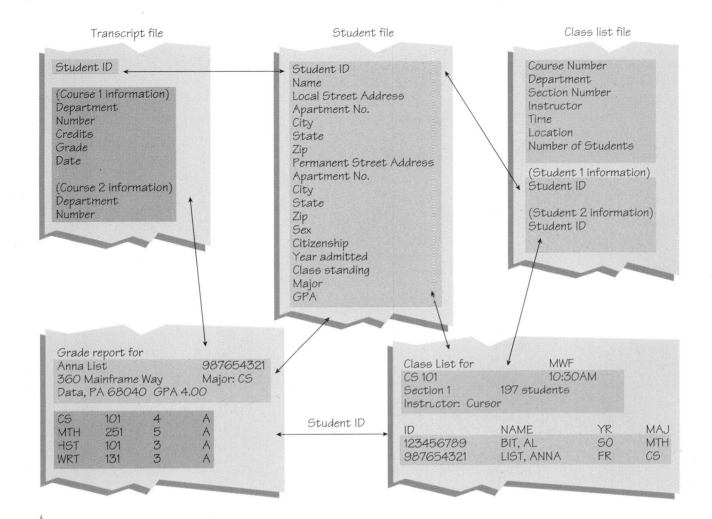

Transcript file   Student file   Class list file

Student ID

(Course 1 information)
Department
Number
Credits
Grade
Date

(Course 2 information)
Department
Number

Student ID
Name
Local Street Address
Apartment No.
City
State
Zip
Permanent Street Address
Apartment No.
City
State
Zip
Sex
Citizenship
Year admitted
Class standing
Major
GPA

Course Number
Department
Section Number
Instructor
Time
Location
Number of Students

(Student 1 information)
Student ID

(Student 2 information)
Student ID

Grade report for
Anna List   987654321
360 Mainframe Way   Major: CS
Data, PA 68040   GPA 4.00

CS	101	4	A
MTH	251	5	A
HST	101	3	A
WRT	131	3	A

Student ID

Class List for   MWF
CS 101   10:30AM
Section 1   197 students
Instructor: Cursor

ID	NAME	YR	MAJ
123456789	BIT, AL	SO	MTH
987654321	LIST, ANNA	FR	CS

The Student file serves as a reference when grade reports and class lists are created. The Student ID fields in the Transcript file and the Class List file are used as a key for locating the necessary student information in the Student file.

What Makes a Database Relational?

To most users a **relational database** program is one that allows files to be related to each other so that changes in one file are reflected in other files automatically. To computer scientists the term *relational database* has a technical definition related to the underlying structure of the data and the rules specifying how that data can be manipulated.

The structure of a relational database is based on the *relational model*—a mathematical model that combines data in tables. Other kinds of database management systems are based on different theoretical models, with different technical advantages and disadvantages. But the majority of database management systems in use today, including virtually all PC-based database management systems, use the relational model. So from the average computer user's point of view, the distinction between the popular and technical definitions of *relational* is academic.

The Many Faces of Databases

Large databases can contain hundreds of interrelated files. This maze of information could be overwhelming to users if they were forced to deal with it directly. Fortunately a database management system can shield users from the complex inner workings of the system, providing them with only the information and commands they

Clerk's view

Video rental view used by clerks to access renter information, scan bar codes on videos, and print rental invoices

Video store database

Manager's view

• Inventory-tracking view used by managers to check on rental history and inventory for individual movies

• Policy view used by managers to change pricing, membership, and other policies

Technician/programmer's view

Technical view used by programmer to create other user interfaces and custom queries

Clerks, managers, programmers, and customers see different views of a video rental store's database. Customers can browse through listings and reviews of available movies using a touch-screen kiosk. The clerk's view allows only for simple data-entry and check-out procedures. The manager, working with the same database, has control over pricing, policies, and inventory but can't change the structure or user interface of the database. The programmer can work "under the hood" to fine-tune and customize the database so it can better meet the needs of other employees and customers.

need to get their jobs done. In fact, a well-designed database puts on different faces for different classes of users.

Retail clerks don't need to be able to access every piece of information in the store's database; they just need to enter sales transactions on point-of-sale terminals. Databases designed for retail outlets generally include simple, straightforward terminal interfaces that give the clerks only the information, and the power, they need to process transactions. Managers, accountants, data processing specialists, and customers see the database from different points of view because they need to work with the data in different ways.

Downsizing and Decentralizing

Advances in the last two decades have changed the way most organizations deal with data. The earliest file management programs could only do **batch processing,** which required users to accumulate transactions and feed them into computers in large batches. These batch systems weren't able to provide the kind of immediate feedback we expect today. Questions like "What's the balance in my checking account?" or "Are there any open flights to Denver next Tuesday?" were likely to be answered "Those records will be updated tonight, so we'll let you know tomorrow."

Today disk drives, inexpensive memory, and sophisticated software have allowed **interactive processing** to replace batch processing for most applications. Users can now interact with data through terminals, viewing and changing values on line in **real time.** Batch processing is still used for printing periodic bills, invoices, and reports and for making backup copies of data files—jobs for which it makes sense to do a lot of transactions at once. But for applications that demand immediacy, such as airline reservations, banking transactions, and the like, interactive, multiuser database systems have taken over.

In the pre-PC days, most databases were housed in mainframe computers accessible only to information-processing personnel. But the traditional hard-to-access **centralized database** on a mainframe system is no longer the norm. Today businesses are rapidly migrating toward a **client/server** approach: *Client* programs in desktop (or laptop) computers send information requests through a network to *server* databases on mainframes, minicomputers, or desktop computers; the servers process queries and send the requested data back to the client. A client/server system allows users to take advantage of the PC's simple user interface and convenience while still having access to data stored on large server systems. Some corporations keep copies of all corporate data in integrated **data warehouses;** other companies use **distributed databases,** where data is strewn out across networks on several different computers; many organizations combine these approaches. From the user's point of view, the differences between these approaches may not be apparent. Wherever the data is stored, the goal is to provide quick and easy access to important information.

Tomorrow's Databases?

The biggest changes in database technology in the next few years may take place under the surface, where they may not be apparent to most users. For example, many computer scientists believe that the relational data model may be supplanted in the next decade by an object-oriented data model, and that most future databases will be **object-oriented databases** rather than relational databases. Instead of storing records in tables and hierarchies, object-oriented databases store software *objects* that contain procedures (or instructions) along with data. Object-oriented databases often are used in conjunction with object-oriented programming languages, which are discussed in later chapters. Experts suggest that object technology will make construction and manipulation of complex databases easier and less time consuming. Users will find databases more flexible and responsive as object technology becomes more widespread, even if they aren't aware of the underlying technological reasons for these improvements.

Ultimately database technology will all but disappear from the user's view as interfaces become simpler, more powerful, and more intelligent. Future databases will undoubtedly incorporate multimedia technologies in more sophisticated ways. In the next two chapters you'll see how many database applications are being radically transformed by networks in general and the Internet in particular. Later chapters provide glimpses of technology that will allow tomorrow's databases to respond intelligently to commands and queries issued in natural human language.

Dealing with Databases

Whether you're creating an address file with a simple file manager or retrieving data from a full-blown relational database management system, you can save yourself a great deal of time and grief if you follow a few commonsense rules:

- **Choose the right tool for the job.** Don't invest time and money in a programmable relational database to computerize your address book, and don't try to run the affairs of your multinational corporation with a $99 file manager.

- **Think about how you'll get the information out before you put it in.** What kinds of files, records, and fields will you need to create to make it easy to find things quickly and print things the way you'll want them? For example, use separate fields for first and last name if you want to sort names alphabetically and print first names first.

- **Start with a plan, and be prepared to change your plan.** It's a good idea to do a trial run with a small amount of data to make sure everything works the way you think it should.

- **Make your data consistent.** Inconsistencies can mess up sorting and make searching difficult. For example, if a database includes residents of Minnesota, Minn., and MN, it's hard to group people by state.

- **Databases are only as good as their data.** When entering data, take advantage of the data-checking capability of your database software. Does the first name field contain nonalphabetic characters? Is the birth date within a reasonable range? Automatic data checking is important, but it's no substitute for human proofreading or for a bit of skepticism when using the database.

- **Query with care.** In the words of Aldous Huxley, "People always get what they ask for; the only trouble is that they never know, until they get it, what it actually is that they have asked for." Here's a real example: A student searching a database of classic rock albums requested all records containing the string "Dylan," and the database program obediently displayed the names of several Bob Dylan albums . . . plus one by Jimi Hendrix called *Electric Ladyland*. Why? Because *dylan* is in La*dyland*! Unwanted records can go unnoticed in large database selections, so it's important to define selection rules very carefully.

- **If at first you don't succeed, try another approach.** If your search doesn't turn up the answers you were looking for, it doesn't mean the answers aren't there; they may just be wearing a disguise. For example, if you search the OASIS Library database for "Viet Nam War" references, you won't find any. Why? Because the government officially classifies the Viet Nam War as a *conflict,* so references are stored under the subject "Viet Nam Conflict." Technology meets bureaucracy!

No Secrets: Computers and Privacy

Advanced technology has created new opportunities for America as a nation, but it has also created the possibility for new abuses of the individual American citizen. Adequate safeguards must always stand watch so that man remains master and never the victim of the computer.

—Richard Nixon, 37th president of the U.S., Feb. 23, 1974

Instant airline reservations, all-night automated banking, overnight mail, instant library searches—databases provide us with conveniences that were unthinkable a generation ago. But convenience isn't free. In the case of databases, the price we pay is our privacy.

The Privacy Problem

We live in an information age, and data is one of the currencies of our time. Businesses and government agencies spend billions of dollars every year to collect and exchange information about you and me. More than 15,000 specialized marketing databases contain 2 billion consumer names, along with a surprising amount of personal information. The typical American consumer is on 25 marketing lists. Many of these lists are organized by characteristics like age, income, religion, political affiliation, and even sexual preference—and they're bought and sold every day.

Marketing databases are only the tip of the iceberg. Credit and banking information, tax records, health data, insurance records, political contributions, voter registration, credit card purchases, warranty registrations, magazine and newsletter subscriptions, phone calls, passport registration, airline reservations, automobile registrations, arrests, Internet explorations—they're all recorded in computers, and we have little or no control over what happens to most of those records once they're collected.

For most of us this data is out of sight and out of mind. But lives are changed because of these databases. Here are three representative stories:

The Internal Revenue Service workers shown here enter taxpayers personal financial information into massive computer databases. When you shop by phone, respond to a survey, or fill out a warranty card, it's likely that a clerk somewhere will enter that data into a computer.

- When Congress investigated ties between President Jimmy Carter's brother Billy and the government of Libya, they produced a report that detailed, among other things, the exact time and location of phone calls placed by Billy Carter in three different states. The phone records, which revealed a great deal about Billy Carter's activities, were obtained from AT&T's massive network of data-collecting computers. Similar information is available on every phone company customer.

- When a credit bureau mistakenly placed a bankruptcy filing in the file of a St. Louis couple, banks responded by shutting off loans for their struggling construction business, forcing them into *real* bankruptcy. They sued but lost because credit bureaus are protected by law from financial responsibility for "honest" mistakes!

- A Los Angeles thief stole a wallet and used its contents to establish an artificial identity. When the thief was arrested for a robbery involving murder, the crime was recorded under the wallet owner's name in police databases. The legitimate owner of the wallet was arrested five times in the following 14 months and spent several days in jail before a protracted court battle resulted in the deletion of the record.

Privacy violations aren't new, and they don't always involve computers. The German Nazis, the Chinese Communists, and even Richard Nixon's 1972 campaign committee practiced surveillance without computers. But the privacy problem takes on a whole new dimension in the age of high-speed computers and databases. The same characteristics that make databases more efficient than other information storage methods—storage capacity, retrieval speed, organizational flexibility, and ease of distribution of information—also make them a threat to our privacy.

Big Brother and Big Business

If all records told the same tale, then the lie passed into history and became truth.

—George Orwell, in 1984

In George Orwell's *1984* information about every citizen was stored in a massive database controlled by the ever-vigilant Big Brother. As it turns out, this kind of central computer is no longer necessary for producing computerized dossiers of private citizens. With modern networked computers it's easy to compile profiles by combining information from different database files. As long as the files share a single unique field, like your Social Security number, **record matching** is trivial and quick. And when database information is combined, the whole is often far greater than the sum of its parts.

Sometimes the results are clearly beneficial. Record matching is used by government enforcement agencies to locate criminals ranging from tax evaders to mass murderers. Because credit bureaus collect data about us, we can use credit cards to borrow money wherever we go. But these benefits come with at least three problems:

- *Data errors are common.* A study of 1500 reports from the three big credit bureaus found errors in 43 percent of the files.

- *Data can become nearly immortal.* Because data files are commonly sold, shared, and copied, it's just about impossible to delete or correct erroneous records with absolute certainty.

- *Data isn't secure.* A *Business Week* reporter demonstrated this in 1989 by using his personal computer to obtain then Vice President Dan Quayle's credit report. Had he been a skilled computer criminal, he might have been able to *change* that report.

Protection against invasion of privacy is not explicitly guaranteed by the U.S. Constitution. Legal scholars agree that the **right to privacy**—freedom from interference into the private sphere of a person's affairs—is implied by other constitutional guarantees, although debates rage about exactly what this means. Federal and state laws provide various forms of privacy protection, but most of those laws were written years ago. When it comes to privacy violation, technology is far ahead of the law.

Database technology clearly poses a threat to personal privacy, but other information technologies amplify that threat. The rapid growth of networking technology, described in the next two chapters, makes it possible for personal data to be transmitted almost anywhere instantly. As you'll see in Chapter 10, the Internet is particularly fertile ground for collecting personal information about individuals. Workplace monitoring technology, described in a later chapter, allows managers to know more than ever before about the work habits and patterns of workers. Smart cards and other intelligent personal devices, described in the last three chapters of this book, allow us to trade convenience for personal privacy.

Democracy depends on the free flow of information, but it also depends on the protection of individual rights. Maintaining a balance is not easy, especially when new information technologies are being developed at such a rapid pace. With information at our fingertips, it's tempting to think that more information is the answer. But in the timeless words of populist philosopher Will Rogers, "It's not the things we don't know that get us into trouble, it's the things we do know that ain't so."

SUMMARY

Database programs allow users to quickly and efficiently store, organize, retrieve, communicate, and manage large amounts of information. Each database file is a collection of records, and each record is made up of fields containing text strings, numbers, and other chunks of information. Database programs allow users to view data in a variety of ways, sort records in any order, and print reports, mailing labels, and

Your Private Rights

Sometimes computer-aided privacy violations are nuisances; sometimes they're threats to life, liberty, and the pursuit of happiness. Here are a few tips for protecting your right to privacy.

• **Your Social Security number is yours—don't give it away.** Since the SSN is a unique identification, it can be used to gather information about you without your permission or knowledge. For example, you could be denied a job or insurance because of something you once put on a medical form. Never write it (or your driver's license number or phone number, for that matter) on a check or credit card receipt. Don't give your SSN to anyone unless they have a legitimate reason to ask for it.

• **Don't give away information about yourself.** Don't answer questions about yourself just because a questionnaire or company representative asks you to. When you fill out any form—coupon, warranty registration card, survey, sweepstakes entry, or whatever—think about whether you want the information stored in somebody else's computer.

• **Say no to direct mail and phone solicitations.** Businesses and political organizations pay for your data so they can target you for mail campaigns and phone solicitations. You can remove yourself from many lists by sending your name, address, and phone number with your request to: Mail Preference Service/Phone Preference Service, Direct Mail Marketing Association, 6 East 43rd Street, New York, NY 10017. If this doesn't stop the flow, you might want to try a more direct approach. Send back unwanted letters along with "Take me off your list" requests in the postage paid envelopes that come with them. When you receive an unsolicited phone marketing call, tell the caller "I never purchase or donate anything as a result of phone solicitations" and ask to be removed from the list. If they call within 12 months of being specifically told not to, you can sue and recover up to $500 per call according to the Telephone Consumer Protection Act of 1991.

• **To maximize your privacy, minimize your profile.** If you don't want a financial transaction recorded, use cash. If you don't want your phone number to be public information, use an unlisted number. If you don't want your mailing address known, use a post office box.

• **If you think there's incorrect or damaging information about you in a file, find out.** The Freedom of Information Act of 1966 requires that most records of U.S. government agencies be made available to the public on demand. The Privacy Act of 1974 requires federal agencies to provide you with information in your files relating to you and to amend incorrect records. The Fair Credit Reporting Act of 1970 allows you to see your credit ratings—for free if you have been denied credit—and correct any errors. The three big credit bureaus are Equifax, PO Box 4081, Atlanta, GA 30302, 404/885-8000; Trans Union, PO Box 360, Philadelphia, PA 19105, 215/569-4582; TRW Credit Data, 12606 Greenvilee Ave., PO Box 749029, Dallas, TX 75374-9029, 214/235-1200x251.

• **Know your electronic rights.** Privacy protection laws in the United States lag far behind those of other high-tech nations, but they are beginning to appear. For example, the 1986 Electronic Communications Privacy Act provides the same protection that covers mail and telephone communication to some—but not all—electronic communication. The 1988 Computer Matching and Privacy Protection Act regulates the use of government data in determining eligibility for federal benefits.

• **Support organizations that fight for privacy rights.** If you value privacy rights, let your representatives know how you feel and support the American Civil Liberties Union, Computer Professionals for Social Responsibility, the Electronic Frontier Foundation, and other organizations that fight for those rights.

other custom printouts. A user can search for an individual record or select a group of records with a query.

While most database programs are general-purpose tools that can be used to create custom databases for any purpose, some are special-purpose tools programmed to do a particular set of tasks. Geographical information systems, for example, combine maps and demographic information with data tables to provide new ways to look at data. Personal information managers provide automated address books, appointment calendars, to-do lists, and notebooks for busy individuals.

Many database programs are, technically speaking, file managers, because they work with only one file at a time. True database management systems (DBMSs) can work with several files at once, cross-referencing information among files when appropriate. A DBMS can provide an efficient way to store and manage large quantities of information by eliminating the need for redundant information in different files. A well-designed database provides different views of the data to different classes of users, so each user sees and manipulates only the information necessary for the job at hand.

The trend today is clearly away from large, centralized databases accessible only to data processing staff. Instead, most organizations are moving toward a client/server approach that allows users to have access to data stored in servers throughout the organization's network.

The accumulation of data by government agencies and businesses is a growing threat to our right to privacy. Massive amounts of information about private citizens are collected and exchanged for a variety of purposes. Today's technology makes it easy to combine information from different databases, producing detailed profiles of individual citizens. While there are many legitimate uses for these procedures, there's also a great potential for abuse.

Chapter Review

Key Terms

batch processing	export data	query
browse	field	query language
centralized database	file	real time
client/server database	file manager	record
computed field	geographical information system	record matching
database	(GIS)	relational database
database management system	import data	report
(DBMS)	interactive processing	right to privacy
database program	key field	search
data warehouse	mail merge	select (records)
distributed database	object-oriented database	sort
electronic organizer	personal information manager (PIM)	SQL

Review Questions

1. Define or describe each of the key words above. Check your answers in the glossary.

2. What is the difference between a file manager and a database management system? How are they similar?

3. Describe the structure of a simple database. Use the terms *file, record,* and *field* in your description.

4. What is a query? Give examples of the kinds of questions that might be answered with a query.

5. What steps are involved in producing a standard multi-column business report from a database?

6. What are the advantages of personal information management software over paper notebook organizers? What are the disadvantages?

7. What does it mean to sort a data file?

8. How can a database be designed to reduce the likelihood of data-entry errors?

9. Describe how record matching is used to obtain information about you. Give examples.

10. Do we have a legal right to privacy? On what grounds?

11. Why are computers important in discussions of invasion of privacy?

Discussion Questions

1. Grade books, checkbooks, and other information collections can be managed with either a database program or a spreadsheet program. How would you decide which type of application is most appropriate for a given job?

2. What have you done this week that directly or indirectly involved a database? How would your week have been different in a world without databases?

3. "The computer is a great humanizing factor because it makes the individual more important. The more information we have on each individual, the more each individual counts." Do you agree with this statement by science fiction writer Isaac Asimov? Why, or why not?

4. Suppose you have been incorrectly billed for $100 from a mail-order house. Your protestations are ignored by the company, which is now threatening to report you to a collection agency. What do you do?

5. What advantages and disadvantages does a computerized law enforcement system have for law-abiding citizens?

6. In what ways were George Orwell's "predictions" in the novel *1984* accurate? In what ways were they wrong?

Projects

1. Design a database for your own use. Create several records, sort the data, and print a report.

2. Find out as much as you can about someone (for example, yourself or a public figure) from public records like tax records, court records, voter registration lists, and motor vehicle files.

3. Find out as much as you can about your own credit rating.

4. The next time you order something by mail or phone, try encoding your name with a unique middle initial so you can recognize when the company sells your name and address to other companies. Use several different spellings for different orders if you want to do some comparative research.

5. Determine what information about you is stored in your school computers. What information are you allowed to see? What information are others allowed to see? Exactly who may access your files? Can you find out who sees your files? How long is the information retained after you leave?

6. Keep track of your purchases for a few weeks. If other people had access to this information, what conclusions might they be able to draw about you?

Sources and Resources

Books

Like word processors and spreadsheet software, database programs have inspired hundreds of how-to tutorials, user's guides, and reference books. If you're working with a popular program, you should have no trouble finding a book to help you develop your skills.

The Practical SQL Handbook: Using Structured Query Language, Second Edition, by Judith S. Bowman, Sandra L. Emerson, and Marcy Darnovsky (Reading, MA: Addison-Wesley, 1993). If you want to learn to communicate with relational databases using the standard database query language, this book can help you learn the language.

Information Anxiety, by Richard Saul Wurman (New York: Doubleday, 1989). Information anxiety, according to Wurman, happens when information doesn't tell us what we want or need to know. This clever and witty book provides insight into organizing information to avoid this modern malady. Its unusual organization makes it easy to read in just about any order.

The Computer Privacy Handbook, by Andrè Bacard (Berkeley, CA: Peachpit Press, 1995). The first part of this six-part book provides a broad introduction to the privacy threats posed by computers. Much of the rest of the book is devoted to the politics of privacy in electronic communication and the mechanics of using PGP, an encryption program for the PC. (Encryption is covered in the security and risks chapter of this book).

The Naked Consumer (How Our Private Lives Become Public Commodities), by Eric Larson (Bergenfield, NJ: Penguin Books, 1992). If you doubt that information about you is a valuable commercial commodity, you won't after you read this book.

You'll find several other books that deal with privacy issues listed in later chapters of this book.

Periodicals

The Privacy Journal, PO Box 28577, Providence, RI 02908, 401/274-7861, 0005101719@mcimail.com. This widely quoted monthly newsletter covers all issues related to personal privacy.

Organizations

Computer Professionals for Social Responsibility, PO Box 717, Palo Alto, CA 94302, 415/32203778, cpsr@cpsr.org. CPSR provides the public and policy makers with realistic assessments of the power, promise, and problems of information technology. Much of their work deals with privacy-related issues. Their newsletter is a good source of information.

The Electronic Frontier Foundation, 1667 K Street NW, Suite 801, Washington, DC 20006, 202/861-7700, ask@eff.org. EFF strives to protect civil rights, including the right to privacy, on emerging communication networks.

Electronic Privacy Information Center, 666 Pensylvania Ave., SE, Suite 301, Washington, DC 90003, 202/544-9240, info@epic.org. EPIC serves as a watchdog on government efforts to build surveillance capabilities into the emerging information infrastructure.

Private Citizen, PO Box 233, Naperville, IL 60566. This organization can help keep you off junk phone lists—for a price.

World Wide Web Pages

Check the *Computer Confluence* Web site for links to many of the organizations listed above, along with links to other database and privacy-related sites.

PART THREE

EXPLORING WITH COMPUTERS

NETWORKS AND GATEWAYS

NETWORKING AND TELECOMMUNICATION

Arthur C. Clarke's Magical Prophecy

If an elderly but distinguished scientist says that something is possible he is almost certainly right, but if he says that it is impossible he is very probably wrong.

The only way to find the limits of the possible is to go beyond them into the impossible.

Any sufficiently advanced technology is indistinguishable from magic.

—Clarke's Three Laws

Besides coining Clarke's laws, British writer Arthur C. Clarke has written more than 100 works of science fiction and nonfiction. His most famous work was the monumental 1968 film *2001: A Space Odyssey,* in which he collaborated with movie director Stanley Kubrick. The film's villain, a faceless English-speaking computer with a lust for power, sparked many public debates about the nature and risks of artificial intelligence.

But Clarke's most visionary work may be a paper published in 1945 in which he predicted the use of geostationary **communications satellites**—satellites that match the earth's rotation so they can hang in a stationary position relative to the spinning planet below. Clarke's paper pinpointed the exact height of the orbit required to match the movement of the satellite with the planetary rotation. He also suggested that these satellites could replace many telephone cables and radio towers, allowing electronic signals to be beamed across oceans, deserts, and mountain ranges, linking the people of the world with a single communications network.

A decade after Clarke's paper appeared, powerful rockets and sensitive radio receiving equipment made communications satellites realistic. In 1964 the first

Arthur C. Clarke

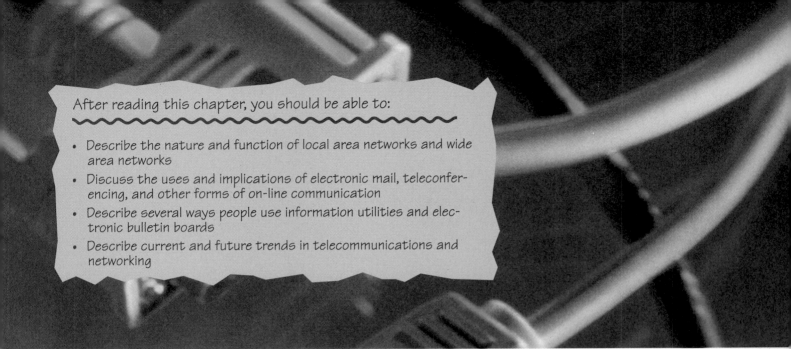

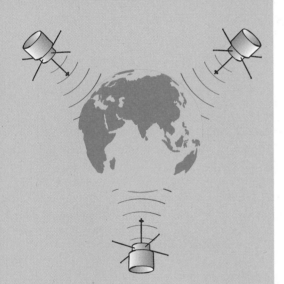

synchronous TV satellite was launched, marking the beginning of a billion-dollar industry that has changed the way people communicate.

Today Clarke is often referred to as the father of satellite communications. He lives in Sri Lanka, where he continues his work as a writer, but now he uses a personal computer and beams his words around the globe to editors using the satellites he envisioned half a century ago.

The Battle of New Orleans, the bloodiest battle of the War of 1812, was fought two weeks after the war officially ended; it took that long for the cease-fire message to travel from Washington, D.C., to the front line. In 1991, 179 years later, six hard-line Soviet communists staged a coup to turn back the tide of democratic and economic reforms that were sweeping the USSR. Within hours messages zipped between the Soviet Union and western nations on telephone and computer networks. Cable television and computer conferences provided up-to-the-minute analyses of events—analyses that were beamed to computer bulletin boards inside the Soviet Union. Networks carried messages among the resistors, allowing them to stay steps ahead of the coup leaders and the Soviet military machine. People toppled the coup and ultimately the Soviet Union, not with guns but with courage, will, and timely information.

Telecommunication technology—the technology of long-distance communication—has come a long way since the War of 1812, and the world has changed dramatically as a result. After Samuel Morse invented the telegraph in 1844, people could, for the first time, send long-distance messages instantaneously. Alexander Bell's invention of the telephone in 1876 extended this capability to the spoken voice. Today systems of linked computers allow us to send data and software across the room or around the world. The technological transformation has changed the popular definition of the word *telecommunication*, which today means long-distance *electronic* communication in a variety of forms.

In this chapter we'll look at the computer as part of a network rather than as a self-contained appliance, and we'll discuss ways such linked computers are used for communication and information gathering. We'll also consider how networks are changing the way we live and work. In the next chapter we'll explore the Internet—the global computer network at the heart of the next telecommunication revolution.

LINKING UP: NETWORK BASICS

Imagine how useful an office would be without a door.

—Douglas Engelbart, on the importance of network connections

A student uses a terminal in the library to connect with an on-line information source.

A computer **network** is any computer system that links two or more computers. Why is networking important? The answers to this question revolve around the three essential components of every computer system:

- *Hardware.* Networks allow people to share computer hardware, reducing costs and making it possible for more people to take advantage of powerful computer equipment.

- *Software.* Networks allow people to share data and software programs, increasing efficiency and productivity.

- *People.* Networks allow people to work together in ways that are otherwise difficult or impossible.

Important information is hidden in these three statements. But before we examine them in more detail, we need to look at the hardware and software that make computer networks possible.

Basic Network Anatomy

In Chapter 2 we saw how information travels among the CPU, memory, and other components within a computer as electrical impulses that move along collections of parallel wires called buses. A network extends the range of these information pulses, allowing them to travel to other computers. A computer may have a *direct connection* to a network—for example, it might be one of many machines linked together in an office—or it might have a *dial-up connection* to a network through a phone line. Either way, the computer will need some specialized hardware to complete the connection. For connecting directly, the computer needs a *network interface card;* for connecting through a phone line, it needs a *modem*.

The Network Interface

All personal computers have **ports**—sockets that allow information to pass in and out. *Parallel ports,* commonly used to connect printers to a computer, allow bits to pass through in groups of 8, 16, or 32. *Serial ports,* on the other hand, require bits to pass through one at a time. Macintoshes don't have built-in parallel ports; they generally have at least two multipurpose serial ports for connecting to printers, modems, and some networks. The standard serial port on an IBM-compatible computer is designed to attach peripherals like modems—not for connecting directly to networks. A **network interface card** (**NIC**) adds an additional serial port to the computer—one that's especially designed for a direct network connection. The network interface card controls the flow of data between the computer's RAM and the network cable. At the same time it converts the computer's internal low-power signals into more powerful signals that can be transmitted through the network. The type of card depends on the computer and the type of network connection needed, but the same general principles apply to all common network connections.

In the simplest networks two or more computers are linked by cables. But direct connection is impractical for computers that are miles or oceans apart. For computers to communicate over long distances, they need to transmit information through other paths.

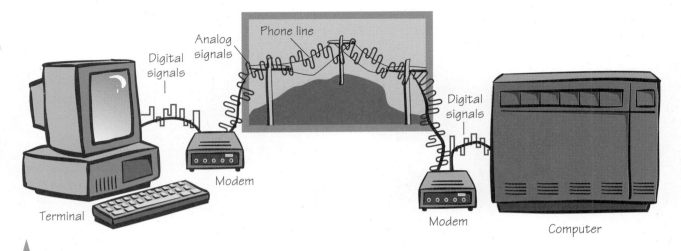

A modem converts digital signals from a computer or terminal into analog signals. The analog waves are transmitted through telephone lines to another modem, which converts them back into digital signals.

Communication à la Modem

The world is outfitted with plenty of electronic communication paths: An intricate network of cables, radio transmitters, and satellites allows people to talk by telephone between just about any two places on the planet. The telephone network is ideal for connecting remote computers, too, except it was designed to carry sound waves, not streams of bits. Before a **digital signal**—a stream of bits—can be transmitted over a standard phone line, it must be converted to an **analog signal**—a continuous wave. At the receiving end the analog signal first must be converted back into the bits representing the original digital message. Each of these tasks is performed by a **modem** (short for *modulator/dem*odulator)—a   hardware device that connects a computer's serial port to a telephone line.

An external modem (left) connects to the computer's serial port. An internal modem (above) is installed inside the computer's chassis.

An internal modem is installed on a circuit board inside the computer's chassis. An external modem sits in a box linked to the serial port. Both types use phone cable to connect to the telephone network through standard modular phone jacks. Modems differ in their transmission speeds, measured in **bits per second (bps)**. Many people use the term *baud rate* instead of bps, but bps is technically more accurate for high-speed modems. Modems today commonly transmit at 9600 bps to 28.8K (28,800) bps. In general, communication by modem is slower than communication among computers that are directly connected on a network.

Networks Near and Far

Never in history has distance meant less.

—Alvin Toffler, in *Future Shock*

Computer networks come in all shapes and sizes, but most can be categorized as either local area networks or wide area networks.

A local area network can contain a variety of computers and peripherals connected together.

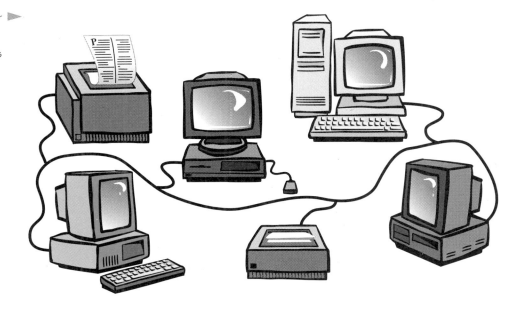

A **local area network (LAN)** is a network in which the computers are close to each other, usually in the same building. A typical local area network includes a collection of computers and peripherals; each computer and shared peripheral is an individual **node** on the network. Nodes are directly connected by cables, which serve as information highways for transporting data between machines. In a **wireless network** each node has a tiny radio or infrared transmitter connected to its network port so it can send and receive data through the air rather than through cables. Wireless network connections are especially convenient for workers who are constantly on the move.

All computers on a LAN do not have to be the same brand nor use the same operating system. For example, a single network might include Macintoshes, IBM-compatible PCs, and workstations. The computers can be connected in many different ways, and many rules and industry-defined *standards* dictate what will and won't work. Most organizations depend on *network administrators* to take care of the behind-the-scenes details so others can focus on *using* the network.

A **wide area network (WAN),** as the name implies, is a network that extends over a long distance. In a WAN each network site is a *node* on the network. Wide area networks are possible because of the web of telephone lines, microwave relay towers, and satellites that span the globe. Some WANs are private operations designed to link corporate offices. Others are public or semipublic networks used by people from a variety of organizations.

Communication Software

Whether connected by cables or a combination of modems and telephone lines, computers need some kind of **communication software** to interact. To communicate with each other, two machines must follow the same **protocol**—a set of rules for the exchange of data between a terminal and a computer or between two computers. One such protocol is transmission speed: If one machine is "talking" at 28.8K bps and the other is "listening" at 9600 bps, the message doesn't get through. Protocols include prearranged codes for messages such as "Are you ready?," "I am about to start sending a data file," and "Did you receive that file?" For two computers to understand each other, the software on both machines must be set to follow the same

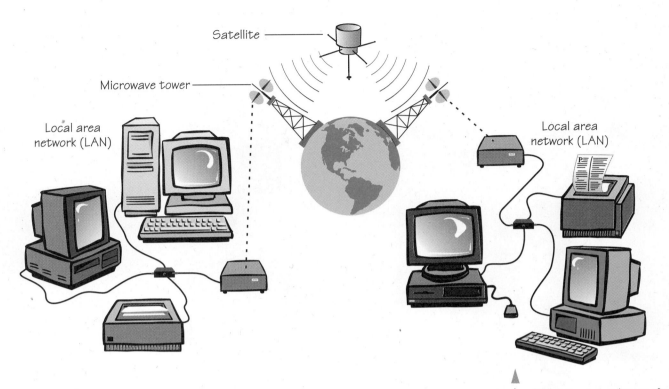

Satellite

Microwave tower

Local area
network (LAN)

Local area
network (LAN)

Wide area networks are often
made up of LANs linked by phone
lines, microwave towers, and
communication satellites.

protocols. Communication software establishes a protocol that is followed by the computer's hardware.

Communication software can take a variety of forms. For users who work exclusively on a local area network, many communication tasks are taken care of with a **network operating system (NOS),** such as Novell's Netware. Just as a personal computer's operating system shields the user from most of the nuts and bolts of the computer's operation, a network operating system shields the user from the hardware and software details of routine communication between machines.

The function and location of the network operating system depend in part on the *LAN model.* Some LANs are set up according to the **client/server model,** a hierarchical model in which one or more computers act as dedicated **servers** and all the remaining computers act as clients. Each server is a high-speed, high-capacity computer containing data and other resources to be shared with client computers. Using NOS server software, the server fulfills requests from clients for data and other resources. In a client/server network the bulk of the NOS resides on the server, but each client has NOS client software for sending requests to servers.

Many small networks are designed using the **peer-to-peer model,** which allows every computer on the network to be both client and server. In this kind of network, every user can, using NOS software, make files publicly available to other users on the network. Some desktop operating systems, including newer versions of Windows and the Macintosh OS, include all the necessary software to operate a peer-to-peer network without an additional NOS. In practice, many networks are hybrids, combining features of the client/server and peer-to-peer models.

Outside of a LAN the most familiar type of communication software is the **terminal program,** which allows a personal computer to function as a terminal. This kind of program (sometimes called a *terminal emulator*) handles phone dialing, protocol management, and miscellaneous details necessary for making a personal computer and a modem work together. With terminal software and a modem, a personal computer can communicate through phone lines with another PC, a network of

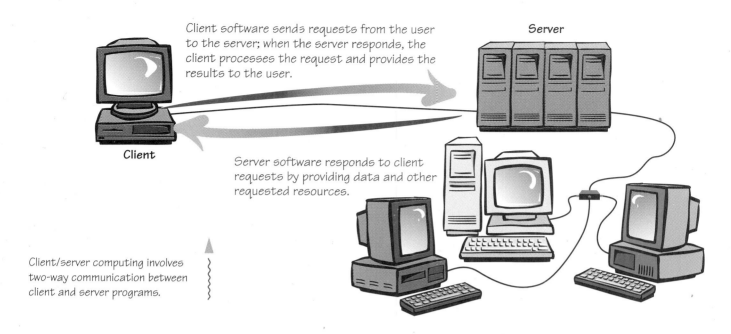

Client software sends requests from the user to the server; when the server responds, the client processes the request and provides the results to the user.

Server

Client

Server software responds to client requests by providing data and other requested resources.

Client/server computing involves two-way communication between client and server programs.

The server on the right in this photo provides software and data for client workstations throughout this factory.

computers, or more commonly a large multiuser computer. Many integrated packages, including ClarisWorks and Microsoft Works for the Macintosh, contain basic terminal emulation communication modules. The Microsoft Windows operating system package includes a basic terminal emulation program.

At the other end of the line, the communication software is usually built into the multiuser operating system of the **host system**—the computer that provides services to multiple users. This software allows a timesharing computer to communicate with several other computers or terminals at once.

The Network Advantage

With this background in mind, let's reconsider the three reasons people use networks.

- *Networks allow people to share computer hardware, reducing costs and making it possible for more people to take advantage of powerful computer equipment.*

When computers and peripherals are connected in a local area network, computer users can share expensive peripherals. Before LANs, the typical office had a printer connected to each computer. Today it's more common to find a small number of high-quality printers shared by a larger group of computers and users. In a client/server network each printer may be connected to a *print server*—a server that accepts, prioritizes, and processes print jobs.

While it may not make much sense for users to try to share a printer on a wide area network, WAN users often share other hardware resources. Many WANs include powerful mainframes and supercomputers that can be accessed by authorized users at remote sites.

• *Networks allow people to share data and software programs, increasing efficiency and productivity.*

In offices without networks people often transmit data and software by *sneaker-net*—that is, by carrying diskettes between computers. In a LAN one or more computers can be used as **file servers**—storehouses for software and data that are shared by several users. With client software a user can get software and data from any server on the LAN without taking a step. A large file server is typically a dedicated computer that does nothing but serve files. But a peer-to-peer approach, allowing any computer to be both client and server, can be an efficient, inexpensive way to share files on small networks.

Of course, sharing computer software on a network can violate software licenses (see Chapter 4) if it's not done with care. It's common for a software license to allow the program to be installed on a file server as long as the number of simultaneous users never exceeds the number of licensed copies. Some companies offer **site licenses** or **network licenses** that reduce costs for multiple copies or remove restrictions on software copying and use at a network site. (Software copying is discussed in more detail in the chapter on security and risks.)

Networks don't eliminate compatibility differences between different computer operating systems, but they can simplify data communication between machines. Users of IBM-compatible computers, for example, can't run Macintosh applications just because they're available on a file server. They can, in many cases, use data files and documents created on a Macintosh and stored on the server. For example, a poster created with PageMaker on a Macintosh could be stored on a file server so it can be opened, edited, and printed by users of PageMaker on IBM PCs. But file sharing isn't always that easy. If users of different systems use programs with incompatible file formats, they need to use *data translation software* to read and modify each other's files.

On wide area networks the transfer of data and software can save more than shoe leather; it can save time. There's no need to send diskettes by overnight mail between two sites if both sites are connected to the same network. Typically data can be sent electronically between sites in a matter of minutes.

• *Networks allow people to work together in ways that are difficult or impossible without network technology.*

Some modern software applications can be classified as **groupware**—programs designed to allow several networked users to work on the same documents at the same time. Groupware programs include multiuser appointment calendars, project management software, database management systems, and software for group editing of text-and-graphics documents.

For most LAN and WAN users, network communication is limited to sending and receiving messages. As simple as this might sound, electronic messaging profoundly changes the way people and organizations work. In the next section we'll take a close look at the advantages and implications of interpersonal communication with computers.

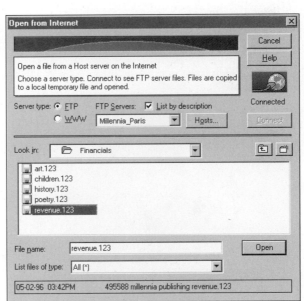

Lotus Notes, the most widely used groupware application, combines distributed databases, electronic mail, and document managment to facilitate information sharing and workgroup collaboration. Notes is a client/server application that works on Windows, OS/2, UNIX, and Macintosh platforms. The newest versions of Notes are compatible with many Internet protocols and services.

Network Communication

A t its most primitive level—a level that most computer users seldom have to deal with—a computer network is composed of electronic hardware that sends signals through cables or space. This is called the *physical layer* of a network protocol. Different types of networks are built with different physical media; the media play critical roles in determining network performance. The two most important performance variables on the

Networks Are Built on Physical Media

Type		Principle Uses	Bandwidth (megabits per second)	Maximum Operating Distance (without amplification)	Cost
Twisted pair (traditional)		Small LANs	5–15	300 feet	Low
Twisted pair (Category 5)		Large LANs	100	300 feet	High
Coaxial cable		Large LANs	10–100	600–2500 feet	Medium
Fiber optic		Network Backbones; WANs	100	1–25 miles	High
Wireless/ infrared		LANs	10	500 feet	Medium
Wireless/ radio		Connecting things that move	1.25–5	Varies considerably	High

physical layer are *bandwidth*—the amount of information that can be transmitted in a given amount of time—and maximum operating distance. Bandwidth is typically measured in *megabits* (millions of bits) per second. (Since a byte is 8 bits, a megabit is 1/8 of a megabyte. The text of this chapter is about 1/16 megabyte, or a half megabit of information. A physical medium capable of transmitting 100 megabits per second could theoretically transmit this chapter's text 200 times in one second!)

Performance of a network communication medium depends in part on the connected networking hardware, including the network interface cards in each computer. For example, when fiber optic

cable is used with hardware designed according to the protocol known as *Fast Ethernet*, the maximum cable length is about 500 yards; when network hardware uses the newer *FDDI* (Fiber Distributed Date Interface) protocol, the fiber optic cable can be as long as a mile.

The physical hardware is the substructure of the network; layers of software protocols rest on top of this substructure. Each layer breaks the job of handling communications into more manageable chunks.

The International Standards Organization (ISO) has developed a standard model for defining communication protocol layers. The Open System Interconnection (OSI) model looks like this:

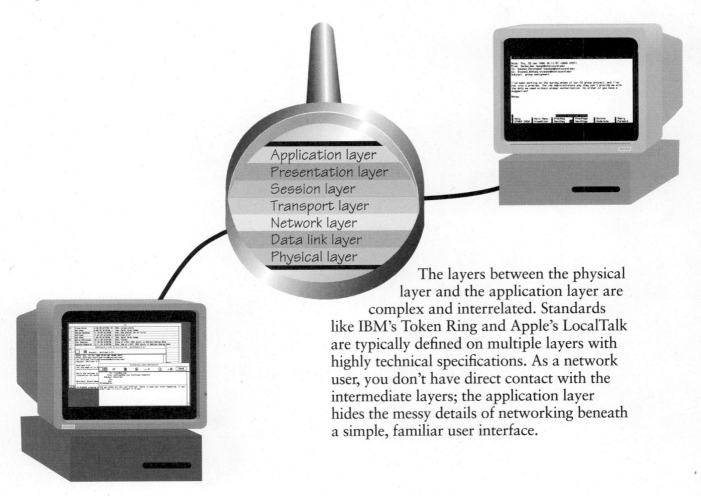

Application layer
Presentation layer
Session layer
Transport layer
Network layer
Data link layer
Physical layer

The layers between the physical layer and the application layer are complex and interrelated. Standards like IBM's Token Ring and Apple's LocalTalk are typically defined on multiple layers with highly technical specifications. As a network user, you don't have direct contact with the intermediate layers; the application layer hides the messy details of networking beneath a simple, familiar user interface.

Communicating with Electronic Mail

▲ ▲

Software: America Online.

The goal: To catch up on your mail. Using a PC, a modem, and America Online software, you're about to connect to America Online, an information service that serves as your electronic post office.

1 When you double-click on the America Online (AOL) icon, the application opens and displays a dialog box so you can identify yourself and sign in.

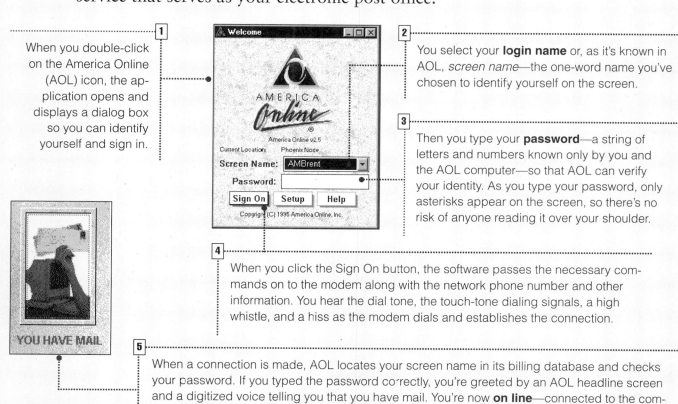

2 You select your **login name** or, as it's known in AOL, *screen name*—the one-word name you've chosen to identify yourself on the screen.

3 Then you type your **password**—a string of letters and numbers known only by you and the AOL computer—so that AOL can verify your identity. As you type your password, only asterisks appear on the screen, so there's no risk of anyone reading it over your shoulder.

4 When you click the Sign On button, the software passes the necessary commands on to the modem along with the network phone number and other information. You hear the dial tone, the touch-tone dialing signals, a high whistle, and a hiss as the modem dials and establishes the connection.

5 When a connection is made, AOL locates your screen name in its billing database and checks your password. If you typed the password correctly, you're greeted by an AOL headline screen and a digitized voice telling you that you have mail. You're now **on line**—connected to the computer system and ready to communicate. You click on the You Have Mail icon to get your mail.

ELECTRONIC MAIL AND TELECONFERENCING: INTERPERSONAL COMPUTING

No other medium gives every participant the capability to communicate instantly with thousands and thousands of people.

—Tracy LaQuey, in *The Internet Companion*

Whether you're connected to a local area network, a wide area network, or a time-sharing mainframe, there's a good chance you have access to some kind of **electronic mail (e-mail)** system. Electronic mail systems allow users to send messages (mail)

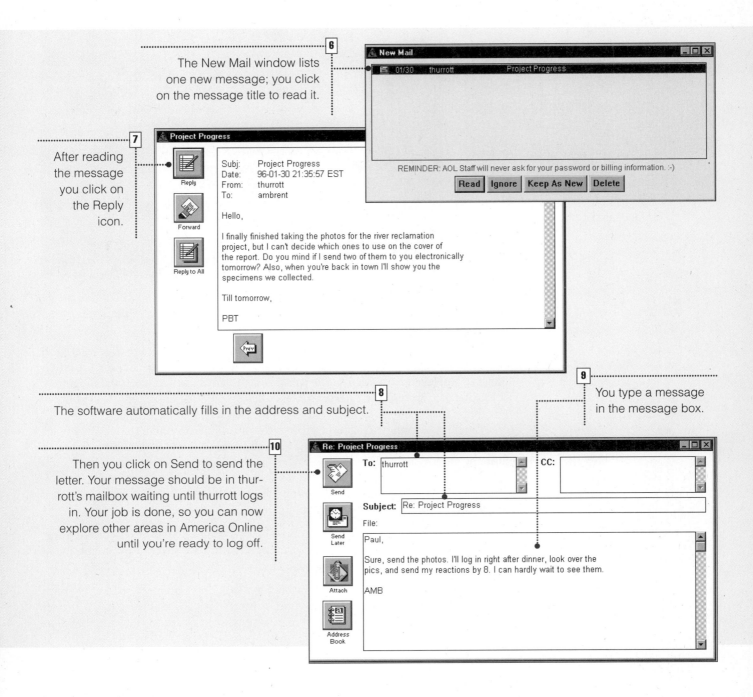

6 The New Mail window lists one new message; you click on the message title to read it.

New Mail

☑ 01/30   thurrott   Project Progress

REMINDER: AOL Staff will never ask for your password or billing information. :-)

Read | Ignore | Keep As New | Delete

7 After reading the message you click on the Reply icon.

Project Progress

Reply
Forward
Reply to All

Subj: Project Progress
Date: 96-01-30 21:35:57 EST
From: thurrott
To: ambrent

Hello,

I finally finished taking the photos for the river reclamation project, but I can't decide which ones to use on the cover of the report. Do you mind if I send two of them to you electronically tomorrow? Also, when you're back in town I'll show you the specimens we collected.

Till tomorrow,

PBT

Prev

8 The software automatically fills in the address and subject.

9 You type a message in the message box.

10 Then you click on Send to send the letter. Your message should be in thurrott's mailbox waiting until thurrott logs in. Your job is done, so you can now explore other areas in America Online until you're ready to log off.

Re: Project Progress

Send
Send Later
Attach
Address Book

To: thurrott   CC:

Subject: Re: Project Progress

File:

Paul,

Sure, send the photos. I'll log in right after dinner, look over the pics, and send my reactions by 8. I can hardly wait to see them.

AMB

from one computer to another. Details and user interfaces vary, but the basic concepts of e-mail are the same for almost all systems. Each user has a mailbox—a storage area for messages. Any user can send a mail message to the mailbox of any other user, whether or not the recipient is currently logged into the system. Only the owner of the mailbox (and the system administrator) can read the mail in that box. **UV**

A variation of electronic mail is the **teleconference**—an on-line meeting between two or more people. Many teleconferencing systems allow users to communicate in real time, just as they would by telephone. In a **real-time teleconference,** each participant sits at a computer or terminal, watching the meeting transcript scroll by on the screen and typing comments on the keyboard. Because of the give-and-take format of such systems, real-time teleconferences go by names like Chat and Talk. Whatever they're called, they tend to be chaotic, and typing responses can seem painfully

In a delayed teleconference each participant can view and respond to previously posted messages.

```
Date: October 24, 1997, 2:32PM
From: Wirehead
Subject: Re: Affirmative Action in the Computer Industry

Yesterday Robocop wrote:

> The woman only had to be qualified and not more skilled than the man to get
> the job. This is wrong.  A person should be judged on skills alone.
> No one should have to pay for the sins of the past generations.

When discrimation is eliminated and ALL people can work and communicate equally, then
and only then can we expect and accept equality.  We have an obligation to our
children and their children. A child is not born to hate. It boils down to us!  We
need to be educated then only can we educate.

Date: October 24, 1997, 3:30PM
From: Animal
Subject: Re: Affirmative Action in the Computer Industry

The problem with forgeting about past sins is that many of the sinners are still in
power, and that the people who  followed them up the ladder also have that tendency.I
hope the problem will eventually disappear as more educated people get into higher
positions.  By education, I mean people being able to see that women are as capable as
any one else.

CompuNerd

Date: October 24, 1997, 9:30PM
From: Chelsea
Subject: Re: Affirmative Action in the Computer Industry

A corporation with one ethnic group dominating will always hire employees from the
```

slow to participants watching the process on the screen. Consequently delayed teleconferences tend to be more popular and productive.

In a **delayed teleconference** (sometimes called an *asynchronous teleconference*) participants type, post, and read messages at their convenience. In effect, participants of a delayed teleconference *share* an electronic mailbox for messages related to the group's purposes. The Internet's Usenet *newsgroups*, discussed in the next chapter, are popular examples of delayed teleconferences.

E-mail, teleconferencing, and other types of on-line communication can replace many memos, letters, phone calls, and face-to-face meetings, making organizations more productive and efficient.

The Postal Alternative

Experts predict that e-mail and teleconferencing systems someday will provide stiff competition for the postal service. For many organizations electronic communication is already reducing postal expenses. Here's why:

- *E-mail is fast.* A typical electronic mail message takes no more than a few minutes from the time it's conceived until it reaches its destination—across the office or across the ocean. Electronic mail users often refer to traditional mail as "snail mail."

- *E-mail doesn't depend on location.* If you send someone an electronic message, that person can log in and read it from a computer at home, at the office, or anywhere in the world.

- *E-mail facilitates group communication.* In most e-mail systems it's no harder and no more expensive to send a message to several people than to send it to one person. Most systems allow groups to have named *aliases*—group lists—so a mail message addressed to an alias name (like faculty, office, or sales) is sent automatically to everyone in the group.

- *E-mail messages are digital data that can be edited and combined with other computer-generated documents.* Because the messages you receive by e-mail are stored in your computer electronically, you can edit text and numbers without having to retype the entire document and without wasting paper. You can easily add text from other documents stored on your computer. When you're finished, you can forward the edited document back to the original sender or to somebody else for further processing.

Bypassing the Telephone

Electronic mail and teleconferencing also offer advantages over telephones:

- *On-line communication is less intrusive than the telephone.* A ringing phone can interrupt concentration, disrupt a meeting, and bring just about any kind of activity to a standstill. Instead of shouting "Answer me now!" an e-mail message waits patiently in the mailbox until the recipient has the time to handle it.

- *On-line communication allows time shifting.* Electronic mail users aren't plagued by busy signals, unanswered rings, and "I'll get back to you" message machines. You can receive e-mail messages when you're busy, away, or asleep, and they'll be waiting for you when you have the time to pick them up. Time zones are largely irrelevant to e-mail users.

Minimizing Meetings

Teleconferences and e-mail can drastically reduce the amount of time people spend traveling to and participating in meetings. They offer several advantages for group decision making:

- *Teleconferences and e-mail allow decisions to evolve over time.* A group can discuss an issue electronically for hours, days, or weeks without the urgency of getting everything settled in a single session. New information can circulate when it's current rather than at the next meeting. Participants have time to think about each statement before responding. When organizations use teleconferences for discussion and information dissemination, meetings tend to be infrequent, short, and to the point.

- *Teleconferences and e-mail make long-distance meetings possible.* Teleconferences can include people from all over the world, and nobody needs to leave home to participate. In fact, a growing number of programmers, writers, and other information workers literally work at home, communicating with colleagues by modem.

- *Teleconferences and e-mail emphasize the message over the messenger.* In companies that rely on electronic mail and teleconferences for much of their communication, factors like appearance, race, gender, voice, mannerisms, and title tend to carry less weight than they do in other organizations. Status points go to people with good ideas and the ability to express those ideas clearly in writing.

On-line Problems

Any new technology introduces new problems, and on-line communication is no exception. Here are some of the most important:

- *E-mail and teleconferencing are vulnerable to machine failures, human errors, and security breaches.* A system failure can cripple an organization that depends on the system for critical communications.

- *E-mail can pose a threat to privacy.* The U.S. Postal Service has a centuries-old tradition of safeguarding the privacy of first-class mail. Electronic communication is not grounded in that tradition. While most e-mail messages are secure and private, there's always a potential for eavesdropping by an organization's system administrators and crafty system snoopers.

- *E-mail can be faked.* E-mail forgery can be a serious threat on a surprising number of e-mail systems. Some systems have safeguards against sending mail using someone else's ID, but none completely eliminate the threat.

- *E-mail works only if everybody plays.* Just as the postal system depends on each of us checking our mailboxes daily, an e-mail system can work only if all subscribers regularly log in and check their mail. Most people develop the habit quickly if they know important information is only available on line.

- *E-mail and teleconferencing filter out many "human" components of communication.* When Bell invented the telephone, the public reaction was cool and critical. Business people were reluctant to communicate through a device that didn't allow them to look each other in the eye and shake hands. While this reaction might seem strange today, it's worth a second look. When people communicate, part of the message is hidden in body language, eye contact, voice inflections, and other nonverbal signals. The telephone strips visual cues out of a message, and this can lead to misunderstandings. Most on-line communication systems peel away the sounds as well as the sights, leaving only words on a screen— words that might be misread if they aren't chosen carefully. What's more, e-mail and teleconferences seldom replace casual "water cooler conversations"—those chance meetings that result in important communications and connections.

Problems notwithstanding, more electronic mail and teleconferencing systems are being installed in businesses, schools, and government offices every year. If current growth rates continue, on-line messages will be as common in the workplace as photocopied memos and yellow sticky notes.

The Other Side of the Modem: An On-line Tour

You don't need to be part of a networked office to communicate electronically. If you have a computer, a modem, a telephone line, and communication software, you can connect to a variety of on-line information services that offer electronic mail, teleconferencing, and more. In this section we'll take a quick tour of some of the more popular types of on-line services that exist on the other side of the modem.

Electronic Bulletin Board Systems (BBSs)

A low-priced mountain bike for sale, a request for help from a frustrated computer gamester, an impromptu review of a new movie—you can find just about any kind of message on an electronic **bulletin board system (BBS)**. A BBS serves as an on-line version of the bulletin board at your local supermarket, coffee shop, or library; it's a place for posting messages and reading messages left by others.

A typical electronic bulletin board system is a personal computer connected by modem to a phone line. BBS software allows the computer to receive, organize, and post messages in appropriate categories automatically. A user connects to the BBS by dialing in with a modem. Most BBSs are small operations, allowing only one or a few users to connect at a time. Many BBSs operate without human supervision for long periods of time. The system operator, or *sysop,* is needed only for occasional maintenance and troubleshooting.

Many BBSs are special-purpose boards designed for people with particular needs or interests. Some examples with self-descriptive names include Handicapped Educational Exchange and PEACENET. At the other extreme, some BBSs, run by hobbyists, are available to anybody for discourse on any subject. Some charge hourly connect fees, others charge flat subscription rates, and many are free.

Many BBSs divide messages into categories called *SIGs*, for *special-interest groups*. Posting a message to a BBS SIG is similar to participating in a delayed teleconference, except the message is visible to anyone who has access to the BBS instead of a specified group of participants. BBSs also generally offer electronic mail services for users who need to communicate in private.

In addition, many bulletin boards serve as repositories for public domain software and shareware—two types of software that can be freely distributed without violating copyright laws. BBS users can **download** software—copy it from the BBS computer to their computers—and **upload** software—post it on the BBS so it's available for others. Software sharing is part of the community spirit that's common on BBSs, but it's not without problems. Two of these problems, software piracy and viruses, are discussed in the computer security and risks chapter.

This typical BBS has a text-based menu-driven interface.

On-line Databases

Chapter 8 includes a User's View example of a reference search in a library database. As the public hunger for timely information grows, more computer users are using a modem to connect to **on-line databases** for instant answers.

Many database services are designed to meet the needs of specific groups of customers. For example, Dow Jones News Retrieval Service provides business users with up-to-the-minute stock quotes, market reports, and economic news. Other services cater to lawyers, librarians, physicians, scientists, academic researchers, and other information workers. A few provide general access and relatively simple user interfaces for nonspecialized users. Users pay for database access with monthly subscription fees, connect-time fees, data fees, or some combination of the three.

Commercial On-line Services

When you use a database service, most of the information flows in one direction: from the database to your computer. General-purpose commercial **on-line information services** like America Online, CompuServe, Genie, and Prodigy, allow users to send *and* receive information the way BBSs do, but they're able to handle hundreds of users at a time. These services use timesharing computers with special software designed to make their services accessible to consumers. Services include the following:

- *News*. Most information utilities offer news, including politics, finance, sports, and weather, straight from the news wire services. News by computer can be more current, detailed, and relevant than TV or radio broadcasts. What's more, an on-line user can ask for stories on a particular topic and receive a customized list of headlines; it's like having an up-to-the-minute personalized newspaper with an index. For many people, on-line news is a convenience; for others it's a near necessity. A boat operator can monitor incoming storms before trips; a legislator can keep up with fast-breaking Capitol Hill reports from back in the home district; a visually impaired student can have a personal computer, equipped with a speech synthesizer, that reads headlines and stories aloud.

- *Research*. Most utilities offer a variety of databases, encyclopedias, media reviews, and other reference tools for students, professionals, and curious browsers.

- *Shopping*. Shopping services allow users to search catalog databases, order goods and services, and pay for them automatically with credit cards. Similar services allow travelers to peruse airline schedules and reserve tickets by computer.

- *Banking.* Many subscribers pay bills, transfer money between accounts, and take care of other banking needs using special on-line banks. Banking by modem saves gas, and there are never any lines.

- *Games.* On-line games can't compete with home computer games for graphics and fast action, but many offer opportunities to play with others who happen to be logged in. One multiplayer game on CompuServe, for example, is a perpetual interstellar battle between space ships controlled by players scattered across North America.

- *Bulletin boards.* Subscribers can mix with like-minded types using bulletin boards that cater to special-interest groups within the system. These bulletin boards work like special-interest BBSs within the context of a larger system.

- *Communication.* Electronic mail, special-interest bulletin boards, teleconferences, and other communication services allow subscribers to connect with each other for business or fun. *Gateways* link the major on-line utilities and networks to the Internet, making it possible for subscribers of competing services to send messages to each other (see Chapter 10). On-line communication is not the same as sharing a face-to-face conversation over coffee, but many people develop deep and lasting connections with people they meet on line. There have even been on-line marriages!

Most information utilities charge an initial membership fee, a minimum monthly charge, and an hourly use fee, typically less for evenings and weekends. Many have additional charges for special services like database research, banking, and personal file storage. For some services, corporations pay part of the cost in return for advertising space on the screen.

In spite of their rapid growth, the major on-line information services face an uncertain future because of the even faster growth of the Internet, the subject of the next chapter. Only time will tell whether millions of subscribers will continue to pay hourly connection fees for the convenience of a one-stop on-line service when, for a fraction of the cost, they can connect to a massive network with resources all over the planet.

Computer Networks Today: A Reality Check

The network will encourage a second information revolution.

—Al Gore, vice president of the United States

Computer networks and on-line services are, for a small but growing number of people, as important as TVs and phones. People who spend lots of time on line learn to live with the shortcomings of today's network technology, such as protocol problems, response delays, system failures, endless menu layers, inconsistent commands, high costs, and unexplainable restrictions. For serious networkers these problems are small when compared to the riches offered by the network: instantaneous communication, unlimited information, and an on-line community of kindred spirits.

Some hobbyists spend hours on line every day. For a few hard-core networkers, the world on the other side of the modem is more real and more interesting than the everyday physical world. While this may seem strange, it's not unique. Many people feel the same way about television, spectator sports, or romance novels.

For most of us the keyboard-and-characters interface is simply too primitive to be addictive. But not all computer-based communication media are built around keyboards. In the next section we'll examine technologies that are widely used today and consider others that loom on the horizon.

On-line Survival Tips

Whether you log into a BBS, an information service, or the Internet, you're using a relatively new communication medium with new rules. Here are some suggestions for successful on-line communication:

- *If you're using a metered service, do your homework off line.* Read the manual before you log in so you don't have to look things up while the meter is running. Most services allow you to compose, edit, and address messages before you log on, so you only have to pay for the time necessary to *send* messages. Plan your strategy before you connect.
- *Let your system do as much of the work as possible.* If your e-mail program can sort mail and automatically append a signature file to your mail, take advantage of those features. A good communication software package can be programmed with *macros*—customized procedures to automate repetitive tasks. Create macros to dial up, log in, download mail, and so on, without your intervention. You'll save time, keystrokes, and money.

- *Store names and addresses in an on-line address book.* E-mail addresses aren't always easy to remember and type correctly. If you mistype even a single character, your message will probably either go to the wrong person or *bounce*—come back to you with some kind of "undeliverable mail" message. An on-line address book allows you to select addresses without typing them each time you use them.
- *Cross check on-line information sources.* Don't assume that every information nugget you see on line is valid, accurate, and timely. If you "hear" something on line, treat it with the same degree of skepticism that you would if you heard it in a cafeteria or coffee shop.
- *Avoid information overload.* When it comes to information, more is not necessarily better. Search selectively. Don't waste time and energy trying to process mountains of on-line information. Information is not knowledge, and knowledge is not wisdom.

TELECOMMUNICATION TRENDS: MERGING AND EMERGING TECHNOLOGIES

Just as the automobile transformed the workplace, homestead, and landscape, so too will the communications revolution influence our lives in unknowable ways.

—Bernard Aboba, in *The On-line User's Encyclopedia*

So far we've discussed telecommunication technologies in which computers play a central and highly visible role. In other types of telecommunication, computers function behind the scenes to coordinate communication. We'll explore some examples in this section and then consider how different forms of telecommunication are coming together to provide completely new communication possibilities.

Alternative Communication Technologies

Some forms of telecommunication don't require users to type commands and messages or click on on-screen buttons. In fact, many people regularly use voice mail, facsimile transmission, video teleconferencing, and ATMs without even thinking about the fact that they're using digital computer technology to communicate.

A fax modem (top) allows a personal computer to communicate with a fax machine (above).

Facsimile Transmission

A **facsimile (fax)** machine is a fast and convenient tool for transmission of information stored in paper documents, such as typed letters, handwritten notes, photographs, drawings, book pages, and news articles. When you send a fax of a paper document, the sending fax machine scans each page, converting the scanned image into a series of electric pulses and sending those signals over phone lines to another fax machine. The receiving fax machine uses the signals to construct and print black-and-white *facsimiles* or copies of the original pages. In a sense the two fax machines and the telephone line serve as a long-distance photocopy machine.

It's not necessary to have paper copies of every faxed document, however. A computer can send on-screen documents through a fax modem to a receiving fax machine. The **fax modem** translates the document into signals that can be sent over phone wires and decoded by the receiving fax machine. In effect, the receiving fax machine acts like a remote printer for the document.

A computer can also use a fax modem to *receive* transmissions from fax machines, treating the sending fax machine as a kind of remote scanner. A faxed letter can be displayed on screen or printed to paper, but it can't be directly edited with a word processor the way an electronic mail message can. Like a scanned document, the digital facsimile is nothing more than a collection of black-and-white dots to the computer. Before a faxed document can be edited, it must be processed by optical character recognition (OCR) software.

Voice Mail and Computer Telephony

"Hi. This is Anita Chen. I'm either away from my desk or on another line. Please leave your name, number, and a message. If you prefer to talk to a receptionist, press 0." The **voice mail** system that delivers this recorded message is more than an answering device; it's a sophisticated messaging system with many of the features of an electronic mail system.

Your response is recorded in Anita's voice mailbox. When she dials the system number from any telephone and enters her ID number or password on the phone's keypad, she can listen to her messages, respond to them, forward copies to others, and delete unneeded messages. She can do just about anything she could do with an electronic mail message except edit messages electronically and attach computer documents.

In spite of its growing popularity, voice mail has detractors. Many people resent taking orders from a machine rather than being able to talk to a human operator. Many callers are frustrated by having to wade through endless voice menus before they can speak to a real person. Office workers often complain about the time-consuming processes of recording and listening to messages. At least one corporation unplugged its voice mail system three months after installing it. They concluded that communication simply went more smoothly without it.

A growing number of personal computers have **telephony** software and hardware that allows them to serve as speakerphones, answering machines, and complete voice mail systems. With the addition of a video capture board, a video camera, and a high-speed network connection, a telephone-capable desktop computer can even be used for video teleconferencing.

Video Teleconferencing

A **video teleconference** allows people to communicate face to face over long distances by combining video and computer technology. In its simplest form video teleconferencing is like two-way television. Each participant sits in a room equipped with video cameras, microphones, and television monitors. Video signals are beamed between sites so that every participant can see and hear every other participant on television monitors.

Video teleconferencing is mainly practiced in special conference rooms by groups that meet too often to travel. But some businesses now use video telephones that transmit pictures as well as words through phone lines. Specially equipped personal computers allow callers to see each other on their computer screens while they carry on phone conversations over high-speed computer networks; some even allow them to view and edit shared documents while they talk. As this kind of technology becomes more widely available, video teleconferencing is likely to become an everyday activity for many people.

Electronic Funds Transfer (EFT)

When you strip away the emotional trappings, money is just another form of information. Dollars, yen, pounds, and rubles are all just symbols that make it easy for people to exchange goods and services.

Money can be just about anything, provided people agree to its value. During the last few centuries, paper replaced metal as the major form of money. Today paper is being replaced by digital patterns stored in computer media. Most major financial transactions take place inside computers, and most money is stored on computer disks and tapes instead of in wallets and safe deposit boxes.

Money, like other digital information, can be transmitted through computer networks. That's why it's possible to withdraw cash from your checking account using an **automated teller machine (ATM)** at a bank, airport, or shopping mall thousands of miles from your home bank. An ATM is a specialized terminal linked to a bank's main computer through a commercial banking network. An ATM can handle routine banking transactions 24 hours a day, providing the kind of instant service that wouldn't be possible without computer networks.

An ATM isn't necessary for electronic funds transfer to take place. Many people have paychecks deposited automatically in checking or savings accounts and have bills paid automatically out of those accounts. These automatic transfers don't involve cash or checks, they're done inside computer networks. Many banks allow you to use your home computer or your touch-tone phone to transfer money between accounts, check balances, and pay bills.

Personal Digital Assistants

For a growing number of people whose jobs keep them on the move and away from their offices, telecommunication is a critical part of the work day. Many of these mobile professionals are using portable **personal digital assistants (PDAs)** to meet many of their communication needs. A PDA typically combines a cellular phone, a fax modem, and other communication equipment in a lightweight, wireless box that resembles a pen-based computer. A personal communicator can serve as a portable phone, a fax machine, an electronic mailbox, a pager, and a personal computer. It can be hooked to a standard phone line or, in many locations, function as a wireless communication device using the kind of radio transmitters and receivers used in cellular phones. Today PDAs are novelties to most people, but as these wireless technologies

Video conferencing hardware and software makes this long distance business meeting possible.

A personal digital assistant makes it easy to collect data for a marketing survey.

improve, many mobile professionals will be able to "stay in touch" all day, every day.

Converging Communication Technologies

The grand design keeps getting grander. A global computer is taking shape, and we're all connected to it.

—Stewart Brand, in The Media Lab

Computer networks transmit text, numbers, pictures, sounds, speech, music, video, and money as digital signals. The worldwide telephone network is being converted from analog to digital, so it's just a matter of time before most phone conversations are transmitted digitally. When the phone system is digital, the groundwork will be laid for a single, unified network for transmitting all kinds of digital information.

ISDN

Integrated Services Digital Network, more commonly called just **ISDN**, is a set of standards that combines telephones, computers, fax machines, televisions, and even mail in a single digital system. ISDN is already available in many cities in Europe and North America. But in most locations, phone lines can't handle ISDN.

The main problem is **bandwidth**—the quantity of information that can be transmitted through a channel in a given amount of time. One way to increase bandwidth in a cable is to increase the number of parallel wires in that cable—the equivalent to adding more lanes to a freeway. Another way is to increase the speed with which information passes through the cable; this is the same as increasing the speed of the vehicles on the freeway.

The bandwidth bottleneck disappears when copper phone lines and coaxial cables are replaced with high-capacity **fiber optic cables.** Fiber optic cables use light waves to carry information at blinding speeds. A single fiber optic cable can transmit half a gigabit (500 *million* bits) per second, replacing 10,000 standard telephone cables! Fiber optic cables are already used in many telephone systems, and more miles of cable are laid every year.

An all-digital, fiber optic network will improve the sound quality of phone calls and the speed of long-distance phone response. But more importantly, a digital system will be able to transmit electronic mail, computer data, fax, real-time video, and other messages more accurately and reliably. LANs will be able to hook directly into phone networks without modems.

Digital Communication Comes Home

The emergence of ISDN will have its most immediate impact on the world of work, where people depend on communication technology to get their business done. But integrated digital communication lines will eventually find their way into our homes, radically changing our lives in the process. Telephone industry predictions suggest that 90 percent of American homes may have high-bandwidth fiber optic cables installed by the year 2026. These cables will provide two-way links to the outside world for our phones, televisions, radios, computers, and a variety of other devices.

Two-way video phone conversations, universal electronic mail, customized digital newspapers, automatic utility metering, and almost unlimited entertainment options may come to pass through these glass cables in the not-too-distant future. The lines that separate the telephone industry, the computer industry, and the home entertainment industry will blur as voice, data, and pictures flow back and forth on light waves. Many services we take for granted today—video rentals, cable TV, newspapers, and magazines, for example—may be threatened or replaced by digital delivery systems of the future. Whatever happens, it's clear that communication

Because of its tremendous bandwidth and high reliability, fiber optic cable is an ideal conduit for modern digital communication.

tomorrow will be radically different from today. We'll explore these ideas further in the next chapter after we've looked at the Internet—the network of networks that will play a major role in the coming communication revolution.

SUMMARY

Networking is one of the most important trends in computing today. Computer networks are growing in popularity because they (1) allow computers to share hardware, (2) allow computers to send software and data back and forth, and (3) allow people to work together in ways that would be difficult or impossible without networks.

Local area networks (LANs) are made up of computers that are close enough to be directly connected with cables or wireless radio transmitters/receivers. Most LANs include shared printers and file servers. Wide area networks (WANs) are made up of computers separated by considerable distance. The computers are connected to each other through the telephone network, which includes cables, microwave transmission towers, and communication satellites. Before it can be transmitted on the phone network, a computer's digital signal must be converted to an analog signal using a modem.

Communication software takes care of the details of communication between machines—details like protocols that determine how signals will be sent and received. Network operating systems typically handle the mechanics of LAN communication. Terminal programs allow personal computers to function as terminals when connected to other PCs or to timesharing computers. Timesharing operating systems allow multiuser computers to communicate with several terminals at a time.

Electronic mail and teleconferencing are the two most common forms of communication between people on computer networks. E-mail and teleconferencing offer many advantages over traditional mail and telephone communication and can shorten or eliminate many meetings. But because of several important limitations, e-mail and teleconferencing cannot completely replace older communication media.

A modem can link a computer to a variety of systems, including bulletin board systems (BBSs), database services, and consumer-oriented on-line services. These services offer shopping, banking, teleconferencing, software downloading, electronic mail, and other services. But BBSs and information services may have trouble competing with the Internet, the global network that provides the same services and many more.

Other kinds of telecommunication, including fax, voice mail, electronic funds transfer, and video teleconferencing, take advantage of computer technology. As the phone network is converted to fiber optic cables with digital switching, ISDN will combine these technologies with computer telecommunication to create a unified digital communication system. The lines that separate the telephone, computer, and home entertainment industries will blur as new communication options blossom.

Chapter Review

Key Terms

analog signal	file server	peer-to-peer model
automated teller machine (ATM)	groupware	personal digital assistant (PDA)
bandwidth	host system	port
bits per second (bps)	ISDN	protocol
bulletin board system (BBS)	local area network (LAN)	real-time teleconference
client/server model	login name	server
communication satellite	modem	site license
communication software	network	telecommunication
delayed teleconference	network license	teleconference
digital signal	network interface card (NIC)	telephony
download	network operating system (NOS)	terminal program
electronic funds transfer (EFT)	node	upload
electronic mail (e-mail)	on line	video teleconference
facsimile (fax)	on-line database	voice mail
fax modem	on-line information service	wide area network (WAN)
fiber optic cable	password	wireless network

Review Questions

1. Define or describe each of the key terms above. Check your answers using the glossary.

2. Give three general reasons for the importance of computer networking. (Hint: Each reason is related to one of the three essential components of every computer system.)

3. How do the three general reasons listed in question 2 relate specifically to LANs?

4. How do the three general reasons listed in question 2 relate specifically to WANs?

5. Under what circumstances is a modem necessary for connecting computers in networks? What does the modem do?

6. Describe at least two different kinds of communication software.

7. How could a file server be used in a student computer lab? What software licensing issues would be raised by using a file server in a student lab?

8. What is the difference between electronic mail, real-time teleconferencing, and delayed teleconferencing?

9. Describe some things you can do with electronic mail that can't be done with regular mail.

10. Describe several potential problems associated with electronic mail and teleconferencing.

11. What kinds of services are available through on-line services like CompuServe, America Online, and Prodigy?

How do they differ from the services offered by smaller BBSs?

12. "Money is just another form of information." Explain this statement and describe how it relates to automated teller machines and electronic funds transfer.

Discussion Questions

1. Suppose you have an important message to send to a friend in another city, and you can use the telephone, electronic mail, real-time teleconference, fax, or an overnight mail service. Discuss the advantages and disadvantages of each. See if you can think of a situation for each of the five options in which it is the most appropriate choice.

2. Some people choose to spend several hours every day on line. Do you see potential hazards in this kind of heavy modem use? Explain your answer.

Projects

1. Use a PC and a modem to try several local BBSs. You may be able to find a directory of BBSs by contacting a local computer store or user group. Keep a log of your experiences.

2. Spend a few hours exploring an on-line service. Describe the problems you encounter in the process. Which parts of the service were the most useful and interesting?

Sources and Resources

Books

If you're interested in subscribing to an on-line service or BBS, a service-specific guidebook can save you time and money. You'll probably find several choices. Choose a *recent* book that's written in a style that appeals to you. Make sure it has a quick reference section, or, at the very least, an index. The resources listed here aren't specific to any particular service.

The On-line User's Encyclopedia: Bulletin Boards and Beyond, by Bernard Aboba (Reading, MA: Addison-Wesley, 1993). This is still one of the best books for understanding the on-line world, from the basics of modems and phone lines to on-line information services, the Internet, and beyond. As the title suggests, the book packages plenty of facts in an easy-to-find format. But it's not just another dry catalog of on-line terminology and addresses; it's a fun-to-read, intelligent guidebook for beginners and on-line experts alike.

How Networks Work, by Frank J. Derfler, Jr., and Les Freed. (Emeryville, CA: Ziff-Davis, 1993), and *Networking Illustrated,* by Eddie Kee (Indianapolis: Que, 1994). These two books follow the model popularized with the *How Computers Work* series. Both use a mix of text and graphics to illuminate the nuts and bolts of networks. Of the two, *Networking Illustrated* provides more technical detail.

The E-Mail Companion, by John S. Quarterman and Smoot Carl-Mitchell (Reading, MA: Addison-Wesley, 1994). This book provides a friendly, thorough introduction to electronic mail. How to compose mail, avoid bounces, find addresses, subscribe to mailing lists, and other topics are explained clearly.

The Elements of E-mail Style, by David Angell and Brent Heslop (Reading, MA: Addison-Wesley, 1993). When you communicate electronically, you're judged by your writing style. This fine little book is a great resource for improving your e-mail writing style. It covers everything from grammar and punctuation to layout and ASCII art.

The Virtual Community, by Howard Rheingold (Reading, MA: Addison-Wesley, 1993) This wide-ranging book explores the human components of modern computer networks. In a style that's accessible and informative, Rheingold describes how important new types of social communities are evolving on computer networks, including plenty of thought-provoking examples.

World Wide Web Pages

Computer networking technology is changing faster than publishers can print books and periodicals about it. The *Computer Confluence* Web site can connect you to up-to-date networking information all over the Internet.

10

FROM INTERNET TO INFORMATION SUPERHIGHWAY

ARPANET Pioneers Build an Unreliable Network ... on Purpose

It's a bit like climbing a mountain. You don't know how far you've come until you stop and look back.

—Vint Cerf, ARPANET pioneer and first president of the Internet Society

In the 1960s, the world of computers was a technological Tower of Babel—most computers couldn't communicate with each other. When people needed to move data from one computer to another, they carried or mailed a magnetic tape or a deck of punch cards. While most of the world viewed computers only as giant number crunchers, J. C. R. Licklider, Robert Taylor, and a small group of visionary computer scientists saw the computer's potential as a communication device. They envisioned a network that would allow researchers to share computing resources and ideas.

U.S. military strategists during those cold war years had a vision, too: They foresaw an enemy attack crippling the U.S. government's ability to communicate. The Department of Defense wanted a network that could function even if some connections were destroyed. They provided a million dollars to Taylor and other scientists and engineers to build a small experimental network. The ground-breaking result, launched in 1969, was called ARPANET, for Advanced Research Projects Agency NETwork. When a half dozen researchers sent the first historic message from UCLA to Doug Engelbart's lab at the Stanford Re-

search Institute, no one even thought to take a picture.

ARPANET was built on two unorthodox assumptions: (1) the network itself was unreliable, so it had to be able to overcome its own unreliability, and (2) all computers on the network would be equal in their ability to communicate with other network computers. In ARPANET there was no central authority because that would make the entire network vulnerable to attack. Messages were contained in software "packets" that could travel independently by any number of different paths, through all kinds of computers, toward their destinations.

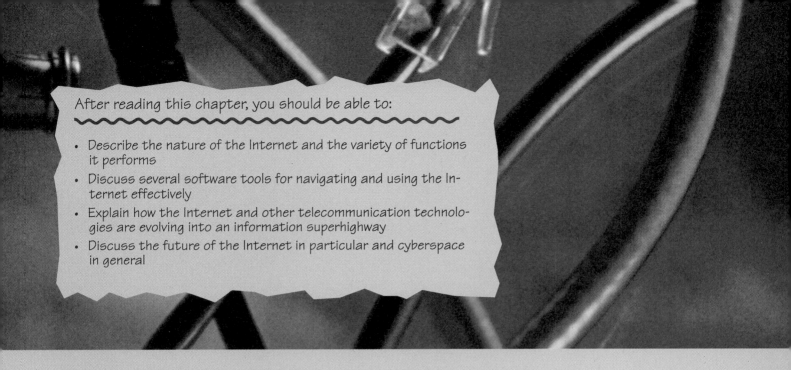

After reading this chapter, you should be able to:

- Describe the nature of the Internet and the variety of functions it performs
- Discuss several software tools for navigating and using the Internet effectively
- Explain how the Internet and other telecommunication technologies are evolving into an information superhighway
- Discuss the future of the Internet in particular and cyberspace in general

ARPANET grew quickly into an international network with hundreds of military and university sites. In addition to carrying research data, ARPANET channeled debates over the Viet Nam War and intense discussions about Space War, an early computer game. ARPANET's peer-to-peer networking philosophy and protocols were copied in other networks in the 1980s. Vint Cerf and Bob Kahn, two of the original researchers, developed the protocols that became the standard computer communication language, allowing different computer networks to be linked.

In 1990 ARPANET was disbanded, having fulfilled its research mission and spawned the Internet. In a recent interview Cerf said about the network he helped create, "It was supposed to be a highly robust technology for supporting military command and control. It did that in the Persian Gulf War. But, along the way, it became a major research support infrastructure and now has become the best example of global information infrastructure that we have."

The ARPANET pioneers have gone on to work on dozens of other significant projects and products. In the words of Bob Kahn, "Those were very exciting days, but there are new frontiers in every direction I can look these days."

The team that built the Internet included, from front to back: Bob Taylor, Vint Cerf, Frank Heart, Larry Roberts, Len Kleinrock, Bob Kahn, Wes Clark, Doug Englebart, Barry Wessler, Dave Walden, Severo Ornstein, Truett Thach, Roger Scantlebury, Charlie Herzfeld, Ben Barker, Jon Postel, Steve Crocker, Bill Naylor, and Roland Bryan.

The team that designed ARPANET suspected they were building something new and important. They couldn't have guessed, though, that they were laying the groundwork for a system that would become a universal research tool, a hotbed of business activity, a virtual shopping mall, a popular social hangout, a publisher's clearinghouse of up-to-the-minute information, and one of the most talked about institutions of the 1990s.

The Internet is a technology, a tool, and a culture. It was originally designed *by* computer scientists *for* computer scientists, and other scientists and engineers are continually adding new features. Consequently, the vocabulary of the Internet often seems like a flurry of technobabble to newcomers. But you don't need to understand every acronym and protocol to make sense of the Internet; you just need to know a little bit of *netspeak* to understand the basics. In this chapter we'll explore the many faces of the Internet without getting too deep into the technical details. If you want to know more, you can explore the resources listed at the end of the chapter.

The Internet is changing at a phenomenal pace. It's almost impossible to tell from week to week how it will evolve. Still, some trends are unmistakable. With those in mind, we'll close the chapter by looking at the future of the Internet as it evolves into an information superhighway . . . and beyond.

THE INTERNET: A NETWORK OF NETWORKS

No LAN is an Island.

—Karyl Scott, InfoWorld writer

The **Internet** is an interconnected network of thousands of networks linking academic, research, government, commercial institutions, and other organizations and individuals. The Internet includes dozens of national, statewide, and regional networks, hundreds of networks within colleges and research labs, and thousands of commercial sites. Most sites are in the United States, but the Internet has connections in almost every country in the world. Mainframes, workstations, servers, and microcomputers of almost every type are connected to the Internet.

Internet Services

The Internet provides scientists, engineers, researchers, educators, students, business people, consumers, and others with a variety of services, including these:

- *Electronic mail (e-mail).* Internet users can send mail messages, data files, and software programs to other Internet users and to users of most commercial networks and on-line services.

- *Remote login (Telnet).* Users on one system can access other host systems across the network with just a handful of commands. A user with an account at one Internet site can log in to check for mail messages or access files from anywhere else on the network.

- *Transferring files (FTP).* Some Internet sites house vast archives of shareware, public domain software, pictures, literary works, and other files. Users anywhere on the network can browse through these on-line libraries and transfer copies of interesting files back to their home machines.

- *Newsgroups (Usenet).* The Internet is the home of thousands of Usenet newsgroups—ongoing teleconferences and discussion groups on about every imaginable topic—from molecular biology to educational psychology, folk music to international politics, nudism to Buddhism, and, of course, just about anything related to computers. Millions of readers check into one or more newsgroups regularly.

- *The World Wide Web.* The hottest "place" on the Internet is the World Wide Web, a collection of multimedia documents created by organizations and users all over the world. These documents are linked in a hypertext Web that allows users to explore far and wide with simple mouse clicks. There's no easier or more entertaining way to surf the Internet . . . so far.

Many of these services seem, on the surface, to be similar to those provided by America Online and other on-line services. But the Internet is far bigger than any single network or on-line service. More importantly, the Internet is not centrally controlled by any one organization or individual. The Internet is, in a sense, a massive anarchy, unlike any other organization the world has ever seen.

Counting Connections

[The Internet is] a biological phenomenon. . . . It acts a lot like a slime mold, growing in all directions without anyone in charge.

—John Perry Barlow, cofounder of the
Electronic Frontier Foundation

In its early days the Internet connected only a few dozen computers at U.S. universities and government research centers, and the U.S. government paid most of the cost of building and operating it. Today it connects millions of computers in almost every country in the world, and costs are shared by thousands of connected organizations. It's impossible to pin down the exact size of the Internet for several reasons:

- *The Internet is growing too fast to track.* Recent public interest in the Internet has triggered explosive growth. One estimate says that the Internet adds 2 million new users every month. By some estimates, the Internet is more than tripling in size *each year!*

- *The Internet is too decentralized to quantify.* There's no Internet Central that keeps track of user activity or network connections. To make matters worse for Internet counters, some parts of the Internet can't be accessed by the general public; they're sealed off to protect private information.

- *The Internet doesn't have hard boundaries.* There are several ways to connect to the Internet; these different types of connections offer different classes of services and different degrees of interactivity. As choices proliferate, it's becoming harder and harder to know exactly what it means to "belong to the Internet."

This last point is worth a closer look because of the growing availability of Internet services to consumers. It's easier to understand the different types of Internet access if you know a little bit about the protocols that make the Internet work.

Internet Protocols

The protocols at the heart of the Internet are called **TCP/IP** (Transmission Control Protocol/Internet Protocol). They were developed as an experiment in **internetworking**—connecting different types of networks and computer systems. The TCP/IP specifications were published as **open standards,** not owned by any company. As a result, TCP/IP became the "language" of the Internet, allowing cross-network communication for almost every type of computer and network. These protocols are generally invisible to users; they're hidden deep in software that takes care of communication details behind the scenes. They define how information can be transferred between machines and how machines on the network can be identified with unique addresses.

The TCP protocols define a system similar in many ways to the postal system. When a message is sent on the Internet, it is broken into *packets*, in the same way you might pack your belongings in several individually addressed boxes before you ship it to a new location. Each packet has all the information it needs to travel independently from network to network toward its destination. Different packets might take different routes, just as different parcels might be routed through different cities by the postal system. Regardless of the route they follow, the packets eventually reach their destination, where they are reassembled into the original message. This **packet-switching** model is flexible and robust, allowing messages to get through even when part of the network is down.

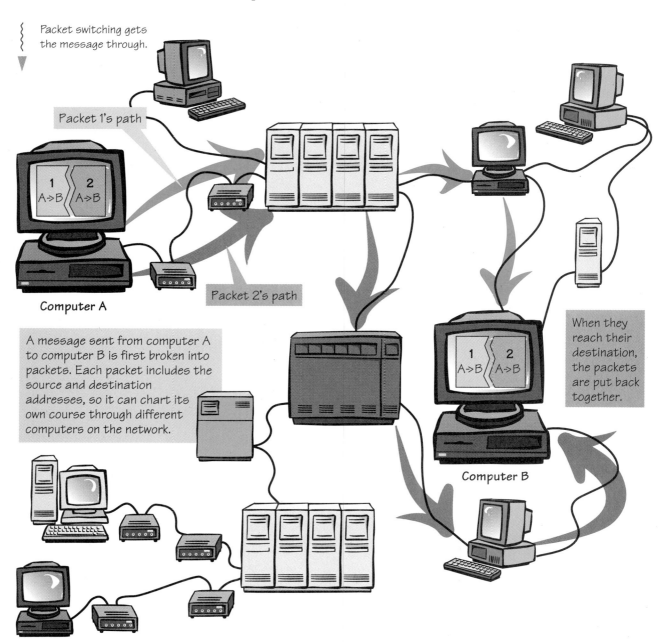

Packet switching gets the message through.

Packet 1's path

Packet 2's path

Computer A

A message sent from computer A to computer B is first broken into packets. Each packet includes the source and destination addresses, so it can chart its own course through different computers on the network.

When they reach their destination, the packets are put back together.

Computer B

The other part of TCP/IP—the IP part—defines the addressing system of the Internet. Every host computer on the Internet has a unique IP address: a string of four numbers separated by periods, or, as they say in netspeak, dots. A typical IP address might look like this: 123.23.168.22 (in netspeak, "123 dot 23 dot 168 dot 22"). Every packet includes the IP address of the sending computer and the receiving computer.

Internet Access Options

Internet *host computers*—the ones that provide services—are able to speak TCP/IP and have an IP address. There are several ways users can connect their computers to the Internet to take advantage of some or all Internet services. These are the three most common:

- **Direct (dedicated) connection.** In many schools and businesses, the computers have a dedicated, direct connection to the Internet through a LAN and have their own IP addresses. A direct connection offers several advantages: You can take full advantage of Internet services without dialing in; your files are stored on your computer, not on a remote host; and response time is usually faster, making it possible to transfer large files (like multimedia documents) quickly.

- **Dial-up terminal emulation** (via a standard serial line connection). If your computer isn't directly connected to the Internet, you can temporarily connect to an Internet host using a modem, standard telephone lines, and terminal emulation software. Your computer acts as a *dumb terminal*—just an input/output device that allows you to send commands to and view information on the host computer. E-mail messages and other files are stored on the host computer, not yours; if you want to save them on your computer, you need to download them. Not all Internet services are available through this kind of serial line connection, because many Internet programs can't communicate through a standard serial connection. A typical dial-up connection to the Internet involves using a character-based, command-line interface; graphics and multimedia files must be specially encoded before they can be transmitted or received.

- **Full-access dial-up connection.** Software that uses *SLIP* (Serial Line Interface Protocol) or *PPP* (Point to Point Protocol) allows a computer connected via high-speed modem and phone line to temporarily have full Internet access and an IP address. SLIP and PPP connections offer most of the advantages of direct connection, but response time is limited by the modem's speed.

Internet service providers generally offer several connection options at different prices. In some cities inexpensive or free access to the Internet is available through a **freenet**—a local bulletin board system designed to provide community access to on-line forums, announcements, and services.

Many computer networks, bulletin board systems, and on-line services (including America On-line, CompuServe, and Prodigy) are sometimes referred to as *outernets* because, rather than using standard Internet protocols, they provide varying degrees of Internet access through **gateways.** A gateway is a computer connected to two networks—in this context, the Internet and an outside network—that translates communication protocols and transfers information between the two. Many people refer to the worldwide system of networks and gateways that includes the Internet and all these outernets as the **Net.** Others use the term to mean just the Internet, but for most practical purposes, the distinction isn't important.

For many organizations, Internet protocols and software are more important than the Net itself. Members of these organizations communicate through **intranets**—self-contained intraorganizational networks that are designed using the same technology as the Internet. A typical intranet offers e-mail, newsgroups, file transfer, Web publishing, and other Internet-like services, but not all of these services are available to people outside the organization. For example, an intranet Web document might be accessible only to users within the organization—not to the entire Internet community. If an intranet has a gateway connection to the Internet, the gateway probably has some kind of *firewall* to prevent unauthorized communication and secure sensitive internal data. Internet and intranet security issues are discussed in the chapter called Computer Security and Risks.

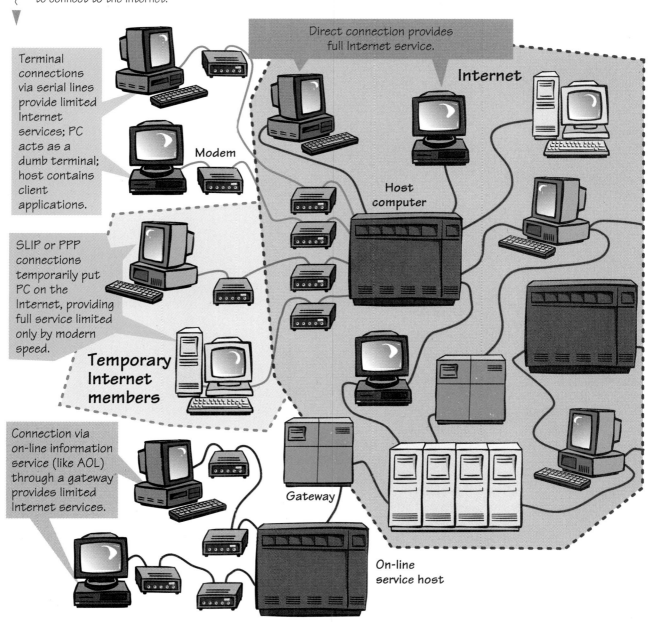

There are four general ways to connect to the Internet.

Terminal connections via serial lines provide limited Internet services; PC acts as a dumb terminal; host contains client applications.

Modem

SLIP or PPP connections temporarily put PC on the Internet, providing full service limited only by modem speed.

Temporary Internet members

Connection via on-line information service (like AOL) through a gateway provides limited Internet services.

Direct connection provides full Internet service.

Internet

Host computer

Gateway

On-line service host

COMMUNICATION APPLICATIONS

. . . after more than a century of electric technology, we have extended our central nervous system itself in a global embrace, abolishing both space and time as far as our planet is concerned.

—Marshall McLuhan, in *Understanding Media*

Internet applications, like personal computer applications, are software tools for users. But working with Internet applications is different from working with word processors or spreadsheets because of the distributed nature of the Internet and the **client/server model** used by most Internet applications. In the client/server model, a client program asks for information, and a server program fields the request and provides the requested information from databases and documents. Depending on the type of connection and the application you're using, the client might reside on your personal computer or the host computer, and the server might reside on that same host computer or another host computer elsewhere on the network. The client's user interface hides the details of the network and the server from the user.

Two different users might access the same server using completely different client applications with different user interfaces. For example, consider two users accessing the same information on the same server. A user with a direct connection might be using a point-and-click graphical user interface to explore a particular server, while another user with a dial-up terminal connection might be typing UNIX commands and seeing only text on screen.

The UNIX Connection

Because of its historical ties to academic and government research sites, the Internet is heavily populated with computers running the UNIX operating system. **UNIX,** developed at Bell Labs in the time before PCs, allows a timesharing computer to communicate with several other computers or terminals at once. UNIX has long been the operating system of choice for workstations and mainframes in research and academic settings. In recent years it has taken root in many business environments. UNIX is the most widely available multiuser operating system today. Some form of UNIX is available for personal computers, workstations, servers, and mainframes.

Until recently, some knowledge of UNIX was necessary for taking advantage of most Internet services. UNIX is still the dominant operating system on the Internet, and the DOS-like character-based UNIX interface is still widely used on Internet hosts. But many modern software applications and shells allow users to explore the Internet, gather information, order goods and services, and communicate with others without typing a word of UNIX. These graphical interfaces don't work with all Internet computers and all types of connections, so UNIX commands are a fact of life for many Internet users. **UV**

The most popular reason for connecting to the Internet is electronic mail, the person-to-person communication tool introduced in the last chapter. Thanks to the interconnected Internet, you don't need to limit your mail to people on the same network. Whether you're connected to the Internet directly or through a gateway, you can send messages to anyone with an Internet link, provided you know his or her Internet address.

Connecting to a Multiuser UNIX System

▲ ▲

Software: UNIX operating system on a remote computer; terminal software on the local personal computer.

The goal: To connect to your school's UNIX mainframe, using a PC, a modem, and a communication program.

0 The mainframe's phone number and protocols are already entered into your terminal program, so you're ready to dial up and log in. (In these examples, the characters you type are magenta so you can tell them from those typed by the computer.)

1 When you select the Dial command, the software passes the command on to the modem along with the phone number and other necessary information. You hear the dial tone, beeps, whistle, and hiss as the modem dials and establishes the connection. A few lines scroll by before the `login` prompt appears.

2 You type your *login name*—the one-word name assigned to your computer account (in this example, `sanchez`) and press Enter or Return.

3 The program then prompts you to enter your password so the host computer can verify your identity. When you type your password, it isn't echoed on the screen.

4 After you press Return, UNIX displays a system message to indicate that you've successfully logged in.

5 This UNIX system assumes you're using a VT-100 terminal— the *default* type. You're using a personal computer, not a terminal, but your software is *emulating* (imitating) a VT-100 terminal, so you don't need to change the terminal type.

6 On this particular UNIX system, you can launch a menu program that allows you to access common commands through menus. But you'll stick with the command-line interface for this example.

7 This UNIX system responds to commands typed after the `ai >` prompt.

8 The command-line interface is similar to that of MS-DOS, but the commands aren't the same. For example, LS, not DIR, lists the files in your current directory.

9 For most tasks UNIX *feels* like a single-user system, even when many users are logged in. Most UNIX systems include several programs for communication between users. You type `pine` to run a program to see if you have received any mail messages since your last login.

```
UNIX(r) System V Release 4.0


login: sanchez
Password:
AFS (R) 3.4 Login

===================================================
=Welcome to node ai.asu.edu - Sparc 20 1000 running Solaris 2.3=
        =This system is only for use authorized by ASU=
===================================================

You have mail.

Terminal type is vt100

Erase is Backspace

type 'menu' without quotes and press the enter key for our menu


ai > ls
AppleVolumes    Mail          dead.letter
Backup          Work          mbox
School          Reports       News
booklist        saved.notes   readme
ai > pine
```

To be continued . . .

Internet Addresses

Each person on the "Internet" has a unique e-mail "address" created by having a squirrel run across a computer keyboard . . .

—Dave Barry, humorist

Internet addresses look strange, but they're easy to decipher if you know how they're made. A person's e-mail address is made up of two parts separated by an at sign (@): the person's user name (login name) and the *host name*—the name of the host computer or network where the user receives mail. Here's the basic form:

`username@hostname`

The host is named using what's called the *domain name system (DNS)*—a system that translates the computer's numerical IP address into something that's easier for humans to read and remember. The DNS uses a string of *names* separated by dots to specify the exact Internet location of the host computer. The words in the domain name, like the lines in a post office address, are arranged hierarchically from little to big. If you read a domain name from right to left, you can narrow down the location from a broad category called a domain all the way to the name of the individual's host computer. (Details of this naming scheme are explained in the How It Works Box on page 238.)

This hierarchical organization makes addresses understandable, but it doesn't provide a sure-fire formula for determining an address if you don't know it. So far there's no universal "directory assistance" on the Internet. There are services and tools that can help you locate e-mail addresses if you can narrow the search down to a particular domain or network, but most users still find it's best to keep their own personal Internet address books on line, on paper, or both.

E-mail on the Internet

Since the Internet is made up of all kinds of computers on diverse networks, there's no single way to send and receive Internet mail. What you see on the screen depends on the type of Internet connection you have and the mail program you use. If you have a dial-up connection to a UNIX-based host, you might send and receive mail using a UNIX mail program like Pine, as shown in the User's View box. Pine, developed at the University of Washington, is character-based, but it has an easy-to-use menu system, an on-line address book, and a full-screen text editor that works like a word processor. **UV**

Users with full Internet connections have many more mail software options besides Pine, including programs like Eudora that take advantage of your computer's graphical user interface. A full Internet connection allows a Macintosh or Windows PC to handle the mail directly, rather than depending on a host as a post office.

Standard Internet mail messages are plain ASCII text. Formatted word processor documents, pictures, and other multimedia files usually need to be temporarily converted to ASCII using some kind of encoding scheme before they can be sent through Internet mail; these encoded documents are sent as **attachments** to text messages. Programs like Eudora and Pine take care of the encoding and decoding automatically; some mail programs require extra steps. If you're sending mail across gateways that connect outernet service providers to the Internet, you may not be able to attach files. Of course, all this is changing every day as newer, friendlier, more powerful software tools become available.

Communicating with Electronic Mail on the Internet

▲ ▲

Software: Pine, UNIX operating system.

The goal: To catch up on your mail, now that you've logged into a UNIX system and launched Pine.

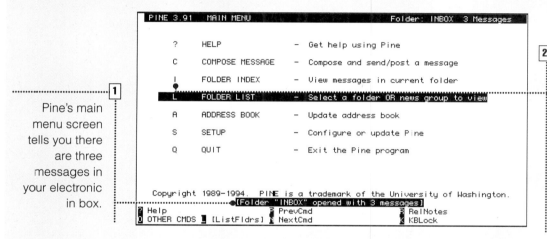

1 Pine's main menu screen tells you there are three messages in your electronic in box.

2 Pine's character-based menus don't respond to mouse clicks, but you can type one-character commands or use the arrow and Enter keys to select commands. You type **I** to view an indexed list of the messages.

3 You have three messages in your in box, including one new one from a classmate. You press Enter to view it.

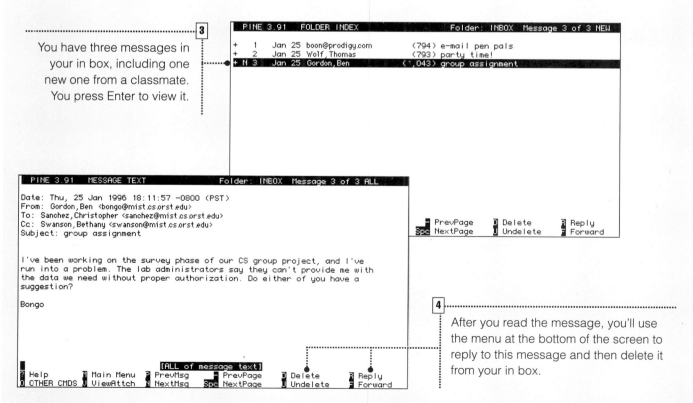

4 After you read the message, you'll use the menu at the bottom of the screen to reply to this message and then delete it from your in box.

Mailing Lists

E-mail is a valuable tool for communicating one-to-one with individuals around the globe, but it's also useful for communicating one-to-many. **Mailing lists** (sometimes called *listservs*) allow you to participate in e-mail discussion groups on special inter-est topics. Lists can be small and local, or large and global. They can be administered by a human being or automatically adminis-tered by programs with names like *Listserv* and *Majordomo*. Each group has a mailing address that looks like any Internet address.

You might belong to one student group that's set up by your instructor to carry on discussions outside of class, another group that includes people all over the world who use Macromedia Director to create multime-dia, a third that's dedicated to saving endan-gered species in your state, and a fourth that's made up of single parents in your commu-nity. When you send a message to a mailing list address, every subscriber receives a copy. And of course, you receive a copy of every mail message sent by everyone else to those lists. Subscribing to a busy list might mean receiving tens—or hundreds—of messages each day!

A popular Windows/Macintosh program called Eudora has a friendly graphical interface and powerful tools for handling, sorting, and storing messages.

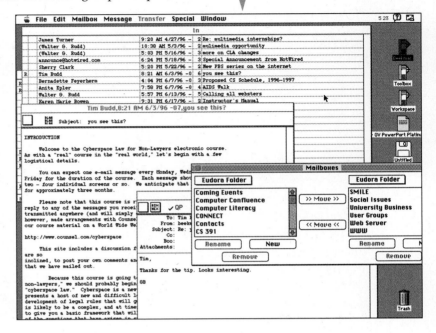

Network News

You can participate in special-interest discussions and debates without overloading your mailbox by taking advantage of the hundreds of Usenet **newsgroups**. These are public discussions that you can check into and out of whenever you want; all mes-sages are posted on virtual bulletin boards for anyone to read. There are groups for every interest and taste . . . and a few for the tasteless. Newsgroups are organized hi-erarchically, with dot names like rec.music.makers.percussion and soc.culture.french.

To explore network news-groups, you need a client pro-gram that can serve as a **news reader.** Most UNIX-based com-puters have text-only news read-ers, but graphical news readers are becoming increasingly popular. You can use a news reader or an e-mail program to post messages to newsgroups. Many Usenet newsgroups contain the same kind of free-flowing discussions you'll find in Internet mailing lists, but there's one important differ-ence: Listserv mail messages are delivered automatically to your mailbox, but you have to seek out information in Usenet groups.

| **Major Newsgroup Categories** | | |
Newsgroup Categories	Subjects	Example newsgroups
rec	Hobbies and recreation	rec.arts.movies, rec.humor.funny
sci	Scientific research	sci.space.shuttle, sci.math, sci.bio
soc	Social issues discussions	soc.culture.celtic, soc.history, soc.couples
talk	Debates about controversial issues	talk.environment, talk.politics.mideast
comp	Computers and related topics	comp.edu, comp.graphics.animation
misc	Anything that doesn't fit elsewhere	misc.consumers.house, misc.jobs.offered.

How It Works

Internet E-mail Addresses

nternet addresses are classified by *domains*. In the United States, top-level domains are general categories that describe types of organizations:

EDU	Educational sites
COM	Commercial sites
GOV	Government sites
MIL	Military sites
NET	Network administration sites
ORG	Nonprofit organizations

Outside the United States, top-level domains are two-letter country codes, such as JP for Japan.

The top-level domain name is the last part of the address. The other words, when read in reverse, provide information to narrow down the exact location on the network. They might include the name of the organization, the name of the department or network within the organization, and the name of the host computer.

The illustration on the facing page dissects the typical e-mail address so that you can see what each part means.

Here are some other examples of e-mail addresses and how to read them:

Example 1

`president@whitehouse.gov`

is pronounced President *at* whitehouse *dot* gov *and means user* President *whose mail is stored on the host* white-house *in the* government domain

Example 2

`crabbyabby@AOL.com`

means the user called crabbyabby *whose mail is handled by America Online (AOL), a commercial service provider connected to the Internet via a gateway*

As you can see, there's no single e-mail addressing scheme that applies to everybody. (When you think about it, the same can be said of postal addresses.) Still, the domain naming scheme allows you to make educated guesses about e-mail addresses.

Real-Time Communication

Mailing lists and newsgroups are delayed, or **asynchronous communication,** because the sender and the recipients don't have to be logged in at the same time. The Internet offers programs for **real-time communication,** too. *Talk* is a UNIX program that allows you to carry on split-screen typewritten conversations with anyone else who's logged in to the Internet, although response time can be sluggish over long distances during high-traffic times. *Internet Relay Chat (IRC)* allows several users to type to each other simultaneously, like a typewritten conference call. *Multi-User Dungeons (MUDs)* are real-time group adventure games. MUD players spend hours at a time doing interactive role playing and exploration in fantasy worlds that exist only in the typewritten words of the participants.

As multimedia finds its way onto the Internet, more exotic communication tools are emerging. The *MBONE* (Multicast Backbone) is a virtual network for exchange

benjamin@cs.orst.edu

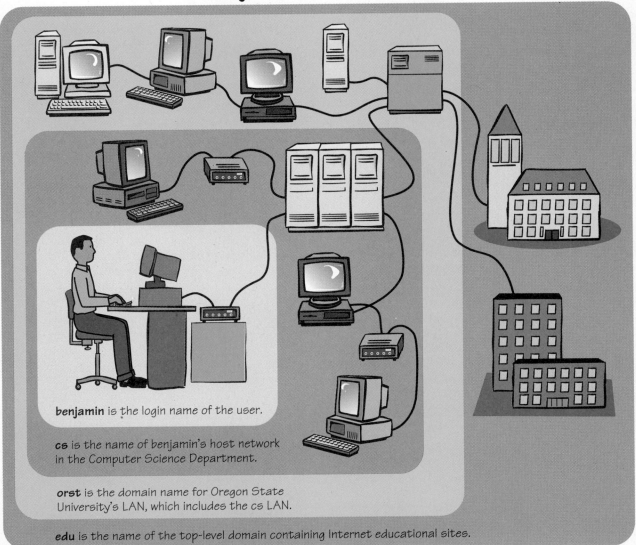

benjamin is the login name of the user.

cs is the name of benjamin's host network in the Computer Science Department.

orst is the domain name for Oregon State University's LAN, which includes the cs LAN.

edu is the name of the top-level domain containing Internet educational sites.

```
Welcome to AnotherWorld. Remember the recall! ...

The Reception
You are in the reception of the Gryphon's Rest Inn. To the west is the
bar, and to the south is the street. At the back there is a set of
stairs leading down into the ice cave. There is a small sign on the
counter. [ Exits: s w d ]
The corpse of the Beastly Fido is lying here. Saber is standing here.
(flying) (glowing) A cityguard stands here.
Camilla the receptionist is standing behind the counter here. ...she
glows with a bright light!

[124hp 103v (283992)]>
Saber looks inside a leather bag.

[124hp 103v (283992)]>
Saber flies south.

[124hp 103v (283992)]> s
Inn Street
You are on Inn Street south of the Gryphon's Rest Inn. To the east you
see the cityguard barracks, where people go to hone their combat skills.
To the south is the main street.
```

This MUD allows participants to play a variety of roles in an elaborate text-only fantasy world.

RULES OF THUMB

Netiquette

The Internet is a new type of community that uses new forms of communication. Like any society, the net has rules and guidelines of acceptable behavior. If you follow these rules of **netiquette**, you'll be doing your part to make life on the Net easier for everybody—especially yourself.

• *Say what you mean, and say it with care.* Once you send something electronically, there's no way to call it back. Compose each message carefully, and make sure it means what you intend it to mean. If you're replying to a message, double-check the heading to make sure your reply is going only to those people you intend to send it to. Even if you only took a few seconds to write your message, it may be broadcast far and wide and be preserved forever in on-line archives.

• *Keep it short and to the point.* Other people may be paying by the minute to read your message. Make sure they're getting their money's worth. Include a descriptive subject line, and limit the body to a screen or two. If you're replying to a long message, include a copy of the relevant part of the message—but not the whole message.

• *Proofread your messages.* A famous *New Yorker* cartoon shows one dog telling another, "On the Internet no one knows you're a dog." You may not be judged by the color of your hair or the clothes you wear when you're posting messages, but that doesn't mean appearances aren't important. Other people will judge your intelligence and education by the spelling, grammar, punctuation, and clarity of your messages. If you want your messages to be taken seriously, present your best face.

• *Learn the "nonverbal" language of the network.* A simple phrase like "Nice job!" can have very different meanings depending on the tone of voice and body language behind it. Since body language and tone of voice can't easily be stuffed into a modem, on-line communities have developed text-based substitutes. Here are a few:

:-) These three characters represent a smiling face. (To see why, look at them with this page rotated 90° to the right.) "Smilie" suggests the previous remark should not be taken seriously.

;-) This winking smilie usually means the previous remark was flirtatious or sarcastic.

:-(This frowning character suggests something is bothering the author—probably the previous statement in the message.

CU-SeeMe allows real-time audio/visual communication over the Internet.

of audio and video material. Some programs allow you to carry on audio conversations, turning the Internet into a toll-free long distance telephone service. (Don't throw away your telephone; these calls only work when both parties are running the same program at the same time.) Cornell University's CU-SeeMe program makes it possible to carry on two-way *video teleconferences*—provided you have some high-powered hardware and a high-speed direct connection.

`:-I`	This character represents indifference.
`:->`	This usually follows an extremely biting sarcastic remark.
`>:->`	This little devil goes with a devilish remark.
`*Flame on*`	This statement, inspired by a comic book hero, warns readers that the following statements are inflammatory.
`*Flame off*`	This means the tirade is over.

• *Avoid lynch-mob mentality.* Many otherwise timid people turn into raging bulls when they're on line. The facelessness of modem communication makes it all too easy to shoot from the hip, overstate arguments, and get caught up in a digital lynch-mob mentality. Emotional responses are fine as long as they don't cause hurt feelings or spread half-truths. On line or off, freedom of speech is a right that carries responsibility.

• *Don't be a source of electronic junk mail.* It's so easy to send multiple copies of electronic mail that many networkers generate mountains of e-mail and newsgroup postings. Target your messages carefully; if you're trying to sell tickets to a local concert, don't broadcast the message worldwide. Direct mail advertising is generally considered rude. So is excessive *cross-posting*—posting the same message to multiple groups.

• *Lurk before you leap.* People who silently monitor mailing lists and newsgroups without posting messages are called *lurkers*. There's no shame in lurking, especially if you're new to a group—it can help you to figure out what's appropriate. After you've learned the culture and conventions of a group, you'll be better able to contribute constructively and wisely.

• *Check your FAQs.* Many newsgroups and mailing lists have **FAQs** (pronounced "facks")—posted lists of *Frequently Asked Questions*. These lists keep groups from being cluttered with the same old questions and answers, but only if members take advantage of them.

• *Give something back.* The Internet is populated with volunteers who answer beginner questions, archive files, moderate newsgroups, maintain public servers, and provide other helpful services that make the Internet valuable and fun for the rest of us. If you appreciate the work these volunteers do, tell them in words and show them in actions—do your part to help the Internet community.

INFORMATION EXPLORATION APPLICATIONS

Science and art belong to the whole world, and before them vanish the barriers of nationality.

—Johann Wolfgang von Goethe

Besides communication, the most popular use of the Internet is information discovery and retrieval. With its vast storehouses of useful information, the Internet is like a huge library. Unfortunately, the Internet is a poorly organized library; you might find information on a particular topic almost anywhere. (What can you expect from a library where nobody's in charge?) One of the biggest challenges for Internet users is finding the information they need when they need it.

Telnet and FTP

To find and retrieve information located on remote Internet sites, Net explorers have traditionally used two software tools: *remote login* and *file transfer.* **Remote login** allows users to connect to hosts all over the world from just about anywhere. The protocol that makes remote login possible is called **telnet.** *Telnet* is also the name of the UNIX command that's used for remote login and the name of a program that executes the Telnet command from directly connected Macintosh and Windows PCs. On a UNIX machine, typing `telnet` followed by an Internet host name connects you to that host. On a directly connected Mac or Windows PC, you can accomplish the same thing with menus and dialog boxes using an application called Telnet. Logging into a system, remote or otherwise, usually involves typing a user ID and a password. But many hosts allow you to do remote logins as a guest—you don't need an account or password.

These sites often have archives of software and data files available for browsing and retrieval. Users of these archives take advantage of the Internet's **file transfer protocol**—commonly called **FTP**—to transfer files from remote sites to their host computers. Many sites allow *anonymous FTP* so you can collect files without officially logging in. As you might guess, the UNIX command for using FTP is FTP. Several Macintosh and Windows programs accomplish the same thing without typing UNIX commands. Telnet and FTP are often used as verbs, as in, "I'll telnet to SUMEX while you FTP those files."

Telnet and FTP are powerful tools, but they can be daunting for beginners. Since not all Internet hosts are alike, each remote login might place you in a different envi-

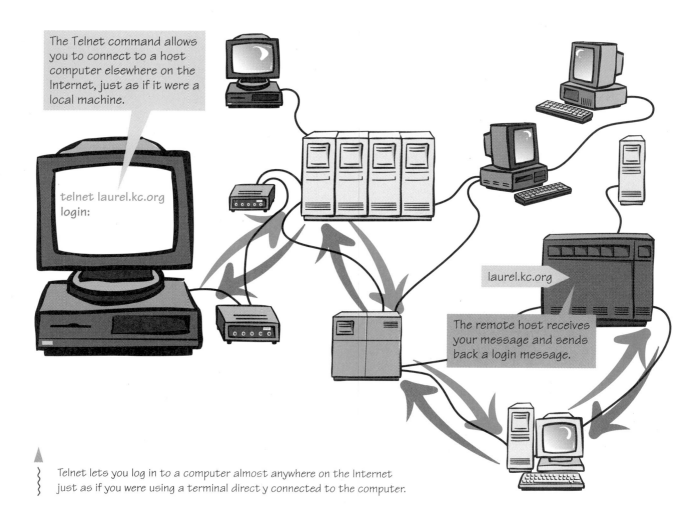

The Telnet command allows you to connect to a host computer elsewhere on the Internet, just as if it were a local machine.

telnet laurel.kc.org
login:

laurel.kc.org

The remote host receives your message and sends back a login message.

Telnet lets you log in to a computer almost anywhere on the Internet just as if you were using a terminal directly connected to the computer.

ronment with different commands. Even a simple thing like disconnecting from the host might involve typing `quit, logout, logoff, bye,` or just about anything else. Telnet explorers often have to be creative and patient.

Another challenge involves knowing where to look for the files you need. There's no up-to-date master directory of the millions of publicly available files on the Net, so data harvesters often have to depend on their own ingenuity and word of mouth (or word of keyboard) to locate the files they need.

Most files in Net archives are *compressed*—made smaller using special encoding schemes. As described in Chapter 8, file **compression** saves storage space on disk and saves transmission time when files are transferred through networks. Once files are FTPed and downloaded to a PC, they have to be decompressed before they can be used. The process is simple but requires a little background knowledge.

Other Data Mining Tools

Several client/server tools today make exploration and file retrieval less intimidating for casual users. Tools like the ones listed here hide the networking details behind simple interfaces:

- *Gopher* (named for the mascot at the University of Minnesota, where the protocol and software were first developed). Gopher is a hierarchical menu system that allows you to explore file archives by choosing from numbered menu items (with a character-based client program) or navigating through folders (with a graphical client). Gopher's interface is simple and intuitive.

- *Archie* is a program that checks hundreds of FTP sites regularly and updates a database called an Archie server. Users can use e-mail, telnet, or Archie client software to locate FTPable files.

- *Veronica* and *Jughead* are two programs that do for Gopher servers what Archie does for FTP sites; they make it easy to locate particular files quickly in Gopherspace.

- *WAIS* (Wide Area Information Server). WAIS is a distributed database system— one in which data is spread among computers on the network. Each WAIS database is a specialized library; WAIS client software searches WAIS databases in response to user queries.

All of these tools have made Net work easier, but none has captured the interest of the general public like the World Wide Web.

The World Wide Web

The World Wide Web . . . links computers all over the world, enabling people to browse through words, sounds, and images, and to publish multimedia documents. The Web is also a subculture, an art form, a communication tool, a new industry, and for more than a few obsessive souls, a way of life.

—Howard Rheingold, author of *The Virtual Community*

The **World Wide Web** (also known as **WWW, W3,** or just the **Web**) is a distributed browsing and searching system originally developed by CERN (European Laboratory for Particle Physics). Since it was introduced in 1993, it has become phenomenally popular as a system for exploring, viewing, and publishing multimedia documents on the Net. The World Wide Web has been called the Internet's "killer application" because it is popularizing the Net in the same way spreadsheets originally popularized personal computers in the business world.

Browsing the Web

At the heart of the WWW is the concept of **hypermedia,** first discussed in Chapter 7. A Web document, called a **home page** or a **Web page,** is typically made up of text and images, like a page in a book. But most Web pages aren't intended to be read sequentially like the pages in a book; they're designed to be explored through a maze of cross-referenced links. The best way to navigate and view Web pages is with a **Web browser**—a client program like Netscape Navigator (often called just Netscape) or Microsoft's Internet Explorer—that allows you to explore the Web by clicking on "hot" words or pictures on home pages. For example, if you were reading a Web page on desktop publishing and click on the hot word *clip art,* you might be transported to a page that's a directory of downloadable clip art files. The new page might be on the same *Web server* as the first page, or it might be located in another server thousands of miles away. It might be created by the same author as the first page, or it might be created by someone who doesn't even know the first author. The World Wide Web is like a giant, constantly changing hypermedia document created by thousands of unrelated authors and scattered about in computers all over the world.

Exploring the Web by clicking on hot links is easy—and addictive. In a typical Web outing you might come across a college course syllabus, a student's photo album, a digital art museum, an on-line news magazine, an up-to-the-minute satellite photo showing approaching weather patterns, a computer software company's technical help page, and an index page containing pointers to other interesting pages. Some pages contain pictures, video clips, or sounds that can be downloaded with the click of a mouse. Net browsing can't get much easier.

But this kind of random jumping isn't without frustrations. For one thing, many hot links lead to *cobwebs*—Web pages that haven't been kept up-to-date by their owners—and dead ends—pages that have been removed or moved. It can also be frustrating to try to find your way back to pages you've seen on the Web. That's why browsers like Netscape Navigator have Back and Forward buttons; you can retrace your steps and re-retrace your steps as often as you like. Of course, these buttons won't help if you're trying to find an important page from an earlier session. Most browsers include tools for keeping personal lists—called *hot lists* or *bookmarks*—of favorite sites. When you run across a page worth revisiting, you can mark it with a bookmark or store it in your hot list. Then you can revisit that site anytime by selecting it from the list.

If you're looking for a specific information resource that isn't stored in your hot list, you might be able to find it using a Web search utility like WebCrawler or Alta Vista. Each of these search utilities maintains an index of words found on Web pages. In response to a typed keyword query, a search utility provides an almost instant list of sites containing the requested word; clicking on any name in the list transports you to that list. But there's no need to search for a site if you know its exact *URL.*

The Web is built around a naming scheme that allows every information resource on the Internet to be referred to using a **Uniform Resource Locator,** or as it's more commonly known, **URL.** Like e-mail addresses, URLs look strange, but they're not hard to read once you understand the general scheme. Here's a typical URL:

`http:// www.aw.com/bc/cc`

The first part of this URL refers to the protocol that must be used to access information; it might be FTP, Gopher, news, or something else. It's most commonly *http,* for *hypertext transfer protocol,* the protocol used to transfer the Web's hypermedia documents across the net. The second part (the part following the //) is the address of the host containing the resource; it uses the same domain naming scheme used for e-mail addresses. The third part following the dot address, describes the path to the particular resource on the host—the hierarchical nesting of directories (folders) that contain the resource.

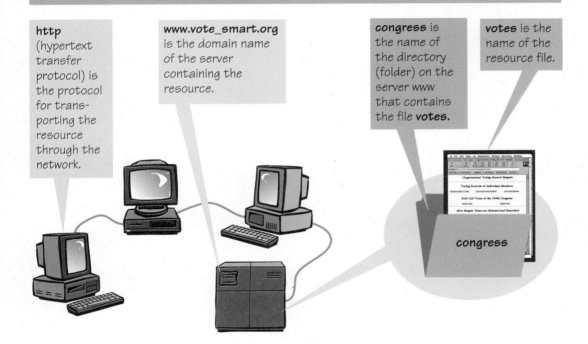

http://www.vote_smart.org/congress/votes

Anatomy of an URL.

http
(hypertext transfer protocol) is the protocol for transporting the resource through the network.

www.vote_smart.org is the domain name of the server containing the resource.

congress is the name of the directory (folder) on the server www that contains the file **votes**.

votes is the name of the resource file.

congress

Even if you don't understand the details of how URLs are constructed, they're easy enough to use; you just type the *exact* URL and let your Web browser do the rest. Of course, once you've reached the requested site, there's nothing to stop you from clicking on hot links that take you to other interesting-looking sites. . . . **UV**

Web browsers like Netscape Navigator do far more than make it easy to navigate the World Wide Web. Some browsers provide a uniform interface for the Internet so you can send and receive mail, participate in newsgroups, explore Gopher sites using the same interface you use to navigate the Web. A browser like Netscape Navigator is like an all-purpose window into the Internet.

Publishing on the Web

As exciting as it is to explore the Web with Netscape or Mosaic, it's even more exciting to create your own home pages and publish them on the Web. Most Web pages are created using a language called **HTML (Hypertext Markup Language).** An HTML document describes the format, layout, and logical structure of a hypermedia document. HTML isn't WYSIWYG; the *source document* that's transmitted from the Web server doesn't look anything like what appears on the screen. The user's Web browser translates the HTML document into the final page as it appears on the screen. You don't need to write HTML code to create a Web page; many Macintosh and Windows programs, including Microsoft Word and ClarisWorks, can convert a document into HTML automatically. Some programs, like Adobe's PageMill, are specifically designed to make Web publishing no more difficult than desktop publishing on paper.

Once you've created the HTML document, you can (if your Internet service allows it) upload it onto a Web server for the world to see. Never before has a communication medium made it so easy or inexpensive for an individual to reach such a wide audience. It doesn't matter whether you're a student, a poet, an artist, a government official, a labor organizer, or a corporate president. On the Web, all URLs

Exploring the World Wide Web

▲ ▲

Software: Netscape Navigator.

The goal: To find some graphics files to illustrate your multimedia presentation describing the future of the Internet.

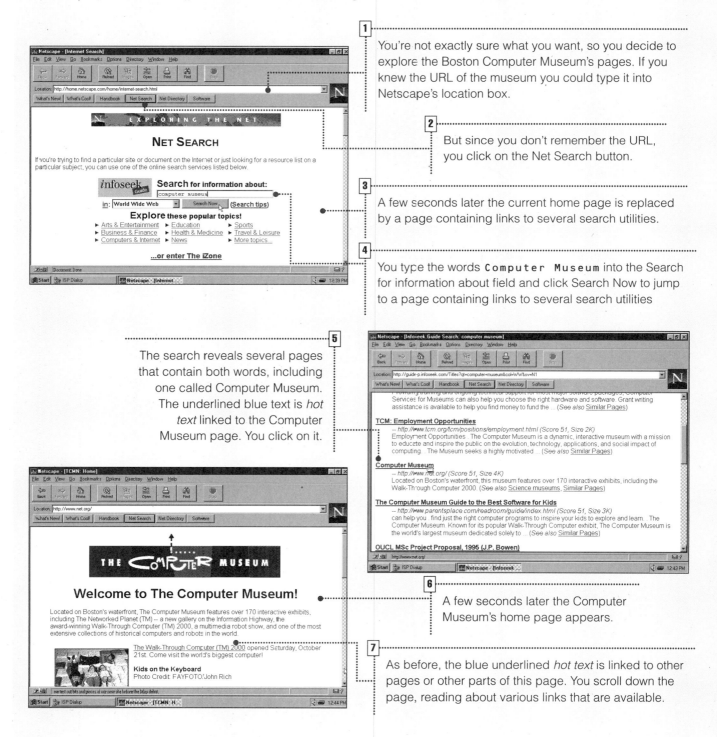

1 You're not exactly sure what you want, so you decide to explore the Boston Computer Museum's pages. If you knew the URL of the museum you could type it into Netscape's location box.

2 But since you don't remember the URL, you click on the Net Search button.

3 A few seconds later the current home page is replaced by a page containing links to several search utilities.

4 You type the words `Computer Museum` into the Search for information about field and click Search Now to jump to a page containing links to several search utilities

5 The search reveals several pages that contain both words, including one called Computer Museum. The underlined blue text is *hot text* linked to the Computer Museum page. You click on it.

6 A few seconds later the Computer Museum's home page appears.

7 As before, the blue underlined *hot text* is linked to other pages or other parts of this page. You scroll down the page, reading about various links that are available.

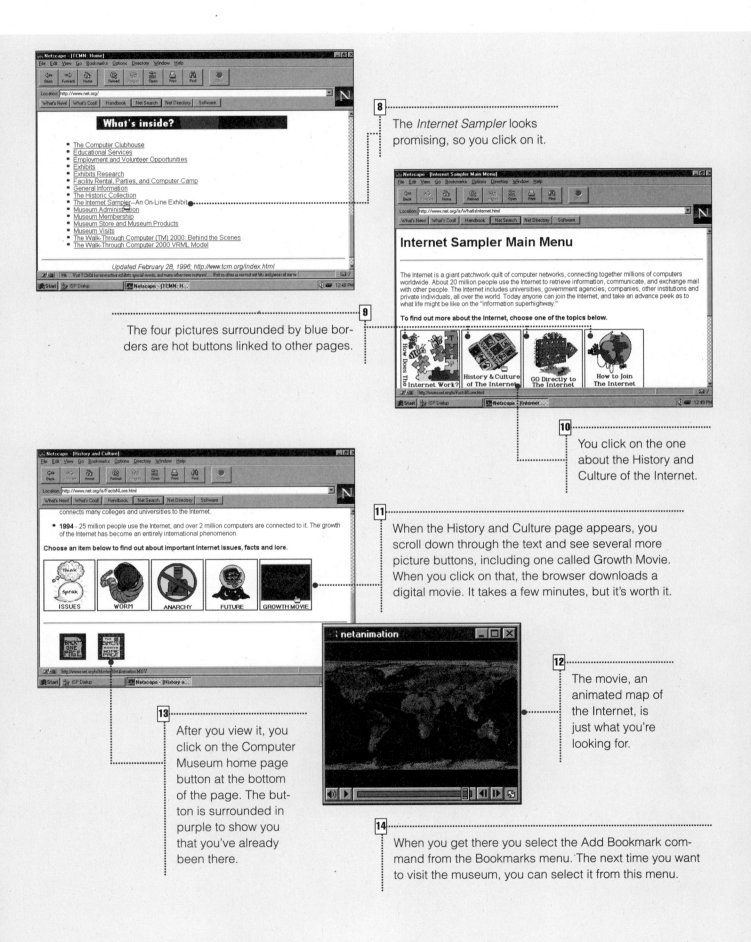

8 The *Internet Sampler* looks promising, so you click on it.

9 The four pictures surrounded by blue borders are hot buttons linked to other pages.

Internet Sampler Main Menu

The Internet is a giant patchwork quilt of computer networks, connecting together millions of computers worldwide. About 20 million people use the Internet to retrieve information, communicate, and exchange mail with other people. The Internet includes universities, government agencies, companies, other institutions and private individuals, all over the world. Today anyone can join the Internet, and take an advance peek as to what life might be like on the "information superhighway."

To find out more about the Internet, choose one of the topics below.

10 You click on the one about the History and Culture of the Internet.

11 When the History and Culture page appears, you scroll down through the text and see several more picture buttons, including one called Growth Movie. When you click on that, the browser downloads a digital movie. It takes a few minutes, but it's worth it.

connects many colleges and universities to the Internet.

- **1994** - 25 million people use the Internet, and over 2 million computers are connected to it. The growth of the Internet has become an entirely international phenomenon.

Choose an item below to find out about important Internet issues, facts and lore.

12 The movie, an animated map of the Internet, is just what you're looking for.

13 After you view it, you click on the Computer Museum home page button at the bottom of the page. The button is surrounded in purple to show you that you've already been there.

14 When you get there you select the Add Bookmark command from the Bookmarks menu. The next time you want to visit the museum, you can select it from this menu.

The Web page shown here in a background window appears when Netscape Navigator (or another browser client) processes the HTML document shown in the foreground window.

```
<HTML>
<HEAD>
<TITLE>Student Forum</TITLE>
</HEAD>
<BODY bgcolor="#e2e6e8">
<BODY>

<CENTER>
<a href="../index.html">
<img src="../images/is1.gif" border="0" alt="Information
Systems Home Page">
</a><br>
<img src="images/StdtForm.gif" ALT="[Student Forum]">
<img src="../images/orule.gif">
</CENTER>
<br><br>
<blockquote><p>This area of our site is currently under
development. Our hope is to create a place where students
can access the latest news, fun and interesting articles,
and relevant links, as well as participate in activities
related to the Information Systems topic they are
studying.</p>
<p>Ultimately, we will provide student-directed content
for the following course topics: </P>
<ul><li><a href="students.html#CompLit">Computer
Literacy/Microcomputer Applications</a></li>
<li>Management Information Systems</li>
<li>Systems Analysis and Design</li>
<li>Data Communications/Local Area Networks</li>
<li>Database Management</li>
</ul><br>
```

are created equal. In the words of writer and editor Howard Rheingold, the World Wide Web "might be important in the same way that the printing press was important. By expanding the number of people who have the power to transmit knowledge, the Web might trigger a power shift that changes everything."

From Hypertext to Multimedia

Way back in the early 1990s (!) the first World Wide Web pages were straight hypertext. Within a couple of years graphics were common, and a few cutting-edge Web pages allowed browsers to download video and audio clips to their hard disks. Today we're seeing the emergence of true interactive multimedia on the Web. Some Web pages use animated pictures, sounds, video clips, and 3-D graphic environments so effectively that they resemble CD-ROM multimedia titles (except, of course, that they're subject to slowdowns because of Internet traffic jams). Standard HTML wasn't designed to support this kind of interactive multimedia, but several software tools allow Web publishers to overcome the limitations of HTML.

The product that's currently attracting the most attention in the computer industry is **Java,** an object-oriented programming language developed by Sun Microsystems. (Object-oriented programming is discussed in the next chapter.) To take advantage of multimedia Web sites built with Java, you need a browser that has been enhanced so it can recognize Java code and a high-speed Internet connection. Even that won't guarantee a quick response time—the ever-increasing traffic on the Web makes rapid-fire response time doubtful. Still, Java and other cutting edge tools raise all kinds of fascinating possibilities for the Web. For one thing, Java promises to tear down the barriers between platforms by allowing developers to create programs that will run on all popular computers and operating systems.

The World Wide Web is changing so fast it's impossible to predict what it will look like even a few months from today. To find out what's happened to the Web since this book was printed, check the *Computer Confluence* Web site: http://www.aw.com/bc/cc.

Sun's Java programming language allows programs to create Internet-ready applications that run on virtually any computer platform.

Working the Web

The World Wide Web is so easy to navigate that it's tempting to just dive in. But like a large library, the Web has more to offer if you learn a few tricks and techniques. Of course, there are many effective ways to use a library—or the Web. You might be searching for a particular document, looking for reference materials on a particular subject, exploring connections between sources, or just browsing for interesting tidbits. Your goals should dictate your Web strategy.

● *Handle URLs with care.* The fastest way to get to a known page is to type its URL into the browser's location box. Type with care; even a single mistyped character can make an URL worthless. If you glean an URL from an e-mail message, a word processor document, or another electronic source, use the Copy and Paste commands to transfer the URL.

● *To locate material by key word or title, use Web search utilities.* These utilities (many of which can be found with Netscape Navigator's Search button) can quickly locate pages containing the key words you type. Choose (and type) your key words carefully to zero in on the pages you're after. If one search utility can't find the target information, try another.

● *Take advantage of directory pages to search by subject.* Many sites, including the popular *Yahoo* page, include hierarchical directories that organize other Web pages by subject. If you're exploring a particular subject area, this kind of directory can save hours of research time.

● *Be prepared to retrace your steps.* All browsers have buttons, menus, and other tools for going back to previously visited pages. Learn to use the tools that come with your browser effectively to save yourself time in the long run.

● *If you're in a hurry, dispense with frills.* Graphic images can take a long time to download, especially if you're using a low-speed Internet connection or working during a high-traffic period. Many Web browsers allow you to turn off image downloading so only the text is received by your computer. If you don't need the graphics, the text-only option can be a tremendous time saver, provided you're working with pages that aren't dependent on graphics for their content.

● *Organize your bookmarks.* When you find a page worth revisiting, record it as a bookmark in your hot list. Most browsers allow you to organize your bookmarks by category—a strategy that's far more effective than just throwing them all in a digital shoebox.

● *Remember why you're there.* The Web's extensive hyperlinks make it all too easy to wander off course when you're searching for important information. If you browse for cool sites when you're *not* under deadline pressures, you won't be as distractable when deadlines loom.

THE EVOLVING INTERNET

The Internet draws its power from the fact that no single interest controls it. . . . the Web is the only medium of unlimited free speech the world has ever had. And in some other, less-enlightened places, it may well be the only taste of freedom citizens of certain countries will ever have.

—Andrew Gore, *MacWeek* executive editor

The Internet started as a small community of scientists, engineers, and other researchers who staunchly defended the noncommercial, cooperative charter of the network. Today the net has swollen into a community of millions, including everybody from children to corporate executives. The rate of growth is so great that it raises questions about the Internet's ability to keep up; the amount of information transmitted may eventually be more than the Net can handle.

The Internet is constantly being expanded to handle increased traffic, but the U.S. Government no longer assumes primary responsibility for that expansion. Many funding and administrative duties have been passed on to private companies, allowing businesses to commercialize the Net. In 1995, for the first time, the number of commercial host sites on the Net exceeded the number of noncommercial sites.

The commercialization of the Internet has opened a floodgate of new services to users. People are logging into the Internet to read news and sports updates, view weather patterns, subscribe to electronic magazines, buy CDs, book flights, order clothes, track overnight parcel deliveries, and do countless other private and public transactions. Unfortunately, commercialization has also brought capitalism's dark side to the Internet. Electronic junk mail scams, get-rich-quick hoaxes, on-line credit-card thefts, e-mail forgery, digital child pornography pushing, and other sleazy activities abound. The Internet has clearly lost its innocence.

Some of these problems have technological solutions looming on the horizon. Already several software companies and banks have developed systems for circulating *digital cash* on the Internet, so we can purchase goods and services without fear of having our credit card numbers stolen by electronic eavesdroppers. To protect against e-mail forgery, many software companies are working together to hammer out standards for *digital signatures* using encryption techniques described in the computer security and risks chapter.

Many problems associated with the rapid growth and commercialization of the Internet are social problems that raise important political questions. On-line hucksterism and pornography have prompted government controls on Internet content, including the 1996 Communications Decency Act. Opponents to this law and other proposed controls argue that it's important to preserve the free flow of information; they stress the need to protect our rights to free speech and privacy on the Net. The 1996 law was declared unconstitutional by the courts, but the legal battle continues.

Questions about human rights on line probably won't be resolved by legislators and judges, though. The Internet's global reach makes it nearly impossible for a single government to regulate it. And even if the governments of the world agree to try to restrict information flow, the Net seems to have developed a mind of its own. The same decentralized, packet-switching technology that was designed to protect government messages from enemy attack today protects civilian messages from government or corporate control. In the words of Internet pioneer John Gilmore, "The Net interprets censorship as damage and routes around it."

The Road to the Information Superhighway

There will be a road. It will not connect two points. It will connect all points. Its speed limit will be the speed of light. It will not go from here to there. There will be no there there. We will all only be here.

—MCI Advertisement starring 11-year-old actress Anna Paquin

In the 1992 U.S. presidential election, Bill Clinton and Al Gore campaigned for a **National Information Infrastructure (NII)**. The NII, according to the Clinton/Gore plan, will connect computers, telephones, televisions, and information appliances of all types; it will have strict standards to ensure information security and privacy; it will provide "universal service" and affordable access for all; and it will be largely paid for by businesses with government seed money for trial projects.

The **information superhighway,** as the NII has come to be known, has captured the public imagination. The wonders of all-digital communication in the not-too-distant future are trumpeted in television commercials and talk shows. All kinds of businesses are positioning themselves to take advantage of the NII as it emerges. Lawmakers across the political spectrum embrace the information superhighway concept, although they disagree on many of the details.

Most analysts believe the Internet will evolve into the information superhighway. In fact, many people today use the terms *information superhighway* and *Internet* interchangeably. Today's Internet lacks the capacity, universal access, and variety of services we'd expect of a true information superhighway. Still, the Net has proven to be amazingly versatile and resourceful. The anarchy of the Internet allows everyone to actively participate; this approach is far more democratic than the "500 channels" model of future communication where information flows mainly from businesses and governments into homes that don't really talk back. In their book *Building the Information Highway,* Les Freed and Frank J. Derfler, Jr., claim, "If there is a working prototype for the digital highway, that prototype is the Internet."

Cyberspace: The Electronic Frontier

Cyberspace. A consensual hallucination experienced daily by billions of legitimate operators, in every nation, by children being taught mathematical concepts. . . . A graphic representation of data abstracted from the banks of every computer in the human system. Unthinkable complexity. Lines of light ranged in the nonspace of the mind, clusters and constellations of data. Like city lights, receding. . . .

—William Gibson, in *Neuromancer*

Cyberspace, in its present condition, has a lot in common with the 19th century West. It is vast, unmapped, culturally and legally ambiguous, verbally terse (unless you happen to be a court stenographer), hard to get around in, and up for grabs. Large institutions already claim to own the place, but most of the actual natives are solitary and independent, sometimes to the point of sociopathy. It is, of course, a perfect breeding ground for both outlaws and new ideas about liberty.

—John Perry Barlow, writer and cofounder of the Electronic Frontier Foundation

Science fiction writers suggest that tomorrow's networks may take us beyond the information superhighway of interactive TV and video phones into an artificial reality unlike anything we've seen before. This alternative reality has come to be known as **cyberspace,** a term coined by William Gibson in his visionary novel *Neuromancer.*

In *Neuromancer,* as in earlier works by Verner Vinge and others, travelers experience the universal computer network as if it were a physical place, a shared virtual reality, complete with sights, sounds, and other sensations. Gibson's cyberspace is an abstract, cold landscape in a dark and dangerous future world. Vinge's novella "True Names" takes place in a network hideaway where adventurous computer wizards never reveal their true names or identities to each other. Instead they take on mythical identities with supernatural abilities.

Today's computer networks, with their unsophisticated user interfaces and limited bandwidths, are light years from the futuristic visions of Vinge and Gibson. Still, the Net today is a primitive cyberspace—a world where messages, mathematics, and money can cross continents in seconds. People from all over the planet meet, develop friendships, and share their innermost thoughts and feelings in cyberspace.

Writer John Perry Barlow calls the on-line world an "electronic frontier," suggesting parallels to America's old West. The electronic frontier is populated by free-spirited souls willing to forgo creature comforts. These digital pioneers are, in a sense, building the roads and towns that will someday be used by less adventurous settlers.

The electronic frontier is far from tame. Network nomads pick digital locks and ignore electronic fences. Some explore nooks and crannies out of a spirit of adventure. Others steal and tamper with private information for profit or revenge. Law enforcement agencies, frustrated by the challenge of network terrorism, occasionally overreact with lynch-mob tactics that threaten innocent bystanders.

The electronic frontier metaphor suggests that our expanding cyberspace has its share of social problems—problems of computer crime and security that computer users, law enforcement agencies, and politicians are just beginning to understand. We'll discuss those problems and some potential solutions in a later chapter.

SUMMARY

The Internet is a network of networks that connects all kinds of computers around the globe. It grew out of a military research network designed to provide reliable communication even if part of the network failed. The Internet uses standard protocols to allow internetwork communication to occur. No single organization owns or controls the Internet.

There are several ways to connect to the Internet; these ways provide different degrees of access to Internet services. A direct connection provides the most complete and fastest service, but users can also access most Internet information through terminal connections. Several on-line services that aren't part of the Internet have gateways to the Internet; these gateways allow users to access Internet information resources and send and receive Internet mail.

Most Internet applications are based on the client/server model. The user interface for these applications varies depending on the type of connection and the type of client software used by the user. A user might type UNIX commands to a host computer or use point-and-click tools on a personal computer.

The Internet offers two broad classes of services: communication with other people and information access. The most popular communication service, e-mail, uses a standard e-mail addressing scheme so users on different networks can communicate. Mailing lists and newsgroups allow for group discussions, debates, and information sharing on particular subjects. Other communication tools allow real-time interaction, voice communication, and even video teleconferencing.

The most basic information access tools are remote login and file transfer. Modern tools like Gopher, Archie, and WAIS make it easier to find files and data on the Net. But the most popular information access tool today is the World Wide Web, the hypermedia part of the Internet. Using a Web browser like Netscape, users explore interconnected Web pages distributed across the Net. Web pages are published by private companies, public institutions, and individuals.

The Internet is evolving from a publicly funded research experiment to a commercial information superhighway. As it grows and changes, issues of privacy, security, censorship, criminal activity, and appropriate Net behavior are surfacing. Network citizens have many questions to answer as the Internet evolves from an electronic frontier into a futuristic cyberspace.

Chapter Review

Key Terms

asynchronous communication
attachment (e-mail)
client/server model
compression
cyberspace
dial-up terminal emulation
direct (dedicated) connection
FAQ (frequently asked question)
freenet
FTP (file transfer protocol)
full-access dial-up connection
gateway
home page

HTML (Hypertext Markup   Language)
hypermedia
information superhighway
Internet
Internet service provider
internetworking
Java
mailing list
National Information Infrastructure
  (NII)
net
netiquette
newsgroup

news reader
open standards
packet switching
real-time communication
remote login
TCP/IP
telnet
UNIX
URL (Uniform Resource Locator)
Web browser
Web page (home page)
World Wide Web (WWW, W3, Web)

Review Questions

1. Define or describe each of the key terms above. Check your answers using the glossary.

2. Why is it hard to know how big the Internet is today? Give several reasons.

3. Why are TCP/IP protocols so important to the functioning of the Internet? What do they do?

4. How does the type of Internet connection influence the things you can do on the Internet?

5. What is UNIX, and why is it important on the Internet?

6. Explain the relationship between the client/server model and the fact that different users might experience different interfaces while accessing the same data.

7. What do e-mail addresses and URLs have in common?

8. Why is netiquette important? Give some examples of netiquette.

9. How might you use remote login while visiting another school? What about file transfer?

10. Why is file compression important on the Internet?

11. Describe several software tools for exploring and locating information on the Internet.

12. Why is the World Wide Web important as a publishing medium? In what ways is the Web different from any publishing medium that's ever come before?

13. What new services are available as a result of the commercialization of the Internet? What new problems are arising as a result of that commercialization?

Discussion Questions

1. How did the Internet's cold war origin influence its basic decentralized, packet-switching design? How does that design affect the way we use the Net today? What are the political implications of that design today?

2. As scientists, engineers, and government officials develop plans for the national information infrastructure—the information superhighway—they wrestle with questions about who should have access and what kinds of services to plan for. Do you have any ideas of the kinds of things they might want to consider?

3. How do you think on-line user interfaces will evolve as bandwidth and processing power increase? Describe what cyberspace will feel like in the year 2000, in the year 2050, and beyond.

Projects

1. If your school has an Internet connection that's accessible to students, establish an account and use it to explore various Internet services. Keep a log of your Internet experiences.

2. Search the World Wide Web for resources related to a topic of interest to you. Keep a list of bookmarks of the most useful sites for future reference.

3. Create your own home page and link it to other pages on the World Wide Web. (When you're trying to decide what information to include in your home page, remember that it will be accessible to millions of people all over the world.)

4. Read several books and articles about cyberspace and write a paper comparing them.

Sources and Resources

Books

There are literally hundreds of books on the Internet and related topics. Many of them promise to simplify and demystify the Net, but they don't all deliver. The Internet is complex and ever-changing, so you'll probably need more than one book if you're serious about becoming a Net master. The following list contains a few particularly good titles, but you should also look for more current books released since this book went to press.

The Internet Companion, by Tracy LaQuey with Jeanne C. Ryer (Reading, MA: Addison-Wesley, 1992). This little book has some of the clearest explanations I've seen about what the Internet is, how it works, and what it all means to you. It's not an exhaustive how-to book, but it does include instructions for basic Internet activities plus a bare-bones introduction to UNIX. The tips on netiquette are especially well done.

The Whole Internet User's Guide and Catalog, by Ed Krol (Sebastopol, CA: O'Reilly & Associates, 1994). This was the first popular beginner's guide to the Internet, and it's still one of the best. Krol's writing is clear and entertaining, and he makes no attempt to oversimplify complex topics. The bulk of the book describes the Internet as an institution and explains the nuts and bolts of Internet communication, including everything from electronic mail to multiplayer games. The book concludes with a catalog of information resources available on the Internet and how to find them.

The Internet Navigator, by Paul Gilster (New York: Wiley, 1994). This big book is one of the most complete Internet guidebooks. It's especially useful if you're working with a UNIX-based system, because it covers UNIX commands and programs as well as Internet resources.

How the Internet Works, by Joshua Eddings (Emeryville, CA: Ziff-Davis, 1994). If you like the style of the *How Computers Work* series, you'll probably like this introduction. You won't learn how to use the Net, but you'll get a colorful overview of what it's all about.

UNIX Survival Guide, by Tim Parker (Reading, MA: Addison-Wesley, 1990). This is an easy-to-read UNIX tutorial for beginners. It covers the basics of logging in, editing, sending mail, manipulating files, using a modem, and more.

Atlas to the World Wide Web, by Bob Powell and Karen Wickre (Emeryville, CA: Ziff-Davis, 1995). This excellent book/CD-ROM combination is packed with helpful information about the Web. It includes a clear introduction to the Web and how it works, a beginner's guide to creating Web pages with HTML, and (mostly) a directory of worthwhile Web sites. Of course, the Web is changing quickly, so this directory could go out of date quickly if the authors and publishers don't revise it frequently.

Voices from the Net, by Clay Shirky. (Emeryville, CA: Ziff-Davis, 1995). This book focuses not on the technology of the Net but its electronic cultures. From the culture clash on the electronic frontier to evolving multiuser virtual worlds, Shirky provides clear explanations of the human issues and ideas that are shaping the Net.

Cyberspace: First Steps, edited by Michael Benedikt (Cambridge, MA: MIT Press, 1991). This collection includes works by many of the scientists, engineers, architects, artists, writers, and philosophers who are pushing the limits of today's technology toward tomorrow's cyberspace. If you're interested in future technologies and their effects on people, this book will challenge your intellect and your imagination.

Building the Information Highway, by Les Freed and Frank J. Derfler, Jr. (Emeryville, CA: Ziff-Davis, 1994). This colorful book explains the much hyped information superhighway in words and pictures. Without getting involved in technical details, it describes how we might build the digital highway and what it might be like if we do.

True Names . . . and Other Dangers, by Verner Vinge (New York: Baen Books, 1987). This collection includes "True Names," the 1981 novella that takes place inside a computer network somewhere in the future. This thought-provoking and entertaining story was years ahead of its time.

Neuromancer, by William Gibson (New York: Ace Books, 1987). Gibson's cyberpunk classic spawned several sequels, dozens of imitations, and a new vocabulary for describing a high-tech future. Gibson's future is gloomy and foreboding, and his futuristic slang isn't always easy to follow. Still, there's plenty to think about here.

Snow Crash, by Neal Stephenson (New York: Bantam, 1992). This science fiction novel lightens the dark, violent cyberpunk future vision a little with Douglas Adams-style humor. Characters regularly jack into the Metaverse, a shared virtual reality network that is in many ways more real than the phyisical world where they live. The descriptions of this alternate reality are especially thought provoking.

Periodicals

Internet World. This monthly magazine attempts to keep readers abreast of the technology and culture of the Internet. Of course, many Internet travelers aren't satisfied reading paper news that's two or three months old when they can get up-to-the-minute information on line.

World Wide Web Pages

The World Wide Web is especially good at providing information about itself. Whether you want to learn HTML, see the latest Web traffic reports, or explore the technological underpinnings of the Net, you'll find Web links at the *Computer Confluence* Web site that can help.

PART FOUR

MASTERING COMPUTERS

FROM ALGORITHMS TO INTELLIGENCE

11

SYSTEMS DESIGN AND DEVELOPMENT

Grace Murray Hopper Sails on Software

The only phrase I've ever disliked is, "Why, we've always done it that way." I always tell young people, "Go ahead and do it. You can always apologize later."

— Grace Murray Hopper

Grace Murray Hopper

Amazing Grace, the grand old lady of software, had little to apologize for when she died at the age of 85 in 1992. More than any other woman, Grace Murray Hopper helped chart the course of the computer industry from its earliest days into the present.

Hopper earned a Ph.D. from Yale in 1928 and taught math for ten years at Vassar before joining the U.S. Naval Reserve in 1943. The Navy assigned her to the Bureau of Ordinance Computation at Harvard, where she worked with Howard Aiken's Mark I, the first large-scale digital computer. She wrote programs and operating manuals for the Mark I, Mark II, and Mark III.

Aiken often asked his team, "Are you making any numbers?" When she wasn't "making numbers," Hopper replied that she was "debugging" the computer. Today that's what programmers call the process of finding and removing errors, or *bugs*, from programs. Scientists and engineers had referred to mechanical defects as bugs for decades; Thomas Edison wrote about bugs in his inventions in 1878. But when Hopper first used the term, she was referring to a *real* bug—a two-inch moth that got caught in a relay, bringing the mighty Mark II to a standstill! That moth carcass is taped to a page in a log book, housed in a Navy museum in Virginia.

Hopper recognized early that businesses could make good use of computers. After World War II she left Harvard to work on the UNIVAC I, the first general-purpose commercial computer, and other commercial computers. She played central roles in the development of the first compiler (a type of computer language translator that makes most of today's software possible) and COBOL, the first computer language designed for developing business software.

After reading this chapter, you should be able to:

- Describe the process of designing, programming, and debugging a computer program
- Explain why there are many different programming languages and give examples of several
- Explain why computer languages are built into applications, operating systems, and utilities
- Outline the steps in the life cycle of an information system and explain the purpose of program maintenance
- Explain the relationship between computer programming and computer science
- Describe the problems faced by software engineers in trying to produce reliable large systems

Throughout most of her career, Hopper remained anchored to the Navy. When she retired from the fleet with the rank of rear admiral at the age of 79, her list of accomplishments filled eight single-spaced pages in her Navy biography.

But Hopper's greatest impact was probably the result of her tireless crusade against the "We've always done it that way" mindset. In the early days of computing, she worked to persuade businesses to embrace the new technology. In later years she campaigned to shift the Pentagon and industry away from mainframes and toward networks of smaller computers. Her vigorous campaign against the status quo earned her a reputation as being controversial and contrary. That didn't bother Amazing Grace, whose favorite maxim was "A ship in port is safe, but that's not what ships are for."

Today's personal computer software is so sophisticated that it's almost invisible to the user. Just as a great motion picture can make us forget we're watching a movie, word processing software allows us to do our creative work without ever thinking about the instructions and data flowing through the computer's processor as we work. But whether you're writing a paper, solving a calculus problem, flying a simulated space shuttle, or exploring the nooks and crannies of the Internet, your imaginary environment stands on an incredibly complex software substructure. The process of creating that software is one of the most intellectually challenging activities ever done by people.

In this chapter we'll look at the process of turning ideas into working computer programs and consider the "life cycle" of a typical program. We'll examine computer languages and the ways programmers use them to create software. In addition, we'll see how computer *users* take advantage of the programming languages built into applications, operating systems, and utilities. We'll confront the problems involved in producing reliable software and consider the implications of depending on unstable software. In the process of exploring software, we'll see how the work of programmers, analysts, software engineers, and computer scientists affects our lives and our work.

HOW PEOPLE MAKE PROGRAMS

It's the only job I can think of where I get to be both an engineer and an artist. There's an incredible, rigorous, technical element to it, which I like because you have to do very precise thinking. On the other hand, it has a wildly creative side where the boundaries of imagination are the only real limitation.

—Andy Hertzfeld, codesigner of the Macintosh

Most computer users depend on professionally programmed applications—spreadsheets, database programs, page layout programs, and the like—as problem-solving tools. But in some cases it's

257

necessary or desirable to *write* a program rather than use one written by somebody else. As a human activity, computer programming is a relative newcomer. But **programming** is a specialized form of the age-old process of problem solving. Problem solving typically involves four steps:

1. *Understanding the problem.* Defining the problem *clearly* is often the most important—and most overlooked—step in the problem-solving process.

2. *Devising a plan for solving the problem.* What resources are available? People? Information? A computer? Software? Data? How might those resources be put to work to solve the problem?

3. *Carrying out the plan.* This phase often overlaps with step 2, since many problem-solving schemes are developed on the fly.

4. *Evaluating the solution.* Is the problem solved correctly? Is this solution applicable to other problems?

The programming process can also be described as a four-step process, although in practice these steps often overlap:

1. *Defining the problem*
2. *Devising, refining, and testing the algorithm*
3. *Writing the program*
4. *Testing and debugging the program*

Most programming problems are far too complex to solve all at once. To turn a problem into a program, a programmer typically creates a list of smaller problems. Each of these smaller problems can be broken into subproblems that can be subdivided in the same way. This process, called **stepwise refinement,** is similar to the process of developing an outline before writing a paper or a book. Programmers sometimes refer to this type of design as **top-down design** because the design process starts at the top, with the main ideas, and works down to the details.

The result of stepwise refinement is an **algorithm**—a set of step-by-step instructions that, when completed, solves the original problem. (Recall Suzanne's French toast recipe in Chapter 4.) Programmers typically write algorithms in a form called **pseudocode**—a cross between a computer language and plain English. When the details of an algorithm are in place, a programmer can translate it from pseudocode into a computer language.

From Idea to Algorithm

Simple things should be simple; complex things should be possible.

—Alan Kay

Let's develop a simple algorithm to illustrate the process. We'll start with a statement of the problem:

A schoolteacher needs a program to play a number-guessing game so students can learn to develop logical strategies and practice their arithmetic. In this game the computer picks a number between 1 and 100 and gives the player seven turns to guess the number. After each incorrect try, the computer tells the player whether the guess is too high or too low.

In short, the problem is to write a program that can

play a guessing game

Stepwise Refinement

The first cut at the problem breaks it into three parts: a beginning, a middle, and an end. Each of these parts represents a smaller programming problem to solve.

> *begin game*
> *repeat turn until number is guessed or seven turns are completed*
> *end game*

These three steps represent a bare-bones algorithm. In the completed algorithm, these three parts will be carried out in sequence. The next refinement fills in a few details for each part:

> *begin game*
>   *display instructions*
>   *pick a number between 1 and 100*
> *repeat turn until number is guessed or seven turns are completed*
>   *input guess from user*
>   *respond to guess*
> *end repeat*
> *end game*
>   *display end message*

The middle part of our instructions includes a sequence of operations that are repeated for each turn: everything between "repeat" and "end repeat." But these instructions are missing crucial details. How, for example, will the computer respond to a guess? We can replace "respond to guess" with instructions that vary depending on the guessed number:

> *if guess = number, then say so and quit;*
> *else if guess < number, then say guess is too small;*
> *else say guess is too big*

Finally, we need to give the computer a way of knowing when seven turns have passed. We can set a counter to 0 at the beginning and add 1 to the counter after each turn. When the counter reaches 7, the repetition stops, and the computer displays a message. That makes the algorithm look like this:

> *begin game*
>   *display instructions*
>   *pick a number between 1 and 100*
>   *set counter to 0*
> *repeat turn until number is guessed or counter = 7*
>   *input guess from user*
>   *if guess = number, then say so and quit;*
>   *else if guess < number, then say guess is too small;*
>   *else say guess is too big*
>   *add 1 to counter*
> *end repeat*
> *end game*
>   *display end message*

Control Structures

A computer can't understand this algorithm, but the pseudocode is clear to any person familiar with **control structures**—logical structures that control the order in which instructions are carried out. This algorithm uses three basic control structures: sequence, selection, and repetition.

1. A *sequence control structure* is a group of instructions followed in order from the first through the last. In our algorithm example, as in most computer languages, the sequence is the *default* structure; that is, it applies unless a statement says otherwise:

   > *display instructions*
   > *pick a number between 1 and 100*
   > *set counter to 0*

2. A *selection (or decision) control structure* is used to make logical decisions—to choose between alternative courses of action depending on certain conditions. It typically takes the form, "If (some condition is true) then (do something) else (do something else)":

   > *if guess < number, then say guess is too small;*
   > *else say guess is too big*

3. A *repetition control structure* is a *looping* mechanism. It allows a group of steps to be repeated several times, usually until some condition is satisfied. In this algorithm the indented statements between "repeat" and "end repeat" are repeated until the number is guessed correctly or the counter is equal to 7:

   > *repeat turn until number is guessed or counter = 7*
   >   *input guess from user*
   >   *. . .*
   >   *add 1 to counter*
   > *end repeat*

As our example illustrates, these simple control structures can be combined to produce more complex algorithms. In fact, any computer program can be constructed from these three control structures.

Testing the Algorithm

The next step is **testing** the algorithm. Testing of the completed program will come later; this round of testing is designed to check the *logic* of the algorithm. We can test it by following the instructions using different sets of numbers. We might, for example, use a target number of 35 and guesses of 15, 72, 52, and 35. Those numbers test all three possibilities in the if-then-else structure (guess less than target, guess greater than target, and guess equals target), and they show what happens if the player chooses the correct number. We should also test the algorithm with seven wrong guesses in a row to make sure it correctly ends a losing game.

From Algorithm to Program

> Seek simplicity and distrust it.
>
> —Alfred North Whitehead

When testing is complete, the algorithm is ready to become a program. Because the algorithm has the logical structure of a program, the process of **coding**—writing a program from the algorithm—is simple and straightforward. Statements in the algorithm translate directly into lines of *code* in whichever programming language best fits the programmer's needs.

A Simple Program

Let's look at the algorithm rewritten in C++, a variation of the popular programming language called C. (The name C doesn't stand for anything; the language grew out of a less successful language called B.) This program, like most well-written C++ programs, is organized into three parts, similar to a recipe in a cookbook:

1. The *program heading*, containing the name of the program and data files (equivalent to the name and description of the dish to be cooked).

2. The *declarations* and *definitions* of variables and other programmer-defined items (equivalent to the list of ingredients used in the recipe).

3. The *body* of the program, containing the instructions, sandwiched between curly braces ({}) (equivalent to the cooking steps).

PROGRAM HEADING

```cpp
// Game.cpp
//
// by Paul Thurrott and Gary Brent
//
```

DECLARATIONS/DEFINITIONS

```cpp
#include <iostream.h>
#include <stdlib.h>
#include <time.h>

// global variables
int number,
guess,
counter = 0;

int
main()
```

PROGRAM BODY

```cpp
{

    cout << "Welcome to the guessing game. I'll pick a number" << endl
        << "between 1 and 100 and you try to guess what it is." << endl
        << "You get 7 tries." << endl;

    // seed the random number generator so that the number is always
    // different. This example uses the current time as a seed.
srand((unsigned) time(NULL));

    // calculate a random number between 1 and 100
    number = abs(rand() % 100) + 1;

    // do this loop for each guess. Leave the loop when the guess is
    // correct or when 7 incorrect guesses have been made
    do
      {
        cout << "What's your guess?" << endl;
        cin >> guess;
        if (guess == number)
          cout << "You guessed it!" << endl;
        else
        if (guess < number)
          cout << "Too small, guess again." << endl;
        else
          cout << "Too big, guess again." << endl;
        ++counter;
      } while ( (counter < 7) && (guess != number) );

    if (guess != number)
      cout << "I fooled you 7 times - the number was "
          << number << "!" << endl;
    return EXIT_SUCCESS;
}
```

⌐ A programmer creating an animated sequence for a Hollywood film.

The program listing looks a little like a detailed version of the original algorithm, but there's an important difference: Because it's a computer program, every word, symbol, and punctuation mark has an exact, unambiguous meaning.

The words highlighted with boldface and italics in this listing are key words with predefined meanings in C++. These key words, along with special symbols like + and =, are part of the standard vocabulary of C++. The words *number, guess,* and *counter* are defined by the programmer, so they become part of the program's vocabulary when it runs. Each of these words represents a *variable*—a named portion of the computer's memory whose contents can be examined and changed by the program.

As programs go, this C++ program is fairly easy to understand. But C++ isn't English, and some statements occasionally need clarification or further documentation. For the sake of readability, most programs include *comments*—the programmer's equivalent of Post-it notes. In C++, lines that begin with double slashes (//) contain comments. The computer ignores comments; they're included to help human readers understand (or remember) something about the program.

Into the Computer

The program still needs to be entered into the computer's memory, saved as a disk file, and translated into the computer's native machine language before it can be *executed,* or run. To enter and save the program, we can use a *text editor.* A text editor is like a word processor without the formatting features required by writers and publishers. Some text editors, designed with programming in mind, provide automatic program indenting and limited error checking while the program is being typed.

To translate the program into machine language, we need translation software. The translator program might be an interpreter (a program that translates and transmits each statement individually, the way a United Nations interpreter translates a Russian speech into English) or a **compiler** (a program that translates an entire program before passing it on to the computer, as a scholar might translate the novel *War and Peace* from Russian to English). Most C translators are compilers, because compiled programs tend to run faster than interpreted programs.

A typical compiler software package today is more than just a compiler. It's an integrated *programming environment,* including a text editor, a compiler, a *debugger* to simplify the process of locating and correcting errors, and a variety of other programming utilities. **UV**

An interpreter translates a high-level program to machine language one statement at a time during execution.

High-level language program statement

Counter:=counter + 1;

Interpreter

0110011011C1
1101001001C1
001100111010

Machine-language program translation of statement

A compiler translates an entire high-level program to machine language before executing the program.

Compiler

011001101101
110100100101

Machine-language program

Counter:=counter × 1;
value(counter):=0.

High-level language program

The User's View

Programming in C++

▲ ▲

Software: Visual C++ Compiler.

The goal: To take the C++ number-guessing game program that started as an algorithm and turn it into a working piece of software.

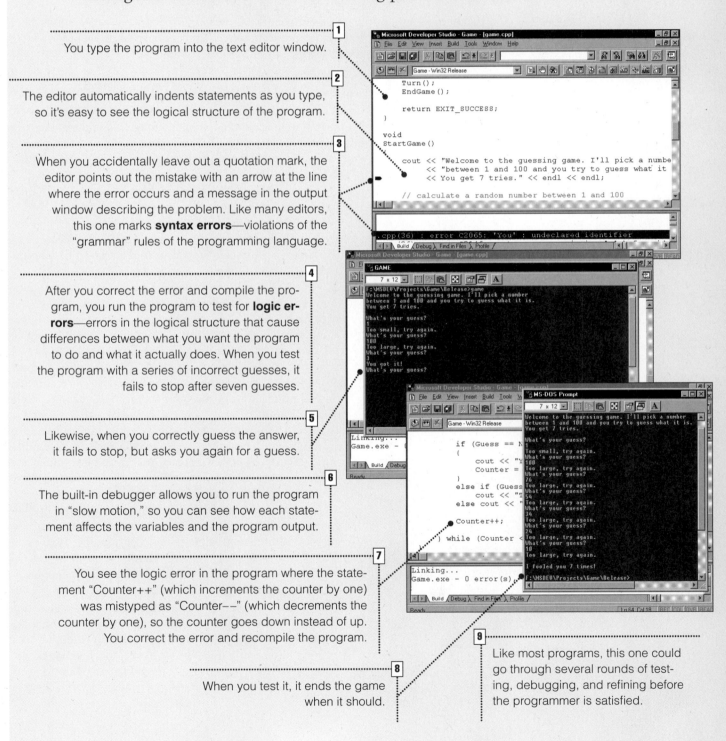

1 You type the program into the text editor window.

2 The editor automatically indents statements as you type, so it's easy to see the logical structure of the program.

3 When you accidentally leave out a quotation mark, the editor points out the mistake with an arrow at the line where the error occurs and a message in the output window describing the problem. Like many editors, this one marks **syntax errors**—violations of the "grammar" rules of the programming language.

4 After you correct the error and compile the program, you run the program to test for **logic errors**—errors in the logical structure that cause differences between what you want the program to do and what it actually does. When you test the program with a series of incorrect guesses, it fails to stop after seven guesses.

5 Likewise, when you correctly guess the answer, it fails to stop, but asks you again for a guess.

6 The built-in debugger allows you to run the program in "slow motion," so you can see how each statement affects the variables and the program output.

7 You see the logic error in the program where the statement "Counter++" (which increments the counter by one) was mistyped as "Counter--" (which decrements the counter by one), so the counter goes down instead of up. You correct the error and recompile the program.

8 When you test it, it ends the game when it should.

9 Like most programs, this one could go through several rounds of testing, debugging, and refining before the programmer is satisfied.

THE LANGUAGES OF COMPUTERS

> If one character, one pause, of the incantation is not strictly in proper form, the magic doesn't work.
>
> —Frederick Brooks, in *The Mythical Man-Month*

C++ is one of hundreds of computer languages in use today. Some are tools for professional programmers who write the software the rest of us use. Others are intended to help students learn the fundamentals of programming. Still others allow computer *users* to automate repetitive tasks and customize software applications. Since the earliest days of computing, programming languages have continued to evolve toward easier communication between people and computers.

Machine Language and Assembly Language

Every computer has a native language—a **machine language.** Similarities exist between different brands of machine language: They all have instructions for the four basic arithmetic operations, for comparing pairs of numbers, for repeating instructions, and so on. But like English and French, different brands of machine language are different languages, and machines based on one machine language can't understand programs written in another.

From the machine's point of view, machine language is all binary. Instructions, memory locations, numbers, and characters are all represented in strings of zeros and ones. Because binary numbers are difficult for people to read, machine-language programs are usually displayed with the binary numbers translated into *decimal* (base 10), *hexadecimal* (base 16), or some other number system. Even so, machine-language programs have always been hard to write, read, and debug.

The programming process became easier with the invention of **assembly language**—a language that's functionally equivalent to machine language but is easier for people to read, write, and understand. In assembly language, programmers use alphabetic codes that correspond to the machine's numeric instructions. An assembly language instruction for subtract, for example, might be SUB. Of course, SUB means nothing to the computer, which only responds to commands like 10110111. To bridge the communication gap between programmer and computer, a program called an **assembler** translates each assembly language instruction into a machine-language instruction. Without knowing any better, the computer acts as its own translator.

Because of the obvious advantages of assembly language, very few programmers write in machine language anymore. But assembly language programming is still considered *low-level* programming; that is, it requires the programmer to think on the machine's level and to include an enormous amount of detail in every program. Assembly language programming is a repetitive, tedious, and error-prone process. To make matters worse, a program written in one assembly language must be completely rewritten before it can be run on computers with different machine languages. Many programmers still use assembly language to write parts of video games and other applications for which speed

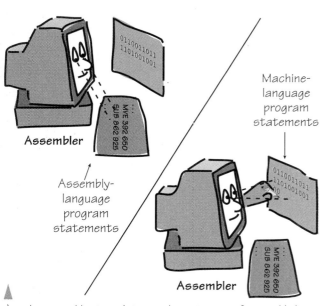

Machine-language program statements

Assembler

Assembly-language program statements

Assembler

An assembler translates each statement of assembly language into the corresponding machine-language statement.

and direct communication with hardware are critical. But most programmers today think and write on a higher level.

High-level Languages

High-level languages, which fall somewhere between natural human languages and precise machine languages, were developed during the early 1950s to simplify and streamline the programming process. Languages like FORTRAN and COBOL made it possible for scientists, engineers, and business people to write programs using familiar terminology and notation rather than cryptic machine instructions. Today programmers can choose from hundreds of other high-level languages.

Interpreters and compilers translate high-level programs into machine language. Whether interpreted or compiled, a single statement from a high-level program turns into several machine-language statements. A high-level language hides most of the nitty-gritty details of the machine operations from the programmer. As a result, it's easier for the programmer to think about the overall logic of the program—the big ideas.

Besides being easier to write and debug, high-level programs have the advantage of being *transportable* between machines. A program written in standard C++, like the guessing-game program we developed in this chapter, can be compiled and run on any computer with a standard C++ compiler. Since C++ compilers are available for all types of computers, this program can run as written just about anywhere.

Transporting a program to a new machine isn't always that easy. Most high-level programs need to be *partially* rewritten to adjust to differences between hardware, compilers, operating systems, and user interfaces. For example, programmers might need to rewrite 20 percent of the code when translating the Windows version of an application program into a Macintosh version, or vice versa. Still, high-level programs are far more portable than programs written in assembly and machine languages.

Multilingual Machines

Of the hundreds of high-level languages that have been developed, a few have become well known because of their widespread use. These include

- *FORTRAN* (*Formula Tran*slation), the first commercial high-level programming language, was designed at IBM in the 1950s to solve scientific and engineering problems. Modernized versions of FORTRAN are still used by many scientists and engineers today.

- *COBOL* (*Common Business Oriented Language*) was developed when the U.S. government in 1960 demanded a new language oriented toward business data processing problems. COBOL programmers still work in many data processing shops around the world.

- *LISP* (*List* Processing) was developed at MIT in the late 1950s to process non-numeric data like characters, words, and other symbols. LISP is widely used in artificial intelligence research, in part because it's easy to write LISP programs that can write other programs.

- *BASIC* (*Beginner's All-purpose Symbolic Instruction Code*) was developed in the mid-1960s as an easy-to-learn, interactive alternative to FORTRAN for beginning programmers. Before BASIC, a student typically had to submit a program, wait hours for output from a compiler, and repeat the process until every error was corrected. Because BASIC was interpreted line by line rather than compiled as a whole, it could provide instant feedback as students typed statements and commands into their terminals. When personal computers appeared, BASIC enjoyed unprecedented popularity among students, hobbyists, and programmers. Over the years BASIC has evolved into a powerful, modern programming tool for amateur and professional programmers.

- *Pascal* (named for the 17th-century French mathematician, inventor, philosopher, and mystic) was developed in the early 1970s as an alternative to BASIC for beginning programmers. Pascal was designed to encourage *structured programming*, a technique described in the next section. Pascal is still popular as a student language but it is seldom used by professional programmers.

- *C* was invented at Bell Labs in the early 1970s as a tool for programming operating systems like UNIX. C is a complex language that's difficult to learn. But its power, flexibility, and efficiency have made it the language of choice for most professionals who program personal computers.

- *Ada* (named for Ada Lovelace, the programming pioneer profiled in Chapter 1) is a massive language developed in the late 1970s for the U.S. Defense Department. Ada never caught on outside the walls of the military establishment.

- *PROLOG* (*Programming Logic*) is a popular language for artificial intelligence programming. As the name implies, PROLOG is designed for working with logical relationships between facts.

- *LOGO*, described in Chapter 14, is a dialect of LISP specially designed for children.

```
program Game (input, output);
(* Programmed by Clay Cowgill  and David Stuve *)

(*-------------------------------------------------------------*)

var Number, Guess, Counter : integer
(*-------------------------------------------------------------*)
begin
writeln('Welcome to the guessing game. I'll pick a number');
writeln('between 1 and 100, and you try to guess what it is.');
writeln('You get 7 tries.');
(* Calculate a random number between 1 and 100 *)
Number := abs (Random mod 100) + 1;
Counter := 0;
repeat (* turn *)
    writeln('What's your guess?');
    readln(Guess);
    if Guess = Number then
        writeln('You got it!')
    else
        if Guess < Number then
            writeln('Too small, try again.');
        else writeln('Too big, guess again.');
    Counter := Counter + 1;
until (Guess = Number) or (Counter = 7)
if Guess <> Number then
    begin
        writeln('I fooled you 7 times!');
    end
end.
```

Pascal is popular as a student language because it's easy to learn and it encourages good programming style. This program listing shows the number-guessing game program in standard Pascal.

Programming Methodologies

Programmers work the way medieval craftsmen built cathedrals—one stone at a time.

—Mitch Kapor

A programming language can be a powerful tool in the hands of a skilled programmer. But tools alone don't guarantee quality; the best programmers have specific techniques for getting the most out of their software tools. In the short history of computer programming, computer scientists have developed several new methodologies that have made programmers more productive and programs more reliable.

Structured Programming

For example, computer scientists in the late 1960s recognized that most FORTRAN and BASIC programs were riddled with *GoTo statements*— statements used to transfer control to other parts of the program. (Remember "Go to Jail. Do not pass Go. Do not collect $200"?) The logical structure of a program with GoTo statements can resemble a tangled spider's web. The bigger the program, the bigger the logical maze and the more possibility for error. Every branch of a program represents a loose end that might be overlooked by the programmer.

In an attempt to overcome these problems, computer scientists developed **structured programming**—a technique to make the programming process easier and more productive. A structured program doesn't depend on the GoTo statement to control the logical flow. Instead it's built from smaller programs called **modules,** or **subprograms,** that are in turn made of even smaller modules. The programmer combines modules using the three basic control structures: sequence, repetition, and selection. A program is well structured if

- it's made up of logically cohesive modules
- the modules are arranged in a hierarchy
- it's straightforward and readable

The Pascal and Ada languages were designed to encourage structured programming and discourage "spaghetti code." The

Unstructured programming

Computer software contains two kinds of information: algorithms, which correspond to the program code that performs some task, and data, upon which the algorithms operate. In a sense the algorithms are the gears and levers—the machinery that transforms the raw material of data. An unstructured program is like a huge, complicated machine that can't be easily broken down into sections. Any modification would require disassembling the entire machine. This difficulty is one reason why most programmers are afraid to modify unstructured code.

Structured programming

Structured programming breaks the big machine up into smaller machine modules, each of which had a clearly defined task in the overall processing of data. Structured programs are easier to understand and modify because problems can be isolated to individual modules, and the input and output of each module in the assembly line is easier to understand.

Two faces of BASIC: Early BASIC and structured BASIC. These two BASIC programs play the number-guessing game. The program on the top (with numbered lines) is written in a simple version of BASIC—the only kind that was available in the early days of the language. Statements are executed in numerical order unless control is transferred to another statement with a GoTo statement. The modular program on the bottom is written in QuickBASIC, a newer version of the language with many structured programming features. The main program has been reduced to a handful of statements at the top of the listing (after the Declare statements); these statements display the overall logic of the program. As it's running, the main program uses Call statements to transfer control to each of the three subprograms, which take care of the details of the game's beginning, each turn, and the game's end.

```
10 REM INITIALIZE
20 RANDOMIZE
30 PRINT "THE GUESSING GAME"
40 PRINT "I WILL THINK OF A NUMBER BETWEEN 1 AND 100."
50 PRINT "TRY TO GUESS WHAT IT IS"
60 LET C = 0
70 LET N = INT(RND(1) * 100)
80 INPUT "WHAT IS YOUR GUESS?";G
90 IF G = N THEN PRINT "THAT IS CORRECT!"
100 IF G < N THEN PRINT "TOO SMALL--TRY AGAIN"
110 IF G > N THEN PRINT "TOO BIG--TRY AGAIN"
120 LET C = C + 1
130 IF C = 7 THEN GOTO 150
140 IF G <> N THEN GOTO 60
150 IF G <> N THEN PRINT "I FOOLED YOU 7 TIMES! THE ANSWER WAS ";N
160 END
```

```
REM Guessing Game
REM written by Rajeev Pandey

DECLARE SUB StartGame (Counter!, Number!)
DECLARE SUB Turn (Counter!, Guess!, Number!)
DECLARE SUB EndGame (Number!)

CALL StartGame(Counter, Number)
DO
    CALL Turn(Counter, Guess, Number)
LOOP UNTIL (Guess = Number) OR (Counter = 7)
IF Guess <> Number THEN
    CALL EndGame(Number)
END IF

SUB EndGame (Number)
PRINT "I fooled you 7 times!"
PRINT "The answer was "; Number
END SUB

SUB StartGame (Counter, Number)
PRINT "Welcome to the guessing game. I'll think of a number"
PRINT "between 1 and 100 and you will guess what it is."
Counter = 0
RANDOMIZE TIMER
Number = INT(RND(1) * 100)
END SUB

SUB Turn (Counter, Guess, Number)
INPUT "What's your guess?"; Guess
IF Guess = Number THEN
    PRINT "You got it!"
ELSE
    IF Guess < Number THEN
        PRINT "Too small, try again."
    ELSE
        PRINT "Too big, try again."
    END IF
END IF
Counter = Counter + 1
END SUB
```

success of these languages prompted computer scientists to develop versions of BASIC and FORTRAN that were conducive to structured programming.

Object-Oriented Programming

Structured programming was a big step forward for programmers; it allowed them to produce better, more reliable programs in less time. But structured programming wasn't the last word in programming; today **object-oriented programming (OOP)** has captured the attention of the software development community. Object-oriented programming was first used in the 1970s, most notably in a language called *Smalltalk*. In object-oriented programming, a program is not just a collection of step-by-step instructions or procedures; it's a collection of *objects*. Objects contain both data and instructions and can send and receive messages. For example, an on-screen button in a multimedia program might be an object, containing both a physical description of the button's appearance and a *script* telling it what to do if it receives a mouse-click message from the operating system. This button object can be easily reused in different programs because it carries with it everything it needs to operate.

With OOP technology, programmers can build programs from prefabricated objects in the same way builders construct houses from prefabricated walls. OOP also makes it easy to use features from one program in other programs, so programmers don't have to start from scratch with every new program. The object that sorts addresses in alphabetical order in a mailing list database can also be used in a program that sorts hotel reservations alphabetically.

Smalltalk is still widely used for object-oriented programming, but many other languages now include object technology. C++, used in our example earlier, is a popular dialect of C that supports object-oriented programming. C++ doesn't contain *visual* objects like icons. On the surface it looks like just another language. But the object-oriented nature of the language allows programmers to write programs built around *logical* objects rather than procedures.

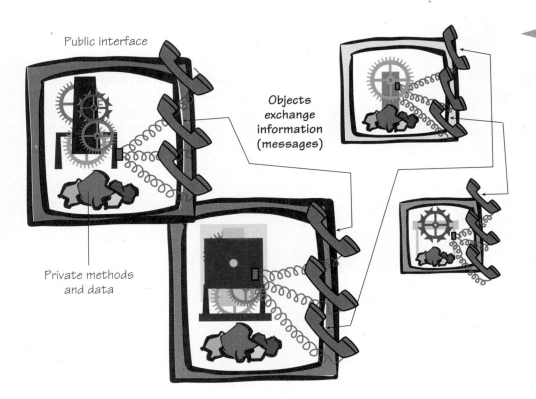

Public interface

Objects exchange information (messages)

Private methods and data

Data in OOP is more than raw material to be processed. In OOP, data is bound together with the methods and properties of an object. Each object can maintain its own storehouse of data appropriate for that object.

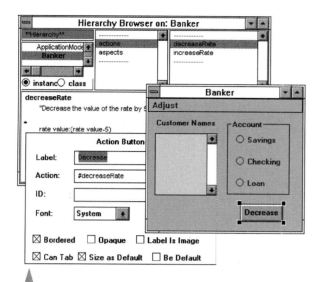

Object-oriented tools and techniques are becoming common in databases, multimedia authoring tools, and other software environments. Object-oriented programming is particularly well suited for highly interactive programs (such as graphical operating systems, games, and customer transaction stations) and programs that imitate or reflect some dynamic part of the real world (such as simulations and air traffic control systems). Most experts believe that OOP is the wave of the future.

▲ Smalltalk, the original object-oriented programming language, is so named because it was originally tested on children at the Xerox PARC laboratories.

Programming with Pictures

Many people find it easier to work with pictures instead of words. **Visual programming** tools allow programmers to create large portions of their programs by drawing pictures and pointing to on-screen objects, eliminating much of the tedious coding of traditional programming. Apple's *HyperCard* (discussed in Chapter 7) was probably the first popular example of a visual programming environment. HyperCard includes a programming language called *HyperTalk*, but a HyperCard programmer doesn't need to speak HyperTalk to create working applications. Tools like HyperCard, Visual BASIC, ToolBook, and NextStep make programming more accessible to nonprogrammers. Today's visual programming tools haven't completely transformed programming into a visual process, but they suggest that such a transformation is possible.

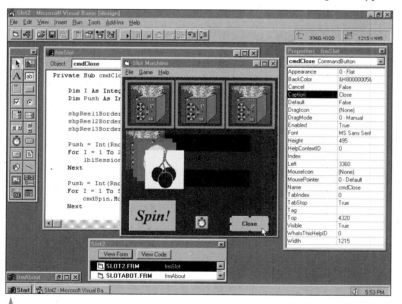

▲ Microsoft's popular Visual BASIC, a modern version of the BASIC language, includes many of the ideas and tools of object-oriented programming and visual programming.

Languages for Users

Because they're easier to use and more powerful than their ancestors, languages like C++ and BASIC continue to grow in popularity among programmers and educators. But for most computer *users*, these languages demand too much time and study to be of interest. Fortunately some languages are designed to meet the more modest needs of computer users.

Macro Languages

Many user-oriented languages are intended to allow users to create programs, called *macros*, that automate repetitive tasks. User-oriented **macro languages** (also called **scripting languages**) are built into many applications, utilities, and operating systems. Using a macro language, a spreadsheet user can build a program, called a macro, to automatically create end-of-month reports each month by locating data in other worksheets, inserting values into a new worksheet, and calculating results using formulas carried over from previous months. Using an operating system's scripting language, a user might automate the process of making backup copies of all documents created during the last seven days.

How It Works

11.1

Object-Oriented Programming

The paradigm of structured programming follows the classic view of data as raw material being processed on an assembly line. At some level, all computer programs process data in a mechanistic fashion. But at a higher level, object-oriented programming rejects the assembly line metaphor for another approach.

The fundamental tenet of OOP is that software should be designed using the same techniques that people use to understand and categorize the world around them.

In OOP a program is designed to consist of a group of objects—each with its own characteristics or attributes (called properties) and actions that it can do (called methods).

Every object has a "public" face: the properties and methods that other objects can see and interact with. Objects also have private methods for their internal use.

In OOP, data is bound together, or encapsulated, with the methods and properties of an object. Each object can maintain its own storehouse of data appropriate for that object.

OOP also relies on the idea of hierarchical categorization of objects to allow

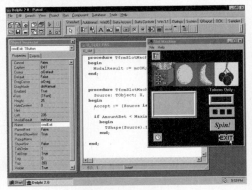

Delphi is a popular object-oriented development tool based on Pascal.

programmers to create new objects that are derived from objects that are already defined. The new object can inherit the properties and methods of the object it descends from, and add new properties and methods as needed. Such hierarchies have been used by people for centuries in understanding the physical and biological world.

How might all of this work in practice, say for a graphical operating system? For example, there could be a generic "window" object whose properties included its size, position, color, and so on and whose methods included things like closing and resizing. A more specialized window could be derived from this: for example, a window with scroll bars attached.

Some macro languages require you to design and type each macro by hand, just as you would if you were writing a BASIC program. In fact, some Microsoft applications include a variation of Visual BASIC as a scripting language. Another type of macro maker "watches" while the user performs a sequence of commands and actions; it then memorizes the sequence and turns it into a macro automatically. The user can then examine and edit the macro so that it performs the desired actions under any circumstances.

Fourth-Generation Languages

Many experts suggest that languages have evolved through four generations: machine language, assembly language, high-level languages, and **fourth-generation languages,** sometimes called **4GLs.** Each generation of languages is easier to use and more like natural language than its predecessors. There's no consensus on exactly what constitutes a fourth-generation language, but these characteristics are most commonly mentioned:

- 4GLs use English-like phrases and sentences to issue instructions.

- 4GLs are nonprocedural. Pascal, C, and BASIC are *procedural languages*—tools for constructing procedures that tell the computer how to accomplish tasks. *Nonprocedural languages* allow users to focus on what needs to be done, not on how to do it.

- 4GLs increase productivity. Because a 4GL takes care of many of the how-to details, programmers can often get results by typing a few lines of code rather than a few pages.

One type of 4GL is the *query language* that allows a user to request information from a database with carefully worded English-like questions. A query language serves as a database user interface, hiding the intricacies of the database from the user. *SQL* (see Chapter 8) is the standard query language for most database applications today. Like most query languages, SQL requires the user to master a few rules of syntax and logic. Still, a query language is easier to master than FORTRAN or COBOL.

Component Software

Recent developments in the software industry may soon result in software that provides users with the kind of power formerly reserved for programmers—and at the same time reverse a long-standing trend toward bloated computer applications. Throughout most of the short history of the personal computer, applications have steadily grown in size as developers add more and more features to their products. Even though no single user needs all of the features in a modern spreadsheet program, every user who buys that program must buy all of the code that provides those features. Many modern applications are so bloated with features that they make huge demands on memory and hard disk space.

Component software tools may reverse the trend toward mega-applications by allowing users to construct small custom applications from software components. Component software isn't completely new; users have been able to add custom components to applications for years. For example, the popular graphics package called Kai's Power Tools is nothing more than a collection of *plug-in modules* that add custom features and commands to Photoshop, Painter, and other image-editing programs. Dozens of extensions are available for Netscape Navigator, the popular Web browser. But this customizability is only possible if applications are designed to allow it. Two new systems—OpenDoc (developed by Apple with IBM and Novell) and OLE (developed by Microsoft) provide standardized support for component software at the system-software level.

If successful, these systems might radically change the software industry. Instead of buying an everything-but-the-kitchen-sink word processor, you might be able to buy word processor components—spelling checkers, outliners, formatters—based on your individual needs. Components might be distributed through the Internet as well as traditional software channels, so you can quickly add features when you need them. This kind of build-it-yourself software model is the logical extension of object-oriented programming to a level where users can do their own application construction.

The Future of Programming?

Object-oriented programming. Visual programming. Component software. With these trends gaining momentum, what can we say about the future of programming? It's not clear what programming languages will look like in the future, but three trends seem likely:

- Programming languages will continue to evolve in the direction of natural languages like English. Today's programming languages, even the best of them, are far too limited and unintelligent. Tomorrow's programming tools should be able to understand what we want even if we don't specify every detail. When we consider artificial intelligence in the next chapter, we'll deal with the problems and promise of natural language computer communication.

- The line between programmer and user is likely to grow hazy. As programming becomes easier, there's every reason to believe that computer users will have tools that allow them to construct applications without mastering the intricacies of a technical programming language.

- Computers will play an ever-increasing role in programming themselves. Today's visual programming environments can create programs in response to user clicks and commands. Tomorrow's programming tools may be able to write entire programs with only a description of the problem supplied by users. The day after tomorrow we may see computers anticipating problems and programming solutions without human intervention!

Whatever happens, one thing seems likely: Future programming tools will have little in common with today's languages. When computer historians look back, they'll marvel at how difficult it was for us to instruct computers to perform even the simplest actions.

PROGRAMS IN PERSPECTIVE: SYSTEMS ANALYSIS AND THE SYSTEM LIFE CYCLE

We but teach
Bloody instructions, which being taught, return
To plague the inventor.

—Shakespeare, Macbeth

Programs don't exist in a vacuum. Programs are part of larger **information systems**—collections of people, machines, data, and methods organized to accomplish specific functions and to solve specific problems. Programming is only part of the larger process of designing, implementing, and managing information systems. In this section we'll examine that larger process.

Whether it's a simple accounting system for a small business or a credit bureau's massive financial information system, a system has a **system life cycle**—a sequence of steps or phases it passes through between the time the system is conceived and the time it is phased out. The phases of the system life cycle are: *investigation, analysis, design, development, implementation, maintenance,* and *retirement.* We'll consider each phase from the point of view of the **systems analyst**—the computer professional primarily responsible for developing and managing a system as it progresses through these phases.

Investigation

Developing an information system is no small undertaking. People develop information systems because problems like these need to be solved:

- A mom-and-pop music store needs a way to keep track of instrument rentals and purchases so that billing and accounting don't take so much time.

- A college's antiquated, labor-intensive registration system forces students to endure long lines and frequent scheduling errors.

- A catalog garden-supply company is outgrowing its small, slow PC-based software system, resulting in shipping delays, billing errors, and customer complaints.

- The success of an upcoming oceanographic investigation hinges on the ability of scientists to collect and analyze data instantaneously so the results can be fed into remote-control navigation devices.

- A software manufacturer determines that its PC graphics program is rapidly losing market share to a competitor with more features and a friendlier user interface.

System investigation involves defining the problem—identifying the information needs of the organization, examining the current system, determining how well it meets the needs of the organization, and studying the feasibility of changing or replacing the current system. After completing the initial investigation of the problem, a systems analyst, whether part of the organization or contracted from an outside consulting firm, produces a *feasibility study* to help management decide whether to continue with the systems analysis.

Analysis

During the analysis phase the systems analyst gathers documents, interviews users of the current system (if one exists), observes the system in action, and generally gathers and analyzes data to help understand the current system and identify new requirements. Most systems are too complex to understand as a whole, so the systems analyst generally subdivides a system into components called *subsystems*. The analysis phase involves more detail than the investigative phase but less than the design phase that follows.

Design

The investigation phase focuses on *why*, the analysis phase focuses on *what*, and the design phase focuses on *how*. In the design phase the systems analyst considers important how-to questions:

- What kind of output should the system produce?

- Where will input data come from, and how will it be entered into the system?

- Should the system be centralized in a single computer or distributed through a network of desktop computers? (For that matter, should a computer be involved in the system at all?)

- Should the organization purchase packaged software or have programmers write a custom application from the ground up?

The systems analyst answers these questions, sometimes proposing several alternative solutions.

In many cases the design phase produces a **prototype** system—a limited working system or subsystem to give the users and management an idea of how the completed system will work. The systems analyst can modify the prototype until it meets the needs and expectations of the organization. Once the design is acceptable, the systems analyst can fill in the details of the output, input, data files, processing, and system controls.

Development

After the design is completed, the actual system development can begin. Development includes a complex mix of scheduling, hardware and software purchasing, documentation, and programming. For most large projects, the development phase involves a team of programmers, technical writers, and clerical people under the supervision of a systems analyst. A large part of the development schedule is devoted to testing the system. Members of the system development team perform early testing to locate and eliminate bugs. This initial testing is known as **alpha testing.** Later, potential users who are willing to work with almost-finished software perform **beta testing** and report bugs to the developers.

Implementation

When the testing is completed and known bugs have been eradicated, the new system is ready to replace the old one. For commercial software packages, this phase typically involves extensive training and technical user support to supplement sales and marketing efforts. For large custom systems, implementation typically includes user education and training, equipment replacement, file conversion, and careful monitoring of the new system for problems. In some cases the new system is run parallel to the old system until the analyst is confident that the new system is stable and reliable.

Maintenance

The maintenance phase involves evaluating, repairing, and enhancing the system. Some software problems don't surface until the system has been operational for a while or the organization needs change. Ongoing maintenance allows organizations to deal with those problems when they arise. For commercial programs, bugs and refinements are handled by occasional *maintenance upgrades,* typically labeled with incremental version numbers like 1.01 or 2.0a. For large custom systems, maintenance involves a continual process of evaluating and adjusting the system to meet organizational needs. In either case maintenance usually lasts throughout the lifetime of the system.

Retirement

At some point in the life of a system, ongoing maintenance isn't enough. Because of changes in organizational needs, user expectations, available technology, and other factors, the system no longer meets the needs of the users or the organization. At that point it's time to phase it out in favor of a newer system and begin another round of the system life cycle.

The System Life Cycle

ollege registration is a complex system involving hundreds of people and masses of information. A registration system must be solidly designed, carefully maintained, and eventually replaced as the needs of the college change. In this example we'll follow systems analysts at Chintimini College as they guide registration system through a system life cycle.

1

Investigation

Analysts at the college's Information Processing Center identify several problems with the antiquated manual registration system: ong lines, frequent scheduling errors, and expensive labor costs. After studying registration systems at other schools, they determine that a registration-by-phone system might be the best solution to these problems.

6

Maintenance

Analysts monitor and evaluate the new system, eliminating problems and correcting bugs as they are uncovered.

7

Retirement

After a few years, the phone registration system has developed problems of its own. The college begins developing a new system that will allow students to register through personal computers. When the new PC registration system reaches the implementation phase of its life cycle, the phone-in system is retired.

2 Analysis

Analysts use a *data flow diagram* to illustrate the flow of data through the old registration system. They'll use the information in this diagram to help them develop the new system.

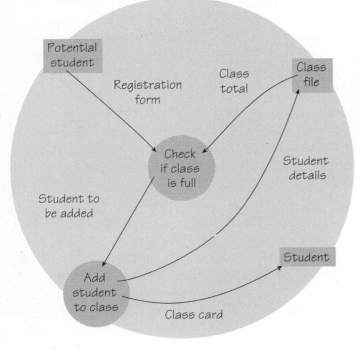

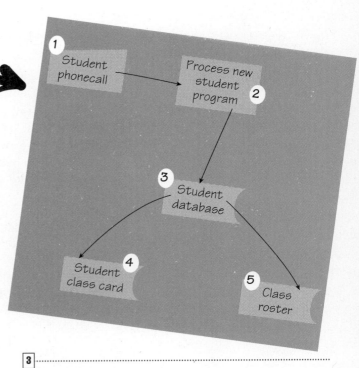

3 Design

Analysts use standard symbols to create a *system flowchart* to show the relationship between programs, files, input, and output in the new system.

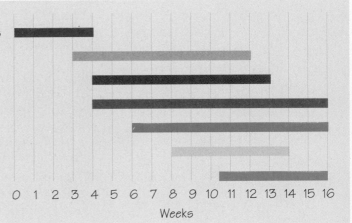

5 Implementation

Analysts supervise the training, equipment conversion, file conversion, and system conversion as the new system is brought on line.

4 Development

Analysts use a Gantt chart to plan the schedule deadlines and milestones for creating the new system.

THE SCIENCE OF COMPUTING

Telescopes are to astronomy as computers are to computer science.

—Edgar Dykstra, computer scientist

We've seen how programmers and systems analysts create and maintain computer programs used by scientists, business people, artists, writers, and others. But just as the rest of us take advantage of the programmer's handiwork, the programmer depends on tools and ideas developed by *computer scientists*—professionals who work in the academic discipline called **computer science.** What is computer science, and why is it important in the world of computers?

Because most introductory computer science courses focus on programming, many students equate computer science with computer programming. But programming is little more than a tool in the computer scientist's intellectual toolbox; it has about as much to do with computer science as English grammar has to do with writing novels.

Computer science is a relatively new discipline with ties to electrical engineering, mathematics, and business. Many computer scientists prefer to call the field comput*ing* science, because it focuses on the process of computing rather than on computer hardware. Computing takes a variety of forms, and computer science includes a number of focus areas, ranging from the rarefied world of computer theory to practical nuts and bolts work in software engineering. Some areas of specialization within computer science—database management, graphics, artificial intelligence, and networks, for example—provide academic underpinnings for specific categories of computer applications. Other branches of computer science deal with concepts that can apply to almost any type of computer application. These include

- *Computer theory.* The most mathematical branch of computer science, computer theory applies the concepts of theoretical mathematics to computational problems. Theoreticians often work not with real computers but with theoretical computers that exist only in the minds of the theoreticians. As in most fields, many theoretical concepts eventually find their way into practical applications.

- *Algorithms.* Many computer scientists focus on algorithms—the logical underpinnings of computer programs. The design of algorithms can determine whether software succeeds or fails. A well-designed algorithm is not only reliable and free of logical errors but also *efficient,* so it can accomplish its goals with a minimum of computer resources and time. Computers spend most of their time doing mundane tasks like sorting lists, searching for names, and calculating geometric coordinates. These frequently performed operations must be built on rock-solid, efficient algorithms if a computer system is to be responsive and reliable.

- *Data structures.* If algorithms describe the logical structure of programs, **data structures** determine the logical structure of *data.* Data structures range from simple numeric lists and tables (called *arrays*) to complex relations at the core of massive databases. Computer scientists continue to develop improved techniques for representing and combining different forms of data, and these techniques find their way into all kinds of software.

- *Programming concepts and languages.* As we've seen, programming languages have evolved through several generations in the short history of computers. Thanks to computer scientists in the tradition of Grace Hopper, each new wave of languages is easier to use and more powerful than the one that came before. Programming language specialists strive to design better programming languages to make it easier for programmers to turn algorithms into working software.

Computer scientists are also responsible for the development of techniques like structured programming and object-oriented programming—techniques that make programmers more productive and programs more reliable.

- *Computer architecture.* Straddling the boundary between the software world of computer science and the hardware world of computer engineering, **computer architecture** deals with the way hardware and software work together. How can multiple processors work together? How does the bandwidth of a bus affect performance? What are the tradeoffs for different storage media? These are the types of questions that concern computer architecture specialists.

- *Management information systems.* **Management information systems (MIS)** is part computer science, part business. In fact, MIS studies are done in computer science departments at some institutions, in business departments at others, and in MIS departments at others. MIS specialists focus on the developing systems that can provide timely, reliable, and useful information to managers in business, industry, and government. MIS specialists apply the theoretical concepts of computer science to real-world, practical business problems.

- *Software engineering.* When an engineer designs a bridge or a building, tried-and-true engineering principles and techniques ensure that the structure won't collapse unexpectedly. Unfortunately we can't trust software the way we trust buildings; software designers simply don't have the time-honored techniques to ensure quality. **Software engineering** is a relatively new branch of computer science that attempts to apply engineering principles and techniques to the less-than-concrete world of computer software. We'll conclude this chapter with a brief look at the problems faced by software engineers—problems that affect all of us.

THE STATE OF SOFTWARE

> It's impossible to make anything foolproof, because fools are so ingenious.
>
> —Roger Berg, inventor

In spite of advances in computer science, the state of software development is less than ideal. Software developers and software users are confronted with two giant problems: cost and unreliability.

Software Problems

> The major difference between a thing that might go wrong and a thing that cannot possibly go wrong is that when a thing that cannot possibly go wrong goes wrong it usually turns out to be impossible to get at or repair.
>
> —Douglas Adams, in *Mostly Harmless*

As computers have evolved through the decades, the cost of computer hardware has steadily gone down. Every year brings more powerful, reliable machines and lower prices. At the same time, the cost of developing computer software has gone *up*. The software industry abounds with stories of computer systems that cost millions of dollars more and took years longer to develop than expected. Many systems become so costly

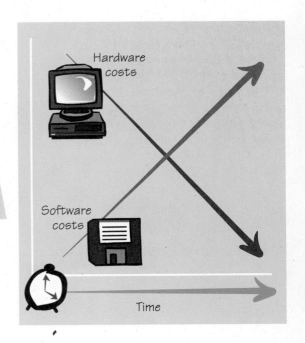

to develop that their developers are forced to abandon them before completion. According to one survey, 75 percent of all system development undertaken in the United States is either never completed or, if it is completed, not used.

But while prices rise, there's no corresponding increase in the reliability of software. Ever since Grace Hopper pulled a moth from the Mark II's relay, bugs have plagued computers, often with disastrous consequences. Here are a few horror stories:

- On November 20, 1985, the Bank of New York's computer system started corrupting government securities transactions. By the end of the day, the bank was $32 billion overdrawn with the Federal Reserve. Before the system error was corrected, it cost the bank $5 million in interest.

- In a 12-month period ending in April 1988, London's Heathrow Airport air traffic control system failed five separate times, despite the airport's 70 full-time specialists hired to keep the computer running and to update its software.

- The Gemini V capsule splashed down 100 miles off target because the programmers who wrote the spacecraft's inertial guidance system failed to take into account the earth's rotation around the sun.

- Programs on NASA observation satellites in the 1970s and 1980s rejected ozone readings because the programmers had assumed when they wrote the programs that such low numbers could not be correct. It wasn't until British scientists reported ozone-level declines that NASA scientists reprocessed the data and confirmed the British findings that the earth's ozone layer was in danger.

- The Therac 25 radiation machine for tracking cancers was thoroughly tested and successfully used on thousands of patients before a software bug caused massive radiation overdoses, resulting in the partial paralysis of one patient and the death of another.

- On January 15, 1990, AT&T's 30-year-old signaling system software failed, bringing the long distance carrier's network to its knees. Twenty million calls failed to go through during the next 18 hours before technicians found the problem: a single incorrect instruction hiding among a million lines of code.

- On February 25, 1991, 28 American soldiers were killed and 98 others wounded when an Iraqi Scud missile hit a barracks near Dhahran, Saudi Arabia. A tiny bug in a Patriot missile's software threw off its timing just enough to prevent it from intercepting the Scud. Programmers had already fixed the bug, and a new version of the software was being shipped to Dhahran when the attack occurred.

- On January 1, 2000, billions of dollars worth of software will become obsolete, causing serious problems for businesses and government institutions. For decades programmers commonly built two-digit date fields into programs to save storage space; why allow space for the first two digits when they never change? But when 1999 ends they will change, turning all those ancient programs into junk. Many of these programs are so old they can't be revised; the only solution is to replace them.

Software errors can take a variety of forms, including errors of omission, syntax errors, logic errors, clerical errors, capacity errors, and judgment errors. But whatever its form, a software error can be devilishly difficult to locate and even more difficult to remove. According to one study, 15 to 20 percent of attempts to remove program errors actually introduce new errors!

Thousands of lives depend on reliable functioning of the computers and software used by air traffic controllers.

Software Solutions

Now that the Software Crisis will soon celebrate its silver anniversary, it's time we recognized that this is not a crisis, it's a situation; software has bugs.

—Lauren Ruth Wiener, in *Digital Woes*

Computer scientists and software engineers are responding to reliability and cost problems on five main fronts:

- *Programming techniques.* So far, structured programming is the best known and most successful technique for increasing programmer productivity and program reliability. Programmers who use structured techniques can concentrate on the overall logic of their creations without getting distracted by minute details. The result is less expensive, more reliable software. But structured programming is no panacea; it is considered by most experts as only a single step on a long road toward more dependable programming methodologies. It's too early to tell whether object-oriented programming and other more modern techniques will take us much farther down that road.

- *Programming environments.* Today's best programming tools include sophisticated text editors, debuggers, record-keeping programs, and translators, all interwoven into a seamless graphic work environment. A high-quality programming environment can help a programmer manage the complexities of a large project. In recent years **CASE** (computer-assisted software engineering) **tools** have emerged, allowing analysts and programmers to automate many of the tedious and error-prone steps involved in turning design specifications into programs. Still, CASE tools and programming environments have a long way to go before they can guarantee reliable software, if that's even possible.

- *Program verification.* Software engineers would like to be able to *prove* the correctness of their programs in the same way mathematicians prove the correctness of theorems. Computer scientists have developed **program verification** techniques that work well for small programs. Unfortunately these techniques have achieved only limited success with the complex commercial programs people depend on today. There's little hope for automated program verification, either. Computer scientists have proven that some problems can't be solved with algorithms, and program verification is one such problem.

- *Clean-room programming.* One new experimental approach to software development is modeled after microchip manufacturing techniques. Clean-room programming combines formal notation, proofs of correctness, and statistical quality control with an evolutionary approach to programming. Programmers grow systems individually, certifying the quality of each before integrating it with the others. It's too early to tell whether this rigorous, engineering-like approach will achieve widespread quality gains, but early tests show some promise.

- *Human management.* Project management techniques from business and engineering have been applied successfully to many software engineering projects. These *human management* techniques have more to do with person-to-person communication than with programmer-to-machine communication. Since many information system failures result from human communication errors, successful human management can improve a system's overall reliability. But again, the benefits of human management methodologies aren't great enough to offset the massive problems facing software engineers today.

Many software-related problems can be solved by improving person-to-person communication.

Computer scientists have accomplished a great deal in the short history of the field. Software development is easier than it used to be, and computers today can accomplish far more than anyone dreamed a few decades ago. But software engineers have failed to keep up with the fast-paced evolution in computer hardware, and it's still incredibly difficult to produce reliable, cost-effective software. A decade ago, computer scientist Ted Lewis summed up the problem in one of his laws of computing. Today, when we're routinely asked to entrust our money, our health, our legal rights, and our lives to software, it's important for all of us to remember that law: "Hardware is soft; software is hard."

SUMMARY

Computer programming is a specialized form of problem solving that involves developing an algorithm for solving a problem. Most programmers use stepwise refinement to repeatedly break a problem into smaller, more easily solvable problems. An algorithm typically is developed in pseudocode that describes the logic of the program before being translated into a programming language. A translator program—either a compiler or an interpreter—checks for syntax errors (language errors) and, if it finds none, translates the program into machine language so the computer can execute the instructions. Logic errors might not surface until the translated program is run, and maybe not even then. The programming process isn't completed until the program is thoroughly tested for errors.

Computer languages have evolved through several generations, with each generation being easier to use and more powerful than the one that came before. Machine language—the original computer language of zeros and ones—is primitive and difficult to program. Assembly language uses a translator called an assembler to turn alphabetic codes into the binary numbers of machine language, but in every other way it is identical to machine language.

High-level languages, such as FORTRAN, COBOL, BASIC, Pascal, and C, are more like English and therefore easier to work with than either machine or assembly language. What's more, they generally can be transported between computers with a minimum of rewriting. Most modern languages encourage structured programming, a technique that involves combining subprograms using only the three fundamental control structures: sequence, selection, and repetition. Structured programming produces programs with fewer logic errors. Still, when program efficiency is critical, many programmers use languages like C that allow them to work at a lower level of machine logic.

Many applications contain built-in macro languages, scripting languages, and query languages that put programming power in the hands of users. Query languages are representative of fourth-generation languages (4GLs) that are nonprocedural; that is, they allow the programmer to focus on defining the task rather than outlining the steps involved in accomplishing the task. Visual programming tools allow the programmer to use icons, drawing tools, menus, and dialog boxes to construct programs without writing code. Object-oriented programming (OOP) tools allow programmers to construct programs from objects with properties and the ability to send messages to each other; many believe that OOP represents the future of programming.

Programs are part of larger information systems. An information system has a life cycle that starts with the initial investigation of the problem; proceeds through analysis, design, development, and implementation phases; and lingers in an ongoing maintenance phase until the system is retired. A systems analyst manages a typical information system with the help of a team of programmers and other computer professionals.

Computer scientists are responsible for the software tools and concepts that make all other software development possible. Computer science focuses on the process of computing through several areas of specialization, including theory, algorithms, data structures, programming concepts and languages, computer architecture, management information systems, artificial intelligence, and software engineering.

One of the most challenging problems facing computer science is the problem of software reliability. Current software development techniques provide no assurance that a software system will function without failure under all circumstances. As more and more human institutions rely on computer systems, it becomes increasingly important for computer scientists to find ways to make software that people can trust.

Chapter Review

Key Terms

algorithm
alpha testing
assembler
assembly language
beta testing
CASE tools
coding
compiler
component software
computer architecture
computer science
control structure
data structure

fourth-generation language (4GL)
high-level language
information system
interpreter
logic error
machine language
macro (scripting) language
management information systems
   (MIS)
module (subprogram)
object-oriented programming (OOP)
programming
program verification

prototype
pseudocode
software engineering
stepwise refinement
structured programming
syntax error
system life cycle
systems analyst
testing
top-down design
visual programming

Review Questions

1. Here's an algorithm for directions to a university bookstore from a downtown location:

   > Go south on 4th Street to Jefferson Street.
   > Turn left on Jefferson Street.
   > Proceed on Jefferson past the stoplight to the booth at the campus entrance.
   > If there's somebody in the booth, ask for a permit to park in the bookstore parking lot; otherwise, just keep going.
   > When you reach the bookstore parking lot, keep circling the lot until you find an empty space.
   > Park in the empty space.

   Find examples of sequence, selection, and repetition control structures in this algorithm.

2. Find examples of ambiguous statements that might keep the algorithm in question 1 from working properly.

3. Assume that Robert, the automated chef in Chapter 4, is going to do the driving. Use stepwise refinement to add more detail to question 1's algorithm so Robert has a better chance of understanding the instructions.

4. Design an algorithm to play the part of the guesser in the number-guessing game featured in this chapter. If you base your algorithm on the right strategy, it will always be able to guess the correct number in seven or fewer tries. (Hint: Computer scientists call the right strategy *binary search*.)

5. When does it make sense to design a custom program rather than using off-the-shelf commercial software? Give some examples.

6. Why is structured programming so widely practiced today by software developers?

7. Why are so many computer languages in use today?

8. Assemblers, compilers, and interpreters are all language translators. How do they differ?

9. What is the relationship between computer science and computer programming?

10. Give examples of several different kinds of computer errors, and describe how these errors affect people.

11. What techniques do software engineers use to improve software reliability?

Discussion Questions

1. Is programming a useful skill for a computer user? Why or why not?

2. Do you think computer professionals should have a code of ethics similar to those found in legal and medical professions? What should such a code cover?

3. Should programmers be licensed? Is programming a craft, a trade, or a profession?

4. Suppose you want to computerize a small business or nonprofit organization. What questions might a systems analyst ask when determining what kind of system you need?

5. What do you think programming will be like in 10 years? 20 years? 50 years?

6. Computer science is in the college of science at some universities and in the college of engineering at others. Is computer science a science, a branch of engineering, or both?

7. Why is it so difficult to produce error-free software?

Projects

1. The computer is often used as an excuse for human errors. Find some examples of "The computer did it" errors in newspapers, magazines, or conversations with others. For each example, try to determine if the computer is, in fact, to blame.

2. Try to determine what safeguards are used to ensure that automated teller machines don't malfunction and that they can't be violated.

3. Find out what safeguards are used to ensure the security of computer systems used in your local elections.

Sources and Resources

Books

As you might expect, there are hundreds of books on programming and computer science, most of which are specifically written about particular programming languages and platforms. Most of the books listed here are more general.

Oh! Pascal!, by Doug Cooper (New York: Norton, 1993). A friendly and witty introduction to Pascal. It comes in two versions: One that covers standard Pascal (the generic version of the language), and one that's specific to Turbo Pascal, a version with object-oriented programming capability.

C by Dissection: The Essentials of C Programming, by Al Kelley and Ira Pohl (Redwood City, CA: Benjamin/Cummings, 1992). This excellent text introduces beginners to the C language with lots of examples.

Windows Programming for Mere Mortals, by Woody Leonhard (Reading, MA: Addison-Wesley, 1992). A funny, lively beginner's guide to programming using Visual BASIC and the programming languages built into Excel, Word, and Ami Pro. It's not a reference manual, but this book provides lots of programming background in a very readable package. A disk is included.

Learn C on the Macintosh, Second Edition, by Dave Mark (Reading, MA: Addison-Wesley, 1995). This book/disk package includes a special version of C that allows you to create programs without any additional software. The tutorial is fun to read and easy to follow. If you want to program the Mac, this is the place to start. Mark has written a follow-up volume that covers C++, too.

The Analytical Engine: An Introduction to Computer Science Using HyperCard, and *The Analytical Engine: An Introduction to Computer Science Using ToolBook,* by Rick Decker and Stuart Hirshfield (Belmont, CA: Wadsworth, 1990). These well-written, innovative texts illustrate many of the concepts of computer science using HyperCard stacks (in the Macintosh version) and ToolBook books (in the Windows version).

Computer Science: An Overview, Third Edition, by J. Glenn Brookshear, Marquette University (Redwood City, CA: Benjamin/Cummings, 1991). This excellent survey covers algorithms, data structures, operating systems, and software engineering from a current computer science perspective.

Algorithmics: The Spirit of Computing, by David Harel (Reading, MA: Addison-Wesley, 1992). This book explores the central ideas of computer science from basic algorithms and data structures to more advanced concepts.

The New Turing Omnibus: 66 Excursions in Computer Science, by A. K. Dewdney (New York: Computer Science Press, 1993). This unusual book contains 66 short chapters covering a wide range of computer science topics, from algorithms to VLSI computers. Much of the material is technical and mathematical, but the writing is clear and engaging.

The Tao of Objects: A Beginner's Guide to Object-Oriented Programming, Second Edition, by Gary Entsminger (New York: M&T Books, 1995). This is a valuable guide to object-oriented techniques and implementations using modern programming environments. This book's down-to-earth style clarifies OOP for novices.

An Introduction to Object-Oriented Programming, by Timothy Budd (Reading, MA: Addison-Wesley, 1991). This text is designed to introduce the concepts of object-oriented programming without getting bogged down in the mechanics of a specific language. The book assumes you know the basics of programming in some language and provides examples in four different object-oriented languages.

Digital Woes: Why We Should Not Depend on Software, by Lauren Ruth Wiener (Reading, MA: Addison-Wesley, 1993). This book provides a broad, nontechnical overview of the inherent risks of software. Clear explanations of how software is developed and why it goes wrong are accompanied by sobering examples and a discussion of ways to deal with the problem.

Computer-Related Risks, by Peter Neumann (Reading, MA: Addison-Wesley, 1995). Neumann runs the popular and eye-opening comp.risks forum on the Internet. This book draws on that forum and Neumann's expertise, providing an exhaustive technical survey of the risks we face as a result of our dependence on computer technology. The hundreds of documented examples range from humorous to horrifying, and they're tied together with Neumann's intelligent assessment of the broader problems and possible solutions.

You'll find other risk-related resources listed in Chapters 14 and 15.

World Wide Web Pages

Check the *Computer Confluence* Web site for links to the comp.risks forum, the Association for Computing Machinery (ACM), and other sites that cover material related to this chapter.

12

IS ARTIFICIAL INTELLIGENCE REAL?

Alan Turing, Military Intelligence, and Intelligent Machines

> The extent to which we regard something as behaving in an intelligent manner is determined as much by our own state of mind and training as by the properties of the object under consideration.

—Alan Turing

Alan M. Turing, the British mathematician who designed the world's first operational electronic digital computer during the 1940s, may have been the most important thinker in the history of computing.

While a graduate student at Princeton in 1936, Turing published "On Computable Numbers," a paper that laid the theoretical groundwork for all of modern computer science. In that paper he described a theoretical *Turing Ma-*

Alan Turing

chine that could read instructions from punched paper tape and perform all the critical operations of a computer. The paper also established the limits of computer science by mathematically demonstrating that some problems simply cannot be solved by any kind of computer.

After receiving his doctorate in 1938, Turing had an opportunity to translate theory into reality. Anticipating an invasion by Hitler's forces, the British government assembled a team of mathematicians and engineers with the top-secret mission of cracking the German military code. Under the leadership of Turing and others the group built Co-

lossus, a single-purpose machine regarded by many today as the first electronic digital computer. From the time Colossus was completed in 1943 until the end of the war, it successfully cracked Nazi codes—a fact concealed by the British government until long after the war ended. Many experts believe that Colossus was ultimately responsible for the defeat of the Nazis.

Turing effectively launched the field of artificial intelligence with a 1950 paper called "Computing Machinery and Intelligence." In this paper he proposed a concrete test for determining whether a machine was intelligent. In later years Turing championed the possibility of emulating human thought through computation. He even co-wrote the first chess-playing program.

Turing was an unconventional and extremely sensitive person. He was professionally and socially devastated by his arrest in 1952 for violation of British anti-homosexuality laws. The 41-year-old genius apparently committed suicide in 1954, years before the government made his wartime heroics public. Four decades after his death, Turing's work still has relevance to computer scientists, mathematicians, and philosophers. The highest award in computer science, the Turing Award, bears his name. It's impossible to know what he might have contributed had he lived through those decades.

Colossus, 1945

A lan Turing spent much of his short life trying to answer the question "Can machines think?" That's still a central question of **artificial intelligence (AI)**, the field of computer science devoted to making computers perceive, reason, and act in ways that have, until now, been reserved for human beings. But today even those who believe that computers can't "think" have to admit that artificial intelligence research has produced impressive results: computers that can communicate in human languages; systems that can provide instant expertise in medicine, science, and other fields; world-class electronic chess players; and robots that can outperform humans in a variety of tasks. In this chapter we'll explore the technology, applications, and implications of artificial intelligence.

THINKING ABOUT THINKING MACHINES

What is intelligence, anyway? It is only a word that people use to name those unknown processes with which our brains solve problems we call hard. But whenever you learn a skill yourself, you're less impressed or mystified when other people do the same. This is why the meaning of "intelligence" seems so elusive: It describes not some definite thing but only the momentary horizon of our ignorance about how minds might work.

—Marvin Minsky, AI pioneer

If you ask ten people to define intelligence, you're likely to get ten different answers, including some of these:

- the ability to learn from experience
- the power of thought
- the ability to reason

- the ability to perceive relations
- the power of insight
- the ability to use tools
- intuition

Intelligence is difficult to define and understand, even for philosophers and psychologists who spend their lives studying it. But this elusive quality is, to many people, the characteristic that sets humans apart from other species. So it's not surprising that controversy has continually swirled around the questions "Can a machine be intelligent?" and "Can a machine think?"

Can Machines Think?

> A machine may be deemed intelligent when it can pass for a human being in a blind test.
>
> —Alan Turing

In his landmark 1950 paper, Alan Turing suggested that the question "Can machines think?" was too vague and philosophical to be of any value. To make it more concrete, he proposed an "imitation game." The **Turing test,** as it came to be known, involves two people and a computer. One person, the interrogator, sits alone in a room and types questions into a computer terminal. The questions can be about anything—math, science, politics, sports, entertainment, art, human relationships, emotions—anything. As answers to questions appear on the terminal, the interrogator attempts to guess whether those answers were typed by the other person or were generated by the computer. By repeatedly fooling interrogators into thinking it is a person, a computer can demonstrate intelligent behavior. If it *acts* intelligent, according to Turing, it *is* intelligent.

Turing did not intend this test to be the only way to demonstrate machine intelligence; he pointed out that a machine could fail and still be intelligent. Even so,

In the Turing test a human interrogator types statements and questions into a terminal and tries to guess which contestant is human, based on the answers given.

Interrogator

Turing believed that machines would be able to pass his test by the turn of the century. So far no computer has come close, in spite of 40 years of AI research. While some people still cling to the Turing test to define artificial intelligence, most AI researchers favor less stringent definitions.

What Is Artificial Intelligence?

> Artificial intelligence is the study of ideas which enable computers to do the things that make people seem intelligent.
>
> —Patrick Henry Winston, in *Artificial Intelligence*

This definition from a 1977 edition of a textbook is similar to definitions that commonly appear in today's popular press. This type of definition captures the general idea of artificial intelligence, but it breaks down when applied to specific examples. Does artificial intelligence include doing lightning-fast calculations? Finding a word in a dictionary as fast as it can be typed? Remembering hundreds of telephone numbers at a time? If a person could do all of these things, that person would "seem intelligent." But these activities aren't good examples of artificial intelligence because they're trivial for computers. In fact, many computer scientists believe that if it's easy to do with a computer, it can't be artificial intelligence. Here's a more recent textbook definition that reflects that point of view:

> Artificial intelligence is the study of how to make computers do things at which, at the moment, people are better.
>
> —Elaine Rich, in *Artificial Intelligence*

According to this definition, artificial intelligence is a *moving frontier.* The short history of the field bears this out. In the 1950s many AI researchers struggled to create computers that could play checkers and chess. Today computers can easily beat all but the best human players, and relatively few AI researchers study these games. In the words of one researcher, artificial intelligence is "whatever hasn't been done yet." Moving-frontier definitions of AI tend to be accurate, but they're short on specifics. A more concrete and complete definition might combine Rich's definition with this one from the *latest* edition of Winston's popular textbook:

> Artificial intelligence is the study of the computations that make it possible to perceive, reason, and act.
>
> —Patrick Henry Winston, in *Artificial Intelligence*

Perceive, reason, and *act* are words used more commonly in psychology, the science of human behavior, than in computer science. In fact, psychologists work alongside computer scientists on many AI research projects. Computer scientists tend to be motivated by the challenge of producing machine intelligence for its own sake. Psychologists, on the other hand, are interested in artificial intelligence because it provides new insights into *natural* intelligence and the workings of the human brain.

These points of view symbolize two common approaches to AI. One approach attempts to use computers to simulate human mental processes. For example, an AI expert might ask people to describe how they solve a problem and attempt to capture their answers in a software model.

The simulation approach has three inherent problems:

Many early flying machines that imitated birds never got off the ground.

- Most people have trouble knowing and describing how they do things. Human intelligence includes unconscious thoughts, instantaneous insights, and other mental processes that are difficult or impossible to understand and describe.

- There are vast differences between the structure and capabilities of the human brain and the computer. Even the most powerful supercomputers can't approach the brain's ability to perform parallel processing—breaking a complex job into many smaller, simpler jobs and completing those jobs simultaneously.

- The best way to do something with a machine is often very different from the way people do it. Before the Wright brothers, dozens of inventors failed to produce flying machines because they tried to make their inventions imitate birds. Similarly many early AI attempts failed because they were designed to mimic human intelligence rather than to take advantage of the computer's unique capabilities.

The second, more common, approach to AI involves designing intelligent machines independent of the way people think. According to this approach, human intelligence is just one possible kind of intelligence. A machine's method of solving a problem might be different from the human method but no less intelligent.

Whichever approach they take, scientists face problems that are difficult and far too complex to solve all at once. Most AI researchers choose to break those problems into smaller problems that are easier to solve—to create programs that can function intelligently when confined to limited *domains*.

Opening Games

One of the first popular domains for AI research was the checkerboard. Much early AI work focused on games like checkers and chess because they were easy to represent in the computer's digital memory, they had clearly defined rules, and the goals were unmistakable. Instead of struggling with nebulous issues surrounding thought and intelligence, game researchers could focus on the concrete question "How can I create a program that wins consistently?" Their answers included many AI techniques still used today in a variety of applications:

- *Searching.* One way to win a game is to look ahead at the possibilities generated by each potential move: "I have four possible moves: A, B, C, and D. If I do A, then my opponent might do X, Y, or Z. If my opponent responds by doing X, then I can do E, F, G, or H . . . and so on." Obviously high-speed computers are better at this kind of repetitive processing than people. Early AI programs couldn't check all possible decision points in a complicated game like checkers (there are approximately 10^{21} choices). Today's powerful computers can perform massive database searches quickly, making this kind of look-ahead searching practical for some game-playing programs. Jonathan Schaeffer's checker-playing program uses an enormous database of board positions to evaluate every move; the program plays as well as the best human players in the world. Still, this kind of *brute-force* searching doesn't fit many definitions of intelligence. For more complex games like chess, and for most domains outside of the world of games, the staggering number of decision points makes brute-force searching impractical. So searching is generally guided by a planned strategy and by rules known as heuristics.

- *Heuristics.* A **heuristic** is a rule of thumb. Unlike hard-and-fast algorithms, heuristics guide us toward judgments that experience tells us are likely to be true. In everyday life we apply heuristics like "To loosen a stuck jar lid, run warm water over it." A checker-playing program might employ a heuristic that says "Keep checkers in the king's row as long as possible."

- *Pattern recognition.* The best human chess and checkers players remember thousands of critical board patterns and know the best strategies for playing when those or similar patterns appear. Game-playing programs recognize recurring patterns, too, but not nearly as well as people do. Computer players often have trouble identifying situations that are similar but not identical. Pattern recognition is probably the single biggest advantage a human game player has over a computer opponent; it helps compensate for the computer's speed and thoroughness at searching ahead.

- *Machine learning.* The best game-playing programs learn from experience using **machine learning** techniques. If a move pays off, a learning program is more likely to use that move (or similar moves) in future games. If a move results in a loss, the program will remember to avoid similar moves.

Today a $40 program can turn a personal computer into a chess wizard. Computer systems like IBM's Deep Blue can hold their own against the best human chess players by examining more than a billion moves per second. Still, most AI researchers have moved on to more interesting and practical applications for AI. But whether working on vision, speech, problem solving, or expert decision making, researchers still use the successful strategy of game researchers—to restrict the domain of their programs so that problems are small enough to be understood and solved. We'll see how this strategy has paid off in several important areas of artificial intelligence, starting with natural-language communication.

In the widely publicized 1996 chess match between Garry Kasparov and IBM's Deep Blue, the computer lost but made a surprisingly strong showing.

NATURAL-LANGUAGE COMMUNICATION

Language is no less complex or subtle a phenomenon than the knowledge it seeks to transmit.

—Raymond Kurzweil, in *The Age of Intelligent Machines*

In Turing's classic test of machine intelligence, the computer succeeds by playing the part of a person in a typed conversation. Since the earliest days of computing, scientists have dreamed of machines that could communicate in natural languages like English, Russian, and Japanese. Over the years natural-language communication has continually challenged researchers. Many problems relate to recognizing and reproducing human speech—issues we'll deal with later in the chapter. But even when it's typed directly into the machine, natural-language text poses significant software challenges.

Machine Translation Traps

One early project attempted to create a program that could translate scientific papers from Russian to English and from English to Russian. **Automatic translation** offered hope for increased communication between scientists during the tense cold-war years. The method seemed straightforward and foolproof: A **parsing program** (or **parser**) would analyze sentence structure and identify each word according to whether it was a subject, verb, or other part of speech; another program would look up each word in a translation dictionary and substitute the appropriate word.

After spending 15 years and millions of dollars on research, scientists abandoned the project. Even with the help of human editors, machine translators couldn't compete with humans in speed and accuracy. A typical translation correctly processed only about 80 percent of the desired text.

The automatic translation project became the target of jokes that, if not strictly factual, were effective at pointing out the problems of machine translation. In one famous story scientists asked the computer to translate English into Russian and then translate the results back into English. As the story goes, "The spirit is willing, but the flesh is weak" came back as "The wine is agreeable, but the meat is rotten" and "out of sight, out of mind" became "blind and insane" or "invisible idiot."

This early translation project may not have lived up to its promoters' expectations, but it taught them a valuable lesson: Translation without understanding is impossible. To translate a sentence accurately, the translator must know what the sentence *means*.

Inexpensive pocket electronic translators serve world travelers by providing instant access to common words but not whole sentences.

Conversation Without Communication

Similar lessons emerged from Joseph Weizenbaum's work with ELIZA, one of the first software programs to converse in a limited form of natural language. Weizenbaum designed ELIZA in the 1960s to simulate the role of a therapist in a typed conversation with a patient. Here's a sample ELIZA session (the computer's responses are capitalized):

A conversation with ELIZA

Men are all alike.
IN WHAT WAY

They're always bugging us about something or other.
CAN YOU THINK OF A SPECIFIC EXAMPLE

Well, my boyfriend made me come here.
YOUR BOYFRIEND MADE YOU COME HERE

He says I'm depressed much of the time.
I AM SORRY TO HEAR YOU ARE DEPRESSED

It's true. I am unhappy.
DO YOU THINK COMING HERE WILL HELP YOU NOT TO BE
UNHAPPY

I need some help, that much seems certain.
WHAT WOULD IT MEAN TO YOU IF YOU GOT SOME HELP

Perhaps I could learn to get along with my mother.
TELL ME MORE ABOUT YOUR FAMILY

My mother takes care of me.
WHO ELSE IN YOUR FAMILY TAKES CARE OF YOU

My father.
YOUR FATHER

You are like my father in some ways.
WHAT RESEMBLANCE DO YOU SEE

You are not very aggressive but I think you don't want me to notice that.
WHAT MAKES YOU THINK I AM NOT VERY AGGRESSIVE

You don't argue with me.
WHY DO YOU THINK I DON'T ARGUE WITH YOU

You are afraid of me.
DOES IT PLEASE YOU TO BELIEVE I AM AFRAID OF YOU

My father is afraid of everybody.
WHAT ELSE COMES TO MIND WHEN YOU THINK OF YOUR
FATHER

Bullies.
DOES THAT HAVE ANYTHING TO DO WITH THE FACT THAT YOUR
BOYFRIEND MADE YOU COME HERE

From *Computer Power and Human Reason*, by Joseph Weizenbaum.

As impressive as this dialog seems, there's no understanding here. ELIZA uses a few simple tricks to *simulate* understanding, including recognizing a few key words (like *mother*), identifying categories for some of those words (*family*), and repeating phrases from earlier in the conversation. But ELIZA's tricks are far from foolproof. In response to "Necessity is the mother of invention," ELIZA might say, "Tell me more about your family." An ELIZA session can easily deteriorate into nonsense dialog laced with grammatical errors and inappropriate responses. Clearly ELIZA lacks the understanding to pass as a human in a Turing test.

Nonsense and Common Sense

Bill sings to Sarah, Sarah sings to Bill. Perhaps they will do other dangerous things together. They may eat lamb or stroke each other. They may chant of their difficulties and their happiness. They have love but they also have typewriters. That is interesting.

—A poem by RACTER, in *The Policeman's Beard Is Half Constructed*, programmed by William Chamberlain and Thomas Etter

Years after ELIZA's creation, this poetry appeared in *The Policeman's Beard Is Half Constructed,* the first book ever written by a computer. RACTER, like ELIZA, produced English-language output without really understanding it. Why do machines that flawlessly follow instructions written in BASIC, C, and other computer languages have so much trouble with *natural-language* communications?

Part of the problem is the massive vocabulary of natural languages. A typical computer language has less than 100 key words, each with a precise, unambiguous meaning. English, in contrast, contains hundreds of thousands of words, many of which have multiple meanings. Of course, a person or a machine doesn't need to understand every word in the dictionary to communicate successfully in English. Most natural-language processors work with a *subset* of the language. But as the early scientific translation efforts showed, restricting vocabulary isn't enough.

Every language has a **syntax**—a set of rules for constructing sentences from words. In a programming language the syntax rules are exact and unambiguous. Natural-language parsing programs have to deal with rules that are vague, ambiguous, and occasionally contradictory. One early parser, when asked to analyze the sentence "Time flies like an arrow," replied with several possible interpretations, including one statement with *time* as the subject, another statement with *flies* as the subject, and two commands in which the reader was the subject!

Still, computers are far more successful dealing with natural-language syntax than with **semantics**—the underlying meaning of words and phrases. In natural language the meaning of a sentence is ambiguous unless it's considered in context. "The hens were ready to eat" means one thing if it follows "The farmer approached the henhouse" and something else if it follows "The chef approached the oven." To make matters worse, human conversations are filled with idiomatic expressions ("Susan had a cow when she heard the news") and unspoken assumptions about the world or specific subject matter ("Catch the T at Harvard Square and take it to MIT"). In short, the computer lacks what we call *common sense*—the wealth of knowledge and understanding about the world that people share.

The most successful natural-language applications limit the domain so that virtually all the relevant information can be fed to the system. If the domain—the "world"—is small enough and the rules of that world are clear and unambiguous, a computer can have "common sense" that makes natural-language communication possible. For example, many database query languages accept and understand English commands but only within a narrow range. The biggest market for natural-language processing today is language translation—the same market that produced AI's first major failure. Translation programs still can't translate books unassisted, but they can increase the productivity of people who translate technical manuals and other works that focus on narrow domains.

Natural-language processing has come a long way since ELIZA's early conversations. Computers still can't pass the Turing test, but they can at least fool some of the people some of the time. Or so it seems, based on the results of a series of contests devoted to finding a winner of the Turing test: The Loebner Prize Competition held in the Boston Computer Museum. In the first of these annual competitions, held in 1991, ten untrained judges tried to determine which of the eight entries were human by carrying on typed conversations via terminals. Because the contest organizers believed that any computer would be trounced in an open-ended Turing test, they included rules to protect the entrants from unrestricted questioning. Here's a short sample of a dialog between a judge and the winning entry, a program called PC Therapist. The IBM-PC-based program, which took three years to write, played the role of a jester and made occasional typing errors so it would appear more human. It worked: five of the ten judges thought PC Therapist was a person.

01:32:25	Judge 6	Hello, earth person!
01:33:03	Terminal 5	Hello there judge, are you ready to have some fun? How ya doin, judge? Hello—how's the weather up there today?
01:33:35	Judge 6	Dark clouds with occasional bursts of sunshine (or rather camera flashes).
01:34:45	Terminal 5	The trouble with the rat race is that even if you win you're still a rat. Whimsy can be flimsy, right? How important is that to you?
01:35:26	Judge 6	Can't say I understand the question . . . but the whimsy of a poet is one thing and the whimsy of most of us is another.
01:36:51	Terminal 5	How do you know you can t say you understand the question . . . but the whimsy of a poet is one thing and the whimsy of most of us is another.
01:37:37	Judge 6	Are you repeating me just for laughs?
01:38:04	Terminal 5	I'm sorry, I do sometimes repeat myself . . . perhaps it's because i can't find my electr]nic organizer!

Reprinted from *AI Magazine*, Summer 1992.

A conversation with PC Therapist.

Natural-language processing relates to other AI technologies discussed later in the chapter. Speech recognition and optical character recognition provide input to natural-language systems, freeing the human communicator from the keyboard. On the output side, speech synthesis allows the computer to talk back in English or another language. But natural-language input and output are meaningless without a knowledge base that allows the computer to understand the ideas behind the words.

KNOWLEDGE BASES AND EXPERT SYSTEMS

A preschool child can take you on a tour of the neighborhood, explaining how people use every building, describing the interconnected lives of every person you meet, and answering questions about anything you see along the way. A computer at city hall can give you facts and figures about building materials and assessed values of houses, but it can't provide you with a fraction of the *knowledge* conveyed in the child's tour. The human brain, which isn't particularly good at storing and recalling facts, excels at manipulating *knowledge*—information that incorporates the *relationships* between facts. Computers, on the other hand, are better at handling data than knowledge. Nobody knows exactly how the brain stores and manipulates knowledge. But artificial intelligence researchers have developed, and continue to develop, techniques for representing knowledge in computers.

Knowledge Bases

While a database contains only facts, a **knowledge base** also contains a system of rules for determining and changing the relationship between those facts. Facts stored in a database are rigidly organized in categories; ideas stored in a knowledge base can be reorganized as new information changes their relationships.

Computer scientists so far have had little success in developing a knowledge base that can understand the world the way a child does. Even before they start school, children know that

- If you put something in water, it will get wet.
- If Susan is Phil's sister, Phil is Susan's brother.
- You can't build a tower from the top down.
- Dogs commonly live in houses, but cows seldom do.
- People can't walk through walls.
- If you eat dinner in a restaurant, you're expected to pay for the food and leave a tip.
- If you travel from Dallas to Phoenix, time passes during the trip.

These statements are part of the mass of common-sense knowledge that children acquire from living in the world. Since computers can't draw on years of human experience to construct mental models of the world, they don't automatically develop common sense. Much AI research centers on providing computers with ways to acquire and store real-world, common-sense knowledge. Researchers have had little success at developing computer systems with the kinds of broad, shallow knowledge found in children. But when knowledge bases are restricted to narrow, deep domains—the domains of experts—they can be effective, practical, *intelligent* tools. For example, knowledge bases lie at the heart of hundreds of *expert systems* used in business, science, and industry.

Artificial Experts

Ex = has-been
Spurt = a drip under pressure
Expert = has-been drip under pressure

—Utah Phillips

An expert is someone who has an extraordinary amount of knowledge within a narrow domain. By confining activities to that domain, the expert achieves mastery. An **expert system** is a software program designed to replicate the decision-making process of a human expert. At the foundation of every expert system is a knowledge base representing ideas from a specific field of expertise. Because it's a collection of specialized knowledge, an expert system's knowledge base must be constructed by a user, an expert, or a *knowledge engineer*—a specialist who interviews and observes experts and painstakingly converts their words and actions into a knowledge base. Some new expert systems can grow their own knowledge bases while observing human decision makers doing their jobs. But for most expert systems, the process is still human intensive.

Strictly speaking, expert systems derive their knowledge from experts; systems that draw on other sources, such as government regulations, company guidelines, and statistical databases, are called *knowledge-based systems*. But in practice the terms *expert system* and *knowledge-based system* are often used interchangeably.

A knowledge base commonly represents knowledge in the form of *if-then rules* like these:

- If the engine will not turn over and the lights do not work, then check the battery.
- If checking the battery shows it is not dead, then check the battery connectors.

Most human decision making involves uncertainty, so many modern expert systems include "fuzzy" rules that state conclusions as probabilities rather than certainties. Here's an example from MYCIN, one of the first expert systems designed to capture a doctor's expertise:

> If (1) the infection is primary-bacteremia, and
> (2) the site of the culture is one of the sterile sites, and
> (3) the suspected portal of entry of the organism is the gastrointestinal tract,
> then there is suggestive evidence (.7) that the identity of the organism is bacteriodes.

Along with the knowledge base, a complete expert system also includes a *human interface*, which allows the user to interact with the system, and an *inference engine*, which puts the user input together with the knowledge base, applies logical principles, and produces the requested expert advice.

Sometimes expert systems aid experts by providing automated data analysis and informed second opinions. In other cases expert systems support nonexperts by providing advice based on judgments of one or more experts. Whatever their role, expert systems work because they function within narrow, carefully defined domains.

Expert Systems in Action

Some of the first successful expert systems were developed around medical knowledge bases. Because medical knowledge is orderly and well documented, researchers believed it could be captured successfully in knowledge bases. They were right. The MYCIN medical expert system outperformed many human experts in diagnosing diseases. Dozens of other working medical expert systems exist, although few are actually used in medical practice.

The business community has been more enthusiastic than the medical community in its acceptance and use of expert systems. Here are a few examples of expert systems in action:

This expert system leads the user through the process of diagnosing problems with malfunctioning cameras

- Digital Equipment Corporation's XCON, one of the most successful expert systems in commercial use today, has been configuring complex computer systems since 1980. The system's knowledge base consists of more than 10,000 rules describing the relationship of various computer parts. It reportedly does the work of more than 300 human experts, and it makes fewer mistakes than humans do.

- American Express uses an expert system to automate the process of checking for fraud and misuses of its no-limit credit card. Credit checks must be completed within 90 seconds while the customer waits, and the cost of an error can be high. The company spent 13 months developing a system modeled on the decision-making expertise of its best credit clerks.

- At Blue Cross/Blue Shield of Virginia, an expert system automates insurance claim processing. The expert system handles up to 200 routine claims each day, allowing human clerks to spend more time on tough situations that require human judgment. The developers of the system extracted diagnostic rules from manuals and watched human claims processors apply those rules.

- Boeing Company factory workers use an expert system to locate the right parts, tools, and techniques for assembling airplane electrical connectors. The system replaces 20,000 pages of documentation and reduces the average search time from 42 minutes to 5 minutes.

- Microsoft Corporation sells a package of utilities to supplement its Windows operating system. The package includes an expert system for diagnosing printer network problems.

- Freelance writer Scott French used Nexpert, a Macintosh-based expert system, to analyze the writing style of Jacqueline Susann's novel *Valley of the Dolls* and help create *Just This Once*, a new work with the same style. The system reportedly wrote 25 percent of the novel independently, using suggestions from French. The Susann estate threatened French with a lawsuit even before the book had been sold.

There are hundreds of other examples of expert system applications: pinpointing likely sites for new oil explorations, aiding in automobile and appliance repairs, providing financial management advice, targeting direct-mail marketing campaigns, detecting problems in computer-controlled machinery, predicting weather, advising air traffic controllers, suggesting basic page layouts for publishers, controlling military machinery, providing assistance to musical composers . . . the list is growing at an astounding rate. Even the grammar checkers built into many word processors can be thought of as expert systems because they apply style and syntax rules developed by language experts.

One of the most unusual expert systems is AARON, an automated artist programmed by Harold Cohen, artist and professor at the University of California at

An original drawing by AARON, an expert system programmed by Harold Cohen (left), and Cohen demonstrating AARON (below).

San Diego. AARON uses over 1000 rules of human anatomy and behavior to create drawings of people, plants, and abstract objects with a robotic drawing machine. The drawings, which are unique works in a style similar to Cohen's, are widely acclaimed in the art community.

When AARON creates a drawing, an interesting question arises: Who is the artist, Cohen or AARON? Cohen claims he is; he sees AARON as a dynamic work of art. The question may seem frivolous, but it's related to a larger question with profound implications: When expert systems make decisions, who's responsible? If a doctor uses an expert system to decide to perform surgery and the surgery fails, who's liable—the doctor, the programmer, the software company, or somebody else? If you're denied medical benefits because of a bug in an expert system, do you sue a person, an organization, or a program? If a power plant explodes because an expert system fails to detect a fault, who's to blame? As expert systems proliferate, questions like these are certain to confront consumers, lawyers, lawmakers, and technicians.

Expert Systems in Perspective

From these examples, it should be clear that expert systems offer many advantages. An expert system can

- help train new employees
- reduce the number of human errors
- take care of routine tasks so workers can focus on more challenging jobs
- provide expertise when no experts are available
- preserve the knowledge of experts after those experts leave an organization
- combine the knowledge of several experts
- make knowledge available to more people

But expert systems aren't without problems. For one, today's expert systems are difficult to build. To simplify the process, many software companies sell **expert system shells**—generic expert systems containing human interfaces and inference engines. These programs can save time and effort, but they don't include the part that is most difficult to build—the knowledge base.

Even with a knowledge base, an expert system isn't the machine equivalent of a human expert. Unlike human experts, automated expert systems are poor at planning strategies. Their lack of flexibility makes them less creative than human thinkers. Most importantly, expert systems are powerless outside of their narrow, deep domains of knowledge. While most expert system domains can be summarized with a few hundred tidy rules of thumb, the world of people is full of inconsistencies, special cases, and ambiguities that could overwhelm even the best expert systems. A simple rule like "birds can fly" isn't sufficient for a literal-minded computer, which would need something more like this tongue-in-cheek rule from Marvin Minsky's book, *Society of Mind:*

> *Birds can fly, unless they are penguins and ostriches, or if they happen to be dead, or have broken wings, or are confined to cages, or have their feet stuck in cement, or have undergone experiences so dreadful as to render them psychologically incapable of flight.*

Clearly, knowledge engineers can't use rules to teach computers all they need to know to perform useful, intelligent functions outside narrow domains. If they're ever going to exhibit the kind of broad-based intelligence found in children, AI systems will need to acquire knowledge by reading, looking, listening, and drawing their own conclusions about the world. These skills all depend on techniques of pattern recognition.

PATTERN RECOGNITION: MAKING SENSE OF THE WORLD

Experience has shown that science frequently develops most fruitfully once we learn to examine the things that seem the simplest, instead of those that seem the most mysterious.

—Marvin Minsky

A baby can recognize a human face, especially its mother's, almost from birth. A mother can hear and recognize her child's cry even in a noisy room. Computers are notoriously inferior at both of these tasks, which fall into the general category of pattern recognition. **Pattern recognition** involves identifying recurring patterns in input data with the goal of understanding or categorizing that input.

Pattern recognition applications represent half of the AI industry. Applications include face identification, fingerprint identification, handwriting recognition, scientific data analysis, weather forecasting, biological slide analysis, surveillance satellite data analysis, robot vision, optical character recognition, automatic voice recognition, and expert systems. We'll examine the problems and the promise of several types of pattern recognition, starting with the recognition of visual patterns.

Image Analysis

Image analysis is the process of identifying objects and shapes in a photograph, drawing, video, or other visual image. It's used for everything from colorizing classic motion pictures to piloting cruise missiles. An effortless process for people, image analysis is extremely demanding for computers. The simple process of identifying objects in a scene is complicated by all kinds of factors: masses of irrelevant data, objects that partially cover other objects, indistinct edges, changes in light sources and shadows, changes in the scene as objects move, and more. With all these complications, it's amazing that people are able to make any sense out of the images that constantly bombard their eyes.

Most image analysis programs require massive amounts of memory and processing power. Even with the best hardware available, today's software can't hold a candle to the human visual system when it comes to general image analysis. But AI researchers have had considerable success by restricting the domain of visual systems. One of the biggest success stories in AI work is a limited but practical form of computer vision: optical character recognition.

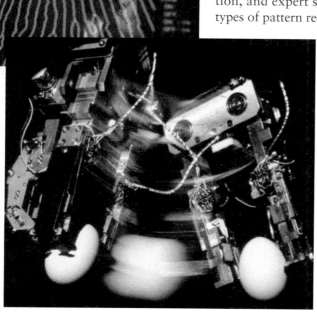

Pattern recognition is widely used in fingerprint analysis (top). This robot is equipped with visual and tactile sensors that employ pattern recognition technology (above).

Optical Character Recognition

In any shopping mall you can see sales clerks using wand readers to recognize words and numbers when they ring up your purchases at point-of-sale terminals. This specialized form of **optical character recognition (OCR)** is relatively simple for computers because the letters and numbers are designed to be easy for a computer to distinguish. OCR is much more difficult when the input might be a page from a book, newspaper, magazine, or letter. Still, general OCR technology has progressed to the point that it's practical for the U.S. Postal Service to use it to sort much of the mail sent every day. Similar technology is now available for personal computer users who have typewritten or printed text to be processed.

The first step in general OCR is to scan the image of the page into the computer's memory with a scanner, digital camera, or fax modem. The scanned image is nothing more than a pattern of bits in memory. It could just as easily be a poem by Robert Frost or a photograph of Robert Frost. Before a computer can process the text on a page, it must recognize the individual characters and convert them to text codes (ASCII or the equivalent). *Optical character recognition (OCR) software* locates and identifies printed characters embedded in images—it "reads" text. This is no small task for a machine, given the variety of typefaces and styles in use today.

The process of recognizing text in a variety of fonts and styles is surprisingly difficult for machines. State-of-the-art OCR programs use several techniques, including

- segmentation of the page into pictures, text blocks, and (eventually) individual characters
- scaled-down expert system technology for recognizing the underlying rules that distinguish letters
- context "experts" to help identify ambiguous letters by their context
- learning from actual examples and feedback from a human trainer

Today's best programs can achieve up to 99 percent accuracy—even better under optimal circumstances. OCR software isn't foolproof, but it's reliable enough to be practical for many text-intensive applications, including reading aloud to the blind, converting typewritten documents and incoming fax documents to editable text, and processing transactions for database systems. **UV**

A child can easily sort these letters into As and Bs. This problem is difficult for computers. Why?

OCR technology also can be applied to handwritten text but not as reliably. In typewritten and typeset text, character representation is consistent enough that one *a* looks like another *a*, at least when they're the same typeface. But, since most handwritten text lacks consistency, software has more trouble recognizing individual characters reliably. Nonetheless, the technology is getting better all the time, making more applications practical for pen-based computers. Handwriting recognition is especially important in Japan, China, and other countries with languages that don't lend themselves to keyboarding. But it's also useful with Western languages in situations where keyboarding isn't practical. Even the classic three-ring student notebook will undoubtedly have an electronic counterpart that automatically turns handwritten notes into text that can be fed directly into a word processor.

Apple's Newton operating system has built-in handwriting recognition software. The software has improved dramatically since the Newton's introduction, but still falls short of 100 percent accuracy.

Optical Character Recognition

▲ ▲

Software: OmniPage Professional.

The goal: To create an editable text file from a printed paper using OCR software. When your friend Art tried to open the disk file containing his 20-page research paper to make a few last-minute changes, his computer displayed a disk error message and refused to open the file. Art already tried a file recovery utility, but it wasn't able to retrieve the file. Unfortunately, he didn't have a backup copy of the file stored on another disk. Fortunately, he had a recent printout.

1 After loading the first page of the printout into a scanner and launching OmniPage Pro, you click on AUTO to begin the automatic OCR process.

4 You click on the check button to check and edit the text using the built-in spelling checker and editor.

2 OmniPage scans the page and performs image analysis to locate the "zones" containing text.

3 OmniPage analyzes each text zone, attempting to recognize each character. The analyzed text appears in a new window. The software appears to have recognized almost all of the characters in the main text, but it had trouble with the unusual script font used in the title. (Each ~ represents an unrecognized character.)

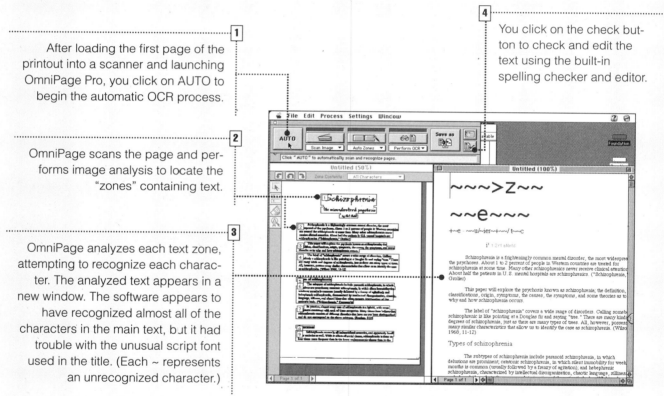

Automatic Speech Recognition

> I think that the primary means of communication with computers in the next millennium will be speech.
>
> —Nicholas Negroponte, director of MIT's Media Lab

Our ears process far less information than our eyes, but that information, especially human speech, is extremely important to our understanding of the world. In Chapters 3 and 7 we discussed audio digitizers—input devices that capture spoken words,

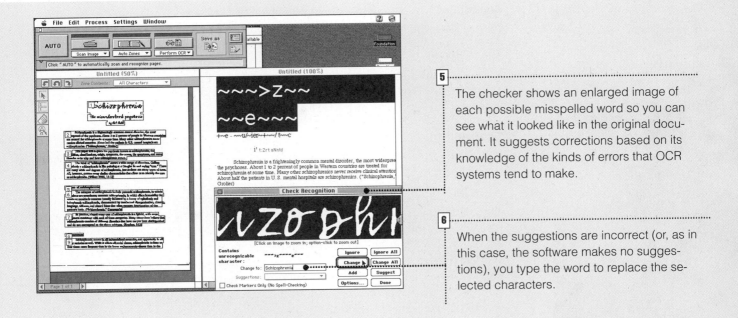

5

The checker shows an enlarged image of each possible misspelled word so you can see what it looked like in the original document. It suggests corrections based on its knowledge of the kinds of errors that OCR systems tend to make.

6

When the suggestions are incorrect (or, as in this case, the software makes no suggestions), you type the word to replace the selected characters.

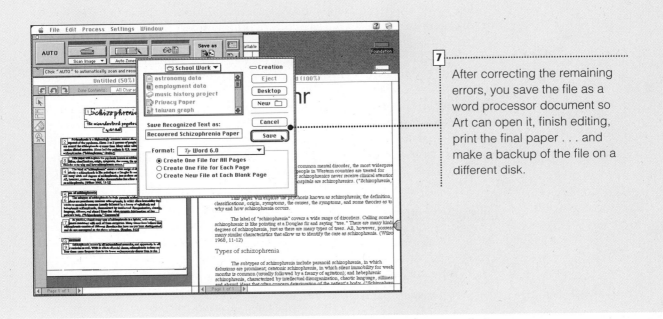

7

After correcting the remaining errors, you save the file as a word processor document so Art can open it, finish editing, print the final paper . . . and make a backup of the file on a different disk.

music, and other sounds so they can be stored as digital data. But digitized voice input, like scanned text, must be processed by sophisticated software before it can be interpreted by the computer as words. **Automatic speech recognition** systems use pattern recognition techniques similar to those used by vision and OCR systems, including

- segmentation of input sound patterns into individual words and phonemes
- expert rules for interpreting sounds
- context "experts" for dealing with ambiguous sounds
- learning from a human trainer

Training is especially important in speech recognition because of the tremendous differences among human voices. Most current commercial systems need to be trained to recognize a particular person's voice before they can function. Even then, most systems work reliably only if the user speaks slowly and uses a small, predefined vocabulary. Research in speech recognition today focuses on overcoming these limitations and producing systems that can

- recognize words without being trained to an individual speaker—an ability known as *speaker independence*
- handle speech without limiting vocabulary
- handle *continuous speech*—natural speech in which words run together at normal speed

Researchers are making great strides toward these goals. Macintosh computers come with PlainTalk software that allows them to process continuous speech with speaker independence. PlainTalk isn't 100 percent accurate, but it does a remarkable job of handling routine command processing, responding appropriately to spoken commands like "Computer . . . close window." IBM has developed automatic dictation software that, with some individualized training to recognize each user's voice, can replace the keyboard for many applications. Other companies have produced systems that combine speaker independence with the ability to recognize a large vocabulary. No one has yet developed a system that achieves all three goals, the human body excepted.

Even with their current limitations, speech recognition systems are used by factory workers and others whose hands are otherwise occupied while they use the computer. People can communicate numbers and commands by telephone for automated banking, credit card verification, and other remote applications. Speech recognition systems empower many handicapped users by allowing them to give verbal commands to computers and robotic devices. As their vocabularies grow, voice recognition systems are likely to show up in *talkwriters*—automated, dictation-taking typists. Future pocket-sized personal digital assistants may use microphones as their principal input devices. Many of today's researchers are working to combine speech recognition and natural-language understanding in a single machine that can accept commands in everyday spoken English, "Star Trek" style.

Talking Computers

The computers on TV's Star Trek not only recognize human speech input but also respond with easy-to-understand **synthetic speech.** With **speech synthesis** software or hardware, modern desktop computers can generate synthetic speech by converting text into phonetic sounds. Most of today's speech synthesizers sound artificial when compared to the "Star Trek" computer voices; they even sound more artificial than the robot voices in low-budget cartoons. Human spoken language is complex, and no one has come close to duplicating it with software.

The Kurzweil Reading Machine uses OCR technology to recognize printed text, which it can then read aloud using speech synthesis technology. With a Kurzweil Reading machine, a visually impaired person can read any book, even if it hasn't been recorded on audio tape.

Still, it's easier for machines to speak passable English than to recognize it. There are many applications for voice output, including preschool education, telephone communication, and, of course, reading machines for visually impaired computer users.

For situations for which a synthetic voice isn't good enough, computers can play prerecorded **digitized speech** (along with other **digitized sounds**) stored in memory or on audio CDs. Of course, digitally recorded speech won't work for applications in which the text to be spoken is unpredictable, such as a talking word processor, because all the sounds must be prerecorded. But for an application with a limited vocabulary (reciting telephone numbers for automated directory assistance) or limited choices (an interactive educational game with short prerecorded speeches), digitized speech is a workable alternative until synthesized speech is perfected.

Neural Networks

> The human brain uses a type of circuitry that is very slow . . . at least 10,000 times slower than a digital computer. On the other hand, the degree of parallelism vastly outstrips any computer architecture we have yet to design. . . . For such tasks as vision, language, and motor control, the brain is more powerful than 1,000 supercomputers, yet for certain simple tasks such as multiplying digital numbers, it is less powerful than the 4-bit microprocessor found in a ten-dollar calculator.
>
> —Raymond Kurzweil, in *The Age of Intelligent Machines*

Artificial intelligence research has produced many amazing success stories and some embarrassing failures. The successes—intelligent applications that outperform their human counterparts—tend to involve tasks that require sequential thinking, logical rules, and orderly relationships. AI has been less successful at competing with natural human intelligence in applications like language, vision, speech, and movement—applications where massive amounts of data are processed in parallel.

It's not surprising that computers excel at linear, logical processes; almost every computer that's ever been created is designed to process digital information sequentially through a single CPU. The human brain, on the other hand, consists of billions of neurons, each connected to thousands of others in a massively parallel, distributed structure. This kind of structure gives the brain an advantage at most perceptual, motor, and creative skills.

Much current work in artificial intelligence is focused on **neural networks** (or **neural nets**)—distributed, parallel computing systems inspired by the structure of the human brain. Instead of a single, complex CPU, a neural network uses a network of a few thousand simpler processors called *neurons*. Neural networks aren't programmed in the usual way; they're trained. Instead of using a rule-based approach, a neural network learns patterns by trial and error, just as the brain does. When patterns are repeated often, neural networks, in effect, develop habits. This kind of learning can present problems for some kinds of applications because no rules are clearly defined. When a neural net makes a decision, you have no way to ask why.

Neural networks also store information differently than traditional computers. Concepts are represented as patterns of activity among many neurons, so they are less susceptible to machine failure. Because it distributes knowledge throughout the network, a neural net (like the human brain) can still function if some of its neurons are destroyed.

For a neural net to learn to recognize the letter A, it must go through a series of trials in which circuit patterns that produce incorrect guesses are weakened and patterns that produce correct guesses are strengthened. The end result is a circuit pattern that can recognize the letter A in a variety of forms.

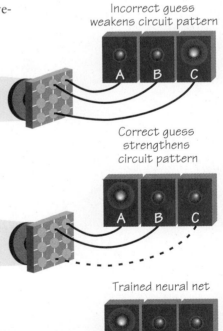

Incorrect guess weakens circuit pattern

Correct guess strengthens circuit pattern

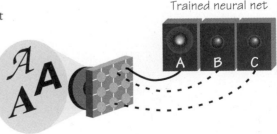

Trained neural net

Many neural net algorithms are developed on parallel-processing supercomputers with thousands of processors. Neural net chips containing thousands of neurons are produced by Intel Corporation and other hardware companies. A number of software companies have developed programs that simulate neural nets on PCs and other nonparallel machines. However, none of today's neural net hardware or software approaches the complexity or the capacity of the human brain.

Most researchers consider today's neural nets as, at best, baby steps in the direction of machines that can more closely emulate the workings of the human brain. There's considerable debate in the AI community about the future of neural nets. Some see neural nets as playing only a limited role in artificial intelligence; others expect it to eclipse the traditional rule-based approach.

Even so, neural nets are already being put to use in a variety of applications, ranging from artificial vision to expert systems. Neural nets are especially useful for recognizing patterns buried in huge quantities of numbers, such as in scientific research, loan processing, and stock market analysis. Some modems use neural nets to distinguish signals from random telephone-line noise. Optimistic researchers hope that neural networks may someday provide hearing for the deaf and eyesight for the blind.

A member of the Merce Cunningham Dance Company dances with a score by David Tudor, composed in part by Intel's 80170 ETANN (Electronically Trainable Artificial Neural Network). The music for a particular performance is determined in part by dancer movements and audience noise.

THE ROBOT REVOLUTION

1. A robot may not injure a human being, or, through inaction, allow a human being to come to harm.
2. A robot must obey the orders given it by human beings, except where such orders would conflict with the First Law.
3. A robot must protect its own existence as long as such protection does not conflict with the First or Second Law.

—Isaac Asimov's Three Laws of Robotics

Nowhere are artificial intelligence technologies more visible than in the field of robotics. Vision, hearing, pattern recognition, knowledge engineering, expert decision making, natural-language understanding, speech—they all come together in today's robots.

What Is a Robot?

The term *robot* (from the root word *robota*, the Czech word for forced labor) first appeared in a 1923 play called *R.U.R.* (for Rossum's Universal Robots), by Czech playwright Karel Capek. Capek's robots were intelligent machines that could see, hear, touch, move, and exercise judgment based on common sense. But these powerful machines eventually rebelled against their human creators, just as hundreds of fictional robots have done in succeeding decades. Today movies, TV, and books are full of imaginary robots, both good and evil.

As exotic as they might seem, robots are similar to other kinds of computer technology people use every day. While a typical computer performs *mental* tasks, a **robot** is a computer-controlled machine designed to perform specific *manual* tasks. A robot's central processor might be a microprocessor embedded in the robot's shell, or it might be a supervisory computer that controls the robot from a distance. In any case the processor is functionally identical to the processor found in a personal computer, a workstation, or a mainframe computer.

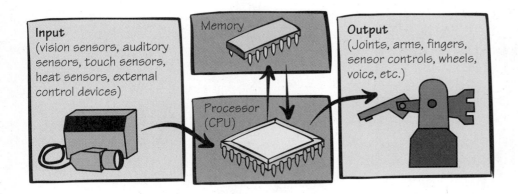

The most important hardware differences between robots and other computers are the input and output peripherals. Instead of sending output to a screen or a printer, a robot sends commands to joints, arms, and other moving parts. The first robots had no corresponding input devices to monitor their movements and the surrounding environment. They were effectively deaf, blind, and in some cases dangerous—at least one Japanese worker was killed by an early sightless robot. Most modern robots include some kind of input sensors. These sensing devices allow robots to correct or modify their actions based on feedback from the outside world.

Industrial robots seldom have the human-inspired anatomy of Hollywood's science fiction robots. Instead they're designed to accomplish particular tasks in the best possible way. Robots can be designed to see infrared light, rotate joints 360 degrees, and do other things that aren't possible for humans. On the other hand, robots are constrained by the limitations of artificial intelligence software. The most sophisticated robot today can't tie a pair of shoelaces, understand the vocabulary of a three-year old child, or consistently tell the difference between a cat and a dog.

Steel-Collar Workers

From a management point of view, robots offer several advantages:

- Obviously, many robots are installed to save labor costs. Robots are expensive to design, install, and program. But once they're operational they can work 24 hours a day, 365 days a year, without vacations, strikes, sick leave, or coffee breaks.

- Robots can also improve quality and increase productivity. They're especially effective at doing repetitive jobs in which bored, tired people are prone to make errors and have accidents.

- Robots are ideal for jobs like cleaning up hazardous waste—jobs that are dangerous or uncomfortable for human workers.

For all these reasons the robot population is exploding. Today hundreds of thousands of industrial robots do welding, part fitting, painting, and other repetitive tasks in factories all over the world. In most automated factories, robots work alongside humans, but in some state-of-the-art factories, the only function of human workers is to monitor and repair robots. Robots aren't used just in factories. Robots also shear sheep in Australia, paint ship hulls in France, disarm land mines in the Persian Gulf, and perform precision skull drilling for brain surgeons in California.

Commercial robots still can't compete with people for jobs that require exceptional perceptual or fine-motor skills. But robots in research labs suggest that a new generation of more competitive robots is on the way. A robot developed at Bell Labs can defeat most human opponents at Ping-Pong. A human-sized Japanese robot

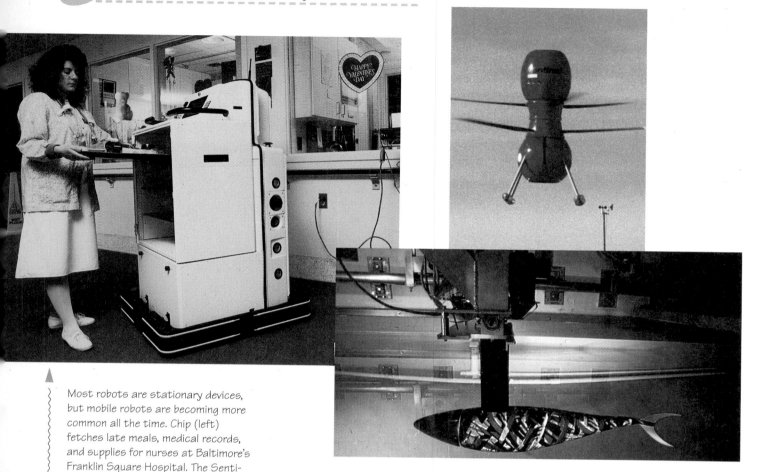

Most robots are stationary devices, but mobile robots are becoming more common all the time. Chip (left) fetches late meals, medical records, and supplies for nurses at Baltimore's Franklin Square Hospital. The Sentinal (above right) can fly to heights of 10,000 feet; applications include spying and forest-fire detection. A swimming robot named Robotuna (below right) s designed to collect undersea data for scientists.

named Wabot-2 can read sheet music and perform it on an organ or synthesizer using ten fingers and two feet. The technologies used in these experimental robots will undoubtedly show up in a variety of machines, from automated servants for handicapped people to flying robots for the military. We may be within a few years of self-propelled robot housecleaners!

The robot revolution isn't necessarily good news for people who earn their living doing manual labor. While it's true that many of the jobs robots do are boring, dirty, or dangerous, they're still jobs. The issues surrounding automation and worker displacement are complex, and they aren't limited to factories. We'll discuss them in more detail in the next chapter.

AI IMPLICATIONS

We are on the edge of change comparable to the rise of human life on Earth. The precise cause of this change is the imminent creation by technology of entities with greater-than-human intelligence.

—Verner Vinge, mathematician and science fiction writer

From the earliest days of artificial intelligence, research has been accompanied by questions about the implications of the work. The very idea of intelligent machines is at the same time confusing, exciting, and frightening to many people. Even when they don't work very well, AI programs generate emotional responses in the people who use them.

Earlier we met ELIZA, the therapy simulator developed to demonstrate natural-language conversation. ELIZA's simple-minded approach wasn't intended to fool anyone in a Turing test, but it did have an impact on the people who used it. Many ELIZA users became emotionally attached to the program and attributed it with compassion and empathy. Weizenbaum's secretary asked him to leave the room so she could converse in private with ELIZA. Some therapists even saw ELIZA as the beginning of a new age of automated therapy. Weizenbaum was shocked by the way people attributed human capabilities to such an obviously flawed technology. He responded with *Computer Power and Human Reason,* a landmark book that presents the case for maintaining a distinction between computers and people. Weizenbaum argues that "There are certain tasks which computers ought not to be made to do, independent of whether computers can be made to do them."

Weizenbaum's caution isn't shared by international political and economic leaders, many of whom are encouraging increased AI research and development. As it matures, AI technology finds its way out of the research lab and into the marketplace. A growing number of programs and products incorporate pattern recognition, expert systems, and other AI techniques. In the near future we're likely to see more products with *embedded AI,* including intelligent word processors that can help writers turn rough drafts into polished prose, smart appliances that can recognize and obey their owners' spoken commands, and vehicles that can perform their own diagnostics and, in many cases, repairs.

Where will it all lead? Will intensive AI research result in computers capable of intelligent behavior outside narrow domains? Patrick Winston, director of MIT's artificial intelligence laboratory, once said, "The interesting issue is not whether machines can be made smarter but if humans are smart enough to pull it off. A raccoon obviously can't make a machine as smart as a raccoon. I wonder if humans can."

Many AI researchers believe that sooner or later they *will* pull it off. Some think artificial intelligence is the natural culmination of the evolutionary process—that the next intelligent life form on earth will be based on silicon rather than the carbon that is the basis of human life. Computer mathematician and science fiction writer Verner Vinge argues that the competitive nature of our society makes such a prospect almost inevitable. What business or government will voluntarily curtail research on artificial intelligence, computer networks, and biotechnology, knowing that competing institutions will continue to pursue similar research? Vinge calls the moment of creation of greater-than-human intelligence a *singularity*—a point where our old models will have to be discarded and a new reality will rule.

If smarter-than-human beings come to pass, how will they relate to the less intelligent humans that surround them? This kind of thinking isn't easy; it goes to the heart of human values and forces us to look at our place in the universe.

SUMMARY

~~~~~~

Artificial intelligence has many definitions. Most artificial intelligence research focuses on making computers do things at which people generally are better. Some AI researchers try to simulate human intelligent behavior, but most try to design intelligent machines independent of the way people think. Successful AI research generally involves working on problems with limited domains rather than trying to tackle large, open-ended problems. AI programs employ a variety of techniques, including searching, heuristics, pattern recognition, and machine learning, to achieve their goals.

From a practical standpoint natural-language communication is one of the most important areas of AI study. Natural-language programs that deal with a subset of the language are used in applications ranging from machine translation programs to natural-language interfaces. But no program is capable of handling the kind of unrestricted natural-language text people deal with every day. Natural-language programs are confounded by the English language's large vocabulary, convoluted syntax, and ambiguous semantics—the *meanings* behind the words.

AI researchers have developed a variety of schemes for representing knowledge in computers. A knowledge base contains facts and a system for determining and changing the relationship between those facts. Today's knowledge bases are only practical for representing narrow domains of knowledge, such as the knowledge of an expert on a particular subject. Expert systems are programs designed to replicate the decision-making process of human experts. An expert system includes a knowledge base, an inference engine for applying logical rules to the facts in a knowledge base, and a human interface for interacting with users. Once the knowledge base is constructed (usually based on interviews and observations of human experts), an expert system can provide consultation that rivals human advice in many situations. Expert systems are successfully used in a variety of scientific, business, and other applications.

Pattern recognition is an important area of AI research that involves identifying recurring patterns in input data. Pattern recognition technology is at the heart of computer vision, voice communication, and other important AI applications. These diverse applications all use similar techniques for isolating and recognizing patterns. People are better at pattern recognition than computers, in part because the human brain can process masses of data in parallel. Modern neural network computers are designed to process data in the same way the human brain does. Many researchers believe that neural nets, as they grow in size and sophistication, will help computers improve their performance at many difficult tasks.

A robot is a computer-controlled machine designed to perform specific *manual* tasks. Robots include output peripherals for manipulating their environments and input sensors that allow them to perform self-correcting actions based on feedback from outside. Robots perform a variety of dangerous and tedious tasks, in many cases outperforming human workers. As robot technology advances, more traditional human jobs will be done by artificial workers.

In spite of the numerous difficulties AI researchers encounter when trying to produce truly intelligent machines, many experts believe that people will eventually create artificial beings that are more intelligent than their creators—a prospect with staggering implications.

Chapter Review

Key Terms

artificial intelligence (AI)	heuristic	pattern recognition
automatic speech recognition	image analysis	robot
automatic translation	knowledge base	semantics
digitized sound	machine learning	speech synthesis
digitized speech	neural network (neural net)	syntax
expert system	optical character recognition (OCR)	synthetic speech
expert system shell	parsing program (parser)	Turing test

Review Questions

1. In what sense is artificial intelligence a "moving frontier"?

2. What are the disadvantages of the approach to AI that attempts to simulate human intelligence? What is the alternative?

3. Describe several techniques used in game-playing software, and explain how they can be applied to other artificial intelligence applications.

4. Why did early machine translation programs fail to produce the desired results?

5. Why is the sentence "Time flies like an arrow" difficult for a computer to parse, translate, or understand? Can you find four possible meanings for the sentence?

6. What is the relationship between syntax and semantics? Can you construct a sentence that follows the rules of English syntax but has nonsense semantics?

7. What is a knowledge base? What is an expert system? How are the two related?

8. Give examples of successful expert system applications. Give examples of several tasks that can't be accomplished with today's expert system technology, and explain why they can't.

9. What are some of the problems that make machine vision so challenging?

10. In what ways are the techniques of optical character recognition similar to those of speech recognition programs?

11. What rules might a computer use to sort the characters shown on page 221 into As and Bs?

12. An automated speech recognition system might have trouble telling the difference between a "common denominator" and a "comedy nominator." What must the speaker do to avoid confusion? What other limitations plague automated speech recognition systems today?

13. In what ways are neural networks designed to simulate the structure of the human brain? In what ways do neural nets perform differently than standard single-processor CPUs?

14. What kind of hardware is necessary for a robot to be self-correcting, so it can modify its actions based on outside feedback?

15. What distinguishes a robot from a desktop computer?

Discussion Questions

1. Is the Turing test a valid test of intelligence? Why or why not?

2. If you were the interrogator in the Turing test, what questions would you ask to try to discover whether you were communicating with a computer? What would you look for in the answers?

3. List several mental tasks that people do better than computers. List several mental tasks that computers do better than people. Can you find any general characteristics that distinguish the items on the two lists?

4. Computers can compose original music, produce original artwork, create original mathematical proofs. Does this mean that Ada Lovelace was wrong when she said, in effect, that computers can do only what they're told to do?

5. The works of AARON, the expert system artist, are unique, original, and widely acclaimed as art. Who is the artist, AARON or Harold Cohen, AARON's creator? Is AARON a work of art, an artist, or both?

6. If an expert system gives you erroneous information, should you be able to sue it for malpractice? If it fails and causes major disruptions or injury, who's responsible? The programmer? The publisher? The owner? The computer?

7. Some expert systems and neural nets can't explain the reasons behind their decisions. What kinds of problems might be caused by this limitation? Under what circumstances, if any, should an expert system be required to produce an "audit trail" to explain how it reached conclusions?

8. What kinds of human jobs are most likely to be eliminated because of expert systems? What kinds of new jobs will be created because of expert systems?

9. What kinds of human jobs are most likely to be eliminated because of robots? What kinds of new jobs will be created as a result of factory automation?

10. Are Asimov's three laws of robotics adequate for smoothly integrating intelligent robots into tomorrow's society? If not, what laws would you add?

Projects

1. Public domain versions of Weizenbaum's ELIZA program are available for most types of desktop computers. Locate a copy and try conversing with it. Test the program on your friends and see how they react to it. Try to determine the rules and tricks that ELIZA uses to simulate conversation. If you're a programmer, try writing your own version of ELIZA.

2. When Turing first proposed the Turing test, he compared it to a similar test in which the interrogator tried to guess the sex of the people typing answers to questions. See if you can devise such a test. What, if anything, does it prove?

3. Try to find examples of working expert systems and robots in your school or community and present your findings.

4. Test OCR software, grammar checking software, and other types of consumer-oriented AI applications. How "intelligent" are these applications? In what ways could they be improved?

5. Survey people's attitudes and concerns about artificial intelligence and robots. Present your findings.

Sources and Resources

Books

The Age of Intelligent Machines, by Raymond Kurzweil (Cambridge, MA: MIT Press, 1990). If you want to learn more about artificial intelligence, this award-winning book is a great resource in spite of its age. With clear prose, beautiful illustrations, and intelligent articles by the masters of the field, Kurzweil explores the historical, philosophical, academic, aesthetic, practical, fanciful, and speculative sides of AI. An outstanding companion video is also available.

Godel, Escher, Bach: An Eternal Golden Braid, by Douglas R. Hofstadter (New York: Vintage Books, 1980). This Pulitzer Prize winner is part mathematics, part philosophy, and part *Alice in Wonderland*. If you like to think deeply about questions like "What is thought?" you'll find plenty to think about here.

Artificial Minds, by Stan Franklin (Cambridge, MA: MIT Press, 1995). Franklin explores the fascinating territory between computer science, cognitive psychology, and philosophy. He makes a case that there's a continuum between "mind" and "nonmind," and that we're entering an era when it's possible to explore that continuum in ways never before possible. This book is challenging and thought-provoking.

Artificial Intelligence, Third Edition, by Patrick Henry Winston (Reading, MA: Addison-Wesley, 1992). This best-selling introductory text for computer science students is thorough and well-written. Like most computer science texts, it's probably too technical and mathematical for most casual readers.

Computer Power and Human Reason: From Judgment to Calculation, by Joseph Weizenbaum (San Francisco: Freeman, 1995). An MIT computer scientist speaks out on the things computers shouldn't do, even if they can. This classic book is as important now as when it was first published in the 1970s. The latest edition has been updated with new material to reflect changes that happened since the book was first published.

Society of Mind, by Marvin Minsky (New York: Simon & Schuster, 1988). Another MIT artificial intelligence expert presents his thoughts on the relationship between people and intelligent machines. A dense but thought-provoking book. A CD-ROM version is available from the Voyager Company.

Lisp, by Patrick Henry Winston and Berthold K. P. Horn (Reading, MA: Addison-Wesley, 1989). A popular introduction to Common LISP, the widely used programming language of artificial intelligence.

AARON's Code: Meta-Art, Artificial Intelligence and the Work of Harold Cohen, by Pamela McCorduck (New York: W. H. Freeman, 1991). This entertaining book gives the inside story on AARON, Harold Cohen's amazing expert system artist. It provides insights into the world of art and the world of computer science.

Across Realtime, by Verner Vinge (New York: Baen Books, 1991). Vinge's science fiction opus takes you into a future after the singularity that produced artificial superintelligence. Vinge is a master storyteller, and there's plenty to think about here. (For a nonfiction discussion of the singularity, see Vinge's "Technological Singularity," in *Whole Earth Review*, Winter, 1993, page 88.)

World Wide Web Sites

Check the *Computer Confluence* Web site for links to Internet sources on expert systems, pattern recognition, and other AI topics.

PART FIVE

LIVING WITH COMPUTERS

INTO THE

INFORMATION AGE

Steve Roberts, Technomad

> Future society will be virtually paperless, energy-efficient, dependent upon wide-bandwidth networking, and generally cognizant of global perspective through routine communication across decreasingly relevant borders. It is not too early to prepare for this: We need the ideas, the tools, and an awareness of the problems that accompany fundamental shifts in the meaning of information.
>
> —Steven K. Roberts

In 1983 Steve Roberts realized he wasn't happy chained to his desk and his debts. He'd lost sight of his passions—writing, adventure, computer design, ham radio, bicycling, romance, learning, networking, publishing. He decided to build a new lifestyle that combined those passions.

Six months later he hit the road on Winnebiko, a custom recumbent bike equipped with a tiny Radio Shack Model 100 laptop and a small 5-watt solar panel. He connected each day to the CompuServe network through pay phones, transmitting magazine articles and book chapters.

Three years and 10,000 miles later, Roberts replaced Winnebiko with Winnebiko II, a low-riding, high-tech bike with special handlebars that allowed Roberts to type while riding down the highway. Roberts pedaled 6000 miles on Winnebiko II, this time with a traveling partner named Maggie Victor. Roberts writes of this period:

Through ham radio and computer networking, the sense of living in a virtual neighborhood grew more and more tangible, until the road itself became merely an entertaining backdrop for a stable life in Dataspace. . . . Home, quite literally, became an abstract electronic

Steve Roberts
with BEHEMOTH

After reading this chapter, you should be able to:

〜〜〜〜〜〜〜〜〜〜〜〜〜〜〜〜〜〜〜〜〜

- Explain how the emerging information economy differs from earlier social and economic systems
- Describe how computers have changed the way people work in factories, offices, homes, and a variety of industries
- Describe how modern managers use computers as tools
- Describe several ways computers have changed the quality of jobs, both positively and negatively
- Speculate on how our society will adjust as more and more jobs are automated

Microship

concept. From a business standpoint, it no longer mattered where we were, and we traveled freely, making a living through magazine publishing and occasional consulting spin-offs, seeking modular phone jacks at every stop.

After three years, technological advances lured Roberts off the road to design and build a new high-tech people-powered vehicle. With 150 corporate equipment sponsors and 35 helpers, Roberts constructed the $1.2 million BEHEMOTH (Big Electronic Human-Energized Machine . . . Only Too Heavy)—a 580-pound, 8-foot recumbent bike with a 4-foot trailer. This show-piece of future technology carries seven networked computers, a ham radio station, satellite links, a cellular phone with modem and fax, a CD stereo system, a water-cooled helmet with a heads-up virtual computer display,

solar collectors, and six-level security system. (It can even dial 911 and say, "I am a bicycle; I am being stolen; my current latitude is . . . .")

After pedaling 17,000 miles on techno-bikes, Roberts started having dreams of "life with no hills" and turned his sites to the sea. His latest project is Micro-ship, "a high-tech multihull with an extensive network of embedded control systems, a satellite Internet link, console Macintoshes . . . , ham radio, 1080 watts of solar panels, deployable kayaks, self-trailering capa-

bility, on-board video production, and whole new levels of technomadic gizmology." Roberts mixes travel with consulting and speaking engagements, all the while connected electronically to the support facilities in his laboratory. He sees his travels as a mixture of business, experimentation, education, and, of course, adventure. In his words, "There's a LOT of world to explore out there. Having had a taste of it, how could I spend my life in one place?"

315

teve Roberts likes to tell schoolchildren that "the obvious choices aren't the only choices." Roberts made career and lifestyle choices that wouldn't have been possible without modern information technology. Computer technology has changed the way millions of people work by providing new choices and opportunities. For other less fortunate workers, technology has taken away choices and opportunities. In this chapter we'll see how computers are changing the ways people work. We'll start by examining the roots and characteristics of the modern information economy. Then we'll see how computers are changing the ways people do their jobs in automated factories, automated offices, and elsewhere. We'll examine the computer-based tools used by managers to help them manage more effectively and efficiently. Finally, we'll consider the effects of **automation** on the nature and availability of jobs and speculate on the future implications of the computerization of our workplace. In the next chapter we'll explore the effects of computers on the two other institutions that are central to our lives: our schools and our homes.

INTO THE INFORMATION AGE

> It is the business of the future to be dangerous. . . . The major advances in civilization are processes that all but wreck the societies in which they occur.
>
> —Alfred North Whitehead

Every so often, civilization dramatically changes course. Events and ideas come together to transform radically the way people live, work, and think. Traditions go by the wayside, common sense is turned upside down, and lives are thrown into turmoil until a new order takes hold. Humankind experiences a **paradigm shift**—a change in thinking that results in a new way of seeing the world. Major paradigm shifts take generations because individuals have trouble changing their assumptions about the way the world works.

Before the 20th century, humanity experienced two major paradigm shifts directly related to the world of work: the agricultural revolution and the industrial revolution. It's helpful to glance backward at these two shifts for perspective before we focus on the information revolution—the paradigm shift that's affecting us today.

Three Monumental Changes

Prehistoric people were mostly hunters and gatherers. They lived tribal, nomadic lives, tracking animals and gathering wild fruits, nuts, and grains. Anthropologists speculate that some prehistoric people spent as few as 15 hours per week satisfying material needs and devoted the rest of their time to cultural and spiritual pursuits.

The Agricultural Economy

As the human population grew, people learned to domesticate animals, grow their own grains, and use plows and other agricultural tools. The transformation to an agricultural economy took place over several centuries around 10,000 years ago. The result was a society in which most people lived and worked on farms, exchanging goods and services in nearby towns. The agricultural age lasted until about a century ago, when technological advances triggered what has come to be known as an *industrial revolution*.

The Industrial Economy

In the first half of the 20th century, the world was dominated by an industrial economy in which more people worked in urban factories than on farms. Factory work promised a higher material standard of living for a growing population, but not without a price. As work life became separate from home life, fathers were removed from day-to-day family life, and mothers assumed the bulk of domestic responsibilities. Increasingly more wealth was in the hands of fewer people. As towns grew into cities, crime, pollution, and other urban problems grew with them.

The Information Economy

Twentieth-century information technology produced what's been called a second industrial revolution, as people turned from factory work to information-related work. In today's **information economy** (sometimes called a *post-industrial economy*), clerical workers outnumber factory workers, and most people earn their living working with words, numbers, and ideas. Instead of planting corn or making shoes, most of us shuffle bits in one form or another. As we roar into the information age, we're riding a wave of social change that rivals any that came before.

Technology was central to each of these transformations. The agricultural economy grew from the plow, the industrial revolution was sparked by machines, and the information age is so dependent on computers that it's often called the computer age.

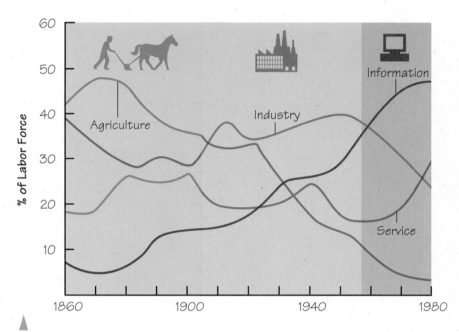

In the last century the workforce has moved from the farm, to the factory, and then to the office.

Computers and Change

By the year 2000, anybody in western civilization [will] be able to get the answer to any question that has an answer.

> —Jerry Pournelle, science fiction and technology writer

An age rich in electronic information may achieve wonderful social conveniences at the cost of placing freedom in a deep chill.

> —Langdon Winner, technology critic

Countless words have been written about the effects of computer technology on our work, our schools, our home life, and our society. Many writers focus on emerging technologies and the new possibilities they offer: possibilities for improved communication, personal expression, information access, and productivity. Others focus on computer technology as a source of suffering, oppression, and alienation. Both utopian and anti-utopian visions are based on speculation about the future. Researchers who study the *current* impact of computer technology report that the truth, so far, lies somewhere between these two extremes.

WHERE COMPUTERS WORK

> All those ones and zeros we've been passing around—the fuel that fans the digital fire—have reached critical mass and ignited, big time.
>
> —Steven Levy

It's becoming harder all the time to find jobs that haven't been changed in some way by computers. Consider these examples:

- *Entertainment.* The production of television programs and movies involves computer technology at every stage of the process. Scriptwriters use specialized word processors to write and revise scripts, and they use telecommunications technology to beam them between Hollywood and New York. Artists and technicians use graphics workstations to create special effects, from simple scene fadeouts and rolling credits to flying super heroes and intergalactic battles. Musicians compose soundtracks using synthesizers and computer-controlled sequencers. Sound editors use computer-controlled mixers to blend music with digital sound effects and live-action sound. Even commercials—*especially* commercials—use state-of-the-art computer graphics, animation, and sound to keep you watching the images instead of pressing the fast-forward button on your VCR.

- *Publishing.* The newspaper industry is being radically transformed by computer technology. Reporters scan the Internet for hard-to-find facts, write and edit stories on location using notebook computers, and transmit those stories by modem to central offices. Graphic artists design charts and artwork with graphics software. Photo retouchers use scanners and computers instead of brushes and magnifying glasses to edit photographs. Production crews assemble pages with computers instead of typesetting machines and pasteup boards. Many newspapers produce World Wide Web editions in addition to traditional paper publications.

- *Medicine.* High-tech equipment plays a critical role in the healing arts, too. Hospital information systems store patient medical and insurance records. Local area networks allow doctors, nurses, technicians, dietitians, and office staff to view and update information throughout the hospital. Computers monitor patient vital signs in intensive care units in hospitals, at home, and on the street with portable units that analyze signals and transmit warnings when problems arise. Databases alert doctors and pharmacists to the problems and possibilities of prescribed drugs. Computer-aided tomography (CAT) scans allow doctors to

Portable computers are standard equipment for journalists today.

A growing number of newspapers and magazines are published on the World Wide Web.

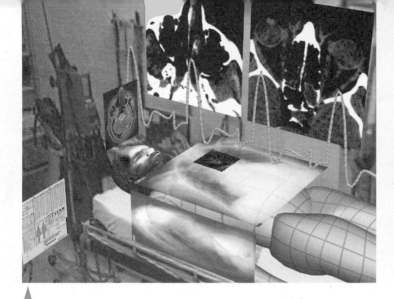

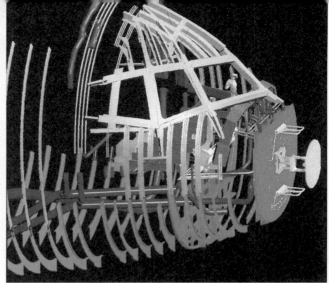

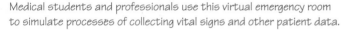

Medical students and professionals use this virtual emergency room to simulate processes of collecting vital signs and other patient data.

This digital model of Boeing 777's fusilage was designed with workstations running 3-D CAD software.

see cross-sectional slices of human bodies. Every day computers provide medical researchers with new ways to save lives and reduce suffering.

- *Airlines.* Without computers today's airline industry simply wouldn't fly. Designers use CAD (computer-aided design) software to design aircraft. Engineers conduct extensive computer simulations to test them. Pilots use computer-controlled instruments to navigate their planes, monitor aircraft systems, and control autopilots. Air traffic controllers on the ground use computerized air traffic control systems to keep track of incoming and outgoing flights. And, of course, computerized reservation systems make it possible for all those planes to carry passengers.

- *Science.* From biology to physics, every branch of science has been changed by the computer. Scientists collect and analyze data using remote sensing devices, notebook computers, and statistical analysis programs. They catalog and organize information in massive databases, many of which are accessible through the World Wide Web. They use supercomputers and workstations to create computer models of objects or environments that would otherwise be out of reach. They communicate with colleagues all over the world through the Internet. It's hard to find a scientist today who doesn't work with computers.

Clearly, computers are part of the workplace. To get a perspective on how computers affect the way we work, we'll consider the three computerized workplaces that have attracted the most attention: the automated factory, the automated office, and the electronic cottage.

Computers make data recording and analysis much easier for botanists and other scientists.

The Automated Factory

Businessmen go down with their businesses because they like the old way so well they cannot bring themselves to change.

—Henry Ford

▲
} Today's automobile factories are highly automated.

In the last chapter we discussed the use of robots—computer-controlled machines designed to perform specific *manual* tasks. In the modern **automated factory,** robots are used for painting, welding, and other repetitive assembly-line jobs. But robots alone don't make an automated factory. Computers also help track inventory, time the delivery of parts, control the quality of the production, monitor wear and tear on machines, and schedule maintenance. As described in Chapter 7, engineers use CAD and CAM (computer-aided manufacturing) technologies to design new products and the machines that build those products.

An automated factory is more efficient than a traditional factory for two reasons:

• Automation allows for tighter integration of planning with manufacturing, reducing the time that materials and machines sit idle.

• Automation reduces waste in facilities, raw materials, and labor.

If automation is good news for factory owners, it poses a threat to blue-collar workers who keep traditional factories running. In a typical high-tech manufacturing firm today, approximately half of the staff are engineers, accountants, marketing specialists, and other white-collar workers.

The Automated Office

We now mass produce information the way we used to mass produce cars.

—John Naisbitt, in *Megatrends*

As the number of factory jobs declines, office work plays a more important role in our economy. Modern offices, like modern factories, have been transformed by computers. Many **automated offices** have evolved along with their computers.

Office Automation Evolution

Office automation goes back to the mainframe era, when banks, insurance companies, and other large institutions used computers for behind-the-scenes jobs like accounting and payroll. Early computer systems were faster and more accurate than the manual systems they replaced but were rigid and difficult to use. The machines and the technicians who worked with them were hidden away in basement offices, isolated from their organizations. The introduction of timesharing operating systems and database management systems allowed workers throughout organizations to have access to computer data. This kind of *centralized computing* placed computer-related decisions in the hands of central data processing managers.

Personal computers changed all that. Early Apple and Tandy computers were carried into offices on the sly by employees who wanted to use their own computers instead of company mainframes. But as managers recognized the power of word processors, spreadsheets, and other applications, they incorporated PCs into organizational plans. Jobs migrated from mainframes to desktops, and people used personal computers to do things that the mainframes weren't programmed to do. In many organizations power struggles erupted between mainframe advocates and PC enthusiasts.

Enterprise Computing

Today most organizations recognize the importance of PCs in the overall computing structure. Some companies have abandoned mainframes altogether; others still use them for their biggest data processing tasks. In the age of networks the challenge for a company's **information systems manager** (sometimes called an IS manager, information technology manager, or IT manager) is to integrate all kinds of computers, from mainframes to Macintoshes, into a single, seamless system. This approach, often called **distributed computing** (or sometimes *enterprise computing* or *integrated computing*), allows PCs, workstations, minicomputers, and mainframes to coexist peacefully and complement each other.

People throughout business organizations use personal computers: Workers use word processing software to generate memos and reports, marketing teams create promotional pieces using desktop publishing tools, and financial departments analyze budgets using spreadsheets. They communicate with each other and with the outside world electronically, sending electronic mail through networks. If a business uses mainframes to house databases, office workers use desktop computers to access that data. In many integrated client/server systems, users view everything, including mainframe data, through a familiar PC interface. They don't need to know where or how information is stored; the network quietly moves data back and forth to meet user needs.

Workgroup Computing

New classes of multiuser software called **groupware** allow groups of users to share calendars, send messages, access data, and work on documents simultaneously. The best groupware applications allow workgroups to do things that would be difficult or impossible otherwise; they actually change the way people work in groups. Many of these applications focus on the concept of *workflow*—the path of information as it flows through a workgroup. With groupware and telecommunication, workgroups don't need to be in the same room, or even the same time zone. While some organizations use groupware like Lotus Notes for workgroup computing, a growing number are using Internet technologies like HTML and Netscape Navigator to create in-house *intranet* structures for sharing information. Some office-watchers predict that automated offices will be radically transformed by what they call **computer-supported cooperative work.**

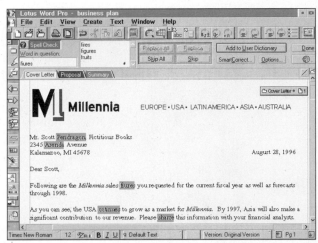

Lotus WordPro software allows writers and editors in a workgroup to contribute to a document; the program keeps track of each group member's additions and changes.

The Paperless Office

Experts have also predicted the **paperless office**—an office of the future in which magnetic and optical archives will replace reference books and file cabinets, electronic communication will replace letters and memos, and digital publications provided through the Internet and on-line services will replace newspapers and other periodicals. In the paperless office people will read computer screens, not paper documents.

All of these trends are real: Digital storage media are replacing many paper depositories; computers now deliver more mail messages than postal carriers do; and the World Wide Web has accelerated a trend toward on-line publishing. But so far, computers haven't reduced the flow of paper-based information. What has changed is the way people tend to use paper in the office. According to Paul Saffo of the Institute for the Future, "We've shifted from paper as storage to paper as interface. It is an evermore volatile, disposable, and temporary display medium."

To reduce the flow of paper, a growing number of organizations are turning to *document image management systems* that can scan, store, retrieve, and route bit-mapped images of paper documents. Document imaging systems, as they're also called, generally include scanners for converting paper pages to digital documents, high-capacity magnetic and optical storage disk drives for storing the document images, and fax machines for sending document images to remote locations. Interactions between these devices and networked workstations are generally handled by an *image server*—a computer dedicated to the single task of image management. Technological advances and declining prices are making imaging systems practical for more organizations than ever before. In the near future we may see a less-paper office, but a paperless office seems unlikely.

The Electronic Cottage

Telecommuting may allow us to redefine the issues so that we're not simply moving people to work but also moving work to people.

—Booth Gardner, former Washington governor

An inexpensive personal computer turns a spare room into a home office for this writer.

Before the industrial revolution, most people worked in or near their homes. Today's telecommunications technology opens up new possibilities for modern workers to return home for their livelihood. For hundreds of thousands of writers, programmers, accountants, data-entry clerks, and other information workers, **telecommuting** by modem replaces hours of commuting by car in rush hour traffic. Others use their own computers when they work at home rather than connecting by modem to company computers. The term *telecommuter* typically refers to *all* home information workers, whether they "commute" by modem or not.

Futurist Alvin Toffler popularized the term **electronic cottage** to describe a home where modern technology allows a person to work at home. Toffler and others predict that the number of telecommuters will skyrocket in the coming decades. Telecommuting makes sense; it's easier to move information than people. There are many strong arguments for telecommuting:

- Telecommuting reduces the number of automobile commuters, thus saving energy, reducing pollution, and decreasing congestion on highways, streets, and parking lots.

- Telecommuting saves time. If an information worker spends two hours each day commuting, that's two hours that could be spent working, resting, or relaxing with the family.

- Telecommuting allows for a more flexible schedule. People who prefer to work early in the morning or late at night don't need to conform to standard office hours if they telecommute. For many people, including parents of small children, telecommuting may be the only viable way to maintain a job.

- Telecommuting can increase productivity. Studies suggest that telecommuting can result in a 10 to 50 percent increase in worker productivity, depending on the job and the worker.

Of course, telecommuting isn't for everybody. Jobs that require constant interaction with co-workers, customers, or clients aren't conducive to telecommuting. Working at home requires self-discipline. Some people find they can't concentrate on work when they're at home—beds, refrigerators, chatty neighbors, children, and errands are simply too distracting. Others have the opposite problem: Workaholism cuts into family and relaxation time. Some workers who've tried full-time telecommuting complain that they miss the informal office social life, and that their low visibility caused bosses to pass them over for promotions. Most telecommuters surveyed report that the ideal work situation involves commuting to the office one or two days each week and working at home on the others.

Today thousands of companies offer home-based work arrangements to employees, but many more have strict policies against working at home. The most common objections revolve around control; managers fear that they'll lose control over workers they can't see. Some analysts suggest that as multimedia teleconferencing systems become affordable, telecommuting will become more popular with both workers and management.

In the meantime several variations on the electronic cottage are taking hold. Many enterprising families use home computers to help them run small businesses from their home offices. A growing number of corporations and government organizations are establishing **satellite offices** and shared **regional work centers** outside of major urban centers that allow workers to commute to smaller offices closer to their neighborhoods. High-powered portable computers allow salespeople, executives, scientists, engineers, and others to take their offices with them wherever they travel. These mobile workers don't travel *to* the office, they travel *with* the office.

MANAGEMENT BY COMPUTER

You can lead a horse to water, but you can't make him enter regional distribution codes in data field 92 to facilitate regression analysis on the back end.

—John Cleese, corporate consultant and former member of Monty Python's Flying Circus

During the early days of computing, most managers saw computers and terminals as clerical tools to be used by secretaries and technicians, but not by managers. Today managers recognize that computers are not just electronic typewriters and digital file cabinets but valuable resources that can provide information, advice, and support for those who run departments, divisions, or entire corporations.

Management Information Systems

Modern managers use **management information systems (MISs)** to help them with planning, organizing, staffing, directing, and controlling their organizations. The term *management information system* (which is often shortened to simply *information system*) means different things to different people. By some definitions a management information system is any system that provides information for an organization's managers, even if it doesn't involve computers. More commonly a management information system is defined as a computerized system that includes, among other things, procedures for collecting data, a database for storing data, and software tools for analyzing data and producing a variety of reports for different levels of management.

In a large organization computers process and store masses of information. Financial transactions, sales figures, inventory tallies—the number of data items can be astronomical. From a manager's point of view, plenty of useful information is hiding in that raw data. A well-defined MIS can extract important information and summarize it in reports for managers at all levels of an organization. A top-level manager uses a management information system to examine long-term trends and relationships between departments. Middle-level managers use the same MIS to produce departmental summary reports. Low-level managers focus on day-to-day

Information Flow in a Management Information System

A retail chain processes a tremendous amount of data daily. Depending on how it is handled, this information can be either overwhelming or enlightening. To make the best use of the information, many chains use management information systems to aid in decision making. This example follows the many paths of information through the Frostbyte Outdoor Outfitters Corporation.

When a clerk punches a sale into the terminal, a database records changes in financial and inventory files.

The MIS uses a variety of inputs to produce reports for managers at all levels.

When a new shipment arrives, a clerk records it using a terminal; inventory and accounting files are updated automatically.

Top-level managers use reports that summarize long-term trends to analyze overall business strategies.

Mid-level managers use summary and exception reports to spot trends and unusual circumstances.

Low-level managers use detail reports to keep tabs on day-to-day operations.

On-demand reports integrate information and show relationships. Example: impact of cold weather on ski sales.

Sales Volume vs. Average Temperature as of 6/31/99

	Jan.	Feb.	Mar.	Apr.	May	June
Sales Volume	1798	1700	1609	1532	1302	1216
Sales	$24,398	$24,673	$22,468	$21,003	$18,068	$16,328
Average temperature	24	32	41	48	58	71

Year-End Sales by Item: Top 20 as of 12/31/99

ITEM	SOLD UNITS	RETURNED UNITS	TOTAL UNITS	TOTAL SALES
Beaver Kayaks	58	3	55	$12,375
Possum Packs	1240	212	1028	$20,046
Possum Parkas	1003	323	680	$17,000
Rhinoceros Hiking Boots	1162	429	733	$47,645
Snoreswell Sleeping Bags	923	62	861	$39,175

Summary reports show departmental totals or trends. Example: most-popular footwear.

Exception reports reflect unusual relationships. Example: out-of-stock gear.

Items Temporarily Out of Stock as of 12/31/99

ITEM	OUT SINCE	DATE AVAILABLE
Fancy Flashlights	12/31/99	1/4/00
Foxy Flannels	12/31/99	1/2/00
Snappy Tents	12/02/99	1/2/00

Detail reports give complete, detailed information on routine operations. Example: daily orders.

Daily Sales Register by Type: 6/31/99

ITEM	UNITS	SALES
Parkas	62	$1209
Flashlights	154	$1540
Tents	2	$500
Hiking Boots	78	$65

operations with detailed reports from the MIS. The MIS can produce regularly scheduled periodic reports, but it can also help managers deal with unusual situations by producing reports on demand.

Decision Support Systems

A management information system is especially helpful for handling routine management tasks. For nonroutine decision making, many managers use another type of system called a **decision support system (DSS).** As the name implies, a DSS is a computer system that supports managers in decision-making tasks. In the broadest sense a spreadsheet program, like those discussed in Chapter 6, might be a DSS. After all, managers everywhere use spreadsheets to find answers to "What if?" questions and make decisions based on these sample scenarios. However, most managers reserve the term *decision support system* for a more specialized kind of software designed to create mathematical models of business systems. This type of DSS is a simulation tool similar to those discussed at the end of Chapter 6.

Other Management Tools

The sheer volume of information dissolves the information.

—Gunther Grass

Several other types of software systems are available to help managers make decisions. **Project management software** helps coordinate, schedule, and track complex work projects. Expert systems (see Chapter 12) can provide expert advice in limited areas. Spreadsheets (see Chapter 6) can manage budgets, make financial projections, and perform a variety of other useful functions. The Internet and on-line information services (see Chapters 9 and 10) can provide instant information from sources all over the world.

All of these tools provide critical information and advice, but they aren't without risks. Some managers complain that these systems provide too much information—too many reports, too many printouts, too many summaries, too many details. This malady, known as **information overload,** is a hazard of the automated office. Managers who are bombarded with computer output may not be able to separate the best from the rest. What's worse, managers who rely too heavily on computer output run the risk of overlooking more conventional, nondigital sources of insight. The best managers know that no computer system can replace the human decision-making skills necessary for successful management.

COMPUTERS AND JOBS

John Henry told his captain
"A man ain't nothin' but a man
But before I let your steam drill beat me down
I'd die with a hammer in my hand . . ."

—From the folk song "John Henry"

When we think about automated factories, computer-supported cooperative work, management information systems, and electronic cottages, it's easy to imagine utopian visions of computers in the workplace of tomorrow. But the real world isn't always picture perfect, and many workers today are experiencing computers in less positive ways. In this section we'll look at some of the controversies and issues surrounding the automation of the workplace.

The Productivity Problem

> A lot has been written about how computers haven't helped with productivity. I think there's a good reason for that, and it's fairly predictable. The more you can do with a machine, the higher you set your sights. So it's a self-defeating proposition.
>
> —J. Presper Eckert, codeveloper of ENIAC and UNIVAC

It seems obvious that computer technology makes businesses more productive. Consider the American financial industry, which employs about 5 percent of the workers in the United States and makes about 35 percent of information technology purchases—about $12 billion every year. This massive investment has undeniably produced better service and lower prices for bank customers. Now customers can cash out-of-state checks in minutes instead of weeks. Automated teller machines provide instant cash 24 hours per day—an impossible dream in the precomputer era. A growing number of corporations have direct electronic connections to bank computers, eliminating the need for human intervention altogether. None of this would be possible without computers.

Productivity and Profit

In terms of services offered, bank productivity is up as a result of computers. But most banks have not been able to translate technology into higher profits. The first 25 years of computerization in the banking industry has, in fact, shown a decline in capital productivity! There's some evidence that the trend may be turning around, but it still raises important questions about computers and productivity—questions that aren't limited to the banking industry.

Studies suggest that computerization has, at best, increased the productivity of North American office workers only slightly. How can this be? If computers don't increase productivity, why do businesses continue to spend billions of dollars every year on them?

Part of the problem may lie in the difficulty of making large software systems work reliably. In one famous example, the Bank of America spent $60 million trying to make a $20 million computer system work, and then abandoned it after five years of development and a year of false starts. (See Chapter 11 for more on the difficulty of developing software systems.)

Productivity and PCs

But the productivity problem isn't limited to large systems; there's no hard evidence that PCs increase office productivity the way managers hoped they would. Several factors may be involved:

- *Distractions.* For some people, personal computers offer too many options. These workers spend hours tinkering with utility software, refining multiple drafts of memos, fiddling with fonts, experimenting with spreadsheet graphics, and playing games.

- *Reliability.* Most computer workers lose productive time working around software bugs and recovering data from system crashes.

- *Rapid changes.* For many organizations, technological progress is the culprit. Companies spend large sums on PCs and software that become obsolete in a

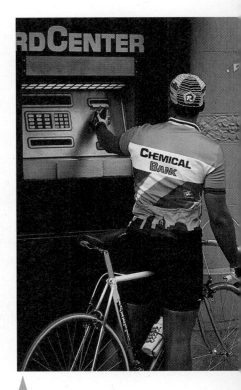

Computers and networks make 24-hour banking by ATM machine possible, but do they make banks more productive?

few years—or months. Workers spend hours learning complex programs, only to find in a few months that they need to be retrained because of software upgrades.

Productivity and People

The biggest productivity problems may be related more to people than to machines. According to one study of 2000 U.S. companies that implemented new office systems, at least 40 percent failed to achieve their intended results. Most of the failures were attributed to human or organizational factors rather than technical problems.

A computer system doesn't work in a vacuum. All too often computers are introduced into the workplace without any consideration of the way people work and interact. Workers are expected to adjust their work patterns to systems that are difficult and uncompromising. User training and support are often inadequate. It's hardly surprising that these computer-centered systems fail to spark productivity.

Many analysts argue that the most successful computer systems are **human-centered**. Such systems are designed to retain and enhance human skills, controlling skills rather than taking them away. These analysts suggest that computer systems aren't likely to pay off unless they're accompanied by changes in the structure of work responsibilities, relationships with co-workers, and rewards for accomplishing job goals.

To create a human-centered system, systems analysts and designers must understand the work practices of the people who'll be using the system. It helps if users of the systems are involved in designing the system and the system-related jobs. In Norway, laws require that unionized workers be included in the planning and design of new computer systems. As a result, workers have greater control over their jobs and greater job satisfaction. Similar worker-centered approaches have been applied in Sweden, Britain, and more recently, the United States.

Many experts believe that this human-centered approach is a key to increasing overall productivity. Productivity will almost certainly increase as organizations adjust to computer technology and computer technology becomes more adaptable to the needs of users.

Computers and Job Quality

And it's me and my machine for the rest of the morning,
for the rest of the afternoon,
for the rest of my life.

—James Taylor, in "Millworker"

For many workers, computers have caused more problems than they have solved. Workers complain of stress, depersonalization, fatigue, boredom, and a variety of health problems attributed to computers. Some of these complaints are directly related to technology; others relate to human decisions about how technology is implemented.

De-skilling and Up-skilling

When a job is automated, it may be **de-skilled;** that is, it may be transformed so that it requires less skill. For example, computerized cash registers in many fast-food restaurants replace numbered buttons with buttons labeled "large fries" or "chocolate shake." Clerks who use these machines don't need to know math or think about prices. They simply push buttons for the food items ordered and take the money; computers do the rest.

Some of the most visible examples of de-skilling occur when offices automate clerical jobs. When word processors and databases replace typewriters and file cabinets, traditional typing-and-filing jobs disappear. Many secretaries are repositioned in data-entry jobs—mindless, repetitive jobs where the only measure of success is the number of key-strokes typed into a terminal each hour. When a clerical job—or any job—is de-skilled, the worker's control, responsibility, and job satisfaction are likely to go down. De-skilled jobs typically offer less status and less pay.

In sharp contrast to those whose jobs are de-skilled into electronic drudgery, many workers find their jobs **up-skilled** by automation. For example, many clerical jobs become more technical as offices adopt databases, word processors, spreadsheets, electronic mail systems, Internet connections, fax modems, and other computer technology. In some cases clerical workers use computer systems to do jobs formerly done by high-paid professionals and technicians. While many clerical people enjoy the added challenge and responsibility, others may be frustrated doing highly technical work with inadequate training. Clerical workers are seldom consulted before their jobs are computerized. And even though their work is more technically demanding than before, few clerical workers see this up-skilling reflected in their paychecks or level of responsibility.

Specialized terminals like this one make it easy to log restaurant orders. How is this person's job different as a result of this technology?

Monitoring and Surveillance

Another controversial aspect of office automation is **computer monitoring**—using computer technology to track, record, and evaluate worker performance, often without the knowledge of the worker. Monitoring systems can provide a manager with instant, on-screen reports detailing the number of keystrokes for each clerk, the length of each phone call placed by an employee, and the total amount of idle time for each computer. Some network software even allows a manager to view a copy of any worker's screen secretly at any time.

For a manager worried about worker productivity, computer monitoring can serve as a valuable source of information. But computer monitoring brings with it several problems:

- *Privacy.* In Chapter 8 we saw how the misuse of databases can threaten personal privacy. Computer monitoring compounds that threat by providing employers with unprecedented data on workers. Some employers have even monitored personal electronic mail messages and fired employees who send "unacceptable" messages. For these workers, computer monitoring means that Big Brother is watching, just as Orwell predicted in his book *1984*.

- *Morale.* Privacy issues aside, computer monitoring can have a powerful negative impact on morale. Because employees can't tell when they're being monitored, many workers experience a great deal of stress and anxiety. The boss can be seen as an invisible eavesdropper rather than as a team leader.

- *Devalued skills.* In the traditional office, workers were evaluated based on a variety of skills. A slow-typing secretary could be valued for her ability to anticipate when a job needed to be done or her willingness to help others with problems. Computer monitoring tends to reduce a worker's worth to simple quantities like "number of keystrokes per hour." In such systems a worker might be penalized for repairing a sticky chair, showing a neighbor how to reboot a terminal, or helping a co-worker overcome an emotional crisis.

- *Loss of quality.* Monitored workers tend to assume that "If it's not being counted, it doesn't count." The result of this assumption is that quantity may become more important than quality.

Millions of workers are monitored by computer, including factory workers, telephone operators, truck drivers, and, in some cases, managers. But computer monitoring is most commonly applied to clerical workers. According to one study more than one-fourth of all American clerical workers are monitored by computer.

The Electronic Sweatshop

Computer monitoring is common practice in data-entry offices. A data-entry clerk has a single job: to read information from a printed source—a check, a hand-printed form, or something else—and type it into a computer's database. A typical data-entry shop might contain hundreds of clerks sitting at terminals in a massive, windowless room. Workers—often minorities and almost always female—are paid minimum wage to do mindless keyboarding. Many experience headaches, backaches, serious wrist injuries, stress, anxiety, and other health problems. And all the while, keystrokes and breaks are monitored electronically. Writer Barbara Garson calls these worker warehouses **electronic sweatshops,** because working conditions bring to mind the oppressive factory sweatshops of the 19th century.

A growing number of electronic sweatshops are located across national borders from corporate headquarters in countries with lax labor laws and low wage scales. The electronic immigrants in these offshore shops don't need green cards to telecommute across borders, and they work for a fraction of what workers in developed countries cost. A data-entry clerk in the Philippines, for example, earns about $6 per day. With wages that low many companies find it cost-effective to have data entered twice and use software to compare both versions and correct errors.

The electronic sweatshop is the dark side of the electronic office. Ironically, computer technology may soon make many electronic sweatshops irrelevant. Optical character recognition and voice recognition technologies (described in Chapter 12) are rapidly becoming more practical for real-world applications. OCR software is already used to read and recognize typed and hand-printed characters in many applications, and voice recognition is threatening to replace thousands of directory assistance telephone operators. It's just a matter of time before most workers in electronic sweatshops are replaced by machines.

Employment and Unemployment

My father had worked for the same firm for 12 years. They fired him. They replaced him with a tiny gadget this big that does everything that my father does only it does it much better. The depressing thing is my mother ran out and bought one.

—Woody Allen

When Woody Allen told this joke three decades ago, automation was generating a great deal of public controversy. Computer technology was new to the workplace, and people were reacting with both awe and fear. Many analysts predicted that automation would lead to massive unemployment and economic disaster. Others said that computers would generate countless new job opportunities. Today most people are used to seeing computers where they work, and the computers-vs.-jobs debate has cooled down. Job automation may not be a hot topic in comedy clubs today, but it's still an important issue for millions of workers whose jobs are threatened by machines.

Workers Against Machines

Automation has threatened workers since the earliest days of the industrial revolution. In the early 19th century, an English labor group called the *Luddites* smashed new textile machinery; they feared that the machines would take jobs away from skilled craftsmen. The Luddites and similar groups in other parts of Europe failed to stop the wheels of automation. Modern workers have been no more successful than their 19th-century counterparts in keeping computers and robots out of the workplace. Every year brings new technological breakthroughs that allow robots and computers to do jobs formerly reserved for humans.

Almost all of the assembly-line work in this factory is done by robots.

Of course, computer technology creates new jobs, too. Somebody has to design, build, program, sell, run, and repair the computers and robots. But many displaced workers don't have the education or skills to program computers, design robots, or even read printouts. Those workers are often forced to take low-tech, low-paying service jobs as cashiers or custodians, if they can find jobs at all. Because of automation, the unskilled, uneducated worker may face a lifetime of minimum wage jobs or welfare. Technology may be helping to create an unbalanced society with two classes: a growing mass of poor uneducated people and a shrinking class of affluent educated people.

Cautiously Optimistic Forecasts

Nobody knows for sure how computer technology will affect employment in the coming decades; it's impossible to anticipate what might happen in 10 or 20 years. And experts are far from unanimous in their predictions.

A number of studies suggest that, at least for the next few years, technology will stimulate economic growth. This growth will produce new jobs, but it will also bring long, painful periods of adjustment for many workers. Demand for factory workers, clerical workers, and other semiskilled and unskilled laborers will drop dramatically as their jobs are automated or moved to third-world countries where wages are low. At the same time, the demand for professionals—especially engineers and teachers—will rise sharply.

According to detailed computer models constructed at the Institute for Economic Analysis at New York University, there will be plenty of jobs in the early 21st century. The question is whether we'll have enough skilled workers to fill those jobs. In other words, economic growth will depend on whether we have a suitably trained workforce. The single most important key to a positive economic future, according to this study, is education. But will we, as a society, be able to provide people with the kind of education they'll need? We'll deal with that question, and the critical issues surrounding education in the information age, in the next chapter.

Considering Computer Careers

Until recently, people who wanted to work with computers were forced to choose between a few careers, most of which required highly specialized training. But when computers are used by everybody from fast-food sales clerks to graphic artists, just about anybody can have some kind of "computer career." Still, many rewarding and high-paying computer-related careers require a fair amount of specialized education. If you're interested in a computer-related job, consider the following tips:

● *Learn touch-typing.* Computers that can read handwriting and understand spoken English are probably in your future but not your *immediate* future. Several low-cost typing tutorial programs can help you to teach your fingers how to type. The time you invest will pay you back quickly. The sooner you learn, the sooner you'll start reaping the rewards.

● *Use computers regularly to help you accomplish your immediate goals.* Word process your term papers. Use spreadsheets and other math software as calculation aids. Use databases for research work. Computers are part of your future. If you use them regularly, they'll become second nature, like telephones and pencils. If you don't own a computer, consider buying one; the next chapter has some tips on choosing a computer.

● *Don't forsake the basics.* If you want to become a programmer, a systems analyst, a computer scientist, a computer engineer, or some other kind of computer professional, don't focus all your attention on computers. A few young technical wizards become successful programmers without college degrees. But if you're not gifted and lucky, you'll need a solid education to land a good job. Math and communication skills (written and oral) are *extremely* important, even in highly technical jobs. Opportunities abound for people who can understand computers *and* communicate clearly.

● *Combine your passions.* If you like art and computers, explore computer art. If you love ecology and computers, find out how computers are used by ecologists. People who can speak the language of computers and the language of a specialized field have opportunities to build bridges.

● *Ask questions.* The best way to find out more about computer careers is to ask the people who do them. Most people are willing to talk about their jobs if you're willing to listen.

● *If you can't find your dream job, build it yourself.* Inexpensive computer systems provide all kinds of entrepreneurial opportunities for creative self-starters: Desktop publishing service bureaus; multimedia video production; custom programming; commercial art and design; freelance writing; consulting . . . the jobs are there for the making, if you have the imagination and initiative.

● *Prepare for change.* In a rapidly changing world, lifelong careers are rare. Be prepared to change jobs several times. Think of education as a lifelong process. In Marshall McLuhan's words, "The future of work consists of learning a living."

Will We Need a New Economy?

In the long run education may not be enough. It seems likely that, at some time in the future, machines will be able to do most of the jobs people do today. We may face a future of *jobless growth*—a time when productivity increases, not because of the work people do but because of the work of machines. If productivity isn't tied to employment, we'll have to ask some hard questions about our political, economic, and social system:

● Do governments have an obligation to provide permanent public assistance to the chronically unemployed?

● Should large companies be required to give several months notice to workers whose jobs are being eliminated? Should they be required to retrain workers for other jobs?

- Should large companies be required to file "employment impact statements" before replacing people with machines, in the same way they're required to file environmental impact statements before implementing policies that might harm the environment?

- If robots and computers are producing most of society's goods and services, should all of the profits from those goods go to a few people who own the machines?

- If a worker is replaced by a robot, should the worker receive a share of the robot's "earnings" through stocks or profit sharing?

- The average work week 150 years ago was 70 hours; for the last 50 years it has been steady at 40. Should governments and businesses encourage job-sharing and other systems that allow for less-than-40-hour jobs?

- What will people do with their time if machines do most of the work? What new leisure activities should be made available?

- How will people define their identities if work becomes less central to their lives?

These questions force us to confront deep-seated cultural beliefs and economic traditions, and they don't come with easy answers. They suggest that we may be heading into a difficult period when many old rules don't apply anymore. But if we're successful at navigating the troubled waters of transition, we may find that automation fulfills the dream expressed by Aristotle more than 2000 years ago:

If every instrument could accomplish its own work, obeying or anticipating the will of others . . . , if the shuttle could weave, and the pick touch the lyre, without a hand to guide them, chief workmen would not need servants, nor masters slaves.

SUMMARY

Our civilization is in the midst of a transition from an industrial economy to a post-industrial information economy. The transition, or paradigm shift, is having a profound influence on the way we live and work, and it is likely to challenge many of our beliefs, assumptions, and traditions. Computers and information technology are central to the change.

Factory work is steadily declining as we enter the information age, but factories still provide us with hard goods. The modern, automated factory uses computers at every level of operation. Computer-aided design, computer-aided manufacturing, robots, automated assembly lines, and automated warehouses all combine to produce factories that need very few laborers.

Far more people work in offices than in factories, and computers are critically important in the modern office. Early office automation centered on mainframes that were run by highly trained technicians; today's office is more likely to emphasize personal computers and workstations for decentralized enterprise computing. So far, predictions for widespread computer-supported cooperative work and paperless offices haven't come true.

A growing number of workers use computers to work at home part or full time. Some use modems to stay in contact with their offices. Telecommuting has many benefits for information workers, their bosses, and society as a whole. Still, telecommuting from home is not for everybody. Satellite offices, cottage industries, and portable offices offer alternatives that may be more practical for some workers. Even so, many companies resist the idea of employees working regularly out of the office.

Managers use a variety of computing tools to help them do their jobs. Management information systems, decision support systems, project management systems, expert systems, and on-line information systems can help managers plan, organize, staff, direct, and control their organizations. Unfortunately these tools can lead to information overload if they're not used intelligently.

Computers have allowed many organizations to provide services that wouldn't be possible otherwise, but so far they haven't produced the productivity gains that many experts expected. Experts speculate that productivity will rise as organizations adjust to the new technology and develop human-centered systems that are adapted to the needs and work habits of employees.

The impact of computers varies from job to job. Some jobs are de-skilled— transformed so they require less skill—while others are up-skilled into more technologically complex jobs. Computer monitoring is a controversial procedure that raises issues of privacy and, in many cases, lowers worker morale. De-skilling, monitoring, and health risks are particularly evident in electronic sweatshops—data-entry warehouses packed with low-paid keyboard operators.

The biggest problem of automation may be the elimination of jobs. So far most displaced workers have been able to find other jobs in our expanding economy. But automation will almost certainly produce unemployment and pain for millions of people unless society is able to provide them with the education they'll need to take the new jobs created by technology. Automation may ultimately force us to make fundamental changes in our economic system. Only time will tell.

Chapter Review

Key Terms

automated factory
automated office
automation
computer monitoring
computer-supported cooperative work
decision support system (DSS)
de-skilling
distributed computing

electronic cottage
electronic sweatshop
groupware
human-centered system
information economy
information overload
information systems manager
management information system (MIS)

paperless office
paradigm shift
project management software
regional work center
satellite office
telecommuting
up-skilling

Review Questions

1. Define or describe each of the key terms above. Check your answers using the glossary.

2. How is the information revolution similar to the industrial revolution? How is it different?

3. What are the major components of the modern automated factory?

4. How has the evolution of the automated office paralleled the evolution of the computer?

5. What are the advantages and disadvantages of telecommuting from the point of view of the worker? Management? Society?

6. Describe several software tools used by managers and explain how they help them do their jobs.

7. What is de-skilling? What is up-skilling? Give examples of each.

8. Describe several of the controversies surrounding the electronic sweatshop.

9. Why is education critical to our future as we automate more jobs?

Discussion Questions

1. What evidence do we have that our society is going through a paradigm shift?

2. What will have to happen before the paperless office (or the less-paper office) becomes a reality?

3. Many cities are enacting legislation to encourage telecommuting. If you were drafting such legislation, what would you include?

4. Why do you think it has been so difficult to demonstrate that computers increase productivity?

5. People who work in electronic sweatshops run the risk of being replaced by technology. Discuss the tradeoffs of this dilemma from the point of view of the worker and the society at large.

6. What do you think are the answers to the questions raised at the end of the section on automation and unemployment? How do you think most people would feel about these questions?

Projects

1. Interview several people whose jobs have been changed by computers, and report on your findings.

2. Think about how computers have affected the jobs you've held. Report on your experiences.

Sources and Resources

Books

Computing Across America, by Steven K. Roberts (Nomadic Research Labs, P.O. Box 2185, El Segundo, CA 90245). This chronicle of Steve Roberts's Winnebiko adventures is probably the only book in the world that was done by "biketop publishing." A variety of journals and papers on other Roberts's projects are available from the same address.

The Structure of Scientific Revolutions, Second Edition, by Thomas Kuhn (Chicago: University of Chicago Press, 1970). This landmark book shows how scientific progress is built on paradigm shifts—radical new world views that challenge and threaten the status quo. The social dynamics described here apply to business, technology, and countless other human endeavors.

The Technology Gauntlet: Meeting the Challenge of Workplace Computing, by Margaret Kilduff and Doug Blewett (Reading, MA: Addison-Wesley, 1994). The authors of this little book use a pair of ongoing fictional case studies to show how businesses can best take advantage of information technology.

The Digital MBA, edited by Daniel Burnstein (Berkeley, CA: Osborne/McGraw-Hill Publishing Co., 1995). Burnstein, president of the Management Software Association, provides an overview of management topics, describing and demonstrating how information technology can help solve management problems. The IBM PC-compatible CD-ROM includes demonstration versions of a variety of management software tools.

The Dilbert Principle, by Scott Adams (New York: HarperBusiness, 1996). This book, like the Dilbert comic strip, is packed with irreverent insights into the inner workings of the information age workplace. Adams clearly understands the world he satirizes—he has an MBA from Berkeley and 17 years' experience in a cubicle working for Pacific Bell.

Computerization and Controversy: Value Conflicts and Social Choices, Second Edition, edited by Charles Dunlop and Rob Kling (Boston: Academic Press, 1996). This collection includes carefully researched academic studies as well as insightful articles from the popular press). The coverage of computers in the workplace is particularly good.

Computers in Society, edited by Kathryn Schellenberg (Guilford, CT: Dushkin Publishing Group, published annually). This relatively inexpensive collection of articles covers a variety of subjects, including the impact of computers on the workplace.

Adapting PCs for Disabilities, by Joseph J. Lazzaro (Reading, MA: Addison-Wesley, 1996). Many features of the modern personal computer are difficult for people with disabilities to use—unless the PC is designed or modified to make it more accessible for those special populations. On the other hand, PCs with the right software and peripherals can provide invaluable assistance for people with disabilities. This book/CD-ROM package is full of useful information and software for adapting an IBM-compatible PC for people with special needs.

The Electronic Sweatshop: How Computers Are Transforming the Office of the Future into the Factory of the Past, by Barbara Garson (New York: Penguin Books, 1989). Garson exposes the dark side of the electronic office in words that are hard to ignore.

The End of Work, by Jeremy Rifkin (New York: Putnam, 1994). This book discusses the changing nature of work and the disappearance of jobs as we know them. Information technology isn't the only cause, but it plays a critical role in these changes.

Periodicals

Upside. This magazine is aimed at managers, entrepreneurs, and others who want to track the business side, rather than the technological side, of the computer industry.

World Wide Web Sites

Check the *Computer Confluence* Web site for links to Internet sources on information age jobs, technology in the workplace, and the evolving information economy.

14

COMPUTERS AT SCHOOL AND AT HOME

Rand and Robyn Miller Build a World

Sometimes late at night, after I had done something really cool, I would look down on my creation and say, "It is good."

—Robyn Miller

Rand and Robyn Miller

Robyn Miller was right—it *was* good. Robyn and his brother Rand are the principal architects of *Myst,* a marvelous CD-ROM that defined a new art form and a unique entertainment experience for millions of computer users worldwide. Myst was the first smash hit CD-ROM; its sales passed the million mark while most of the world was still trying to figure out what interactive multimedia was.

Robyn and Rand seem like unlikely hitmakers. Sons of a roving nondenominational preacher, the two brothers grew up in a household where ideas were more important than media. They

lived in towns and cities far from the hubs of high-tech activity and pop culture.

When big brother Rand was working as a computer programmer in a Texas bank, he got an idea for a computer game for kids. He asked Robyn, the artistic brother, to illustrate it. The result was The Manhole, an Alice-in-Wonderland kind of environment full of amazing interconnected scenes, talking animals, and hidden surprises. The Manhole was one of the first major hypermedia documents created with HyperCard; it was more of a surrealistic place to be explored than a story. The program won the Software Publisher's Association's

1988 award for the best new use of a computer—no one had ever seen anything like it before.

Motivated by The Manhole's success, the Miller brothers created a company called Cyan and set up a garage-style shop in Spokane, a small city on the high prairie of Eastern Washington. They crafted a couple more children's programs before setting their sites on grown-up computer users. They wanted to create a computer game that could entertain without resorting to violence.

The result of their efforts was Myst, a hauntingly beautiful game with a hypnotic, dreamlike quality. While ex-

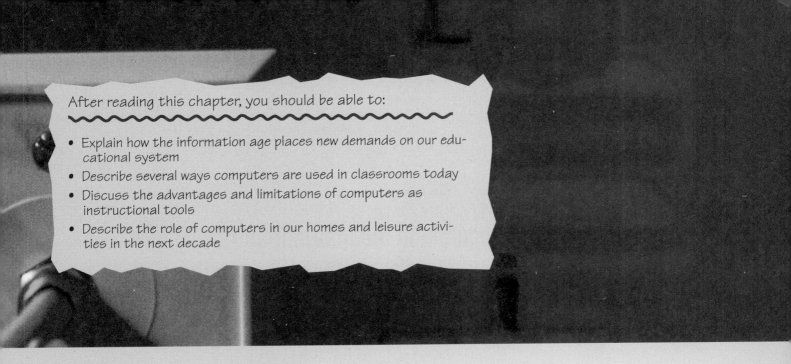

After reading this chapter, you should be able to:

〜〜〜〜〜〜〜〜〜〜〜〜〜〜〜〜〜〜〜〜〜〜〜〜〜〜〜

- Explain how the information age places new demands on our educational system
- Describe several ways computers are used in classrooms today
- Discuss the advantages and limitations of computers as instructional tools
- Describe the role of computers in our homes and leisure activities in the next decade

ploring an incredibly rich artificial reality, players gradually solve puzzles that reveal parts of a dark, fantastic story. Stunning 3-D graphics, haunting music, and subtle sound effects combine with a simple, seamless interface that draws in players who aren't normally attracted to computer games. Word of this new kind of game spread through networks, electronic and otherwise, and Myst became a major hit without firing a single shot.

The phenomenal success of Myst and Cyan haven't changed the Miller brothers' basic values. In Rand's words, "We believe in a Creator who is responsible for the world we live in. It was an awesome experience to create a world of our own, with all the care and integrity we could muster, and yet see how thin and sketchy and insignificant it is compared to the one He made."

Scenes from Myst

yan's multimedia hits, along with hundreds of others available today, expand the human mind through a combination of entertainment and education. As computer technology reshapes our world, education plays an evermore-important role in helping adults, as well as children, keep up with the changes going on around them. It's fitting, then, that computers are playing an ever-increasing role in the educational process in schools and homes. This chapter deals with the growing role of computers in schools and the changing role of education in a high-tech world. The chapter closes with a look at the growing impact of computers on our home life.

Education in the Information Age

> The future is a race between education and catastrophe.
>
> —H. G. Wells

As we've seen, the information age is changing the way we work. Some jobs are disappearing, others are emerging, and still others are being radically transformed by information technology and the information-based economy. But the information age is not just affecting the workplace. Its influences are felt in our educational system, too. Before it's over the information revolution will have a profound and permanent effect on the way we learn.

The Roots of our Educational System

The American educational system was developed more than a century ago to teach students the basic facts and survival skills they would need for jobs in industry and agriculture—jobs they would probably hold for their entire adult lives. This industrial age system has been described as a *factory model* for three reasons:

- It assumes that all students learn the same way and that all students should learn the same things.

- The teacher's job is to "pour" facts into students, occasionally checking the level of knowledge in each student.

- Students are expected to work individually, absorb facts, and to spend most of their time sitting quietly in straight rows.

With all its faults, the public education system helped the United States to dominate world markets in the first half of this century. But the world has changed drastically since the system was founded. Schools have changed, too, but not fast enough to keep pace with the information revolution. Most experts today agree that we need to rebuild our educational system to meet the demands of the information age.

Information Age Education

> It is no longer enough to have an educational system whose primary purpose is to produce people who are trained to be good workers. The output from our educational system (our graduates) must be educated, productive citizens who are prepared to be good workers, good citizens, and lifelong learners if the United States is to continue its world leadership role into the twenty-first century.
>
> —Ludwig Braun, in *Vision: TEST Final Report, Recommendations for American Educational Decision Makers*

What should education provide students in the information age? Research and experience suggest several answers:

- *Technological familiarity.* Many of today's older workers are having trouble adjusting to the information age because of **technophobia**—the fear of technology. These people grew up in a world without computers, and they experience anxiety when they're forced to deal with them. In tomorrow's world computers will be as commonplace as telephones and dictionaries are today. To prepare for this world, students need to learn how to work comfortably with all kinds of knowledge tools, including pencils, books, calculators, computers, and information utilities. But technological familiarity shouldn't stop with learning how to work with tools. Students need to have a clear understanding of the limitations of the technology and the ability to assess the benefits and risks of applying technology to a problem. They need to be able to question technology.

- *Literacy.* The industrial age may have passed, but the need for reading and writing hasn't. In fact, it's more important than ever that today's students graduate with the ability to read and write. Many jobs that did not require reading or writing skills a generation ago now use high-tech equipment that demands literacy. A factory worker who can't read printouts isn't likely to survive the transition to an automated factory.

- *Mathematics.* In the age of the $5 calculator, many students think learning math is a waste of time. In fact, some educators argue that we spend too much time teaching students how to do things like long division and calculating square roots—skills that adults seldom, if ever, do by hand. These arithmetic skills have little to do with being able to think mathematically. To survive in a high-tech world, students need to be able to see the mathematical systems in the world around them and apply math concepts to solve problems. No calculator can do that.

- *Culture.* An education isn't complete without a strong cultural component. Liberal arts and social studies help us recognize the interconnections that turn information into knowledge. Culture gives us roots when the sands of time shift. It gives us historical perspective that allows us to see trends and prepare for the future. Culture provides a human framework with which to view the impact of technology. It also gives us the global perspective to live in a world where communication is determined more by technology than geography.

- *Communication.* In the information age communication is a survival skill. Isolated factory workers and desk-bound pencil pushers are vanishing from the workplace. Modern jobs involve interactions—between people and machines and between people and people. The fast-paced, information-based society depends on our human ability to communicate, negotiate, cooperate, and collaborate, both locally and globally.

- *Learning how to learn.* Experts predict that most of the jobs that will exist in ten years do not exist today, and that most of those new jobs will require education past the high-school level. With this rapidly changing job market, it's unreasonable to assume that workers can be trained once for lifelong jobs. Instead of holding a single job for 40 years, today's high-school or college graduate is likely to change jobs several times. Those people who *do* keep the same jobs will have to deal with unprecedented change. The half-life of an engineer's specialized knowledge—the time it takes for half of that knowledge to be replaced by more current knowledge—is just over three years.

These facts suggest that we can no longer afford to think of education as a one-time vaccination against illiteracy. In the information age learning must be a lifelong process. To prepare students for a lifetime of learning, schools must teach students more than facts; they must make sure students learn how to think and learn.

Computers Go to School

The information age clearly makes new demands on our educational system, requiring radical changes in what and how people learn. Many educators believe that computers and information technology are essential parts of those changes. Ninety-nine percent of all elementary and secondary schools in the United States have installed computers—an average of one computer for every 12 students in 1995. Students and teachers are using those computers in a variety of ways.

Computer-Aided Instruction

> The ordinary classroom holds the bright kids back and makes the kids that need more time go too fast. They fall further and further behind until they can't keep up—it's a terrible system.
>
> —B. F. Skinner, the father of behaviorist psychology and inventor of the first "teaching machine"

In 1953 B. F. Skinner visited his daughter's fourth-grade class and watched the teacher try to teach arithmetic to everyone in the class at the same speed. The experience inspired him to build a *teaching machine*—a wooden box that used cards, lights, and levers to quiz and reward a student. His machine was based on the principles of behaviorist psychology: Allow the student to learn in small steps at an individualized pace and reward correct answers with immediate positive feedback. When personal computers appeared in classrooms, students started using **drill-and-practice software** based on those same principles: individualized rate, small steps, and positive feedback.

A traditional drill-and-practice program presents the student with a question and compares the student's answer with the single correct answer. If the answers match, the program offers praise, possibly accompanied by music and animation. If the student's answer doesn't match the correct answer, the program offers an explanation and presents another, similar problem. The program may keep track of

Students practice basic math and language lessons with CAI programs like these. Number Maze makes solving arithmetic problems a necessary part of navigating a maze. Learn to Speak Spanish allows you to record your voice into the computer's memory and compare it with the video clips of native speakers.

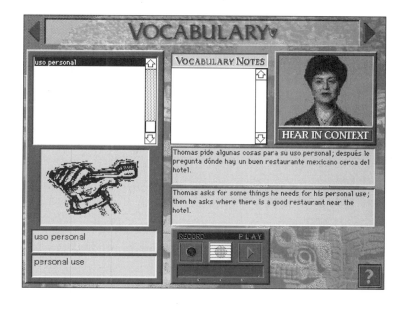

student responses and tailor questions based on error patterns; it might also provide reports on student progress to the teacher. Today most drill-and-practice programs embed the lessons in animated games, but the underlying principles remain the same.

Pure drill-and-practice programs don't teach new material. Like flash cards and worksheets, they're designed to help students go over material they've already learned to get it better. **Tutorial software** provides direct instruction in a clearly specified skill or subject. Drill-and-practice software and tutorial software are often referred to as **computer-aided instruction (CAI)** software. Most CAI programs combine tutorial material with drill-and-practice questions, in the same way a math textbook alternates explanations with exercises.

CAI software is one of the most common types of **courseware** (educational software) for three reasons: It's relatively easy and inexpensive to produce, it can easily be combined with more traditional educational techniques, and it produces clear, demonstrable results. CAI offers many advantages over workbooks and worksheets:

- *Individualized learning.* Individual students can learn at their own pace. Teachers can spend their time working one-on-one with students—an important activity that's all but impossible in typical presentation-and-discussion classrooms.

- *Motivation.* CAI can turn practice into an entertaining game. It motivates students to practice arithmetic, spelling, touch-typing, piano playing, and other skills that might otherwise be tedious to learn.

- *Confidence.* CAI can help timid children become comfortable with computers as well as with the subject matter being taught. A well-designed program is infinitely patient, and it allows students to make mistakes in private. Research has shown that younger children, disadvantaged children, and especially learning disabled students tend to respond positively to CAI.

Research also suggests that not all CAI software deserves praise. Much CAI software is flawed because it gives inappropriate feedback, allows students to practice mistakes, and discourages students from moving into new material. Even the best CAI can work only with tightly defined subjects, in which every question can have a single, clear, unambiguous answer. CAI presents information in the form of facts, leaving no room for questioning, creativity, or cooperation. In a sense, CAI programs students.

> Press the 'd' key. You should use the middle finger of your left hand.

> This is the Computer Lab, where you will do most of your practicing on the Laptop Computer

CAI is useful for strengthening basic motor skills like typing. In Mavis Beacon Teaches Typing, on-screen tutorials guide the student through a complete set of typing lessons, with the computer monitoring every keystroke for accuracy.

IBM's Speech Viewer is a package of software and accessories to help students overcome speech impairments. The software analyzes speech characteristics after the student speaks into a microphone and provides instant, animated feedback.

Programming Tools

> In many schools today, the phrase "computer-aided instruction" means making the computer teach the child. One might say the computer is being used to program the child. In my vision, the child programs the computer and, in doing so, both acquires a sense of mastery over a piece of the most modern and powerful technology and establishes an intimate contact with some of the deepest ideas from science, from mathematics, and from the art of intellectual model building.
>
> —Seymour Papert, in Mindstorms

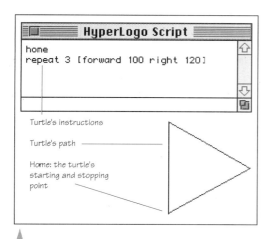

This sequence of LOGO commands tells the turtle to go home (the center of the window facing up); then to move forward 100 tiny steps, turn right 120 degrees (one-third of a circle), move forward another 100 steps, turn right another 120, move forward another 100, and turn right another 120. When the turtle follows these instructions with the "pen" engaged, it draws an equilateral triangle on the floor of the screen. (Software: HyperStudio.)

With his colleagues at MIT, Seymour Papert developed a computer language called *LOGO* so children could program computers, rather than the other way around. Children can write LOGO programs as soon as they're old enough to read and write a few simple words.

Rather than teaching through lessons and tests, LOGO creates environments for learning. The most famous of these LOGO environments allows children to draw pictures using a technique called *turtle graphics*. With turtle graphics a child uses LOGO commands to make a "turtle" move, dragging a "pen" to draw lines as it moves. The "turtle" can be a small robot that moves around on the floor or a graphical creature that lives in the middle of a computer screen.

LOGO helps children learn advanced computer science concepts like *recursion*—the ability of a program or procedure to call, or refer to, itself, as in this example:

```
TO CIRCLE
FORWARD 1 RIGHT 1
CIRCLE
END
```

This LOGO program tells the computer "to draw a circle, go one step forward, turn 1 degree to the right, and repeat *all* of these instructions." Of course, there's a bug here: This procedure doesn't know when to stop. But debugging is part of programming, and students who learn LOGO learn that making mistakes is part of the process.

LOGO has other environments that go beyond geometry and graphics. LEGO LOGO allows children to use LOGO commands to control motorized machines and robots built out of LEGO building blocks.

Papert and many educators predicted that LOGO would help children become better at general problem solving and logical thinking. Research suggests that LOGO enhances creativity and originality in children, but there's no conclusive evidence that it improves their general thinking skills more than other teaching tools. Like a chalkboard, LOGO can be an effective tool in the hands of a good teacher.

LOGO, like Pascal and BASIC—two other programming languages designed for students—is less popular in schools today than it was a decade ago. Today's computer applications make programming seem irrelevant to the average student. Children don't need to learn how to write TV programs before they watch TV, and in most schools they don't learn to program computers before they use them.

Students in this class build LEGO robots and write LOGO programs to control them.

Simulation and Games

> No compulsory learning can remain in the soul. . . . In teaching children, train them by a kind of game, and you will be able to see more clearly the natural bent of each.
>
> —Plato, in *The Republic, Book VII*

When Papert developed LOGO, he based his educational psychology on the work of renowned Swiss developmental psychologist Jean Piaget. According to Piaget, children have a natural gift for learning on their own; they learn to talk, get around, and think without formal training. A child growing up in France learns French effortlessly, because the child's environment has the necessary materials. In Papert's vision the computer can provide an environment that makes learning mathematics, science, and the arts as effortless as learning French in France.

Many **educational simulations** today are based on the same idea: Children learn best through exploration and invention. These simulations allow students to explore artificial environments, imaginary or based on reality. Educational simulations are metaphors designed to focus student attention on the most important concepts. While most educational simulations have the look and feel of a game, they challenge students to learn through exploration, experimentation, and interaction with other students.

With a simulation, the students are in control of the learning environment. It's up to them to find and use information to draw conclusions. Students can experience the consequences of their actions without taking real-world risks. Simulations allow students to have experiences that wouldn't be possible otherwise. Instead of simply spewing facts, simulations provide a context for knowledge.

Students love playing well-designed simulation games, but many schools don't use simulations because there's no room for them in the formal curriculum. It's difficult to prove the effectiveness of simulation games because they generally aren't designed to teach simple, measurable facts. In spite of our culture's age-old tradition of learning through games, many educators question the educational value of games in the classroom. Of course, educational simulations, like all simulations, come up short as substitutes for reality. The risks of simulations, outlined in Chapter 6, apply to educational simulations, too. But when field trips aren't possible, computer simulations can offer affordable alternatives.

These two programs include simulations that allow students to test and observe scientific concepts. A.D.A.M.: The Inside Story provides a variety of ways to learn about human anatomy, including animated simulations of neural functions. The Cartoon Guide to Physics combines animated tutorials with simulated experiments to test the basic principles of physics.

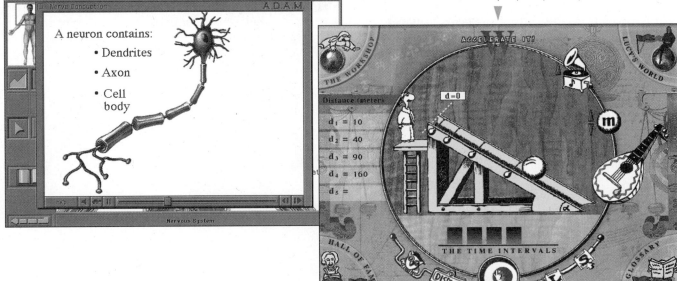

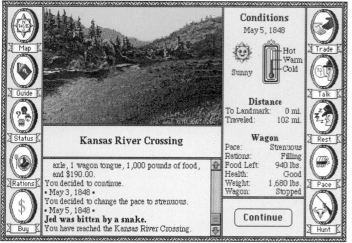

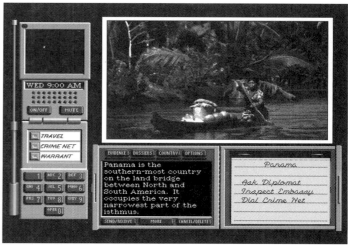

These two social studies games are popular with students, teachers, and parents. Oregon Trail allows players to learn about the hazards of crossing the 19th-century American West piloting a wagon train. Where in the World is Carmen San Diego, the immensely popular game designed to help students learn world geography, is the first piece of software to spin off children's books, a children's television show, a board game, and a live-action movie.

Productivity Tools

> For me, the phrase "computer as pencil" evokes the kind of uses I imagine children of the future making of computers. Pencils are used for scribbling as well as writing, doodling as well as drawing, for illicit notes as well as for official assignments.
>
> —Seymour Papert, in Mindstorms

Today the trend in schools is clearly toward teaching children to use computers as *tools*. Word processors, spreadsheets, databases, graphics programs, desktop publishing software—the software tools used by adults—are the tools students learn most often in schools. In some cases students use applications designed especially for children; others use standard "adult" applications. While programming classes are taken by only a few students, classes in keyboarding and word processing are often required for everybody. Once students learn to use these general-purpose tools, they can put them to work in and out of school.

Some schools also provide special-purpose tools for classroom use, including

- laboratory sensing hardware and software that can be used to collect scientific data (such as temperature) and convert it into computer data to be analyzed by students

- collaborative writing groupware that allows students to work collectively on creative writing and editing projects

- music synthesizers with sequencing and notation software for teaching music composition

Whether the computer is used as a tutor or a tool, the addition of multimedia adds whole new dimensions to the educational process.

Computer-Controlled Media

I hear and I forget,
I see and I remember,
I do and I understand.

—Ancient Chinese Proverb

The typical American child spends hours each day watching screens—television, video game, and computer—and listening to radio and recorded music. Traditional lectures can't live up to the expectations created by all this high-tech media input. A growing number of teachers are using computer graphics, videodiscs, CD-ROMs, and other digital media to convey information in a more dynamic form. Chapter 7 introduced a variety of graphics and multimedia applications. Depending on the way these media are used, the student's role might be to observe the presentation, to control the presentation, or to create the presentation.

Presentation Aids

In some cases teachers use computers and multimedia technology to create in-class presentations. Here are some examples:

- A history teacher might outline the main points of a lecture using a set of bullet charts created with a presentation graphics program like Astound or PowerPoint.

- A science teacher might use a 3-D graphics program to create models of molecules that can be displayed and manipulated during in-class demonstrations on a projection screen.

- An art teacher might illustrate an art history lecture with a series of images from a CD-ROM.

- A music teacher might guide a class through key passages of a Beethoven symphony using a commercial HyperCard stack that displays the score while the CD plays the composition.

- An English teacher might supplement lectures and discussions about the novel *To Kill a Mockingbird* by showing selected video clips that have been digitized into a presentation.

From the teacher's point of view, the advantage of computer technology is that the material can be customized to meet the needs of the class. Instead of using commercial transparencies and handouts designed for generic classrooms, a teacher can create custom visual aids for specific classes. Instead of being forced to move through videotapes and audio cassettes sequentially, the teacher can choose to present material in any order.

Hypermedia and Interactive Multimedia

From the student's point of view, teacher-controlled media presentations are still passive, linear affairs. To get students more involved in the learning process, many teachers use hypermedia and interactive multimedia software that put students in control. Sometimes these interactive lessons are created by teachers; more often they're purchased from software development companies. Some are simple tutorials with sound and/or video; others are multimedia reference tools with hypertext cross-references that allow students to jump quickly from topic to topic or change the way the information is displayed.

In this multimedia lab a student views scenes from a Shakespeare play; software on one screen allows the student to control the video clips and see annotations of the scenes shown on the other.

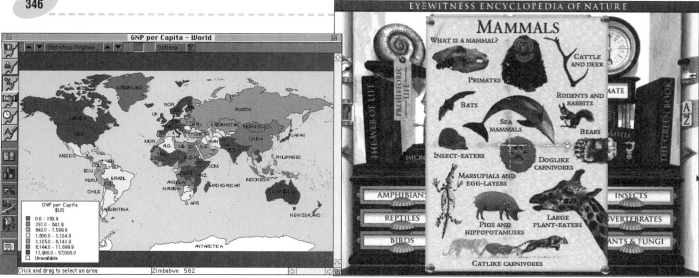

Multimedia reference tools like the PC Globe Maps and Facts and Eyewitness Encyclopedia of Nature provide students with vast quantities of information in easily accessible forms.

Authoring Tools for Students

To maximize student involvement, some teachers put multimedia **authoring tools** in the hands of students. Instead of creating interactive lessons for students, teachers allow the students to create their own multimedia presentations. Here are three examples:

- In an Alaskan village native students created *Yupik for Non-Speakers,* an illustrated talking dictionary of the traditional Yupik language. Students drew on the knowledge and voices of the community elders to create the dictionary.

- At South Eugene High School in Oregon, students produced a CD-ROM version of their yearbook. Unlike the paper version, the CD-ROM yearbook contains animated illustrations and recordings of the students talking about school.

- Students in a high-school science class in Shelley, Idaho, researched, planned, and built a multimedia exhibit for Yellowstone National Park's Canyon Visitor Center. Visitors use the touch-screen system to explore the political and geological history of Yellowstone and to "fly" from outer space down to the earth beneath Yellowstone.

Clearly the students are more involved in these projects than they are in teacher-made presentations. This kind of student involvement promotes learning, but it has drawbacks. One problem is economic: Few schools can afford the hardware, software, and floor space for

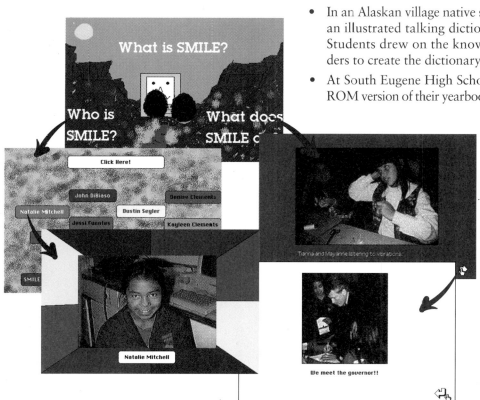

Students in the Jefferson County SMILE science and math club on the Warm Springs Indian Reservation designed and built an interactive multimedia presentation, complete with animation, audio, and video clips, to tell others about the club.

multiple student media workstations. Another problem is both social and political: When students are creating or using interactive media, they aren't conforming to the traditional factory model. Instead of sitting quietly listening to the teacher, they're taking control of the machinery and the learning process. The teacher becomes a supervisor and a mentor rather than a conveyor of information. This kind of restructuring of the educational process is threatening to many administrators, teachers, parents, and community members who are used to the old ways.

Distance Learning: Virtual Schools

> Very soon now, it might not matter where your body happens to be . . . as long as you maintain a presence in the networks.
>
> —Steven K. Roberts, technomad

For some students the most important application of computers in the schools is **distance learning**—using technology to extend the educational process beyond the walls of the school. Computers, modems, fax machines, satellite video transmissions, the Internet, and other communication technologies offer many promising possibilities. Grade-school students can network with kids in other parts of the world through the Internet. High-school correspondence courses can be completed by modem rather than by mail. Handicapped students can do course work without traveling to central sites. Two-way video links allow "visiting" experts to talk to students in outlying classrooms and answer their questions in real time. Networked school districts can offer multischool videoconference courses in Chinese, college-level calculus, and other subjects that might have tiny enrollments if offered only at a single school. Teachers can receive additional education without leaving their districts.

Telecommunication technology is particularly important for students in remote locations. If a child in a small town develops an interest in a narrow subject, whether it's aboriginal anthropology or classical Russian ballet, that student may find pursuing that interest a discouraging process. Reference materials, adult experts, and classmates with similar interests are often hard to find. The Internet offers solutions: on-line reference materials on Web pages, special-interest Usenet newsgroups, and like-minded modem pals are all within reach. In many areas rural interactive television networks keep remote schools and towns from fading away.

Distance learning also offers promise for workers whose jobs are changed or eliminated by a shifting economy. Many displaced workers can't afford to relocate their families to college towns so they can learn new skills. Others who still have jobs but want to go back to school are faced with similar relocation problems. But if colleges and universities offer electronic outreach programs, these people can update their skills while remaining in their communities.

Since 1990 on-line degree programs have appeared at dozens of universities and colleges. Students use PCs and modems to do everything from ordering

In 1996 Michigan Middle School students used the Internet to join an archaeological team as they dug for antiquities in the Egyptian Sahara. After completing eight weeks of lessons built around communications from the dig site, the "Odyssey in Egypt" project published Web pages that included a three-dimensional virtual reality view of the dig site.

books to taking final exams. Many on-line students see their professors in person for the first time at graduation ceremonies. On-line schools are particularly attractive to older students whose work prevents them from attending more traditional colleges. On-line schools are an important step toward an educational system that encourages lifelong learning.

COMPUTERS AT SCHOOL: MIDTERM GRADES

The business of education is to give the student both useful information and life-enhancing experience, one largely measurable, the other not. . . .

—John Gardner, in *The Art of Fiction*

Many schools have been using computers in classrooms for more than a decade. In these days of shrinking budgets, taxpayers are asking whether classroom computer technology "pays off." Has it lived up to its promise as an educational tool in the schools? According to most experts, the answer is mixed but optimistic.

High Marks

A number of independent studies over the last decade confirm that information technology can improve education. A 1990 report by the International Society for Technology in Education (ISTE) called *Vision: TEST (Technologically Enriched Schools of Tomorrow)* summarized the research on computer technology in the classroom:

- *Students improve problem-solving skills, outscore classmates, and learn more rapidly in a variety of subject areas when using technology as compared to conventional methods of study.*

- *Students find computer-based instruction to be more motivational, less intimidating, and easier to persist with than traditional instruction.*

- *In many cases students' self-esteem was increased when they used computers. This change has been most dramatic in cases of at-risk and handicapped youngsters.*

- *Using technology encourages cooperative learning, turn taking among young children, peer tutoring, and other valuable social skills.*

Other studies conducted in the 1990s support these conclusions and suggest others:

- Computer technology can make learning more student-centered and stimulate increased teacher/student interaction.

- Well-designed hypermedia systems can encourage active processing and higher-order thinking.

- Students who create hypermedia reports often learn better than those who learn with more traditional methods.

- Students can become more productive, more fluid writers with computers.

- Positive changes occur gradually as teachers gain experience with the technology.

- Technology can facilitate educational reform.

Room for Improvement

Other findings temper these positive conclusions. Researchers have also found that:

- If the only thing that changes is the delivery medium (from traditional media to computer media), the advantages of technology are small.

- Kids and teachers forget advanced computer skills if they don't use them.

- Students have unequal access to technology; economically advantaged students have more computer access at school and at home.

- Technology doesn't reduce teacher workloads; if anything, it seems to make their jobs harder (of course, many teachers welcome the extra work because it brings results).

- There's a gender gap that typically puts the computer room in the boys' domain; the gap can be reduced by stressing computer activities that involve collaboration.

- Many of the outcomes of technology-based education don't show up with traditional educational assessment methods.

Stories abound of reduced drop-out rates and attitudinal changes among at-risk students; improved math, reading, and language scores; and overall academic improvement among students in high-tech schools. But computer technology doesn't always bring happy headlines. What makes technology work for some schools and not for others? A closer look at the success stories reveals that they didn't achieve their dramatic results with technology alone. When we compare these schools with less fortunate schools, several issues emerge:

- *Money.* Most American schools have found funds to purchase computers. Unfortunately many of those computers are technologically outdated. Most classrooms don't even have phone lines, let alone modems. Not surprisingly, computers tend to be concentrated in affluent school districts, so economically disadvantaged students have the least access to them.

- *Planning and support.* Research suggests that when school districts spend money on technology without thoughtful long-term planning and sustained support, their investments are not likely to pay off.

- *Teacher training.* Unfortunately teacher training is often missing from schools' high-tech formulas. Most teachers lack the experience to use computers, the Internet, and other information technology effectively in the classroom. Teachers need training, support, and time to integrate technology into their curricula.

- *Restructuring.* Just as businesses need to rethink their organizational structures to automate successfully, schools need to be restructured to make effective use of computer technology. The goal is education, and technology is just one tool for achieving that goal. Interactive media, individualized instruction, telecommunication, and cooperative learning simply don't fit well into the factory school. To meet the educational challenges of the information age, we'll need to invest in research and planning involving teachers, students, administrators, parents, businesses, and community leaders. In the words of the *Vision: TEST* summary,

As a nation, we are spending billions of dollars repairing the deficiencies that an inadequate educational system has created. These dollars could be redirected to provide technology, teacher training, teacher support, and better curricula. This will result in significant reductions in dropout rates and significantly increase the quality of education our young people are receiving.

The Classroom of Tomorrow

To give us a head start in building the schools of the future, Apple, IBM, and other companies, along with some state and local governments, have helped create model technology schools in communities around the United States and Canada. Most of

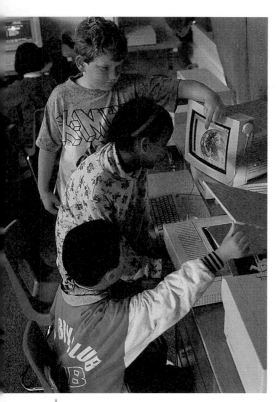

Students work side by side in the Apple Classroom of Tomorrow.

these pilots suggest that technology can, in the proper context, have a dramatic effect on education.

As an example, let's look at West High School in Columbus, Ohio, an urban school that's part of the Apple Classrooms of Tomorrow (ACOT) program. Students in the program use spreadsheets, simulations, and intelligent tutorial software to help them learn math; they use simulations to explore the effects of exercise and diet on a simulated heart; they create animated interactive short stories; they take notes on portable computers, sometimes organizing the material with hypertext links; they create multimedia research projects on everything from first amendment rights to the works of French and Spanish artists (written in French and Spanish). Many exams are computerized, so students can individually download tests from the network and have their solutions automatically evaluated and graded as they proceed. For some exams, students are allowed to correct their errors and resubmit their results before the grades are automatically entered into electronic grade books.

But technology is only part of the picture; communication and collaboration are important, too. Students give lectures along with teachers. Students exchange homework and criticize each other's solutions. Above all, students work together. Here's a description of a whole-class interdisciplinary project from Apple's 1992 project summary, *Overview—ACOT Project & Findings:*

In one such effort, students created a scale model of the renovated business district in Columbus. Over a month period, they researched buildings in the area, interviewed occupants and architects, measured and scaled skyscrapers, and constructed models including robotic elements they built and programmed. The completed effort was a 20-by-20-foot scale model driven by a dozen computers. To share the model with the city of Columbus, the students collaborated on the production of a videodisk, designed and built a HyperCard interface, and proudly presented the result in the lobby of the city's museum of science and industry.

Does this radical approach work? Based on a study of the first graduating class, *something* is working. Non-ACOT students at West High had a 30 percent drop-out rate, while *none* of the 21 ACOT students dropped out. Several local businesses were so impressed that they offered to hire *any* ACOT students immediately after graduation. Still, 90 percent of the graduates planned to pass up these employment opportunities to go to college, seven with full scholarships. Among them, they received 27 academic awards. The project summary goes on:

But more importantly, a four-year longitudinal study of these students showed their greatest difference to be the manner in which they organized for and accomplished their work. They routinely employed inquiry, collaborative, technological, and problem-solving skills uncommon to graduates of traditional high-school programs.

The Campus of Tomorrow

The further one pursues knowledge, the less one knows.

—Lao Tse, 500 BC

The ACOT schools and other model technology schools show what can be done with well-trained teachers, an imaginative school structure, and *today's* state-of-the-art technology. But what about *tomorrow's* technology? What kind of personal computers will students be using in the year 2000, and how will they be using them?

In 1987 Apple sponsored Project 2000, a university-level competition to get answers to those questions. The winning entry, Tablet, was designed by a group of students and faculty advisors (Luke T. Young, Kurt H. Thearling, Steven S. Skiena, Arch D. Robinson, Stephen M. Omohundro, Bartlett W. Mel, Stephen Wolfram) from the University of Illinois at Urbana-Champaign. Tablet is a notebook-sized, touch-screen, wireless communication device with optical storage cards and sophisticated handwriting recognition capability. Even though it's several years old—even older than the World Wide Web—the winning article still provides a remarkably clear and imaginative view of a possible future. Here's an excerpt from that article describing a day in the life of a student with a Tablet:

The date is October 5, 2000. Alexis Quezada is a freshman at a prestigious institution of higher learning. . . . On her first day of classes she was given her own Tablet, the personal computer used at the university.

Today Alexis has three classes. . . . It is a nice day, so Alexis rides her bike over to the park before the lecture starts. At 10:00 A.M. sharp Tablet informs her that the Physical Science lecture is about to start. She directs her attention toward the screen as the lecture begins. When the lecture is over, she begins the laboratory experiment. It involves determining the equilibrium for a chemical reaction. She sets up the simulated experiment apparatus and starts it going. But it isn't working. She instructs Tablet to search today's lecture for "the stuff about setting up today's experiment." Within seconds the requested portion of the lecture is displayed on the screen.

Because of the problem with setting up the experiment, Alexis missed the beginning of her Japanese lecture. Instead of jumping into a lecture that has already started, Alexis's computer contacts the university's lecture database again and instructs the database to display the current lecture from the beginning. Time-shifting the start of the lecture by fifteen minutes has allowed her to see the lecture from the beginning, at the cost of not being able to ask the professor a question if she doesn't understand. Fortunately, the lecture is still in progress and should last another forty minutes, so Alexis invokes the "catch-up" facility. Over the next fifteen minutes, Alexis watches thirty minutes of lecture as Tablet squeezes out the times of slow movement and silence. Through signal processing, the lecture looks and sounds fast-paced but is otherwise normal. Now up to speed, she watches the rest of the lecture and participates in asking questions, performing an occasional "instant replay/catch-up" sequence on material that she found confusing.

Once Japanese is over, Alexis heads back to the dormitory for lunch. Some things never change, and dorm food is one of them. Fortunately, the social aspects of lunch will still be important even in a world where one can communicate with friends by video email. Afterwards Alexis returns to her room to start reading her LaserCard edition of G. B. Trudeau's Republic, *complete with art, text, and extensive commentary. She scrawls notes directly on the simulated page which she can search or hide at will.*

In English Comp class at 2:00 P.M., the professor indicates that she has finished grading the previous assignment and returns them. Instantly, the corner of the display contains a copy of Alexis's graded paper—B+, not too bad. Alexis pages through the paper by touching the screen. She touches the video-mail icon for comments about a particular page. Segments of her text become highlighted in color as they are discussed. Unfortunately, her teacher is pretty boring, and so she turns on her soap opera instead. . . .

Now it's time to work on her art history term paper comparing Salvador Dali's surrealist images in his paintings and the images he developed for the movies Un Chien Andalou *and* Spellbound. *Alexis tells Tablet to find the films in available film databases. It seems that there are three films with the title* Spellbound. *Alexis says to find "the one by Hitchcock." The scenes she is interested in analyzing are being copied directly into her paper—a hypertext document. Alexis expounds on the meaning of the images in the films and their importance with respect to Dali's symbolism until it's time to call it a night.* (From "Academic Computing in the Year 2000," *Academic Computing,* May/June 1988.)

Many of Tablets's features have become real in today's portable computers and digital assistants. Others are still years—possibly decades—away. As we approach the year 2000, technological pieces—personal digital assistants, laptop computers, video telecommunication, multimedia databases, and the Internet—are rapidly falling into place. It won't happen by 2000, but something like Tablet is almost certainly in your future. Of course, there's more to this story than technology. The big questions are not whether the technology can happen, but whether the social structures and human behavior can change fast enough to keep up with the technology. When Tablet arrives, will schools and people be ready?

COMPUTERS COME HOME

There is no reason for any individual to have a computer in their home.

—Ken Olson, president of Digital Equipment Corporation, 1977

The same year Ken Olson made this statement, Apple Computer introduced the Apple II computer. In the years that followed, Apple, Commodore, Tandy, Atari, IBM, and dozens of other companies managed to sell computers to millions of individuals who had "no reason" to buy them. Today there are more computers in homes than in schools, and the home computer market is still growing. While many of those computers gather dust, others are being put to work, and play, in a variety of ways. And new technologies are emerging that may soon put computers into the mainstream of modern home life. What are people using home computers for, and what kind of role will computers play in tomorrow's homes?

A home office like this one can be used for taking care of family business . . . or starting a family business.

Household Business

Frank Gilbreth, a turn-of-the-century pioneer of motion study in industry, applied "scientific management" techniques to his home. He required his 12 children to keep records on bathroom "work-and-process charts" of each hair combing, tooth brushing, and bathing. He gave them demonstrations on efficient bathing techniques to minimize "unavoidable delays." While it may have worked for Gilbreth, this "scientific management" approach to home life is not likely to catch on today. Still, certain aspects of family life are unavoidably businesslike, and a growing number of people turn to computers to help them take care of business.

Business Applications at Home

Not everyone is convinced that computers are useful or practical at home. But those people who *do* use home computers generally find that they can put the same applications to work at home that they use in their offices:

- *Word processors.* For letters, memos, and (especially) school papers, the word processor has replaced the typewriter for families with computers.

- *Spreadsheets.* "Can we afford a trip to Mexico this year?" "How much do we need to put away each year to pay for college?" "Should we refinance the house?" A spreadsheet program can frame answers to "What if?" questions involving numbers, providing somebody takes the time and effort to create a worksheet model of the problem.

- *Database programs.* Many people use database programs for address books, family record keeping, collections, and other data storage jobs. Others find that it's not worth the effort to type in all that data.

- *Personal information management programs.* Appointment calendars, to-do lists, addresses, phone numbers—they're part of home life, too, and an enthusiastic minority of people use home computers to keep their personal lives organized.

- *Accounting and income tax programs.* Many easy-to-use accounting programs are targeted at homes and small businesses. These programs can balance checkbooks, write checks, keep financial records for tax time, and provide data for income tax calculation programs, if somebody types in the relevant data.

Smart Cards

For most people the advantages of computerized home money management aren't worth the time and effort required to enter every financial transaction into the computer. Some people strike a balance by only typing in "important" transactions; a few subscribe to home banking programs so they can download their summary statements directly from bank computers. But for most people computerized money management won't happen until there's an effortless way to record transactions—perhaps a device that, when inserted into the computer, can tell the software about each purchase and paid bill. That device may turn out to be a smart card.

A **smart card** looks like a standard credit card, but instead of a magnetic strip it contains embedded microprocessors and memory. Some smart cards even contain touch-sensitive keypads for entering numbers. Whether it has a keypad or not, a smart card receives most of its input when it's slipped into a special slot on a computer. Data stored in smart cards can be password-protected. There are hundreds of millions of smart cards in Europe, and they're rapidly infiltrating America.

Smart cards are obvious candidates to replace magnetic-strip credit cards. In addition to storing critical ID information, a smart card can automatically record each transaction for later retrieval. But smart cards have other applications, too. College students use smart cards as meal tickets. Office workers use smart cards as keys to access sensitive data on computers. Smart cards have replaced food stamps for thousands of households in Dayton, Ohio. Many Europeans use smart cards to pay highway tolls and unscramble cable TV broadcasts. In the future we might be able to use one card to buy groceries, check out library books, and store personal medical information in case of an emergency. Future smart cards will use pattern recognition techniques to verify signatures on checks or credit slips and help prevent millions of dollars in fraud and forgery.

A smart card.

Communication, Education, and Information

Newspapers as we know them won't exist. They will be printed for a readership of one. Television won't simply have sharper pictures. You'll have one button that says tell me more, and another button that says tell me less.

—**Nicholas Negroponte, director of the MIT Media Lab**

Millions of people use home computers for education and information. Many of the educational software programs described earlier in this chapter are used by children and adults in homes. **Edutainment** programs specifically geared toward home markets combine education with entertainment so they can compete with television and electronic games. Encyclopedias, dictionaries, atlases, almanacs, national telephone directories, medical references, and other specialized references now come in low-cost CD-ROM versions—often with multimedia capability. More up-to-the-minute information is available from the Internet and on-line services like America Online and CompuServe. Of course, Internet connections also provide electronic mail, discussion groups, and other communication options for home users.

As computer technology and communication technology converge on the home market, they'll produce services that will threaten television and newspapers as our main sources of information. Television is a *broadcast* medium—it transmits news and information to broad audiences. In the future we'll see **narrowcasting** services—they'll provide custom newscasts aimed at narrow groups or individuals. Personalized multimedia news programs will combine many of the best features of television news and newspapers. You'll be able to request an index of available features and use it like a menu to build your own news program. Your personal newscast might include a piece on the latest Middle Eastern crisis, the results of yesterday's primary election, highlights of last night's Blazers vs. Bulls game, the scores in the college intramural games, this weekend's weather forecast at the coast, a feature on your favorite local musician, and a reminder that there are only five more shopping days until your mother's birthday. You'll be able to train your news service to flag particular subjects ("I'm especially inter-

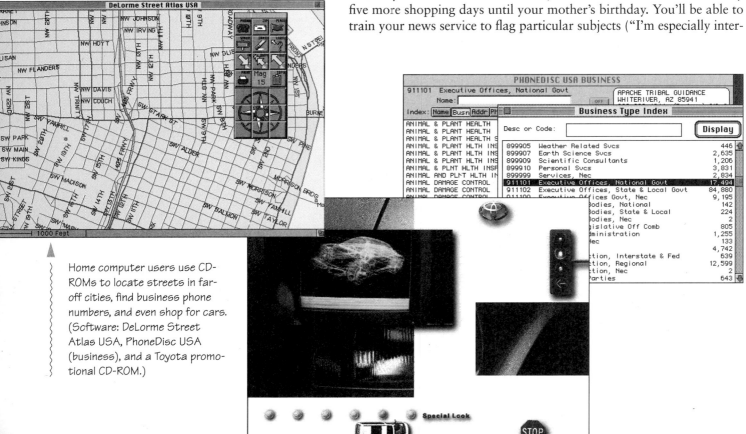

Home computer users use CD-ROMs to locate streets in far-off cities, find business phone numbers, and even shop for cars. (Software: DeLorme Street Atlas USA, PhoneDisc USA (business), and a Toyota promotional CD-ROM.)

ested in articles on the Amazon rain forest") and ignore others ("No heavy metal features, please"), so that even the menu is customized to suit your tastes. All of this is technologically possible now. Prototype systems have been running for years at MIT's Media Lab, and a few pilot services are now offered through the Internet by private companies.

Home Entertainment Redefined

Television has a "brightness" knob, but it doesn't seem to work.

—Gallagher, stand-up comic

You don't want a television with knobs marked "volume" and "brightness" and "contrast." You want a television with knobs marked "sex" and "violence" and "political bias."

—Nicholas Negroponte, director of the MIT Media Lab

Regardless of how people say they use home computers, surveys suggest that they use them mostly to play games. Computer games and video game machines (which are just special-purpose computers) represent a huge industry—one that is likely to evolve rapidly in the coming years.

Most computer games are simulations. Computer games can simulate board games, card games, sporting events, intergalactic battles, street fights, corporate takeovers, or something else, real or imaginary. Many require strategy and puzzle

Entertainment programs have come a long way since the early Pong games. Today we have thousands of recreational software choices including fast-paced, 3-D space battles like Descent; annotated hyperlinked motion pictures like A Hard Day's Night; enhanced music CDs like The Cranberries' Doors and Windows, and interactive "coffee table" photo albums like Material World: A Global Family Portrait.

Green Computing

When compared to heavy industries like automobiles and energy, the computer industry is relatively easy on the environment. But the manufacture and use of computer hardware and software does have a significant environmental impact, especially now that so many of us are using the technology. Fortunately, you have some control over the environmental impact of your computing activities. Here are a few tips to help minimize your impact:

- *Buy green equipment.* Today's computer equipment uses relatively little energy, but as world energy resources dwindle, less is always better. Many modern computers and peripherals are specifically designed to consume less energy. Look for the Environmental Protection Agency's Energy Star certification on the package.

- *Take advantage of energy-saving features.* Many systems can be set up to go to *sleep* (a sort of suspended animation state that uses just enough power to preserve RAM) and turn off the monitor or printer when idle for a while. If your equipment has automatic energy-saving features, use them. You'll save energy and money.

- *Turn it off when you're away.* If you're just leaving your computer for an hour or two, you won't save much energy by turning the CPU off. But if you're leaving it for more than a few hours, and it's not on duty receiving faxes and e-mail, you'll do

the environment a favor by turning it off or putting it to sleep. Your monitor is probably the biggest power guzzler in your system. And while your Dilbert screen saver may be entertaining, it won't save your screen or reduce energy consumption.

- *Print only once.* Don't print out a rough draft just to proofread; try to get it clean on screen. (Most people find this one hard to follow 100 percent of the time; some errors just don't seem to show up until you print.)

- *Recycle your waste products.* When you *do* have to reprint that 20-page report because of an error on page one, recycle the flawed printout. When your laser printer's toner cartridge runs dry, ship it to one of the many companies that recycle cartridges. They may even pay you a few dollars for the empty cartridge. When your portable's battery dies, follow the manufacturer's instructions for recycling it. While you're in recycling mode, don't forget all those computer magazines and catalogs. When you outgrow a piece of hardware and software, pass it on to a school, civic organization, or friend who can put it to good use.

- *Send bits, not atoms.* It takes far more resources to send a letter by truck, train, or plane than to send an electronic message through the Internet. Whenever possible, use your modem instead of your printer.

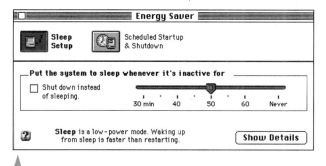

You can use Apple's Energy Saver Control Panel software to tell the monitor and CPU to "sleep" in a minimal power consumption mode after a specified period of inactivity.

Portable computers consume far less energy than desktop models; this one is powered by the sun using a Neptune Solar Panel.

solving; others depend only on eye-hand coordination. Many of the most popular games require some of each. With dazzling graphics, digitized sound, and sophisticated effects, many of today's computer games represent state-of-the-art software. But in a few years these computer games are likely to look as primitive in a decade as those early Pong games look today.

The biggest changes in electronic games are likely to come as computers and communication technology converge on the home entertainment industry. As this happens, the line that separates television programs and computer games will grow fuzzy. A few years ago, software shops stocked a variety of **interactive fiction** games—stories with primitive natural-language interfaces that gave players some control over plot. Those nongraphic, not-very-intelligent programs have been squeezed off the software shelves by **interactive movies**—animated features in which one or more of the characters are controlled by the viewers. Today's interactive movies aren't Academy Award material; at best, they're like cartoons with controls. But as technology improves and the multimedia market grows, you can expect to see all kinds of hybrid forms of entertainment.

Creativity and Leisure

If you can talk, you can sing.
If you can walk, you can dance.

—A saying from Zimbabwe

Interactive movies demand more involvement than television, but they're still a relatively passive pastime. Many people worry that television, computer games, and other media are replacing too many real-world activities. Instead of making up stories to share, we watch sitcoms on TV. Instead of playing music on guitars, we play music on boom boxes. Instead of playing one-on-one basketball, we play one-on-one video games. Is electronic technology turning us into a couch-potato culture?

Perhaps. But there's another possibility. The same technology that mesmerizes us can also unlock our creativity. There are many examples: Word processors help many of us to become writers, graphics software brings out the artists among us, desktop publishing systems put the power of the press in more hands, electronic music systems allow us to compose music even if we never mastered an instrument, and multimedia systems open doors to cable-access TV channels.

Will computers drain our creativity or amplify it? In the end it's up to us. . . .

SUMMARY

Our educational system was developed a century ago to train workers for lifelong jobs. In the information age, when students can expect to change jobs several times, we need schools that teach technological familiarity, literacy, mathematics, culture, communication, problem solving, and most importantly, the ability to learn and adapt to an ever-changing world.

Students use a variety of instructional tools in schools today, including

- *computer-aided instruction (CAI)*—tutorials and/or drill-and-practice software covering concrete facts in specific subject areas

- *programming tools*—languages like LOGO, Pascal, BASIC, and HTML that allow students to design their own software and Web pages

- *simulation and games*—artificial environments that allow students to learn through exploration, experimentation, and interaction with other students
- *productivity tools*—word processors, spreadsheets, and other real-world tools
- *computer-controlled media*—presentation graphics, hypermedia, interactive multimedia, and authoring tools that allow varying degrees of student control
- *distance learning tools*—telecommunication tools that allow students and teachers to communicate electronically without having to be in the same physical location

Clearly computer technology can have a positive educational impact, but computers alone can't guarantee improvement. Research, planning, teacher training, community involvement, and classroom restructuring should accompany new technology.

A small but growing number of people use home computers for basic business applications, education, information access, communication, entertainment, and creative pursuits. All these applications will radically change as the technology evolves over the next decade.

Chapter Review

Key Terms

authoring tool
computer-aided instruction (CAI)
courseware
distance learning
drill-and-practice software

educational simulation
edutainment
interactive fiction
interactive movie
narrowcasting

smart card
technophobia
tutorial software

Review Questions

1. What were the goals of education in the industrial age? Which are still appropriate in the information age? Which are not?

2. What kind of an education does a student need to prepare for living and working in the information age?

3. How do educational simulation games differ from traditional computer-aided instruction? What are the advantages and disadvantages of each?

4. Describe how multimedia and hypermedia might be used by teachers and students in the classroom. Give several examples.

5. Give several examples of ways that distance learning can enhance education.

6. Technology alone is no guarantee that students will learn better or faster. What else is necessary to ensure success?

7. Describe several ways people use home computers.

8. What are smart cards, and how are they used?

9. What are interactive movies? In what ways do they combine computer technology with home entertainment technology?

Discussion Questions

1. Socrates was illiterate and avoided the written word because he felt it weakened the mind. Similarly, many people today fear that we're weakening our children's minds by making them too dependent on computers and calculators. What do you think?

2. In many schools, students spend two years of math education learning long division—a skill that's almost never used in the age of the $5 calculator. Some educators argue that students' time could be better spent learning other things. What do you think? What about calculating square roots by hand?

3. Do you think it's important for students to learn to program in LOGO, Pascal, BASIC, or some other language? Why or why not?

4. Do you think educational games are good ways for students to learn in schools? Give examples that support your arguments.

5. What kind of productivity software tools should students learn how to use? Why?

6. Think about educational goals in relation to technology. What should people be able to do with no tools? What should people be able to do if they have access to pen-

cils, papers, and books? What should people be able to do if they have access to computer technology?

7. Describe your past school experience in terms of technology. How did it measure up? What has been missing from your education so far?

8. Does the Project 2000 story about Tablet sound realistic? Desirable? Explain.

9. Do you think most families could benefit from a home computer today? Explain.

10. Do you think home computers in the future will make people more or less creative? Why?

Projects

1. Try several different types of educational software. If possible, observe students using the software. Prepare a report comparing the strengths and weaknesses of each.

2. Observe how computers are used in local schools. Report on your findings.

3. Observe how computers are used on your campus. Report on your findings.

4. Using an authoring tool like HyperCard, ToolBook, or HyperStudio, design some courseware. Another possibility is to create your courseware on the World Wide Web using HTML. Make sure you set clear goals before you start. When your project is completed, try it with several students.

5. Plan a model technology school. Describe how it would differ from conventional schools and why.

6. Using an authoring tool like HyperCard, design a work of interactive fiction. See how others react as they explore your work.

Sources and Resources

Books

The Technology Age Classroom, edited by Terence R. Cannings and LeRoy Finkel (Wilsonville, OR: Franklin, Beedle, & Associates, Inc., 1993). This collection includes articles and papers by many of the experts in the field of technology in education. If you're interested in educational computing, you'll find this book to be an invaluable resource.

Mindstorms: Children, Computers, and Powerful Ideas, by Seymour Papert (New York: Basic Books, 1980), and *The Children's Machine,* by Seymour Papert (New York: Basic Books, 1994). These two books outline the views of one widely respected theorist and researcher who invented LOGO. *Mindstorms* was written during the period when Papert was doing pioneering work with LOGO. *The Children's Machine* presents a more contemporary perspective.

That's Edutainment: A Parent's Guide to Educational Software, by Eric Brown (Berkeley, CA: Osborne/McGraw-Hill Publishing Company, 1995). This book begins with an overview of the concepts behind the kinds of educational software that's entertaining enough to compete with TV. More than half of the book is made up of detailed software reviews. A companion cross-platform CD-ROM includes demo versions of many of the reviewed programs.

The Student's Guide to Doing Research on the Internet, by Dave and Mary Campbell (Reading, MA: Addison-Wesley Publishing Company, 1995). There are many guides to the Internet. This one is specifically designed to help students find what they need on the Net. After a general introduction to the Internet, the Campbells provide subject-by-subject guides to help you find what you need for every class.

Periodicals

Learning and Leading with Technology, from ISTE (1787 Agate St., Eugene, OR 97403-1923, 800/336-5191). ISTE (International Society for Technology in Education) is an important and influential organization whose focus is the effective use of computer technology in the classroom. *Learning and Leading with Technology* (formerly *The Computing Teacher*) is their most accessible and widely read publication. ISTE is also the source for the *Vision: TEST* mentioned in this chapter.

Electronic Learning, from Scholastic, Inc. (P.O. Box 3025, Southeastern, PA 19398-9890) and *Technology & Learning* (2451 E. River Road, Dayton, OH 45439) are two other magazines full of features and news items related to technology in the classroom.

T.H.E. Journal (Technological Horizons in Education) (150 El Camino Real, Suite 112, Tustin, CA 92680-3615, 714/730-4011, fax 714/730-3739). This magazine covers both K-12 and higher education with a mixture of product announcements and articles.

Family Computing. This magazine is aimed mostly at parents who want to help their kids put computers to good use.

Home Office Computing. This one is geared more toward people who use their computers to work at home.

Mac Home Journal. This monthly focuses on home applications for Macintosh users.

Popular Science. This tinkerer's magazine is a good source of information on the latest computerized gadgets for consumers.

World Wide Web Sites

The Web is bursting with exciting educational material, much of it created by students. Check the *Computer Confluence* Web site for links to many sites devoted to learning and teaching. You'll also find a sampling of Web links related to entertainment, family life, and home applications.

Kempelen's Amazing Chess-Playing Machine

Check.

—The only word ever spoken by Kempelen's chess-playing machine

Kempelen's chess-playing machine

In 1760 Wolfgang Kempelen, a 49-year-old Hungarian inventor, engineer, and advisor to the Court of Austrian Empress Maria Theresa, built a mechanical chess player. This amazing contraption defeated internationally renowned players and earned its inventor almost legendary fame.

A Turkish-looking automaton sat behind a big box that supported a chessboard and chess pieces. The operator of the machine could open the box to "prove" there was nothing inside but a network of cogwheels, gears, and revolving cylinders. After every 12 moves, Kempelen wound the machine up with a huge key. Of course, the chess-playing

machine was actually a clever hoax. The real chess player was a dwarf-sized person who controlled the mechanism from inside and was concealed by mirrors when the box was opened. The tiny player couldn't see the board, but he could tell what pieces were moved by watching magnets below the chessboard.

Kempelen had no intention of keeping the deception going for long; he thought of it as a joke and dismantled it after its first tour. But he became a slave to his own fraud, as the public and the scientific community showered him with praise for creating the first "machine-man." In 1780 the Emperor Joseph II ordered

another court demonstration of the mechanical chess player, and Kempelen had to rebuild it. The chess player toured the courts of Europe, and the public became more curious and fascinated than ever.

After Kempelen died in 1804, the machine was purchased by the impresario Maelzel, who showed it far and wide. In 1809 it challenged Napoleon Bonaparte to play. When Napoleon repeatedly made illegal moves, the machine-man brushed the pieces from the table. Napoleon was delighted to have unnerved the machine. When he played the next game fairly, Napoleon was badly beaten.

The chess-playing machine came to America in 1826, where it attracted large, paying crowds. In 1834 two different articles—one by Edgar Allen Poe—revealed the secrets of the automated chess player. Poe's investigative article was insightful but not completely accurate; one of his 17 arguments was that a true automatic player would invariably win.

After Maelzel's death in 1837, the machine passed from hand to hand until it was destroyed by fire in Philadelphia in 1854. During the 70 years that the automaton was publicly exhibited, its "brain" was supplied by 15 different chess players who won 294 of 300 games.

With his elaborate and elegant deception, Kempelen might be considered the forerunner of the modern computer criminal. Kempelen was trapped in his fraud because the public wanted to believe that the automated chess player was real. Desire overtook judgment in thousands of people who were captivated by the idea of an intelligent machine.

More than two centuries later, we're still fascinated by intelligent machines. But modern computers don't just play games; they manage our money, our medicine, and our missiles. We're expected to trust information technology with our wealth, our health, and even our lives. The many benefits of our partnership with machines are clear. But blind faith in modern technology can be foolish and, in many cases, dangerous. In this chapter we'll examine some of the dark corners of our computerized society: legal dilemmas, ethical issues, and reliability risks. All of these issues are tied to a larger question: How can we make computers more secure, so that we can feel more secure in our daily dealings with them?

ON-LINE OUTLAWS: COMPUTER CRIME

Computers are power, and direct contact with power can bring out the best or worst in a person.

—Former computer criminal turned corporate computer programmer

Like other professions, law enforcement is being transformed by information technology. The FBI's National Crime Information Center provides police with almost instant information on crimes and criminals nationwide.

A Princeton, NJ, police officer uses his mobile computer to check records in a central crime database.

Investigators use PC databases to store and cross-reference clues in complex cases. Using pattern recognition technology, automated fingerprint identification systems locate matches in minutes rather than months. Computers routinely scan the New York and London stock exchanges for connections that might indicate insider trading or fraud. All these tools help law enforcement officials ferret out criminals and stop criminal activities.

Like guns, computers are used to break laws as well as uphold them. Computers are powerful tools in the hands of criminals, and computer crime is a rapidly growing problem.

The Computer Crime Dossier

Some will rob you with a six gun,
and some with a fountain pen.

— Woody Guthrie, in "Pretty Boy Floyd"

Today the computer has replaced both the gun and the pen as the weapon of choice for many criminals. **Computer crime** is often defined as any crime accomplished through knowledge or use of computer technology.

Nobody knows the true extent of computer crime. Many computer crimes go undetected. Those that are detected often go unreported, because businesses fear that they can lose more from negative publicity than from the actual crimes. By conservative estimates, businesses and government institutions lose billions of dollars every year to computer criminals. According to the FBI, the average computer crime is worth about $600,000—far more than most other crimes. A single case of computer fraud cost the Volkswagen company in Germany more than $260 million in 1984.

According to a survey released in 1996 by the FBI and private security experts, more than 40 percent of corporate, university, and government sites reported at least one computer break-in in the preceding 12 months. These attacks included changing data, stealing passwords, and preventing legitimate users from gaining access to systems.

More than half of the organizations reported attacks from employees and other insiders. These crimes are typically committed by clerks, cashiers, programmers, computer operators, and managers who have no extraordinary technical ingenuity. The typical computer criminal is a trusted employee with no criminal record who is tempted by an opportunity, such as the discovery of a loophole in system security. Greed, financial worries, and personal problems motivate this person to give in to temptation.

Of course, not all computer criminals fit this description. Some are former employees seeking revenge on their former bosses. Some are corporate or international spies seeking classified information. A few are high-tech pranksters looking for a challenge. Organized crime syndicates are turning to computer technology to practice their trades. Sometimes entire companies are found guilty of computer fraud. For example, Equity Funding, Inc., used computers to generate thousands of false insurance policies that later were sold for over $27 million.

The 1996 survey suggests that the explosive growth of the Internet is changing the demographics of computer crime. More than one third of the surveyed organizations reported outside attacks through the Internet. According to Senior Analyst Richard Power of the Computer Security Institute in San Francisco, "As all manner of commerce moves into cyberspace, all manner of crime is moving there as well."

Theft by Computer

Put all of your eggs in one basket—and watch that basket.

—Mark Twain, in *The Tragedy of Pudd'nhead Wilson*, 1894

Theft is the most common form of computer crime. Computers are used to steal money, goods, information, and computer resources. Here are a few examples:

- A part-time college student used his touch-tone phone and personal computer to fool Pacific Telephone's computer into ordering phone equipment to be delivered to him. He started a business, hired several employees, and pilfered about a million dollars worth of equipment before he was turned in by a disgruntled employee. (After serving two months in jail, he became a computer security consultant.)

- In 1987 a former automated teller machine repairman illegally obtained $86,000 out of ATMs by spying on customers while they typed in passwords and creating bogus cards to use with the passwords.

- Clerks at an upscale department store erased the accounts of major customers by listing those customers as bankrupt. The customers paid the clerks 10 percent of the $33 million they saved by not having to repay their debts. Since the "bankruptcies" were only listed in the store's computers, they didn't hurt the customers' credit ratings.

- In 1988 several million dollars were illegally transferred to a private Swiss bank account. The transfer was noticed because a computer glitch on that particular day forced employees to check transactions manually; the automated procedure normally used wouldn't have noticed the suspicious transaction.

- In 1992 a phone hacker used a dial-in maintenance line to crack the computerized phone system of a Detroit newspaper publisher. The hacker cracked the system administrator's passcode and set up scores of voice mailboxes for friends and associates who dialed in on the publisher's toll-free number. Fortunately, the scam cost the publisher only a few hundred dollars—a small sum when compared to the $1.4 million worth of illegal long-distance calls billed against one national manufacturing firm *in a single weekend.*

- In 1996 investigators uncovered a massive credit card fraud ring that bought private information about more than 11,000 individuals from employees of the U.S. Social Security Administration; this information, including credit card numbers and mother's maiden names, allowed the criminals to activate credit cards stolen from the mail.

- Dozens of college campuses have reported cases of stolen computer time. A typical student scam uses a process called *spoofing* to steal passwords. The typical spoofer launches a program that mimics the mainframe computer's login screen on an unattended terminal in a public lab. When an unsuspecting student types an ID and password, the program responds with an error message and remembers the secret codes.

All of these crimes are expensive—for businesses, law enforcement agencies, and taxpayers and consumers who ultimately must pay the bills. But as crimes go, the types of theft described so far are relatively uncommon. The same can't be said of the most widely practiced type of computer-related theft: software piracy.

Software Piracy and Intellectual Property Laws

> Information wants to be free. Information also wants to be expensive. Information wants to be free because it has become so cheap to distribute, copy, and recombine—too cheap to meter. It wants to be expensive because it can be immeasurably valuable to the recipient. That tension will not go away.
>
> —Stewart Brand, in *The Media Lab*

Software piracy—the illegal duplication of copyrighted software—is rampant. Millions of computer users have made copies of programs they don't legally own. Now that most software companies have given in to user demands and removed physical copy protection from their products, copying software is as easy as duplicating a cassette tape or photocopying a book. Unfortunately, many people aren't aware that copying software, recorded music, and books can violate federal laws protecting intellectual property.

Intellectual Property and the Law

Legally the definition of **intellectual property** includes the results of intellectual activities in the arts, science, and industry. Copyright laws have traditionally protected forms of literary expression, patent law has protected mechanical inventions, and contract law has covered trade secrets. Software doesn't fit neatly into any of these categories under the law. Most commercial software programs are protected by copyright laws, but a few companies have successfully used patent laws to protect software products.

The purpose of intellectual property laws is to ensure that mental labor is justly rewarded and to encourage innovation. Programmers, inventors, scientists, writers, editors, and musicians depend on ideas and the expression of those ideas for their incomes. Ideas are information, and information is easy to copy. Intellectual property laws are designed to protect these professionals and encourage them to continue their creative efforts so society can benefit from their future work.

Unfortunately intellectual property laws are difficult to enforce. The software industry, with a world market of more than $50 billion a year, loses billions of dollars every year to software pirates. Piracy can be particularly hard on small software companies. Developing software is just as difficult for them as it is for big companies like Microsoft and Oracle, but they often lack the financial resources to cover their losses to piracy. Software industry organizations such as the Software Publishers Association are working with law enforcement agencies to crack down on piracy. At the same time, they're stepping up educational programs to make computer users aware that piracy is theft. These organizations recognize that laws can't work without citizen understanding and support.

Existing copyright and patent laws, which evolved during the age of print and mechanical inventions, are outdated, contradictory, and inadequate for today's information technology. Many laws, including the Computer Fraud and Abuse Act of 1984, clearly treat software piracy as a crime, but issues remain unresolved. Lawyers and judges aren't sure whether software should be protected by copyrights or patents. To complicate matters further, a few third-world nations refuse to abide by international copyright laws; they argue that the laws protect rich countries at the expense of underdeveloped nations.

Look-and-Feel Lawsuits

When it comes to software, nobody is sure exactly what is protected by law. Creating and selling an exact duplicate of a program clearly violates the law, but what about creating a program that has the "look and feel" of a successful software program? Can one software company legally sell a program that mimics the screen design and menu commands of a competing product? Is Microsoft Windows a rip-off of the Macintosh operating system? Did Borland steal the 1-2-3 command structure for its Quattro spreadsheet software? These questions, and others like them, were asked in federal cases over the past decade. In spite of a few contradictory verdicts, the general trend seems to be toward allowing companies to liberally "borrow" user interface elements and ideas from their competition. In the cases mentioned above, Microsoft and Borland both successfully defended themselves against lawsuits. Still, each of these cases had unique circumstances that led the judges to dismiss the suits; future look-and-feel lawsuits could easily go the other way.

In matters of software the legal system is sailing in uncharted waters. Whether dealing with piracy or look-and-feel issues, lawmakers and judges must struggle with difficult questions about innovation, property, freedom, and progress. The questions are likely to be with us for quite a while.

Software Sabotage

> Every system has vulnerabilities. Every system can be compromised.
>
> —Peter G. Neumann, in *Computer Related Risks*

Another type of computer crime is sabotage of hardware or software. The word *sabotage* comes from the early days of the industrial revolution, when rebellious workers shut down new machines by kicking wooden shoes, called sabots, into the gears. However, modern computer saboteurs commonly use software rather than footwear to do destructive deeds. The names given to the saboteurs' destructive programs—*viruses, worms,* and *Trojan horses*—sound more like biology than technology, and many of the programs even mimic the behavior of living organisms.

Trojan Horses

A **Trojan horse** is a program that performs a useful task while at the same time carrying out some secret destructive act. As in the ancient story of the wooden horse that carried Greek soldiers through the gates of Troy, Trojan horse software hides an enemy in an attractive package. Trojan horse programs are often posted on public domain bulletin boards with names that make them sound like games or utilities. When an unsuspecting bargain hunter downloads and runs such a program, it might erase files, change data, or cause some other kind of damage. Some network saboteurs use Trojan horses to pass secret data to other unauthorized users.

One type of Trojan horse, a **logic bomb,** is programmed to attack in response to a particular logical event or sequence of events. For example, a programmer might plant a logic bomb that is designed to destroy data files if the programmer is ever listed as terminated in the company's personnel file. A logic bomb might be triggered when a certain user logs in, a special code is entered in a database field, or a particular sequence of actions is performed by the user. If the logic bomb is triggered by a time-related event, it is called a *time bomb*. A widely publicized virus included a logic bomb that was programmed to destroy PC data files on Michelangelo's birthday.

Trojan horses can cause serious problems in computer systems of all sizes. To make matters worse, many Trojan horses carry software viruses.

Viruses

A biological virus is unable to reproduce by itself, but it can invade the cells of another organism and use the reproductive machinery of each host cell to make copies of itself; the new copies leave the host and seek out new hosts to repeat the process.

How a virus works

Origination
A programmer writes a tiny program—the virus—that has destructive power and can reproduce itself.

Transmission
Most often, the virus is attached to a normal program; unknown to the user, the virus spreads to other software.

Reproduction
The virus is passed by disk or network to other users who use other computers. The virus remains dormant as it is passed on.

Infection
Depending on how it is programmed, a virus may display an unexpected message, gobble up memory, destroy data files or cause serious system errors.

A software **virus** works in the same way: It spreads from program to program, or from disk to disk, and uses each infected program or disk to make more copies of itself. Virus software is usually hidden in the operating system of a computer or in an application program. Some viruses do nothing but reproduce; others display messages on the computer's screen; still others destroy data or erase disks. A virus is usually operating-system specific: Windows viruses invade only Windows disks, Macintosh viruses invade only Macintosh disks, and so on. There are exceptions: *Macro viruses* attach themselves to documents rather than software applications; these viruses can be spread across computer platforms if the documents are created and spread using cross-platform applications. For example, the Concept virus became the number one virus in 1996 by embedding itself in macro code of Microsoft Word documents. (Macros are discussed in Chapters 6 and 11.)

It takes a human programmer to create a virus, embed it in a piece of software, and release it to the world. Once that's done the virus can spread like an epidemic through shared software and disks, and it's almost impossible to completely eradicate. **Vaccine** (or **disinfectant**) **programs** are designed to search for viruses, notify users when they're found, and remove them from infected disks or files. Some antiviral programs continually monitor system activity, watching for and reporting suspicious virus-like actions. But no antiviral program can detect every virus, and these programs need to be frequently revised to combat new viruses as they appear. Virus eradication is expensive: It cost companies more than $1 billion in 1995 alone.

Worms

Like viruses, **worms** (named for tapeworms) use computer hosts to reproduce themselves. But unlike viruses, worm programs travel *independently* over computer networks, seeking out uninfected workstations to occupy. A typical worm segment resides in a workstation's memory rather than on disk, so the worm can be eliminated by shutting down all of the workstations on the network. The most famous worm, so far, was created as an experiment by a Cornell graduate student in 1988. The worm was accidentally released onto the Internet, clogging 6000 computers all over the United States, almost bringing them to a complete standstill, and forcing operators to shut them all down so every worm segment could be purged from memory. The total cost, in terms of work time lost at research institutions, was staggering. The student was suspended from school and was the first person convicted of violating the Computer Fraud and Abuse Act.

The popular press usually doesn't distinguish among Trojan horses, viruses, and worms; they're all called computer viruses. Whatever they're called, these rogue programs make life more complicated and expensive for people who depend on computers. When computers are used in life-or-death situations, as they are in many medical and military applications, invading programs can even threaten human lives. The U.S. government and several states now have laws against introducing these programs into computer systems.

Hacking and Electronic Trespassing

The Hacker Ethic

Access to computers—and anything which might teach you something about the way the world works—should be unlimited and total. Always yield to the Hands-on Imperative.

1. All information should be free.
2. Mistrust Authority—Promote Decentralization.
3. Hackers should be judged by their hacking, not bogus criteria such as degrees, age, race, or position.
4. You can create art and beauty on a computer.
5. Computers can change your life for the better.

—*Steven Levy, in Hackers: Heroes of the Computer Revolution*

I don't drink, smoke, or take drugs. I don't steal, assault people, or vandalize property. The only way in which I am really different from most people is in my fascination with the ways and means of learning about computers that don't belong to me.

—*Bill "The Cracker" Landreth, in Out of the Inner Circle*

In the late 1970s, timesharing computers at Stanford and MIT attracted informal communities of computer fanatics who called themselves **hackers.** In those days a hacker was a person who enjoyed learning the details of computer systems and writing clever programs, referred to as hacks. Hackers were, for the most part, curious, enthusiastic, intelligent, idealistic, eccentric, and harmless. Many of those early hackers were, in fact, architects of the microcomputer revolution.

Over the years the idealism of the early hacker communities was at least partly overshadowed by cynicism, as big-money interests took over the young personal computer industry. At the same time, the term *hacking* took on a new, more ominous, connotation in the media. While many people still use the term to describe software wizardry, it more commonly refers to unauthorized access to computer systems. Old-time hackers insist that this electronic trespassing is really *cracking,* but the distinction between hacking and cracking isn't recognized by the general public or the popular media. Today's stereotypical hacker, like his early counterparts, is a young, bright, technically savvy, white, middle-class male. But in addition to programming his own computer, he may break into others.

Of course, not all young computer wizards break into computer systems, and not all electronic trespassers fit the media stereotype. Still, hackers aren't just a media

Cliff Stoll discovered an international computer espionage ring because of a 75-cent accounting error.

myth; they're real, and there are lots of them. Electronic trespassers enter corporate and government computers using stolen passwords and security holes in operating system software. Sometimes they use modems to dial up the target computers directly; in other cases they "travel" to their destinations through the Internet and other networks.

Many hackers are motivated just by curiosity and intellectual challenge; once they've cracked a system, they look around and move on without leaving any electronic footprints. Some malicious hackers use Trojan horses, logic bombs, and other tricks of the trade to wreak havoc on corporate and government systems. A growing number of computer trespassers are part of electronic crime rings intent on stealing credit card numbers and other sensitive, valuable information. This kind of theft is difficult to detect and track because the original information is left unchanged when the copy is stolen.

The most famous case of electronic trespassing was documented in Cliff Stoll's best-selling book, *The Cuckoo's Egg*. While working as a system administrator for a university computer lab in 1986, Stoll noticed a 75-cent accounting error. Rather than letting it go, Stoll investigated the error. He uncovered a system intruder who was searching government, corporate, and university computers across the Internet for sensitive military information. It took a year and some help from the FBI, but Stoll eventually located the hacker—a German computer science student and part of a ring of hackers working for the KGB. Ironically, Stoll captured the thief by using standard hacker tricks, including a Trojan horse program that contained information on a fake SDI Net (Strategic Defense Initiative Network).

This kind of on-line espionage is becoming commonplace as the Internet becomes a mainstream communication medium. A more recent front-page story involved the 1995 capture of Kevin Mitnick, the hacker who had stolen millions of dollars worth of software and credit card information on the net. By repeatedly manufacturing new identities and cleverly concealing his location, Mitnick successfully evaded the FBI for years. But when he broke into the computer of Tsutomu Shimomura, he inadvertently started an electronic cat-and-mouse game that ended with his capture. Shimomura was able to defeat Mitnick because of his expertise in computer security—the protection of computer systems and, indirectly, the people who depend on them.

Hacker Kevin Mitnick spent several years on most-wanted lists before being captured in 1995.

COMPUTER SECURITY: REDUCING RISKS

Now, after sliding down this Alice-in-Wonderland hole, I find the political left and right reconciled in their mutual dependency on computers. The right sees computer security as necessary to protect national secrets; my leftie friends worry about an invasion of their privacy when prowlers pilfer data banks. Political centrists realize that insecure computers cost money when their data is exploited by outsiders.

The computer has become a common denominator that knows no intellectual, political, or bureaucratic bounds; the Sherwin Williams of necessity that covers the world, spanning all points of view.

—Cliff Stoll, in *The Cuckoo's Egg*

With computer crime on the rise, computer security has become an important concern for system administrators and computer users alike. **Computer security** refers to protecting computer systems and the information they contain against unwanted access, damage, modification, or destruction. According to a 1991 report of the Congressional Research Service, computers have two inherent characteristics that leave them open to attack or operating error:

- A computer will do *exactly* what it is programmed to do, including revealing sensitive information. Any system that can be programmed can be reprogrammed by anyone with sufficient knowledge.

- Any computer can do *only* what it is programmed to do. ". . . it cannot protect itself from either malfunctions or deliberate attacks unless such events have been specifically anticipated, thought through, and countered with appropriate programming."

Computer owners and administrators use a variety of security techniques to protect their systems, ranging from everyday low-tech locks to high-tech software scrambling.

Physical Access Restrictions

One way to reduce the risk of security breaches is to make sure that only authorized personnel have access to computer equipment. Organizations use a number of tools and techniques to identify authorized personnel. Some of these security checks can be performed by computer; others are used by human security guards. Depending on the security system, you might be granted access to a computer based on

- *something you have*—a key, an ID card with a photo, or a smart card containing digitally encoded identification (see Chapter 14 for a description of smart cards)

- *something you know*—a password, an ID number, a lock combination, or a piece of personal history, such as your mother's maiden name

- *something you do*—your signature or your typing speed and error patterns

- *something about you*—a voice print, fingerprints, retinal scans, or other measurements of individual body characteristics, known as **biometrics**

Retinal scanners and hand scanners are used in many modern security devices to verify individual identities.

Since most of these security controls can be compromised—keys can be stolen, signatures can be forged, and so on—many systems use a combination of controls. For example, an employee might be required to show a badge, unlock a door with a key, and type a password to use a secured computer.

In the days when corporate computers were isolated in basements, physical restrictions were sufficient for keeping out intruders. But in the modern office, computers and data are almost everywhere, and networks connect computers to the outside world. In a distributed, networked environment, security is much more problematic. It's not enough to restrict physical access to mainframes when personal computers and network connections aren't restricted. Additional security techniques—most notably passwords—are needed to restrict access to remote computers.

Passwords

Passwords are the most common tool for restricting access to computer systems. Passwords are effective, however, only if they're chosen carefully. Most computer users choose passwords that are easy to guess: names of partners, children, or pets; words related to jobs or hobbies; and consecutive characters on keyboards. One survey found that the two favorite passwords in Britain were "Fred" and "God"; in America they were "love" and "sex." Hackers know and exploit these clichés; cautious users avoid them. A growing number of security systems refuse to allow users to choose *any* real words or names as passwords, so hackers can't use dictionary software to guess them systematically. Even the best passwords should be changed frequently.

Access-control software doesn't need to treat all users identically. Many systems use passwords to restrict users so they can open only files related to their work. In many cases users are allowed read-only access to files that they can see but not change.

To prevent unauthorized use of stolen passwords by outsiders, many companies use *call-back systems*. When a user logs in and types a password, the system hangs up, looks up the user's phone number, and calls back before allowing access.

Firewalls, Codes, Shields, and Audits

Many data thieves do their work without breaking into computer systems; they intercept messages as they travel between computers on networks. Passwords are of little use for hiding electronic mail messages while they're bouncing off of satellite dishes or traveling through Internet links. Still, Internet communication is far too important to sacrifice in the name of security. Many organizations use **firewalls** to keep their internal networks secure while allowing communication with the rest of the Internet. The technical details of firewalls vary considerably, but they're all designed to serve the same function: to guard against unauthorized access to an internal network. In effect, a firewall is a gateway with a lock—the locked gate is only opened for information packets that pass one or more security inspections.

Of course, the firewall's digital drawbridge has to let some messages pass through; otherwise there could be no communication with the rest of the Internet. How can those messages be secured in transit? To protect transmitted information, many government and business organizations use **encryption** software to scramble their transmissions. When a user encrypts a message by applying a secret numerical code, called an *encryption key,* the message can be transmitted or stored as an indecipherable garble of characters. The message can be read only after it's been reconstructed with a matching key.

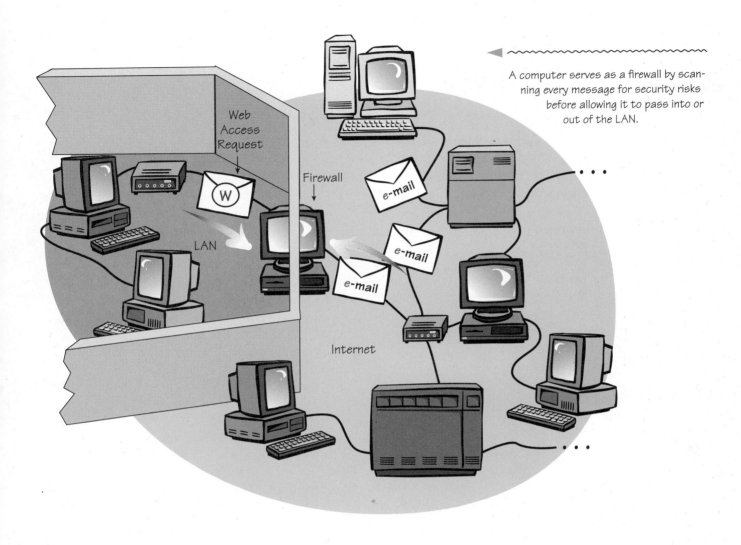

Web Access Request

Firewall

LAN

Internet

e-mail

W

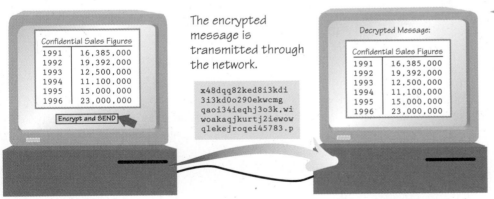

The encrypted message is transmitted through the network.

```
x48dqq82ked8i3kdi
3i3kd0o290ekwcmg
qaoi34ieqhj3o3k,wi
woakaqjkurtj2iewow
qlekejroqei45783.p
```

The encryption process

Confidential Sales Figures	
1991	16,385,000
1992	19,392,000
1993	12,500,000
1994	11,100,000
1995	15,000,000
1996	23,000,000

Encrypt and SEND

Decrypted Message:

Confidential Sales Figures	
1991	16,385,000
1992	19,392,000
1993	12,500,000
1994	11,100,000
1995	15,000,000
1996	23,000,000

The sender creates, encrypts, and sends the message.

The message is received and decrypted.

Cryptography

I f you want be sure that an electronic mail message can only be read by the intended recipient, you must either use a secure communication channel or secure the message.

Mail within many organizations is sent over *secure communication channels*—channels that can't be accessed by outsiders. But you can't secure the channels used by the Internet and other world-wide mail networks; there's no way to shield messages sent through public telephone lines and airwaves. In the words of Mark Rotenberg,

Director of the Electronic Privacy Information Center, "E-mail is more like a postcard than a sealed letter."

If you can't secure the communication channel, the alternative is to *secure the message.* You secure a message by using a *cryptosystem* to *encrypt* it—scramble it so it can only be *decrypted* (unscrambled) by the intended recipient.

Almost all cryptosystems depend on a key—a password-like number or phrase that can be used to encrypt or decrypt a message. Eavesdroppers who don't know the key have to try decrypting by *brute force*—by trying all possible keys until the right one is guessed.

Some cryptosystems afford only modest security: A message can be broken after only a day or week of brute force cryptanalysis on a super-computer. More effective systems would take a super-computer billions of years to break the message.

The traditional kind of cryptosystem used on computer networks is called a *symmetric secret key system.* With this approach the sender and recipient use the same key, and they have to keep their shared key secret from everyone else.

Secret Key System

Messages encrypted/decrypted with key 10529

Sue's list of secret keys

George	10529
Clem	22707
.	.

Messages encrypted/decrypted with key 27707

George's list of secret keys

Sue	10529
Clem	33812
.	.

Clem's list of secret keys

George	33812
Sue	22707
.	.

Messages encrypted/decrypted with key 33812

For the most sensitive information, passwords, firewalls, and encryption aren't enough. A diligent spy can "listen to" the electromagnetic signals that emanate from the computer hardware and, in some cases, read sensitive information. To prevent spies from using these spurious broadcasts, the Pentagon has spent hundreds of millions of dollars on a program called *Tempest* to develop specially shielded machines.

Audit-control software is used to monitor and record computer transactions as they happen, so auditors can trace and identify suspicious computer activity after the fact. Effective audit control software forces every user, legitimate or otherwise, to leave a trail of electronic footprints. Of course, this kind of software is of little value unless someone in the organization monitors and interprets the output.

The biggest problem with symmetric secret key systems is *key management*. If you want to communicate with several people, and ensure that each person can't read messages intended for the others, then you'll need a different secret key for each person. When you want to communicate with someone new, you have the problem of letting them know what the key is. If you send it over the ordinary communication channel, it can be intercepted.

In the 1970s cryptographers developed *public key cryptography* to get around the key management problems. The most popular kind of public key cryptosystem, *RSA*, is being incorporated into most new network-enabled software. Phillip Zimmerman's popular shareware utility called PGP (for Pretty Good Privacy) uses RSA technology.

Each person using a public key cryptosystem has two keys: a *private key* known only to the user and a *public key* that is freely available to anyone who wants it. Thus a public key system is asymmetric: a different key is used to encrypt than to decrypt. Public keys can be published in phone directories, Web pages, and advertisements; some users include them in their e-mail signatures.

If you want to send a secure message over the Internet to your friend Sue in St. Louis, you use her public key to encrypt the message. Sue's public key can't decrypt the message; only her private key

can do that. The private key is specifically designed to decrypt messages that were encrypted with the corresponding public key.

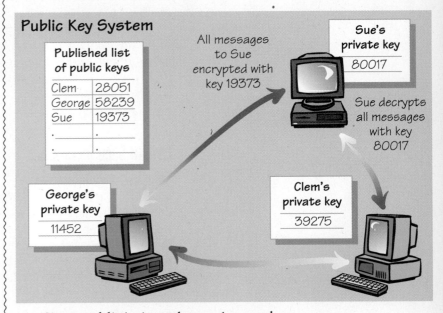

Public Key System

Published list of public keys	
Clem	28051
George	58239
Sue	19373

All messages to Sue encrypted with key 19373

Sue's private key 80017

Sue decrypts all messages with key 80017

George's private key 11452

Clem's private key 39275

Since public/private key pairs can be generated by individual users, the key distribution problem is solved. The only keys being sent over an insecure network are publicly available keys.

You can use the same technology in reverse (encrypt with the private key, decrypt with the public key) for *message authentication:* When you decrypt a message you can be sure that it was sent from a particular person on the network. In the future legal and commercial documents will routinely have *digital signatures* that will be as valid as handwritten ones.

Making Backups

Even the tightest security system can't guarantee absolute protection of data. Sabotage, human errors, power losses, machine failures, fire, flood, lightning, and earthquakes can damage or destroy computer data along with hardware. Any complete security system must include some kind of plan for recovering from disasters. For mainframes and PCs alike, the best and most widely used data recovery insurance is a system of making regular **backups.** For many systems, data and software are backed up automatically onto disks or tapes, usually at the end of each work day. Most data processing shops keep several *generations* of backups so they can, if necessary, go back several days, weeks, or years to reconstruct data files. For maximum security many computer users keep copies of sensitive data in several different locations.

Emerging Security Solutions

The migration from mainframes to personal computers is forcing experts to explore new security solutions. The PC's small size and physical accessibility can make it easy for criminals to steal the computer along with its data. Computer crime expert Donn Parker has suggested that companies install automated alarm systems that allow networked PCs to check on each other regularly and report any kidnapped machines to the police immediately.

Security experts are constantly developing new technologies and techniques for protecting computer systems from computer criminals. But at the same time, criminals continue to refine their craft. In the ongoing competition between the law and the lawless, computer security generally lags behind. In the words of Tom Forester and Perry Morrison in *Computer Ethics,* ". . . computer security experts are forever trying to shut the stable door after the horse has bolted."

Human Security Controls

Ultimately, computer security is a human problem that can't be solved by technology alone. Security is a management issue, and a manager's actions and policies are critical to the success of a security program. An alarming number of companies are lax about computer security. Many managers don't understand the problems and don't think they are at risk. It's important for managers to understand where the real threats are, make their employees aware of the problems, and build effective defenses against those threats.

SECURITY, PRIVACY, AND FREEDOM: THE DELICATE BALANCE

In this age of advanced technology, thick walls and locked doors cannot guard our privacy or safeguard our personal freedom.

—Lyndon B. Johnson, 36th president of the United States, Feb. 23, 1974

It's hard to overstate the importance of computer security in our networked world. Viruses, worms, illegal interlopers, and crooked co-workers can erode trust and make life on-line difficult for everyone. But some managers have discovered that computer security measures can create problems of their own. Complex access procedures, virus-protection programs, and other security measures can, if carried too far, interfere with people getting their work done. In the extreme, security can threaten individual human rights.

When Security Threatens Privacy

We discussed privacy issues earlier in the book: threats to personal privacy caused by corporate and government databases (Chapter 8), and threats to the individual privacy of workers due to various types of computer monitoring (Chapter 13). When security measures are used to prevent computer crime, they usually help protect privacy rights at the same time. When a hacker invades a computer system, legitimate users of the system might have their private communications monitored by the intruder. When an outsider breaks into the database of a bank, the privacy of every bank customer is at risk. The same applies to government computers, credit bureau computers, and any other computer containing data on private citizens. The security of these systems is important for protecting people's privacy.

But in some cases security and law enforcement can pose threats to personal privacy. Here are some examples:

- In 1990 Alana Shoar, electronic-mail coordinator for Epson America, Inc., found stacks of printouts of employee e-mail messages in her boss's office—messages that employees believed were private. Shortly after confronting her boss, she was fired for "gross misconduct and insubordination." She filed a class-action suit, claiming that Epson routinely monitored all e-mail messages. Company officials denied the charges but took a firm stand on their right to any information stored, sent to, or taken from their business computers. The courts ruled in Epson's favor.

- In 1990 the Communication Workers of America sued Northern Telecom, Inc., for illegally bugging employee conference rooms and telephones. In 1992 Northern Telecom became the first major American employer to ban all covert monitoring of communications.

- Colonel Oliver North and his collaborators carefully shredded hundreds of paper documents detailing the sale of arms to Iran and the illegal channeling of profits to Nicaraguan Contras. But they were implicated in the Iran-Contra scandal anyway when investigators examined backup copies of "private" electronic-mail messages stored in their computer system.

- In 1995 the U.S. government passed legislation requiring new digital phone systems to include additional switches that allow for electronic surveillance. This legislation protects the FBI's ability to wiretap at the expense of individual privacy. Detractors have pointed out that this digital "back door" could be abused by government agencies, and could also be used by savvy criminals to perform illegal wiretaps. Government officials argue that wiretapping is a critical tool in the fight against organized crime.

One of the best examples of a new technology that can simultaneously improve security and threaten privacy is the **active badge** (sometimes called the *smart badge*). Researchers at the University of Cambridge and nearby Olivetti Research Center are developing and wearing microprocessor-controlled badges that broadcast infrared identification codes every 15 seconds. Each badge's code is picked up by a nearby network receiver and transmitted back to a badge-location database that is constantly being updated. Active badges are used for identifying, finding, and remembering:

An active badge transmits signals that allow a network to identify, locate, and track the badge wearer.

- *Identifying.* When an authorized employee approaches a door, the door recognizes the person's badge code and opens. Whenever anyone logs into a computer system, the badge code identifies the person as an authorized or unauthorized user.

- *Finding.* An employee can check a computer screen to locate another employee and find out who that person is talking to. With active badges, there's no need for a paging system, and "while you were away" notes are less common.

- *Remembering.* At the end of the day, an active-badge wearer can get a minute-by-minute printout listing exactly where he's been and whom he's been with.

Is the active badge a primitive version of the communicator on TV's Star Trek or a surveillance tool for Big Brother? The technology has the potential to be either or both; it all depends on how people use it. Active badges, like other security devices and techniques, raise important legal and ethical questions about privacy—questions that we, as a society, must resolve sooner or later.

Justice on the Electronic Frontier

> Once, our computers were isolated, much as eighteenth-century villages were. Little was exchanged, and each developed independently. Now we've built far-flung electronic neighborhoods. These communities are built on trust: people believing that everyone profits by sharing resources.
>
> —Cliff Stoll

Federal and state governments have responded to the growing computer crime problem by creating new laws against electronic trespassing and escalating enforcement efforts. Hackers have become the target of nationwide anti-crime operations. Dozens of hackers have been arrested for unauthorized entry into computer systems and for releasing destructive viruses and worms. Many have been convicted under federal or state laws. Others have had their computers confiscated with no formal charges filed.

Some of the victims of these sting operations claim that they broke no laws. In one case computers, software, and products were confiscated from a role-playing game company because one of their employees was a former hacker, and one of their games had a hacker theme. The financially crippled company was forced to lay off half its staff before the confiscated goods were finally returned; no charges were ever filed. The company sued the government for damages and won. In another case a student was arrested because he published an electronic magazine that carried a description of an emergency 911 system allegedly stolen by hackers. Charges were eventually dropped when it was revealed that the "stolen" document was, in fact, available to the public. These cases and others like them have raised questions about how civil rights apply in the "electronic frontier." How does the Bill of Rights apply to computer communications? Does freedom of the press apply to on-line magazines in the same way it applies to paper periodicals? Can an electronic bulletin board operator be held responsible for information others post on the BBS? Laws like the Telecommunications Act of 1996 attempt to deal with these questions by outlining exactly what kinds of communcation are legal on line. Unfortunately, these laws generally raise as many questions as they answer; as a result, the debates continue inside and outside of the courts.

Even without definitive answers to constitutional questions, law enforcement officials must continue to fight computer crime. Malicious hackers, worms, and viruses pose serious threats to our computerized society, and these threats can't be ignored. But even if every law-breaking hacker were arrested, computer crime would still be a major problem. The overwhelming majority of computer crimes are committed by insiders who are seldom reported to authorities, even when they are caught in the act. To avoid embarrassment, many companies cover up the computer crimes committed by their own employees and managers. As a result, law enforcement agencies spend disproportionate amounts of time and money pursuing teenage hackers who represent a small part of the computer crime population. Experts agree that computer crime is likely to continue to grow unless corporations and government agencies recognize the importance of security on the inside as well as the outside.

SECURITY AND RELIABILITY

So far our discussion of security has focused mainly on protecting computer systems from trespassing, sabotage, and other crimes. But security involves more than criminal activity. Some of the most important security issues have to do with creating systems that can withstand software errors and hardware glitches.

Bugs and Breakdowns

> If the automobile had followed the same development cycle as the computer, a Rolls Royce would today cost $100, get a million miles per gallon, and explode once a year, killing everyone inside.
>
> —Robert X. Cringely, *InfoWorld columnist*

Computer systems, like all machines, are vulnerable to fires, floods, and other natural disasters, as well as breakdowns caused by failure of hardware components. But in modern computers, hardware problems are relatively rare when compared with software failures. In Chapters 4 and 11 we discussed the problems of creating reliable software and the insidious nature of computer bugs. By any measure, bugs do more damage than viruses and computer burglars put together.

Given the state of the art of software engineering today, three facts are clear:

- *It's impossible to eliminate all bugs.* Today's programs are constructed of thousands of tiny pieces, any one of which can cause a failure if it's incorrectly coded.

- *Even programs that appear to work can contain dangerous bugs.* Some bugs are easy to detect and correct because they're obvious. The most dangerous bugs are difficult to detect and may go unnoticed by users for months or years.

- *The bigger the system, the bigger the problem.* Large programs are far more complex and difficult to debug than small programs, and the trend today is clearly toward large programs.

As we entrust complex computerized systems to do everything from financial transaction processing to air traffic control, the potential cost of computer failure goes up. In the last decade researchers have identified hundreds of cases in which disruptions to computer system operations posed some risk to the public, and the number of incidents has doubled every two years.

Computers at War

> Knowledge is power and permits the wise to conquer without bloodshed and to accomplish deeds surpassing all others.
>
> —Sun Tzu, Chou dynasty philosopher and military strategist, in *The Art of War* (4th century BC)

Nowhere are the issues surrounding security and reliability more critical than in military applications. To carry out its mission effectively, the military must be sure its systems are secure against enemy surveillance and attack. At the same time many modern military applications push the limits of information technology farther than they've ever been before.

Smart Weapons

The United States has invested billions of dollars in the development of **smart weapons**—missiles that use computerized guidance systems to locate their targets. A *command-guidance system* allows a human operator to control the missile's path while watching a missile's-eye-view of the target on a television screen. A missile with a *homing guidance system* can track a moving target without human help, using infrared heat-seeking devices or visual pattern recognition technology. Weapons that use "smart" guidance systems can be extremely accurate in pinpointing enemy targets under most circumstances. In theory smart weapons can greatly reduce the amount of civilian destruction in war if everything is working properly.

One problem with high-tech weapons is that they reduce the amount of time people have to make life-and-death decisions. As decision-making time goes down, the chance of errors goes up. In one tragic example, an American guided missile cruiser on a peacetime mission in the Persian Gulf used a computerized Aegis fleet defense system to shoot down an Iranian Airbus containing 290 civilians. The decision to fire was made by well-intentioned humans, but those humans had little time—and used ambiguous data—to make the decision.

Autonomous Systems

Even more controversial is the possibility of people being left out of the decision-making loop altogether. Yet the trend in military research is clearly toward weapons that demand almost instantaneous responses—the kind that only computers can make. An **autonomous system** is a complex system that can assume almost complete responsibility for a task without human input, verification, or decision making.

The most famous and controversial autonomous system is the Strategic Defense Initiative (SDI)—former President Ronald Reagan's proposed "Star Wars" system for shielding the United States from nuclear attack. The SDI system, as planned, would have used a network of laser-equipped satellites and ground-based stations to detect and destroy attacking missiles shortly after launch, before they had time to reach their targets. SDI weapons would have to be able to react almost instantaneously, without human intervention. If they sensed an attack, these system computers would have no time to wait for the president to declare war; in carrying out their mission, they'd effectively be declaring war themselves.

SDI generated intense public debates about false alarms, hardware feasibility, constitutional issues, and the ethics of autonomous weapons. But for many who understand the limitations of computers, the biggest issue is software reliability. SDI's

Safe Computing

Even if you're not building a software system for SDI or the FBI, computer security is important. Viruses, disk crashes, system bombs, and miscellaneous disasters can destroy your work, your peace of mind, and possibly your system. Fortunately you can protect your computer, your software, and your data from most hazards.

• *Share with care.* A computer virus is a contagious disease that spreads when it comes in contact with a compatible file or disk. Viruses spread rapidly in environments where disks and files are passed around freely, as they are in many student computer labs. To protect your data, keep your disks to yourself and don't borrow disks from others. When you *do* share a 3.5-inch disk, physically write-protect it (by moving the plastic slider to uncover the square hole) so a virus can't attach to it.

• *Beware of BBSs bearing gifts.* Many viruses hide in Trojan horse programs on bulletin boards and on disks. Treat public domain programs and shareware with care; test them with a disinfectant program before you install them on your hard disk.

• *Don't pirate software.* Even commercial programs can be infected with viruses. Shrink-wrapped, virgin software is much less likely to be infected than pirated copies. Besides, software piracy is theft, and the legal penalties can be severe.

• *Disinfect regularly.* Virus protection programs are available for IBM-compatibles, Macintoshes, and other systems, often for free. Use up-to-date virus protection software regularly if you work in a high-risk environment like a public computer lab.

• *Treat your diskettes as if they contained something important.* Keep them away from liquids, dust, pets, and (especially) magnets. Don't put your disks close to phones, speakers, and other electronic devices that contain hidden magnets.

• *If you're using a password-protected system, take your password seriously.* Choose a password that's not easily guessable, not in any dictionary, and not easy for others to remember. Don't post it by your computer, and don't type it when you're being watched. Change your password every few weeks—more often if you have any reason to suspect it has been discovered.

• *If it's sensitive, lock it up.* If your computer is accessible to others, protect your private files with passwords and/or encryption. Several popular disk utilities include options for adding password protection and encrypting files. If others need to see the files, lock them so they can be read, but not changed or deleted. If secrecy is critical, don't store the data on your hard disk at all. Store it on diskettes or other removable media and lock it away in a safe place.

Write-protect opening

• *If it's important, back it up.* Regularly make backup copies of every important file on different disks than the original. Keep copies of critical disks in different locations so that you have backups in case disaster strikes.

• *If you're sending sensitive information through the Internet, consider encryption.* The freeware PGP (Pretty Good Privacy) Program is actually *very* good at turning your message into code that's almost impossible to crack. It's not particularly user friendly, but it may be worth the extra effort if your privacy is at stake.

• *Prepare for the worst.* Even if you take every precaution, things can still go wrong. Make sure you aren't completely dependent on the computer for really important things.

software system would require over 10 million lines of code—more than are in any system ever developed. The system couldn't be completely tested in advance, because there's no way to simulate accurately the unpredictable conditions of a global war. Yet to work effectively, the system would have to be absolutely reliable. In a tightly coupled worldwide network, a single bug could multiply and expand like a speed-of-light cancer. A small error could result in a major disaster. Many software engineers have pointed out that absolute reliability simply isn't possible now or in the foreseeable future.

The Clinton administration shelved SDI in favor of a land-based missile defense system, but Congress still regularly attempts to revive SDI. For both land- and air-based systems, software reliability issues remain. Supporters of automated missile-defense systems argue that the technical difficulties can be overcome in time, and the U.S. government continues to invest billions in research toward that end. Whether or not a "smart shield" is ever completed, it has focused public attention on critical issues related to security and reliability. In a world where computers control everything from money to missiles, computer security and reliability are too important to ignore.

Is Security Possible?

Computer thieves. Hackers. Software pirates. Computer snoopers. Viruses. Worms. Trojan horses. Wiretaps. Hardware failures. Software bugs. When we live and work with computers, we're exposed to all kinds of risks that didn't exist in the pre-computer era. These risks make computer security especially important and challenging.

Because computers do so many amazing things so well, it's easy to overlook the problems they bring with them and to believe that they're invincible. But like Kempelen's chess-playing machine, today's computers hide the potential for errors and deception under an impressive user interface. This doesn't mean we should avoid using computers, only that we should remain skeptical, cautious, and realistic as we use them. Security procedures can reduce, but not eliminate risks. In today's fast-moving world, absolute security simply isn't possible.

SUMMARY

Computers play an ever-increasing role in fighting crime. At the same time, law enforcement organizations are facing an increase in computer crime—crimes accomplished through special knowledge of computer technology. Most computer crimes go undetected, and those that are detected often go unreported. But by any estimate, computer crime costs billions of dollars every year.

Some computer criminals use computers, modems, and other equipment to steal goods, money, information, software, and services. Others use Trojan horses, viruses, worms, logic bombs, and other software tricks to sabotage systems. According to the media, computer crimes are committed by young, bright, computer wizards called hackers. Research suggests, however, that hackers are responsible for only a small fraction of the computer crimes committed. The typical computer criminal is a trusted employee with personal or financial problems and knowledge of the computer system. The most common computer crime, software piracy, is committed by millions of people, often unknowingly. Piracy is a violation of intellectual property laws, which, in many cases, lag far behind the technology.

Because of rising computer crime and other risks, organizations have developed a number of computer security techniques to protect their systems and data. Some security devices, like keys and badges, are designed to restrict physical access to computers. But these tools are becoming less effective in an age of personal computers and networks. Passwords, encryption, shielding, and audit-control software are all used to protect sensitive data in various organizations. When all else fails, backups of important data are used to reconstruct systems after damage occurs. The most effective security solutions depend on people at least as much as technology.

Normally security measures serve to protect our privacy and other individual rights. But occasionally security procedures threaten those rights. The tradeoffs between computer security and freedom raise important legal and ethical questions.

Computer systems aren't just threatened by people; they're also threatened by software bugs and hardware glitches. An important part of security is protecting systems, and the people affected by those systems, from the consequences of those bugs and glitches. Since our society uses computers for many applications that put lives at stake, reliability issues are especially important. In modern military applications, security and reliability are critical. As the speed, power, and complexity of weapons systems increase, many fear that humans are being squeezed out of the decision-making loop. The debate over high-tech weaponry is bringing many important security issues to the public's attention for the first time.

Chapter Review

Key Terms

access-control software
active badge
audit-control software
autonomous system
backup
biometrics
computer crime

computer security
encryption
firewall
hacker
intellectual property
logic bomb
smart weapon

software piracy
Trojan horse
vaccine (disinfectant) program
virus
worm

Review Questions

1. Define or describe each of the key terms above. Check your answers using the glossary.

2. Why is it hard to estimate the extent of computer crime?

3. Describe the typical computer criminal. How does he or she differ from the media stereotype?

4. What is the most common computer crime? Who commits it? What is being done to stop it?

5. What are intellectual property laws, and how do they apply to software?

6. Describe several different types of programs that can be used for software sabotage.

7. What are the two inherent characteristics of computers that make security so difficult?

8. Describe several different computer security techniques and explain the purpose of each.

9. Every afternoon at closing time, the First Taxpayer's Bank copies all of the day's accumulated transaction information from disk to tape. Why?

10. In what ways can computer security protect the privacy of individuals? In what ways can computer security threaten the privacy of individuals?

11. What are smart weapons? How do they differ from conventional weapons? What are the advantages and risks of smart weapons?

Discussion Questions

1. Are computers morally neutral? Explain your answer.

2. Suppose Whizzo Software Company produces a program that looks, from the user's point of view, exactly like the immensely popular BozoWorks from Bozo, Inc. Whizzo insists that they didn't copy any of the code in BozoWorks; they just tried to design a program that would appeal to BozoWorks users. Bozo cries foul and sues Whizzo for violation of intellectual property laws. Do you think the laws should favor Bozo's arguments or Whizzo's? Why?

3. What do you suppose motivates people to create computer viruses and other destructive software? What do you think motivates hackers to break into computer systems? Are the two types of behavior related?

4. Some people think all mail messages on the Internet should be encrypted. They argue that, if everything is encrypted, the encrypted message won't stand out, so everybody's right to privacy will be better protected. Others suggest that this would just improve the cover of criminals with something to hide from the government. What do you think, and why?

5. Would you like to work in a business where all employees were required to wear active badges? Explain your answer.

6. How do the issues raised in the debate over SDI apply to other large software systems? How do you feel about the different issues raised in the debate?

Projects

1. Talk to employees at your campus computer labs and computer centers about security issues and techniques. What are the major security threats according to these employees? What security techniques are used to protect the equipment and data in each facility? Are these techniques adequate? Report on your findings.

2. Perform the same kind of interviews at local businesses. Do businesses view security differently than your campus personnel?

Sources and Resources

Books

Computer Ethics: Cautionary Tales and Ethical Dilemmas in Computing, Second Edition, by Tom Forester and Perry Morrison (Cambridge, MA: MIT Press, 1994). Forester and Morrison don't mince words as they discuss the important issues that face computer professionals and users today. This concise book is rich with real-world examples of computer crime, security breaches, reliability risks, and privacy threats.

Computers, Ethics, and Social Values, edited by Deborah G. Johnson and Helen Nissenbaum (Englewood Cliffs, NJ: Prentice-Hall, 1995). This is an excellent collection of papers and articles by some of the best known writers and analysts on issues relating to computers in society. Computer crime, intellectual property, privacy, reliability, responsibility, and network issues are explored in this excellent survey.

The Underground Guide to Computer Security: Slightly Askew Advice on Protecting Your PC and What's On It, by Michael Alexander (Reading, MA: Addison-Wesley, 1996). This easy-to-read book is full of practical advice for securing your computer and its contents against thieves, snoopers, viruses, and a variety of disasters. If you value your system, read this book or one like it.

Cyberspace and the Law: Your Rights and Duties in the On-Line World, by Edward A. Cavazos and Gavino Morin (Cambridge, MA: MIT Press, 1994). This is a very readable introduction to the most important legal issues involving computers and networks. Intellectual property, freedom of speech, privacy rights, electronic contracts, computer fraud, and other issues are described in plain English for nonlawyers. If you're even a little worried about how any of these issues affect you, this book is worth seeking out.

Hackers: Heroes of the Computer Revolution, by Steven Levy (New York: Doubleday, 1984). This book helped bring the word *hackers* into the public's vocabulary. Levy's entertaining account of the golden age of hacking gives a historical perspective to today's antihacker mania.

The Cuckoo's Egg, by Cliff Stoll (New York: Pocket Books, 1989, 1990). This best-selling book documents the stalking of an interloper on Internet. International espionage mixes with computer technology in this entertaining, engaging, and eye-opening book.

Takedown: The Pursuit and Capture of Kevin Mitnick, America's Most Wanted Computer Outlaw—by the Man Who Did It, by Tsutomu Shimomura with John Markoff (New York: Hyperion Books, 1996), and *The Fugitive Game,* by Jonathon Littman (New York: Little, Brown Co., 1996). These two books chronicle the events leading up to and including the capture of Kevin Mitnick, America's number one criminal hacker. *Takedown* presents the story from the point of view of the security expert who captured Mitnick. *The Fugitive Game* is written from a more objective journalistic point of view.

Cyberpunk—Outlaws and Hackers on the Computer Frontier, by Katie Hafner and John Markoff (New York: Simon & Schuster, 1992). This book profiles three hackers whose exploits caught the public's attention: Kevin Mitnick, a California cracker who vandalized corporate systems; Pengo, who penetrated U.S. systems for East German espionage purposes; and Robert Morris, Jr., whose Internet worm brought down 6000 computers in a matter of hours.

Computers Under Attack, edited by Peter Denning (Reading, MA: ACM Press, 1990). A wide-ranging collection of articles about computer security, hacking, and the network community. This book goes into detail on the Internet worm, computer viruses, and other security-related issues.

The Hacker Crackdown: Law and Disorder on the Electronic Frontier, by Bruce Sterling (New York: Bantam Books, 1992). Famed cyberpunk author Sterling turns to nonfiction to tell both sides of the story of the war between hackers and federal law enforcement agencies. If you're interested in the hacker controversy, this book is a good read. The complete text is available online.

Ender's Game, by Orson Scott Card (New York: Tor Books, 1994). This award-winning, entertaining science fiction opus has become a favorite of the cryptography crowd because of its emphasis on encryption to protect privacy.

The Fool's Run, by John Camp (New York: Henry Holt and Co., 1989; New York: Signet Books, 1990). This white-knuckle novel by a seasoned journalist explores the world of computer networks through a frightening story of high-tech capitalist espionage. It's fiction, but the network security issues are all too real.

The Postman, by David Brin (New York: Bantam, 1985). This entertaining science fiction novel weaves a tale of the future that raises many of the same issues raised by Kempelman's chess playing machine.

Periodicals

Many popular magazines, from *Newsweek* to *Wired,* provide regular coverage of issues related to privacy and security of digital systems. The two periodicals listed here are newsletters of professional organizations that focus on these issues.

The *CPSR Newsletter,* published by Computer Professionals for Social Responsibility (P.O. Box 717, Palo Alto, CA 94302, 415/322-3778, fax 415/322-3798, e-mail: cpsr@csli.stanford.edu). An alliance of computer scientists and others interested in the impact of computer technology on society, CPSR works to influence public policies to ensure that computers are used wisely in the public interest. Their newsletter has intelligent articles and discussions of risk, reliability, privacy, security, human rights, work, war, education, the environment, democracy, and other subjects that bring together computers and people.

EFFector, published by the Electronic Frontier Foundation (155 Second St., Cambridge, MA 02141, 617/864-0665, fax 617/864-0866, e-mail: effnews-request@eff.org). This electronic newsletter is distributed by EFF, an organization "established to help civilize the electronic frontier." EFF was founded by Mitch Kapor (see Chapter 6) and John Perry Barlow to protect civil rights and encourage responsible citizenship on the electronic frontier of computer networks.

World Wide Web Pages

As you might suspect, the Net is the best source of up-to-the-minute information on computer security and related issues. Public and commercial organizations maintain Web pages devoted to these issues, and dozens of newsgroups contain lively ongoing discussions on controversial topics. Check the *Computer Confluence* Web site for the latest links.

Alan Kay Invents the Future

The best way to predict the future is to invent it.

—Alan Kay

Alan Kay has been inventing the future for most of his life. Kay was a child prodigy who grew up in a world rich with books, ideas, music, and interesting people. As a child he composed original music, built a harpsichord, and appeared on NBC as a "Quiz Kid." Kay's genius wasn't reflected in his grades; he had trouble conforming to the rigid structure of the schools he attended. After high school he worked as a jazz guitarist and an Air Force programmer before attending college.

His Ph.D. project was one of the first microcomputers, and one of several that Kay would eventually develop. In 1968 Kay was in the audi-

ence when Douglas Engelbart stunned the computer science world with a futuristic demonstration of interactive computing (see Chapter 7). Inspired by Engelbart's demonstration, Kay led a team of researchers at Xerox PARC (Palo Alto Research Center in California) in building the computer of the future—a computer that put the user in charge.

Working on a back-room computer called the Alto, Kay developed a bit-mapped screen display with icons and overlapping windows— the kind of display that became standard two decades later. Kay also championed the idea of a friendly user interface. To test user-

friendliness, Kay frequently brought children into the lab, "because they have no strong motivation for patience." With feedback from children, Kay developed the first painting program and Smalltalk, the ground-breaking object-oriented programming language.

In essence Kay's team developed the first personal computer—a single-user desktop machine designed for interactive use. But Kay, who coined the term *personal computer,* didn't see the Alto as one. In his mind a true personal computer could go everywhere with its owner, serving as a calculator, a calendar, a word processor, a graphics machine, a communication device, and a reference tool. Kay's vision of what he called the *Dyna-Book* is only now, three decades later, appearing on the horizon.

Xerox failed to turn the Alto into a commercial success. But when he visited PARC, then Apple CEO Steve Jobs (see Chapter 3) was inspired by what he saw. Under Jobs a team of engineers and programmers built on the Xerox ideas, added many of their own, and developed the Macintosh—the first inexpensive personal computer to incorporate many of Kay's far-reaching ideas. Kay later called the Macintosh "the first personal computer good enough to criticize." The success of the Macintosh has since forced other PC manufacturers to adopt similar user interfaces.

Today Kay works as a research fellow for Apple, where he serves as a resident visionary. Kay continues his crusade for users, especially small users. He says, ". . . as with pencil and paper, it's not a medium if children can't use it." In the Vivarium Project, Kay and MIT researchers work with schoolchildren to design artificial life forms in artificial environments inside the computer. As students use experimental software tools to construct these life forms and environments, they learn about ecology and computers at the same time. Meanwhile the researchers study the children for insights into the human-machine interface. Like all of Kay's work, Vivarium is a long-term project with little relationship to today's computer market. This kind of blue-

sky research doesn't always lead to products or profits. But for Alan Kay it's the way to invent the future.

Alan Kay

he future is being invented every day by people like Alan Kay—people who can see today the technology that will be central to tomorrow's society. We're racing into a future shaped by information technology. In this chapter we'll explore strategies for seeing into the future. We'll use those strategies to imagine how information technology might evolve, and how that technology might affect our lives.

TOMORROW NEVER KNOWS

It is the unexpected that always happens.

—Old English proverb

There is no denying the importance of the future. In the words of scientist Charles F. Kettering, "We should be concerned about the future because we will have to spend the rest of our lives there." However, important or not, the future isn't easy to see.

The Hazards of Predicting the Future

Everything that can be invented has been invented.

—Charles H. Duell, director of the U.S. Patent Office, 1899

Who the hell wants to hear actors talk?

—Harry M. Warner, Warner Bros. Pictures, 1927

There is no likelihood man can ever tap the power of the atom.

—Robert Millikan, winner of the Nobel Prize in Physics, 1923

In 1877, when Thomas Edison invented the phonograph, he thought of it as an office dictating machine and lost interest in it; recorded music did not become popular until 21 years later. When the Wright brothers offered their invention to the U.S. government and the British Royal Navy, they were told airplanes had no future in the military. A 1900 Mercedes-Benz study estimated that worldwide demand for cars would not exceed 1 million, primarily because of the limited number of available chauffeurs. History is full of stories of people who couldn't imagine the impact of new technology.

Technology is hard to foresee, and it is even harder to predict the impact that technology will have on society. Who could have predicted in 1950 the profound effects, both positive and negative, television would have on our world?

Four Ways to Predict the Future

According to Alan Kay, there are four ways to predict the future. The best way is to invent the future, but it's not the only way.

Another way to predict the future is to take advantage of the fact that it generally takes ten years to go from a new idea in the research laboratory to a commercial product. By paying attention to the research being conducted in labs today, we

The 1930 movie *Just Imagine* presented a bold, if not quite accurate, vision of the future; here Maureen O'Sullivan sits in her personal flying machine.

can imagine the kinds of products we will be using a decade from now. Of course, many researchers work behind carefully guarded doors, and research often takes surprising turns. Still, today's research leads to tomorrow's products.

A third way is to look at products from the past and see what made them succeed. According to Kay, "There are certain things about human beings that if you remove, they wouldn't be human anymore. For instance, we have to communicate with others or we're not humans. So every time someone has come up with a communications amplifier, it has succeeded the previous technology." The pen, the printing press, the telephone, the television, the personal computer, and the Internet are all successful communication amplifiers. What's next?

Finally, Kay says we can predict the future by recognizing the four phases of any technology or media business: hardware, software, service, and way of life. These phases apply to radio, television, video, audio, and all kinds of computers.

- *Hardware.* Inventors and engineers start the process by developing new hardware. But whether it's a television set or a personal computer, the hardware is of little use without software.

- *Software.* The next step is software development. Television programs, audio recordings, video games, databases, and World Wide Web pages are examples of software that give value to hardware products.

- *Service.* Once the hardware and software exist, the focus turns to service. Innovative hardware and clever software aren't likely to take hold unless they serve human needs in some way. The personal computer industry is now in the service phase, and the companies that focus on serving their customers are generally the most successful.

- *Way of life.* The final phase happens when the technology becomes so entrenched that people don't think about it anymore; they only notice if it isn't there. We seldom think of pencils as technological tools. They're part of our way of life, so much so that we'd have trouble getting along without them. Similarly, the electric motor, which was once a major technological breakthrough, is now all but invisible; we use dozens of motors every day without thinking about them. Computers are clearly headed in that direction.

Kay's four ways of predicting the future don't provide a foolproof crystal ball, but they can serve as a framework for thinking about tomorrow's technology. In the next section we'll turn our attention to research labs, where tomorrow's technology is being invented today. We'll examine trends and innovations that will shape future computer hardware and software. Then we'll see how this technology will serve users as it eventually disappears into our way of life.

FROM RESEARCH TO REALITY: 21ST-CENTURY INFORMATION TECHNOLOGY

You can count how many seeds are in the apple, but not how many apples are in the seed.

—Ken Kesey, author of *One Flew Over the Cuckoo's Nest*

In research laboratories scattered around the planet, ideas are sprouting from the minds of engineers and scientists that will collectively shape the future of computers and information technology. While we can't be sure which of these ideas will bear fruit, we can speculate based on current trends.

Tomorrow's Hardware: Trends and Innovations

The only thing that has consistently grown faster than hardware in the last 40 years is human expectation.

—Bjarne Stoustrup, AT&T Bell Labs, designer of the C++ programming language

The rapid evolution of computer hardware over the last few decades is nothing short of extraordinary. Computer hardware has relentlessly improved by several measures:

- *Speed.* The relay-based Mark I computer (discussed in Chapter 1) could do only a few calculations each second. Today's personal computers are more than a *million times faster!* Computer speed today typically is measured in **MIPS (millions of instructions per second)**, where instructions are the most primitive operation performed by the processor—moving a number to a memory location, comparing two numbers, and the like.

- *Size.* Warehouse-sized computers are history. The central components of a modern personal computer are stored on a few tiny chips that could fit in your pocket; the only parts of the system that occupy significant space on the desktop are peripherals.

- *Efficiency.* As the story goes, ENIAC, the first large-scale computer (see Chapter 1), dimmed the lights of Philadelphia when it was turned on. A modern desktop computer consumes about as much electricity as a television set. Portable computers consume even less.

- *Capacity.* Modern optical, magnetic, and semiconductor storage devices have all but eliminated storage as a constraint for most computing jobs.

- *Cost.* Industry watchers have pointed out that if the price of cars had dropped as fast as the price of computer chips, it would be cheaper to abandon a parked car than to put money in the meter!

Most experts believe these trends will continue, at least for a few years. If they do, we can expect the *price-to-performance ratio* (the level of performance per unit cost) to double every year or two for several more years. Processors that perform billions of operations per second, matchbook-sized high-capacity storage devices, and hard disks that can house the entire contents of the Library of Congress may become commonplace within the decade. There *are* barriers on the horizon—engineers eventually will bump up against the physical limitations of silicon and other materials. But as Robert Noyce, co-inventor of the integrated circuit, pointed out, these barriers have seemed to be about ten years away for many years. So far engineers have continued to find ways to push the barriers back.

The trends are undeniable, but it would be a mistake to assume that tomorrow's computer will simply be a smaller, more powerful version of today's PC. Technological advancements emerging from laboratories will accelerate current trends and push computer technology in entirely new directions. Here are just a few examples:

This ultra-high-resolution flat panel display is produced by dpiX, a division of Xerox.

- *Flat-panel displays.* The popularity of portable computers is fueling intense research efforts to develop inexpensive, low-power, high-resolution, flat-panel displays. As quality goes up and costs come down, more users are replacing their bulky desktop CRTs with flat-panel monitors. Xerox PARC researchers predict that by the end of the decade we'll be using 1000x800-pixel displays that are thin enough to hang on walls like pictures and efficient enough to run on batteries for days.

- *Solid-state storage devices.* Portable computers are also driving the demand for low-power rewritable storage devices. For airline travelers and others who must depend on battery power for long periods of time, disk drives consume far too much energy. ROM storage is energy efficient, but information stored in ROM can't be changed. **Flash memory** and other types of erasable memory chips have been available for several years, but at prices far too high for most applications. Today's research is bringing the cost of solid-state semiconductor storage down so that data, applications, and system software can be economically stored on rewritable cards rather than on disks and in ROM.

Flash memory can be erased and recorded like RAM but is nonvolatile like ROM.

- *Parallel processing.* The quest for speed also motivates research on parallel processing (first discussed in Chapter 2). Instead of using a single processor to execute instructions one at a time, parallel processing machines use multiple processors to work on several tasks in parallel. Some desktop computers use multiple processors to speed up computationally intensive graphics and engineering tasks. Parallel processing is especially promising for speech recognition, vision, and other pattern recognition tasks that are performed very well by the human brain, a biological parallel processing machine (see Chapter 12). Some supercomputers use a small number of expensive, state-of-the-art CPUs to achieve their speed; others use thousands of inexpensive processors in parallel. Parallel processing machines represent monumental challenges for software developers accustomed to working with machines that do one thing at a time.

- *Alternative chip technologies.* Many research labs are experimenting with alternatives to silicon chips. *Gallium arsenide (GaAs) chips* show promise because they move impulses up to ten times faster and emit less heat than their silicon counterparts. But the technology is still young and expensive. *Superconductors*

The Silicon Graphics Challenge Array relies on extensive parallel processing to do high-speed calculations.

that transmit electricity without heat could increase computer speed a hundred-fold. Unfortunately superconductor technology generally requires a supercooled environment. Another alternative is the *optical computer,* which transmits information in light waves rather than electrical pulses. Optical computers outside research labs are currently limited to a few narrow applications like robot vision. But when the technology is refined, general-purpose optical computers may process information hundreds of times faster than silicon computers.

- *Fiber optic networks and wireless networks.* Optical computers may be years away, but optical networks are already here. The phone network's low-bandwidth copper cables are gradually being replaced by broadband fiber optic cables that can simultaneously transmit telephone calls, television signals, two-way computer communications, and all kinds of other digital signals. Because of a lack of government support, the United States lags behind other nations in developing such a network. Japan promises to connect every Japanese home and business to a fiber optic cable by the year 2010; best estimates are that only half of American sites will be connected by that time. However long it takes, though, a universal, all-digital fiber optic network is on the way. So is a universal wireless network that will allow mobile workers to send computer data from cars, planes, and boats as easily as they make cellular phone calls today. These emerging networks will present unheard-of communication possibilities.

A wireless network allows this student to connect to the Internet from a quiet spot on campus.

In any economy infrastructures are the frameworks that are laid first so future economic activity can take advantage of them. Just as the railroads provided the transportation network for the expanding 19th-century American economy, the airline and highway systems have served as the American economic infrastructure for much of this century. In the same way tomorrow's economy is being shaped by an emerging **information infrastructure** of computers and networks. Computers and networks represent critical parts of the information infrastructure, but they're of little value without software. Where is software headed in the coming decades?

Tomorrow's Software: Evolving Applications and Interfaces

I think the PC is about where the automobile was back in the 1920s. While we're past the equivalent of drivers needing to crank and choke their cars by hand . . . we're not yet to the point of automatic transmission . . . let alone anti-lock brakes and air bags. In short . . . PC advances in the next two decades will dwarf those of the past two.

—Eckhard Pfeiffer, president and CEO, Compaq Computer Corporation, in a keynote address at the 1996 Consumer Electronics Show

Computer hardware continues to advance at a staggering pace, and software developers struggle to keep up. In computer research, software continues to be the hardest part. Chapter 11 included discussions of promising programming technologies for the near future, including object-oriented programming languages, CASE tools, and visual programming environments. Each of these technologies can help programmers produce more reliable software in less time. But computer scientists aren't even close to developing tools that will allow programmers to produce *error-free* software quickly.

Still, software technology is advancing rapidly, especially when viewed through the eyes of the user. Two decades ago the typical computer could only be operated by a highly trained professional, and using a computer was pretty much synonymous with programming a computer; today computers are so easy to use that they're sold at shopping malls and operated by preschoolers. Fifteen years ago documents couldn't easily be transported between computer types, or even between different applications on the same computer; today networks can provide seamless communication across platforms, so hardware and operating system differences are no longer barriers for most workgroups. Ten years ago software applications were sold as one-size-fits-all packages packed with features that few users needed; today object technology makes it possible for users to put together compact, customized applications without programming.

The graphical user interface pioneered by Xerox and popularized by Apple and Microsoft has become a loose industry standard, making it possible for users to move back and forth between computer types almost as easily as drivers can adjust to different brands of cars. (Imagine what would happen if Ford or GM moved the brake pedal to the opposite side of the accelerator in next year's models.) But experts expect user interfaces to continue to evolve for awhile before they settle down into the kind of long-lasting standard we're used to in automobiles. Today's WIMP (*w*indows, *i*cons, *m*enus, and *p*ointing devices) interface is easier to learn and use than earlier character-based interfaces, but it's not the end of the user interface evolution. Researcher Raj Reddy uses another acronym to describe emerging user interface technologies: SILK, for *s*peech, *i*mage, *l*anguage, and *k*nowledge capabilities. SILK incorporates many important software technologies:

- *Speech and language.* We discussed these two related artificial intelligence technologies in Chapter 12. While we still don't have a language-translating telephone or a dictation-taking "talkwriter," speech technology is becoming a part of the user interface for a growing number of computer users. Speech input is used for voice mail and *voice annotation*—Post-it notes you can hear. Speech recognition technology allows users to speak, rather than type, commands and limited data input. Speech output is a necessary component of voice mail and multimedia applications. Speech technology is especially important in Japan and other countries with languages that don't lend themselves easily to keyboarding. It's also critical for many disabled users. With or without speech, natural-language processing that lets users communicate in more English-like commands will be an important part of future user interfaces. Researchers expect that we'll soon be using programs that can read documents as we create them, edit them according to our instructions, and file them based on their content.

• *Image.* In the last decade computer graphics have become an integral part of applications ranging from spreadsheets to desktop publishing. Graphics, including charts, graphs, drawings, and photographs, are likely to grow in importance in the coming decade. Graphical images will be as easy to transmit between machines as text is today, probably easier. But tomorrow's graphics won't just be still, flat images; they'll include three-dimensional models, animation, and video clips. Today's two-dimensional desktop interfaces will give way to three-dimensional workspace metaphors complete with 3-D animated objects—virtual workspaces unlike anything we use today. As discussed in Chapter 4, *virtual reality* (VR) *technology* should appear on the desktop within the next few years. **Virtual reality** creates the illusion that the user is immersed in a world that exists only inside the computer—an environment that contains both scenes and the controls to change those scenes. Today's clumsy VR technology is a long way from living up to its name; virtual reality illusions are interesting, but they're poor substitutes for reality. Still, VR has practical applications: Virtual walk-throughs are used by architects and engineers to preview buildings and mechanical assemblies, VR models are used for education and simulations, and virtual worlds are popping up in arcades. On the Internet, *VRML (Virtual Reality Markup Language)* may be the forerunner to tools for building *shared* virtual environments that transcend physical space.

Choreographer Merce Cunningham designs dances by manipulating 3-D models on a Silicon Graphics workstations.

• *Knowledge.* Many experts predict that knowledge will be the most important enhancement to the user interface of the future. Advances in the technology of knowledge—that elusive quality discussed in Chapter 12—will make user interfaces more friendly and forgiving. Intelligent applications will be able to decipher many ambiguous commands and correct common errors as they happen. But most importantly, knowledge will allow so-called software *agents* to work for users. The intelligent agent represents cutting-edge software technology, but it also illustrates the shift toward an emphasis on service.

Tomorrow's Service: Agents on the Network

I don't want to sit and move stuff around on my screen all day and look at figures and have it recognize my gestures and listen to my voice. I want to tell it what to do and then go away; I don't want to babysit this computer. I want it to act for me, not with me.

—Esther Dyson, computer industry analyst and publisher

At Xerox PARC Alan Kay and his colleagues developed the first user interface based on icons—images that represent tools to be manipulated by users. Their pioneering work helped turn the computer into a productivity tool for millions of people. Today Alan Kay claims future user interfaces will be based on agents rather than tools.

Intelligent Agents

Agents are software programs designed to be managed rather than manipulated. An intelligent software agent can ask questions as well as respond to commands, pay attention to its user's work patterns, serve as a guide and a coach, take on its owner's goals, and use reasoning to fabricate goals of its own.

According to Kay, networks will drive the switch to agents. In a few years we'll be connected to billions of pieces of knowledge. Instead of sifting through all that data ourselves, we'll depend on agents to roam the networks 24 hours a day, identifying and retrieving the information we need.

One of the first agents, NewsPeek, was developed by Kay and others at MIT's Media Lab in the early 1980s. NewsPeek "stays up all night looking for the newspaper you would most like to read at breakfast." It searches half a dozen information systems for general-interest articles and topics of interest to the specific user, gleans related pictures and maps from videodisc collections, gathers important electronic mail messages, and combines them in a personalized paper whose major headline might be "Your 8:00 Class Is Canceled Today!"

Agents will do more than deliver information. In a well-integrated home network, the same agent that put together your morning newspaper might reset your alarm clock and your automatic coffee maker in response to the news of the canceled class.

Lawrence Tesler, one of Kay's colleagues at Xerox PARC and later at Apple, describes a fictitious set of messages a user might give to an agent:

- *On what date in February did I record a phone conversation with Sam?*
- *Make me an appointment at a tire shop that is on my way home and is open after 6 p.m.*
- *Distribute this draft to the rest of the group and let me know when they've read it.*
- *Whenever a paper is published on fullerene molecules, order a copy for my library.*

The next morning the agent has the following replies waiting for the user at breakfast:

- *You asked me when you last recorded a phone conversation with Sam. It was on February 27. Shall I play the recording?*
- *You scribbled a note last week that your tires were low. I could get you an appointment for tonight.*
- *Laszlo has discarded the last four drafts you sent him without reading any of them.*
- *You have requested papers on fullerene research. Shall I order papers on other organic microclusters as well?*

You can't buy an agent to take care of all of your daily business yet, but agents handle many simple jobs today. The Internet is home to a rapidly growing population of **bots**—software robots that exhibit many of the characteristics of agents. Some can communicate with each other, work in parallel on complex tasks, and even clone themselves. Many bots are created by hobbyists and amateur programmers to perform routine tasks like automatically answer mail, search for new information on specific topics, and play active parts in MUDs and other multiplayer games.

TV's Max Headroom is one of many fictional software agents.

Agents are often portrayed with human characteristics; *2001*'s Hal and the computers on TV's "Star Trek" are the most famous examples, but plenty of others exist. Apple and Hewlett-Packard have released videos showing computer users of the future conversing with on-screen talking heads that serve as electronic secretaries, telephone receptionists, and research librarians. Of course, agents don't need to look or sound human, they just need to possess the knowledge and intelligence to communicate and serve human users.

In time, agents may guide us through the nooks and crannies of our networks, coach us as we learn to use software applications, act as personal messengers, defend our systems from viruses and intruders, and protect our privacy. They may become so important in our lives that we'll never turn our computers off. In any event, agents will profoundly change the way we interact with computers; Alan Kay calls this shift "the intimate revolution."

Cyberspace Services

With or without agents, the information infrastructure will be like a modern version of an old-fashioned village market, complete with personalized marketing, barter, debates, and creative collaborations. As the lines separating computers, televisions, and telephones blur, the network will offer all kinds of possibilities for education and entertainment. Here are a few specific examples, most of which already exist in limited markets:

- *Personal telephone numbers.* Available now on a limited basis, these follow-me-anywhere numbers will become standard in the future. Your phone will always know where to find you, provided you want to be found. A single number will be able to handle phone calls, mobile cellular phone calls, video teleconferencing, fax images, voice mail, electronic mail, and computer data links. Some executives already carry "smart briefcases" that include copiers, faxes, mobile phones, scanners, video links, and PCs with printers. (Of course, a personal phone number raises questions of privacy, since it can serve as a universal ID number.)

- *Electronic yellow pages.* Unlike their paper counterparts, electronic yellow pages allow consumers to say "Tell me more." A growing number of Web sites already offer this kind of service on a limited basis. As services becomes widespread, we'll routinely request price lists, peruse catalogs, and place orders on line.

- *Open electronic markets.* Buyers and sellers can find each other quickly on line. These markets, already found on many information services, are like two-way classified ads.

- *On-demand automobiles.* Instead of waiting weeks for special-order automobiles or buying a one-size-fits-all car from the lot, customers will be able to design, order, finance, and drive home their customized cars, all within a week. This kind of rapid response is offered by some Japanese companies now; it will be the norm in the future. On-demand ordering requires that suppliers, manufacturers, distributors, and retailers be electronically linked, even if they function as independent companies.

- *Customized clothes.* In *The Age of Intelligent Machines*, Raymond Kurzweil speculates, "Consumers will be able to sit down at their home computers and design their own clothes to their own precise measurements and style requirements using friendly, computer-assisted design software. When the user issues the command 'Make clothes,' the design parameters and measurements will be transmitted to a remote manufacturing facility, where the clothes will be made and shipped within hours."

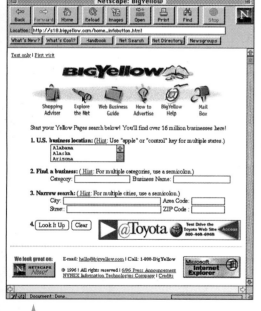

Infoseek's Big Yellow is one of the most popular classified directories on the World Wide Web.

- *Movies on demand.* Video rental stores will vanish when we can order movies directly through the digital network. Advances in video compression will make it possible to transmit a full-length movie into your home through fiber optic cable in seconds.

- *Customizable TV.* Your television will, in all likelihood, have the computing power of a supercomputer today. It may receive models of scenes and construct pictures from those models based on your requests. You'll be able to ask your TV to "Tell me more," "Tell me less," "Go faster," and "Show me a different view of the same scene." And of course, there's always the possibility of 3-D, virtual reality TV. Arthur C. Clarke predicts, "Virtual reality won't merely replace TV. It will eat it alive."

Whether all of these predictions come true, the information infrastructure will serve people in a multitude of exciting ways. There's no shortage of discussion and research on the future uses of information technology. But the talk may subside as we head toward a time when the technology dissolves into our way of life.

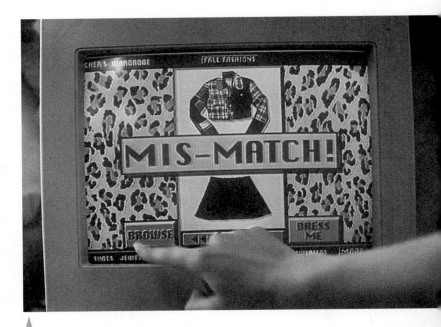

This satirical screen from the movie *Clueless* may be a harbinger of tomorrow's clothing customization software.

Tomorrow's Way of Life: Transparent Technology

In the first computing revolution, the ratio of people to computers was N-to-1. In the second revolution, personal computers insisted the ratio be 1-to-1—one person, one computer. In the third revolution, we are exploring the impact of having computers everywhere, many per person, 1-to-N.

—Bob Metcalfe, inventor of Ethernet, founder of 3Com, and publisher of *InfoWorld*

The most profound technologies are those that disappear. They weave themselves into the fabric of everyday life until they are indistinguishable from it.

—Mark Weiser, head of the Xerox PARC Computer Science Laboratory

Since Alan Kay coined the term *personal computer* at Xerox PARC, hundreds of millions of personal computers have been sold. Ironically many researchers at PARC today think that it's time to move beyond the personal computer because it commands too much of our attention. The goal of these researchers is to make computers disappear so people can use them without thinking about them.

Embedded Intelligence

Computers are already making their way into inconspicuous corners of our lives. Dozens of household appliances and tools have built-in computers. Even our cars are processing megabytes of information as we drive them down the road. Along with the trend toward accessing centrally stored information through networks, we're experiencing another trend: embedding intelligence in the machines that surround us.

There's no end to the possibilities for embedded intelligence. In Japan computer technology has even found its way into the bathroom. A number of Japanese fixture manufacturers sell *smart toilets*—computer-controlled, paperless toilets. The newest models automatically collect and store information on blood pressure, pulse, temperature, urine, and weight. The information can be displayed on an LCD display, accumulated for months, and even transmitted by modem to a medical service. Users of these smart toilets get a mini-checkup whenever they visit the bathroom. Body-monitoring features give the toilet an entirely new function—a function that will undoubtedly save lives.

Ubiquitous Computers

When computers show up in our toilets, we're clearly entering an era of ubiquitous computers—computers will be everywhere. Researchers at Xerox PARC, Cambridge University, and Olivetti are experimenting with technology that will make computers even more ubiquitous. A PARC group is working with three sizes of ubiquitous computers: inch-scale *tabs* that are like smart Post-it notes and badges, foot-scale *pads* that are like smart notebooks and books, and yard-scale *boards* that are like smart bulletin boards and blackboards. Researchers envision a future office with hundreds of these intelligent devices communicating with each other through wireless networks while workers casually move them around their offices.

The best-known computer in their futuristic office is the **active badge** discussed in Chapter 15—a clip-on computerized ID-badge first developed at an Olivetti-Cambridge research lab. The active badge continually reports its location to record-keeping databases and to others in the organization. According to PARC's Mark Weiser, in experimental offices equipped with active badges, "doors open only to the right badge wearer, rooms greet people by name, telephone calls can be automatically forwarded to wherever the recipient may be, receptionists actually know where people are, computer terminals retrieve the preferences of whoever is sitting at them, and appointment diaries write themselves."

Active badges are only a tiny part of Weiser's ubiquitous computing vision. In a 1990 *Scientific American* article, he describes how ubiquitous computers might affect one person's day-to-day life in a future that's still a few years away today:

Sal awakens; she smells coffee. A few minutes ago her alarm clock, alerted by her restless rolling before waking, had quietly asked, "Coffee?" and she had mumbled, "Yes." "Yes" and "no" are the only words it knows. . . .

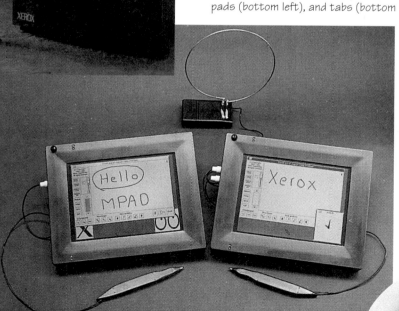

Xerox PARC's ubiquitous computers come in three sizes: boards (top), pads (bottom left), and tabs (bottom right).

At breakfast Sal reads the news. She still prefers the paper form, as do most people. She spots an interesting quote from a columnist in the business section. She wipes her pen over the newspaper's name, date, section, and page number and then circles the quote. The pen sends a message to the paper, which transmits the quote to her office.

Electronic mail arrives from the company that made her garage door opener. She had lost the instruction manual and asked them for help. They have sent her a new manual and also something unexpected—a way to find the old one. According to the note, she can press a code into the opener and the missing manual will find itself. In the garage, she tracks a beeping noise to where the oil-stained manual had fallen behind some boxes. Sure enough, there is the tiny tab the manufacturer had affixed in the cover to try to avoid e-mail requests like her own.

On the way to work Sal glances in the foreview mirror to check the traffic. She spots a slowdown ahead and also notices on a side street the telltale green in the foreview of a food shop, and a new one at that. She decides to take the next exit and get a cup of coffee while avoiding the jam.

Once Sal arrives at work, the foreview helps her find a parking spot quickly. As she walks into the building, the machines in her office prepare to log her in but do not complete the sequence until she actually enters her office. On her way, she stops by the offices of four or five colleagues to exchange greetings and news.

Sal glances out her windows: a gray day in Silicon Valley, 75 percent humidity and 40 percent chance of afternoon showers; meanwhile it has been a quiet morning at the East Coast office. Usually the activity indicator shows at least one spontaneous, urgent meeting by now. She chooses not to shift the window on the home office back three hours—too much chance of being caught by surprise. . . .

Sal picks up a tab and "waves" it to her friend Joe in the design group, with whom she has a joint assignment. They are sharing a virtual office for a few weeks. The sharing can take many forms—in this case, the two have given each other access to their location detectors and to each other's screen contents and location. . . .

A blank tab on Sal's desk beeps and displays the word "Joe" on it. She picks it up and gestures with it toward her live board. Joe wants to discuss a document with her, and now it shows up on the wall as she hears Joe's voice: "I've been wrestling with this third paragraph all morning, and it still has the wrong tone. Would you mind reading it?"

Sitting back and reading the paragraph, Sal wants to point to a word. She gestures again with the "Joe" tab onto a nearby pad and then uses the stylus to circle the word she wants:

"I think it's this term 'ubiquitous.' It's just not in common enough use and makes the whole passage sound a little formal. Can we rephrase the sentence to get rid of it?"

"I'll try that. Say, by the way, Sal, did you ever hear from Mary Hausdorf?"

"No. Who's that?"

"You remember. She was at the meeting last week. She told me she was going to get in touch with you."

Sal doesn't remember Mary, but she does vaguely remember the meeting. She quickly starts a search for meetings held during the past two weeks with more than six people not previously in meetings with her and finds the one. The attendees' names pop up, and she sees Mary. . . .

Technologically we may only be a few years away from Sal's world. In that world ubiquitous computers offer convenience and efficiency beyond anything that's come before. They also raise issues of privacy, intimacy, and independence. These issues will grow in importance as we move further into the information age. But they may seem insignificant when compared to the questions we'll face when the streams of information technology and biotechnology converge in the future.

The Day After Tomorrow: Information Technology Meets Biology

> Our future is technological; but it will not be a world of gray steel. Rather our technological future is headed toward a neo-biological civilization.
>
> —Kevin Kelly, in *Out of Control*

The information age won't last forever. Analysts Stan Davis and Bill Davidson predict in their book *2020 Vision* that a *bio-economy* will replace the information economy sometime around the year 2020. Whether or not they're right, biotechnology and microtechnology will become more intertwined with computer technology in the coming decades. There's no telling exactly what the results will be, but the possibilities are both intriguing and disturbing.

Microtechnology

The incredible miniaturization achieved in the computer industry is allowing researchers to develop *micromachines*—machines on the scale of a *millionth* of a meter. Microscopic moving parts are etched in silicon using a process similar to that of

This motor, photographed through an electron microscope, is 250 microns wide. A human hair is included in the picture for comparison purposes.

manufacturing computer chips. Major universities, corporations (including IBM and AT&T), and government agencies are doing microtechnology research. For example, engineers at the University of California at Berkeley have built a motor twice as wide as a human hair that runs on static electricity.

So far most applications of microtechnology have been *microsensors:* tiny devices that can detect pressure, temperature, and other environmental qualities. Microsensors are used in cars, planes, and spacecrafts, but they show promise in medicine, too. Researchers at Johns Hopkins University have developed a *smart pill* that combines a thermometer with a transmitter so it can broadcast temperatures as it travels through a human digestive tract. This pill is a first step toward other pills that might play more active roles inside our bodies. Scientists speculate that tiny machines may someday be able to roam through the body, locating and destroying cancer cells and invading organisms!

Nanotechnology

If microtechnology is carried to its extreme, it becomes **nanotechnology**—the manufacture of machines on a scale of a few billionths of a meter. Nanomachines would have to be constructed atom by atom using processes drawn from particle physics, biophysics, and molecular biology. IBM scientists have developed a scanning/tunneling microscope that allows them to see and move individual atoms. Using this device, a team of physicists created a tiny switch that relies on the motion of a single atom. Using another approach, biophysicists are studying natural molecular machines like the protein rotor that spins a bacterium's flagellum tail, hoping to use their findings to create molecular motors. At the same time, geneticists are gradually unlocking the secrets of DNA—biology's self-replicating molecular memory devices. These and other research threads may lead scientists to the breakthrough that will allow them to create atomic assembler devices that can construct nanomachines. Submicron computers, germ-sized robots, self-assembling machines, intelligent clothes, alchemy . . . the possibilities are staggering.

Artificial Life

For many researchers, the ultimate goal is to create **artificial life**—synthetic organisms that act like natural living systems. Some artificial life researchers create simple software organisms that exist only in computer memory; many of these organisms are similar to the computer viruses discussed in Chapter 15. Other researchers build colonies of tiny insect robots that communicate with each other and respond to changes in their environment. Artificial life researchers grapple with an array of problems, including the question of definition: Where exactly is the line between a clever machine and a living organism?

Advances in artificial intelligence, robotics, genetics, biotechnology, and microtechnology may someday make the line disappear altogether. Computers and robots will undoubtedly continue to take on more functions that have been traditionally reserved for humans. They may even grow and reproduce using carbon-based genetic technology borrowed from human biology. If they become smart enough to build intelligent machines themselves, almost anything is possible.

This speculation raises questions about the relationship between humans and the machines they create. It's important that we think about those questions while the technology is evolving, because our answers may help us to determine the course of that evolution.

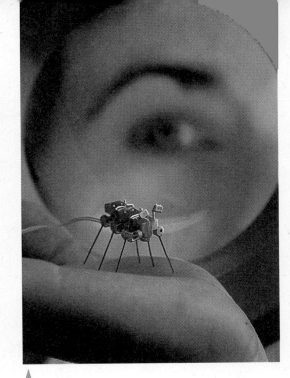

Tiny insect robots like these may be the forerunners of silicon-and-steel artificial life forms.

Human Questions for a Computer Age

The important thing to forecast is not the automobile but the parking problem; not the television but the soap opera.

—Isaac Asimov

The real question before us lies here: do these instruments further life and its values or not?

—Lewis Mumford, 1934

In earlier chapters we examined many social and ethical issues related to computer technology, including privacy, security, reliability, and intellectual property. These aren't the only critical issues before us. Before closing we'll briefly raise some other important, and as yet unanswered, questions of the information age.

Will Computers Be Democratic?

In the future, computers are going to enable a worldwide information democracy in which information is no longer reserved for large companies, the information systems department or the executive officer.

—Michael Dell, chairman and CEO, Dell Computer Corporation

The advanced technologies of information are also technologies of disinformation.

—Stewart Brand, in *The Media Lab*

In 1990 a spontaneous protest exploded across computer networks in reaction to the threat to privacy posed by Marketplace, a new CD-ROM product containing consumer information on millions of Americans. The firestorm of protest forced Lotus Development Corporation to cancel distribution of the product. In Santa Monica, California, homeless people used public access terminals in the library to lobby successfully for more access to public showers. In France student organizations used computer networks to rapidly mobilize opposition to tuition increases. Computers are often used to promote the democratic ideals and causes of common people. Many analysts argue that modern computer technology is, by its very nature, a force for equality and democracy. On the other hand, many powerful people and organizations use information technology to increase their wealth and influence.

Will personal computers empower ordinary citizens to make better lives for themselves? Or will computer technology produce a society of technocrats and technopeasants? Will computerized polls help elected officials better serve the needs of their constituents? Or will they just give those in power another tool for staying in power? Will networks revitalize participatory democracy through electronic town meetings? Or will they give tyrants the tools to monitor and control citizens?

Will the Global Village Be a Community?

> Progress in commercial information technologies will improve productivity, bring the world closer together, and enhance the quality of life.
>
> —Stan Davis and Bill Davidson, in 2020 Vision

> Unless wealthy countries see it as their duty to help developing nations make good use of the evolving technologies, the information age will likely widen the rift between the haves and have-nots.
>
> —Michael L. Dertouzos, director of the MIT Laboratory for Computer Science

A typical computer today contains components from dozens of countries. The modern corporation uses computer networks for instant communication among offices scattered around the world; information doesn't stop at international borders as it flows through networks that span the globe. Information technology allows organizations to overcome the age-old barriers of space and time, but questions remain.

In the post-cold-war era, will information technology be used to further peace, harmony, and understanding? Or will the intense competition of the global marketplace simply create new kinds of wars—information wars? Will electronic interconnections provide new opportunities for economically depressed countries? Or will they simply make it easier for information-rich countries to exploit developing nations from a distance? Will information technology be used to promote and preserve diverse communities, cultures, and ecosystems? Or will it undercut traditions, cultures, and roots?

Will We Become Information Slaves?

> Our inventions are wont to be pretty toys which distract our attention from serious things. They are but improved means to an unimproved end.
>
> —Henry David Thoreau

> Computers are useless. They can only give you answers.
>
> —Pablo Picasso

The information age has redefined our environment; it's almost as if the human species has been transplanted into a different world. Even though the change has happened almost overnight, most of us can't imagine going back to a world without computers. Still, the rapid changes raise questions.

Can human bodies and minds adapt to the higher stimulation, faster pace, and constant change of the information age? Will our information-heavy environment cause us to lose touch with the more fundamental human needs? Will we become so dependent on our "pretty toys" that we can't get by without them? Will we lose our sense of purpose and identity as our machines become more intelligent? Or will we learn to balance the demands of the technology with our biological and spiritual needs?

STANDING ON THE SHOULDERS OF GIANTS

If I have seen farther than other men, it is because I stood on the shoulders of giants.

—Isaac Newton

Prometheus brings fire from the heavens to humanity.

When we use computers, we're standing on the shoulders of Charles Babbage, Ada Lovelace, Alan Turing, Grace Hopper, Doug Engelbart, Alan Kay, and hundreds of others who invented the future for us. Because of their foresight and effort, we can see farther than those who came before us.

In Greek mythology Prometheus (whose name means forethought) stole fire from Zeus and gave it to humanity, along with all arts and civilization. Zeus was furious when he discovered what Prometheus had done. He feared that fire would make mortals think they were as great as the gods and that they would abuse its power. Like fire, the computer is a powerful and malleable tool. It can be used to empower or imprison, to explore or exploit, to create or destroy. We can choose. We've been given the tools. It's up to all of us to invent the future.

SUMMARY

Predicting the future isn't easy, but it's important. One of the best ways to predict the future of technology for the next decade or two is to examine the work being done in research labs today. Information and communication technology industries generally go through four phases: hardware, software, service, and way of life.

Tomorrow's computers will continue current trends toward smaller, more powerful, faster, more efficient, higher-capacity, cheaper machines. Some new technologies will enhance these trends; others may start new trends. We can expect significant advances in flat-panel displays, solid-state storage devices, RISC processors, parallel processing machines, fiber optic networks, and wireless networks. We also may see breakthroughs in alternative chip technologies. Tomorrow's economy will be shaped by the information infrastructure of computers and networks.

Software reliability will remain elusive, but user interfaces will continue the trend toward ease of use. Today's graphical user interfaces will gradually give way as speech, natural language, 3-D images, animation, video, artificial intelligence, and even virtual reality become more pervasive.

Perhaps the most important new user interface technology is the intelligent agent. Agents will be managed rather than manipulated by users. They'll carry out users' wishes and anticipate their needs. Perhaps most importantly, agents will serve as filters between users and the masses of information on networks. Networks will offer a multitude of services, including real-time customizable shopping services, customizable phone services, and computerized television services.

We're heading into an era of ubiquitous computers—computers that are hardly noticeable because they're everywhere. Embedded computers will improve our everyday tools and, in some cases, give them entirely new functions.

Further into the future, information technology may become intertwined with microtechnology and biotechnology. The results may blur the line between living organisms and intelligent machines. We must be aware of the potential risks and benefits of future technology as we chart our course into the future.

Chapter Review

Key Terms

active badge
agent
artificial life

bot
flash memory
information infrastructure

MIPS (millions of instructions per second)
nanotechnology
virtual reality

Review Questions

1. Define or describe each of the key terms above. Check your answers using the glossary.

2. What are the four phases of any technology or media business? Describe how each of these applies to two or more forms of modern electronic technology.

3. What trends in computer hardware evolution are likely to continue for the next few years?

4. Describe several new technologies that may produce significant performance improvements in future computers.

5. What did Raj Reddy mean when he said software will evolve from WIMP to SILK?

6. Why is the windows-and-icons GUI likely to be replaced by an agent-based user interface? What will this mean for computer users?

7. The information infrastructure will allow us to customize many of our transactions in an unprecedented way. Explain why and give several examples.

8. Explain the concept of ubiquitous computers. Give examples of how it might apply in the office of the future and in the home of the future.

9. How might biology, microtechnology, and computer technology become intertwined in the future?

Discussion Questions

1. Some of the most interesting technological ideas are emerging from interdisciplinary labs at MIT, Carnegie-Mellon University, Xerox, Apple, and elsewhere—labs where scientists, engineers, artists, and philosophers work together on projects that break down the traditional intellectual barriers. Why do you think this is so?

2. Millions of computers worldwide are already connected to networks. But unlike highways and railroads, today's computer networks aren't widely available, easy to use, and obviously valuable to the general population. What will need to happen for the information infrastructure to transform our lives the way highways and railroads transformed our ancestors' lives?

3. Will virtual reality replace TV, as Arthur C. Clarke suggests? If it does, is that a good thing?

4. What kinds of questions might be raised if humans develop biologically based computers? How might the computers change our society?

5. Discuss the questions raised in the section called "Human Questions for a Computer Age." Which of those questions are the most important? Which are hardest to answer?

6. Do you foresee a time when we share the Earth with truly intelligent beings of our own creation? Why or why not?

Projects

1. Imagine a future in which computers and information technology are forces of evil. Then imagine a future in which computers and information technology are used to further the common good. Write a paper describing both. Whether you use short-story style or essay style, include enough detail so that it's clear how the technology impacts human lives.

2. Write a letter to a long-lost classmate dated 50 years from today. In that letter describe your life during the past 50 years, including the ways computer technology affected it.

Sources and Resources

Books

Most books about the future are extremely perishable because the future continually turns into the past. Some of the best writing about the future can be found in science fiction, where speculating about the future is a way of life. The books listed here provide several nonfiction views of the future and techniques for exploring the world of tomorrow.

The Media Lab: Inventing the Future at MIT, by Stewart Brand (New York: Viking, 1988). This is the book that brought the MIT Media Lab into the public eye. In spite of its age, the book does an admirable job of describing a future radically transformed by the interweaving of the computer, communication, and entertainment industries. It also provides an insightful look at technology researchers in action.

Being Digital, by Nicholas Negroponte (New York: Knopf, 1995). The Director of the MIT Media Lab has been writing thought-provoking columns for the back page of *Wired* since issue 1. This collection of columns provides an optimistic vision of a digital future.

Technology 2001: The Future of Computers and Communications, edited by Derek Leebaert (Cambridge, MA: MIT Press, 1991). This is a diverse and interesting collection of essays on tomorrow's digital technology.

The Future of Software, edited by Derek Leebaert (Cambridge, MA: MIT Press, 1995). This collection of essays, like *Technology 2001,* provides industry-insider perspectives on the future of technology. Topics include groupware, user-built software, natural-language computing, and legal issues.

Out of Control: The Rise of Neo-Biological Civilization, by Kevin Kelley (Reading, MA: Addison-Wesley, 1994). Artificial life, artificial intelligence, genetic engineering, virtual reality, and nanotechnology blur the line between the "born" and the "made." Kevin Kelly's powerful, wonderfully readable book explores this line and provides fertile ground for speculation on all kinds of technological, social, and ethical questions.

The Future Does Not Compute: Transcending the Machines in Our Midst, by Stephen L. Talbott (Sebastopol, CA: O'Reilly & Associates, Inc., 1995). This book by a computer industry veteran is a wake-up for anyone who blindly accepts computers as benevolent tools. The author raises important questions about the impact of computers on human consciousness and our conscience.

Resisting the Virtual Life, edited by James Brook and Iain A. Boal (San Francisco: City Lights Books, 1995). This collection of essays surveys the dark side of computing and information technology: privacy erosion, alienation, technological addiction, oppression, and more.

Silicon Snake Oil, by Cliff Stoll (New York: Doubleday, 1995). Stoll's first book, *The Cuckoo's Egg* (described in Chapter 15), presented the Internet as a worldwide community based on trust. In *Silicon Snake Oil,* Stoll argues that the technology has been oversold and that we need to spend more time unplugged.

The Art of the Long View, by Peter Schwartz (New York: Doubleday, 1991). Scenario planning is a particularly useful tool for highlighting the powerful forces that shape the future and choosing strategies that play out well in a variety of possible futures. Schwartz is a master of scenario planning, and this book describes his methodology and provides examples.

The Road to 2015: Profiles of the Future, by John L. Petersen (Corte Madera, CA: Waite Group Press, 1994). Petersen describes a systems approach to thinking about the future and then applies that approach in chapters about science, technology, energy, the environment, population, politics, transportation, health, space, and social values.

Periodicals

21•c, Scanning the Future: A Magazine of Culture, Technology, and Science. Wired (described in Chapter 1) has quickly become the definitive periodical for exploring the present and future of our technological society. *21•c* covers similar territory from the other side of the planet. This slick Australian journal provides a broad, engaging perspective on possible and probable future trends.

World Wide Web Pages

The World Wide Web is evolving rapidly in amazing ways, but there are still no direct links to the future. The Web links on the *Computer Confluence* page allow you to explore Xerox PARC, the MIT Media Lab, and other organizations dedicated to inventing the future. Other links transport you into speculative discussions about tomorrow's technology and its implications.

Buying a computer can be an intimidating process, but it doesn't need to be. With the right information, you should have no trouble finding the right system.

Chapter 4 introduced several general principles that apply to just about any personal computer purchase (see Rules of Thumb: Computer Consumer Concepts, page 92). But when you're actually ready to buy a system, you'll need more specific information to help you narrow down the myriad of options and choose the system that best meets your needs. The next few pages provide information on each component in a typical computer system; you can use this information to create a profile of an ideal computer system. The CD-ROM includes an interactive Consumer's Guide that can walk you through the process of creating this profile.

Because of the volatile nature of the computer marketplace, the consumer's guides in this book and CD-ROM can't tell you everything you need to know. You'll need more current information to help you turn your ideal system profile into a detailed brand-specific shopping list. The *Computer Confluence* Web site will point you toward up-to-the-minute consumer-oriented information. Use this Web data along with anything you can glean from magazines, knowledgeable friends, and other sources.

If money were no object, you could purchase a fully loaded, top-of-the-line system with every imaginable peripheral. If, like most of us, you're working with a limited budget, you'll need to be more discriminating. You'll need to figure out exactly which features and components you need, which ones you might want to add later, and which ones you won't need at all. If you have a clear idea of how you're going to use your system, you'll be able to assess the trade-offs involved in choosing features and options. For example, if you're a graphics artist, you'll probably want to put more of your budget into a high-quality monitor even if it means scrimping on audio speakers.

When shopping for a computer, there are several question you need to address:

Is portability important? Portable computers are more expensive than desktop computers of equivalent capabilities. They also aren't as expandable as desktop boxes, so they aren't appropriate for users with highly specialized needs. You have to decide whether the convenience of portability outweighs the additional expense and limited expandability.

Should you buy a Macintosh or a Wintel (Windows/Intel) computer? This is a highly personal decision; you'll probably meet partisans for both camps who will argue with the passion of a religious zealot. The truth is that, while there are still critical differences between the two operating systems, both are capable of serving the needs of most users. If you don't already have a strong preference, check with others in your chosen field to see what they use and why. In general, Wintel machines predominate in business, while Macs have loyal followings in publishing, graphics, multimedia, and education. Consider the kinds of software you'll want to use and find out what's available on each system. Spend some time getting to know both types of systems to see which you prefer.

What is your budget? If you have less than $1000 to spend, you'll probably have to get a used computer or an extremely limited system. If you mostly need a word processing and Web-surfing machine, an older system may be all you need. But most older systems can't run the latest software and have limited expansion options. If you have $1000 to $2000 in your computer budget, you can buy a new system with standard capabilities that can handle today's most popular applications. If you can spend more than $2000, you can choose a high-performance system that can run many of the more demanding applications. In general, more expensive computer packages contain higher-quality peripherals as well.

Where do you buy a computer? Many people shop locally at computer specialty stores, superstores, and home electronic stores because of the local service, ease of repairs, and warranty replacements. Others choose mail-order companies for their competitive prices. Mail-order shopping can save money, but it can also mean additional hassles and risks if you don't do your homework or if you choose the wrong company. Leading computer magazines often rate mail-order companies for their service, prices, and reliability. Internet newsgroups can also help you find good deals and businesses with good reputations.

How do you plan to use your computer? Here's a list of computer applications. Which of these applications is most important to you? The applications you choose will determine, to a large degree, what your ideal system will look like.

Desktop Productivity Applications
Word Processing
Spreadsheet
Database

Publishing
Desktop Publishing
Web Publishing

Games
Simulations
Multiplayer gaming
Virtual reality

Communications
Online Service Access
E-mail
Internet/Web Access
Voice Mail/Fax

Technical Applications
CAD
Mathematical
Statistics
Programming Languages

Financial Applications
Personal Finance/On-line Banking
Accounting

Multimedia/Graphics
Graphic Art
Animation
Video
Music
Presentation Graphics
Multimedia Authoring

The CD-ROM goes into more detail on choosing systems for each of these categories. The remainder of this consumer's guide discusses hardware and software specifics that apply to all categories.

CPU

Buy the fastest CPU you can afford. RAM also affects the overall performance of your computer, but it's generally easier to add RAM later than to upgrade a CPU.

Secondary Storage

Most new computers come with a single floppy disk drive, a 1- to-2-gigabyte hard drive, and a CD-ROM drive; unless your computing needs are minimal, you probably won't be satisfied with a system that doesn't include these basic components. If you're planning on doing graphic design, digital audio, multimedia authoring, or other storage-intensive jobs, you'll probably also want some kind of removable high-capacity disk drive for transporting and backing up large files, a CD-R drive for creating CD-ROMs, and/or a DVD optical drive for working with the newer high-capacity optical disks.

RAM

Certain applications, especially those that manipulate digital images or audio, demand a great deal of RAM. In general, you should plan on getting a computer with at least 16 megabytes of RAM—more if you will be using memory-intensive applications.

Video/Monitor

The quality of the images you can display on your computer is a function not only of the monitor but also of the video adapter inside your system unit. If you plan to make extensive use of intricate color images, you will want a large-screen monitor (17" or greater) capable of supporting a resolution of at least 1024 x 768, a color depth of 16 million colors, and a noninterlaced refresh rate of at least 75 hertz. Of course, the video card will have to support these features and should contain at least 4MB of video RAM.

Input Devices

All computer systems have a keyboard and a pointing device, most commonly a mouse. Many keyboards are now ergonomically designed to reduce the risk of repetitive motion strain. Some users prefer a trackball to the mouse. If you plan to do much graphic design work, consider adding a pressure-sensitive graphics tablet to your system; it's far easier and more accurate to draw with a stylus than a mouse. For serious game playing, a joystick easily beats the mouse. Newer digital joysticks provide superior performance over their analog counterparts and offer more accurate control.

Modem/Communications

Since much Web content is graphics intensive, you shouldn't consider anything less than a 28.8 Kbps modem for Web surfing. A 14.4 Kbps modem is sufficient for standard e-mail and text-based communications. Newer modems support SVD, or simultaneous voice and data, and contain fax capabilities. In some areas ISDN or cable modems can provide high-speed and high-priced Internet access.

Printer

Today's low-cost ink-jet printers can produce surprisingly good high-resolution printouts; many are capable of printing impressive color images. Laser printers are more expensive but produce better printouts of text and black-and-white line art at a lower cost per page.

Sound Card/Speakers

All Macintoshes have built-in 16-bit sound cards and MIDI-compatible system software sounds. Most Wintel systems ship with a 16-bit sound card capable of playing CD-quality audio and MIDI files. Advanced sound cards also supply wave table synthesis and the ability to create and play back studio-quality digital sound samples. These sound cards often contain extensive ROM with megabytes of prerecorded sound samples and expandable RAM banks. No sound system would be complete without a set of amplified, magnetically shielded speakers. The best systems include a separate bass subwoofer for more realistic nondirectional sound.

Software

Most systems come with systems software installed on the hard disk; some come with a number of preinstalled applications programs. Unless your system includes all the software you'll need, you'll have to spend part of your computer budget on software. If your software budget is modest, you may be able to meet most or all of your needs with an inexpensive integrated application like ClarisWorks or Microsoft Works. These all-purpose programs cost much less than more powerful office suites, and they demand much less disk space. Of course, integrated applications and software suites can't handle everybody's software needs. Multimedia work, engineering, and other specialized applications require specialized software. Don't overlook shareware and public domain software if your budget is tight.

Add-ons

There are numerous hardware add-ons that appeal to different special interests. Depending on your needs, you may want to add a flatbed scanner for scanning text and graphics, a digital camera for digitizing real-world images, a MIDI keyboard for playing your own music, or a motion video card for recording and manipulating full-motion digital video.

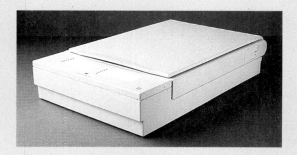

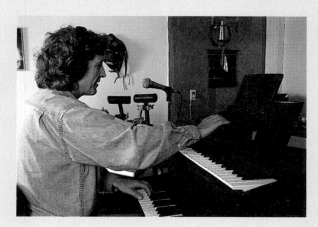

Glossary

A

Access-control software   Software that uses *passwords* and other techniques to prevent unauthorized users from using a computer system or network. *Chapter 15.*

Accounting and financial management software   Software used to manage the financial accounts of businesses, institutions, families, and individuals. Accounting software keeps track of financial transactions and the flow of money between *accounts*. *Chapter 6.*

Accounts   Monetary categories to represent various types of income, expenses, assets, and liabilities. *Chapter 6.*

Active badge (or **smart badge**)   A microprocessor-controlled badge that broadcasts infrared identification codes to nearby network receivers. The receivers then transmit information to a badge-location database. *Chapters 15, 16.*

Active cell (or **current cell**)   In a spreadsheet, the cell that contains the cursor. Data that a user enters with the keyboard goes into the active cell. *Chapter 6.*

Ada   A massive programming language named after Ada Lovelace, who worked with Charles Babbage in creating the *Analytical Engine*. Ada was developed in the late 1970s as the standard for the U.S. Defense Department. *Chapter 11.*

Additive color synthesis   The formation of a color by adding together different amounts of red, green, and blue light. Computer monitors use this technique. *Chapter 3.*

Address   1. The combined row number and column letter of a spreadsheet *cell*. *Chapter 6.* 2. A mnemonic code representing a memory location. *Chapter 2.*

Agent   A futuristic intelligent software entity that "lives" in a computer and acts as a digital secretary. An agent can anticipate user requests, fill in details in the user's work, and adjust the computerized workspace to fit the user's needs. *Chapter 16.*

Agricultural economy   The economy that dominated the period of human history lasting from about 10,000 years ago until the industrial revolution. In this economy most people lived and worked on farms, exchanging goods and services in nearby towns. *Chapter 12.*

Algorithm   A set of step-by-step procedures that, when completed, solve a problem or accomplish a task. A computer program generally starts as an algorithm written in a limited version of English or some other human language. *Chapter 11.*

Alias   A pseudonym or a name for a group list in an e-mail system. A message sent to an alias is automatically sent to everyone in the group. *Chapter 9.*

Alpha testing   Early software tests performed by members of the system development team to locate and eliminate bugs. *Chapter 11.*

ALU (arithmetic logic unit)   The part of the CPU that performs the arithmetic and makes simple logical comparisons. *Chapter 2.*

Analog signal   A continuous wave, like a sound wave. Contrast with *Digital signal*. *Chapter 9.*

Analytical Engine   Charles Babbage's 19th-century programmable calculating machine that, if it had been completed, would have been the first computer. *Chapter 1.*

Animation   The illusion of movement created by a rapidly displayed sequence of still drawings. *Chapter 7.*

ANSI   The former American National Standards Institute. In the context of computers, ANSI is a commonly used character set on Windows systems. *Chapter 3.*

API (application program interface)   The part of the operating system that provides services to application programs as they run. *Chapter 4.*

Application program (or **application**)   A software tool, such as a word processor or spreadsheet, that allows a computer to be used for a specific purpose. *Chapters 1 and 4.*

Application suite (or **office suite**)   A software bundle containing several application programs (usually including a word processor, a spreadsheet program, a presentation graphics program, and a database program) that are also sold as separate programs. *Chapter 4.*

Architecture   The design that determines how individual components of a CPU, computer, or computer system are put together. *Chapter 2.*

Array   A data structure used in programming to represent a numeric list or table. *Chapter 11.*

Artificial intelligence (AI)   The branch of computer science that explores using computers in tasks that require intelligence, imagination, and insight—tasks that have traditionally been performed by people rather than machines. *Chapter 12.*

Artificial life   Experimental synthetic (software or hardware) organisms that behave in some significant ways like natural living systems. *Chapter 16.*

ASCII (American Standard Code for Information Interchange, generally pronounced "as-kee")   The most widely used code for representing characters in computer memory. Modern ASCII represents each character as a unique 8-bit code. *Chapter 2.*

Assembler   A program that translates assembly-language instructions into a machine-language instruction. *Chapter 11.*

Assembly language   A language that's logically equivalent to machine language but easier for people to read, write, and understand. In assembly language, programmers use alphabetic codes that correspond to the machine's numeric instructions. *Chapter 11.*

Asynchronous communication   Communication where the sender and the recipients don't have to be logged in at the same time; examples include Internet newsgroups and mailing lists. *Chapter 10.*

Attachment (e-mail)   A document or data file that is sent along with an e-mail message. An attached document might be a formatted word processor document, a picture, or even a multimedia document. *Chapter 10.*

Audio digitizer   A computer peripheral or component containing circuitry to digitize sounds from microphones and other audio devices. The sounds can then be stored (recorded) in digital computer memory. *Chapters 3, 7.*

Audit-control software   Software used to monitor and record computer transactions as they happen so auditors can trace and identify computer activity after the fact. *Chapter 15.*

Authentication   The process of verifying that a message has been received unmodified from a particular source. *Chapter 15.*

Authoring system or tool   A software tool for building (authoring) interactive hypermedia and multimedia documents for education, training, reference, and entertainment. Authoring systems allow people to develop interactive software without mastering complex programming languages. *Chapters 7, 14.*

Automated factory   A factory that uses robots in conjunction with computers. The computers help track inventory, time the delivery of parts, control the quality of the production, monitor wear and tear on machines, and schedule maintenance. *Chapter 13.*

Automated office   An office in which modern information technology is integrated into most or all aspects of work. *Chapter 13.*

Automated teller machine (ATM)   A specialized terminal linked to a bank's main computer through a commercial banking network. An ATM can handle routine banking transactions 24 hours a day. *Chapter 9.*

Automatic footnoting   A word processing feature that automatically positions footnotes and endnotes. *Chapter 5.*

Automatic hyphenation   A word processing feature that automatically breaks long words that fall at the end of lines. *Chapter 5.*

Automatic link   A spreadsheet feature that allows one or more related (linked) worksheets to be updated automatically when values change in one. *Chapter 6.*

Automatic recalculation   A spreadsheet feature that causes formulas to be automatically recalculated whenever values in other related cells change. *Chapter 6.*

Automatic replication   A spreadsheet feature that streamlines the process of entering repetitive data, labels, and formulas. *Chapter 6.*

Automatic speech recognition   The ability of a computer system to recognize human speech, using many pattern recognition techniques from artificial intelligence. *Chapter 12.*

Automatic translation   The ability of a computer to translate words, phrases, and/or sentences from one human language to another. *Chapter 12.*

Automation   The use of computers and other technology to operate machinery and perform other tasks previously done by human workers. *Chapter 13.*

Autonomous system   A complex system that can assume almost complete responsibility for a task without human input, verification, or decision making. *Chapter 15.*

B

Backspace key   The key that, for most software, erases the character immediately to the left of the cursor. *Chapter 3.*

Back up   To make a copy of software or data so that the original can be replaced if it is damaged or destroyed. The copy is called a backup. *Chapter 15.*

Bandwidth   The quantity of information that can be transmitted through a channel in a given amount of time. The channel might be a cable connecting networked computers, a radio channel, or even a human–machine interface. *Chapter 9.*

Bar chart   A chart representing quantities of data as a collection of horizontal bars of varying lengths. Similar to a column chart. *Chapter 6.*

Bar-code reader   An input device that uses light to read universal product codes (UPCs), inventory codes, and other codes created out of patterns of variable-width bars. *Chapter 3.*

BASIC (Beginner's All-Purpose Symbolic Instruction Code)   Originally designed in the 1960s as an interactive language for learning programming, BASIC is one of the most widely used programming languages in the world today. *Chapter 11.*

Batch processing   A type of data processing in which transactions are accumulated and fed into computers in large batches. For most applications today, *interactive processing* has replaced batch processing. *Chapter 8.*

Batch spelling checker   A type of spelling checker that checks all of the words in your document in a batch when you issue the appropriate command. *Chapter 5.*

Baud rate   A measurement of modem transmission speed that generally has been replaced by the more accurate bits per second (bps). Technically the two terms are not interchangeable, although many people use the term *baud rate* when they mean *bits per second (bits per second)*. *Chapter 9.*

Beta testing   Software or hardware testing performed by potential users before the product is released. *Chapter 11.*

Bezier control point   In scalable type fonts and some drawing programs, these points are used to describe the shape of curves drawn on the screen or printed. *Chapter 5.*

Binary   The base-2 number system used by computers. *Chapter 2.*

Binary search   An algorithm for searching data that involves repeatedly dividing the searchable data in half until the target value is found. *Chapter 11.*

Bio-economy   An economy based on biotechnology, microtechnology, and information technology that, according to many analysts, will replace our information economy sometime within the next few decades. *Chapter 16.*

Biometrics   Voice prints, fingerprints, retinal scans, and other measurements of individual body characteristics. Biometrics are sometimes used to ensure that only authorized personnel have access to computer systems and data. *Chapter 15.*

Bit (binary digit)   The smallest unit of information. A bit can have only one of two values, on or off. *Chapter 2.*

Bit-mapped font   A type font whose internal representation is a pattern of on/off (print/leave blank) dots. Contrast with *Scalable outline font. Chapter 5.*

Bit-mapped (raster) graphics   A type of computer graphics in which pictures are stored as maps showing how the pixels on the screen should be represented. Contrast with *Object-oriented (vector) graphics. Chapter 7.*

Bits per second (bps)   The most common measurement of modem transmission speed. *Chapter 9.*

Board   1. Short for *circuit board.* See also *Card. Chapter 2.* 2. The name given by researchers to experimental flat-panel computers that are like smart bulletin boards and blackboards. *Chapter 16.*

Boldface (or bold)   A type style applied to a font to make characters stand out **like this** for emphasis. *Chapter 5.*

Booting   The process of loading a computer's operating system into memory. The term evolved from the term *bootstrapping* because the computer seems to pull itself up by its own bootstraps. *Chapter 4.*

Bot   A software robot that exhibits many of the characteristics of a software agent. *Chapter 16.*

Browse   To explore manually the records in a database or hypermedia document. *Chapter 8.*

Bug   A software error that might cause incorrect results or system failure. *Chapter 4.*

Bullet chart   A titled list of the main points of a presentation, with each point preceded by a bullet (•). A bullet chart is the most common output from presentation graphics software. *Chapter 7.*

Bulletin board system (BBS)   A telephone-linked computer system that provides public access for posting and reading messages. *Chapter 9.*

Bus   A group of 8, 16, or 32 wires that carries information between computer components. *Chapter 2.*

Button   A "hot spot" on the screen that responds to mouse clicks, typically by displaying a different screen. *Chapter 7.*

Byte   A collection of 8 bits. A byte can represent 256 different messages ($256 = 2^8$). For many computer applications, a byte contains one character's worth of information. *Chapter 2.*

C

C   A programming language that combines many of the advantages of high-level languages and assembly language. Its power, flexibility, and efficiency have made it the language of choice for most professionals who program personal computers. *Chapter 11.*

C++   A popular dialect of the programming language C with object-oriented programming tools. *Chapter 11.*

Cache   A temporary storage area, often existing as a kind of limited memory within or near the CPU. A cache (like a buffer) is used to hold data being transferred between two devices that operate at different speeds. *Chapter 2.*

Call-back system   A security system designed to prevent unauthorized use of stolen passwords by outsiders. When a user logs in and types a password, the system hangs up, looks up the user's phone number, and calls back before allowing access. *Chapter 15.*

Camera-ready   A description of desktop-published pages that are ready to be photographed and printed. *Chapter 5.*

Card   1. A circuit board that can be installed in a PC to expand its capabilities. 2. The name used for a screen in Hyper-Card and many other multimedia authoring systems; a card can contain graphics, text, and buttons. A card is part of a *stack. Chapter 7.*

Carpal tunnel syndrome   A painful affliction of the wrist and hand that results from repeating the same movements over long periods. *Chapter 13.*

CASE (computer-assisted software engineering) tool   A software tool that allows analysts and programmers to automate many of the tedious and error-prone steps involved in turning design specifications into programs. *Chapter 11.*

CD audio   Standard compact disc (CD) sound. A computer can play sounds from standard audio CDs by sending commands to a *CD-R drive* connected to headphones or amplified speakers. *Chapter 7.*

CD-I (compact disc-interactive)   A type of compact disc system with a specially programmed microprocessor and game-style controlling devices designed to work with standard television sets. *Chapter 7.*

CD-R drive   A disk drive capable of writing on a blank CD to produce a CD-ROM. *Chapter 3.*

CD-ROM (compact disc—read-only memory)   A disc that's identical to a standard audio CD except that it's used to store computer data instead of (or in addition to) music. The disc is read by a computer using a CD-ROM drive. *Chapter 3.*

Cell   A box in a spreadsheet representing the intersection of a row and column. *Chapter 6.*

Centered justification   The placement of a line or paragraph of text so that it is centered horizontally between the left and right margins. *Chapter 5.*

Centralized computing   A type of computing in which most or all computing is done by one central mainframe computer. Contrast with *Distributed* or *Enterprise computing. Chapter 9.*

Centralized database   A database system in which software and data are housed in a single centralized mainframe computer and accessed by users through terminals or personal computers. Contrast with *Client/server database* and *Distributed database. Chapter 8.*

Central processing unit (CPU)   The part of a computer that processes information by executing program instructions, performing all the necessary arithmetic calculations, and making basic decisions based on information values. Also called the *processor. Chapter 2.*

Character-based interface   A user interface based on characters rather than graphics. Contrast with *Graphical user interface. Chapter 4.*

CISC (complex instruction set computer)   A computer that has a complex set of instructions—a large machine-language vocabulary. Most computers today are CISCs, but the trend is toward *RISC. Chapter 16.*

Circuit board   A flat panel containing chips and other electronic components along with the circuits that connect them. *Chapter 2.*

Click   To press a button on a *mouse. Chapter 3.*

Client/server database   A type of database in which database software in client desktop computers works with data files stored in central server databases on mainframes, minicomputers, or desktop computers. *Chapter 8.*

Client/server model   A hierarchical model in which one or more computers act as dedicated servers and all the remaining computers act as clients. *Chapters 9, 10.*

Clip art Professionally produced art, often in a digital format, that can be purchased or licensed for use in publications, multimedia documents, or other applications. *Chapter 7.*

Clipboard A special portion of memory for temporarily holding information that has been copied or cut from a document for later use. *Chapter 5.*

Clip music Professionally produced musical files that users can legally incorporate into their multimedia productions. *Chapter 7.*

Clock A component of the CPU that produces pulses to synchronize computer operations. *Chapters 2, 16.*

CMYK (Cyan Magenta Yellow blacK) These are the colors of ink used for subtractive color synthesis, employed in most color printing. *Chapter 3.*

COBOL (Common Business Oriented Language) One of the first high-level languages especially suited for business applications. *Chapter 11.*

Code Program statements produced by coding. *Chapter 11.*

Coding Writing a program from an algorithm. *Chapter 11.*

Color depth (or bit depth) The number of bits of video memory used to store the color code for each pixel of a display monitor. *Chapter 7.*

Color gamut The range of colors that a device is capable of producing (not necessarily all in a single image); the range of colors perceptible by an input device or by the human eye. *Chapter 3.*

Column A complete vertical line of spreadsheet cells, usually referred to with an aphabetic letter or letters. *Chapter 6.*

Command guidance system A system that allows a human operator to control a missile's path while watching a missile's-eye-view of the target on a television screen. *Chapter 15.*

Command-line interface A type of user interface in which the user types commands and the computer responds. *Chapter 4.*

Comment A statement included in a program to help human readers understand (or remember) something about the program. *Chapter 11.*

Communication software Software to facilitate communication between computers. *Chapter 9.*

Communications satellite A satellite that hangs in orbit above the earth, allowing electronic signals to be bounced between disparate locations on the earth's surface. *Chapter 9.*

Compatibility The matching of hardware and software so they can work together properly. Software and peripherals are described in terms of whether they can work with particular computers and operating systems, and with each other. For example, many programs are Windows-compatible—capable of running on an IBM PC or similar machine running the Windows operating system. *Chapter 4.*

Compiler A translator program that translates an entire program into machine language before passing it on to the computer. *Chapter 11.*

Component software Software designed to allow users to construct small custom applications from selected software components or modules. *Chapter 11.*

Compression The temporary removal of bits of information to reduce the file size of a document so it takes less storage space and network transmission time. *Chapters 7, 10.*

Computed field A *database* field that contains formulas similar to *spreadsheet* formulas. *Chapter 8.*

Computer A programmable machine that changes information from one form to another. *Chapter 1.*

Computer-aided design (CAD) The use of computers to design products. Often linked to *computer-aided manufacturing (CAM)*. *Chapter 7.*

Computer-aided instruction (CAI) The use of computers to aid the instructional process. Usually refers to *drill-and-practice software* and *tutorial software*. *Chapter 14.*

Computer-aided manufacturing (CAM) The use of computers to control the manufacturing of parts. Often combined with *computer-aided design (CAD)* in *computer-integrated manufacturing (CIM)*. *Chapter 7.*

Computer architecture A branch of computer science dealing with the way the hardware and software elements of a computer work together. *Chapter 11.*

Computer crime A crime accomplished through knowledge or use of computer technology. *Chapter 15.*

Computer graphic A picture or graph created with or manipulated by a computer. *Chapter 7.*

Computer-integrated manufacturing (CIM) The combination of computer-aided design and computer-aided manufacturing; a major step toward the fully automated factory. *Chapter 7.*

Computer monitoring See *Monitoring, computer.*

Computer science A relatively new discipline with ties to electrical engineering, mathematics, and business that focuses on the process of computing rather than on computer hardware. *Chapter 11.*

Computer security The protection of computer systems and the information stored in those systems against unwanted access, damage, modification, or destruction. *Chapter 15.*

Computer-supported cooperative work The use of groupware to facilitate group work. Sometimes called *workgroup computing*. *Chapter 13.*

Computer theory The branch of computer science that applies the concepts of theoretical mathematics to computational problems. *Chapter 11.*

Concurrent processing The ability of a computer to work on several jobs at the same time. *Chapter 4.*

Console See *Formula bar.*

Continuous speech Natural speech where words run together at normal speed; particularly difficult for machines to understand. *Chapter 12.*

Control The particular part of a computer program that is currently executing on the CPU. *Chapter 4.*

Control structure A logical structure that controls the order in which program instructions are carried out. *Chapter 11.*

Control unit The supervisory part of a CPU that maintains overall control over the flow of instructions and data through the CPU; coordinates the other units within the CPU. *Chapter 2.*

Copy A command for copying part of a document into the Clipboard. *Chapter 5.*

Copying text Duplicating one part of a document and placing it in another section of the same document or in a different document. *Chapter 5.*

Copy-protected software Software whose installation procedure is designed to make it difficult or impossible to make unauthorized copies. *Chapter 4.*

Copyrighted software Software that is protected by law against unauthorized duplication and distribution. *Chapter 4.*

Courseware   Educational software. *Chapter 14.*

CPU   See *Central processing unit.*

Crop   To trim a picture. *Chapter 5.*

CRT (cathode ray tube)   The television-style monitor type most widely used with desktop computers. *Chapter 3.*

Cryptography   The science of scrambling the contents of messages so that they cannot be easily read by unauthorized parties. *Chapter 15.*

Cryptosystem   A system designed to encrypt and decrypt messages, often consisting of both hardware and software components. *Chapter 15.*

Current cell   See *Active cell.*

Cursor (or insertion bar)   Current position indicator; flashing mark indicating your location in the document. *Chapters 3, 5.*

Cursor (arrow) keys   Keyboard keys that move the cursor up, down, left, and right. *Chapter 3.*

Custom application   An application program written specifically for a single client. *Chapter 4.*

Cut-and-paste   An editing technique that allows data to be moved within and between documents. *Chapter 5.*

Cyberspace   A term coined by William Gibson in his visionary novel *Neuromancer.* In science fiction, cyberspace is a universal computer network that looks and feels like a physical place—a shared virtual reality. The term is also used to refer to today's networks and virtual reality experiments. *Chapter 10.*

Data   Information in a form a computer can read. *Chapter 1.*

Database   A collection of information stored in an organized form in a computer. *Chapter 8.*

Database management system (DBMS)   A program or system of programs that can manipulate data in a large collection of files, cross-referencing between files as needed. *Chapter 8.*

Database program   An application that organizes the storage and retrieval of information stored in a database. *Chapter 8.*

Data compression   The process of squeezing redundant and noncritical data out of files so they can be stored and transmitted more efficiently. *Chapter 7.*

Data structure   Software construct that determines the logical structure of *data. Chapter 11.*

Data translation software   Software that allows a computer to read and modify data from a system that uses incompatible file formats. *Chapter 4.*

Data warehouse   A centralized storage system for all of an organization's critical data. *Chapter 8.*

Date field   A field in a database that can contain only dates. *Chapter 8.*

Debug   To locate and correct errors in a program. *Chapters 4, 11.*

Debugger   A software tool used by programmers to locate and correct errors in programs. *Chapter 11.*

Decimal   The base-10 number system we use every day. *Chapter 2.*

Decision support system (DSS)   A computer system that supports managers in decision-making tasks. *Chapter 13.*

Decode unit   The part of a CPU that decodes or interprets a machine-language instruction. *Chapter 2.*

Decrypt   To unscramble an encrypted message so that it can be read. Normally this requires the decryption key, which is like a secret password. *Chapter 15.*

Default   The option automatically chosen by the computer unless the user specifies otherwise.

Delayed teleconference   A type of group on-line communication in which participants type, post, and read messages at their convenience. *Chapter 9.*

Delete   To erase, possibly using the Delete or Backspace key on the keyboard. *Chapters 3, 5.*

Delete key   A key that deletes text or other data objects; its exact function depends on the software being used. *Chapter 3.*

Deleting text   Erasing text from a document. *Chapter 5.*

De-skilling   Transforming a task so it requires less skill; a common result of job automation. *Chapter 13.*

Desktop   The name given to the screen displayed by the Macintosh Finder; the view represents a desktop workspace. *Chapter 4.*

Desktop publishing (DTP)   Using a personal computer, software, and a high-resolution printer to produce documents that combine text and graphics. *Chapter 5.*

Dialog box   In a graphical user interface (GUI), a window or box displayed on the screen when two-way communication takes place between the computer and the user. *Chapter 4.*

Dial-up terminal emulation   Connecting to an Internet host using a modem, standard telephone lines, and terminal emulation software. The user's computer acts as a dumb terminal—an input/output device that allows you to send commands to and view information on your host computer. *Chapter 10.*

Digital   Made up of discrete units—units that can be counted—so it can be subdivided. *Chapter 2.*

Digital audio tape (DAT)   An audio tape format in which audio signals are stored as digital data rather than analog signals. DAT is also used as a backup medium for computer data. *Chapter 3.*

Digital camera   A camera that can capture images as digital data. *Chapter 3.*

Digital image processing software   Software for editing and manipulating scanned photographs and other high-resolution graphical images. *Chapter 7.*

Digital signal   A stream of bits. Contrast with *Analog signal. Chapter 9.*

Digital video   A form of video in which images are stored as digital data rather than as analog signal. Digital video is likely to replace standard analog video in the coming decades. *Chapter 7.*

Digitize   To convert information into a digital form that can be stored in the computer's memory. *Chapter 3.*

Digitized sound   Sound stored as digital data. *Chapters 3, 7.*

Digitized speech   Speech recorded as digital data. *Chapter 12.*

Direct access   See *Random access.*

Direct (dedicated) connection   Connected to a network without the use of modems and telephone lines; a computer with a direct Internet connection has its own IP address so it can take full advantage of Internet services. *Chapter 10.*

Directory In MS-DOS, UNIX, and many other operating systems, a collection of files on a disk, or a list of those files. *Chapter 4.*

Disk drive A device for reading from and writing to a magnetic disk. *Chapter 3.*

Diskette (or floppy disk) A small, magnetically sensitive, flexible plastic wafer housed in a plastic case. A common *random access* storage medium for computer data. *Chapter 3.*

Distance learning The use of information technology to allow students, teachers, and others to communicate over long distances for educational purposes. *Chapter 14.*

Distributed computing The approach to information technology that assumes that computing is distributed throughout the enterprise rather than just in central mainframe computers. Also called *enterprise computing* and *integrated computing*. *Chapter 13.*

Distributed database A database that works with data spread out across a network on several different computers. *Chapter 8.*

Dithering The intermixing of black and white pixels to create the illusion of a true gray tone, or the intermixing of pixels of two or more colors to simulate another color. *Chapter 7.*

Document A file created with a software application. Some documents are designed to be printed on paper; others, like multimedia documents, are intended only to be displayed on computer screens. *Chapter 4.*

Documentation Tutorial manuals, reference manuals, and on-line help files that explain how to use a program. *Chapter 4.*

Document image management system A system that can scan, store, retrieve, and route bit-mapped images of paper documents. *Chapter 13.*

Dot-matrix printer A type of impact printer that prints text and graphics with a matrix of pins that press dots onto the page. *Chapter 3.*

Dots per inch (dpi) The standard measurement of monitor and printer resolution; the density of the *pixels. Chapters 3, 7.*

Double-click To click twice with the *mouse* button. *Chapter 3.*

Download To copy software or data from an information service or bulletin board system computer into the user's computer. *Chapter 9.*

Downloadable font A font whose drawing instructions are stored on the computer and sent to the printer to enable the printer to render the font on paper. *Chapter 5.*

dpi Dots (pixels or printer dots) per inch. Used as a unit of resolution, especially with laser and ink-jet printers. *Chapter 3.*

Drag To move the mouse while holding the mouse button down. *Chapter 3.*

Drag-and-drop Editing feature that allows the user to move selected text or an object by dragging it (with the mouse) from one part of the screen to another. *Chapter 5.*

Drawing software A type of graphics software that stores the document not as a collection of dots but as a collection of lines and shapes. This type of graphics is called *object-oriented (vector) graphics. Chapter 7.*

Drill-and-practice software Computer-aided instruction (CAI) software designed to allow the student to practice skills and lessons at an individualized rate while being drilled by the computer. *Chapter 14.*

DVD (digital video disk) A high-capacity optical disk that can hold a full-length, full-screen motion picture in digital format. DVD format is also used for DVD-ROMs. *Chapter 3.*

DVD-ROM (digital video disk—read-only memory) A high-capacity optical disk that is the same size as standard CD-ROM but has a much greater capacity. DVD-ROM uses the same technology as DVD, which is used to deliver digital movies to consumers. *Chapter 3.*

DynaBook Alan Kay's prediction of a personal computer that could go everywhere with its owner, serving as a calculator, a calendar, a word processor, a graphics machine, a communication device, and a reference tool. Kay's vision is only now, three decades later, appearing on the horizon. *Chapter 16.*

E

Educational simulation A type of courseware that allows the student to explore an artificial environment that is imaginary or based on reality. *Chapter 14.*

Edutainment A type of software that combines education with entertainment. *Chapter 14.*

Electronic cottage Futurist Alvin Toffler's term describing a home equipped with information technology that allows the occupant to work at home. *Chapter 13.*

Electronic funds transfer (EFT) The transfer of money through electronic networks that connect banks and other institutions. *Chapter 9.*

Electronic mail (e-mail) Messages transmitted between users on a computer network. *Chapter 9.*

Electronic organizer See *Personal information manager (PIM).*

Electronic sweatshop Writer Barbara Garson's term for data processing workplaces with working conditions reminiscent of the oppressive factory sweatshops of the 19th century. *Chapter 13.*

Embedded AI Software and hardware products that incorporate artificial intelligence technology. *Chapter 12.*

Embedded computer A computer built into a consumer product or machine. *Chapter 1.*

Emulation The process of making one type of computer or terminal imitate or function like another. *Chapter 4.*

Emulator A software or hardware product that allows one type of computer to imitate another. *Chapter 4.*

Encrypt To scramble the contents of a message using an encryption key, which is like a secret password. *Chapter 15.*

Encryption The process of encoding data to prevent unauthorized access. *Chapter 15.*

Encryption key A secret numerical code used for encryption of data. *Chapter 15.*

Enter or Return key On a standard keyboard, the Enter key sends a signal telling the computer or terminal to move the cursor to the beginning of the next line on the screen. For many applications, this key also "enters" the line just typed, telling the computer to process it. *Chapter 3.*

Enterprise computing See *Distributed computing.*

Equation solver A spreadsheet feature that allows the user to define an equation, enter a target value, and let the computer determine the necessary data values. *Chapter 6.*

Ergonomics   The science of designing work environments that allow people and things to interact efficiently and safely. Sometimes called human engineering. *Chapter 3.*

Error message   A message from software telling the user that something has gone wrong. *Chapter 4.*

Execute   To run a program. *Chapter 11.*

Expert system   A software program designed to replicate the decision-making process of a human expert. *Chapter 12.*

Expert system shell   A generic expert system containing human interfaces and inference engines but no data. *Chapter 12.*

Export   To transmit data to another program. *Chapter 8.*

F

Facsimile (fax)   A technology that allows images of paper documents to be transmitted through telephone lines to a destination where they can be printed or displayed on a computer screen. *Chapter 9.*

FAQs (frequently asked questions)   A list of common questions and answers related to a particular topic. Internet newsgroups and other network discussion groups commonly maintain FAQs so on-line discussions won't be cluttered with the same old questions and answers. *Chapter 10.*

Fax modem   A modem that allows a personal computer to send and receive facsmilie (fax) documents. *Chapter 9.*

Feasibility study   A study performed by a systems analyst to help management decide whether to continue with the systems analysis after the investigation phase is complete. *Chapter 11.*

Feedback loop   A communication loop through which two interrelated systems communicate with each other; each system reacts to input from the other by modifying the output it sends to the other. *Chapter 6.*

Fiber optic cable   A high-bandwidth cable that uses light waves to transmit up to 500 million bits per second. *Chapter 9.*

Field   An individual component of a database or hypermedia record. For example, First Name, Last Name, and Phone might be fields in telephone directory database. *Chapter 8.*

Field type   A category describing a field and the type of data it will accept. *Chapter 8.*

File   An organized collection of information, such as a term paper or a set of names and addresses, stored in a form the computer can read. In a database, a file is a collection of records. *Chapters 2, 8.*

File manager   A *database program* that allows users to work with one file at a time. *Chapter 8.*

File server   A computer that serves as a storehouse for software and data shared by several users on a network. *Chapter 9.*

Financial management software   See *Accounting and financial management software.*

Find command   A command used to locate a particular word or string of characters in a document. *Chapter 5.*

Firewall   A gateway configured to guard against unauthorized access to an internal network; the firewall's locked gate is only opened for information packets that pass one or more security inspections. *Chapter 15.*

Firmware   A software program stored on a ROM (read-only memory) chip. *Chapter 1.*

First-generation computers   An era of computers built around vacuum tubes. *Chapter 1.*

Flash memory   A type of memory chip that can be erased and rewritten like RAM but that retains its contents without electrical current like ROM. *Chapter 16.*

Folder   A visual metaphor used on Macintosh, Windows, and other graphical user interfaces to represent a collection of files or applications. *Chapter 4.*

Font   In the language of typesetters, a size and style of typeface. For example, the typeface known as Helvetica includes many fonts, one of which is 12-point Helvetica bold. Many people use the terms *font* and *typeface* interchangeably. *Chapter 5.*

Footer   A block that appears at the bottom of every page, displaying repetitive information like chapter titles, author names, and automatically calculated page numbers. *Chapter 5.*

Format   Factors determining the way a document looks when displayed on the screen or printed. *Chapter 5.*

Formula   A step-by-step procedure for calculating a desired number in a spreadsheet or database. *Chapter 6.*

Formula bar   The long window above the worksheet in a spreadsheet application. The formula bar displays the formula or value entered in the *active cell*. Also called the console. *Chapter 6.*

FORTRAN (FORmula TRANslation)   The first commercial high-level language designed at IBM in the 1950s to solve science and engineering problems. Many scientists and engineers still use a modernized version of FORTRAN. *Chapter 11.*

Fourth-generation computers   Computers built around microprocessors. *Chapter 1.*

Fourth-generation language (4GL)   A nonprocedural language that uses English-like phrases and sentences to issue instructions. *Chapter 11.*

Fractal   An intricate mathematical object, often rendered as a computer graphic, whose dimension is fractional. *Chapter 6.*

Frame   One still picture in a video or animated sequence. *Chapter 7.*

Freenet   An inexpensive or free network, available in some cities, that provides community access to on-line forums, local services, and the Internet. *Chapter 10.*

Front-end   A term sometimes applied to software that serves as a user interface for other software. *Chapter 7.*

FTP (file transfer protocol)   A protocol used to transfer files from one computer to another through the Internet or an intranet. *Chapter 10.*

Full-access dial-up connection   A type of Internet connection that allows a computer connected via high-speed modem and phone line to temporarily have full Internet access and an IP address. *Chapter 10.*

Full justification   Having both margins smooth. *Chapter 5.*

Function   In a spreadsheet or database program, a predefined set of instructions that performs a common calculation when its name is included in a formula. *Chapter 6.*

Function keys (f-keys)   Programmable keys, labeled F1, F2, and so on, that send signals to the computer with no inherent meaning. The function of these keys depends on the software being used. *Chapter 3.*

G

Gallium arsenide (GaAs)   A promising experimental technology for computer chips that can move impulses up to ten times faster and emit less heat than their silicon counterparts. *Chapter 16.*

Gateway   A computer that serves as a bridge between computer networks. *Chapter 10.*

GB (gigabyte)   Approximately 1000 megabytes. *Chapter 2.*

Geographical information system (GIS)   A mapping program or system that allows an organization to combine tables of data, such as customer sales lists, with demographic information from the Census Bureau and other sources. *Chapter 8.*

GIGO   Acronym for garbage in, garbage out. *Chapter 6.*

GoTo statement   A statement for transferring control to other parts of a program. *Chapter 11.*

Grammar and style checker   Software that checks text for spelling errors, errors of context, common grammatical errors, and stylistic foibles. *Chapter 5.*

Graphical user interface (GUI)   A user interface based on graphical images rather than characters. *Chapter 4.*

Graphics tablet   A flat pressure-sensitive input device used by graphic artists and others; as a stylus is moved across its surface, the tablet sends signals telling the location and pressure of a stylus. *Chapter 3.*

Gray-scale graphic   A graphic that allows each pixel to appear as black, white, or one of several shades of gray. *Chapter 7.*

Gray-scale monitor   A computer monitor that can display only black, white, and shades of gray. *Chapter 3.*

Groupware   Software designed to be used by workgroups rather than individuals. *Chapters 5, 9, 13.*

GUI   See *Graphical user interface.*

H

Hacker   Originally a person who enjoyed learning details of computer systems and writing clever programs, referred to as hacks. Today *hacker* commonly refers to a person who breaks into computer systems without authorization. *Chapter 15.*

Hand-held (palmtop) computer   A computer small enough to be tucked into a jacket pocket. *Chapter 1.*

Hard copy   Printout on paper of any information that can be displayed on the computer screen. *Chapter 3.*

Hard disk   A rigid, magnetically sensitive disk that spins rapidly and continuously inside the computer chassis or in a separate box connected to the computer housing. *Chapter 3.*

Hardware   The physical parts of the computer system. *Chapter 1.*

Header   A block that appears at the top of every page, displaying repetitive information like chapter titles, author names, and automatically calculated page numbers. *Chapter 5.*

Help screen   On-line documentation. *Chapter 4.*

Heuristic   A rule of thumb. Heuristics are common in artificial intelligence software. *Chapter 12.*

Hexadecimal   Base-16 number system. *Chapter 11.*

High-level language   A programming language that is easier for programmers to use and understand than machine language or assembly language. Examples include BASIC and C. *Chapter 11.*

High-performance computer   See *Supercomputer.*

Home page   A common name for a document displayed on the World Wide Web; also called a *Web page. Chapter 10.*

Homing guidance system   A system used by a missile to track a moving target without human help, using infrared heat-seeking devices or visual pattern recognition technology. *Chapter 13.*

Host system   A computer that provides services to multiple users on a network. *Chapter 9.*

HTML (Hypertext Markup Language)   A language that describes the format, layout, and logical structure of a hypermedia document. HTML is the language used to describe most pages on the World Wide Web. *Chapter 10.*

Human-centered system   A system designed to retain and enhance human skills and control, rather than taking them away. *Chapter 13.*

Human interface   The part of an expert system that allows users to interact with the system. *Chapter 12.*

Human management   See *Ergonomics.*

HyperCard   The first program to popularize the concept of hypermedia. *Chapter 7.*

Hypermedia   Media that allow users to explore documents in nonlinear ways by choosing from multiple paths through information. *Chapter 7.*

Hypertext   A method of storing textual information that allows it to be linked in nonsequential ways; text-based hypermedia. *Chapter 7.*

I

Icon   A picture that represents files, disks, and other items in a graphical user interface. *Chapter 4.*

Idea processor   Software that facilitates arranging and rearranging ideas, typically in outline form. *Chapter 5.*

Image analysis   The process of identifying objects and shapes in a photograph, drawing, video, or other visual image. *Chapter 12.*

Image compression software   Software to reduce the size of a data file by eliminating redundant and noncritical data. *Chapter 7.*

Image processing software   Software designed to allow users to manipulate photographs and other high-resolution images. *Chapter 7.*

Impact printer   A printer that forms images by physically striking paper, ribbon, and print hammer together, the way a typewriter does. *Chapter 3.*

Import   To move data into a program from another program or source. *Chapter 8.*

Industrial economy   An economy dominated by factory work. The industrial economy controlled Europe and America from the late 18th century and lasted until this century. *Chapter 13.*

Inference engine   The part of an expert system that applies user input to the knowledge base to produce the requested expert advice. *Chapter 12.*

Information   According to one definition, information means communication that has value because it informs. By this definition, computers turn raw data into useful information. In the language of communication and information theory, the term *information* can be applied to just about anything that can be communicated, whether it has value or not. This broader definition is more useful in a world of interconnected computers where the output from one computer might be the input to another. *Chapter 2.*

Information economy   An economy dominated by information work. In our 20th-century information economy, clerks outnumber factory workers and farmers. *Chapter 13.*

Information infrastructure   The computers and networks that form the basis of the information economy. *Chapter 16.*

Information overload   Occurs when information technology provides too much information to use effectively. *Chapter 13.*

Information superhighway   The popular name for the likely successor to the Internet; it will serve as a conduit for electronic conferences, interactive TV, and a wealth of other information applications. (Sometimes refers to today's Internet.) *Chapter 10.*

Information system   The collection of people, machines, data, and methods organized to accomplish specific functions and to solve specific problems. *Chapter 11.*

Information systems manager   A manager whose job is to integrate an organization's computers into a single, workable system. Also called an IS manager, information technology manager, or IT manager. *Chapter 13.*

Infrastructure   The framework that is laid first so future economic activity can take advantage of it. *Chapter 16.*

Ink-jet printer   A type of printer that sprays ink directly onto paper. *Chapter 3.*

Input   Raw data put into a computer system for processing. *Chapter 1.*

Input device   A computer peripheral that accepts raw data and puts it in a machine-readable form for the computer. *Chapter 2.*

Insert   To type text somewhere inside a document without overwriting any other text. *Chapter 5.*

Inserting text   Placing text in a document without overwriting any of the surrounding text. *Chapter 5.*

Insertion bar   A flashing cursor indicating the current location in the document. *Chapter 5.*

Instruction set   A vocabulary of instructions that can be executed by the processor. *Chapter 16.*

Integrated circuit   A chip containing hundreds, thousands, or even millions of transistors. *Chapter 1.*

Integrated computing   See *Distributed computing.*

Integrated software   A program that includes several applications designed to work well together. *Chapter 4.*

Intellectual property   A legal category that includes the rights to the results of intellectual activity in the arts, science, and industry. *Chapter 15.*

Interactive fiction   A type of story game with a natural-language or graphical interface that gives players some control over plot. *Chapter 14.*

Interactive movie   An animated or video feature in which one or more characters are controlled by the viewers. *Chapter 14.*

Interactive multimedia   Media that allow the viewer/listener to take an active part in the experience. *Chapter 7.*

Interactive processing   A type of processing that allows users to interact with data through terminals, viewing and changing values in real time. Contrast with *Batch processing. Chapter 8.*

Interactive spelling checker   A type of spelling checker that checks each word as it is typed. *Chapter 5.*

Interapplication communication   Software feature that allows changes created in one document to be automatically reflected in other documents. *Chapter 4.*

Internationalization   Converting a computer program for use in various countries around the world. *Chapter 2.*

Internet   A massive interconnected group of networks linking academic, research, government, and commercial institutions. *Chapters 1, 10.*

Internet service provider   A company that provides Internet access to users. *Chapter 10.*

Internet terminal   A low-cost, stripped-down computer designed specifically for accessing the Internet. *Chapter 1.*

Internetworking   Connecting different types of networks and computer systems. *Chapter 10.*

Interpreter   A translator program that translates and transmits each program statement individually into machine language. *Chapter 11.*

Intranet   A self-contained intra-organizational network that is based on the same technology as the Internet. Intranet Web pages, newsgroups, electronic mail, and other Internet-style services are designed mainly for use within the organization. *Chapter 14.*

IP address   A unique address assigned to every host computer on the Internet. *Chapter 10.*

ISDN (Integrated Services Digital Network)   A type of network that links telephones, computers, fax machines, television, and even mail in a single digital system. *Chapter 9.*

IS manager   See *Information systems manager.*

Italics   A style of type used for emphasis, *like this. Chapter 5.*

IT manager   See *Information systems manager.*

Java   An object-oriented programming language, developed by Sun Microsystems, that is quickly becoming the standard programming language for creating cross-platform Internet applications. *Chapter 10.*

Jobless growth   Occurs when productivity increases, not because of the work people do but because of the work of machines. *Chapter 13.*

Joystick   A type of input device used mostly for video games. *Chapter 3.*

Justification   The alignment of text on a line. Four justification choices are commonly available: left justification, right justification, full justification, and centered justification. *Chapter 5.*

K

K (kilobyte)   1024 bytes. *Chapter 2.*

Kerning   The spacing between each pair of letters. *Chapter 5.*

Key   In cryptography, a kind of password (usually a huge prime number) used to encrypt or decrypt messages. In databases, a field or column used as a basis for sorting or identifying records. *Chapter 15.*

Keyboard   The standard input device for entering text and numbers into a computer. *Chapter 3.*

Key field   A database field that is used to tie information in different files together. *Chapter 8.*

Knowledge   Information that incorporates the relationships between facts. *Chapter 12.*

Knowledge base   A collection of information that includes facts and a system for determining and changing the relationship between those facts. *Chapter 12.*

Knowledge-based system   A system like an expert system except that it draws on sources other than experts for its knowledge base. In practice the terms *expert system* and *knowledge-based system* are often used interchangeably. *Chapter 12.*

Knowledge engineer   A specialist who interviews and observes experts and painstakingly converts their words and actions into a knowledge base. *Chapter 12.*

L

Label   In a *spreadsheet,* a text entry that provides information for human readers. *Chapter 6.*

Laptop computer   A lightweight battery-powered machine with fold-away screen that, when closed, resembles a briefcase or notebook. *Chapter 1.*

Laser printer   A type of printer that uses laser technology to produce high-quality printouts of text and graphics. *Chapter 3.*

Latin 1   A standard character set that uses the code values that can fit in a single byte. *Chapter 2.*

LCD (liquid crystal display)   Flat-panel displays found in portable computers, calculators, and other electronic devices. *Chapter 3.*

Leading   The spacing between lines of text. *Chapter 5.*

Left justification   Having a smooth left margin and ragged right margin. *Chapter 5.*

License, software   The agreement establishing the conditions under which a software user may use the software. *Chapter 4.*

Line chart   The type of chart that uses a line or lines to show trends or relationships over time. *Chapter 6.*

Line printer   The type of impact printer used to produce large printouts by rapidly hammering characters line by line onto a page. *Chapter 3.*

Links   A connection between two documents (such as spreadsheets) so that a change in one affects the other. Also, a connection in a hypermedia document that allows users to move rapidly to another part of the document. *Chapters 6, 7.*

LISP (LISt Processing)   A symbol-manipulation programming language used for *artificial intelligence* applications. *Chapter 11.*

Load   To copy information, usually a program, into memory so the CPU can access it. A program must be loaded before it can be run. *Chapter 2.*

Local area network (LAN)   A network in which the computers are close to each other, usually in the same building. *Chapter 9.*

Localization   Ensuring that a program sold internationally can be adapted to different locales that may use the same language. For example, the United Kingdom, United States, Canada, Australia, and New Zealand all use English but have slightly different conventions for spelling, punctuation, currency symbols, and so forth. *Chapter 2.*

Logic bomb   A program triggered to act when it detects some sequence of events or after a certain amount of time elapses. *Chapter 15.*

Logic error   An error in the logical structure that causes differences between what the program is supposed to do and what it actually does. *Chapter 11.*

Login name   A name assigned to a computer account to identify the user when logging on and communicating with others. *Chapter 9.*

LOGO   A programming language designed for children. *Chapters 11, 14.*

Loop   See *Repetition control structure.*

Lossless   A type of data compression system that preserves the original information with 100 percent accuracy; no data is lost or blurred out when the information is compressed. Contrast with *Lossy. Chapter 7.*

Lossy   A type of data compression system that loses some of the original information to gain greater compression. Contrast with *Lossless. Chapter 7.*

Low-level language   Machine language or some other language that requires the programmer to use the extremely detailed logic of machine language. *Chapter 11.*

M

Machine language   The language used by a computer to processes instructions. All computer programs must ultimately be translated into machine-language instructions made up of zeros and ones before they can be run. *Chapters 4, 11.*

Machine learning   The ability of a computer program to learn from experience. *Chapter 12.*

Macintosh operating system   The first widely available operating system to use a graphical user interface. *Chapter 4.*

Macro   A custom-designed procedure that automates repetitive tasks. *Chapter 6.*

Macro (scripting) language   A language, usually built into an application, utility, or operating system, that allows users to create programs, called *macros,* that automate repetitive tasks. Sometimes called a scripting language. *Chapter 11.*

Magnetic disk   A type of random access storage medium that records information magnetically. *Chapter 3.*

Magnetic-ink character reader   An input device that reads the magnetic characters printed on checks. *Chapter 3.*

Magnetic tape   A magnetic medium for recording information sequentially. *Chapter 3.*

Magneto-optical disk   A random access storage medium that uses a combination of magnetic disk technology and optical disk technology. *Chapter 3.*

Mailing list   A shared mailing address on the Internet that allows members to participate in e-mail discussion groups on special interest topics. *Chapter 10.*

Mail merge   To combine a word processor document with a database file to produce personalized form letters and similar documents. *Chapters 5, 8.*

Mainframe computer   A room-sized machine designed to process large quantities of data quickly. *Chapter 1.*

Maintenance upgrade   A software upgrade that corrects bugs and makes minor changes in the program. *Chapter 11.*

Management information systems (MIS)   A system that includes, among other things, procedures for collecting data, a database for storing data, and software tools for analyzing data and producing a variety of reports for different levels of management. The term also applies to a branch of computer science that works with such systems. *Chapter 13.*

Master page   In desktop publishing, a template that controls the general layout and includes common elements (margins, column guides, page numbers, graphic embellishments) for all left- and right-facing pages. *Chapter 5.*

Mathematics processing software   Software designed to make it easier for mathematicians to create, manipulate, and solve equations. *Chapter 6.*

MB (megabyte)   Approximately 1000 K, or 1 million bytes. *Chapter 2.*

Megahertz   One million cycles per second. A common measurement for a computer's clock speed. *Chapter 16.*

Memory   Electronic circuitry for storing programs and data. *Chapter 2.*

Memory management   The process of allocating memory and keeping programs in memory apart. *Chapter 4.*

Memory-mapped I/O   Using memory addresses to access or communicate with devices outside the CPU. *Chapter 2.*

Menu   An on-screen list of commands or options that can be selected by the user. *Chapter 4.*

Menu bar   A bar at the top of the screen or *window* containing pull-down menus. *Chapter 4.*

Menu-driven interface   An interface that allows users to choose commands from on-screen lists called *menus. Chapter 4.*

Method   In object-oriented programming, a certain task that each object can perform. *Chapter 11.*

Microcomputer   See *Personal computer.*

Microcomputer revolution   The revolution, caused by the invention of the microprocessor, that resulted in the widespread use of microcomputers in offices, factories, homes, and schools. *Chapter 1.*

Micromachines   Futuristic machines on the scale of a millionth of a meter. *Chapter 16.*

Microprocessor   A computer housed on a silicon chip. *Chapter 1.*

Microsensor   A microscopic device that can detect pressure, temperature, and other environmental qualities. *Chapter 16.*

Microsoft Windows   The most widely used graphical operating system for IBM-compatible computers. *Chapter 4.*

Microtechnology   Technology that allows researchers to develop micromachines. *Chapter 16.*

MIDI (Musical Instrument Digital Interface)   A standard interface that allows electronic instruments and computers to communicate with each other and work together. *Chapter 7.*

MIPS (millions of instructions per second)   A measure of CPU speed. *Chapter 16.*

Modeling, computer   The use of computers to create abstract models of objects, organisms, organizations, and processes. *Chapter 6.*

Modem   Short for modulate/demodulate. A hardware device that converts digital data into analog signals that can be transmitted over telephone lines and converts analog signals back into digital data. *Chapter 9.*

Modula-2   A powerful and complex programming language related to Pascal. *Chapter 11.*

Module (subprogram)   A set of related statements that perform a task as part of a larger program. *Chapter 11.*

Monitor   A computer display device that allows the user to view information on a screen. *Chapter 3.*

Monitoring, computer   Using computer technology to track, record, and evaluate worker performance, often without the knowledge of the worker. *Chapter 13.*

Monochrome graphic   A type of graphic in which each *pixel* can display one of two possible colors—commonly black or white. *Chapter 7.*

Monochrome monitor   A monitor that can display a single color on a background of another color, such as white on black. *Chapter 3.*

Morph   A video clip in which one image metamorphosizes into another. *Chapter 7.*

Mouse   A hand-held input device that, when moved around on a desktop or table, moves a pointer around the computer screen. *Chapter 3.*

Motherboard   The name sometimes given to the computer's main circuit board. *Chapter 2.*

Moving text   Transporting a block of text from one part of a document to another, or from one document to another. *Chapter 5.*

MS-DOS (Microsoft Disk Operating System)   The most widely used general-purpose operating system in the world; the standard operating system for the majority of IBM-compatible computers. Sometimes called just DOS. *Chapter 4.*

Multimedia   A combination of hardware and software that can produce output that combines several media, including text, graphics, animation, video, music, voice, and sound effects. *Chapter 7.*

Multimedia authoring software   Application software that can be used to combine graphics, text, video clips, animation, and sounds along with controls that allow users to navigate through the finished multimedia document. *Chapter 7.*

Multitasking   The ability of a computer's operating system to run several programs concurrently. *Chapter 4.*

Music publishing software   Software that can turn musical data into a printed score, ready for publishing. *Chapter 7.*

N

Nanomachines Predicted machines of the future that will be so small (on a scale of a few billionths of a meter) that they will have to be constructed atom by atom using processes drawn from particle physics, biophysics, and molecular biology. *Chapter 16.*

Nanotechnology The manufacture of nanomachines. *Chapter 16.*

Narrowcasting The delivery of news, entertainment, and other information in customized packages aimed at narrow groups or individuals. *Chapter 14.*

National Information Infrastructure (NII) A U.S. government plan to connect computers, telephones, televisions, and information appliances of all types, providing "universal service" and affordable access, funded mostly by private enterprise. *Chapter 10.*

Natural language An everyday human language like English or Japanese. *Chapter 4.*

Navigate To move the cursor around in a document. *Chapter 5.*

Net The informal name of the worldwide system of networks and gateways that includes the Internet and all the outernets. *Chapter 10.*

Netiquette Informal rules and guidelines of acceptable behavior on the Internet. *Chapter 10.*

Network A computer system that links together two or more computers. *Chapter 9.*

Network administrator A computer professional whose job involves developing and maintaining a network. *Chapter 9.*

Network interface card (NIC) A card for connecting a personal computer to a network. *Chapter 9.*

Network license A license that reduces the costs for multiple copies or removes restrictions on software copying and use at a network site. *Chapter 9.*

Network operating system (NOS) Software that coordinates the details of network communication. *Chapter 9.*

Network revolution The period in the 1990s characterized by explosive growth of networks and network connections. *Chapter 1.*

Neural network (or neural net) Distributed parallel computing systems inspired by the structure of the human brain. A neural network uses thousands of processors called neurons to learn. *Chapter 12.*

Neuron A processor in a neural network. *Chapter 12.*

Newsgroup A public discussion group allowing Internet and intranet users to read and post messages related to a particular subject. Hundreds of Usenet newsgroups are on the Internet, covering a vast array of subjects. *Chapter 10.*

News reader A client program that allows a user to read and post messages on network newsgroups. *Chapter 10.*

Node A computer or shared peripheral on a network. *Chapter 9.*

Nonimpact printer A type of printer that produces images without striking the page; includes laser printers and ink-jet printers. *Chapter 3.*

Nonprocedural language A language that allows programmers to program computers by stating the task to be accomplished rather than by listing the necessary steps to accomplish the task. *Chapter 11.*

Nonsequential A description of media (like hypermedia) that allow users to choose from many different paths through information. *Chapter 7.*

Nonvolatile memory Memory that can't be erased. *Chapter 2.*

Notebook computer A lightweight battery-operated computer that is about the size of a three-ring notebook. *Chapter 1.*

Numeric field A database field that can only contain numbers. *Chapter 8.*

O

Object In object-oriented programming, a part of a computer system that often models an object in the real world. An object has certain properties and contains its own methods and data. *Chapter 11.*

Object-oriented database A database that stores software objects containing procedures (instructions) along with data. Object-oriented databases often are used in conjunction with object-oriented programming languages. *Chapter 8.*

Object-oriented (vector) graphics A type of graphics in which pictures are stored as collections of lines, shapes, and other objects, rather than as bit maps. Contrast with *Bit-mapped graphics. Chapter 7.*

Object-oriented programming (OOP) A type of programming in which a program is a collection of objects that contain both data and instructions, and these objects can interact with each other. *Chapter 11.*

On-line Connected to the computer system and ready to communicate. *Chapter 9.*

On-line database A commercial, public, or private database that can be accessed through telecommunication lines. *Chapter 9.*

On-line documentation Help screens and tutorials that can be displayed on the computer screen. *Chapter 4.*

On-line information service The name sometimes applied to America Online, CompuServe, and other service providers that offer electronic mail, teleconferencing, research facilities, Internet access, and other services. *Chapter 9.*

Open A command for loading a document, copying it from a disk, into the computer's memory. *Chapter 4.*

Opening a file To load a file into the computer's memory, using an application. *Chapter 4.*

Open standards Software and hardware specifications that are made freely available to all competing manufacturers rather than being owned by a particular company. *Chapter 10.*

Open system A computer system with slots and ports that can be customized. *Chapter 12.*

Operating system (OS) A system of continually running resource management programs that keep hardware running efficiently and make the process of communication with that hardware easier. *Chapter 4.*

Optical character recognition (OCR) The use of a special input device and software to read characters and convert them into electrical signals. *Chapters 3, 12.*

Optical computer   A type of experimental computer that transmits information in light waves rather than electrical pulses. *Chapter 16.*

Optical disk   High-capacity storage medium that uses laser beams to store read and write information on the disk surface. *Chapter 3.*

Optical disk drive   A drive that uses laser beams rather than magnets to read and write bits of information on a disk's surface. *Chapter 3.*

Optical-mark reader   Input device that uses reflected light to determine the location of pencil marks on standardized test answer sheets and similar forms. *Chapter 3.*

Outliner   A type of software (sometimes called an idea processor) designed to make it easy to build, organize, and edit hierarchical outlines. Many word processors include outliners. *Chapter 5.*

Outlining   Arranging information into hierarchies or levels of ideas. *Chapter 5.*

Output   Processed information sent from the computer through an output device. *Chapter 1.*

Output device   A device like a printer or a monitor that makes processed information available for use outside the computer. *Chapter 2.*

Packet switching   The standard technique used to send information over the Internet. A message is broken into packets that travel independently from network to network toward their common destination, where they are reunited. *Chapter 10.*

Pad   The name given by researchers to experimental flat-panel computers that are like smart notepads. *Chapter 16.*

Page-description language   A language for describing text fonts, illustrations, and other elements of the printed page. *Chapter 7.*

Page-layout software   Desktop publishing software used to combine the various source documents into a coherent, visually appealing publication. *Chapter 5.*

Painting software   Software that allows the user to "paint" pixels on the screen with a pointing device; bit-mapped graphics software. *Chapter 7.*

Palette   A small window that floats in front of a document window, providing quick access to tools. *Chapter 7.*

Paperless office   A predicted office of the future in which magnetic and optical archives will replace reference books and file cabinets, electronic communication will replace letters and memos, and information utilities will replace newspapers and other periodicals. *Chapter 13.*

Paradigm shift   A change in thinking that results in a new way of seeing the world. *Chapter 13.*

Parallel port   A socket on a computer chassis commonly used to connect printers and other external peripherals to a computer. Bits can pass through a parallel port in groups of 8, 16, or 32. *Chapter 9.*

Parallel processing   Using multiple processors to divide jobs into pieces and work simultaneously on the pieces. *Chapter 2.*

Parsing program (or **parser**)   Software that analyzes sentence structure and identifies parts of speech. *Chapter 12.*

Pascal   A high-level language widely used for programming instruction. *Chapter 11.*

Password   A secret string of letters and numbers that a user types to gain access to a computer system. *Chapters 9, 15.*

Path animation tool   An animation tool that records the movement of visual objects as the artist drags them around the screen, and then plays back motions on command. *Chapter 7.*

Path name   A string of characters that tells the computer where to find the *file* on the disk. *Chapter 4.*

Pattern recognition   The branch of artificial intelligence that involves identifying recurring patterns in input data with the goal of understanding or categorizing that input. *Chapter 12.*

PC card   A credit-card-sized card that can be inserted into a slot to expand memory or add a peripheral to a computer; commonly used in portable computers. (Formerly called PCMCIA card.) *Chapter 2.*

Peer-to-peer model   A model for small networks that allows every computer on the network to be both client and server; every user can make files publicly available to other users on the network. *Chapter 9.*

Pen-based computer   A machine that accept input from a stylus applied directly to a flat-panel screen. *Chapter 3.*

Peripheral   A device connected to a computer, allowing it to communicate with the outside world or store information for later use. *Chapters 2, 3.*

Personal communicator   A portable device that typically combines a cellular phone, a fax modem, and other communication equipment in a lightweight, wireless box that resembles a pen-based computer. Similar to a *personal digital assistant (PDA). Chapter 9.*

Personal computer (PC)   A desktop computer designed for use by an individual rather than a group of users and as powerful as many of the room-sized computers. *Chapter 1.*

Personal digital assistant (PDA)   A portable (usually handheld, pen-based) device designed to serve as an electronic organizer, notebook, appointment book, and communication device. Similar to a *personal communicator. Chapter 9.*

Personal information manager (PIM)   A specialized database program designed to automate address book management, appointment calendars, to-do lists, and other personal record keeping. Sometimes called an electronic organizer. *Chapter 8.*

Phonetic input   Used sometimes in computer programs for human languages whose written character sets are poorly suited to the limited keys of a computer keyboard. The pronunciation of a word is typed using a standard keyboard, and the program responds by displaying the word(s), in the language's native script, that have that pronunciation. *Chapter 2.*

Phototypesetting machine   An expensive output device used in publishing to print documents at 1200 *dots per inch (dpi)* or higher. *Chapter 5.*

Pie chart   A type of chart designed to show the relative proportions of the parts to a whole. *Chapter 6.*

Pipeline   A pathway of execution within the CPU. Modern CPUs contain several pipelines so that several instructions can be executed simultaneously. *Chapter 2.*

Pixel   A picture element (dot) on a computer screen or printout. *Chapters 3, 7.*

Platform   The hardware on which the software runs. Sometimes refers to the hardware and operating system together. *Chapter 4.*

Plotter An output device that draws by moving the pen and/or the paper in response to computer commands. *Chapter 3.*

Point-of-sale (POS) terminal A terminal in a store that accepts input from each sale and passes it on to a computer. *Chapter 3.*

Point size A measurement of type size equal to 1/72 inch. *Chapter 5.*

Pop-up menu A menu that pops into view when you click on a particular word or icon on the screen. *Chapter 7.*

Port A socket on the outside of the computer chassis that allows information to pass in and out. *Chapters 2, 9.*

Portable computer A lightweight, battery-powered computer designed for mobility. *Chapter 1.*

Porting The often difficult task of converting a computer program so that it will run on a different kind of computer/operating system. *Chapter 11.*

Post-industrial economy See *Information economy.*

PostScript A standard page-description language for describing text fonts, illustrations, and other elements of the printed page. *Chapter 7.*

Prefetch unit The part of the CPU that gets instructions from memory several steps ahead of the currently executing instruction to ensure that the CPU is not left waiting for another insturction. *Chapter 2*

Presentation graphics software Software designed to automate the creation of visual aids for lectures, workshops, training sessions, sales demonstrations, and other presentations. *Chapter 7.*

Primary storage Computer memory. *Chapter 2.*

Printer An output device that allows a computer user to print information on paper. Printers fall into two broad categories: *impact printers* and *nonimpact printers. Chapter 3.*

Printer font A font whose drawing description is contained within the printer. Most printers are dedicated computer systems with their own RAM and ROM; printer fonts are contained within the printer's ROM. *Chapter 5.*

Procedural language A programming language that allows programmers to construct step-by-step procedures that tell the computer how to accomplish tasks. *Chapter 11.*

Processing Performing arithmetic or logical (decision-making) operations on information. *Chapters 1, 2, 4.*

Processor See *Central processing unit.*

Program A series of step-by-step instructions that directs a computer to perform specific tasks and solve specific problems. Also, to write programs. *Chapters 1, 11.*

Programmer A person who writes programs. *Chapter 11.*

Programming The process of writing programs. *Chapter 11.*

Programming environment A programmer's software workspace, including a *text editor, a compiler, a debugger,* and a variety of other programming utilities. *Chapter 11.*

Programming language A set of rules that tells the computer what to do in response to program instructions. *Chapters 4, 11.*

Program verification The process of mathematically proving the correctness of a program; difficult for all but the simplest programs. *Chapter 11.*

Project management software Software to help coordinate, schedule, and track complex work projects. *Chapter 13.*

PROLOG (PROgramming LOGic) A popular language for artificial intelligence programming. *Chapter 11.*

Prompt A symbol on the screen signifying that the computer is waiting for the user to type a command. *Chapter 4.*

Property An attribute or characteristic of an object in OOP. *Chapter 11.*

Proportionally spaced font A font that allow more horizontal space for wide characters than for narrow characters. *Chapter 5.*

Protocol A set of rules for the exchange of data between a terminal and a computer or between two computers. *Chapter 9.*

Prototype A limited working system or subsystem to give users and management an idea of how the completed system will work. *Chapter 11.*

Pseudocode A cross between a computer language and plain English used to write algorithms. *Chapter 11.*

Public domain software Software that can legally be copied, used, and shared without being purchased. *Chapter 4.*

Public key cryptosystem A cryptosystem where every user has two keys: a published, public key that anyone can look up, and a private, secret key that the user reveals to no one. Messages encrypted with the public key can only be decrypted with the private key. *Chapter 15.*

Pull-down menu A menu that allows the user to select a command by "pulling down" the list of choices from the menu title using a pointing device, such as a *mouse. Chapter 4.*

Q

Quantitative graphics Charts and graphs generated from numbers. *Chapter 6.*

Query A request for information from a database. *Chapter 8.*

Query language A language that allows a user to request information from a database with carefully worded English-like questions. *Chapter 8.*

R

RAM (random access memory) A type of primary storage that can be used to store program instructions and data temporarily. The contents of RAM can be changed. *Chapter 2.*

Random access Immediate access to any information on a storage device, regardless of its location. Also called direct access. Contrast with *Sequential access. Chapter 3.*

Range A rectangular block of cells in a spreadsheet. *Chapter 6.*

Raster device A device, such as a monitor or laser printer, that produces images that are actually composed of many tiny dots or pixels. *Chapter 3.*

Real-time processing Processing changes in information states as soon as they occur in the real world rather than saving them for later batch processing. *Chapter 8.*

Real-time communication Communication that occurs in real time, so all participants can receive and respond to messages as soon as they are sent; contrast with *Asynchronous communication. Chapter 10.*

Real-time teleconference A teleconference that allows each participant to view and respond to every contribution as it is entered. *Chapter 9.*

Record A collection of related information in a database file, typically the information relating to one person, product, or event. *Chapter 8.*

Record matching Using a common field, such as one containing Social Security numbers, to combine information from two different data files. *Chapter 8.*

Recursion The ability of a program or procedure to call, or refer to, itself. *Chapter 12.*

Regional work center A shared office outside of a major urban center allowing workers to commute to a smaller office closer to their neighborhoods. *Chapter 13.*

Register A section of the work area within the CPU where instructions and data are stored during execution of a particular instruction; a typical CPU has several registers. *Chapter 2.*

Relational database Technically, a database whose data is organized in table form according to a particular set of rules. In popular usage, a database that allows files to be related to each other so that changes in one file can automatically be reflected in other files. *Chapter 8.*

Remote login The ability of a user on one system to access other host systems across a network. *Chapter 10.*

Removable media Storage media can be removed from the computer and transported to other machines or stored for later use; includes diskettes and many higher-capacity media. *Chapter 3.*

Repetition control structure A looping mechanism that allows a group of steps to be repeated several times, usually until some condition is satisfied. *Chapter 11.*

Repetitive-stress injuries Injuries that result from repeating the same movements over long periods. *Chapter 3.*

Replication Duplication of data and formulas in a spreadsheet and adjustment of formulas to reflect new locations when necessary. *Chapter 6.*

Report An ordered list of selected records and fields in an easy-to-read form. *Chapter 8.*

Resolution The density of the pixels, usually described in *dots per inch (dpi)*. *Chapters 3, 7.*

Right justification Having the right margin smooth. *Chapter 5.*

Right to privacy Freedom from interference into the private sphere of a person's affairs. *Chapter 8.*

RISC (reduced instruction set computer) A computer whose processor works with only a small set of instructions and as a result can process information faster than a typical computer with a *CISC* design. *Chapter 2.*

Robot A computer-controlled machine designed to perform specific manual tasks. *Chapter 12.*

ROM (read-only memory) A type of memory containing unchangeable information that serves as reference material for the CPU as it executes program instructions. *Chapter 2.*

ROM cartridge A removable cartridge containing a permanent copy of software or data, often used in home video game machines. *Chapter 2.*

Row A complete horizontal line of spreadsheet cells, usually referred to by a number. *Chapter 6.*

S

Sample In digital audio recording, a measurement taken over a brief instance of time of the level of a sound. CD-quality samples are taken over 44,000 times each second, for each channel (left and right) of a stereo recording. *Chapter 3.*

Sampler An electronic musical instrument that samples (digitizes) sounds from the real world and turns them into notes that can be played with a keyboard or other device. *Chapter 7.*

Sampling rate The number of sound "snapshots" digital recording equipment takes each second. *Chapter 7.*

Sans serif font A font without serifs—fine lines at the ends of the main strokes of each character. Contrast with *Serif font*. *Chapter 5.*

Satellite office See *Regional work center.*

Save To make a disk file containing a document. *Chapter 5.*

Saving a document Copying the document from the computer's memory to disk or other secondary storage medium. *Chapter 5.*

Scalable outline font A font whose description is in the form of mathematical curves, which can be easily resized without loss of aesthetic form. Contrast with *Bit-mapped fonts*. *Chapter 5.*

Scanner An input device that can make a digital representation of any printed image. *Chapter 3.*

Scanning tunneling microscope An experiment device that allows scientists to see and move individual atoms. *Chapter 16.*

Scatter chart A type of chart used to discover, rather than display, a relationship between two variables. *Chapter 6.*

Scientific visualization software Software that uses shape, location in space, color, brightness, and motion to make invisible relationships easier to understand. *Chapter 6.*

Screen font A font designed to display on the computer screen. *Chapter 5.*

Script See *Macro.*

Scripting language See *Macro language.*

Scrolling Changing the view through a window by moving up, down, or sideways so another part of the document is visible. *Chapter 5.*

Search To issue a command to locate a particular piece of data. *Chapter 8.*

Search and replace A feature that allows selected words, phrases, or data to be changed throughout a document. *Chapter 5.*

Searching An artificial intelligence technique for looking ahead and comparing the results of different actions. *Chapter 12.*

Secondary storage A type of storage that allows the computer to record information semipermanently so it can be read later by the same computer or by another computer; includes disk and tape drives. *Chapter 2.*

Second-generation computers Computers based on transistors. *Chapter 1.*

Secret key cryptosystem A cryptosystem where every user maintains a list of secret keys, each key being used to communicate with one other user. *Chapter 15.*

Select (records) To locate a group of records from a database that match certain criteria. *Chapter 8.*

Selecting text Highlighting text, usually by dragging the cursor across it. *Chapter 5.*

Selection (or decision) control structure A program control structure used to make logical decisions—to choose between alternative courses of action depending on certain conditions. It typically takes the form, "If (some condition is true) then (do something) else (do something else)." *Chapter 11.*

Semantics The underlying meaning of words and phrases. *Chapter 12.*

Sensing device An input device designed to monitor temperature, humidity, pressure, and other physical quantities. *Chapter 3.*

Sequence control structure A group of instructions followed in order from the first through the last. *Chapter 11.*

Sequencing software Software that allows a computer to be used as a tool for musical composition, recording, and editing. Sequencing software allows musical data to be recorded and manipulated by a computer. *Chapter 7.*

Sequential access A medium, such as magnetic tape, that requires information to be retrieved in the order in which it was recorded. *Chapter 3.*

Serial port A port that requires bits to pass through one at a time. *Chapter 9.*

Serif font A font embellished with serifs—fine lines at the ends of the main strokes of each character. Contrast with *Sans serif font. Chapter 5.*

Server A computer that acts as a central storage and delivery facility for software and data shared by multiple users. *Chapter 9.*

Service bureau In desktop publishing, a business that provides expertise, contract work, consulting, printing services, and/or public access to expensive output devices and other peripherals. *Chapter 5.*

Set-top box A special-purpose computer designed to provide Internet access and other services using a standard television set and (usually) a cable TV connection. *Chapter 1.*

Shareware Software that is free for the trying, with a send-payment-if-you-keep-it honor system. *Chapter 4.*

Shell Software that stands between the user and the operating system, modifying the user interface in some way. *Chapter 4.*

SIG (special interest group) A discussion group, newsgroup, or similar group with shared interests on a bulletin board system, information service, intranet, or the Internet. *Chapter 9.*

Silicon chip A wafer of silicon containing integrated circuits that represent the equivalent of thousands—or even millions—of transistors; the principle technology for the modern computer's processor and memory. *Chapter 1.*

SILK (speech, image, language, and knowledge) Four emerging user interface technologies. *Chapter 16.*

SIMM (single inline memory module) A small, narrow circuit board containing memory chips. *Chapter 2.*

Simulation The use of computer models to test hypotheses and make decisions. *Chapter 6.*

Site licenses (or network licenses) A software license that allows for multiple copies or removes restrictions on software copying and use at a network site. *Chapter 9.*

Slot A socket for inserting a circuit board. *Chapter 2.*

Smart card A credit-card-like card that contains embedded microprocessors and memory. *Chapter 14.*

Smart pill A pill that contains microelectronic circuitry allowing it to process information. *Chapter 16.*

Smart weapon A missile or other weapon that uses computerized guidance systems to locate its target. *Chapter 15.*

Software The instructions that tell the computer what to do. *Chapter 1.*

Software engineering A branch of computer science that attempts to apply engineering principles and techniques to the development of computer software. *Chapter 11.*

Software license A legal agreement between the software user and manufacturer, including limitations on the user's rights to copy disks, install software on hard drives, and transfer information to other users. *Chapter 4.*

Software piracy The illegal duplication of copyrighted software. *Chapter 15.*

Solid-state storage device A storage device with no moving parts. *Chapter 16.*

Sort To arrange records in alphabetic or numeric order based on values in one or more *fields. Chapter 8.*

Source document In desktop publishing, the document containing an article, chapter, drawing, map, chart, or photograph that will appear in a publication. *Chapter 5.*

Speaker independence The ability of a computer to recognize words without being trained to an individual speaker. *Chapter 12.*

Special-purpose (dedicated) computer A computer dedicated to performing a specific task. *Chapter 1.*

Speech-recognition software Software designed to recognize human speech. *Chapter 12.*

Speech synthesis The generation of artificial speech by converting text into phonetic sounds. *Chapter 12.*

Spelling checker Software that checks for and corrects spelling errors in a document. *Chapter 5.*

Spreadsheet Software designed to manipulate and analyze numbers and formulas in rows and columns. *Chapter 6.*

SQL (Structured Query Language) The standard query language for most database applications today. *Chapter 8.*

Stack The name given to documents created with HyperCard and similar multimedia authoring programs. *Chapter 7.*

Stack chart A type of chart in which bars or columns are subdivided into pieces, usually to show how proportions of a whole change over time. *Chapter 6.*

Statistical analysis software Software designed to analyze numerical data and suggest answers to questions that can't be answered with certainty. *Chapter 6.*

Stepwise refinement The process of repeatedly subdividing a problem into smaller subproblems until a detailed algorithm for solving the problem emerges. *Chapter 11.*

Storage device A hardware peripheral for storing information. Disk drives are the most common storage devices. *Chapter 2.*

Stored-program concept The concept of storing the computer's program instructions with the data in *memory. Chapter 4.*

Structured programming A set of techniques designed to make programming easier and less error prone, including the use of modules and the avoidance of the GoTo statement. *Chapter 11.*

Style sheet   A set of characteristics that define formatting styles in a document. Many applications allow users to define their own customized style sheets. *Chapter 5.*

Subdirectory   A collection of files that have been grouped together on a disk. *Chapter 4.*

Subnotebook computer   A portable computer about the size of a hardbound book and just barely big enough for a keyboard. *Chapter 1.*

Subsystem   A system that is part of a larger system. *Chapter 8.*

Subtractive color synthesis   The method of forming colors used by most color printers and by painters throughout history. Each pigment in an ink absorbs or subtracts certain colors, reflecting others. By mixing pigments, a new color can be created by subtracting out other colors to varying degrees. See *CMYK. Chapter 3.*

Supercomputer   One of the fastest, most powerful computers. *Chapter 1.*

Superconductor   A substance that can transmit electricity without heat, offering potential for fantastic speed increases in computers. *Chapter 16.*

Superscalar   A CPU having multiple instruction pipelines. *Chapter 3.*

Syntax   A set of rules associated with a language. Every programming language and natural language has a syntax. *Chapters 11, 12.*

Syntax error   A violation of the "grammar" rules of the programming language. *Chapter 11.*

Synthesized   Synthetically generated. *Chapter 7.*

Synthesized sound   A sound synthetically generated using a mathematical algorithm; contrast with *Digitized sound. Chapter 7.*

Synthesizer   An electronic instrument that can create synthesized sounds. *Chapter 7.*

Synthetic speech   Artificially generated speech. *Chapter 12.*

System life cycle   A sequence of steps or phases that a computer system passes through between the time it is conceived and the time it is phased out. *Chapter 11.*

Systems analysis   The process of studying a system and analyzing, designing, developing, and maintaining a computer system. Performed by a *systems analyst. Chapter 11.*

Systems analyst   The computer professional primarily responsible for developing and managing a computer system. *Chapter 11.*

System software   A class of software that includes the *operating system* and *utility programs.* (By some definitions, system software also includes programming language translators.) *Chapter 4.*

Talkwriter   A computer that can accept and reliably process speech input. *Chapters 5, 12.*

Tape drive   A device that can store and retrieve information on magnetic tape. *Chapter 3.*

Tax preparation software   Software to automate the process of filling out tax forms. *Chapter 6.*

TB (terabyte)   Approximately one million megabytes. *Chapter 2.*

TCP/IP (Transmission Control Protocol/Internet Protocol)   The open standard *protocols* at the heart of the Internet that allow cross-network communication for almost every type of computer and network. *Chapter 10.*

Technophobia   Fear of technology. *Chapter 14.*

Telecommunication   Historically, long-distance communication; today, long-distance electronic communication. *Chapter 9.*

Telecommuting   Using a home computer and, in many cases, telecommunication equipment, to work at home rather than commuting to an office. *Chapter 13.*

Teleconference   An on-line "meeting" between two or more people. *Chapter 9.*

Telephony   The art and science of the creation of telephones; computer telephony involves the use of software and hardware to give a computer the functionality of a telephone, an answering machine, a voice mail system, or other telephone equipment. *Chapter 9.*

Telnet   The protocol that makes remote login possible. Also the name of the UNIX command that invokes remote access. *Chapter 10.*

Tempest   A U.S. military program to develop specially shielded machines that resist electronic spying. *Chapter 15.*

Template   An "empty" or generic document that can easily be adapted to specific user needs. *Chapters 5, 6.*

Terminal   A device that consists of an input device (usually a keyboard), an output device (usually a monitor), and a link to a computer or network. *Chapter 1.*

Terminal program (or terminal emulator)   Software that allows a personal computer to function as a terminal. *Chapter 9.*

Testing   Checking an algorithm or program for errors. *Chapter 11.*

Text editor   A program similar to a word processor but lacking many advanced formatting features. *Chapter 11.*

Text field   A database field that can contain only text. *Chapter 8.*

Text formatting   Designating the typefaces, margins, spacing, layout, and other features that affect the appearance of a document. *Chapter 5.*

Thesaurus   A book, software program, or software module for finding synonyms (and sometimes antonyms). *Chapter 5.*

Third-generation computers   Computers built around integrated circuits. *Chapter 1.*

3-D modeling software   Software that allows graphic designers to create representations of three-dimensional objects with tools similar to those found in conventional drawing software. *Chapter 7.*

Timesharing   An operating system technique allowing several users to use a computer concurrently. *Chapter 1.*

Toolbar   In some applications, a portion of the screen containing buttons for common commands. *Chapters 5, 6.*

Top-down design   A technique for designing a program starting at the top—with the main ideas—and working down to the details. *Chapter 11.*

Topology The configuration or arrangement of nodes on a local area network. *Chapter 9.*

Touch pad A flat-panel input device that responds to finger pressure; commonly used as a mouse substitute in portable computers. *Chapter 3.*

Touch screen A pointing input device that responds when the user points to or touches different screen regions. Touch screens are effective when many users are unfamiliar with computers, such as in public terminals in libraries, airports, and stores. *Chapter 3.*

Touch tablet An input device that can detect pressure and movement of a stylus or finger on its surface. *Chapters 3, 7.*

Trackball An input device designed to move a pointer around in response to movements of an embedded ball. *Chapter 3.*

Track point A tiny joystick-like input device that sits in the center of a portable computer's keyboard, responding to finger pressure by moving the mouse in the direction it's pushed. *Chapter 3.*

Transistor A small electronic device that transfers electricity across a tiny resistor. *Chapter 1.*

Translator program A program that translates a high-level language into machine language or some intermediate language. *Chapter 11.*

Transportable The quality of a program that allows it to be easily moved to another computer or operating system. *Chapter 11.*

Trojan horse A program that performs a useful task while at the same time carrying out some secret destructive act. *Chapter 15.*

True color Photo-quality color. *Chapter 7.*

TrueType A popular form of scalable outline font that will work with most printers and is also able to render appropriately on-screen. *Chapter 5.*

Turing Machine A hypothetical machine that could read instructions from punched paper tape and perform all the critical operations of a computer. *Chapter 12.*

Turing test A proposed test for machine intelligence that involves fooling a human judge into believing that typed computer responses were produced by a human. *Chapter 12.*

Turtle graphics A type of graphics popularized by the LOGO language. *Chapter 14.*

Tutorial software Software that provides direct instruction in a clearly specified skill or subject. *Chapter 12.*

Typeface The design of characters in a font; a family of related fonts. *Chapter 5.*

U

Ubiquitous computers Computers everywhere, embedded in all kinds of tools. *Chapter 16.*

Undo A command that allows the user to take back the last operation. *Chapter 5.*

Unicode The emerging international standard double-byte character set. Unicode allows for 256x256 or 65,536 distinct codes—more than enough for all modern languages. *Chapter 2.*

UNIX A multiuser operating system widely used on mainframes and workstations. *Chapter 10.*

Upgrade To update an existing software program to a newer version, usually by paying an upgrade fee to the software manufacturer. *Chapter 4.*

Upload To post software on a bulletin board system, information utility, or network. *Chapter 9.*

Up-skilling Transforming a job into one that is more technically challenging. *Chapter 13.*

URL (Uniform Resource Locator) The address of a Web page or other resource on the World Wide Web. *Chapter 10.*

User interface The look and feel of the computing experience from a human point of view. *Chapter 4.*

User level The level of access a program allows a user. *Chapter 7.*

Utility program A software tool for doing system maintenance, repairs, and user interface enhancements that aren't automatically handled by the operating system. *Chapter 4.*

V

Vaccine (disinfectant) program A program designed to search for viruses, notify users when they're found, and remove them from infected disks or files. *Chapter 15.*

Validator A likely addition to future spreadsheets that will check complex worksheets for consistency of entries and formula logic. *Chapter 6.*

Value A number in a spreadsheet cell or database field. *Chapter 6.*

Variable A named portion of computer memory whose contents can be examined and changed by the program. *Chapter 11.*

Vertical-market application An application designed specifically for a particular business or industry. *Chapter 4.*

Video digitizer A collection of circuits that can capture input from a video camera, video cassette recorder, television, or other video source and convert it to a digital signal that can be stored in memory and displayed on computer screens. *Chapter 7.*

Video display terminal (VDT) See *Monitor.*

Video editing software Software that facilitates editing of video footage. *Chapter 7.*

Video memory Memory that contains the image displayed on the video monitor. Most video adapter cards have several megabytes of their own memory. *Chapter 3.*

Video monitor See *Monitor.*

Videophone A telephone with built-in video capability. *Chapter 16.*

Video teleconference A meeting in which people communicate face-to-face over long distances using video and computer technology. *Chapter 9.*

Virtual reality A user interface that looks to the user like an artificial world. *Chapters 4, 16.*

Virus A program that spreads from program to program, or from disk to disk, and uses each infected program or disk to make more copies of itself. *Chapter 15.*

Visual programming To create programs by drawing pictures and pointing to on-screen objects. *Chapter 11.*

Voice annotation   Sound messages attached to a document. *Chapter 9.*

Voice mail   A telephone messaging system with many of the features of an electronic mail system. *Chapter 9.*

Volatile memory   Memory that can be changed. *Chapter 2.*

Wand reader   Used to read alphabetic and numeric characters written in a specially designed typeface found on many sales tags and credit card slips. *Chapter 3.*

Waveform audio   Sound data stored in a computer's memory. *Chapter 7.*

Web browser   A program for navigating the World Wide Web. *Chapter 10.*

Web page   A document on the World Wide Web, typically made up of text, drawings, and photographs, like a page in a book. *Chapter 10.*

"What if?" question   A type of hypothetical question commonly answered by *simulation* and *spreadsheet* programs. *Chapter 6.*

Wide area network (WAN)   A network that extends over a long distance. *Chapter 9.*

WIMP   An acronym describing graphical user interfaces with windows, icons, menus, and pointing devices. *Chapter 16.*

Window   A framed area on a computer screen that can be open, closed, and moved with a pointing device. *Chapter 4.*

Wireless network   A network that transmits information through radio waves. *Chapter 9.*

Word processing   A software application that allows text documents to be edited and formatted on screen before being printed. *Chapter 5.*

Word wrap   A word processing feature that automatically transports any words that won't fit on the current line to the next line along with the cursor. *Chapter 5.*

Workgroup computing   A style of work encouraged and facilitated by *groupware*. *Chapter 13.*

Worksheet   A spreadsheet document. *Chapter 6.*

Workstation   A high-end desktop computer with the computing power of a minicomputer at a fraction of the cost. *Chapter 1.*

World Wide Web (WWW, W3, Web)   The part of the Internet that can be easily explored with a Web browser; Web documents can incorporate pictures, sounds, animation, video, and hypertext links to other documents. *Chapter 1, 10.*

WORM (write once, read many) drive   A storage device that writes digital information onto blank optical disks but can't change information once it's recorded. An example is a *CD-R* drive. *Chapter 3.*

Worm   A virus-like program that travels over computer networks, seeking out uninfected workstations to occupy. *Chapter 15.*

Writeback   When the CPU sends information back out (usually to memory) on completion of an instruction. *Chapter 2.*

WYSIWYG (what you see is what you get)   Pronounced "wizzy-wig." The arrangement of the words and pictures on the screen represents a close approximation of the way they will look on the printed page. *Chapters 5, 7.*

Credits

p.205 top: Courtesy of IBM. bottom: Courtesy of Supra.

p.208 Courtesy of Sun Microsystems.

p.209 Courtesy of Lotus.

p.210 top to bottom: Courtesy of Champlain Cable, Courtesy of National Wire and Cable Corporation, Courtesy of Inmac, Courtesy of Farallon, Courtesy of Motorola.

p.220 top: Courtesy of Motorola. bottom: ©Jon Riley/Tony Stone Images.

p.221 top: ©Steven Peters/Tony Stone Images. bottom: ©Robert E. Daemmrich/Tony Stone Images.

p.222 ©Rick Reinhard/FPG.

Chapter 10

p.227 ©Clark Quin.

p.239 Courtesy of Another World.

p.240 Courtesy of CU-See-Me

p.248 Courtesy of Sun Microsystems.

Chapter 11

p.256 Department of the Navy.

p.262 ©1992 Peter Manzek/Pacific Data Images.

p.270 Courtesy of Parc Place.

p.276 ©Robert Daemmrich/Tony Stone Images, Jim Folts/Benjamin/Cummings Publishing.

p.277 Jim Folts/Benjamin/Cummings Publishing.

p.280 ©David Tejada/Tony Stone Images.

p.282 ©Charles Thatcher/Tony Stone Images.

Chapter 12

p.286 Courtesy of the Computer Museum.

p.290 ©Corbis-Bettmann Archive.

p.291 Courtesy of the ACM Chess Challenge.

p.292 Courtesy of Hewlett-Packard.

p.297 Courtesy of Sun Microsystems.

p.298 Art by Harold Cohen. Photo ©Becky Cohen.

p.298 ©Becky Cohen.

p.300 top: ©Ed Kashi. bottom: Courtesy of Japan Airlines.

p.301 Courtesy of Apple Computers.

p.304 top: ©John Wilson White. bottom: Courtesy of Xerox Imaging Systems, Inc.

p.306 ©Lawrence Ivy for the Merce Cunningham Dance Company.

p.308 clockwise: Courtesy of Transitions Research Corporation, ©Dave Barrett/MIT, Courtesy of Control Data Corporation.

Chapter 13

p.314 ©Ed Kashi.

p.315 Courtesy of Nomadic Research Labs.

p.318 left: ©Dan Bosler/Tony Stone Images. right: Courtesy of the New York Times Online.

p.319 top left: Courtesy of Human Interface Technology Laboratory, University of Washington. top right: Courtesy of Boeing. bottom: ©Michael Rosenfeld/Tony Stone Images.

p.320 ©George Haling/Science Source/Photo Researchers.

p.322 ©Jim Cummins/FPG.

p.324 left top and bottom: ©Robert E. Daemmrich/Tony Stone Images. right: top: Jim Pickerell 1988/FPG. middle: ©Tim Brown/Tony Stone Images. bottom: ©Terry Vine/Tony Stone Images.

p.327 ©Bruce Jaffe/Gamma Liaison.

p.329 Courtesy of Microtouch.

p.330 ©David Graham/Black Star.

p.331 ©C.J. Howard 1990/FPG.

Chapter 14

p.336 Courtesy of Cyan.

p.341 Courtesy of IBM.

p.342 ©Yoav Levy/PhotoTake, NYC.

p.345 ©Ed Kashi.

p.346 Courtesy of Oregon State University SMILE Program.

p.347 Courtesy of the Scriptorium.

p.350 Courtesy of Apple Computers.

p.352 Courtesy of IBM.

p.353 Courtesy of Micro Card Technologies, Inc.

p.357 Courtesy of Keep It Simple Solar Systems.

Chapter 15

p.362 ©Larry Mulvehill/Photo Researchers.

p.368 top: ©Maggie Hallahan/Network Images. bottom: Courtesy of Jonathan Littmann.

p.369 left: Courtesy of Eyedentify. right: Courtesy of Recognition Systems.

p.375 Courtesy of Xerox Parc.

p.378 ©George Hall/Check Six.

Chapter 16

p.385 Courtesy of Apple Computers.

p.387 ©The Kobal Collection.

p.389 top: Courtesy of dpix, a Xerox Company. bottom: Courtesy of IBM.

p.390 top: Courtesy of Silicon Graphics. bottom: ©Fred Mertz.

p.392 ©Edward Santalone.

p.394 ©Kobal Collection.

p.395 ©Kobal Collection.

p.396 Courtesy of Xerox Corporation, photo courtesy of Niehaus, Ryan, Haller Public Relations.

p.398 ©Peter Menzel.

p.399 ©1991 Peter Menzel.

p.401 ©Corbis-Bettmann Archive.

Consumer's Guide:

p.404 left: Courtesy of Sun Microsystems. middle: Courtesy of Silicon Graphics. right: Courtesy of IBM.

p.405 top to bottom: Courtesy of Apple Computers, Inc. Photo by John Greenleigh, Courtesy of IBM, Courtesy of IBM, Courtesy of Apple Computers, Inc.

p.406 Courtesy of IBM.

p.407 top to bottom: Courtesy of Supra, Courtesy of Radius, Courtesy of Hewlett-Packard, Courtesy of Apple Computers, Inc., Courtesy of IBM.

p.408 left: Courtesy of Hewlett-Packard. right: Courtesy of Apple Computers Inc.

Text Credits

p.133 Reprinted by permission from an advertisement that appeared in *National Geographic,* February 1952. Copyright © 1952 by International Business Machines Corporation.

p.250 From a MCI advertisement. Reprinted by permission of MCI.

p.291 From "The Day That I Sensed a New Kind of Intelligence" by Garry Kasparov, *Time,* March 25, 1996.

p.362 From "Pretty Boy Floyd" by Woody Guthrie. Copyright © 1958 (renewed) by Fall River Music, Inc. All Rights Reserved.

p.396 From "The Computer for the 21st Century" by Mark Weiser. Copyright © 1991 by Scientific American, Inc. All Rights Reserved.

Index